LAND AND SOCIETY IN EARLY SOUTH ASIA

This volume explores the process of social changes which unfolded in rural society of early medieval Bengal, especially the formation of stratified land relations and occupational groups which later got systematised as *jātis*.

One of the first books to systematically reconstruct the early history of the region, this book presents a history of the economy, polity, law, and social order of early medieval Bengal through a comprehensive study of land and society. It traces the changing power relations among constituents of rural society and political institutions, and unravels the contradictions growing among them. The author describes the changing forms of agrarian development which were deeply associated with these overarching structures and offers an in-depth analysis of a wide range of textual sources in Sanskrit and other languages, especially contemporary inscriptions pertaining to Bengal.

The volume will be an essential resource for researchers and academics interested in the history of Bengal, and the social and economic history of early South Asia.

Ryosuke Furui is Associate Professor at the Institute for Advanced Studies on Asia, The University of Tokyo, Japan.

LAND AND SOCIETY IN EARLY SOUTH ASIA

Eastern India 400–1250 AD

Ryosuke Furui

Routledge
Taylor & Francis Group
LONDON AND NEW YORK

First published 2020
by Routledge
2 Park Square, Milton Park, Abingdon, Oxon OX14 4RN

and by Routledge
605 Third Avenue, New York, NY 10017

First issued in paperback 2021

Routledge is an imprint of the Taylor & Francis Group, an informa business

British Library Cataloguing-in-Publication Data
A catalogue record for this book is available from the British Library

Library of Congress Cataloging-in-Publication Data
A catalog record for this book has been requested

Typeset in Sabon
by Apex CoVantage, LLC

ISBN 13: 978-0-367-78592-5 (pbk)
ISBN 13: 978-1-138-49843-3 (hbk)

TO JAE EUN

CONTENTS

ILLUSTRATIONS

Map

Tables

PREFACE

The present work is based on my PhD thesis submitted to Jawaharlal Nehru University in 2007. The unnecessarily long time taken for revising – rather rewriting – it for publication is to some extent due to my laziness. To larger extent, however, it is because of the reconsideration and reworking necessitated by the discoveries of new evidences and the reinterpretations of known sources, to both of which I myself made some contributions. I have no regret for those additional years so far as they deepened my understanding and improved the present work.

My experiences in discovering and deciphering new inscriptions and re-reading old ones told me how easily a single discovery can smash a widely accepted theory and compel us to construct a new one. Accordingly, what is explicated in this book cannot help being a provisional theory susceptible to changes forced by future discoveries, for which I will surely continue my efforts. Still, I believe it worth presenting the result of my research to the academic society in the current form. I hope that this book can live a long life through the discussions among my present and future academic colleagues.

The present work owes much to the academic interactions with my teachers and friends all over the world. Before anybody else, I would like to thank Prof. B. D. Chattopadhyaya, my supervisor, for all his advices and encouragements since my days in Jawaharlal Nehru University. The interactions with him were always inspiring and made me realise many possibilities hidden in the sources. I hope that I could repay some portion of my debt to him by this book. I would also like to thank Prof. Kunal Chakrabarti, my second supervisor, for his help and guidance. The valuable comments by Dr. Gouriswar Bhattacharya and Prof. Arun K. Nag enriched the present work. I am grateful to them.

My sincere thanks go to late Prof. Gen'ichi Yamazaki, who initiated me to the study of early South Asian history and taught me the importance of primary sources. It is my gravest regret that he could not see the publication of this book. Prof. Toshio Yamazaki introduced me to South Asian epigraphy through his works and gave me much insight through our conversations. I thank him and look forward to his comments on my works to come, including the present one. My interest in Bengal was aroused by Prof. Nariaki Nakazato, whose excellent works on the modern history of Bengal and beyond showed me the standard to aspire to. I thank him and hope that the present work could somehow alleviate his concern about the slow progress of my work, even though it may not be up to his mark. This book could never have been born without the trainings in Sanskrit at the University of Tokyo, for which I would like to express my gratitude to late Prof. Katsuhiko Kamimura and Prof. Ryutaro Tsuchida. I am also grateful to Prof. Harry Falk, who gave me an opportunity to stay in Berlin and see the high standard of Indological studies in Europe including his own.

I was fortunate enough to have close association with Prof. Krishna Mohan Shrimali and to receive enormous help from Prof. Gautam Sengupta in my research in India. I thank them for their help and encouragement. I am also grateful to Dr. J. E. Dowson, Mr. Tejpal Singh, Dr. Sharmila Saha, Mr. Satyakam Sen, Ms. Srabanti Sardar, Mr. Indrajit Chowdhury, Mr. Sadhan Deb, Drs Enamul Haque, Md. Shafiqul Alam, Swapan Kumar Biswas, Md. Monirul Hok, Md. Abdul Kuddus, Ms. Afroza Khan Mita, Mr. Tauhiddun Nabi, Mr. Mahabubul Alam and Mr. Sadequzzaman for their help in my researches in Delhi, West Bengal and Bangladesh. I would like to express my gratitude to Profs Abdul Momin Chowdhury, Suresh Chandra Bhattacharya, Bhairabi Prasad Sahu and Ranabir Chakravarti for the fruitful discussions with them.

The associations with my friends were always inspiring and refreshing. I would especially like to thank Arlo Griffiths for his critical and encouraging comments which enormously improved my discussions. I have no word to express my gratitude to Annette and Rainer Schmiedchen for their kind regards and helps in many occasions in my life. My thanks also go to Subir Sarkar, Suchandra Ghosh, Susmita Basu Majumdar, Sayantani Pal, Rajat Sanyal, Kaushik Gangopadhyay and Sayan Bhattacharya, conversations with whom always made my researches in Kolkata fruitful and enjoyable. On the other side of the border, I would like to thank Swadhin Sen for always giving me inspirations by the latest result of his vigorous research works in northern Bangladesh. I am grateful to Gerd Mevissen for the precious information given from his vast knowledge on images and other objects on both sides of Bengal. I also thank Jesse Ross Knutson, care-free academic interactions with whom widened my view to the history and culture of Bengal. Daily interactions with my colleagues, especially Kazuo Morimoto and Norihisa Baba, were thought-provoking. I would like to express my sincere thanks to them.

At last but least, I would like to thank Jae Eun Shin, my wife, to whom the present book is dedicated. But for her, my world, both academic and otherwise, could have been a narrow one.

In different stages, my research culminated in the present form has been funded by Japan Society for Promotion of Science (Grant-in-Aid for Young Scientists (Start-up) 20820015, Grant-in-Aid for Young Scientists (B) 22720264, Grant-in-Aid for Young Scientists (A) 26704008). I thank the society for the financial help provided by it.

ACKNOWLEDGEMENTS

Some parts of the present book were published earlier in the following articles in different forms:

> 'Finding Tensions in the Social Order: a Reading of the Varṇasaṃkara Section of the Bṛhaddharmapurāṇa', in Suchandra Ghosh, Sudipa Ray Bandyopadhyay, Sushmita Basu Majumdar and Sayantani Pal (eds), *Revisiting Early India: Essays in Honour of D. C. Sircar*, Kolkata: R. N. Bhattacharya, 2013, pp. 203–18.
>
> (Chapter 6, the last section)
>
> 'Characteristics of Kaivarta Rebellion Delineated from the Rāmacarita', *Proceedings of Indian History Congress*, 75, 2015, pp. 93–98.
>
> (Chapter 5, the last section)
>
> 'Variegated Adaptations: State Formation in Bengal from the Fifth to the Seventh Century' (rev.), in Karashima Noboru and Hirosue Masashi (eds), *State Formation and Social Integration in Premodern South and Southeast Asia: A Comparative Study of Asian Society*, Tokyo: The Toyo Bunko, 2017, pp. 73–87.
>
> (Map 2.1)

I herewith acknowledge their reproduction to the editors, publishers and associations related to them.

ABBREVIATIONS

BS	Bengal Samvat (594 AD~).
CBI	Ramaranjan Mukherjee and Sachindra Kumar Maity (eds), *Corpus of Bengal Inscriptions: Bearing on History and Civilization of Bengal*, Calcutta: Firma K. L. Mukhopadhyay, 1967.
CII 3 (rev.)	D. R. Bhandarkar (rev.), B. Ch. Chhabra and G. S. Gai (eds), *Corpus Inscriptionum Indicarum, vol. 3 (rev.): Inscriptions of the Early Guptas*, New Delhi: Archaeological Survey of India, 1981.
CPI	copper plate inscription.
CPS	Kamalakanta Gupta (ed.), *Copper-Plates of Sylhet, vol. 1 (7th – 11th Century A. D.)*, Sylhet: Lipika Enterprises, 1967.
EDEP	D. C. Sircar, *Epigraphic Discoveries in East Pakistan*, Calcutta: Sanskrit College, 1973.
GE	Gupta Era (319–20 AD~).
GL	Akshay Kumar Maitreya (ed.), *Gauḍalekhamālā*, Rajshahi: The Varendra Research Society, 1912 (reprint, Kolkata: Sanskrit Pustak Bhandar, 2004).
IAA	Mukunda Madhava Sharma, *Inscriptions of Ancient Assam*, Gauhati: Department of Publication, Gauhati University, 1978.
IB	Nani Gopal Majumdar, (ed.), *Inscriptions of Bengal Volume III: Containing Inscriptions of the Chandras, the Varmans and the Senas, and of Īśvaraghosha and Dāmodara*, Rajsahi: The Varendra research Society, 1929.
IEG	D. C. Sircar, *Indian Epigraphical Glossary*, Delhi: Motilal Banarsidass, 1966.
IO	Snigdha Tripathy (ed.), *Inscriptions of Orissa vol. 1: Circa Fifth-Eighth Centuries A. D.*, Delhi: Motilal Banarsidass, 1997.
RE	Regnal Era.
SE	Śaka Era (78 AD~).

SI 1	D. C. Sircar (ed.), *Select Inscriptions Bearing on Indian History and Civilization Vol. 1: From the Sixth Century B. C. to the Sixth Century A. D.* (2nd ed.), Calcutta: University of Calcutta, 1965.
SI 2	D. C. Sircar (ed.), *Select Inscriptions Bearing on Indian History and Civilization Vol. 2: From the Sixth to the Eighteenth Century A. D.*, Delhi: Motilal Banarsidass, 1983.
STP	D. C. Sircar, *Śilālekha-Tāmraśāsanādir Prasaṅga*, Calcutta: Sahityaloka, 1982.
VE	Vikrama Era (58–57 BC~).

1

INTRODUCTION

Theme and aims of research

The regions of South Asia show diverse social profiles matching their diverse environments and histories. The two elements which contribute the most to this social diversity are the power relations around control over land and the configurations of caste groups, more precisely *jāti*s, in particular orders. Bengal, an eastern region approximating the present territories of Republic of Bangladesh and Indian state of West Bengal, is no exception. Throughout the modern period, it has seen a stratified land system consisting of layers of tenure holders and subordinate cultivators embedded in a particular power relation.[1] Its society, at least its Hindu half, is characterised by the bipolar division of *jāti*s into the two *varṇa* categories of *brāhmaṇa* and *śūdra*, and the superior *kulīna* status given to some sections of *brāhmaṇa*s and *kāyastha*s.[2]

The establishment of this social order owed much to the early modern development, namely, the formulation of social outlook and its imposition by *brāhmaṇa*s and its acceptance by the other social groups, which manifested itself in the creation of origin myth and the textual composition of genealogies called the *Kulagrantha*s.[3] The same can be said of the land system characterised by landholders called *zamindar*s, to which the Mughal rule made a great contribution.[4] These developments, however, must have been conditioned by the historical change in the previous period, which predisposed them to certain directions. Therefore, the delineation of the process of social change in the earlier period is crucial in understanding the society of Bengal, and the present study, which deals with the long period over 800 years between the early fifth and the mid-13th centuries AD, attempts at it.

The period of study mostly overlapped with the one labelled early medieval in the current historiography. It is deemed to be the period of great transformation, or transition, when new power relations and social structures emerged and regions in the subcontinent were moulded into distinct contours. In this period, diverse regions of North India saw the hierarchised political structure consisting of the king and his subordinate rulers and the stratified agrarian society made of landed magnates and subject cultivators, of which all the constituents had differential control over and interest in land. The society of these regions witnessed the emergence of *jāti*s resulting from the organisation of professional groups and the incorporation of new social groups, especially non-sedentary groups, into its margins. Early medieval Bengal and its society also experienced such phenomena. The present study attempts to delineate and understand the overall process of historical changes connected with them.

What is to be delineated in the present study as the process of historical change is a structural transformation of the society with emphasis on the changing power relations among its constituents. Due to the involvement of diverse social groups with different material bases and cultural backgrounds, the process would inevitably be a complex one, though the sources limited in both quantity and quality entice us to search for a rather simplistic causation. My proposition is to understand the complexity of historical change as dynamics generated by agencies and interactions of the social groups at the particular historical conjunctures, which are in turn transformed by their agencies. In other words, I take their agencies and interactions as the prime causes of change while recognising the limitations imposed on them by the contemporary political context and material conditions.

The proposition made above on the relation between historical conjunctures and agencies of social groups, and on the historical change brought out by the latter, is based on the theory of practice developed by Pierre Bourdieu to transcend antinomies of structuralism and subjectivism.[5] According to him, 'the structures constitutive of a particular type of environment' produce in an agent '*habitus*, systems of durable, transposable *dispositions*, structured structures predisposed to function as structuring structures' adjusted to the structures which generated it.[6] *Habitus* produces 'practices which tend to reproduce the regularities immanent in the objective conditions of the production of their generative principle',[7] namely the practices conforming to the requirement of existing structure. At first glance, this configuration of *habitus* and practices seems to deny the ability of agencies to transform the structure, while it can well explain the durability of a system. However, as *habitus* is deemed to be an endless capacity to engender thoughts, perceptions, expressions, actions whose limits are set by historically and socially situated conditions of its production,[8] and the dialectical relationship between *habitus* and an objective event is considered to constitute the conjuncture capable of transforming practices into collective action,[9] this theory of practice enables us to consider the capacity of agencies of social groups to transform the social structure within a certain limit imposed by the objective conditions generating their *habitus*. Each social group located in a particular social context acquires certain principles, behavioural manners and aspirations adjusted to the context. The agencies of those groups would in turn transform their social context and structure within a limit imposed by the *habitus* generated by their past experiences.

For discussing the historical conjunctures which limit agencies of social groups, on the other hand, the Marxist concept of social formation is invoked. It entails a complex structure of social relations and a unity of economic, ideological and political structural levels in which the role of the economy is determinant.[10] By invoking this concept, we can configure the social context of agencies of social groups in its complexity, incorporating various elements while emphasising the economic conditions. However, the invocation of the concept never means to put a label of particular social formation, like feudal, on each phase of historical change in early Bengal. As will be clear from the historiography in the next section, such an exercise had led us to an impasse through the inflation of concepts. I would rather use the concept as a guideline in analysing elements of a historical conjuncture including relations of production in a certain historical phase.

Following the aforementioned theoretical framework, the present study explores the social formation including political context and economic conditions, the character of social groups constituting this formation and their power relations, and the agencies and interactions of those groups and their effects on the social formation in each phase of the early history of Bengal.

With the theme and aims stated, I would like to proceed to the discussion on historiography, of which the current state further necessitates the present study.

Historiography

In the middle of the last century, some phenomena related to land and society in early medieval South Asia like land relation and *jāti*s were studied by scholars who dealt with them as some of diverse aspects of the socio-economic history, with undue emphasis on the issue of land ownership and casual application of European concepts like feudalism and manorial system.[11] A qualitative change was brought about by the almost contemporary works of D. D. Kosambi and R. S. Sharma, who tried to comprehend the historical change of the period as a long term socio-economic process through the application of the Marxist concept of feudalism. Since then, the understanding of the socio-economic change has been the main concern of researches for a substantial period and several theories have been proposed for that. Among them, the most important and influential were the three, namely, Indian Feudalism, Segmentary State and Integrative Polity on which following discussions were centred.[12]

The earliest theorisation of feudalism by Kosambi and Sharma took different forms. Kosambi proposed the theory of 'Feudalism from above' and 'Feudalism from below,' by which he supposed the two stages of development, namely, the decentralisation of administration by subordinate rulers and the rise of intermediaries within villages.[13] Denying Kosambi's proposition of feudalism from below, Sharma fully theorised Indian Feudalism by envisaging the closed economy resulting from the decline of Roman trade and monetary economy, and the feudal political and social setups, namely the rise of intermediaries and the subjection of peasants, mainly generated by land grants.[14] It was the latter conceptualisation of Indian Feudalism which was enriched by the works of Sharma himself and the other scholars following his line of reasoning.[15]

The theory of Indian Feudalism provoked vigorous discussions and invited criticisms on both empirical and theoretical grounds. The most questioned of its empirical validity was the supposed closed economy. D. C. Sircar first raised the question, and the works of B. D. Chattopadhyaya, M. R. Tarafdar and B. N. Mukherjee on the continuing monetary economy and trade then disproved it in regional contexts.[16] John S. Deyell, who extensively studied the early medieval North Indian coin hoards by the thorough application of Kosambi's numismatic methodology,[17] cast a serious doubt on the supposed paucity of coins and gave a persuasive interpretation of the circulation of debased coins as a measure to supply currency for vigorous trade against a dwindling silver supply.[18] The works of Ranabir Chakravarti also showed the thriving condition of foreign and inter-regional trade in the early medieval period.[19]

A severe criticism on theoretical ground came from Harbans Mukhia. Based on his understanding of European feudalism in terms of modes of production, he questioned its applicability to Indian history, which had different agrarian conditions. He denied the subjection of peasants in the early medieval South Asia and proposed the production based on economically free peasants. He also criticised the attribution of the establishment of feudalism to state action by proponents of Indian Feudalism.[20] His criticism was, however, not without problems either. He was right in bringing back modes of production, which was not discussed properly in Indian Feudalism, to the centre stage and in pointing out the peculiar conditions of West European feudalism in terms of ecology and relations of production. But his formulation of the pre-modern Indian economy as stable free peasant production without much technological progress is unacceptable as it is based on the juxtaposition of sources of different periods and on the agrarian situation mostly limited to western India, ignoring ecological diversity within the subcontinent and stratifications among agriculturalists in the early medieval period.[21]

B. D. Chattopadhyaya, on the other hand, criticised Indian Feudalism for its emphasis on a total bipolarity between the early historical and early medieval periods, which presupposed the presence of centralised political power and monetised economy characterised by foreign trade and urbanisation for the former and their absence for the latter.[22] He claimed that the construct of Indian Feudalism based on an assumed binary opposition bypassed the long term processes characterising South Asian history in general, namely, transformations of pre-state society to state society, and of tribes to peasants.[23]

Confronted with those criticisms, Sharma and his followers made efforts to refine the theory of Indian Feudalism. Criticised for superficial comparisons with West European feudalism and dependence on external elements like the decline of foreign trade, they tried to uphold their theory by emphasising the inner dynamics of Indian history. But their construct was a simplistic causality in which royal land grants resulted in the political decentralisation and the supposed urban decay led to the ruralisation.[24] They also had recourse to the contradictory notion of Kaliyuga crisis,[25] which took a Brahmanical perception of catastrophe for an actual social crisis and made the symptoms of Kaliyuga both cause and content of the new formation.[26]

A more serious problem of the followers of Indian Feudalism was, however, that they did not deepen the discussion on modes of production and their inherent contradictions which led to the rise of feudalism and its decline. Though Sharma vigorously defended his position against criticisms and D. N. Jha followed his suit, their answers were rather evasive.[27] As a result, the discussion on Indian Feudalism became stagnant, though it continued persistently towards the end of the last century. This is clear from the publication of the two article collections,[28] of which the contents mostly overlapped with the earlier publications on the same topic.[29] If the debate on Indian Feudalism was to go into another round, its proponents should squarely answer the raised questions and seriously engage in the discussion on modes of production and comparison at a deeper level of historical dynamics, not at the level of superficial phenomena. The works of Rajan Gurukkal and Kesavan Veluthat could be the initiator of a new round of discussions for their intensive treatments of social formation.[30]

In spite of all those empirical and theoretical problems, the enormous contribution of Indian Feudalism to the study of the early medieval history of South Asia is undeniable. It totally smashed the imperialist assumption of unchanging Indian villages and made it impossible for any serious historians to discuss the historical change without considering the transformation of society.

The vigorous discussions around Indian Feudalism gave rise to the alternative ways of understanding the early medieval society from the 1970s onwards. They were characterised by the focus on particular regions. The most prominent, but controversial at the same time, were the works of Burton Stein. He tried to apply the model of Segmentary State, which had been developed by Aiden Southall for the pre-state society of Alurs in East Africa, to the history of South India, especially the Tamil region, from the Pallava to Vijayanagara period. He conceived *nāḍu* as an autonomous agrarian unit with political authority constituted by the alliance of *brāhmaṇa*s and higher peasants, over which the king could wield limited power verging on only a ritual sovereignty.[31] His model was severely criticised on both empirical and theoretical grounds, especially for his inadequate use of inscriptional evidences and the theory of Brahman-peasant alliance.[32] The applicability of the model proposed for a pre-state society of Africa to the medieval Indian history was also questioned seriously.[33] In the attempts to revise his theory, Stein ignored all the criticisms on the validity of his evidences and evaded the theoretical ones.[34] While the model was dismissed by Indian scholars in near totality, it still found a resonance in the works of American scholars on South India in their undue emphasis on the ideological dimension, namely, the centrality of kingship and its pervasive ritual authority, in spite of the improvement made by them in the other aspects to be discussed below.[35]

The other alternative can be called the theory of Integrative Polity, though the scholars subscribing to this form of theorisation did not share a particular terminology or constitute a school. In the context of Orissa, Hermann Kulke considered the historical process of early medieval South Asia a process of the establishment of state at the nuclear region and its integration of peripheral regions. He regarded the legitimatisation of kingship through settling of *brāhmaṇa*s and construction of royal temples, and the integration of local cults to a royal cult as a system of state integration.[36] B. D. Chattopadhyaya perceived the expansion of agrarian and state society towards areas in pre-state condition as a continuous process of the early South Asian history and interpreted the historical change of the early medieval period as its intensification.[37] His studies on Rajasthan exhibited the interrelation of state formation through the formation of Rajput lineages, agrarian expansion through the development of irrigation facilities and flourishing commercial activities through the making of new urban centres.[38]

The discussions around those theories brought out consensus on some phenomena of the early medieval history, even though each theory gave different interpretations to them. The first is the agrarian expansion, which denotes the expansion of sedentary agriculture and agrarian society across the diverse terrains of South Asia. For the Integrative Polity model presupposing the presence of the non-sedentary, non-state society in periphery to be integrated through the expansion of both agriculture and state system, the agrarian expansion constitutes one of its core concepts. For Indian Feudalism, on the other hand, it is a phenomenon contingent to the de-urbanisation and closed economy. In both strands, it is accepted that the agrarian expansion entails the incorporation of non-agrarian tribal people into sedentary agrarian society as subordinate cultivators. The second is the decentralised hierarchical power structure. Indian Feudalism, which presupposes the presence of centralised state in the earlier period, interprets it as a result of disintegration of such a state and attributes its emergence to royal land grants. In contrast, Integrative Polity model takes it as a consequence of the process of secondary state formation and political integration, in which tribal chiefdoms grew to kingdoms by the expansion of state system from the nuclear region and were integrated to the central kingdom with their chiefs acquiring the position of subordinate rulers. In case of Segmentary State model, decentralised power structure is presupposed in its configuration of *nāḍu* as an autonomous political unit with its chiefs acknowledging only ritual sovereignty of the king.

Based on such consensus, the recent studies on the society of early medieval South Asia saw a renewed emphasis on regional history. This was due to the realisation of geographical diversity and peculiar historical condition of South Asia where social groups belonging to different levels of material and cultural life have existed synchronically and influenced each other. While the realisation of the former was enhanced by the recent surge of studies on environmental history,[39] that of the latter was already latent in Kosambi's conceptualisation of 'living prehistory' in hindsight.[40] In contrast to the regional histories written earlier, which presupposed the existence of particular regions in an essentialist way, the new regional history concerned itself with the process of the formation of a region and its identity.[41]

Thanks to the enormous number of inscriptions and the relative ease in locating settlements and land plots mentioned in them, a substantial number of researches in the line of regional history was made on South India, especially Tamil area. While the earlier works, in their efforts to criticise and overcome Stein's Segmentary State, intensively discussed the stratified agrarian relations with varying shades of rights over land and its produce and the social groups and institutions around them,[42] the recent works tried to delineate the process of agrarian expansion and regional integration in a more concrete way, based on the recognition of inner ecological diversity by identifying poetic *tiṇai* stereotypes with micro-eco-zones.[43] The most notable among them were the works of James Heitzman and Cynthia Talbot. By statistically analysing the inscriptional data with mapping of land plots through intensive fieldwork, Heitzman minutely traced the agrarian expansion through the extension of irrigation facilities, centred on particular temples in the four sample areas of Coḷamaṇḍalam with different ecological settings.[44] Following him, Talbot made a statistical analysis of Kākatīya inscriptions with consideration of the ecological diversity and delineated the agrarian expansion from coastal to interior Andhra.[45] Both of them emphasised agency of local rulers and so did Veluthat in his study on the political system under the Coḷas.[46]

Studies on the history of the other regions, which were not favoured by abundant epigraphic sources, were pursued with various degrees of success. In those works, the interpretative strategy for reading limited sources was crucial as attested by the different results from the same sets of sources. In his studies on early medieval Orissa, Bhairabi Prasad Sahu traced the process of agrarian expansion through the settling of *brāhmaṇa*s by land grants and the resultant peasantisation of tribal groups, with a consideration of the ecological diversity within the region.[47] In contrast, Upinder Singh did not consider geographical elements in analysing the distribution of inscriptions in her otherwise highly sophisticated study on the same region and failed to detect the interaction of agrarian and tribal societies.[48] We can similarly compare Nayanjot Lahiri's works on early medieval Assam, which argued for geographical uniformity of the Assam valley and relative changelessness for eight centuries, with the work of Chitrarekha Gupta which delineated the process of agrarian and settlement expansion from lower to upper Assam.[49]

One of the best works in this category was the monograph of Nandini Sinha Kapur on the medieval history of Mewar, the southern sub-region of Rajasthan. Following the works of B. D. Chattopadhyaya on Rajasthan,[50] she described the state formation of the Guhila lineage and the making of the sub-region in relation to the settlement expansion incorporating hilly forest tracts inhabited by Bhil tribes, the integration of various social groups including the other Rajput lineages, Jain merchants and Bhils, and the strategy of royal lineage in its legitimisation through legend and religious symbols.[51]

In case of the history of Bengal, Niharranjan Ray first went beyond the framework of conventional history, in which dynastic history constituted main parts, and some aspects of the society was described in a separate chapter without much consideration of change.[52] He delineated the historical change of Bengal society in terms of caste and class. He explained the growing rigidity of caste system by relating it with the progress of Aryanisation and the change of regimes from the Buddhist Pālas and Candras to the strictly Brahmanical Varmans and Senas. Regarding the class, he related the fluctuation of the social rank of each occupational class with the shift of economic importance from commerce to agriculture.[53] Though it was the great departure at the time of its first publication in 1949, some notions like Aryanisation and the overemphasis of religious affiliation of dynasties became obsolete and should be overcome by a better framework for the social change.

The next remarkable contributions were made by Puspa Niyogi and Barrie M. Morrison through their extensive analyses of Bengal inscriptions. Niyogi researched on the expansion of Brahmanic settlements and Brahmanism by donations from the Gupta period onwards in each sub-division of Bengal.[54] Morrison envisaged sub-divisions of the region by plotting find-spots and issuing places of the copper plate inscriptions and by analysing their geographical distributions. He also analysed the shapes, forms and contents of copper plate inscriptions and sorted them into the four categories, and claimed the correlation of these categories with the political history and the character of governments in Bengal.[55] It is remarkable that both were conscious of sub-regional diversity within Bengal and the process of settlement expansion and regional integration, while not concerned much with the contemporary discussions around Indian Feudalism.

The studies more concerned with some aspects of rural society in early medieval Bengal and its historical transformation appeared in 1980s and 1990s, with due attention to the discussions on the early medieval historical change. In a series of articles, Chitrarekha Gupta investigated the land system and process of agrarian expansion in each period of early medieval Bengal based on the analysis of copper plate inscriptions.[56] B. D. Chattopadhyaya studied rural settlements and society of Bengal with refined frameworks in analysing copper plate inscriptions. He delineated the general settlement patterns through the analysis of geographical information in the inscriptions and pointed out the spatial and social interrelation among settlements. He also argued the supra-village social relationship of peasants in the Gupta period and its change in the Post-Gupta period, especially the rise of local magnates.[57] His insights afforded clues to the interpretation of inscriptional data in the general context of agricultural and societal expansion in the early medieval period.

Adding to those works based on the inscriptional evidences, the monograph of Kunal Chakrabarti made a quite different but fruitful approach to the formation of Bengal as a region. He envisaged the process of cultural interaction and making of regional tradition called 'Puranic Process,' in which *brāhmaṇa*s tried to incorporate local cultures through the composition of localised *Purāṇa*s, with the aim to maintain their hegemony over other social groups.[58] Though he basically followed the old paradigm of Niharranjan Ray in understanding the contemporary society of Bengal, without incorporating the results of works based on inscriptional evidences mentioned above, his overall framework on the process of region formation in Bengal, especially the hegemony and agency of *brāhmaṇa*s as a group, was valid and quite valuable in delineating their involvement in the social change in early medieval rural Bengal.

The historiography discussed above have shown the direction which the present and future studies on the historical change of early medieval South Asia should take, namely, the research on the process of agrarian expansion and political and social integration in particular regions or sub-regions. A systematic attempt in this direction, however, is yet to come for the history of early medieval Bengal. The present study also tries to answer this historiographical requirement.

Sources and their interpretations

The scarcity of sources, the inherent problem of early South Asian history, renders their strategic reading crucial for any studies, including the present one. It is all the more so for almost all the available sources, both epigraphic and textual, were written in Sanskrit, which had ceased to be the language of everyday life long before the concerned period.[59] In this section, I will discuss the types and characteristics of sources used in this book and the strategies taken for their interpretation. I start the discussion by locating our mostly Sanskrit sources in their historical context, where wider social space for Prakrit and other non-Sanskrit languages can be supposed.

Sanskrit had been used for almost all the inscriptions of Bengal from royal grants to private votive records since its first use so far confirmed in the mid-fourth-century Susuniya hill rock inscription.[60] The address of grants including rural residents and the involvement of their influential section in issuing some of the grants allude to the presence of rural population with Sanskrit literacy. The upper section of peasant householders and local literates like *kāyastha*s, who were involved in the procedures around land sale grants, belonged to this category. On the other hand, the use of non-Sanskrit terms for some border landmarks and place names in inscriptions indicates daily use of non-Sanskrit languages by local population. Because an attempt at literary employment of the Bengali language started as late as the period between 950 and 1200 AD with the use of Old Bengali for the composition of verses called *Caryāgīti* under the strong influence of Western or Śaurasenī Apabhraṁśa,[61] we have to suppose mostly non-literary condition of the local languages in the concerned period.

From those points, we can infer the presence of literate groups with access to both languages who mediated the written communication through Sanskrit and the oral one through local languages. Their mediation facilitated transmission of orders and information written in Sanskrit to the wider section of rural population illiterate of this language through oral channels. Such mediation and oral communication seem to have been presupposed by the issuers of grants and the composers of texts like the *Purāṇa*s. In the case of the grants, their continuous issue in Sanskrit endorses this conjecture. In the case of the *Purāṇa*s, the texts themselves prescribed their oral communication through recital at special occasions like *vrata*s.[62] The interpretations and explanations in vernacular languages accompanying the *Purāṇa* recital can also be guessed from the modern account.[63] We can thus assume that those Sanskrit texts contain what their composers expected rural populace to comprehend, in spite of the illiteracy of the latter. We can read some aspects of rural society in those texts, as long as we keep in our mind that the images depicted in them are the ones held by the composers and shared by the dominant section of rural society.

The sources used in the present study can be divided into the categories of inscriptions, Brahmanical texts and the other texts. Inscriptions, especially the ones pertaining to rural society and landscape, constitute the main source of the present study.[64] The most important among them are copper plate inscriptions. They are documents issued by particular authority, mainly the king, to announce the transfer of landed property or right over incomes from particular space mostly as grants to *brāhmaṇa*s or the other religious agents. The transfer is often accompanied by privileges including immunity from revenue and other charges. The documents are addressed to relevant personnel and local residents who are requested to protect the donated property or the right of donees and observe the prescribed terms. Apart from the details of donations, procedures taken on these occasions are also recorded in them. The inscriptions follow particular formats which are somehow fixed but differ according to issuing authorities.[65]

The factual matters recorded in the documents including donated tracts, donees and conditions of donations are important in themselves as precious information on some aspects of rural settlements and society like environmental condition and forms of agrarian management. Copper plate inscriptions, however, can give us more insights into the changing relation between political authority and rural settlement and the internal organisation of the latter, when their components with radical change, including changing phraseology, are read carefully.[66] It can be further claimed that the attentive reading of procedures recorded in the inscriptions and minute analysis of their formats would shed light on power relations surrounding rural society.

In early medieval Bengal, we have two types of copper plate inscriptions according to their issuing authorities, namely, land sale grants issued by the local body called *adhikaraṇa* or people related with it, and royal grants issued by kings or subordinate rulers. The majority of grants from the second quarter of the fifth century to the early seventh century belong to the first category. They were issued to announce purchases and donations of land plots by certain individuals.[67] As they minutely record procedures in which various sections of rural society were involved, we can read mutual relations of those groups and power relations surrounding them in those inscriptions.

Royal grants, of which the earliest belongs to the early sixth century, became the norm from the mid-seventh century onwards. They are royal edicts that unilaterally inform donations made by the king, sometimes petitioned by his family members or subordinates, and request protection of donated property and service to donees. They were issued to royal subordinates including officials and subordinate rulers, and local residents who were related to the donated tracts. Though some grants of the sixth and seventh centuries were issued by subordinate rulers, the issue of grants became the royal monopoly or the privilege of independent rulers from the eighth century onwards.

Royal grants are highly formalised, and references to rural society are limited to the particular sections like address, privileges conferred on donees and stipulations for cultivators. Those descriptions are stereotypical and common to almost all the grants of a particular dynasty. They may not necessarily reflect the reality at the ground level. However, the slight differences of contents, like constituents of addressees or additional privileges pertaining to particular cases, show some recognition of change and difference in each locality by the authority involved in drafting such documents. Those differences should be investigated with sensitivity to understand the conditions and changes in rural society through royal grants.

Monopolisation of the issue of grants, on the other hand, shifted the focus of copper plate inscriptions to political authorities including the king, his administrative apparatus and subordinate rulers. The royal claim of overarching control over rural society, the intention of political powers to enhance their presence in rural society and the power relation between the king and his subordinate rulers became visible in those grants. Religious authorities including *brāhmaṇa* donees and their relation with temporal powers also became conspicuous in those documents. We can discern the relation between those authorities and rural society in these inscriptions and comprehend the power relation in which the latter was located.

The other inscriptions include eulogies and votive inscriptions. The first records pious deeds of influential people like kings, subordinate rulers and highly qualified *brāhmaṇa*s with lengthy verses adoring their deeds and genealogies. Though embellished with stereotypical expressions,[68] eulogies show how those people perceived and tried to represent themselves and their past. They are especially important for tracing activities of subordinate rulers called *sāmanta*s and networking of *brāhmaṇa*s, as will be shown below. Genealogy is not limited to families, and one inscription records genealogy of a particular religious sect closely connected with temporal powers.[69]

Votive inscriptions engraved on images and the other objects of donations are rather short. Basic information contained in them include names and titles of the donors. Occasionally, they refer to genealogy, relatives and residential place of the donors, and names of the reigning kings and dates in their regnal era. As they record donations of moderate scale, a wider range of social groups is mentioned in this genre of inscriptions. Though information is limited, references to those social groups are precious and the way of their representation can show some aspects of social relations among them.

Apart from them, there is a stone inscription recording agreement by a merchant association based in rural landscape in relation to a local shrine, which shed light on activity and organisation of a particular social group.[70]

Brahmanical texts used in this research are *Purāṇa*s and *dharma* texts composed in early medieval Bengal. They are categorised as such due to the purpose of their composition to propagate particular values associated with *brāhmaṇa*s and Brahmanical traditions.

The *Purāṇa*s mainly used in this research are the *Mahābhāgavatapurāṇa*, the *Devībhāgavatapurāṇa* and the *Bṛhaddharmapurāṇa*, which were composed in the period from the 11th century to the second half of the 13th century.[71] The *Kālikāpurāṇa*, which was more associated with contemporary Kāmarūpa,[72] is also consulted for comparison. The composers of those *Purāṇa*s tried to represent themselves as highly qualified *śrotriya brāhmaṇa*s differentiated from low rank *brāhmaṇa*s called either 'nominal *brāhmaṇa*' (*brahmabandhu*) or 'fallen *brāhmaṇa*' (*patita*),[73] while the language of the texts show a strong local influence.[74] Their intention to distinguish themselves from the other social groups is also discernible in the prescription for *brāhmaṇas* to speak in Sanskrit when they are greeted by the other three *varṇas*.[75] Such tendencies indicate the correspondence between the composition of those *Purāṇas* and the making of clearer identity of *brāhmaṇa*s and settling of their highly qualified section in rural society through network buildings.[76]

We can read in those *Purāṇa*s the perception of social reality held by the *brāhmaṇa*s with their own framework. Their intention of social reorganisation and systematisation based on Brahmanical social view is also detectable in the texts. Such aspects are especially clear in Puranic festivals aiming at social cohesion and the narrative on *Varṇasaṃkara* in the *Bṛhaddharmapurāṇa*.[77]

Dharma texts mainly used in this research are *Dharmanibandha*s or digests of *dharma* composed in Bengal in the 11th and 12th centuries. They were composed by the highly qualified *brāhmaṇa*s associated with the Varman and Sena courts to explicate certain topics related to *dharma* with ample citations from the older *dharma* texts and *Purāṇas*.[78] In case of the Senas, kings themselves were involved in the composition.[79] In this early phase, *Dharmanibandha*s were mainly concerned with particular Brahmanical rituals or codes of conduct for *brāhmaṇa*s. What transpire from them are the self-perception of *brāhmaṇa*s and their connection with kingship through ritual services. Those points are connected with the establishment of Brahmanical authority, which became clear in the 12th century.[80]

The other texts include Sanskrit texts without clear intention of Brahmanical propagation, Old Bengali verses compiled as the *Caryāgīti* and foreign accounts. The most important text in the first category is the *Kṛṣiparāśara*, a Sanskrit agricultural text composed in Bengal in the mid-11th century.[81] As an intended agricultural manual, it contains descriptions of rural society. It seems to have been composed by a person belonging to local *brāhmaṇa* or other moderately literate groups residing in a rural area.[82] He constructed the intended audience of the text as cultivators cum householders with a cultural and intellectual background similar to his own. The social categories that can fit into such a construction are peasant householders from local *brāhmaṇa* and other intellectual groups like *kāyastha*s.[83] Thus the image of rural society depicted in the text can be a cognition or an idealised image shared by rural literate groups, who made up a part of local notables. On the other hand, consideration of the historical context, in which the text was composed, indicates another aspect of the composition, namely, an attempt at social reorganisation by local notables.[84]

Another genre of texts included in the first category is *kāvya*s written in Bengal. Though they were mainly composed by court poets for consumption by circle of courtiers, some works offer a glimpse of life in rural society perceived by those elites. Especially important among them are the *Subhāṣitaratnakoṣa* of Vidyākara and the *Saduktikarṇāmṛta* of Śrīdharadāsa, the anthologies of Sanskrit verses compiled in Bengal.[85] The former seems to have been compiled at some Buddhist monastery, which can be Jagaddalamahāvihāra in Varendra, about 1100 AD,[86] and the latter was compiled at the court of Lakṣmaṇasena in 1205 AD.[87] Though some verses incorporated in these anthologies are those of the earlier poets like Kālidāsa and Bāṇa, the others seem to have been composed by near contemporary poets living in Bengal.[88] The latter include many verses depicting life in rural landscape, which would give us a glimpse of the contemporary rural society.[89] The most important feature is subordinate cultivators called *pāmara*s, who never appear in the contemporary inscriptions.

Though stereotypical, those verses represent the elite cognition of rural society. The location of Buddhist monasteries in rural space and their presence as large-scale landholders point to the actual contact with rural society and the cognition based on it. A peculiar concern on reality held by the Sena court poets also gives their verses on rural society some credentials as representation.[90]

Another *kāvya* text important for the present study is the *Rāmacarita* of Sandhyākaranandin.[91] This is a work which narrates in double entendre a summarised version of the *Rāmāyaṇa* and the deeds of the Pāla king Rāmapāla and his descendants simultaneously. It was composed by Sandhyākaranandin, a court poet of Madanapāla, during the latter's reign in the mid-12th century. The narrative centres on the *Kaivarta* rebellion, which temporarily ousted the Pālas from Varendra. This text, especially with its contemporary commentary written by an anonymous author, offers a minute account of the event, which can be interpreted as a culmination of several contradictions in contemporary rural society, if we read it in the historical context constructed by the inscriptions and the other contemporary sources.

The *Caryāgīti* is the collection of verses composed in Old Bengali and considered to be the first attempt to employ this language for literary use.[92] Those verses were composed by *siddhācārya*s of Sahajiyā Buddhist sect, which belonged to a Tantric strand.[93] They are written in a cryptic language called *sandhābhāṣā*, which would convey esoteric meaning to the initiates of the sect who learned how to decode them.[94] Descriptions of daily life in contemporary rural society are often employed in those verses as metaphors.[95] Those descriptions, which were supposed to work as metaphors, must have been fully understood by the intended audience, who were prospective devotees and members of the sect living in rural space, so that we can interpret them as expressing some aspects of social reality recognised by members of sedentary society.

Foreign accounts mainly consist of the travel and geographical accounts written by Chinese Buddhist monks and Arab/Persian merchants and geographers. Their itineraries and records attest to the connection of Bengal with inter-regional trade networks and show some aspects of economic life like use of cowries as currency in the region. The account of military expedition by Muhammad Ba<u>kh</u>tiyār <u>Kh</u>aljī recorded in the *Tabakāt-i-Nāsirī*, the chronicle written by Minhāj al-Sirāj Jūzjānī, also sheds light on those phenomena at the beginning of the 13th century.[96] They are further confirmed by another account of Ibn Baṭṭūṭa, which belongs to slightly later period.[97]

The accounts of Chinese Buddhist monks also give us interesting information on some aspects of Buddhist *vihāra*s including life of monks residing there. The most relevant for the present study is the emergence of those *vihāra*s as large-scale landholders and their relation with temporal powers. The history of Buddhism by Tāranātha, which was written in Tibet around 1600 AD, is also useful for investigating the last point, as it contains legends connecting the Pāla kings with the establishment of the eminent Buddhist *mahāvihāra*s in eastern India.[98] Those accounts complement the information obtained from the inscriptions.

In addition to the textual sources, some archaeological data consisting of reports of excavations and surface explorations are used as subsidiary sources.

Structure of chapters

In the present study, the historical change of rural society of early medieval Bengal is delineated in chronological order. The concerned period is divided into four, to which one each of the main chapters is devoted. The periodisation follows the observed historical changes, so it does not necessarily agree with dynastic divisions adopted by the earlier scholars.

The third chapter covering the period between circa 400 and 550 AD deals with the social and power relations within rural society and its negotiation with the state power focused on the local body called *adhikaraṇa* in Puṇḍravardhana, North Bengal, and the form of agrarian development based on the family labour of peasant householders called *kuṭumbin*s and its inherent contradictions. It also discusses the cases in Samataṭa, a subregion of eastern Bengal which saw different contours of state formation and agrarian development.

The fourth chapter covering the period between circa 550 and 800 AD is devoted to the discussions on the changed power relations around *adhikaraṇa*, characterised by ascendancy of local notables called *mahattara*s, under the rules of emergent sub-regional kingdoms in Vaṅga, Rāḍha and Puṇḍravardhana, respectively southern, western and northern subregions, in which subordinate rulers generally called *sāmanta*s started to show their presence. It also deals with the contemporary agrarian development overcoming the earlier contradiction in these sub-regions, the state formation and agrarian expansion in the eastern sub-regions of Samataṭa, Śrīhaṭṭa and Harikela and the emergence of religious institutions as large-scale landholders.

The fifth chapter covering the period between circa 800 and 1100 AD discusses the growing contradictions in the power relations among (1) rural society which saw the stratification of its members, (2) regional kingships with their administrative apparatus which established their rules over plural sub-regions and were strengthening their control over rural society, and (3) subordinate rulers who tried to enhance their power through the negotiation with the kingship. The focus of the contention between the last two agents was religious institutions and highly qualified migrant *brāhmaṇa*s building up their networks. The agrarian development in the changed power configuration, a new phenomenon of commercialisation of rural economy and the two forms of social reorganisation attempted in this period, namely the maintenance of inner cohesion of cultivators and the organisation of groups based on occupations, are also delineated. This chapter ends with the discussion on the *Kaivarta* rebellion as the culmination of the contradictions observed in this period.

The sixth chapter covering the period between circa 1100 and 1250 AD describes the efforts towards enhanced control by the kingships, especially the Senas through the assessment of production in a currency unit, and the changed position of subordinate rulers under them. It also describes the establishment of authority of *brāhmaṇa*s both at royal courts and in rural society, the development of the earlier tendencies of social stratification and organisation of occupational groups, and the agrarian development and commercialisation of rural economy proceeding in different sub-regions. It finally discusses the progress of the forms of social reorganisation observed in the previous period under the Brahmanical hegemony, which manifested itself as the Puranic festivals with elements of social gathering and subversion of normal order and the attempted systematisation of *jāti* order discernible in the narrative of *Varṇasaṃkara*.

The seventh chapter concludes the book by reviewing the historical processes delineated through the previous chapters and providing the prospect for the change in the following period. The list of inscriptions follows it as an appendix.

Before the main discussions, geographical characters of Bengal and its sub-regions will be discussed in the second chapter as a preamble.

Notes

1 For layers of land tenures observed in modern Bengal, see Rajat Ray and Ratna Ray, 'Zamindars and Jotedars: A Study of Rural Politics in Bengal', *Modern Asian Studies*, 1975, 9(1): 81–102; Ratnalekha Ray, *Change in Bengal Agrarian Society: c1760–1850*, New Delhi: Manohar, 1979.

2 For these phenomena and their supposed history, see Nripendra Kumar Dutt, *Origin and Growth of Caste in India, vol.2: Castes in Bengal*, Calcutta: Firma KL Mukhopadhyay, 1965 (reprinted as combined volume with vol.1, 1986).

3 As an attempt to understand the development of *jāti* system in late medieval Bengal based on the *Kulagranthas*, see Ronald B. Inden, *Marriage and Rank in Bengali Culture: A History of Caste and Clan in Middle Period Bengal*, New

Delhi: Vikas Publishing House, 1976. For *Kulagranthas*, see Kumkum Chatterjee, 'Communities, Kings and Chronicles: The *Kulagranthas* of Bengal', *Studies in History, New Series*, 2005, 21(2): 173–213.

4 Tapan Raychaudhuri, *Bengal under Akbar and Jahangir: An Introductory Study in Social History*, New Delhi: Munshiram Manoharlal, 1969.

5 Pierre Bourdieu, Richard Nice (tr.), *Outline of a Theory of Practice*, Cambridge: Cambridge University Press, 1977; idem, *The Logic of Practice*, Stanford, CA: Stanford University Press, 1990.

6 Bourdieu, *Outline of a Theory of Practice*, p. 72.

7 *Ibid.*, p. 77.

8 *Ibid.*, p. 95.

9 *Ibid.*, pp. 82–83.

10 Barry Hindess and Paul Q. Hirst, *Pre-Capitalist Modes of Production*, London, Henley and Boston: Routledge and Kegan Paul, 1975, p. 13.

11 Bhakat Prasad Mazumdar, *Socio-Economic History of Northern India: 1030–1194 A.D., Calcutta*: Firma KLM, 1960, pp. 1–41, 77–124; Lallanji Gopal, *The Economic Life of Northern India: c. A.D. 700–1200*, Delhi: Motilal Banarsidass, 1965, pp. 1–31; B. N. S. Yadava, *Society and Culture in Northern India in the Twelfth Century*, Allahabad: Central Book Depot, 1973, pp. 1–111, 140–200.

12 For the historiography, see Hermann Kulke, 'Introduction: The Study of the State in Pre-modern India', in idem (ed.), *The State in India 1000–1700*, Delhi: Oxford University Press, 1995, pp. 1–47.

13 D. D. Kosambi, *An Introduction to the Study of Indian History* (Revised 2nd ed.), Bombay: Popular Prakashan, 1975, pp. 295–405.

14 R. S. Sharma, *Indian Feudalism: c. AD 300–1200*, Calcutta: Calcutta University Press, 1965.

15 Ex. R. S. Sharma, *Social Changes in Early Medieval India (circa A. D. 500–1200)*, New Delhi: People's Publishing House, 1969; B. N. S. Yadava, 'The Problem of the Emergence of Feudal Relations in Early India', in D. N. Jha (ed.), *The Feudal Order: State, Society and Ideology in Early Medieval India*, New Delhi: Manohar, 2000, pp. 249–301 (Originally Presidential Address, Ancient India Section, Indian History Congress, 41st session, 1980); Ramendra Nath Nandi, *State Formation, Agrarian Growth and Social Change in Feudal South India: c. A. D. 600–1200*, New Delhi: Manohar, 2000.

16 D. C. Sircar, *Landlordism and Tenancy in Ancient and Medieval India as Revealed by Epigraphical Records*, Lucknow: University of Lucknow, 1969, pp. 60–61; B. D. Chattopadhyaya, 'Trade and Urban Centres in Early Medieval North India', *Indian Historical Review*, 1974, 1: 203–19; idem, 'Currency in Early Bengal', *Journal of Indian History*, 1977, 55(3): 41–60; M. R. Tarafdar, 'Trade and Society in Early Medieval Bengal', *Indian Historical Review*, 1978, 4(2): 274–86; B. N. Mukherjee, 'Commerce and Money in the Western and Central Sectors of Eastern India (c. A. D. 750–1200)', *Indian Museum Bulletin*, 1982, 17: 65–83.

17 D. D. Kosambi, 'Scientific Numismatics', in idem, *Indian Numismatics*, New Delhi: Orient Longman, 1981, pp. 145–56.

18 John S. Deyell, *Living without Silver: The Monetary History of Early Medieval North India*, Delhi: Oxford University Press, 1990.

19 Ranabir Chakravarti, *Trade and Traders in Early Indian Society*, New Delhi: Manohar, 2002.

20 Harbans Mukhia, 'Was There Feudalism in Indian History?', in Kulke (ed.), *The State in India*, pp. 86–133 (originally Presidential Address, Medieval Section, Indian History Congress 40th Session, 1979).

21 *Ibid.*; Harbans Mukhia, 'Peasant Production and Medieval Indian Society', *The Journal of Peasant Studies*, 1985, 12(2–3): 228–51.
22 B. D. Chattopadhyaya, 'Introduction: The Making of Early Medieval India', in idem, *The Making of Early Medieval India*, Delhi: Oxford University Press, 1994, pp. 1–37.
23 Idem, 'State and Economy in North India: Fourth Century to Twelfth Century', in Romila Thapar (ed.), *Recent Perspectives of Early Indian History*, Bombay: Popular Prakashan, 1995, pp. 309–37.
24 R. S. Sharma, *Urban Decay in India (c.300–c.1000)*, New Delhi: Munshiram Manoharlal, 1987.
25 Idem, 'The Kali Age: A Period of Social Crisis', in S. N. Mukherjee (ed.), *India: History and Thought (Essays in Honour of A. L. Basham)*, Calcutta: Subarnarekha, 1982, pp. 186–203; B. N. S. Yadava, 'The Accounts of the Kali Age and the Social Transition from Antiquity to the Middle Ages', *Indian Historical Review*, 1979, 5(1–2): 31–63.
26 Chattopadhyaya, 'State and Economy in North India', p. 330.
27 R. S. Sharma, 'How Feudal was Indian Feudalism? (revised and updated, 1992)', in Kulke (ed.), *The State in India*, pp. 48–85; idem, *Early Medieval Indian Society: A Study in Feudalisation*, New Delhi: Orient Longman, 2001; D. N. Jha, 'Editor's Introduction', in idem (ed.), *The Feudal Order* pp. 1–58.
28 Harbans Mukhia (ed.), *The Feudalism Debate*, New Delhi: Manohar, 1999; Jha (ed.), *The Feudal Order.*
29 *The Journal of Peasant Studies*, 1985, 12(2–3) (Terence J. Byers and Harbans Mukhia (ed.), Special Issue: Feudalism and Non-European Societies); D. N. Jha (ed.), *Feudal Social Formation in Early India*, Delhi: Chanakya Publications, 1987.
30 Rajan Gurukkal, *Social Formations of Early South India*, New Delhi: Oxford University Press, 2010; Kesavan Veluthat, *The Early Medieval in South India*, New Delhi: Oxford University Press, 2009.
31 Burton Stein, 'The Segmentary State in South Indian History', in Richard G. Fox (ed.), *Realm and Region in Traditional India*, New Delhi: Vikas Publishing House, 1977, pp. 3–51; idem, *Peasant State and Society in Medieval South India*, Delhi: Oxford University Press, 1980.
32 R. Champakalakshmi, 'Peasant State and Society in Medieval South India', *The Indian Economic and Social History Review*, 1981, 18(3–4): 411–26; D. N. Jha, 'Relevance of Peasant State and Society to Pallava-Cola Times', *Indian Historical Review*, 1981–82 (1982), 8(1–2): 74–94; Kesavan Veluthat, *The Political Structure of Early Medieval South India* New Delhi: Orient Longman, 1993, pp. 250–55.
33 For the problem of African models in reference to the historical background of their creation by social anthropologists, see Bernard S. Cohn, 'African Models and Indian Histories', in Fox (ed.), *Realm and Regions in Traditional India*, pp. 90–98.
34 Burton Stein, 'The Segmentary State: Interim Reflections', in Kulke (ed.), *The State in India*, pp. 134–61.
35 James Heitzman, *Gifts of Power: Lordship in an Early Indian State*, Delhi: Oxford University Press, 1997; Cynthia Talbot, *Precolonial India in Practice: Society, Region and Identity in Medieval Andhra*, New Delhi: Oxford University Press, 2001.
36 Hermann Kulke, 'Royal Temple Policy and the Structure of Medieval Hindu Kingdom', in Anncharlott Eschmann, Hermann Kulke and Gaya Charan Tripathi (eds), *The Cult of Jagannath and the Regional Tradition of Orissa*, New Delhi: Manohar, 1978, pp. 125–37; idem, 'The Early and the Imperial Kingdom:

A Processural Model of Integrative State Formation in Early Medieval India', in idem (ed.), *The State in India*, pp. 233–62.

37 B. D. Chattopadhyaya, 'Political Process and the Structure of Polity in Early Medieval India', in idem, *The Making of Early Medieval India*, pp. 183–222 (originally Presidential Address, Ancient India Section, Indian History Congress 44th session, 1983); idem, 'Introduction: The Making of Early Medieval India'.

38 Chattopadhyaya, *The Making of Early Medieval India*, pp. 38–119.

39 Ex. Madhav Gadgil and Ramachandra Guha, *This Fissured Land: An Ecological History of India*, Delhi: Oxford University Press, 1992.

40 D. D. Kosambi, 'Living Prehistory in India', in idem, B. D. Chattopadhyaya (comp., ed., intro.), *The Oxford India Kosambi: Combined Methods in Indology and Other Writings* (2nd ed.), New Delhi: Oxford University Press, 2009, pp. 30–48.

41 Ex. Eschmann, Kulke and Tripathi (eds), *The Cult of Jagannath*; Karine Shomer, Joan L. Erdman, Deryck O. Lodrick and Lloyd I. Rudolph (eds), *The Idea of Rajasthan: Explorations in Regional Identity*, 2 vols, New Delhi: Manohar, 2001.

42 Noboru Karashima, *South Indian History and Society: Studies from Inscriptions, A.D. 850–1800*, Delhi: Oxford University Press, 1984; R. Tirumalai, *Land Grants and Agrarian Reactions in Coḷa and Pāṇḍya Times*, Madras: University of Madras, 1987; Kesavan Veluthat, 'The Structure of Land-rights and Social Stratification in Early Medieval South India', in Vijay Kumar Thakur and Asok Aounshuman (eds), *Peasants in Indian History vol. 1: Theoretical Issues and Structural Enquiries (Essays in Memory of Professor Radhakrishna Chaudhary)*, Patna: Janaki Prakashan, 1996, pp. 312–30.

43 K. Sivathamby, 'Early South Indian Society and Economy: The Tinai Concept', *Social Scientist*, 1974, 3(5): 20–37; Rajan Gurukkal, 'From Clan and Lineage to Hereditary Occupations and Caste in Early South India', *Indian Historical Review*, 1993–94 (1996), 20: 22–33.

44 Heitzman, *Gifts of Power*.

45 Talbot, *Precolonial India in Practice*.

46 Veluthat, *Political Structure*.

47 Bhairabi Prasad Sahu, 'Aspects of Rural Economy in Early Medieval Orissa', *Social Scientist*, 1993, 21(1–2): 48–68; idem, 'Agrarian Changes and the Peasantry in Early Medieval Orissa (c. A. D. 400–1100)', in Thakur and Aounshuman (eds), *Peasants in Indian History*, pp. 283–311; idem, *The Changing Gaze: Regions and the Constructions of Early India*, New Delhi: Oxford University Press, 2013.

48 Upinder Singh, *Kings, Brāhmaṇas and Temples in Orissa: An Epigraphic Study AD 300–1147*, New Delhi: Munshiram Manoharlal, 1994.

49 Nayanjot Lahiri, 'Landholding and Peasantry in the Brahmaputra Valley C. 5th–13th Centuries AD', *Journal of the Economic and Social History of Orient*, 1990, 33(2): 157–67; idem, *Pre-Ahom Assam: Studies in the Inscriptions of Assam between the Fifth and the Thirteenth Centuries AD*, New Delhi: Munshiram Manoharlal, 1991; Chitrarekha Gupta, 'Evolution of Agrarian Society in Kamarupa in Early Medieval Period', *Indian Historical Review*, 1992–93 (1996), 19(1–2): 1–20.

50 Chattopadhyaya, *The Making of Early Medieval India*, pp. 38–119; idem, *Aspects of Rural Settlements and Rural Society in Early Medieval India*, Calcutta: K P Bagchi, 1990, pp. 70–92.

51 Nandini Sinha Kapur, *State Formation in Rajasthan: Mewar during the Seventh-Fifteenth Centuries*, New Delhi: Manohar, 2002.

52 Ex. R. C. Majumdar (ed.), *History of Bengal vol. 1: Hindu Period*, Dacca: The University of Dacca, 1943, pp. 557–622; idem, *History of Ancient Bengal*, Calcutta: Bharadwaj & Co., 1971, pp. 413–505.
53 Niharranjan Ray, J. W. Hood (tr.), *History of Bengali People (Ancient Period)*, Calcutta: Orient Longman, 1994 (Originally published in Bengali as *Bāṅgālīr Itihās: Ādi Parva*).
54 Puspa Niyogi, *Brahmanic Settlements in Different Subdivisions of Ancient Bengal*, Calcutta: Indian Studies: Past and Present, 1967.
55 Barrie M. Morrison, *Political Centers and Cultural Regions in Early Bengal*, Tucson: University of Arizona Press, 1970.
56 Chitrarekha Gupta, 'Early Brahmanic Settlement in Bengal – Pre Pala Period', in B. N. Mukherjee, D. R. Das, S. S. Biswas and S. P. Singh (eds), *Sri Dinesacandrika: Studies in Indology (Shri D. C. Sircar Festschrift)*, Delhi: Sundeep Prakashan, 1983, pp. 215–24; idem, '"Khila-kṣetra" in Early Bengal Inscriptions', in Debala Mitra and Gouriswar Bhattacharya (eds), *Studies in Art and Archaeology of Bihar and Bengal: Nalīnikānta Śatavārṣikī: Dr. N. K. Bhattasali Centenary Volume (1888–1988)*, Delhi: Sri Satguru Publications, 1989, pp. 271–83; idem, 'Land-measurement and Land-revenue System in Bengal under Senas', in Debala Mitra (ed.), *Explorations in Art and Archaeology of South Asia: Essays Dedicated to N. G. Majumdar*, Calcutta: Directorate of Archaeology and Museums, 1996, pp. 573–93.
57 Chattopadhyaya, *Aspects of Rural Settlements*, pp. 18–69.
58 Kunal Chakrabarti, *Religious Process: the Purāṇas and the Making of a Regional Tradition*, New Delhi: Oxford University Press, 2001.
59 Madhav M. Deshpande, *Sociolinguistic Attitudes in India: An Historical Reconstruction*, Ann Arbor: Karoma Publishers, 1979, pp. 11–13.
60 *SI* 1, pp. 351–52.
61 Suniti Kumar Chatterji, *The Origin and Development of the Bengali Language*, New Delhi: Rupa & Co., 1993 (reprint), pp. 116, 123.
62 Chakrabarti, *Religious Process*, pp. 236–37.
63 Ludo Rocher, *The Purāṇas*, Wiesbaden: Otto Harrassowitz, 1986, pp. 57–59.
64 For the list of those inscriptions, see Appendix.
65 For forms and contents of copper plate inscriptions, see Bahadur Chand Chhabra, 'Diplomatic of Sanskrit Copper-plate Grants', *The Indian Archives*, 1951, 5(1): 1–20; D. C. Sircar, *Indian Epigraphy*, Delhi: Motilal Banarsidass, 1965, pp. 120–50.
66 Chattopadhyaya, *Aspects of Rural Settlements*, p. 36.
67 For the contents and characters of land sale grants, see Toshio Yamazaki, 'Some Aspects of Land-Sale Inscriptions in Fifth and Sixth Century Bengal', *Acta Asiatica*, 1982, 43: 17–36.
68 This is connected with the emergence of 'Sanskrit Cosmopolis' proposed by Sheldon Pollock, where Sanskrit functioned as the sole language of political expression and particular rhetoric was shared by elites of a wide geographical stretch. Sheldon Pollock, 'The Sanskrit Cosmopolis, 300–1300: Transculturation, Vernacularization, and the Question of Ideology', in Jan E. M. Houben (ed.), *Ideology and Status of Sanskrit: Contributions to the History of the Sanskrit Language*, Leiden: E. J. Brill, 1996, pp. 197–247; idem, *The Language of the Gods in the World of Men: Sanskrit, Culture, and Power in Premodern India*, Delhi: Permanent Black, 2007.
69 D. C. Sircar, 'Bāṇgaḍh Stone Inscription of the Time of Nayapāla', *Journal of Ancient Indian History*, 1973–74 (1975), 7: 135–58; idem, 'Mūrtiśiva's Bangarh

Prasasti of the Time of Nayapāla', *Journal of Ancient Indian History*, 1980–82 (1983), 13: 34–56.

70 Ryosuke Furui, 'Merchant Groups in Early Medieval Bengal: With Special Reference to the Rajbhita Stone Inscription of the Time of Mahīpāla I, Year 33', *Bulletin of the School of Oriental and African Studies*, 2013, 26(3): 391–412.

71 R. C. Hazra, *Studies in the Upapurāṇas*, vol. 2, Calcutta: Sanskrit College, 1963, p. 282 (*Mahābhāgavata*); pp. 346–47 (*Devībhāgavata*); p. 461 (*Bṛhaddharma*).

72 *Ibid*., pp. 232, 245.

73 Haraprasad Shastri (ed.), *Bṛhaddharmapurāṇam* (2nd ed.), Varanasi: Krishnadas Academy, 1974, 3. 14. 75 (*patita, brahmabandhu*); *Śrīmaddevībhāgavatapurāṇam*, Delhi: Nag Publishers, 1986 (reprint), 1. 3. 21 (*dvijabandhu*).

74 For the minute analysis of the language used in those *Purāṇas*, see Hazra, *Studies in Upapurāṇas*, vol. 2, pp. 278–79 (*Mahābhāgavata*); pp. 353–55 (*Devībhāgavata*); pp. 449–50 (*Bṛhaddharma*).

75 *Bṛhaddharma*, 3. 1. 26–28ab.

76 For this process, see Ryosuke Furui, '*Brāhmaṇas* in Early Medieval Bengal: Construction of their Identity, Networks and Authority', *Indian Historical Review*, 2013, 40(2): 223–48.

77 Infra Chapter 6.

78 For the authors of *Dharmanibandhas*, see P. V. Kane, *History of Dharmaśāstra*, vol. 1, pt. 2 (2nd ed.), Poona: Bhandarkar Oriental Research Institute, 1975, pp. 639–52 (*Bhaṭṭa* Bhavadeva), pp. 699–713 (Jīmūtavāhana), pp. 727–30 (Aniruddha), pp. 622–39 (Halāyudha).

79 *Ibid*., pp. 730–35.

80 Furui, '*Brāhmaṇas* in Early Medieval Bengal', pp. 236–44.

81 Girija Prasanna Majumdar and Sures Chandra Banerji (ed., tr.), *Kṛṣi-Parāśara*, Calcutta: The Asiatic Society, 2001 (reprint). For its provenance, see *ibid*., introduction, pp. xix–xxi. For its date, see Lallanji Gopal, 'The Date of the Krsi-Parasara', *Journal of Indian History*, 1973, 50: 151–68.

82 Ryosuke Furui, 'The Rural World of an Agricultural Text: A Study on the *Kṛṣiparāśara*', *Studies in History, New Series*, 2005, 21(2): 153–60.

83 *Ibid*., pp. 160–63.

84 *Ibid*., pp. 164–69.

85 D. D. Kosambi and V. V. Gokhale (eds), *The Subhāṣitaratnakoṣa*, Cambridge, MA: Harvard University Press, 1957; Sures Chandra Banerji (ed.), *Sadukti-Karṇāmṛta of Śrīdharadāsa*, Calcutta: Firma KLM, 1965.

86 *Subhāṣitaratnakoṣa*, introduction, pp. xxxi–xxxix.

87 *Saduktikarṇāmṛta*, introduction, p. viii.

88 For authors and their identities, see *Subhāṣitaratnakoṣa*, introduction, pp. lxxi–cvi; *Saduktikarṇāmṛta*, author index, pp. 1–28.

89 For such verses in the *Subhāṣitaratnakoṣa*, see Daniel H. H. Ingalls, 'A Sanskrit Poetry of Village and Field: Yogeśvara and His Fellow Poets', *Journal of the American Oriental Society*, 1954, 74: 119–31.

90 For 'realism' in the Sena court poetry, see Jesse Ross Knutson, *Into the Twilight of Sanskrit Court Poetry: The Sena Salon of Bengal and Beyond*, Berkeley, Los Angeles and London: University of California Press, 2014, especially Chapters 3 and 4.

91 Haraprasad Sastri (ed.), Radhagovinda Basak (rev., tr., notes), *Rāmacaritam of Sandhyākaranandin*, Calcutta: The Asiatic Society, 1969.

92 Chatterji, *Origin and Development*, p. 116.

93 For their philosophy and practices, see Shashibhushan Dasgupta, *Obscure Religious Cults* (3rd ed.), Calcutta: Firma KLM, 1969, pp. 35–50, 87–109.

94 Atindra Mojumdar (ed., tr.), *The Caryāpadas* (2nd ed.), Calcutta: Nayaprokash, 1973, pp. 93–102.
95 *Ibid.*, pp. 10–26.
96 H. G. Raverty, (tr.), *Tabakat-i-Nasiri: A General History of the Muhammadan Dynasties of Asia Including Hindustan from A. H. 194 (810 A. D.) to A. H. 658 (1260 A. D.) and the Irruption of the Infidel Mughals in Islam*, 2 vols, Calcutta: The Asiatic Society, 1995 (reprint), pp. 548–76.
97 Mahdi Husain (tr., comm.), *The Reḥla of Ibn Baṭṭūṭa: India, Maldive Islands and Ceylon*, Baroda: Oriental Institute, 1953.
98 Debiprasad Chattopadhyaya (ed.), Lama Chimpa and Alaka Chattopadhyaya (trs), *Tāranātha's History of Buddhism in India*, Delhi: Motilal Banarsidass, 1990.

2

GEOGRAPHICAL DELINEATION

Bengal as a region

Bengal geographically consists of alluvial plains and deltas surrounded clockwise from the west to the south by Chotanagpur and Rajmahal hills, Meghalaya plateau, Tripura and Chittagong hill tracts and the Bay of Bengal. As a region with some of the biggest rivers and the largest delta of the world, variations in its geographical features mostly come from the activity of those rivers and their tributaries. Such variations can entail as many as 24 geographical sub-regions on the Bangladesh side alone.[1] According to Spate, this 'Bengal Delta' can be subdivided into five sub-regions, namely, (1) the sub-montane terai (Duars), (2) the northern paradeltas (the Ganga-Brahmaputra Doab) and the Barind, (3) the eastern margins: the Surma valley and the plains along the Meghna and the Chittagong coast, (4) the western margins: largely lateritic piedmont plain between the Hooghly and the Peninsular Block, and the Contai coastal plain and (5) the Ganga Delta proper between Hooghly-Bhagirathi, Padma-Meghna and the sea, including moribund, mature and active sections.[2] If we add Madhupur tract, Haor basin in central Sylhet and Tippera surface,[3] they more or less cover the geographical features relevant to our research. From those features, we can deem Bengal to be a geographical region constituted by deltas and relatively higher old alluvium surrounding them, which are further surrounded by hill tracts. This geographical entity is open to the outside through coastal strips at its south-west and south-east corners, Ganga and Brahmaputra valleys in the Garo-Rajmahal gap to the north-west, Bay of Bengal to the south and several passes going through the hill tracts.

The most prominent geographical feature in this low land is its river system constituted by the Ganga, the Brahmaputra, and their tributaries and distributaries. Those rivers divide the land into four major divisions,[4] while their watercourses function as channels of communication. The courses of those rivers have never been stable and changed through the ages, due to tectonic activities and diluvial land formations. Though the precise delineation of the old courses is difficult, a few important changes can be noted from the historical sources. First, the southward channel of the Ganga, roughly represented by the present Bhagirathi-Hooghly and a moribund channel called the Adiganga, was a strong current and the main course of the river.[5] Another channel, the Padma flowing south-eastward, was narrower and became the main course only in the early 14th century, though its importance had already been recognised in the 12th century.[6] In addition, the Ganga after passing Rajmahal hill took the course cutting across the present Malda district through the river Karindri and lower course of the Mahananda, and passed the eastern side of the ruins of Gaur.[7] Second, the Tista, which flows through Jalpaiguri and Rangpur into the Jamuna, the present main course of the Brahmaputra, had been flowing through the Purnabhava, Atrai and Karatoya until floods of 1787 changed its course.[8] Accordingly, the Karatoya, which is a shallow and narrow stream at present, was a mighty river as attested by a verse in the *Āryāsaptaśatī* of Govardhana which calls it ever flooded,[9] and formed the eastern border of northern sub-region of Puṇḍravardhana with Kāmarūpa, western Assam.[10] Third, the Brahmaputra, of which the Jamuna is currently the main channel, flowed through the south-eastward channel now called the Old Brahmaputra before 1787.[11]

The recognition of this geographical stretch as a region is a relatively new phenomenon. Bengali language, one of the most important elements of the regional identity, established its distinction from Assamese, another descendant of Eastern Magadhan, only in the 15th century.[12] Bengal had never constituted a political unit before it was made a province (*sūbah*) under the Mughals, though it had already been deemed a distinct territory by the mid-14th century.[13] The use of the term 'Bengala' to denote the affinity of whole the region was rather initiated by foreign travellers with much uncertainty from the 13th century onwards.[14] Bhattacharyya even speculates that the term Bengala gained currency through these foreigners and the whole of Bengal came to be known as Bangala/Bengala/Bengal in consequence.[15] Before that, Vaṅgāla, an antecedent of the term, denoted south-eastern part differentiated from Vaṅga,[16] a sub-region of Bengal. As Kunal Chakrabarti shows, the making of the cultural formation which would be considered typical of Bengal may trace its inception from the 'Puranic Process' in the early medieval period, with local *brāhmaṇa*s as its agents.[17] But its culmination through vernacular literary culture and new religious movements were witnessed in the early modern period,[18] and the making of Bengali identity is rather a process intensified through the complicated experience of colonial modernity, in relation to the wider notion of nationhood.[19]

The imposition of Bengal as a region onto this geographical stretch in the early medieval period is a retrospective exercise, and the historical subregions like Vaṅga had more relevance then, as Barrie M. Morrison discusses on the basis of inscriptional evidence.[20] The validity of the region as an object of research, however, can still be claimed for the following reasons. First, the sub-regions of Bengal had interacted with each other in many respects. Though political powers were based on each of them and none could integrate all, some could extend their influence beyond one sub-region, resulting in the wider geographical areas connoted by the terms like Gauḍa and Vaṅga. As the rivers demarcating the sub-regions also worked as channels of communication, non-political interactions like trade may have also been prevalent among them. Second, those sub-regions shared some historical phenomena and changes, which will be discussed in the following chapters. It is therefore still valid to use Bengal as a geographical framework as long as we keep its arbitrariness in our mind.

Sub-regions of Bengal and their characters

While dealing with Bengal as a region, it is still necessary to consider its early history in terms of its constituent sub-regions. The four of them, Puṇḍravardhana or Varendra, Rāḍha, Vaṅga and Samataṭa, constituted the main parts of the region. Courses of the rivers Bhagirathi, Ganga-Padma, Karatoya and Meghna demarcated them from each other (Map 2.1). Their borders and extent were not fixed and prone to change by geological events or political situations. Nevertheless, we can still delineate those sub-regions and their characters with some historical implications in general terms for our discussion.

Puṇḍra or Puṇḍravardhana, to be called Varendra in the later period, is located in northern Bengal. In geographical terms, it mainly consists of Barind tract, one of the several Pleistocene terraces within the Bengal Basin,[21] and the mostly old floodplains of the rivers Padma, Mahananda, Purnabhava, Atrai, Tista and Karatoya.[22] The Padma and Karatoya demarcate it from the other sub-regions, as inferable from a description in the *Rāmacarita* of Sandhyākaranandin written in the mid-12th century.[23]

It was administratively organised as Puṇḍravardhanabhukti under the Guptas[24] and remained as such until the end of the Pāla rule. When the jurisdiction of Pauṇḍravardhanabhukti, a unit covering Samataṭa and Śrīhaṭṭa established under the Candras in the early tenth century, extended to Vaṅga and Puṇḍravardhana under the Sena rule,[25] this sub-region was reorganised as Varendrī belonging to the *bhukti*. The city of Puṇḍravardhana or Puṇḍranagara, identified with the present site of Mahasthangarh near Bogra, had been the centre of the sub-region from the third century BC onwards, as indicated by the Mahasthan stone inscription.[26] Koṭivarṣa, represented by the site of Bangarh near Gangarampur in South Dinajpur district, was the secondary centre whose jurisdiction covered a *viṣaya* of its namesake.

Adjacent to Aṅga and Videha, respectively the eastern and northern parts of present Bihar, Puṇḍravardhana received the cultural inflow from the Mid-Ganga heartland earlier than any other sub-regions. The aforementioned inscription from Mahasthan is one evidence. It is the oldest inscription in

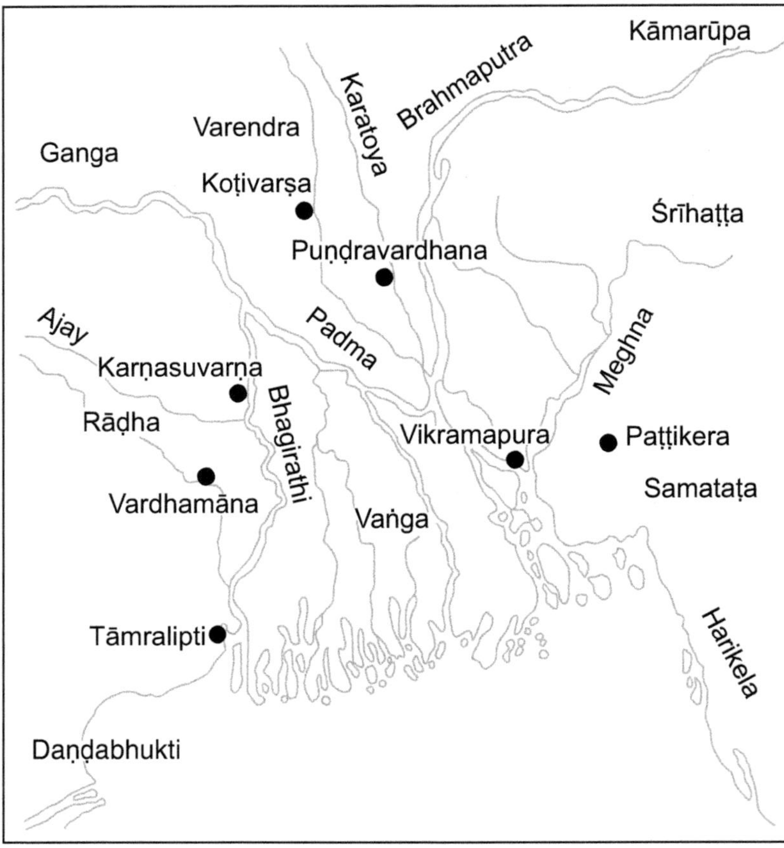

Map 2.1 Bengal and its sub-regions

Source: (Reproduced from Fig 4.1 in Ryosuke Furui, 'Variegated Adaptations: State Formation in Bengal from the Fifth to the Seventh Century' (rev.), in Karashima Noboru and Hirosue Masashi (eds), *State Formation and Social Integration in Pre-modern South and Southeast Asia: A Comparative Study of Asian Society*, Tokyo: The Toyo Bunko, 2017, p. 75.

Bengal, written in Brāhmī script assignable to the third century BC, and it attests to the existence of urban settlement in this early period and its interaction with the sedentary agrarian society. It also reveals the political authority of the Mauryas or the other Magadhan dynasties over this sub-region with Puḍanagala (Puṇḍranagara) as its administrative centre.

The political connection of the sub-region and the powers in Magadha continued in the later period. As Puṇḍravardhanabhukti, it remained under the Gupta rule from the second quarter of the fifth century to the middle of the sixth century. It had been the core territory of the Guptas until the end of their rule. Conversely, the Pālas, who originated from Varendra according to Sandhyākaranandin,[27] extended their control to Magadha region and held the latter as their stronghold until the end of their rule.[28] Thus during the concerned period, 'the political relations of' Puṇḍravardhana 'with the territories lying further up the Gangetic plain were much closer than its relations with the other sub-regions of the Delta', and this sub-region 'might be characterized as a buffer zone between the North Indian dynastic territories and the dynastic territories of the kingdoms centred further down the Ganges-Padma Rivers.'[29]

Rāḍha is located in western Bengal. It consists of lateritic old alluvium flanked by the coalesced fans of the rivers Ajay, Damodar, Rupnarayan and Kasai, and the moribund and mature deltas along the Bhagirathi-Hooghly.[30] It is bordered by the Rajmahal and Chotanagpur hill tracts to the west. The Ganga and Bhagirathi demarcate it from the other sub-regions. This sub-region is further divided into Dakṣiṇa (South) and Uttara (North) Rāḍha with the Ajay River as their border.[31] The former was called Suhma in the earlier period, and Tāmralipti, a famous ancient sea port identified with present Tamluk, was sometimes incorporated into it.[32]

The administrative unit corresponding to this sub-region was Vardhamānabhukti, of which the earliest appearance was in the Mallasarul copper plate inscription of the mid-sixth century.[33] This *bhukti* was also divided into the *maṇḍala*s of Uttara Rāḍha and Dakṣiṇa Rāḍha, as suggested by the reference to the former in the Naihati grant of Vallālasena.[34] During the reign of Lakṣmaṇasena, the northern part of this sub-region was reorganised as Kaṅkagrāmabhukti incorporating Uttara Rāḍha.[35] The southernmost part of this sub-region was known as Daṇḍabhukti in the copper plate inscriptions of the sixth and seventh centuries.[36] This *bhukti* corresponds to the southern part of former Medinipur district of West Bengal and Baleswar district of Orissa.[37] It was incorporated into Vardhamānabhukti as Daṇḍabhuktimaṇḍala by the second half of the tenth century, as attested by the copper plate inscriptions of the Kāmboja king Nayapāla.[38]

The sub-region of Rāḍha witnessed the earliest occurrences of proto-historic settlements with evidence of agriculture, characterised by the Black and Red Ware. This is indicated by the archaeological sites scattered all over the area, especially along the Ajay and Damodar valleys.[39] The growth of sedentary agrarian society and the early state formation accompanying it in the subsequent period are indicated by the Susuniya rock inscription, which attests to the existence of a kingdom on the Damodar valley in the mid-fourth century.[40] Expansion of rural settlements towards the western fringe of the sub-region is also suggested by the Mallasarul grant, which records land purchase and donation in the forest area locatable within present Galsi subdivision of Bardhaman district.[41] Both processes were gradual and continuous. The state formation in the western fringe continued under the Pāla rule as inferable from the names of *sāmanta*s listed in the *Rāmacarita*[42] and even until the 17th century in its westernmost part, where a number of tribal kingdoms beginning with Mallabhūm emerged.[43] The agrarian expansion, especially the peasantisation of lower class members of the society, proceeded from the 16th century onwards in tandem with the new religious tendencies represented by the Neo-Vaiṣṇava movement of Caitanya and the popular cults of Dharma and other minor deities.[44]

In the coastal area of Rāḍha, the urban settlements with implications of thriving seaborne trade rose up at the estuary of Ganga and its distributaries from the third century BC onwards, according to the available archaeological data.[45] The period between the second century BC and the second century AD marked the most active phase of those settlements,[46] while the lively trade activity in Tāmralipti was witnessed by Chinese monks who visited there from the beginning of the fifth century to the end of the seventh century.[47]

Another place name associated with this sub-region is Gauḍa. At first, it consisted of areas corresponding to the present district of Murushidabad and the southernmost part of Malda district, with Karṇasuvarṇa, represented by the ruin of Rajbadidanga, as its centre.[48] Thus it mostly overlapped with Uttara Rāḍha. As the political power based in this region extended its sway over the other sub-regions of Bengal and some parts of present Bihar and Orissa, especially after the rise of Śaśāṅka at the beginning of the seventh century, the term Gauḍa attained wider connotation denoting the western part of Bengal or eastern India in general.[49]

Towards the end of the Pāla rule, the area around present Gaur in Malda district, namely the northernmost part of Gauḍa demarcated from Puṇḍravardhana by the old course of the Ganga, became the centre of western and northern Bengal following the establishment of the city of Rāmāvatī by Rāmapāla in the late 11th century. Lakṣmaṇasena also constructed Lakṣmaṇāvatī in the same area and it continued to be the political centre of Bengal in the early phase of the Turkish rule.[50]

Vaṅga occupied the southern part of Bengal. It is constituted by the Ganga Delta proper, which can be further subdivided into the moribund, mature and active,[51] or the moribund, mature, immature and active deltas.[52] The area surrounded by the rivers Bhagirathi, Padma and Meghna constitutes the main part of this sub-region, while its boundaries oscillated through the ages.[53] In the early medieval period, it included the present districts of Dhaka, Manikganj, Narayanganj and Munshiganj of Bangladesh apart from its core part mentioned above.

There is no administrative division denoting whole the sub-region. In the sixth century, a unit called Navyāvakāśikā covered the southern part of present Dhaka division, especially the area around Gopalganj district.[54] In the period between the tenth and 13th centuries, this sub-region first came under the jurisdiction of Pauṇḍrabhukti in the reigns of the Candra and Varman kings, and then of Pauṇḍravardhanabhukti under the Senas.[55] In this period, Vaṅga was subdivided into Vikramapurabhāga, Nāvya and the other smaller units.[56] Vikramapurabhāga, named after the political centre of those three dynasties and identified with the area around Rampal in Munshiganj district, may have corresponded to the central part of present Dhaka division, as it included parts of the present districts of Dhaka, Shariatpur and Gopalganj according to the distribution of the inscriptions mentioning this administrative unit.[57] Nāvya, meaning navigable, included at least the area around Gaurnadi *upazila* of Barishal district. It may have denoted present Barishal subdivision, 'which abounds in creeks and rivers and is navigable (*nāvya*) all through the year.'[58]

The *Baudhāyanadharmasūtra*, datable to the period from the beginning of the third century to the middle of the second century BC,[59] mentions Vaṅga together with Puṇḍra as one of the groups of people living outside Āryāvarta: a visit to their lands would necessitate purification rites.[60] It indicates a certain level of social organisation reached by local population, at which they could be perceived as ethnic groups with some territoriality. The growth of such an organisation may be attested by the description of the conquest of Vaṅga people in Kālidāsa's *Raghuvaṃśa* and the Mehrauli iron pillar inscription of king Candra, both assignable to the beginning of the fifth century.[61] In the latter, king Candra is said to have defeated allied enemies in Vaṅga.[62] This sub-region witnessed the rise of an independent kingdom in the mid-sixth century. Between the tenth and 13th centuries, it was under the successive rules of the Candras, the Varmans and the Senas. As the core territory of those dynasties, Vaṅga became the most important sub-region of Bengal, just as Vikramapura, its centre, can be considered the capital of the Bengal Delta.[63]

Vaṅgāla is a place name which has an intricate relation with Vaṅga through the history. Originally, it denoted the coastal regions of south-eastern Bengal.[64] It may have overlapped with Nāvya subdivision of Vaṅga, and this possibility is confirmed by an inscription in which Vaṅgālavaḍā is mentioned as a locality within Rāmasiddhipāṭaka of Nāvya.[65] In this light, D. C. Sircar's interpretation of the term as the combination of Vaṅga and Prakrit suffix *-āla* in the sense of a notable district belonging to Vaṅga seems to be correct.[66] This area may have been co-extensive with Candradvīpa, which was the stronghold of the Candras before the expansion of their rule to the whole of Vaṅga.[67] Following the expansion of their dominion to the wider areas of south-eastern Bengal, the connotation of Vaṅgāla also expanded to the extent that all the parts of eastern Bengal came to be denoted by the name, especially in the inscriptions discovered outside Bengal.[68]

Samataṭa is on the eastern fringe of Bengal, flanked by sub-regions of Śrīhaṭṭa and Harikela to its north and south respectively. It is a low land constituted by a delta and floodplains made by the activities of the rivers Surma and Meghna, and Tippera surface, with low hill range of Lalmai on its eastern end.[69] The area around Lalmai hill was known as Paṭṭikera from the eighth century onwards, according to the inscriptions and coins discovered there.[70] Śrīhaṭṭa corresponds to the depression called Haor basin in present Sylhet division,[71] and Harikela to the coastal area of present Chittagong district.[72] The Meghna constitutes the border between Samataṭa and Vaṅga,[73] while the borders demarcating the former from Śrīhaṭṭa and Harikela are not so clear.

It is assumed from the third plate of Vainyagupta containing the grant of Nāthacandra that a part of this sub-region was divided into *maṇḍala*s of four cardinal directions as early as in the early fifth century.[74] An administrative unit denoting whole the sub-region appeared only in the 11th century. In the inscriptions of the Candras, this sub-region was under the jurisdiction of Samataṭamaṇḍala of Pauṇḍrabhukti.[75] Śrīhaṭṭa also constituted a *maṇḍala* of Pauṇḍravardhanabhukti under the Candras.[76] Harikelamaṇḍala, on the other hand, is mentioned in the Chittagong plate of Kāntideva, which belongs to the first half of the ninth century.[77]

The king of Samataṭa is mentioned in the Allahabad pillar inscription of Samudragupta, belonging to the mid-fourth century, as one of the peripheral kings (*pratyantanṛpati*) who acknowledged his suzerainty.[78] The continued presence of local kings with hierarchy of rulers under them from the early fifth century to the early sixth century are attested by the Gunaighar grant and the third plate of Vainyagupta, respectively dated years 188 and 184 GE, and by a grant of Nāthacandra dated year 91 GE copied on the latter.[79] The following three centuries saw the development of such political powers in both Samataṭa and the neighbouring sub-regions with more complicated relations among rulers.[80] From the tenth century to the third decade of the 13th century, Samataṭa was ruled by the kings based in Vaṅga like the Candras and the Senas.

One characteristic of those sub-regions was their marginality with much room for reclamation. It is attested by the cases of large-scale grants to the enormous number of *brāhmaṇa*s or religious organisation in forest tracts.[81] They indicate the ongoing process of reclamation and agricultural expansion, which would further intensify in the following period.[82]

There are two sections of Bengal which were not included in any of the sub-regions discussed above. They are the area to the south of the Ganga reaching the Sundarbans contained in the present districts of Kushtia, Jessore and Khulna, and another stretching from the northern part of Dhaka district up to the Meghalaya plateau, which includes the Madhupur jungle tract and the low marshy lands lying at the foot of the western part of the plateau. As Morrison discussed, no copper plate inscriptions were recovered from those areas.[83] Those tracts, which were covered with dense forest and marshy lands, may not have been reclaimed and settled by sedentary agrarian society whose landscape would be recorded in the textual sources. However, the copper plate inscriptions of the 13th century pertaining to the lower Bhagirathi estuary including Sundarbans and present Gazipur district close to Madhupur tract mark the beginning of agrarian expansion towards the aforementioned areas to be pursued intensively in the following period.[84]

The sub-regions of Bengal have interacted with each other, while keeping their own characters. One form of interaction was the political expansion of sub-regional powers. The Pālas, who originated from Puṇḍravardhana, extended their rule to Rāḍha in the early phase. The Candras, who started as the rulers of Candradvīpa, expanded their territory to the whole of Vaṅga and then to Samataṭa. The Senas, who migrated from Karṇāta and became the subordinate rulers in Rāḍha, spread their power over Vaṅga and Puṇḍravardhana, with their centre shifted to Vikramapura in the former.

The traffics among those sub-regions can be assumed as they were mostly located in the low land without obstacles and rivers dividing them were navigable. The itinerary of Xuanzang, a Chinese Buddhist monk who visited South Asia in the first half of the seventh century, offers a glimpse of such traffics. According to his biography written by Huili and Yancong, he travelled from Kajaṅgala, present Rajmahal, to Puṇḍravardhana. From there he proceeded to Karṇasuvarṇa, then to Samataṭa and finally to Tāmralipti.[85] On the other hand, the account of Xuanzang edited by Bianji mentions the route from Puṇḍravardhana to Kāmarūpa, then going south to Samataṭa. It goes from there to Tāmralipti and then to Karṇasuvarṇa.[86] From these descriptions, the following routes can be reconstructed as a whole: (1) running from Kajaṅgala to Kāmarūpa through Puṇḍravardhana, (2) from Puṇḍravardhana to Tāmralipti via Karṇasuvarṇa, probably along the Bhagirathi, (3) connecting Kāmarūpa with south-east Bengal, probably through the Brahmaputra, (4) between Karṇasuvarṇa and Samataṭa, probably along the Padma channel and (5) passing through coastal Bengal, which linked south-east and south-west Bengal. In terms of the sub-regions discussed above, the fifth route is the one which connects Samataṭa and Dakṣiṇa Rāḍha or Suhma through lower Vaṅga. From those routes, we can assume that the traffics most likely connected the sub-regions for trade, as the Chinese monk could not have travelled off the beaten tracks. Such traffics went beyond Bengal and connected it with the neighbouring regions.

Interactions with neighbouring regions

Bengal is connected with neighbouring regions by several channels. They consist of land and river routes provided by the rivers beginning with the Ganga and the Brahmaputra, narrow passes cutting across hill ranges and coastlines on the shore of the Bay of Bengal. Sea lane of the bay also facilitated the traffics not only to neighbouring regions but also to and from regions further to the south and southeast.

The historical regions of Bihar, especially Magadha, had close relation with Bengal as discussed above. The main route of traffics connecting them went along the Ganga passing by Rajamahal hill. Faxian and Xuanzang took this route when they respectively travelled from Campā to Tāmralipti or to Puṇḍravardhana via Kajaṅgala.[87] The former may have taken the route along the Ganga and the Bhagirathi. It indicates the existence of a trade route along the Ganga and its channel through which the regions in Bihar and far up the stream were connected with the sea ports in coastal Rāḍha and with the larger seaborne trade network. This route may have been taken by the merchant Udayamāna and his brothers who were said to have been to Tāmralipti from Ayodhyā for trade, according to the Dudhpani rock inscription of the eighth century.[88] Apart from trade, this route facilitated the military expedition from both sides. Śaśāṅka and Dharmapāla, both of whom got involved in the struggles over the control of Kānyakubja, may have taken this route in view of their centres located on the banks of the Bhagirathi and the Ganga. Vijayasena also made naval expedition along the Ganga, according to his Deopara inscription.[89] On the other hand, political powers based in Bihar and upper Ganga basin like the Later Guptas, Harṣavardhana and Yaśovarman used this route for their expeditions to Bengal.

Another route which connected both regions passed through Chotanagpur hills and the forest of Hazaribagh. Yijing took this route on his way from Tāmralipti to Rājagṛha and on his way back from Nālandā to Tāmralipti.[90] On his way, he joined a party consisting of several hundred merchants and around 20 residential monks of Nālandā.[91] It shows that this route was frequented by merchants for their trade, while facilitating the network connecting Buddhist *vihāra*s in Magadha and Rāḍha.[92] Yijing also narrates his encounter with a band of brigands on this hilly route.[93] He was robbed again on his way back.[94] The presence of brigands on this route is an indicator of the brisk trade and traffic, without which there may not have been any incentive for them to waylay travellers.

The political relation between powers in Bengal and Assam was rather hostile. In the seventh century, Śaśāṅka, the king of Gauḍa, and Bhauma-Varman kings of Kāmarūpa had protracted conflicts culminating in the temporary occupation of Karṇasuvarṇa by Bhāskaravarman.[95] The Mlecchas or the Śālastambhas, who ruled Kāmarūpa from the middle of the seventh century to the end of the ninth century, fought with the Pālas of Bengal.[96] The Pālas of Kāmarūpa were at war with both the Pālas and the Candras of Bengal from the tenth century to the 12th century.[97]

The main route for the traffics between Bengal and Assam might have been the one which crossed the river Karatoya and connected the cities of Puṇḍravardhana and Prāgjyotiṣa. The account of Xuanzang mentions this route as discussed above. Bhāskaravarman seems to have taken the same route to join Harṣavardhana's camp at Kajaṅgala with his fleet and elephants.[98] Military engagements between the powers in Kāmarūpa and those in Gauḍa and Puṇḍravardhana may have also been made through this route. It is further connected with Tibet. According to the *Tabakāt-i-Nāsirī* of Minhāj al-Sirāj Jūzjānī, Muhammad Bakhtiyār Khaljī made his ill-fated expedition to Tibet by the route from Lakhnawatī through Kāmrūd

(Kāmarūpa).[99] He also mentions horses sold in Lakhnawatī imported by the mountainous passes through Kāmrūd and Tirhut.[100]

Another route connected Kāmarūpa with Samataṭa, as mentioned in the account of Xuanzang.[101] It probably went along the Brahmaputra. In his *Kitāb al-Masālik wa'l-Mamālik* (*The Book of Roads and Kingdoms*) written by 846–7 AD, Ibn Khurdādhbih, a Persian geographer living in Iraq, stated that aloes-wood was brought from Kāmarūn (Kāmarūpa) through 15 to 20 days' river journey to Samundar, a port in coastal Bengal.[102] Though the location of Samundar is yet to see the agreement of scholars,[103] the river mentioned in the account is identifiable with the Meghna. Accordingly, Samundar can be located around its estuary. Ibn Baṭṭūṭa, who visited Bengal in 1346 AD, travelled from Chittagong to mountains of Kāmarū (Kāmarūpa), probably indicating the area around the present Sylhet, and went back to Sonargaon through the river identifiable with the Meghna.[104] He saw innumerable boats commuting on this river.[105] Those descriptions show the thriving condition of trade activities between Kāmarūpa and Samataṭa from, at the latest, the ninth century onwards. Apart from it, there might have been another route which went through the valleys cutting across hilly tracts of present Assam and Meghalaya.

The interaction between Bengal and Orissa was facilitated by the route along coastline of the present Baleswar district of the latter. This border land was controlled by the political powers which ruled Daṇḍabhukti like Gopacandra, Śaśāṅka and the Kāmbojas.[106] Śaśāṅka extended his political influence through this route to Koṅgoda, the coastal area of southern Orissa, as attested by the acknowledgement of his suzerainty by Mādhavarāja, the Śailodbhava king.[107] This route was taken by the kings of Orissa like the Eastern Gangas[108] and possibly of South India like Rājendra Coḷa and Western Cālkyan Vikramāditya VI for their military expedition to Bengal.[109]

The interaction between both regions through this route was not limited to military expeditions. Xuanzang took this way to travel from Tāmralipti to Oḍra, then to Koṅgoda and Kaliṅga subsequently.[110] This route may have been frequented by the other travellers like traders.

The last region to mention for its interaction with Bengal is Burma. Both were connected by several routes cutting across mountainous ranges, which further lead to the south-western frontier of China.[111] The coastline of Chittagong may also have contributed to this interaction.

The interaction between the political authorities on both sides is indicated by the probable use of Burma era in the metal vase inscription of Devātideva belonging to the eighth-century Harikela[112] and the appearance of a peculiar name ending Eva, characteristic of Burmese names, in the Mainamati plate of Dadhieva, dated year 1141 SE (1220 AD).[113] It is also possible that the Candras of south-eastern Bengal were associated with the Candras of Arakan.[114] All those cases suggest a close connection between Arakan on the one hand and Samataṭa and Harikela on the other hand.

Their economic connection is attested by a series of small silver coins with high purity found in south-eastern Bengal, which circulated mainly in Harikela and Samataṭa from the seventh to the tenth century.[115] Early specimens of those Harikela coins are typologically and metrologically related to the coins of the Candra dynasty of Arakan and might have been acceptable in Arakan region too.[116] Circulation of such currencies may be prompted by the close economic relation between those regions. The connection between Samataṭa and kingdoms located in the coastal areas of present Burma, like Śrīkṣetra, Kāmalāṅkā and Dvāravatī, is alluded to by the account and biography of Xuanzang, though he did not visit these places and depended his statements on hearsay.[117]

The Bay of Bengal, demarcating the southern limit, facilitated the far-reaching seaborne connections of Bengal with wider areas. It connected the region with coastal Orissa and Burma through littoral routes on the one hand and with the vast trade network covering the ports of South India, Siṃhala and Southeast Asia on the other hand.

The most important port from the earliest time to the eighth century was Tāmralipti in Suhma or Dakṣiṇa Rāḍha. As mentioned above, this port was connected with regions of the Mid-Ganga plain through the Ganga and its Bhagirathi channel. The thriving condition of the trade between Tāmralipti and Siṃhala in the fifth century, which further reached islands of Southeast Asia, is attested by the account of Faxian. He embarked on a large merchant-vessel at the port and went to Siṃhala.[118] After staying there for two years, he took another merchant-vessel for Java.[119] The continuance of the route connecting Tāmralipti and Siṃhala in the seventh century is confirmed by the reference to it in the biography of Xuanzang.[120] It is also shown by the itinerary of the Vietnamese monk Dachengdeng.[121] His encounter with pirates in the estuary nearby the port may also indicate brisk trade attracting them.

Another route connecting Tāmralipti with Southeast Asia linked it with Kedah, the port city facing Malacca strait on the side of Sumatra Island, via Andaman-Nicobar Islands. Yijing travelled by this route and left a minute account of transactions between the merchants and the islanders.[122]

While Tāmralipti still held its position as a prominent port, another port involved with the trade network in the Bay of Bengal emerged in the seventh century. Two of the Chinese monks, whose biographies were compiled by Yijing, disembarked at Harikela. Among them, Tanguang travelled from China to Harikela through Southeast Asia, though his itinerary was not minutely recorded.[123] Another monk Wuxing travelled from Kedah to Nāgapattinam, Siṃhala and then Harikela.[124] The itinerary of the latter shows the involvement of Harikela with the commercial network connecting eastern Bengal with South India and Siṃhala. Though it is unclear which port is meant by Harikela in those accounts, the rising importance of this sub-region for trade network in the Bay of Bengal is confirmed by the account of Sulaymān and other Arab merchants compiled in 851 AD, in which they called the bay 'Sea of Harkandh.'[125] The shift of trade centres to eastern Bengal is also attested by the mention of Samundar on the Meghna estuary as a trade centre in another account of Persian geographer,[126] or references to Sudkāwāṅ (Chittagong) and Sunurkāwāṅ (Sonargaon) by Ibn Baṭṭūṭa.[127] The latter travelled to Chittagong from the Maldives and embarked on the ship to Java at Sonargaon in 1346 AD.[128]

What should be noted is that this network, with which Bengal was involved, was linked to the wider commercial networks which covered the whole of Indian Ocean connecting the Mediterranean world, West Asia and Ethiopia to the west, and Southeast Asia and southern China to the east. The early trade contact with the 'West' is recorded in the Greek classical accounts, especially in the works like the *Periplus Maris Erythraei* belonging to the second half of the first century.[129] The last text shows that the port called Ganges at the estuary of the Ganga, which could be located somewhere in the coastal West Bengal, was well-embedded in the trade network which connected the Roman Empire with South Asia.[130] This trade network was maintained by various participants like Persian merchants even after the decline of the Roman Empire.[131] The active role played by the Arab merchants in this trade network in the later period is obvious in their accounts cited above. The trade network with Southeast Asia and southern China is also attested by the accounts of Chinese Buddhist monks.

In the discussion made above, I tried to make a general delineation of the geographical character of Bengal, its sub-regions and their interactions with each other and with the neighbouring regions. With them, I would like to proceed to my main discussions.

Notes

1 Haroun Er Rashid, *Geography of Bangladesh* (2nd ed.), Dhaka: University Press Ltd., 1991, pp. 9–42.
2 O. H. K. Spate and A. T. A. Learmonth, *India and Pakistan: A General and Regional Geography* (3rd ed.), Delhi: Munshiram Manoharlal, 1984 (reprint), pp. 572–73.
3 For these features, see Rashid *Geography of Bangladesh*, pp. 22–26, 28–29.
4 Amitabha Bhattacharyya, *Historical Geography of Ancient and Early Medieval Bengal*, Calcutta: Sanskrit Pustak Bhandar, 1977, pp. 11–13.
5 *Ibid.*, pp. 14–20.
6 *Ibid.*, pp. 23–25.
7 D. C. Sircar, *Studies in the Geography of Ancient and Medieval India* (2nd ed.), Delhi: Motilal Banarsidass, 1971, pp. 120–21.
8 Bhattacharyya, *Historical Geography*, pp. 28–29.
9 Durga Prasad, Kasinath Pandurang Parab and Vasudev Laxman Sastri Pansikar (eds), *The Āryāsaptaśatī of Govardhanāchārya with the Commentary Vyaṅgyārtha-dīpanā of Ananta=Paṇḍit*, Delhi: Nag Publishers, 1988, v. 224.
10 Bhattacharyya, *Historical Geography*, pp. 29–30.
11 Rashid, *Geography of Bangladesh*, pp. 18–19 and p. 23, Map 2.4. Bhattacharyya claims the present Jamuna to be the principal course of Brahmaputra in the

early medieval period, on the basis of Yaśodhara's mention of Vaṅga to the east of the Lauhitya in his commentary on the *Kāmasūtra*. Bhattacharyya, *Historical Geography*, pp. 32–33. As he admits, it is highly doubtful whether Yaśodhara had a clear conception of the geographical denotation of Vaṅga. As the zone of subsidence between Barind and Madhupur tract can be a long term cause of the shift of the Brahmaputra, it is more plausible that the river had flowed through its old course before the shift.

12 More precisely, North Bengal dialect got differentiated from Assamese. Suniti Kumar Chatterji, *The Origin and Development of the Bengali Language*, New Delhi: Rupa & Co., 1993 (reprint), pp. 98–99.

13 Richard M. Eaton, *The Rise of Islam and the Bengal Frontier, 1204–1760*, Berkeley: University of California Press, 1993, p. 41. For the conquest of Bengal by the Mughals and the consolidation of their rule, see *ibid*., pp. 137–58.

14 Bhattacharyya, *Historical Geography*, pp. 2–5.

15 *Ibid*., p. 5. In the original text Bangala is mistakenly put as Bengala.

16 *Ibid*., pp. 62–65.

17 Kunal Chakrabarti, *Religious Process: The Purāṇas and the Making of a Regional Tradition*, New Delhi: Oxford University Press, 2001.

18 *Ibid*., pp. 297–305. For the social change in early modern Bengal delineated from vernacular *Maṅgalakābya*s, see David L. Curley, *Poetry and History: Bengali Mangal-kābya and Social Change in Precolonial Bengal*, New Delhi: Chronicle Books, 2008.

19 Swarupa Gupta, *Notions of Nationhood in Bengal: Perspectives on Samaj, c. 1867–1905*, Leiden: Brill, 2009.

20 Barrie M. Morrison, 'Region and Subregion in Pre-Muslim Bengal', in David Kopf (ed.), *Bengal Regional Identity*, East Lansing, MI: Asian Studies Center, Michigan State University, 1969, pp. 3–19.

21 Rashid, *Geography of Bangladesh*, pp. 13–15.

22 *Ibid*., pp. 12–13, 15–20.

23 Haraprasad Sastri (ed.), Radhagovinda Basak (rev., tr., notes), *Rāmacaritam of Sandhyākaranandin*, Calcutta: The Asiatic Society, 1969, 3. 10.

24 Bhattacharyya, *Historical Geography*, pp. 73–75.

25 Puṇḍravardhanabhukti and Pauṇḍravardhanabhukti are differentiated in the Pāla and Candra inscriptions. This point is overlooked by Bhattacharyya. *Ibid*., pp. 75–78.

26 *SI* 1, pp. 79–80.

27 *Rāmacarita*, 1. 38.

28 Abdul Momin Chowdhury, *Dynastic History of Bengal (c. 750–1200 A. D.)*, Dacca: The Asiatic Society of Pakistan, 1967, pp. 133–35.

29 Barrie M. Morrison, *Political Centers and Cultural Regions in Early Bengal*, Tucson: University of Arizona Press, 1970, p. 152.

30 Spate and Learmonth, *India and Pakistan*, pp. 586–88.

31 Bhattacharyya, *Historical Geography*, p. 51.

32 *Ibid*., pp. 45–48.

33 *SI* 1, pp. 372–77.

34 Bhattacharyya, *Historical Geography*, p. 81.

35 *Ibid*., pp. 82–83.

36 Jayarampur CPI of the time of Gopacandra, year 1, *IO*, pp. 174–79; Antla CPI of Śubhakīrtti, year 8, *SI* 2, pp. 24–25; Antla CPI of Somadatta, year 19, *ibid*., pp. 26–27.

37 Bhattacharyya, *Historical Geography*, pp. 81–82.

38 *Ibid.*, p. 82; N. G. Majumdar, 'Irda Copper-plate of the Kamboja King Nayapaladeva', *Epigraphia Indica*, 1933–34 (1984), 22: 150–59; K. V. Ramesh and S. Subramonia Iyer, 'Kalanda Copper Plate Charter of Nayapāladeva', *Epigraphia Indica*, 1975–76 (1989), 41: 199–205.
39 Arun K. Nag, 'Spatial Analysis of Pre- and Proto-Historic Sites in Ajay-Damodar Valley', in B. M. Pande and B. D. Chattopadhyaya (eds), *Archaeology and History: Essays in Memory of Shri A. Ghosh*, Delhi: Agam Prakashan, 1987, pp. 265–80; Dilip K. Chakrabarti, Gautam Sengupta, R. K. Chattopadhyay and Nayanjot Lahiri, 'Balck-and-Red Ware Settlements in West Bengal', *South Asian Studies*, 1993, 9: 123–35.
40 *SI* 1, pp. 351–52.
41 Chitrarekha Gupta, 'Bengal Art and Bengal Inscriptions: An Approach Towards Co-relation – A Case Study with Punchra: A Village in the Vardhaman District, West Bengal', *Journal of Bengal Art*, 2002, 7: 86–87.
42 *Ibid.*, p. 87.
43 Hitesranjan Sanyal, 'Mallabhum', in Surajit Sinha (ed.), *Tribal Polities and State Systems in Pre-Colonial Eastern and North-Eastern India*, Calcutta: K P Bagchi, 1987, pp. 73–142.
44 Jawhar Sircar, *The Construction of the Hindu Identity in Medieval Western Bengal?: The Role of Popular Cults*, Kolkata: Institute of Development Studies, 2005.
45 Gautam Sengupta, 'Archaeology of Coastal Bengal', in Himanshu Prabha Ray and Jean-François Salles (eds), *Tradition and Archaeology: Early Maritime Contact in the Indian Ocean*, New Delhi: Manohar, 1996, pp. 115–28.
46 *Ibid.*, p. 120.
47 *Ibid.*, p. 124.
48 Sircar, *Studies in Geography*, pp. 121–22.
49 *Ibid.*, pp. 122–28.
50 A. B. M. Husain, 'History, Society and Culture', in A. B. M. Husain, M. Harunur Rashid, Abdul Momin Chowdhury and Abu H. Imamuddin (eds), *Gawr-Lakhnawati*, Dhaka: Asiatic Society of Bangladesh, 1997, pp. 9–18.
51 Spate and Learmonth, *India and Pakistan*, p. 588.
52 Rashid, *Geography of Bangladesh*, pp. 29–34.
53 For somewhat inconclusive explanation on this issue, see Bhattacharyya, *Historical Geography*, pp. 56–62.
54 *Ibid.*, pp. 78–79. Bhattacharyya overlooked the fact that Navyāvakāśikā is mentioned as the highest administrative unit in the inscriptions from Kotalipada area.
55 Pauṇḍrabhukti and Pauṇḍravardhanabhukti are differentiated in the Candra and Varman inscriptions. This point is also overlooked by Bhattacharyya. *Ibid.*, pp. 75–77.
56 *Ibid.*, pp. 60–62.
57 Idilpur CPI of Viśvarūpasena, year 3(?), *IB*, pp. 118–31; D. C. Sircar, 'Madanapada Plate of Visvarupasena', *Epigraphia Indica*, 1959–60 (1987), 33: 315–26; Madhyapada CPI of Viśvarūpasena, years 13 and 14, *IB*, pp. 140–48.
58 Bhattacharyya, *Historical Geography*, p. 61.
59 Patrick Olivelle (ed., note, tr.), *Dharmasūtras: The Law Codes of Āpastamba, Gautama. Baudhāyana, and Vasiṣṭha*, Delhi: Motilal Banarsidass, 2000, p. 10.
60 *Baudhāyanadharmasūtra*, 1. 2. 14, in *ibid.*, p. 198.
61 C. R. Devadhar (ed.), *Raghuvaṃśa of Kālidāsa*, Delhi: Motilal Banarsidass, 1985, 4. 36; *SI* 1, pp. 283–85. There is a controversy over the identity of this king. For several theories on it, see Ashvini Agrawal, *Rise and Fall of Imperial Guptas*, Delhi: Motilal Banarsidass, 1989, pp. 177–85.

62 *SI* 1, p. 283, l. 1.
63 Morrison, *Political Centers*, pp. 152–53.
64 Bhattacharyya, *Historical Geography*, pp. 62–63.
65 Madhyapada CPI of Viśvarūpasena, year 13 and 14, *IB*, p. 146, ll. 42–43.
66 Sircar, *Studies in Geography*, p. 140.
67 *Ibid.*, p. 133.
68 Bhattacharyya, *Historical Geography*, pp. 62–63.
69 Rashid, *Geography of Bangladesh*, pp. 28–29, 36.
70 Bhattacharyya, *Historical Geography*, pp. 70–71.
71 Rashid, *Geography of Bangladesh*, pp. 24–26.
72 Bhattacharyya, *Historical Geography*, pp. 69–70.
73 *Ibid.*, p. 67.
74 The grant of Nāthacandra, dated year 91 GE, mentions Pūrva- and Dakṣiṇamaṇḍala. Ryosuke Furui, 'Ājīvikas, Maṇibhadra and Early History of Eastern Bengal: A New Copperplate Inscription of Vainyagupta and its Implications', *Journal of the Royal Asiatic Society*, 2016, 26(4): 674.
75 Mainamati CPIs of Laḍahacandra, year 6, nos1 and 2, *EDEP*, p. 73, l. 36, p. 75, l. 8; Mainamati CPI of Govindacandra, *ibid.*, p. 80, l. 35.
76 Paschimbhag CPI of Śrīcandra, year 5, *ibid.*, pp. 63–69.
77 R. C. Majumdar, 'Chittagong Copper-plate of Kantideva', *Epigraphia Indica*, 1941–42 (1985), 26: 317, l. 16.
78 *SI* 1, p. 265, l. 22.
79 *Ibid.*, pp. 340–45; Furui, 'Ājīvikas'.
80 Ryosuke Furui, 'Agrarian Expansion and Local Power Relation in the Seventh and Eighth Century Eastern Bengal: A Study on Copper Plate Inscriptions', in Ratnabali Chatterjee (ed.), *Urbanity and Economy: The Pre Modern Dynamics in Eastern India*, Kolkata: Setu Prakashani, 2013, pp. 103–6.
81 *Ibid.*, pp. 97–100.
82 For the agricultural expansion and Islamisation in East Bengal, see Eaton, *Rise of Islam*, especially pp. 194–227.
83 Morrison, 'Region and Subregion in Pre-Muslim Bengal', p. 5.
84 Infra Chapter 6.
85 Kiyoyoshi Utsunomiya (ed.), *Daitou Daijionji Sanzouhoushi Den Oyobi Koui Sakuin*, Kyoto: Houyu Shoten, 1979, fasc. 4, pp. 2–4, Li Rongxi (tr.), *A Biography of the Tripiṭaka Master of the Great Ci'en Monastery of the Great Tang Dynasty: Translated from the Chinese of Śramaṇa Huili and Shi Yancong (Taishō, Volume 50, Number 2053)*, Berkeley: Numata Center for Buddhist Translation and Research, 1995, pp. 109–10.
86 Kyoto Teikoku Daigaku Bunka Daigaku (ed.), *Daitou Saiiki Ki*, Tokyo: Tosho Kankoukai, 1972 (reprint), fasc. 10, pp. 8–9, 12–14, Li Rongxi (tr.), *The Great Tang Dynasty Record of the Western Regions: Translated(sic.) by the Tripiṭaka-Master Xuanzang under Imperial Order Composed by Śramaṇa Bianji of the Great Zongchi Monastery (Taisho, Volume 51, Number 2087)*, Berkeley: Numata Center for Buddhist Translation and Research, 1996, pp. 297–99, 301–3.
87 Kazutoshi Nagasawa, (ed., tr., annot.), *Hokkenden Yakuchu Kaisetsu: Hokusou-bon, Nansou-bon, Kourai Daizoukyou-bon, Ishiyamadera-bon Yonshu Eiin To Sono Hikaku Kenkyu*, Tokyo: Yuzankaku, 1996, p. 108, Li Rongxi (tr.), 'The Journey of the Eminent Monk Faxian: Translated from the Chinese of Faxian (Taishō Volume 51, Number 2085)', in *Lives of Great Monks and Nuns (BDK English Tripiṭaka 76-III, IV, V, VI, VII)*, Berkeley: Numata Center for Buddhist Translation and Research, 2002, p. 203; *Daitou Daijionji*, fasc. 4, pp. 1–3, Li, *Biography of the Tripiṭaka Master*, pp. 107–9.

88 F. Kielhorn, 'Dudhpani Rock Inscription of Udayamana', *Epigraphia Indica*, 1894 (1984), 2: 343–47.
89 Chowdhury, *Dynastic History of Bengal*, p. 223; *IB*, p. 47, ll. 20–21.
90 Kiroku Adachi (ed., tr., annot.), *Daitou Saiiki Guhou Kousou Den*, Tokyo: Iwanami Shoten, 1942, pp. 139–40, I-Ching, Latika Lahiri (tr.), *Chinese Monks in India: Biography of Eminent Monks Who Went to the Western World in Search of the Law During the Great T'ang Dynasty*, Delhi: Motilal Banarsidass, 1986, pp. 79–80.
91 *Ibid.*
92 For the networks of Buddhist monasteries, see Infra Chapter 4.
93 Adachi, *Daitou*, pp. 139–40, I-Ching, Lahiri, *Chinese Monks*, pp. 79–80.
94 Adachi, *Daitou*, p. 140, I-Ching, Lahiri, *Chinese Monks*, pp. 82–83.
95 D. C. Sircar, 'Political History', in H. K. Barpujari (ed.), *The Comprehensive History of Assam vol. 1: Ancient Period*, Guwahati: Publication Board Assam, 1990, pp. 108–9, 114–17.
96 *Ibid.*, p. 138.
97 *Ibid.*, pp. 144, 147, 161–65.
98 *Daitou Daijionji*, fasc. 5, p. 5, Li, *Biography of the Tripiṭaka Master*, p. 142.
99 H. G. Raverty (tr.), *Tabakat-i-Nasiri: A General History of the Muhammadan Dynasties of Asia Including Hindustan from A. H. 194 (810 A. D.) to A. H. 658 (1260 A. D.) and the Irruption of the Infidel Mughals in Islam*, vol. 1, Calcutta: The Asiatic Society, 1995 (reprint), pp. 560–72.
100 *Ibid.*, pp. 567–68.
101 *Daitou Saiiki Ki*, fasc. 10, p. 12, Li, *Great Tang Dynasty Record*, p. 301.
102 *Al-Masālik wa'l-Mamālik*, XIII, in S. Maqbul Ahmad (tr.), *Arabic Classical Accounts of India and China*, Shimla: Indian Institute of Advanced Study, 1989, p. 5.
103 For these opinions, see Shahnaj Husne Jahan, 'Samandar: An Important Centre for Maritime Activities in Bengal', *Journal of Bengal Art*, 2000, 5: 223–43. Her opinion mainly based on the geographical and satellite data is not convincing either.
104 Mahdi Husain, (tr., comm.), *The Reḥla of Ibn Baṭṭūṭa: India, Maldive Islands and Ceylon*, Baroda: Oriental Institute, 1953, pp. 237–38, 241.
105 *Ibid.*, p. 241.
106 Jayarampur CPI of the time of Gopacandra, year 1, *IO*, pp. 174–79; Antla CPIs of Śubhakīrtti, year 8 and of Somadatta, year 19, *SI* 2, pp. 24–27; Majumdar, 'Irda Copper-plate', pp. 150–59; Ramesh et al., 'Kalanda Copper Plate', pp. 199–205.
107 E. Hultzsch, 'Plates of the Time of Sasankaraja; Gupta-Samvat 300', *Epigraphia Indica*, 1900–01 (1981), 6: 144, ll. 1–3.
108 Chowdhury, *Dynastic History of Bengal*, pp. 127–28.
109 Bhattacharyya, *Historical Geography*, p. 105.
110 *Daitou Daijionji*, fasc. 4, pp. 4–5, Li, *Biography of the Tripiṭaka Master*, pp. 110–11.
111 Himanshu Bhusan Sarkar, 'Bengal and Her Overland Routes in India and Beyond', *Journal of the Asiatic Society*, 1974, 16: 104–14.
112 Gouriswar Bhattacharya, 'A Preliminary Report on the Inscribed Metal Vase from the National Museum of Bangladesh', in Debala Mitra (ed.), *Explorations in Art and Archaeology of South Asia: Essays Dedicated to N. G. Majumdar*, Calcutta: Directorate of Archaeology and Museums, 1996, pp. 237–47.
113 Dinesh Chandra Bhattacharyya, 'The Maināmati Copper-plate of Raṇavaṅkamalla Harikāladeva (1141 Śaka)', *The Indian Historical Quarterly*, 1933, 9(1): 282–89.

114 Chowdhury, *Dynastic History of Bengal*, pp. 162–65.
115 B. N. Mukherjee, 'A Survey of the Samataṭa and Harikela Coinages', *Journal of Bengal Art*, 2003, 8: 199–212.
116 *Ibid.*, pp. 203, 205.
117 *Daitou Saiiki Ki*, fasc. 10, p. 13, Li, *Great Tang Dynasty Record*, p. 302; *Daitou Daijionji*, fasc. 4, p. 4, Li, *Biography of the Tripiṭaka Master*, p. 110.
118 Nagasawa, *Hokkenden*, pp. 108–9, Li, 'Journey of the Eminent Monk Faxien', p. 203.
119 Nagasawa, *Hokkenden*, pp. 118, 121, Li, 'Journey of the Eminent Monk Faxien', pp. 210–11.
120 *Daitou Daijionji*, fasc. 4, p. 4, Li, *Biography of the Tripiṭaka Master*, pp. 110–11.
121 Adachi, *Daitou*, p. 78, I-Ching, Lahiri, *Chinese Monks*, p. 41.
122 Adachi, *Daitou*, p. 139, I-Ching, Lahiri, *Chinese Monks*, pp. 78–79.
123 Adachi, *Daitou*, p. 123, I-Ching, Lahiri, *Chinese Monks*, p. 70. Lahiri misunderstood this portion to mean that Tanguang first arrived at western India.
124 Adachi, *Daitou*, p. 174, I-Ching, Lahiri, *Chinese Monks*, pp. 94–95.
125 *Akhbār Al-Ṣīn wa'l-Hind* ('An Account of China and India') in Maqbul Ahmad, *Arabic Classical Accounts*, pp. 34–35, 38.
126 *Al-Masālik wa'l-Mamālik* in *ibid.*, p. 5.
127 Husain, *Reḥla of Ibn Baṭṭūṭa*, pp. 235–36, 241.
128 *Ibid.*, Introduction, pp. lxix–lxx.
129 Lionel Casson (ed., tr., intro., comm.), *The Periplus Maris Erythraei*, Princeton, NJ: Princeton University Press, 1989, pp. 89, 91.
130 *Ibid.*, 63, p. 47; Bhattacharyya, *Historical Geography*, pp. 36–40.
131 Sachindra Kumar Maity, *Economic Life in Northern India in the Gupta Period (Cir. A. D. 300–550)* (2nd ed.), Delhi: Motilal Banarsidass, 1970, pp. 175–81.

3

RURAL SOCIETY AND INNER CONTENTIONS

c. 400–550 AD

In spite of the archaeological data attesting to the presence of sedentary agrarian society in the earlier period, it was only from the early fifth century onwards that some aspects of the rural society in Bengal got accessible for minute scrutiny, thanks to the commencement of the issue of copper plate inscriptions under the Gupta administration.

The beginning of the Gupta rule over Bengal is not clear. The reference to Candravarman as one of the kings annihilated by Samudragupta in the Allahabad pillar inscription may indicate his annexation of western Bengal,[1] if the former was identical with *mahārāja* Candravarman of the Susuniya rock inscription.[2] On the other hand, the reference to the conquest of Vaṅga by king Candra, who could be identified as Candragupta II, in the Meharauli iron pillar inscription may point to the further expansion of the Gupta rule towards the coastal area of Bengal.[3] What was certain was that the Gupta rule of Puṇḍravardhana had been established by the time of Kumāragupta I in the first half of the fifth century. Since then, the Guptas had kept hold of it until the end of their rule in the mid-sixth century. Meanwhile, Samataṭa saw the state formation under the rulers subordinate to the Guptas from the fourth century onwards, culminating in the semi-independent power of Vainyagupta in the early sixth century.

The two sub-regions witnessed the different forms of agrarian development and rural social relations, discernible in the two distinctive groups of copper plate inscriptions. On rural society of Puṇḍravardhana, the land sale grants issued by local bodies called *adhikaraṇa* shed light. They minutely record procedures related to land sale and donation, which are characterised by the involvement of individuals and social groups with their own interests and stakes in each locality. In spite of the limited context of land sale and donation, we can detect in these procedures some aspects of social relations surrounding rural society, including collaboration, domination and subordination, negotiation, and possible conflict over authority or even clash of interests. These aspects were also related to the forms of agrarian management and development, and their inherent contradiction. The royal grants of Vainyagupta, on the other hand, tell us of different power relations and agrarian development in a peripheral kingdom of Samataṭa. In this chapter, I will first discuss some aspects of rural society and agrarian development in Puṇḍravardhana, and then the situation in Samataṭa in comparison.

Cases in Puṇḍravardhana: characters of land and tenure

The cases of land sale and donation in this period pertained to Puṇḍravardhana. So far 12 copper plates, including one from the present Monghyr area of Bihar, are known to have recorded these cases. The basic pattern of procedures recorded in the documents is as follows: an organisation called *adhikaraṇa* is approached by individual or collective petitioners. The petitioners ask it to give them land plots with tenure called *akṣayanīvī* or *nīvīdharma* against the payment of money counted in *dīnāra*s and *rūpaka*s, units of gold and silver currencies used under the Gupta rule,[4] for donation to a *brāhmaṇa* or other religious agents, or for their own subsistence in case the petitioners themselves are *brāhmaṇa*s. The *adhikaraṇa* refers this petition to *pustapāla*s (record keepers) and the latter verify its conformity to the local custom and assure its validity. With their verification, the *adhikaraṇa* gives, or asks residents of the locality to measure, divide and give, the land to the petitioners. Then the latter give it to the donee. The *adhikaraṇa* asks present and future administrators and residents to protect the donated land.

As indicated by this basic pattern, purchase of land plots and their donation to religious agents by individual or collective petitioners were enacted through these procedures. The analysis of these procedures and their participants would give us insights into the social relation among the latter. The comprehension of social relation and context would in turn make us understand the meaning of this transaction and the pattern of agrarian relation and development which enabled and necessitated it. Before the analysis, however, some clarifications on the character of land plots transferred in these procedures and the tenure of their enjoyment are required.

In almost all the cases, the transferred land plots are called *khilakṣetra*. Following Sachindra Kumar Maity, Chitrarekha Gupta interprets it as cultivable fallow on the basis of a verse in the *Nāradasmṛti* which says that the land uncultivated for three years is fallow while uncultivated for one year is half fallow (*ardhakhila*).[5] Toshio Yamazaki, on the other hand, considers it to be uncultivated land.[6] He based his opinion on the description of the land plots as 'uncultivated' (*aprahata*) in some inscriptions and their location at the outskirts of the village. He also criticises Maity and interprets the concerned phrase in the *Nāradasmṛti* to mean that the land uncultivated for three years is the same as uncultivated waste.[7] His view is shared by Barrie M. Morrison who interprets it as waste land.[8] Some of the descriptions in the copper plate inscriptions in this period surely support Yamazaki's view. In the Baigram plate of year 128 GE and the Nandapur plate of year 169 GE, *khilakṣetra* is prefixed by the term *ādyastamba*, which seems to mean 'covered with original shrubs'.[9] In case of the Damodarpur plates of years 124 and 224 GE, it is prefixed by 'uncultivated' (*aprahata*).[10] However, the location of the land at the outskirts of a village does not necessarily indicate its character as uncultivated waste, as it can rather indicate nucleation of settlements in which both cultivated and uncultivated land plots are located on the periphery.[11] The border demarcation of a plot in the Jagadishpur plate shows that *khilakṣetra* could exist side by side with the land plot and pond belonging to individuals.[12] As for the verse in the *Nāradasmṛti*, Yamazaki's interpretation is correct as far as the verse itself is concerned, for its latter half runs 'the land wasted for five years is the same as forest.'[13] However, the preceding verses, which concern the right of landowner (*kṣetrika*) over the land abandoned by him and cultivated by another, treat the land as *khila*, by prescribing that the original owner can get its ownership back only after giving the cultivator *khilopacāra*, that is, paying him for attending *khila* land.[14] From these points, we may conclude that *khilakṣetra* in this period includes both uncultivated waste land and cultivable fallow without clear differentiation. This situation may be explained by the precarious condition of cultivation in which fallow land abandoned of cultivation was the same as uncultivated waste. A case of land donated to Śvetavarāhasvāmin in the Damodarpur plates of the time of Budhagupta and year 224 GE alludes to such a condition. In the first inscription, the temple of Śvetavarāhasvāmin was established beside (*samīpya*) the land formerly donated to the deity. However, the temple of the same deity is said to be 'in the forest of this locality' in the second plate, after more than 50 years.[15] It means that the donated land reverted to forest within a few decades after its abandonment.

Apart from *khilakṣetra* to be converted to cultivated tract, another category of land is mentioned in some cases. It is homestead land generally called *vāstu*, which is given for accommodating house or garden in donations to religious institutions. In the Baigram plate, two plots of raised homestead land (*sthalavāstu*) are given for house and garden.[16] In the Jagadishpur plate of year 128 GE, one land plot was given nearby a temple of the Sun for the purpose of flower garden and house.[17] Similarly, a plot of homestead land was given for house and garden of a Jain *vihāra* in the Paharpur plate of year 159 GE.[18] In the case of the Damodarpur plate of the reign of Budhagupta without date, the donation of land plots was made for providing homestead land of two temples and two small storehouses attached to them.[19] It is notable that *vāstu* fetches the same price as *khilakṣetra* in these cases and that the custom pertaining to land sales in the Baigram and Jagadishpur plates mentions only the latter, assuming that the former is included in the same category.[20] Thus *vāstu* in these cases was waste land unsuitable for paddy cultivation and donated to be converted to either homestead land or a garden.

The size of the donated plot is measured by units called *kulyavāpa*, *droṇavāpa* and *āḍhavāpa*. One *kulyavāpa* is equated with eight *droṇavāpa*s and one *droṇavāpa* equals four *āḍhavāpa*s, according to the descriptions in the Paharpur plate.[21] Etymologically, these units can denote area of land required for sowing particular amount of seeds, namely, *kulya*, *droṇa* and *āḍhaka*. However, the measurement in this period was made by a linear standard called *nala*, of which several kinds are mentioned in the inscriptions.[22] The scholars have made several attempts to ascertain the size of land denoted by these units through the etymological interpretation, the estimation of the length of *nala* and the comparison with modern units used in the area. Among them, Morrison's approach through the consideration of a specific function for which a particular measure of land was donated is important, though his conclusion that 1 *kulyavāpa* approximately equals 3 *bigha*s is untenable as it is based on his wrong assumption that a *brāhmaṇa* donee would live only with his immediate family and that 3 *kulyavāpa*s corresponds to a self-sufficient family holding in the present, namely 7 to 10 *bigha*s.[23]

Among the cases in this period, seven are donations to individual *brāhmaṇa*s. In the three cases, each *brāhmaṇa* acquired 1 *kulyavāpa*. It is clearly mentioned in the Damodarpur plate of year 163 that the donation is made for settling a *brāhmaṇa*, while *brāhmaṇa*s themselves are the petitioners in the other two cases.[24] These cases show that 1 *kulyavāpa* of land is sufficient for providing residence and subsistence to a *brāhmaṇa* and his family, which could be an extended one. The other cases call for some explanations. In the Kalaikuri plate, three *brāhmaṇa*s received 5, 2 and 2 *kulyavāpa*s respectively.[25] As I will explain below, these land plots seem to have been managed by the ten petitioners and the donees got a part of income from them. In case of the Damodarpur grant of year 128, a *brāhmaṇa* purchased 5 *droṇavāpa*s of land with *haṭṭa* (market) and *pānaka* (water place), so that the additional income from these facilities may have compensated for small size of the plot.[26] The donee of the Nandapur plate, an *agrahārika*, acquired 4 *kulyavāpa*s from a *viṣayapati*, while a *brāhmaṇa* of Kautsa *gotra* and Vājasaneya school, who belonged to the community of *cāturvidya*s in Mahatīraktamālāgrahāra, was given 2 *kulyavāpa*s by a *mahāmātra* in another plate of the same year.[27] The donees of both cases seem to have already kept some landholdings either as *agrahārika* or a member of *brāhmaṇa* community residing in an *agrahāra* and been donated additional tracts with arrangement of their cultivation, most probably by the donors who were officials. Thus, the last four cases have reasons for their rather smaller or larger size of plots and do not contradict the previous conclusion that 1 *kulyavāpa* of land is sufficient for supporting a *brāhmaṇa* family.

This conclusion draws our attention to the opinion of D. C. Sircar. On the basis of the later lexicographers and authorities on *Dharmaśāstra*s in Bengal, Sircar shows that the mutual relation of three weight standards of *kulya*, *droṇa* and *āḍhaka* corresponds to that of the three area units and that a *kulya* of paddy seeds is equal to 12 *maunds* 32 *seers* or 16 *maunds* in the modern weight measure. He calculates 1 *kulyavāpa* to be 38 to 48 *bighas*, 1 *droṇavāpa* to be 4 1/2 to 6 *bighas*, and 1 *āḍhavāpa* to be 1 1/8 to 1 1/2 *bighas*.[28] It is noteworthy that the size of a *kulyavāpa* of land conjectured by Sircar tallies well with the size of land categorised as 'a fair-sized, comfortable holding' by modern revenue collectors in the corresponding districts of Bengal, namely, from 25 to 50 *bighas* or 8 to 17 acres.[29] It also corresponds to the conclusion that 1 *kulyavāpa* of land was enough for a *brāhmaṇa* and his family. As was the case of modern *bigha*, the size denoted by a *kulyavāpa* may have varied in each locality, for *nala* on which the land is measured has variations according to local customs. The size of land required for cultivation in this period may also have been different from that in the modern age if we count on the enhancement of productivity by the improvement of agricultural technologies including species, manure and so on. Nevertheless, the calculation by Sircar can provisionally be taken as an approximation in the absence of clearer evidences.

In almost all the cases, the land plots are purchased by payment of money in gold or silver currencies. Such transactions presuppose the spread of money as means of exchange and its acceptance as a denominator of the accumulated wealth. However, the price of land plot is decided by local customs, rather than by its exchange value. It indicates still premature condition of the monetary economy in rural society, where the land had not yet become commodity in a strict sense.

The land plots are donated with the tenure called *nīvīdharma* or *akṣayanīvī*. In the *Amarakośa*, as Maity discusses, *nīvī* is synonymous with *paripaṇa* and *mūladhana*, meaning the capital or principal in sale and purchase and other transactions, while *akṣaya* literally means 'indestructible' or 'perpetual.'[30] Accordingly, when it is applied to the monetary endowment to religious institutions, *akṣayanīvī* means the arrangement in which the necessary expenditure is met by the interest from the endowed money without reducing the original amount. The money endowment with *akṣayanīvī* tenure mentioned in the Nasik cave inscription of the time of Nahapāna in the early second century conforms to this interpretation. In this case, a Buddhist *saṃgha* was given 3,000 *kahāpaṇas* of money, which was deposited to merchant groups and interest accruing from which would pay for provisions of the monks.[31] The presence of similar arrangements in the fifth century North India is also proved by the Indor copper plate inscription of Skandagupta, year 146 GE, in which money was given to the Sun temple to which the community of oil pressers was obliged to supply a certain amount of oil from the interest of the original money.[32] On the analogy of these cases, *akṣayanīvī* in land donation seems to denote the tenure with which the donees could enjoy the land perpetually without any power to alienate it by sale, mortgage or otherwise.[33] The cases encountered in land sale grants do not contradict this interpretation. Such tenure presupposes that the donated land plots would be cultivated and yield product to be enjoyed by the donee, in case of fallow land, or used for accommodating some buildings, in case of homestead land.

As is clear from the discussions made above, what is initiated by the transaction is the conversion of fallow/waste land into agrarian tract and homestead land. This can be a form of agrarian expansion prescribed by the contemporary social conditions. Some aspects of these conditions are represented in the *adhikaraṇa*.

Adhikaraṇa and the Gupta administration

What is conspicuous in the procedure of land purchase and donation is the function and authority of the *adhikaraṇa*. The term can denote any office, as shown by the contemporary clay seals and sealings excavated from Basarh and the other sites.[34] But in the contemporary land sale grants, it exclusively means a particular kind of office established at a certain administrative division. They were *adhiṣṭhānādhikaraṇa*, *viṣayādhikaraṇa*, *vīthyadhikaraṇa* and *aṣṭakulādhikaraṇa*. At different levels of the administrative hierarchy, they performed the same function of receiving petition for land sale and authorising the immunity of donated land from revenue charges. They were constituted by local influential people with different regularity and membership depending on the administrative division and location to which they belonged.

The administration which is present all through this period and constantly appears in our sources is the Gupta provincial administration. North Bengal in this period was under the jurisdiction of Puṇḍravardhanabhukti. For most of the period, it was governed by a governor called *uparika*, who was appointed by the Gupta kings according to the description in the Damodarpur plates.[35] The three *uparika*s except *rājaputra* Devabhaṭṭāraka, the last *uparika* in the Gupta period,[36] shared the same name ending of Datta.[37] It implies hereditary character of this position. They may have been either members of a local influential lineage who were nominated to this position, or officials who established their hereditary position as a result of nomination. From the reign of Budhagupta, their title changed to *uparikamahārāja*,[38] suggesting that members of this lineage established themselves as local subordinate rulers.

Under the *bhukti*, several administrative divisions functioned at supravillage level. It was this level at which the *adhikaraṇa* was constituted and the administration worked in close interaction and connection with local influential groups through it.

An administrative division which regularly appears in the contemporary inscriptions of North India as a sub-division of *bhukti* is *viṣaya*.[39] In North Bengal under the Guptas, we have the three *viṣaya*s mentioned in the copper plate inscriptions, namely, Koṭivarṣaviṣaya, Pañcanagarīviṣaya and Khādāpāraviṣaya,

Koṭivarṣaviṣaya can be located around present South Dinajpur district of West Bengal and Dinajpur district of Bangladesh. It included at least the areas around Bangarh, the ruin of the city of Koṭivarṣa,[40] and Damodarpur, the findspot of the five copper plates around 30 km to the east-northeast of the former.[41] It was governed by administrators appointed by *uparikas*.[42] They held titles of *kumārāmātya*, *āyuktaka* or *viṣayapati* in each case and 'manage' the *adhiṣṭhānādhikaraṇa* 'with' (*saṃvyavaharati*) the members of the *adhikaraṇa*.[43]

The *adhiṣṭhānādhikaraṇa*, the city office, of Koṭivarṣaviṣaya is mentioned in the four Damodarpur plates of years 124 and 128, Budhagupta's reign without date and year 224.[44] It had functioned for a long period of 100 years at Koṭivarṣa, the centre of the *viṣaya*. It witnessed a stable participation by the influential section of city dwellers as shown by its seats occupied by people with almost the same designations all through the period (**Table 3.1**).

A case of the same people having been members for at least four years also confirms the stability and fixity of its membership.[45] This *adhikaraṇa* thus seems to have been a regular organisation. The members who constituted the *adhikaraṇa* were *nagaraśreṣṭhin* (city merchant), *sārthavāha* (caravan trader), *prathamakulika* (chief artisan) and *prathamakāyastha* (chief scribe). They were leaders of mercantile, artisanal and scribal groups in urban settlements. Among these groups, *śreṣṭhin*, *sārthavāha* and *kulika* were known for running a guild-like organisation called *nigama* alone or jointly at Vaiśālī, as indicated by the contemporary clay sealings found at Basarh in North Bihar.[46] Existence of the composite *nigama* consisting of several groups alludes to the interaction and connection among them for daily businesses and other transactions. Though it is not clear whether such an organisation existed in Koṭivarṣa, as no seals of this kind have yet been reported from the excavation,[47] it is probable that mercantile and artisanal groups of the city also interacted with each other on a daily basis. As mercantile transactions require documents, their regular interaction with

Table 3.1 Members of the *Adhiṣṭhānādhikaraṇa* of Koṭivarṣaviṣaya

Year 124 GE (*SI* 1, p. 291, ll. 4–6.)
nagaraśreṣṭhin Dhṛtipāla, *sārthavāha* Vandhumitra, *prathamakulika* Dhṛtimitra, *prathamakāyastha* Śāmbapāla.
Year 128 GE (*SI* 1, p. 293, ll. 4–5.)
nagaraśreṣṭhin Dhṛtipāla, *sārthavāha* Vandhumitra, *prathamakulika* Dhṛtimitra, *prathamakāyastha* Śāmbapāla.
Budhagupta's reign, No Date (*SI* 1, p. 337, ll. 3–4.)
nagaraśreṣṭhin Ribhupāla, *sārthavāha* Vasumitra, *prathamakulika* Varadatta, *prathamakāyastha* Viprapāla.
Year 224 GE (*SI* 1, pp. 347–48, ll. 4–5.)
āryanagaraśreṣṭhin Ribhupāla, *sārthavāha* Sthāṇudatta, *prathamakulika* Matidatta, *prathamakāyastha* Skandapāla.

kāyasthas is also inferable. The *adhiṣṭhānādhikaraṇa* may have been organised on the basis of such interaction and connection among those influential urban groups. With the sanction and collaboration of the administrators of the *viṣaya*, they regularly assembled and solved the administrative matters in the city. Petitions of land purchase and donation might have been one of matters which they dealt with. It is noteworthy that the jurisdiction of this *adhikaraṇa*, which was located in the city, covered rural area in the *viṣaya*.

Pañcanagarīviṣaya mentioned in the Baigram plate was different from Koṭivarṣaviṣaya in terms of its administrative arrangement. This *viṣaya* included at least the area around Baigram, the findspot of the copper plate located 35 km to the south-east of Damodarpur.[48] It was also governed by a *kumārāmātya*. But he was appointed by a *bhaṭṭāraka* who could be the Gupta king, and there is no reference to the higher administrative division or a superior administrator in the plate.[49]

Viṣayādhikaraṇa appears only in this inscription. The *adhikaraṇa* of the Nandapur plate of year 169, which has no specification, may also be a *viṣayādhikaraṇa* as it works at the level of *viṣaya*.[50] In both cases, there is no specific indication of their membership, while they may have plural members as indicated by the use of plural form for the verb 'inform' or 'inform and inscribe' in each inscription.[51] The latter expression indicates the presence of scribes among the *adhikaraṇa* members, though we have no other clues. The *adhikaraṇa* in the former inscription worked with the *kumārāmātya*, the administrator of the *viṣaya*, for the both acted as issuers.[52] There is no reference to administrators in the latter inscription, and the *adhikaraṇa* was a sole issuing authority.[53] In both cases, the *adhikaraṇa* notified and ordered *kuṭumbins* including *samvyavahārins*.[54] As I will explain in the next section, *kuṭumbins* were peasant householders, the main constituents of rural society, and *samvyavahārins* were their upper section who worked or collaborated with the administration for management of local affairs. Thus, the notification and order in the Baigram and Nandapur plates was addressed to *kuṭumbins* including their dominant section. It suggests that the *viṣayādhikaraṇa* did not include dominant section of *kuṭumbins* as members and was rather present outside the locality in the same way as *adhiṣṭhānādhikaraṇa*. Its members accordingly consisted of outsiders of rural society.

The Khādāpāraviṣaya is mentioned in the Dhanaidaha plate.[55] Its administration is unclear and the *aṣṭakulādhikaraṇa*, which will be discussed below, settled the case of land sale and donation for which the grant was issued.

Another lower administrative division present in North Bengal was *vīthī*. It was a supra-village administrative unit placed between *bhukti* and *grāma*, parallel to *viṣaya*. We have three, Śṛṅgaveravīthī, Dakṣiṇāṃśakavīthī and Madhyamaṣaṇḍikavīthī, mentioned in the contemporary inscriptions.

Śṛṅgaveravīthī appears in the Kalaikuri-Sultanpur and Jagadishpur plates. It may be located around present Rajshahi and Natore districts in

Bangladesh, in consideration of the findspot of the second inscription.[56] It had Pūrṇakauśikā as its headquarter and was governed by *āyuktaka* Acyutadāsa or Acyuta, who seems to have been one and the same person.[57] According to the second inscription, he was appointed by the king.[58] He acted as an issuer of the grants with the *adhikaraṇa* of *vīthī*. Though there is no reference to the higher administrative division or a superior administrator, the villages where petitioners lived are said to belong to Puṇḍravardhana in the second plate.[59] It suggests that this *vīthī* was under the jurisdiction of Puṇḍravardhanabhukti.

The *adhikaraṇa* of Śṛṅgaveravīthī is well recorded in the aforementioned inscriptions of years 120 and 128 GE,[60] both of which are related to the same locality within the relatively short period of eight years. It consists of *mahattara*s and *kuṭumbin*s of the *vīthī*.[61] As I will discuss in the next section, *mahattara*s are within the upper section of *kuṭumbin*s, who have superiority in terms of authority. There are an enormous number of members of the *adhikaraṇa* whose names are listed in both cases. The names of eight *mahattara*s and 80 *kuṭumbin*s are listed in the first case, while four *mahattara*s and 28 *kuṭumbin*s listed in the second, with the overlap of 24 (**Table 3.2**).

Fluctuation of the number may be due to the difference in number of the villages involved in each case: five in the former and two in the latter, of

Table 3.2 Members of the *Vīthyadhikaraṇa* of Śṛṅgaveravīthī

Year 120 GE (*SI* 1, p. 353, ll. 4–12.)
-*Vīthīmahattara* (8): Kumāradeva, Gaṇḍa, Prajāpati, Umayaśas, Rāmaśarman, Jyeṣṭhadāman, Svāmicandra, Harisiṅha.
-*Kuṭumbin* (80): Yaśoviṣṇu, Kumāraviṣṇu, Kumārabhava, Kumārabhūti, Kumārayaśas, Gupta, Vailiṇaka, Śivakuṇḍa, Vasu, Śiva, Aparaśiva, Dāmarudra, Prabhamitra, Kṛṣṇamitra, Maghaśarman, Īśvaracandra, Rudra, Bhava, Svāmideva, Śrīnātha, Hariśarman, Guptaśarman, Suśarman, Hari, Alātasvāmin, Brahmasvāmin, Mahāsenabhaṭṭa, Ṣaṣṭhirā-ta, Gu-śarman, Uṇṭaśarman, Kṛṣṇadatta, Nandadāman, Bhavadatta, Ahiśarman, Somaviṣṇu, Lakṣmanaśarman, Kānti, Dhovvoka, Kśemaśarman, Śukraśarman, Sarppapālita, Kaṅkuṭi, Viśva, Śaṅkara, Jayasvāmin, Kaivartaśarman, Himaśarman, Purandara, Jayaviṣṇu, Uma –, Siṅhadatta, Bonda, Nārāyaṇadāsa, Vīranāga, Rājyanāga, Guha, Mahi, Bhavanātha, Guhaviṣṇu, Śarvvayaśoviṣṇu, Ṭakka, Kuladāman, – va, Śrīguhaviṣṇu, Rāmasvāmin, Kāmanakuṇḍa, Ratibhadra, Acyutabhadra, Loḍhaka, Prabhakīrtti, Jayadatta, Kāluka, Acyuta, Naradeva, Bhava, Bhavarakṣita, Piccakuṇḍa, Pravarakuṇḍa, Śarvadāsa, Gopāla.
Year 128 GE (*EDEP*, p. 61, ll. 4–8.)
-*Vīthīmahattara* (4): Kumāradeva, Gaṇḍa, Prajāpati, Jeṣṭhadāman
-*Kuṭumbin* (28): Yaśoviṣṇu, Umayaśas, Hariśarman, Sarppapālita, Hiraṇyagupta, Kumārayaśas, Kumārabhūti, Śivakuṇḍa, Śiva, Aparaśiva, Somaviṣṇu, Satyaviṣṇu, Kaṅkuṭi, Nandadāman, Vīranāga, Nārāyaṇadāsa, Rudra, Bhava, Guha, Acyuta, Kuvera, Śarvanāga, Bhavanāga, Śrīdatta, Bhavadatta, Dhanaviṣṇu, Guṇaratha, Naradeva.

* Underlined names (24) are mentioned in both inscriptions

which two are common.[62] The overlap of both village and personal names leads us to the conclusion that people mentioned in both grants belonged to these two villages. It means that this *adhikaraṇa* was not a regular body based on fixed membership but a temporary one constituted each time by the dominant section of *kuṭumbin*s belonging to the villages involved in such a case.

The character of their participation is shown by the way of their representation. In both cases, all the participants are classified into the two broad categories, namely, *mahattara*s and *kuṭumbin*s of the *vīthī*. The diversity of their social background is alluded to by their names, which include names with typical *brāhmaṇa* name endings like Śarman, Deva and Svāmin, names constituted by a single Sanskrit word or name of deity, and names difficult to comprehend as a Sanskrit word like Kaṅkuti and Bonda (**Table 3.2**). Adding to this, they might belong to different villages under the jurisdiction of the *vīthī*. Regardless of their social backgrounds or residential villages, all of them are represented as *mahattara*s and *kuṭumbin*s of the *vīthī*. It can be interpreted as the participation at supra-village level based on the minimal commonality as *mahattara* and *kuṭumbin*, with the temporary suppression of inner differences. The participation is limited to *kuṭumbin*s with *mahattara*s as a part of them, excluding other social groups in the locality. It presupposes the dominance of *kuṭumbin*s over the others, which will be discussed in the next section, and their horizontal social interaction and network. On the other hand, there are unnamed *kuṭumbin*s mentioned as addressees[63] and ones named as petitioners but not included in the *adhikaraṇa* members.[64] It implies the relation of domination and subordination present even among *kuṭumbin*s, though members of the *adhikaraṇa*, who may have dominance over the other *kuṭumbin*s, rather represent themselves as a homogeneous entity.

Dakṣiṇāṃśakavīthī is mentioned in the Jagadishpur and Paharpur plates. If we consider the finspot of the second inscription, it may be located around the border between present Naogaon and Joypurhat districts in Bangladesh.[65] In the first plate, this administrative division is said to have contained settlement Mecikāmra, where the abode of *siddha*s (*siddhāyatana*) lay.[66] In the second, it is described as an administrative division to which Nāgiraṭṭamaṇḍala, including several village clusters, belonged.[67] As *āyuktaka*s and the *adhiṣṭhānādhikaraṇa* of Puṇḍravardhana issued the grant to several villages belonging to these village clusters, this *vīthī* was under the jurisdiction of Puṇḍravardhanabhukti. This *adhikaraṇa* had *āryanagaraśreṣṭhin* as a member or members.[68] The last seems to be the same as *nagaraśreṣṭhin*, for both are used interchangeably in the Damodarpur plates of Budhagupta's reign and year 224 (**Table 3.1**). He or they may also have been the influential person of the urban settlement and functioned with the sanction and collaboration of administrators, as *āyuktaka*s and the *adhikaraṇa* issued the grant together. It is remarkable that the authority of administrators and the *adhikaraṇa* of the city bypassed any administrative settings of *vīthī* and *maṇḍala*, though we have no clue to the latter.

Madhyamaṣaṇḍikavīthī is mentioned in the Mahatiraktamala plate dated year 159 GE. The plate is soldered with a seal of the *adhikaraṇa* of the *āyuktaka* of the *vīthī*.[69] The intervention of Brahmadatta, the *uparika* of Puṇḍravardhanabhukti, mentioned in the plate suggests that this *vīthī* was under the jurisdiction of the *bhukti*.[70] The plate was issued from Mahatīraktamālāgrahāra by *kumārāmātya* Yūthapati, appointed by the king, and an unspecified *adhikaraṇa* to *kuṭumbin*s of Khuḍḍīraktamālikā, which seems to have been a hamlet adjacent to the *agrahāra*.[71] If the *āyuktaka* of the seal was identical with Yūthapati, he was the administrator of the *vīthī* and he and his *adhikaraṇa* issued the grant when they visited the *agrahāra*, where the petitioner lived, on circuit. Thus, this *adhikaraṇa* seems to be an organisation attached to the administrator, which functions with him in administrative dealings. It is different from the *vīthyadhikaraṇa* mentioned in both Kalaikuri and Jagadishpur plates, though we have no clue to its membership. As its despatched members worked with '*kuṭumbin*s of noble family of *viṣaya*' (*viṣayakulakuṭumbin*),[72] the organisation seems not to have included the latter as its members.

There are cases in which *aṣṭakulādhikaraṇa* located in a particular village, not at the level of lower administrative division, presided over matters of another village or functioned at the supra-village level. *Aṣṭakulādhikaraṇa* or *grāmāṣṭakulādhikaraṇa* is mentioned in the Dhanaidaha plate and the Damodarpur grant of year 163.[73] As indicated by a word *grāma*, it is placed at a certain village. Palāśavṛndaka, from which the second grant was issued, must be one of such villages. It literally means 'office of eight families' and may originally have been a village organ composed of representatives of several families,[74] though its character has already changed in this period. It functions at supra-village level, as is shown by a mention of the custom followed in a *viṣaya*,[75] and by the fact that the jurisdiction of the *adhikaraṇa* located in Palāśavṛndaka covered Caṇḍagrāma.[76] It could have been 'a link between upper tiers of local political organization and villages interconnected in its network.'[77]

Regarding membership, these two cases show some differences. In the first case, the *adhikaraṇa* was constituted by more than 18 people categorised as *kuṭumbin*s with subcategories of *brāhmaṇa*, *mahattara* and *goṣṭhaka* (**Table 3.3**). The order of precedence and disproportionate numbers show superiority of *brāhmaṇa*s and *mahattara*s over *goṣṭhaka*s, which may denote *kuṭumbin*s with *adhikaraṇa* membership according to the context.[78] Their distinction from ordinary *kuṭumbin*s is clear from the reference to neighbouring *kuṭumbin*s who were just informed of the petition, agreed with it and measured the land to be donated.[79]

In the second case, the members of the *adhikaraṇa* are just mentioned as 'beginning with *mahattara*s,'[80] and consisted of '*adhikaraṇakuṭumbin*s

Table 3.3 Members of the *Grāmāṣṭakulādhikaraṇa* in Dhanaidaha CPI, year 113 GE (*SI* 1, p. 288, ll. 3–6.)

-*Kuṭumbi – brāhmaṇa* (2): Śivaśarman, Nāgaśarman
-*Maha(ttara?)* (2): – vakīrtti, Kṣemadatta.
-*Goṣṭhaka* (13): Vargapāla, Śuṅkuka, Kala –, – viṣṇu, Devaśarman, Viṣṇubhadra, Khāsaka, Rāmaka, Gopāla, Śrībhadra, Somapāla, Rāma

beginning with *mahattaras*,' who worked as executors of the transaction, that is, fulfilled the duty of inspection and measurement of the land to be donated.[81] What was common to the *adhikaraṇa* of these two cases was its membership consisting of a part of *kuṭumbins* excluding the others. In both cases, *mahattaras* are mentioned as the foremost among them. It means that the *adhikaraṇa* was an organisation where such a dominant section of the peasants came together and presided over matters related to the administration. It presupposed horizontal relation among upper rung of *kuṭumbins* and their dominance over other *kuṭumbins* and social groups. The case of the Damodarpur plate of year 163 shows the inequality among rural settlements in addition. It is clearly indicated by the fact that the *aṣṭakulādhikaraṇa* in Palāśavṛndaka presided over a matter concerning Caṇḍagrāma, where such an organisation did not exist.[82] From these points, *aṣṭakulādhikaraṇa* can be interpreted as an organisation through which the upper strata of *kuṭumbins* collectively decide on the administrative matters related to their own and other settlements at supra-village level covering several villages.

As described above, the administrative settings at supra-village level show diversity and complexity. Even the same category of divisions had different administrative apparatuses in different localities. Matters in Koṭivarṣaviṣaya were under the jurisdiction of the *adhiṣṭhānādhikaraṇa* of Koṭivarṣa, while a case in Pañcanagarīviṣaya was decided by the *viṣayādhikaraṇa*. For one of the Damodarpur grants was issued in the same year as the Baigram plate, namely year 128 GE, these cases show the synchronic diversity in administrative arrangements even among the *viṣayas* in some proximity. Similarly, Śṛṅgaveravīthī had its *vīthyadhikaraṇa* as an authority, while the *adhiṣṭhānādhikaraṇa* of Puṇḍravardhana presided over a case in Dakṣiṇāṃśakavīthī. The latter also had a *maṇḍala* at the level between *vīthī* and village, while the former did not. In Madhyamaṣaṇḍikavīthī, the *āyuktaka* and his *adhikaraṇa* decided on the case of land sales.

The cases mentioned above show that the diversity in the administration was mostly due to the different organisations of the *adhikaraṇa*. It was organised on the basis of existing social relations among dominant social groups. The *adhiṣṭhānādhikaraṇa*, located in urban settlements, was based on daily interactions of urban elites. The *aṣṭakulādhikaraṇa* and *vīthyadhikaraṇa*, located in a rural area, presupposed horizontal social networks and solidarity of dominant *kuṭumbins*, and their dominance over ordinary *kuṭumbins* and other social groups. The *aṣṭakulādhikaraṇa* was based on a village and worked at the supra-village level[83] because of the hierarchical relation among those villages. The *vīthyadhikaraṇa* worked at the supra-village level and was based on the identity of members as *mahattaras* and *kuṭumbins* of the *vīthī*. As the existing social relations and dominant social groups varied in each locality, so did the organisational principles of *adhikaraṇas* and its location in the administrative divisions. In view of this, the administrative arrangement at supra-village level through the organisation of *adhikaraṇas* can be interpreted as an adjustment of state apparatus to local social relations. What necessitated this adjustment were the dependence of the administration on local influential groups in different degrees and the relative weakness of the state control which could not impose the uniform system on its entire territory.

The character of the *adhikaraṇas*, especially their relations with rural society, was various. According to their location in relation to rural society, they can be classified into the two broad categories, namely, the ones located within rural society and the others outside it.

The *aṣṭakulādhikaraṇa* and *vīthyadhikaraṇa* belonged to the first category. They were occasional gatherings of the dominant section of peasant householders dealing with matters within rural society. As its dominant groups, they represented interest of rural society to the state through the *adhikaraṇa*. On the other hand, they took part in the administration as members of the *adhikaraṇa*, and this form of involvement gave them the authority to preside over some important matters in the locality like land sale and donation. It also offered them an occasion to congregate and reconfirm their solidarity, and to enhance their dominance over the other social groups. Through the *vīthyadhikaraṇa*, *kuṭumbins* scattered around several villages came together and reconfirmed their cohesion as *mahattaras* and *kuṭumbins* of the *vīthī*, and asserted their dominance by excluding the other groups in the *vīthī*. In case of the *aṣṭakulādhikaraṇa*, what was reconfirmed was the cohesion of dominant *kuṭumbins* in a village and their dominance over the other social groups. It also gave participants the authority to preside over matters in another settlement, at least in case of the Damodarpur plate of year 163 mentioned above. Thus, dominant *kuṭumbins* acquired the position to mediate interests of rural society and state through their involvement with the *adhikaraṇa*. Their position in relation to the administration was relatively strong and can be called autonomous. In the case of Śṛṅgaveravīthī recorded in the Kalaikuri and Jagadishpur plates, it was members of the *adhikaraṇa*, the named *mahattaras* and *kuṭumbins*, who took initiatives in making decisions. This point is indicated by the fact that 'we,' indicating the *adhikaraṇa* consisting of these members, were the acceptant of the petitions and the authority over the cases recorded in these inscriptions.[84] In the cases of *aṣṭakulādhikaraṇa*,[85] there is no mention of administrators even as issuing authorities. The *adhikaraṇa* and a section of *kuṭumbins* issued the grant in one case.[86]

The *adhiṣṭhānādhikaraṇa* and *viṣayādhikaraṇa* belonged to the second category, namely, the ones located outside rural society. The *vīthyāyuktakādhikaraṇa* of Madhyamaṣaṇḍikavīthī can be included in this category. The *adhiṣṭhānādhikaraṇa* was a regular organisation consisting of the representatives of urban elite groups. The *viṣayādhikaraṇa* did not see the participation by the dominant section of *kuṭumbin*s, though its membership was unclear. As members of these *adhikaraṇa*s were outsiders, it seems to have been their association with administration which gave them authority to preside over rural affairs, while they did not have any capacity to represent the interest of rural society. This point is shown by their closer relation with administrators, in which the latter 'manage' the *adhiṣṭhānādhikaraṇa* together 'with' the urban elites on regular basis.[87] As a part of the administration, the *adhikaraṇa* and its participants had to deal with rural society including its dominant section. In this exercise, they could not impose their decision unilaterally and should rather negotiate with rural population and respect the local situation. One aspect of the negotiation was the land measurement and demarcation by local *kuṭumbin*s, to be discussed in the next section. Their respect for local situation is shown by their adherence to local custom incorporated as customs of particular administrative divisions. As the *adhikaraṇa* members, the influential groups outside rural society also mediated between the society and state, but on the side of the latter.

In different degrees, the two categories of the *adhikaraṇa* represented interests of both rural society and state. In the first category, the dominant *kuṭumbin*s represented the interest of rural society while enhancing their authority through their involvement with state administration. In the second, the urban elites and the other outside groups confronted and dealt with rural society as a part of administrative agency, while they had to respect local interests in negotiation. This aspect of the *adhikaraṇa*s is attested by the verification by *pustapāla*s, which formed a basis of their decision.

*Pustapāla*s, record keepers, appeared in almost all the cases as verifiers of the petition of land purchase and donation.[88] They seem to have constituted a part of administration as professionals of recordkeeping. On the other hand, their proximity to, or rather inclusion in, rural society is attested by the case of the Kalaikuri plate. In this case, *pustapāla*s collectively made petition for land purchase and donation with a *kulika* and *kāyastha*s of the *vīthī*.[89] In other words, they had connection with the other professional groups of the same *vīthī* with whom they gathered wealth and shared interest in landed property in rural settlements. Thus, *pustapāla*s can be considered members of rural society involved in the administration and mediating between both at each level together with *adhikaraṇa*s.

What *pustapāla*s verified was the conformity of petitions and price of the land to a particular custom (*maryādā*) of village, *vīthī*, *viṣaya* and the city office.[90] Among them, the custom of village was clearly a local custom. Other customs rather seem to belong to administrative divisions. However, their contents concerning the sale of *khila* land with *akṣayanīvī* tenure and its price are almost the same as the custom of village. It seems that local customs were incorporated into the customs of these administrative divisions. The local character of these customs is shown by the emphasis on the words 'here' (*iha*) and 'your/our' (*yuṣmākam*, *yuṣmad/asmad*) attached to these divisions.[91] On the other hand, *pustapāla*s also verified that there was no loss of profit but the acquisition of the one sixth of merit by the king from the donation, in cases of the Paharpur, Nandapur and Damodarpur plates of years 163 and 224.[92] Thus interests of both rural society and state were considered in these verifications.

In terms of land sale and donation, or rather transfer of land, what is represented here is the control over fallow/waste land by rural society and the state claim over territorial land. Rural society as a community still seems to have kept control over *khila* land as their commons, while each *kuṭumbin* held his own land as a unit of production. This fact authorised its dominant section as the *adhikaraṇa* members to preside over disposal of such land, as long as the decision conformed to the local custom. On the other hand, the state claim of land control was enhanced along with the entrenchment of the Gupta administration in some parts of North Bengal.

The case recorded in the Mahatiraktamala plate, year 159 GE, attests to the overlapping presence of both powers and their contradiction verging on an occasional clash. Nandabhūti, a *brāhmaṇa* donee, was given 2 *kulyavāpa*s of *khila* land plot in Govardhanakagrāma by Suvarcasadatta, *mahāmātra* of Puṇḍravardhana who purchased it presumably from the *adhikaraṇa* of the *āyuktaka* of Madhyamaṣaṇḍikavīthī in the year 157. However, the king donated Govardhanakagrāma to a group of *brāhmaṇa*s residing in Dugdhotikā in the year 159, and Nandabhūti's right over the aforementioned plot was infringed upon in consequence. Nandabhūti informed *uparika* Brahmadatta, the governor of Puṇḍravardhanabhukti, of the infringement, and the governor, who after consulting with his own *adhikaraṇa*, gave his instruction through *deśoparika* Svāmicandra to the *adhikaraṇa* at the *vīthī*. On his instruction, the *adhikaraṇa* gave the donee another plot of the same size at Khuḍḍīraktamālikā.[93] Thus the royal territorial claim, which manifested itself in the donation of a whole village, clashed with the land control of the *adhikaraṇa* at the *vīthī* and overrode the latter's decision on the sale of a *khila* land plot. Their clash caused friction in the locality which necessitated the intervention of another power, the governor of *bhukti*, and the issue of the other grant.

In different degrees, both remnant of communal control and emerging state claim over the land were represented through the *adhikaraṇa,* and this composite character gave it the authority to preside over land transactions. The difference in degrees was expressed by the two categories of *adhikaraṇa*s discussed above. As the social relation and power structure were different in each locality and the degree of state control over it varied, the *adhikaraṇa*s were located at different administrative levels, while fulfilling the same function as an authority over land transactions.

The *adhikaraṇa* discussed above can be interpreted as a conjunction of the state authority represented by the administration and the local interests represented by the influential groups who constituted or interacted with it. It worked as an arena of negotiation among the people with different interests and power relations, who were involved in the transactions of land sale and donation in different capacities.

Participants and their power relations

The cases of land sale and donation can be divided into the two categories according to the location of *adhikaraṇa*s in relation to rural society, namely, whether they were located within or outside it. While the first category reveals the power relation within rural society, the second adds another angle of its relation with outside powers.

The most conspicuous social category recognisable in the rural landscape of those cases is *kuṭumbin*. As a derivative from *kuṭumba*, 'house,' it literally means 'one having household' and denotes a householder. It was mainly used for a peasant householder while its synonym *gṛhapati* (*gahapati* in Middle Indo-Aryan like Pali) rather denoted a householder with vast wealth and social pre-eminence in the earlier period, from the first century BC to the third century AD.[94]

From the fourth century onwards, *kuṭumbin* became a regular figure in copper plate inscriptions as a category of rural residents to whom the inscriptions were addressed. Its connotation of a peasant householder with his own house and land is indicated by a passage in the contemporary *Nāradasmṛti*, which mentions house and land as essentials for subsistence of *kuṭumbins*.[95] The descriptions of *kuṭumbin*s in the land sale grants mentioned above also conform to this connotation. Their engagement in agriculture is attested by an expression 'neighbouring *kuṭumbin*s cultivating land' in the Dhanaidaha plate,[96] and by references to *kuṭumbin*s requested to measure, divide and give land in an area that would not disturb their own cultivation in the Baigram, Paharpur and Nandapur plates.[97]

As a social category, *kuṭumbin* had a comprehensive character. It included *mahattara*s, *samvyavahārin*s and *brāhmaṇa*s as its foremost section as attested by the expressions like 'village *kuṭumbin*s beginning with *brāhmaṇa*s', 'village *kuṭumbin*s, of whom *brāhmaṇa*s are foremost, headed by *samvyavahārins*,' 'prominent *kuṭumbin*s beginning with *brāhmaṇa*s' and '*kuṭumbin*s beginning with *mahattara*s, of whom *brāhmaṇa*s are foremost' in the address of the grants.[98] Their difference in terms of economic condition, social prestige and authority is also recognisable. Some of them were resourceful enough to purchase land for donation, while others were simply not. There was some variation even among the first group. The *kuṭumbin* brothers Bhoyila and Bhāskara, petitioners of the Baigram plate, belonged to an affluent section. Their father was wealthy enough to build a temple, and they themselves could afford the expenditure of six *dīnāra*s and eight *rūpaka*s.[99] On the other hand, three *kuṭumbin*s of the Jagadishpur plate could spend only two *dīnāra*s, though they must have been still better off than the others.[100]

The difference of social prestige and authority is clearly shown by their association with *adhikaraṇa*s. It has already been mentioned in the previous section that only a part of *kuṭumbin*s were members of an *adhikaraṇa*. Here, we can detect domination and subordination among them in different degrees. In the Dhanaidaha plate, neighbouring *kuṭumbin*s, who seemed to have been informed and consulted by the *adhikaraṇakuṭumbin*s, agreed with them about the petition, measured and gave the land.[101] In this case, the position of non-*adhikaraṇa*-member *kuṭumbin*s in relation to member *kuṭumbin*s seems to have been relatively strong.

The inner difference of *kuṭumbin*s was growing in the later period, as attested by the Mahatiraktamala plate of year 159 which is addressed to *kuṭumbin*s 'with small and prominent ones and so on.'[102] The same plate also indicates the differentiation of *kuṭumbin*s accruing from the association with an *adhikaraṇa*. The *viṣayakulakuṭumbin*s worked with despatched members of the *adhikaraṇa*.[103] Though they were not members of the *adhikaraṇa*, these eminent *kuṭumbin*s were differentiated from residential *kuṭumbin*s of Khuḍḍīraktamālikā mentioned as addressees only.[104] It was their association with the *adhikaraṇa* which made them distinct from residential *kuṭumbin*s and involved in the affair of a settlement where they did not reside.

The case of the Damodarpur grant of year 163 shows in similar terms a complicated gradation of power among *kuṭumbin*s with three categories. The first was *adhikaraṇakuṭumbin*s constituting the *aṣṭakulādhikaraṇa*. The second was *grāmikakuṭumbin*s who notified about the donation and acted as receivers of the petition together with the *adhikaraṇa*.[105] Both of them seem to have belonged to village Palāśavṛndaka. The third was *kuṭumbin*s of Caṇḍagrāma beginning with *brāhmaṇa*s, who were just notified about the donation and had no other role in the procedure described in the plate.[106] *Adhikaraṇakuṭumbin*s including *mahattara*s wielded authority as members of the *adhikaraṇa*. The *grāmikakuṭumbin*s listed as co-issuers of the grant were not the members of the *adhikaraṇa*, but their superiority to *kuṭumbin*s of Caṇḍagrāma was obvious and it may have come from their association with the *adhikaraṇa*. *Grāmika* can be interpreted as 'a village headman.'[107] But in view of the context in which it is used to denote *kuṭumbin*s seemingly inferior to *adhikaraṇakuṭumbin*s, it may mean 'belonging to village' and *grāmikakuṭumbin* must have been a *kuṭumbin* belonging to the village which had the *adhikaraṇa*, in this case, Palāśavṛndaka. Finally, *kuṭumbin*s of Caṇḍagrāma, with other residents, had no authority over the matters related to their own village.

Mahattaras, in morphological terms a comparative degree of the adjective *mahat*, 'large', denotes a part of *kuṭumbins* which had some kind of superiority. Their superiority is indicated by the fact that they are mentioned as the foremost among *kuṭumbins* or ahead of them in address,[108] and by their smaller number compared with *kuṭumbins* in the Kalaikuri and Jagadishpur plates (**Table 3.2**).[109] Their distinction from *kuṭumbins* is not solely based on the better economic condition, even though the superiority in terms of landholding may be the precondition. This point is illustrated by the case of the Baigram plate, in which brothers Bhoyila and Bhāskara are not called *mahattara* in spite of their wealth enough to purchase 3 1/4 *kulyavāpas* of *khila* land.[110] The superiority of *mahattaras* rather seems to have been a matter of their authority based on the family background, knowledge, fame and so on, though there is no clear indication.

The distinction between *mahattaras* and other *kuṭumbins*, at least their upper section, was not rigid in this period. Umayaśas figured as a member of the *adhikaraṇa* of Śṛṅgaveravīthī as *mahattara* in the Kalaikuri plate and as *kuṭumbin* in the Jagadishpur grant.[111]

The noun *samvyavahārin* is derived from the verb *saṃ-vy-ava-√hṛ* meaning 'to have intercourse or business with.'[112] This verb is used for *kumārāmātya* and other administrators who managed *adhiṣṭhānādhikaraṇa* with the influential urban groups in the Damodarpur plates.[113] Thus *samvyavahārin* in this period and region may have meant 'a person who manages together.' The fact that *samvyavahārin* constituted a part of *kuṭumbins* is deduced from the expression '*grāmakuṭumbins* headed by *samvyavahārins*' and '*kuṭumbins* beginning with *samvyavahārins*' in the Baigram and Nandapur plates.[114] While they worked with *kuṭumbins* for the practical part of donation, namely land measurement and border fixation by the order of the *adhikaraṇa*,[115] *samvyavahārins* were especially asked to protect the donation in those inscriptions.[116] They were also asked to protect or to agree with the donation in the other grants.[117] In the Kalaikuri and Jagadishpur plates, they were requested to protect the donation along with *viṣayapatis*, *āyuktakas*, *kuṭumbins* and *adhikaraṇikas*.[118] Considering all these references, I may conclude that *samvyavahārins* were the upper section of *kuṭumbins* who worked or collaborated with the administration for management of local affairs.

Brāhmaṇas mentioned as a part of *kuṭumbins* were the ones living in rural area. The cases of *brāhmaṇas* who themselves purchased land and who were settled through land donation indicate the process through which they settled down and got incorporated into rural society.[119] They may have engaged in agriculture as *kuṭumbins*, though whether they themselves tilled land cannot be ascertained.[120] Their identity as *brāhmaṇas* comes to fore almost exclusively when they are mentioned as donees. In other contexts, they are included in the categories of *kuṭumbin* and *mahattara*, as names of the members of Śṛṅgaveravīthyadhikaraṇa show (**Table 3.2**). Even when their identity is mentioned, they are just called *brāhmaṇa*,[121] at most with reference to the Vedic school and residential place,[122] with the exception of the two mentioned with their *gotra*s, of whom one is described as belonging to a community of *brāhmaṇa*s studying the four Vedas and the other with the title of *agrahārika*.[123] As donees, their presence in rural area may have been strong with their landholding and privileges which included right over income from market and place of drinking water for cattle in one case.[124] However, their rise and distinction as a social group would become clearer in the following period together with the ascendancy of *mahattara*s, though the two groups of *brāhmaṇa*s respectively residing in Mahatīraktamālāgrahāra and Dugdhotikā mentioned in the Mahatiraktamala plate show the early symptom of such a tendency.[125]

The horizontal social relation or network based on locality is recognisable among *kuṭumbin*s who appear in these grants. The organisation of *adhikaraṇa*s in rural area was based on it, as discussed in the previous section. The case of the Jagadishpur plate, in which three *kuṭumbin*s residing in two villages collectively made land purchase and donation, indicates the existence of such a relation among residents of neighbouring villages.[126] These relations could be constructed within or beyond a single village, as was the case of *aṣṭakulādhikaraṇa* and *vīthyadhikaraṇa*.[127] Although the familial relation, which can be the basis of daily life and agricultural operation of *kuṭumbin*s, is recognisable in cases of the Baigram plate in which the petitioners were brothers,[128] and the Paharpur plate in which a *brāhmaṇa* and his wife made a petition together,[129] we have no further information on kin and family networks.

The other groups in rural area whose activity can be glimpsed from contemporary inscriptions are *kulika*, *kāyastha* and *pustapāla*. They collectively made a petition in the Kalaikuri plate as a *kulika*, *kāyastha*s and *pustapāla*s of the *vīthī*.[130] Their association, in which they accumulated their wealth together and probably shared interest in the donated landed property, indicates the existence of a relation based on locality among these professional groups like that of *kuṭumbin*s mentioned above. Some of them were involved in the process of land purchase and donation in the other ways apart from being petitioners. *Kulika* Bhīma acted as a cashier receiving money from the petitioners in the Jagadishpur plate.[131] *Pustapāla*s Siṁhanandin and Yaśodāman verified the petitions in both Kalaikuri and Jagadishpur grants.[132] In spite of their involvement in the process, they were not members of the *adhikaraṇa*. *Pustapāla*s had some authority as they carried out administrative function and made verification of petitions. However, the initiative was taken by the *adhikaraṇa*, which referred cases to them and made decision. It shows dominance of the upper strata of *kuṭumbin*s over the other groups in rural area, maintained through the *adhikaraṇa*.

The discussions on participants in the transactions of land sale and donation made above show the dominance of the upper strata of *kuṭumbin*s over the other *kuṭumbin*s and social groups in rural area. For the maintenance of their dominance, they had to show their cohesion and solidarity against other groups by temporarily suppressing their inner difference, no matter how different they were within. Their involvement in the administration as members of the *adhikaraṇa* gave them an opportunity to reconfirm their cohesion and enhance their dominance. In the case of the *aṣṭakulādhikaraṇa*, the cohesion of dominant *kuṭumbin*s in a village and their dominance over the other social groups and rural settlements was reconfirmed. The relation with the *adhikaraṇa* defined the three categories of *kuṭumbin*s and their hierarchical order in the case of the Damodarpur plate of year 163.[133] Through the *vīthyadhikaraṇa*, *kuṭumbin*s living in several villages came together and reconfirmed their cohesion as *mahattara*s and *kuṭumbin*s of the *vīthī*, and asserted their dominance by excluding other groups.

The participation in the transaction also provided dominant *kuṭumbin*s with an opportunity to extend their own interest. *Grāmika* Nābhaka, who seems to have been one of the *grāmikakuṭumbin*s associated with the *aṣṭakulādhikaraṇa* of Palāśavṛndaka, could acquire some landed interest in Caṇḍagrāma through the transaction, of which his brethren tacitly approved.[134]

For the other groups who were forced to comply with the authority of dominant *kuṭumbin*s, the *adhikaraṇa* became an arena where they negotiated their relation with the latter. The collective petitions of land purchase and donation by *kulika* Bhīma, seven *kāyastha*s and two *pustapāla*s in the Kalaikuri plate and the three *kuṭumbin*s in the Jagadishpur grant, can be interpreted as attempts of non-dominant but still resourceful and influential groups to achieve personal and collective profit through the negotiation.[135]

Another type of negotiation is detectable in the Dhanaidaha plate, in which neighbouring *kuṭumbin*s seem to have agreed with the *adhikaraṇa* on the petition and executed the practical part of donation, namely, the measurement of the land to be donated.[136] This situation was analogous to the cases in which local *kuṭumbin*s measured the land plot and demarcated its border in an area that would not disturb their own cultivation. As I will discuss below, it alludes to the right of local *kuṭumbin*s to choose the plot to be donated, and the similar description in the Dhanaidaha plate indicates that the same right was retained by the ordinary *kuṭumbin*s against the authority of their dominant section wielded through the *adhikaraṇa*. This case alludes to the negotiation with the latter by the *kuṭumbin*s who were neither dominant nor resourceful. They could at least keep some right through the negotiation, though they were unable to defy the authority of the *adhikaraṇa*.

In contrast, the land measurement and border demarcation were executed by the *adhikaraṇakuṭumbin*s beginning with *mahattara*s in the Damodarpur plate of year 163.[137] This can be a case in which the power balance tilted towards the dominant *kuṭumbin*s, who encroached upon the domain previously held by subordinate *kuṭumbin*s.

The outside powers which interacted with rural society through the *adhikaraṇas* were the urban elites and the lower rank officials. In urban landscape, *kuṭumbins* were conspicuous by their absence,[138] in contrast to urban elites. As discussed above, the latter may have had daily interactions on which the *adhiṣṭhānādhikaraṇa* was organised. Through the *adhikaraṇa*, they wielded authority over affairs in the rural area under their jurisdiction. The involvement with the *adhikaraṇa* also gave them an opportunity to extend their personal interest in rural area. The case of *nagaraśreṣṭhin* Ribhupāla, mentioned in the Damodarpur plate of Budhagupta's reign, is an example.

Ribhupāla, a member of the *adhiṣṭhānādhikaraṇa* of Koṭivarṣa, petitioned for sale and donation of land plots to construct two temples and two small storehouses for the deities Kokāmukhasvāmin and Śvetavarāhasvāmin in the vicinity of plots which he had previously donated to them in Doṅgāgrāma.[139] According to Sircar, Kokāmukha was a *tīrtha* (place of pilgrimage) located in the eastern part of present Nepal, and Ribhupāla may have been there on pilgrimage and donated a large area of land in his native district to the two deities of the *tīrtha* after his return.[140] Then he made two temples of the same deities and two storehouses nearby the donated tract, due to the difficulty to send the income from the land to the *tīrtha* in Nepal.[141] In both occasions, Ribhupāla may have been deeply involved in management of the land and forwarding of the income from it to the temples. Through these acts, he could establish strong presence and influence in the village, while keeping his own interest in the city. Whole the procedure suggests that the *adhikaraṇa* members did favour to their colleague with some formality on the one hand, and that the authority of the *adhikaraṇa* and its protocol were too forceful even for an influential person like Ribhupāla to bypass on the other hand. In any case, he could establish in a village the two temples and their landed property, in which he may have kept vested interest, through the procedure at the *adhikaraṇa*, especially with the tacit consent of his colleagues.

The extent of his success is shown by the Damodarpur plate of year 224 GE.[142] It records the purchase and donation of several land plots located in five settlements to the deity Śvetavarāhasvāmin by Amṛtadeva, 'a son of noble family' (*kulaputra*). This deity may have been identical with the one mentioned in the earlier grant, and his temple located in the forest nearby must have been one of the temples constructed by Ribhupāla. It indicates that the authority of the deity and his temple had been established in the locality within 50 years or so,[143] while the destiny of Kokāmukhasvāmin, the other deity, and his temple is unclear. Śvetavarāhasvāmin obtained several land plots located in five settlements other than his original location, Doṅgāgrāma, and this may indicate spread of his authority within the *viṣaya*. One of the members of the *adhiṣṭhānādhikaraṇa* was *āryanagaraśreṣṭhin* Ribhupāla.[144] If he was identical with his namesake mentioned in the earlier

Damodarpur plate, he could have been in this position at least for 50 years and must have been quite old. He might also have been a descendant with the same name. In either case, Ribhupāla himself or his namesake, as the foremost member of the *adhikaraṇa*, did a favour to the temple in which he had vested interest as a progenitor or his descendant. The other members were complicit with him on this matter.

As for the authority of urban elites over rural society, what was important was its relation with the authority of dominant *kuṭumbin*s, which could overlap with it. In all the cases related to the *adhiṣṭhānādhikaraṇa* of Koṭivarṣa, the lack of references to *kuṭumbin*s is conspicuous.[145] Only *samvyavahārin*s are asked to agree with the donation in the Damodarpur plates of year 128, Budhagupta's reign and year 224.[146] It gives an impression that the procedures were undertaken by the *adhikaraṇa* bypassing *kuṭumbin*s. On the other hand, the Paharpur plate related to the *adhiṣṭhānādhikaraṇa* of Puṇḍravardhana mentions local *kuṭumbin*s as addressees and records their involvement in the procedure. Similar descriptions are found in the Baigram and Nandapur grants, both of which are related to *viṣayādhikaraṇa*s, and the Mahatiraktamala plate issued by a *vīthyāyuktakādhikaraṇa*. These cases pertaining to the *adhikaraṇa*s located outside rural society show one aspect of the relation between outside powers and the latter, namely, negotiation.

In the Baigram, Paharpur and Nandapur plates, the rural residents notified by the *adhikaraṇa* were ordered to divide, demarcate and give the land to be donated at the place which would not disturb their own cultivation.[147] It means that they implemented the practical part of donations. What to note is the constituents of the rural residents who were notified. In the Baigram and Nandapur plates, they were '*grāmakuṭumbin*s, of whom *brāhmaṇa*s are foremost, headed by *samvyavahārin*s' and '*kuṭumbin*s beginning with *saṃvyavahārin*s, of whom *brāhmaṇa*s are foremost' respectively.[148] Similarly, the Paharpur grant was addressed to '*kuṭumbin*s beginning with *mahattara*s, of whom *brāhmaṇa*s are foremost'.[149] As discussed above, both *mahattara*s and *samvyavahārin*s belonged to the influential section of *kuṭumbin*s. It means that the rural residents who executed the order of the external *adhikaraṇa* were *kuṭumbin*s with their dominant section. The description in the inscriptions cited above shows that these local *kuṭumbin*s still retained the right to choose land plots to be given, while they had to comply with the order of the *adhikaraṇa*. We can detect here the tension and negotiation between outside dominant groups, who tried to exercise their control over rural area through the *adhikaraṇa*, and *kuṭumbin*s including their dominant section, who tried to retain their power on local matters. The special references to the standard *nala* for measurement in these cases indicate the attempt of the former to restrict the agency of the latter by its imposition,[150] while such references in the Dhanaidaha plate and the Damodarpur grant of year 163 allude to the similar attempt by the dominant *kuṭumbin*s against other *kuṭumbin*s of their own village or residents of another under their control.[151]

In the Mahatiraktamala plate, the *kuṭumbins* residing in Khuḍḍīraktamālikā were ordered to measure, demarcate and give the land plot to the donee with an *adhikaraṇa* despatched by Yūthapati and his *adhikaraṇa*, which probably consisted of some members of the latter organisation, and *kuṭumbins* of noble family of a *viṣaya*.[152] The residential *kuṭumbins* still retained their right to choose land, but it was restricted and infringed upon by the imposition of some *adhikaraṇa* members and eminent *kuṭumbins* from outside. This case shows the weak position of the concerned settlement and its residents in relation to the outside authority.

The presence of both cases of bypassing and negotiating with *kuṭumbins* indicates diverse power equations between outside authority and rural society. It should however be noted that the acceptance of the authority of the outside *adhikaraṇa* by rural residents was presupposed in both cases.

Another external power interfering with rural society through the *adhikaraṇa* was lower rank officials. As administrators at the supra-village level, they were closely involved with the *adhikaraṇa* especially in its function as an issuing authority of grants. Apart from such a public association, they had personal stakes and interests in rural society through the mediation of the *adhikaraṇa* both within and outside; this is shown by the cases of the Dhanaidaha, Mahatiraktamala and Nandapur plates in which such officials are the petitioners for land sale and donation.[153] In all those cases, it is probable that they obtained some right over donated land. An *āyuktaka* confronted the dominant *kuṭumbins* through the *aṣṭakulādhikaraṇa*in the first plate. In the second case, a *mahāmātra* of Puṇḍravardhana purchased a plot in Govardhanakagrāma by applying to the *vīthyāyuktakādhikaraṇa*, though the decision was later overturned by the village grant by the king. The last plate shows a *viṣayapati* of another *viṣaya* confronted with rural society with the sanction of the *viṣayādhikaraṇa*.[154] It means that they had to accept the authority of the *adhikaraṇa* and comply with its procedural protocols in their relation with rural society as both state agents and interested section, no matter whether the *adhikaraṇa* was located within or outside it.

A change in this relation is detectable in the later phase. Nandabhūti, the donee of the Mahatiraktamala plate of year 159, retained his land right, which was infringed upon by the royal village grant, in a form of alternative land plot by appealing to *uparika* Brahmadatta for intervention. The latter imposed his decision on *kumārāmātya* Yūthapati and his *adhikaraṇa* as an instruction (*ādeśa*) conveyed by *deśoparika* Svāmicandra.[155] We can detect in this chain of command the interference of higher administrative echelon with the functioning of a lower *adhikaraṇa* confronting with rural society, unheard of in the earlier period. It should be reminded that Brahmadatta held the title of *uparikamahārāja* in the other plate dated year 163.[156] The enhanced presence of administrative machinery detectable in the Mahatiraktamala plate can thus be connected with his acquisition of the status of a subordinate ruler and attempt to strengthen local control by interfering with function of the *adhikaraṇa*. Such an attempt is also detected among the lower level administrators. In the Damodarpur plate of year 224, it is mentioned as a part of verification by *pustapāla*s that any obstacle should not be made by a *viṣayapati*.[157] It suggests that there was some attempt by the administrator to interfere with the affair of land purchase and donation, which had been exclusively decided by the *adhikaraṇa*s with the verification of *pustapāla*s. Here we can detect the rise of some section of administrators who would defy the authority of the *adhikaraṇa*s.

Contradictions in agrarian relations and their implications

The discussions made above clarified the position of the *adhikaraṇa*s and its basis within and outside rural society, and the participants and their power relations observable in the transactions at these organisations. Now I would like to examine the meaning of land purchase and donation in view of those discussions, the pattern of agrarian relations inferable from it and the contradictions inherent in this pattern.

In all the cases but one, the land purchase and donation was claimed to be a pious deed.[158] In the cases in which *brāhmaṇa*s themselves were petitioners cum recipients, the land was said to be purchased for their daily rituals.[159] This can be an expression suggesting that the purpose of land purchase was subsistence of these *brāhmaṇa*s in rural society. The donations to *brāhmaṇa*s for their daily rituals or settling were the same in this respect.[160] In the other cases, the land purchase and donation was claimed to be made either for the acquisition of religious merit (*puṇya*) by petitioners or their parents,[161] or for the maintenance of religious institutions.[162] The acquisition of prestige and distinction in rural society may have been intended by the petitioners in these acts. The minute analysis of these cases, however, points to the economic aspect of land purchase and donation.

According to petitioners and size of land, cases can be divided into the two categories. First to mention is the case of residents or would-be residents of locality applying for a small-scale land purchase. In the Damodarpur plates of years 124 and 128, the petitioners were *brāhmaṇa*s most probably engaged in cultivation of the land.[163] In the other cases, the petitioners seem to have been involved in management of donated tracts. In the Baigram plate, *kuṭumbin* brothers Bhoyila and Bhāskara purchased 3 *kulyavāpa*s of *khilakṣetra* and 2 *droṇavāpa*s of *vāstu* land for maintenance of the Sun temple built by their father. It is clearly mentioned which plots in two villages were given to Bhoyila and Bhāskara respectively,[164] while they collectively paid money for all the plots.[165] It suggests that they would respectively cultivate or manage these newly acquired land plots and allocate a part of their product for maintenance of the temple. The cases of the Jagadishpur and Paharpur plates were similar. In the former, the 6 *droṇavāpa*s of land assigned to *śramaṇakācārya* Balakuṇḍa for maintenance of the Buddhist *vihāra*s was said to belong to the three petitioners, while 2 *dropnavāpa*s of the Sun temple belonged to one of them.[166] In the latter, *brāhmaṇa* Nāthaśarman and his wife Rāmī acquired land plots 1 1/2 *kulyavāpa*s in total for their use in a manner requested by themselves, namely, for maintenance of a Jain *vihāra*.[167] In these cases, the petitioners may have managed the donated land plot and enjoyed its product on the condition that they would transfer a part of it to the donees for stipulated purposes. In case of the Kalaikuri plate, the petitioners consisting of a *kulika*, seven *kāyastha*s and two *pustapāla*s purchased 9 *kulyavāpa*s of land plots and donated them to the three *brāhmaṇa*s. While the donees acquired 5, 2 and 2 *kulyavāpa*s respectively, land plots were scattered around the four settlements as 1 *kulyavāpa* in Dhānyapāṭalikagrāma, 2 *droṇavāpa*s in Gulmagandhika, and 7 *kulyavāpa*s and 6 *droṇavāpa*s in the three hamlets belonging to Hastiśīrśa and Vibhītaka.[168] It means that each donee held several separate land plots distributed over those settlements and had them cultivated by local residents. It is possible that the petitioners were involved in the management of donated tracts, even though they were not directly engaged in cultivation.

From the discussion made above, we can assume that those donated tracts were managed by the petitioners. The size of plot for each petitioner ranged from 1/3 *kulyavāpa* in the Jagadishpur plate to 1 5/8 *kulyavāpa*s in the Baigram plate. As the petitioners must have their own landholdings which enabled them to accumulate enough wealth to purchase *khila* land plots, the involvement in the management of the donated plots could be additional and interpreted as an extension of agrarian management through the reclamation of *khilakṣetra*. From the rough estimation of the size of a *kulyavāpa*, we can conclude that what was added to the landholdings of petitioners was rather moderate.

Another category is the purchase and donation of relatively large land plots by outsiders, which was witnessed in the later phase from the reign of Budhagupta onwards. In the Mahatiraktamala plate, *mahāmātra* Suvarcasadatta purchased 2 *kulyavāpa*s of land plot to donate it to a *brāhmaṇa* belonging to a community of *cāturvidya*s, while *viṣayapati* Chattramaha in the Nandapur plate purchased 4 *kulyavāpa*s for a *brāhmaṇa* with the title of *agrahārika*.[169] In case of the Damodarpur plate without date, *nagaraśreṣṭhin* Ribhupāla donated 11 *kulyavāpa*s of land plots previously and homestead land for two temples and two small storehouses further to the deities Kokāmukhasvāmin and Śvetavarāhasvāmin.[170] *Kulaputra* Amṛtadeva, the petitioner of the Damodarpur plate of year 224, purchased 5 *kulyavāpa*s of *khilakṣetra* and donated it to the last deity.[171] It is not clear which side, petitioners or donees, was involved in the management of the donated tracts. At least in the third case, it was plausible that the petitioner Ribhupāla was involved in the management of these temples and their landholdings, as discussed in the previous section. No matter which took charge, both petitioners and donees had to organise reclamation and cultivation of the donated *khilakṣetra* by mobilising local residents.

In both categories of land purchase and donation, one economic aspect, namely, the acquisition or extension of resource base is recognisable as an intension of petitioners. What compelled them to take this form to accomplish their purposes? One answer lay in the contemporary agrarian relation.

The presence of *kuṭumbin*s as a main component of rural society indicates the production based on family labour of their household as a dominant form. It had reached the level well beyond subsistence, at which some could accumulate enough wealth to purchase land plots. Both in terms of wealth and authority, the differentiation among *kuṭumbin*s was in progress as discussed above. However, it had not yet gone far enough to generate a sharp division among cultivators and a separation of landholding and cultivation. In this condition, the extension of agrarian management was possible for some members of rural society only through the acquisition of additional land plot and its cultivation by family labour, limited size of which inevitably resulted in the moderate scale of management. The limitation was the same for influential outsiders who should depend on the additional labour of *kuṭumbin*s for the extension of their agrarian base and its management, in the absence of any alternative way of labour mobilisation. They had to negotiate with *kuṭumbin*s, especially their dominant section, for this purpose.

Another answer can be found in the discussions on the *adhikaraṇa* made above. The *adhikaraṇa* wielded the authority to preside over the matters related to *khilakṣetra* as an organisation representing both remnant of communal control and emerging state claim over land in different degrees. It was necessary for the dominant sections both within and outside rural society to overcome the restrictions imposed by community and state for extending their resource base through the reclamation and cultivation of waste/fallow land. Their petition for land purchase and donation can be understood as a way to legitimately overcome both restrictions in the name of religious endowment. In this respect, religious agents were important as providers of legitimacy. These agents were in turn beneficiaries of the transactions, partaking of product from the donated tracts.

The agrarian relation and manner of expansion discussed above had inherent contradictions. Though the production was beyond subsistence, the potential of further agrarian expansion was limited by available labour power confined to that of family members. The relation of *kuṭumbin*s to rural society and community was also contradictory. As just discussed above, the remnant of communal control over land was an obstacle to the extension of their resource base, at least for their dominant section. However, their dominance and eminence in rural society was based on their capacity to represent its interest. It was also necessary for them to keep their solidarity as a community to confront the external authority, as was attested by the cases of them retaining some right over the execution of land donation against the authority of the external *adhikaraṇa*.[172]

These contradictions were to be resolved by the stratification of cultivators, growth of landed magnates and establishment of their dominance, and weakening of communal restriction all of which would result in a new agrarian relation with subjection of cultivators. Some symptoms in this direction were present in the later phase of this period. More complicated gradation of *kuṭumbin*s found in the Mahatiraktamala plate and the Damodarpur plate of year 163 was one of them.[173] The most notable, however, was a new pattern of land purchase and donation involving outsiders and relatively large plots represented by the second category mentioned above. Their involvement in land management dependent on labour of *kuṭumbin*s indicates the tendency towards higher land rights separated from cultivation. The same can be said of the religious institutions accumulating land plots, which had potential to grow to large-scale landholders. This new pattern also suggests the growing presence of authorities outside rural society, of which the emergence of state officials interfering with rural society overriding or defying the authority of *adhikaraṇa*, detectable in the Mahatiraktamala plate and the Damodarpur plate of year 224 GE, may be one symptom.[174] In spite of those developments, the limit imposed by labour shortage and communal control remained, as shown by the continuance of the same form of agrarian expansion and the procedure centred on the *adhikaraṇa*. The resolution of aforementioned contradictions would be seen in the following period in a different social and political context.

Samataṭa: agrarian development and emergence of local kingship

Samataṭa witnessed a form of political power and a pattern of agrarian development different from those in Puṇḍravardhana. The process of state formation in this sub-region had started by the mid-fourth century, as its king is mentioned in the Allahabad pillar inscription of Samudragupta as one of the peripheral kings (*pratyantanṛpati*) who acknowledged his suzerainty.[175] The continued presence of a subordinate king under the Guptas is attested by the grant of *mahārāja maheśvara* Nāthacandra, dated year 91 GE, which is copied on the copper plate grant of Vainyagupta dated year 184. It records the royal donation of vast land tract, 1,355 *droṇavāpa*s in total, and 19 kinds of movables to the Ājīvikas.[176] The titles of *mahāsāndhivigrahika* and *kumārāmātya* held by Mādhavadatta, an official whose approval was given for engraving the grant of Nāthacandra, hint at an attempt of the early Samataṭa kings to introduce a bureaucratic apparatus modelled on the Gupta one,[177] to be developed further by the time of Vainyagupta. The appearance of Pūrva- and Dakṣiṇamaṇḍalas in the same grant suggests the establishment of administrative divisions consisting of *maṇḍala*s of the four cardinal directions.[178] The Uttaramaṇḍala mentioned in the Gunaighar plate of Vainyagupta, dated year 188 GE, confirms it.[179] These aspects attest to some level of state formation reached by the early fifth century.

The grant of Vainyagupta, which approves the previous grant to Ājīvikas made by Nāthacandra, proves the continued presence of subordinate rulers of Samataṭa under the Gupta suzerainty until the early sixth century, though nothing can be known from this plate on the political situation in the interval of the reigns of the two kings, covering 90 years or so. However, it gives us better information on Vainyagupta's rule and the changing character of his power. His status as a subordinate ruler under an overlord is clear from the phrase *paramabhaṭṭārakapādānudhyāta* attached to him and his titles of *pañcādhikaraṇoparika*, *mahāpratīhāra* and *mahārāja*.[180] In contrast, his Gunaighar grant, dated year 188 GE, does not contain any expressions indicating his subordinate status, except the title *mahārāja* and dating in the Gupta Era. The word *paramabhaṭṭāraka* in the phrase of subordination is replaced by Bhagavan Mahādeva, with which the overall expression rather conveys his claim of acceptance by god Śiva.[181] Vainyagupta seems to have attained the position verging on semi-independence in the period of around four years between year 184 GE, Caitra 13 and year 188 GE, Pauṣa 24, the dates of his two plates. The enhancement of his power is suggested by the presence of subordinate rulers wielding the title of *mahārāja* under him. *Mahārāja* Rudradatta, the applicant for donation, was called 'servant of our feet' (*asmatpādadāsa*), while *mahārāja* Vijayasena acted as a messenger (*dūtaka*) of the royal order.[182] Suggestively, the titles held by the king in the earlier grant were then borne by Vijayasena, whose titles include *mahāpratīhāra*, *mahāpīlupati*, *pañcādhikaraṇoparika*, *pāṭyuparika*, *purapāloparika*, *mahārāja* and *mahāsāmanta*.[183]

The agrarian development in Samataṭa was in progress in this political context, namely, the formation of subordinate kingdom and its growth towards semi-independence. The descriptions of donated land plots in the copied grant of Nāthacandra indicate the relatively high level of agrarian development and settlement formation from the early period (**Table 3.4**). In Jayanāṭana of Pūrvamaṇḍala, a large tract of 1,235 *droṇavāpa*s in size consisting of 28 land plots were procured from the 46 individual landholders scattered around the 16 settlements, mostly through purchase in the 12 occasions, for each of which names of one to five witnesses are mentioned (**Table 3.4, Plots 1–28**). Though it was large, this tract must have been only a part of the entire cultivated area, and 13 more settlements are mentioned as either residential villages of witnesses or neighbouring settlements.[184] It should be added that another land plot of 120 *droṇavāpa*s in Taralacaṇḍa of Dakṣiṇamaṇḍala (**Table 3.4, Plot 29**), which could belong to the king himself,[185] was also donated to the Ājīvika *saṃgha*.

Geographical context of the agrarian development is discernible in the inscription. Minute descriptions of the 28 land plots in Jayanāṭana are

Table 3.4 Land plots, landholders and witnesses in the third CPI of Vainyagupta, year 184 GE (Ryosuke Furui, 'Ājīvikas, Maṇibhadra and Early History of Eastern Bengal: A New Copperplate Inscription of Vainyagupta and its Implications', *Journal of the Royal Asiatic Society*, 2016, 26(4): 660–61, ll. 15–41, 662, l. 43.)

Plot	*Location*	*dro*	*Dī*	*Landholders*	*Remarks*
Land Plots in Jayanāṭana of Pūrvamaṇḍala					
Occasion 1 witnesses: Siddhagodama (Heṣamakhalla), Śrīvilāla (Jayanāṭana), Usalamanaśācāra (Do.)					
1	Jakkanaśāṭi	40	4	Poyāvādappa, Paḍakhāsika	
2	Do.	15	1 1/2	Dharmadevavilāla, Kantārakarmāntika	
3	Do.	15	1 1/2	Umalavaṅgāla, Utpalavaṅgālaka	
	Sum	70	7		
Occasion 2 witnesses: Oghāgrāmanaśācāra, Guṇamāne . . . (Jakkanaśāṭi), Mattenapalagāla, Vondorakarmāntika (Do.)					
4	Pāyanāṭana	10	1	Paḍakhāsiyāka	
5	Do., in a forest (*vanaka*)	20	2	Akkihoravaḍḍi, Paṭṭiyāka	
	Sum	30	3		
Occasion 3 witnesses: Khedamanaśācāravaḍḍidaṇḍa (Ulagiuccālikā)					
6	Jakkanaśāṭi	30		Bhivaravaḍḍi, Siddhavaṅgāla	donated as gift
7	Pāyanāṭana	40		Ghidharāvadda	belonging to (*santaka*)
8	Ulagiuccālikā	100		*tasya* (=Ghidharāvadda), Sivaravela	belonging to (*santaka*)
9	Do.	20	2	Kopanikheda, Kāyaśāka	
	Sum	190	2		
Occasion 4 witnesses: Gomapoya, Devavaṅgāla, Malliyāka (Jakkanaśāṭi)					
10	Jakkanaśāṭi	30	3	Ajarudra, Nadiyāka	
11	Do.	20	2	Ammadeva, his son Siddhāka	
12	Do.	40	4	Pūdanikā's sons Usalāka, Grodāka, Pokkaka	
	Sum	90	9		

(*Continued*)

Table 3.4 (Continued)

Plot	*Location*	*dro*	*Dī*	*Landholders*	*Remarks*
Occasion 5 witnesses: Bhīmavilāla (Peraññaśaka), Jaḍḍavaṅgāla, Iṭṭahāni (Arīuccāli)					
13	Peraññaśaka	40	4	Virimaināri, Mamipraka, Vaḍidakṣi . . .	
Occasion 6 witnesses (for 15 and 16): Paṭṭivaṅgāla, Bhondoravilāla (Nāgapaṭṭoccālikā)					
14	Kheṇṭavilla	15		Vokkicandā . . .	belonging to (*santaka*)
15	Nagnapaṭṭoccālikā	80	8	Jaḍḍolakarmāntika	
16	Nāgapaṭṭoccālikā	20	2	Ugeyā	
	Sum	115	10		
Occasion 7 witnesses: with Paṭṭimatta, Mūladevākavaṅgāla (Gothāna), Ghomaśāka, Ekhada (Tyugroccālikā)					
17	Maramallatuṣappa	40		Śrīmatta, Kaḍḍaparamatta	divided into half and donated
18	Ūracaṇḍoccālikā	40	4	Siddhakeppaśreṣṭhin	
	Sum	80	4		
Occasion 8 witnesses: Nāgolakarmānti, Posagavilāla (Heṣamakhalla), Dvādaśācaṇḍika (Peratyugra), Ambukarmāntika, Kelāmeṭa (Khaddatyugra)					
19	Tyugroccālikā	60	6	Jaḍḍolakarmāntika, Khedāka	
20	Do.	90	30	Yuṅgipunnakakāra, Gadollavilāla, Hakkavaḍḍika	after attaching to Nāgolārikhāṭa
21	Marameṭa		18	Jaḍḍolakarmāntika, Indiramanaśācāra	Four houses
	Sum	150	54		
Occasion 9 witnesses: Dīmmittrajyeṣṭhaka, Drapadhelagodama (Peragodamakoṭṭa)					
22	Khaddamattanoccālikā	80	8	Goyolakarmāntikavilāla's son Khavatti, Mayīpaṭyāla, Jannaka	Caturvargikakṣetra

Occasion 10 witnesses: Khāḍupolasoriyāka (Bhāśilaśāṭi), Pradyumna, Nademaka, Dīvamanaśācāra (Ma . . . śola), with Paṭṭimatta					
23	Udyāttaśāṭi	50		Danta	of Danta residing there
24	Peravakaṭi	100	20	Nīleśva . . . nāgika, Āśriyākapaṭyāla	to the north of Uraṅgi-paccālāgrahāra in a cluster with Bheḍavilla
	Sum	150	20		
Occasion 11 witnesses: Laṅkānātha, Bhollabappa (Ūracaṇḍa), Paccālaka (Vendāsyagrahāra)					
25	Godhānikā	40	4	Paṭṭivādappa	to the east of Ūracaṇḍa
Occasion 12 witnesses: Paṭṭinamaga (no mention), Nāgolakarmāntika (Khaddhatyugra)					
26	Ketogapaṭṭoccālikā	60	6	Vilālameḍi, Attapoya	with the land of Nalāmātya
27	Do.	40	4	Paṭṭinamaga of Phalaśapaṭṭikṣetra	
28	Do.	100	10	Manuvilāla of Bhīmārikṣetra	
	Sum	200	20		
	Sum total	1,235	145		
A Land Plot in Dakṣiṇamaṇḍala					
29	Taralacaṇḍa	120			belonging to (*santaka*)
	Total	1,355			

followed by reference to the two large tracts of land. They are a) 717 *droṇavāpa*s in Svākagileraka belonging to Vātagaṅgā, making a cluster with Sakeḍḍikoṭṭa, with homestead land and cultivated land, and b) 518 *droṇavāpa*s of land in Vātagaṅgā, in Unnatasāra bordering the storehouse (*bhāṇḍāra*) and cremation ground (*śmaśāna*).[186] The sum of both tracts, 1,235 *droṇavāpa*s, equals the sum of all the 28 land plots listed in the previous section. It seems to mean that the land described in this section is actually the same as all the plots listed in the previous section combined. We find here the sum of land plots divided into two groups according to a different criterion. The division seems to be based on the location of land plots in relation to particular geographical features including a river, fort, storehouse and cremation ground. Centrality of Vātagaṅgā, a river, for both tracts suggests concentration of settlements and progress of reclamation in the area along this river.[187]

Somewhat different degree of agrarian development is discernible in the Gunaighar plate of Vainyagupta, year 188. It also records the royal land donation of relatively large size, 11 *pāṭaka*s of *khila* land in five plots in Kānteḍadakagrāma of Uttaramaṇḍala.[188] As a *pāṭaka* in this plate equals 40 *droṇavāpa*s,[189] 11 *pāṭaka*s are equal to 440 *droṇaavāpa*s. All the border landmarks of these plots, except the neighbouring settlements and a pond,[190] consist of cultivated land (*kṣetra*) prefixed with the term *rājavihāra*,[191] personal name or names,[192] or the term denoting a profession.[193] They attest to some degree of agrarian development, at which varieties of landholders were engaged in cultivation, directly or indirectly. It should however be noted that the donated tract was categorised as *khila*, uncultivated or fallow. The availability of a large expanse of uncultivated or fallow land side by side with many cultivated land plots within the same village indicates room for further agrarian expansion. From these points, the agrarian development in this village is deemed to have been at the early stage where the expansion of cultivation had not exhausted its potential, and reclamation of uncultivated tracts was still on the way.

The ecological context of this early phase of agrarian development is shown by the border demarcation of the low land (*talabhūmi*) and the marshy *khila* land (*hajjikakhilabhūmi*) of the *vihāra*, which are mentioned additionally and seem to be in the vicinity of the other plots. The former was surrounded on the three sides by watercourse (*jolā*) and canal (*khāṭa*) with boat-landings (*nauyoga*),[194] and the latter had Hacāta river (*gaṅga*) on its west side.[195] Their location on the riverside connected with other areas through watercourses is clear in this description. It suggests that the early agrarian expansion in this area was undertaken by reclaiming riverine tracts.

Both cases discussed above suggest agrarian development in riverine tracts. The symptom of ongoing reclamation found in the Gunaighar grant points to the wave of agrarian expansion arriving at the area in Uttaramaṇḍala later in the early sixth century, while the enormity of donated plots in the

Nāthacandra's grant attests to the intensive cultivation under which the riverine tracts along Vātagaṅgā were put by the early fifth century. It seems that the intensive cultivation was limited to such tracts in a particular area in the early period and that the further agrarian expansion was facilitated by the following reclamation of similar riverine tracts in the other areas. This form of agrarian development would be followed by another, the reclamation of vast forest tracts in the period from the seventh century onwards, enabled by a changed power relation to be discussed in the next chapter minutely.

The people most closely connected with agrarian development and management were landholders. In the grant of Nāthacandra, their inner difference is detectable in the size of land plots procured from them, ranging between 10 and 100 *droṇavāpa*s, which were held singularly or collectively (**Table 3.4**). Though these plots must not have been all the landed properties held by them, the size of each plot tells us how much were alienable for different landholders and can be taken as an indicator of their respective wealth. While two pairs of them, the Dharmadevavilāla and Kantārakarmāntika in the one case and Umalavaṅgāla and Utpalavaṅgālaka in another, sold only 15 *droṇavāpa*s each (**Table 3.4, Plots 2, 3**), Jaḍḍolakarmāntika sold 80 *droṇavāpa*s alone (**Table 3.4, Plot 15**). The latter also sold 60 *droṇavāpa*s of land plot and four houses with the other holders (**Table 3.4, Plots 19, 21**).[196] Such difference in wealth among landholders confirms the ongoing process of agrarian development which would result in concentration of landed properties in fewer hands. The coexistence of both individual and collective landholdings among the plots mentioned as border landmarks in the Gunaighar plate also suggests similar difference among landholders.[197]

The difference is not limited to their wealth. The names of landholders in both inscriptions show diverse social groups included in this category. The names suffixed with *karmāntika* (artisan) and *śreṣṭhin* (merchant) in Nāthacandra's grant suggest inclusion of some professional groups in the circle of rural residents with substantial landholdings and respectability.[198] The names ending in *vilāla*, literally meaning 'machine' or 'cat,'[199] can also denote such a professional group, namely, artisans specialised in particular mechanical devices.[200] The landholdings by professional groups are also confirmed by the cultivated lands (*kṣetra*) of Viṣṇuvardhaki (carpenter), Miduvilāla, Pakkavilāla and *vaidya*s (physicians) mentioned in the Gunaighar plate as border landmarks.[201] The land of *khaṇḍa* Viḍuggurika mentioned in the last plate suggests inclusion of some local functionaries in this circle.[202] On the other hand, the name ending Vaṅgāla, the same as the toponym denoting the coastal region of south-east Bengal, found in the first grant alludes to their origin as migrants from this area.[203]

The forms of agrarian managements by those landholders also show some diversity. The reference to father and son or children of a particular person as collective landholders attest to a family holding and its cultivation with family labour (**Table 3.4, Plots 11–12, 22**),[204] while the collective holdings by seemingly unrelated people indicates joint holding and cultivation by neighbouring residents (**Table 3.4, Plots 1–2, 5–6, 8–10, 13, 19–21, 24, 26**). The professional groups and officials may have others cultivate their land plots, though the deployment of their own family members cannot be ruled out.

In spite of their diversity, especially in terms of their wealth, no hierarchical divisions seem to have developed among landholders, unlike *mahattaras* and several categories of *kuṭumbins* in Puṇḍravardhana. The superiority of peasant householders over other social groups witnessed in the last subregion was also absent, at least among those named in the inscriptions. Even witnesses in Nāthacandra's grant mentioned as verifiers of transference of land plots did not show any substantial difference from landholders. Both shared common name endings,[205] and Paṭṭinamaga appeared as both landholder and witness.[206] What the listed names of witnesses represent can be concluded as mutual confirmation by rural residents of more or less the same status. It made a stark contrast with procedures surrounding *adhikaraṇas* in Puṇḍravardhana discussed above, in which complicated power relations among urban and rural residents were detected. Thus, the social relation of rural residents in Samataṭa, at least their landed sector, was less hierarchical. On the other hand, their horizontal relation beyond one village was attested by the witnesses residing in different villages acting together.[207]

The character of social relation among landholders seems not to have changed substantially in the later period, as far as discernible from the border demarcations in the Gunaighar plate. Landholders including professionals continued to hold land plots individually or collectively, without any clear indication of their stratification.

Rural society without sharp stratification was overborne by the power and authority of the king and the state apparatus under him. From the earliest time, he had been the sole authority to issue a land grant and to authorise revenue exemption. The orders of both Nāthacandra and Vainyagupta were addressed to their present and future subordinates, without any reference to local residents.[208] However, Nāthacandra still had to purchase most of land plots from individual or collective landholders spending as much as 145 *dīnāras* with only a few cases of possible confiscation (**Table 3.4**).[209] Though the large amount of gold coins paid for land plots indicates his power to extract from rural society and accumulate enormous wealth, he was yet to claim overarching right over land superseding the proprietary right of landholders. In contrast, Vainyagupta as both receiver of petition and donor wielded the overarching authority over land in his own territory in the Gunaighar plate, even though it was limited to *khila* land. It tallied well with his status enhanced towards semi-independence.

The growth of kingship accompanied more complicated relation within the state apparatus, represented by the conspicuous presence of subordinate rulers in the case recorded in the Gunaighar grant. The role of *mahārāja mahāsāmanta* Vijayasena as a messenger conveying the grant and his titles connoting both military and administrative capacities allude to the employment of these subordinate rulers as state functionaries.[210] The three *kumārāmātyabhogikas* Revajjasvāmin, Bhāmaha and Vatsa, who executed the royal order, also seem to have been such functionaries, as their title *bhogika* indicates their position of enjoying some land assignment.[211] On the other hand, the activity of *mahārāja* Rudradatta, who petitioned the king for land donation to Buddhist *saṃghas*, shows another aspect of the relation between the king and subordinate rulers, which involved religious agents.

The presence of religious agents as an authority above local residents was pronounced in case of the Ājīvika *saṃgha*, which was the donee of enormous size of land tracts in plots scattered around 17 settlements. For their management, it needed to mobilise labour power of its own servants, if any, or local residents by exerting some authority. The grant by Nāthacandra and its approval by Vainyagupta indicate the royal authority empowering the *saṃgha* to employ necessary labour power. The landholdings and control by the *saṃgha* in turn enabled the king to extend and entrench his authority over rural society by its exercise through the network of the *saṃgha* and its territory. The incentive for large-scale grant and its maintenance by those kings may have lain in this point.

The growth of state apparatus inducing complicated relation between the king and his subordinate rulers, detectable in the Gunaighar plate, gives another angle to the comprehension of religious institutions: they became focuses of the contention between those political powers. Rudradatta, the petitioner of donation in the Gunaighar plate, seems to have had a personal connection with *ācārya* Śāntideva, under whose name he was building a *vihāra*.[212] His construction of the *vihāra* and the land donation to its Buddhist *saṃghas* petitioned by him may have contributed to the enhancement of his presence and authority in the locality. This was the case in which a subordinate ruler tried to legitimately enhance his power with royal sanction in the name of religious endowment. The petition must be entertained as far as it conformed to the norm of charitable act and respected the royal authority over the land in own territory. The grudge with which the king accepted the petition could be detected in the phrase 'accepting the pain/burden by oneself' mentioned in his considerations on the merit of land donation.[213] The king had to donate land plots while anticipating a loss.

Further evidence of the contention around religious institutions is found in the description of border landmarks including a temple (*devakula*) of Pradyumneśvara and three Buddhist *vihāras*. Their patronage by different political authorities is detectable at least for the Buddhist *vihāras*. Rājavihāra, whose land plot bordered the first and second donated plots,[214] seems to have been established by the king. The *vihāra* which received land donations in the grant was constructed by Rudradatta in the name of Śāntideva. The other *vihāra* of Buddhist monk Jitasena, of which the land plot bordered marshy *khila* land belonging to the last *vihāra*,[215] may have been established by another authority in the name of this monk. It is remarkable that the landholdings of these religious institutions existed side by side in the same village. The land plot of the shrine of Pradyumneśvara was located between low land and marshy *khila* land of the *vihāra* of Rudradatta.[216] The competing presence of religious institutions patronised by the king and subordinate rulers alludes to their competition over the local influence through the establishment of these institutions and their landed properties. Though his overarching authority was acknowledged, the king still needed to extend his influence in this way. Together with the case of petition by Rudradatta, it shows a precarious balance with which the king kept his authority over subordinate rulers and the effort of the latter to negotiate their position with him.

Samataṭa in this period saw intensive agrarian development in particular riverine tracts with room for further agrarian expansion. Rural society in the region can be considered the one consisting of less stratified landholders, imposed of the control of religious institutions and state apparatus with inner contention among its constituents, the king and subordinate rulers. While the accumulation of landed property by rural landholders, though in progress, did not result in the emergence of local landed magnates, the superimposition of religious institutions and political powers on rural society gave rise to the superior right over particular land plots. Further developments in those aspects will be seen in the next period, with more diversity within.

Notes

1 *SI* 1, p. 265, l. 21.
2 *Ibid.*, p. 351, l. 2.
3 *Ibid.*, p. 283, l. 1.
4 According to the evidence of Baigram CPI, one *dīnāra* is equal to 16 *rūpaka*s. *Ibid.*, p. 357, note 1. For currencies mentioned in the inscriptions from Bengal, see B. D. Chattopadhyaya, 'Currency in Early Bengal', *Journal of Indian History*, 1977, 55(3): 41–60.
5 Chitrarekha Gupta, '"Khila-kṣetras" in Early Bengal Inscriptions', in Debala Mitra and Gouriswar Bhattacharya (eds), *Studies in Art and Archaeology of Bihar and Bengal: Nalinīkānta Śatavārṣikī, Dr. N. K. Bhattasali Centenary Volume (1888–1988)*, Delhi: Sri Satguru Publications, 1989, p. 272. Cf. Sachindra Kumar Maity, *Economic Life in Northern India in the Gupta Period (Cir. A. D. 300–550)* (2nd ed.), Delhi: Motilal Banarsidass, 1970, p. 35.
6 Toshio Yamazaki, 'Some Aspects of Land-Sale Inscriptions in Fifth and Sixth Century Bengal', *Acta Asiatica*, 1982, 43: 20–21.
7 Idem, '5, 6 Seiki Bengal No Tochibaibaimonjo Ni Tsuiteno Jakkan No Kousatsu' (Some considerations on the land sale documents of the fifth and sixth century Bengal) (in Japanese), *Toyo Bunka Kenkyujo Kiyo*, 1959, 18: 104, note 3.
8 Barrie M. Morrison, *Political Centers and Cultural Regions in Early Bengal*, Tucson: University of Arizona Press, 1970, p. 85.

9 *SI* 1, p. 356, l. 5, p. 357, l. 11, p. 382, l. 5, p. 383, l. 9. Cf. *Ibid.*, p. 382, note 4.
10 *Ibid.*, p. 292, l. 7, p. 348, l. 6.
11 B. D. Chattopadhyaya, *Aspects of Rural Settlements and Rural Society in Early Medieval India*, Calcutta: K P Bagchi, 1990, pp. 20–24.
12 *dhanaviṣṇupuṣkiriṇyā, nābhrakasatakasīmā*, *EDEP*, p. 62, l. 21. *Sataka* seems to be a colloquial form of *svatvaka*, meaning 'own land' in this context.
13 *pañcavarṣāvasannaṃ tu syāt kṣetram aṭavīsamam*, Richard W. Lariviere (ed., tr., annot.), *The Nāradasmṛti*, Philadelphia: Department of South Asia Regional Studies, Pennsylvania University, 1989, 11. 23cd.
14 *aśaktapretanaṣṭeṣu kṣetrikeṣv anivāritaḥ | kṣetraṃ ced vikṛṣet kaścid aśnuvīta ca tatphalam || vikṛṣyamāṇe kṣetre cet kṣetrikaḥ punar āvrajet | khilopacāraṃ tat sarvaṃ dattvā svakṣetram āpnuyāt ||*, *ibid.*, 11. 20–21.
15 *tatkṣettrasamīpyabhūmau*, *SI* 1, p. 337, l. 7; *atrāraṇye*, *ibid.*, p. 348, l. 8.
16 *Ibid.*, p. 357, ll. 8–9, p. 358, ll. 15–17.
17 *EDEP*, p. 62, ll. 18–19.
18 *SI* 1, p. 360, l. 7, p. 361, l. 14.
19 *Ibid.*, p. 338, ll. 8–9, ll. 11–12.
20 *Ibid*, pp. 356–57, ll. 4–6, p. 357, ll. 11–12; *EDEP*, pp. 61–62, ll. 12–13; *SI* 1, p. 360, ll. 4–5.
21 *Ibid.*, pp. 359–63.
22 (*aṣṭakana*)*vakanalā*[*bhyā*]*m apaviñchya*, Dhanaidaha CPI, *SI* 1, p. 288, l. 11; *darvvīkarmmahastenāṣṭakanavakanalābhyām apaviñcchya*, Baigram CPI, *ibid.*, p. 358, ll. 18–19, Nandapur CPI, *ibid.*, p. 383, l. 14; *ṣaṭkanaḍair apaviñcchya*, Paharpur CPI, *ibid.*, p. 362, ll. 19–20; (*a*)*ṣṭakanavakanavakanalābhyām apaviñchya*, Damodarpur CPI, year 163 GE, *ibid.*, p. 334, l. 10. *naitikakuddālakhātikaratnyāṣṭakanavakanalābhyām apaviñcchya*, Arlo Griffiths, 'New Documents for the Early History of Puṇḍravardhana: Copperplate Inscriptions from the Late Gupta and Early Post-Gupta Periods', *Pratna Samiksha: A Journal of Archaeology, New Series*, 2015, 6: 20, l. 21.
23 Morrison, *Political Centers and Cultural Regions*, pp. 88–89.
24 Dhanaidaha CPI, *SI* 1, pp. 287–89; Damodarpur CPI, year 124 GE, *ibid.*, pp. 290–92; Damodarpur CPI, year 163 GE, *ibid.*, pp. 332–34.
25 *Ibid.*, pp. 354–55, ll. 25–27.
26 *Ibid.*, pp. 292–94.
27 *Ibid.*, pp. 382–84; Griffiths, 'New Documents', p. 19, ll. 3–6.
28 D. C. Sircar, *Indian Epigraphy*, Delhi: Motilal Banarsidass, 1965, pp. 413–14.
29 W. W. Hunter, *A Statistical Account of Bengal, vol. 7: Districts of Maldah, Rangpur, and Dinajpur*, Delhi: Concept Publishing Company, 1984 (reprint), pp. 74–75 (Maldah, 30–50 *bighas*), p. 263 (Rangpur, about 25 *bighas*), p. 395 (Dinajpur, 3 ploughs = 15 acres = 45 *bighas*); idem, *A Statistical Account of Bengal, vol. 8: Districts of Rajshahi and Bogra*, Delhi: Concept Publishing Company, 1984 (reprint), p. 65 (Rajshahi, about 35 *bighas*), p. 203 (Bogra, average-sized farm consists of 30 *bighas*).
30 Maity, *Economic Life in Northern India*, pp. 37–39.
31 *SI* 1, pp. 164–66.
32 *Ibid.*, pp. 318–20.
33 Gupta, 'Khila-kṣetras', p. 273.
34 Ex. *śrīpara*[*mabhaṭṭāraka*]*pādīyakumārāmātyādhikaraṇa*, T. Bloch, 'Excavations at Basarh', *Annual Report of Archaeological Survey of India*, 1903–04: 108, no. 8; *śrīyuvarājabhaṭṭārakapādīyabalādhikaraṇasya*, *ibid.*, no. 12, Pl. 40.5.
35 Ex. *para*[*madaiva*]*taparamabhaṭṭārakamahārājādhirāja*[*śrīkumāragupte*] *pṛthivīpatau* [*tatpāda*]*parigṛhītasya pu*[*ṇḍra*]*vardhanabhuktāv upa*[*rikaci*]*rāta*

datta[sya] bhogenānuvahamānaka, Damodarpur CPI, year 128, *SI* 1, p. 293, ll. 1–3.

36 *Ibid.*, p. 347, ll. 2–3 (year 224).

37 *Ibid.*, p. 291, l. 3, p. 293, l. 2 (Cirātadatta, years 124 and 128), p. 333, l. 2 (Brahmadatta, year 163), p. 336, l. 2 (Jayadatta, in the time of Budhagupta, ND). Brahmadatta also appears as *uparika* in the Mahatiraktamala CPI. Griffiths, 'New Documents', p. 19, l. 8.

38 Damodarpur CPI, year 163, *SI* 1, p. 333, l. 2.

39 For *viṣaya*s mentioned in the contemporary inscriptions, see Parmeshwari Lal Gupta, *The Imperial Guptas*, vol.2, Varanasi: Vishwavidyalaya Prakashan, 1979, pp. 29–30.

40 For the limited but well-conducted excavation of the site, see Kunja Govinda Goswami, *Excavations at Bangarh (1938–41)*, Calcutta: University of Calcutta, 1948. For the recent excavation, see T. J. Baidya and Shantanu Maity, 'Excavation at Bangarh 2008–2009', *Pratna Samiksha: A Journal of Archaeology, New Series*, 2010, 1: 35–37.

41 This village is identified with present Uttara Damodarpur in Eluari union, Phulbari *upazila*, Dinajpur district. Ayoub Khan, 'Bengal Copperplates: Provenances and Preservation Data', *Pratnatattva*, 2007, 13: 6.

42 Ex. *tanniyuktakaku[mā]rāmātyave[tra]varmmaṇi*, Damodarpur CPI, year 128, *SI* 1, p. 293, ll. 3–4.

43 *Ibid.*, p. 291, l. 4, p. 293, l. 3 (*kumārāmātya*, years 124 and 128), p. 337, l. 3 (*āyuktaka*, in the time of Budhagupta, ND), p. 347, l. 4 (*viṣayapati*, year 224).

44 *Ibid.*, p. 291, ll. 3–4, p. 293, ll. 3–4, p. 337, l. 3, p. 347, ll. 3–4. It has often been mistaken for *viṣayādhikaraṇa*. Cf. Chattopadhyaya, *Aspects of Rural Settlements*, p. 39. However, it is clearly called *adhiṣṭhānādhikaraṇa*. *Viṣayādhikaraṇa* is a different category mentioned in the Baigram plate. *SI* 1, p. 356, l. 1.

45 Table 3.1, years 124 and 128 GE.

46 *śreṣṭhinigama*, D. B. Spooner, 'Excavations at Basarh, 1911–1912', *Annual Report of Archaeological Survey of India*, 1913–14: 126, nos 36 and 53, 140, no. 286 etc.; *śreṣṭhisārtthavāhanigama*, Bloch, 'Excavations at Basarh', p. 111, no. 40; *śreṣṭhisārtthavāhakulikanigama*, *ibid.*, p. 110, no. 28 etc.

47 The seals excavated from the site mostly belong to the earlier period. Goswami, *Excavations at Bangarh*, pp. 12–13.

48 Baigram is located in Present Boaldar union, Hakimpur *upazila*, Dinajpur district. Khan, 'Bengal Copperplates', p. 6, no. 5.

49 *bhaṭṭārakapādānudhyātaḥ kumārāmātyakulavṛddhir*, *SI* 1, p. 356, l. 1.

50 *Ibid.*, p. 382, l. 1; *yuṣmad viṣaye*, *ibid.*, l. 5; *iha viṣaye*, *ibid.*, p. 383, l. 8.

51 *bodhayanti*, *ibid.*, p. 356, l. 3; *bodhayanti likhanti ca*, *ibid.*, p. 382, l. 2.

52 *Ibid.*, p. 356, l. 1.

53 *Ibid.*, p. 382, l. 1.

54 *Ibid.*, p. 356, l. 2, p. 358, ll. 18–19; p. 382, ll. 1–2, p. 383, ll. 13–15.

55 *Ibid.*, p. 288, l. 7.

56 Jagadishpur belongs to Silmaria union, Puthia *upazila*, Rajshahi district. Khan, 'Bengal Copperplates', p. 6, no. 4.

57 Kalaikuri CPI, *SI* 1, p. 352, l. 1; Jagadishpur CPI, *EDEP*, p. 61, l. 1.

58 *bhaṭṭārakapādānuddhyātaḥ āyuktaka acyutaḥ*, *EDEP*, p. 61, l. 1.

59 *Ibid.*, l. 3.

60 Kalaikuri CPI, *SI* 1, p. 352, l. 1; Jagadishpur CPI, *EDEP*, p. 61, ll. 1–2.

61 Chattopadhyaya considers them not constituents of the *adhikaraṇa*, while being associated with its functioning. Chattopadhyaya, *Aspects of Rural Settlements*, p. 40. However, the use of the term *puroga*, which is used in the four Damodarpur

plates to indicate members of *adhiṣṭhānādhikaraṇa*, and the context show that they were members of the *adhikaraṇa* and took the initiative in the procedure.

62 Hastiśīrṣa, Vibhītakī, Gulmagandhikā, Dhānyapāṭalikā, Saṃgohāli in Kalaikuri CPI, *SI* 1, p. 352, ll. 1–2; Gulmagandhika, Saṅgohālika in Jagadishpur CPI, *EDEP*, p. 61, l. 2.

63 Kalaikuri CPI, *SI* 1, p. 352, ll. 1–2; Jagadishpur CPI, *EDEP*, p. 61, l. 2.

64 Bhoyila and Mahīdāsa, the residential *kuṭumbins* of Gulmagandhika, Jagadishpur CPI, *EDEP*, p. 61, ll. 3–4.

65 Paharpur belongs to Jagadishpur union, Badalgachi *upazila*, Naogaon district. Khan, 'Bengal Copperplates', p. 6, no. 7.

66 *EDEP*, p. 61, ll. 8–9.

67 *SI* 1, pp. 359–60, ll. 1–3.

68 *āryyanagaraśreṣṭhipurogañ cādhiṣṭhānādhikaraṇam*, *ibid*., p. 359, l. 1.

69 *maddhyamaṣaṇḍikavīthyāyuktakādhikaraṇasya*, Griffiths, 'New Documents', p. 19, main seal, ll. 1–2.

70 *Ibid*., p. 19, l. 8, p. 20, l. 16.

71 *Ibid*., p. 19, l. 1.

72 *Ibid*., p. 20, ll. 20–22.

73 *SI* 1, p. 288, l. 6, p. 333, ll. 2–3.

74 Yamazaki, 'Some Aspects of Land-Sale Inscriptions', p. 28.

75 Dhanaidaha CPI, *SI* 1, p. 288, l. 7.

76 Damodarpur CPI, year 163, *ibid*., pp. 332–34.

77 Chattopadhyaya, *Aspects of Rural Settlements*, p. 39.

78 *Goṣṭhaka* can be the same as *goṣṭhika*, meaning 'member of a committee or assembly'. *IEG*, p. 119.

79 *SI* 1, p. 288, ll. 9–11.

80 *mahattarādy*, *ibid*., p. 333, l. 2.

81 *Ibid*., p. 334, ll. 9–10.

82 Chattopadhyaya, *Aspects of Rural Settlements*, p. 38.

83 *Ibid*., p. 39.

84 Kalaikuri CPI, *SI* 1, pp. 352–55; Jagadishpur CPI, *EDEP*, pp. 61–63.

85 Dhanaidaha CPI, *SI* 1, pp. 287–89; Damodarpur CPI, year 163, *ibid*., pp. 332–34.

86 Damodarpur CPI, year 163, *ibid*., p. 333, ll. 2–3.

87 Damodrpur CPIs, *ibid*., p. 291, l. 6 (year 124), p. 293, l.5 (year 128), p. 337, l. 4 (in the time of Budhagupta, ND), p. 348, l. 5 (year 224). Also, Paharpur CPI, *ibid*., pp. 359–63.

88 In the Dhanaidaha CPI, the part related to the verification is unclear due to corrosion. *Ibid*., p. 288, l. 10. The Mahatiraktamala CPI does not contain any reference to the process of verification but mentions *pustapāla* Manorathadāsa soldering the seal. Griffiths 'New Documents', p. 20, ll. 25–26.

89 *SI* 1, pp .352–53, ll.3–4.

90 *grāma*: Damodarpur CPI, year 163, *ibid*., p. 333, l. 5. *vīthī*: Kalaikuri CPI, *ibid*., p. 353, ll. 12–13, p. 354, ll. 18–19; Jagadishpur CPI, *EDEP*, pp. 61–62, ll. 12–13. *viṣaya*: Baigram CPI, *SI* 1, pp. 356–57, ll. 4–6, p. 357, ll. 11–12; Nandapur CPI, *ibid*., pp. 382–83, ll. 5–6, p. 383, ll. 8–9; Damodarpur CPI, year 224, *ibid*., p. 348, ll. 6–7. *adhiṣṭhānādhikaraṇa*: Paharpur CPI, *ibid*., p. 360, ll. 4–5, p. 361, ll. 11–12.

91 *iha*: Dhanaidaha CPI, *ibid*., p. 288, l. 7; Kalaikuri CPI, *ibid*., p. 353, l. 12, p. 354, l. 18; Baigram CPI, *ibid*., p. 356, l. 4, p. 357, l. 11; Paharpur CPI, *ibid*., p. 360, l. 4; Nandapur CPI, *ibid*., p. 383, l. 8. *yuṣmākam*, *yuṣmad / asmad*: Jagadishpur CPI, *EDEP*, p. 61, l. 12, p. 62, l. 15; Paharpur CPI, *SI* 1, p. 360, l. 4, p. 361, l. 11; Nandapur CPI, *ibid*., p. 382, l. 5.

92 *Ibid.*, p. 362, ll. 16–17, p. 383, ll. 10–11, p. 333, l. 7, p. 349, ll. 12–13.
93 Griffiths, 'New Documents', pp. 19–20, ll. 3–22.
94 Ranabir Chakravarti, 'Kutumbikas of Early India', in Vijay Kumar Thakur and Ashok Aounshuman (eds), *Peasants in Indian History vol. 1: Theoretical Issues and Structural Enquiries (Essays in Memory of Professor Radhakrishna Chaudhary)*, Patna: Janaki Prakashan, 1996, p. 183.
95 *gṛhaṃ kṣetraṃ ca vijñeyaṃ vāsahetuḥ kuṭumbinām* | *tasmāt tan nākṣiped rājā tad dhi mūlaṃ kuṭumbinām* ||, Lariviere, *Nāradasmṛti*, 11. 37.
96 *[kṣetra]karaprativeśikuṭumbibhiḥ*, *SI* 1, p. 288, l. 9, note 8.
97 *Ibid.*, p. 358, ll. 18–19, p. 362, ll. 19–20, p. 383, ll. 13–15.
98 *brāhmaṇādīn grāmakuṭumbi[naḥ]*, Kalaikuri CPI, *ibid.*, p. 352, l. 2; *brāhmaṇottarān samvyavahāripramukhān grāmakuṭumbinaḥ*, Baigram CPI, *ibid.*, p. 356, l. 2; Cf. *brāhmaṇottarān saṃvyavahāryādikuṭumvinaḥ*, Nandapur CPI, *ibid.*, p. 382, ll. 1–2; *vrāhmaṇādīn pradhānakuṭu[mbi]naḥ*, Jagadishpur CPI, *EDEP*, p. 61, l. 2; *brāhmaṇottarān mahattarādikuṭumbinaḥ*, Paharpur CPI, *SI* 1, p. 360, l. 3.
99 *Ibid.*, pp. 355–59.
100 *EDEP*, pp. 61–63. Bhoyila, one of those three *kuṭumbin*s, may not have been identical with his namesake mentioned in the Baigram CPI. They lived in different localities and it is difficult to suppose that he shifted from one place to another within a short period of two months, from Māgha 19 to Caitra 20 of year 128 GE.
101 *SI* 1, pp. 288–89, ll. 9–13.
102 *sakṣudrapradhānādikuṭumbino*, Griffiths, 'New Documents', p. 19, l. 2.
103 *Ibid.*, p. 20, ll. 20–22.
104 *Ibid.*, p. 19, l. 2.
105 *SI* 1, p. 333, ll. 2–3.
106 *Ibid.*, ll. 3–4.
107 *IEG*, p. 121.
108 Paharpur CPI, *SI* 1, p. 360, l. 3; Damodar CPI, year 163, *ibid.*, p. 334, l. 10.
109 Ranabir Chakravarti calculates their ratio as nearly one to nine in the Kalaikuri CPI and one to seven in the Jagadishpur CPI. Chakravarti, 'Kutumbikas of Early India', p. 190. In my own reading, the number in the former case is *mahattara* eight and *kuṭumbin* 80. Accordingly, the ratio is one to ten.
110 Yamazaki, 'Some Aspects of Land-Sale Inscriptions', p. 27.
111 He is listed as the fourth *mahattara* in the former and the second *kuṭumbin* in the latter (**Table 3.2**). Chattopadhyaya, *Aspects of Rural Settlements*, p. 43. In his critical review of the work of Chattopadhyaya, Vishwa Mohan Jha objects to the identification of Umayaśas in both plates. Vishwa Mohan Jha, 'Settlement, Society and Polity in Early Medieval Rural India', *Indian Historical Review*, 1996, 20: 50–51. If we consider concurrence of as many as 24 names in both records and their mostly corresponding order, and the common location, it is more plausible that he is one and the same person.
112 Monier Monier-Williams, *A Sanskrit-English Dictionary: Etymologically and Philologically Arranged with Special Reference to Cognate Indo-European Languages* (new ed.), Oxford: Oxford University Press, 2000 (reprint), p. 1117, col. 1.
113 *SI* 1, p. 291, ll. 4–6 (year 124), p. 293, ll. 3–5 (year 128), p. 337, ll. 3–4 (the time of Budhagupta, ND), pp. 347–48, ll. 4–5 (year 224).
114 *Ibid.*, p. 356, l. 2, p. 382, ll. 1–2.
115 *Ibid.*, p. 358, ll. 18–19, 23, p. 383, ll. 13–15.
116 *Ibid.*, pp. 358–59, ll. 20–21, p. 383, l. 16.

117 Damodarpur CPI, year 163, *ibid.*, p. 334, l. 11 (*pratipālanīya*), Damodarpur CPI, year 128, *ibid.*, p. 294, ll. 10–11, Damodarpur CPI, in the time of Budhagupta, ND, *ibid.*, p. 338, l. 15, Damodarpur CPI, year 224, p. 349, l. 19 (*anumantavya*).
118 *viṣayapatayaḥ āyuktakāḥ kuṭumbinodhikaraṇikā vā* [*samvyava*]*hāriṇo*, *ibid.*, p. 355, ll. 28–29, *EDEP*, pp. 62–63, ll. 22–23.
119 Damodarpur CPIs, year 124, *SI* 1, pp. 290–92, year 128, *ibid.*, pp. 292–94; Damodarpur CPI, year 163, *ibid.*, pp. 332–34.
120 Chakravarti, 'Kutumbikas of Early India', pp. 188–89.
121 Dhanaidaha CPI, *SI* 1, p. 288, l. 3; Damodarpur CPI, year 124, *ibid.*, p. 291, l. 6; Paharpur CPI, *ibid.*, p. 360, ll. 3–4.
122 Dhanaidaha CPI, *ibid.*, p. 288, l. 11; Kalaikuri CPI, *ibid.*, p. 353, ll. 14–15.
123 Griffiths, 'New Documents', p. 19, l. 3, p. 20, l. 15; Nandapur CPI, *SI* 1, p. 382, ll. 3–4.
124 Damodarpur CPI, year 128, *ibid.*, p. 294, l. 10.
125 Griffiths, 'New Documents', p. 19, ll. 3, 7, p. 20, l. 18.
126 *EDEP*, pp. 61–63.
127 Dhanaidaha CPI, *SI* 1, pp. 287–89; Damodarpur CPI, year 163, *ibid.*, pp. 332–34; Kalaikuri CPI, *ibid.*, pp. 352–55; Jagadishpur CPI, *EDEP*, pp. 61–63.
128 *SI* 1, p. 356, l. 3.
129 *Ibid.*, p. 360, ll. 3–4.
130 *Ibid.*, pp. 352–53, ll. 3–4.
131 *kṣemākabhoyilamahidāsayor hastāt kulikabhīmenopasaṃgṛhī*(*ta*)*kadīnāra*, *EDEP*, p. 62, l. 16.
132 *SI* 1, p. 354, ll. 17–18; *EDEP*, p. 62, ll. 14–16.
133 *SI* 1, pp. 332–34.
134 Damodarpur CPI, year 163, *Ibid.*
135 *Ibid.*, pp. 352–55; *EDEP*, pp. 61–63.
136 *SI* 1, pp. 288–89, ll. 9–13.
137 *Ibid.*, p. 334, ll. 9–10.
138 Chakravarti, 'Kutumbikas of Early India', p. 189.
139 *SI* 1, pp. 336–39.
140 D. C. Sircar, *Studies in the Geography of Ancient and Medieval India* (2nd ed.), Delhi: Motilal Banarsidass, 1971, pp. 280–81.
141 *Ibid*, p. 281.
142 *SI* 1, pp. 346–50.
143 The reign of Budhagupta so far known was from the year 157 to 175 GE. Ashvini Agrawal, *Rise and Fall of Imperial Guptas*, Delhi: Motilal Banarsidass, 1989, pp. 226–28. Accordingly, when the donation was made in the year 224 GE, 49 to 67 years had passed since the establishment of the temple.
144 *SI* 1, p. 347, l. 4.
145 Damodarpur CPIs, *ibid.*, pp. 290–92 (year 124), 292–94 (year 128), 336–39 (in the time of Budhagupta, ND), 346–50 (year 224).
146 *Ibid.*, p. 294, ll. 10–11, p. 338, l. 15, p. 349, l. 19.
147 *Ibid.*, p. 358, ll. 18–19, p. 362, ll. 19–20, p. 383, ll. 13–15.
148 *Ibid.*, p. 356, ll. 2–3, p. 382, ll. 1–2.
149 *Ibid.*, pp. 359–60, ll. 1–3.
150 Baigram CPI, *ibid.*, p. 358, ll. 18–19; Nandapur CPI, *ibid.*, p. 383, l. 14; Paharpur CPI, *ibid.*, p. 362, ll. 19–20.
151 *Ibid.*, p. 288, l. 11, p. 334, l. 10.
152 Griffiths, 'New Documents', p. 20, ll. 20–22.
153 *SI* 1, p. 288, ll. 7, 11; Griffiths, 'New Documents', p. 19, ll. 4–6; *SI* 1, p. 382, l. 2.

154 *Viṣayapati* Chattramaha, the petitioner, mentions the *viṣaya* as 'your *viṣaya*' (*yuṣmadviṣaye*). *Ibid*., p. 382, l. 4.
155 Griffiths, 'New Documents', pp. 19–20, ll. 8–18.
156 Damodarpur CPI, year 163, *SI* 1, p. 333, l. 2.
157 *nā(ttra vi)ṣayapatinā kaścid virodhaḥ kevalaṃ*, *ibid*., pp. 348–49, ll. 11–12.
158 The purpose of the petitioner in the Dhanaidaha CPI is not clear due to corrosion.
159 *agnihotra*: Damodarpur CPI, year 124, *SI* 1, p. 292, l. 7; *pañcamahāyajña*: Damodarpur CPI, year 128, p. 293, l. 6.
160 *pañcamahāyajña*: Kalaikuri CPI, *ibid*., p. 353, l. 15, p. 355, l. 27; settling: Damodarpur CPI, year 163, *ibid*., p. 333, l. 4.
161 Kalaikuri CPI, *ibid*., p. 353, ll. 13–14, p. 354, l. 25; Damodarpur CPIs, year 163, *ibid*., p. 333, l. 4, year 224, *ibid*., p. 348, ll. 7–8; Nandapur CPI, *ibid*., p. 382, l. 3; Griffiths, 'New Documents', p. 19, l. 9.
162 Baigram CPI, *SI* 1, p. 356, ll. 3–4, p. 357, ll. 7–8; Jagadishpur CPI, *EDEP*, p. 61, ll. 8–11; Paharpur CPI, *SI* 1, p. 360, ll. 5–7, p. 361, ll. 12–14; Damodarpur CPIs, in the time of Budhagupta, ND, *ibid*., p. 337, ll. 7–8, year 224, *ibid*., p. 348, ll. 8–9.
163 *Ibid*., pp. 290–92, 292–94.
164 *Ibid*., p. 358, ll. 15–17.
165 *(a)vayos sakāśāt ṣaḍ dīnārān aṣṭa ca rūpakān āyī[kṛ]tya*, *ibid*., p. 357, ll. 6–7.
166 *EDEP*, p. 62, ll. 17–19.
167 *SI* 1, pp. 359–63.
168 *Ibid*., p. 354, ll. 21–25, pp. 354–55, ll. 25–27.
169 Griffiths, 'New Documents', pp. 19–20; *SI* 1, pp. 382–84.
170 *Ibid*., pp. 336–39.
171 *Ibid*., pp. 347–50.
172 Supra.
173 Supra.
174 Supra.
175 *SI* 1, p. 265, l. 22.
176 Ryosuke Furui, 'Ājīvikas, Maṇibhadra and Early History of Eastern Bengal: A New Copperplate Inscription of Vainyagupta and Its Implications', *Journal of the Royal Asiatic Society*, 2016, 26(4): 660–62, ll. 10–47.
177 *Ibid*., p. 662, ll. 46–47. Titles of *sāndhivigrahika* and *kumārāmātya* were held by Hariṣeṇa, the composer of Samudragupta's *praśasti* engraved on the Allahabad stone pillar. *SI* 1, p. 268, l. 32.
178 Furui, 'Ājīvikas', p. 660, l. 15, p. 662, l. 43.
179 *SI* 1, p. 342, l. 7.
180 Furui 'Ājīvikas', p. 659, l. 1. For the meaning of the term *pādānudhyāta* 'favoured by the feet of . . . (or respected . . .) ', indicating delegation of power by gods, overlords, kings or father, see Cédric Ferrier and Judit Törzsök, 'Meditating on the King's Feet? Some Remarks on the Expression *pādānudhyāta*', *Indo-Iranian Journal*, 2008, 51(2): 100–2.
181 *bhagavanmahādevapādānuddhyāto*, *SI* 1, p. 342, l. 1.
182 *Ibid*., p. 341, l. 3 (Rudradatta), p. 343, ll. 15–16 (Vijayasena).
183 *Ibid*.
184 They are Heṣamakhalla, Jayanāṭana, Ṣollavillagrāma, Arīucāli, Gothāna, Peratyugra, Khaddatyugra, Peragodamakoṭṭa, Uraṅgipaccālāgrahāra, Bhāśilaśāṭi, Ma . . . śola, Ūracaṇḍa, and Vendāsyagrahāra. Furui, 'Ājīvikas', p. 660, ll. 17–18, p. 661, ll. 26, 29, 32–38.

185 *Ibid.*, p. 662, l. 43. The plot is just prefixed with *santaka*, without any personal name indicating the person to whom it belongs. It is speculated that it was unnecessary to mention the person from whom the plot was transferred.
186 Furui, 'Ājīvikas', pp. 661–62, ll. 41–43.
187 Vātagaṅgā later appears as name of a *viṣaya*. S. C. Bhattacharyya, 'Mainamati Copper Plate of Vīradharadeva', *Journal of Ancient Indian History*, 1983–84 (1984), 14(1–2): 26, l. 11.
188 *SI* 1, p. 342, ll. 7–8.
189 *Ibid.*, p. 342, note 4.
190 Guṇekāgrahāragrāma is to the east of the first and second plots and Nādaḍadakagrāma to the north of the fifth. *Ibid.*, p. 343, ll. 18–19, p. 344, ll. 21, 27. Ḍoṣībhogapuṣkariṇī constitutes the northern border of the first plot. *Ibid.*, p. 344, l. 20.
191 To the south of the first plot and the west of the second. *Ibid.*, p. 343, l. 19, p. 344, l. 22.
192 Viṣṇuvardhaki and Miduvilāla, east and south of the first plot. *Ibid.*, p. 343, l. 19; Pakkavilāla, south of the first. *Ibid.*, p. 344, ll. 21–22; Jolāri, west of the third. *Ibid.*, l. 24; Buddhāka, Kālaka, Sūryya, Mahīpāla, east, south, west, north of the fourth. *Ibid.*, l. 25; *khaṇḍa* Viḍuggūrika, east of the fifth. *Ibid.*, l. 26; Maṇibhadra, south of the fifth. *Ibid.*, ll. 26–27; Yajñarāta, west of the fifth. *Ibid.*, l. 27; Sūrī-Nāsī-Rampūrṇṇeka, west of the first plot. *Ibid.*, pp. 343–44, ll. 19–20; Piyāk-Āditya-Vandhu, north of the first. *Ibid*, p. 344, l. 20; Nāgī-Joḍāka, north of the third. *Ibid.*, l. 24. Maṇibhadra may rather indicate the *yakṣa* worshiped by the Ājīvikas and others in this locality. Furui, 'Ājīvikas', pp. 672–74.
193 *Vaidya*, north of the second plot. *SI* 1, p. 344, l. 22.
194 *Jolā* in the middle of *nauyoga*s of Cūḍāmaṇi and Nagaraśrī. *Ibid.*, p. 344, l. 28; *naukhāṭa*, *ibid.*; Praḍāmāranauyogakhāṭa, *ibid.*, l. 29.
195 *Ibid.*, p. 345, l. 31.
196 The former with Khedāka and the latter with Indiramanaśācāra.
197 Supra note 192.
198 Table 3.4, Plots 2, 15, 19, 21–22, witnesses of occasions 2, 8, 12 (*karmāntika*), Plot 18 (*śreṣṭhin*).
199 Monier-Williams, *Sanskrit-English Dictionary*, p. 985, col. 2.
200 Table 3.4, Plots 2, 20, 22, 28, witnesses of occasions 1, 5–6, 8.
201 *SI* 1, p. 343, l. 19, p. 344, ll. 21–22.
202 *Ibid.*, p. 344, l. 26. *Khaṇḍa* seems to be an abbreviation of *khaṇḍarakṣa*, 'swordsman'. *IEG*, p. 155. Its synonym *khāḍgin* appears in the Mallasarul plate, which pertains to the 6th century Rāḍha, as a local military functionary. *Ibid.*, p. 374, l. 7.
203 Table 3.4, Plots 3 and 6, witnesses of occasions 4–7. For geographical connotation of Vaṅgāla, see supra Chapter 2.
204 Furui, 'Ājīvikas', p. 661, l. 24 (Ammadeva and his son Siddhāka), ll. 24–25 (Pūdanikā's sons Usalāka, Grodāka and Pokkaka), ll. 33–34 (Goyolakarmāntikavilāla's sons Khavatti, Mayīpaṭyāla and Jannaka).
205 Table 3.4, Plots 3, 6, witnesses of occasions 4–7 (*vaṅgāla*), Plots 2, 20, 22, 28, witnesses of occasions 1, 5–6, 8 (*vilāla*), Plots 2, 15, 19, 21–22, witnesses of occasions 2, 8, 12 (*karmāntika*), Plots 4–5, 9–12, 19, 24, witnesses of occasions 4, 7, 10 (*āka* / *yāka*).
206 *Ibid.*, Plot 27, one of the witnesses of occasion 12.
207 *Ibid.*, occasions 1, 5, 7–8, 10–12.

208 Nāthacandra: *bhaviṣyān itastyāṃ rājñonyāṃś ca rājapādopajīvinaḥ*, Furui, 'Ājīvikas', p. 660, l. 11; Vainyagupta: *itastyāṃ bhaviṣyāṃ vā ānyāṃś ca tatpādopajīvinaḥ*, *ibid*, l. 2, *svapādopajīvinaś ca*, *SI* 1, p. 341, l. 2. The last *akṣara*s in the Gunaighar plate is preceded by some eight lost *akṣara*s, which Sircar guesses to be *brāhmaṇādīn kuṭumbinaḥ* or *samavetān kuṭumbinaḥ*. *Ibid*., note 5. The case of the plate of year 184 rather suggests words connoting the present and future.

209 Plots 7–8, 14 are denoted only as 'belonging to' (*santaka*) particular landholders without any indication of the form of transference. As donations did not accompany monetary payment or voluntary donation by landholders, it is surmised that the king donated these plots after confiscating them from original owners for some reasons.

210 *SI* 1, p. 343, ll. 15–16.

211 *Ibid*., l. 17.

212 *Ibid*., p. 341, ll. 3–4.

213 *svatas tu pīḍām apy ūrīkṛtya*, *ibid*., p. 342, ll. 9–10.

214 *Ibid*., p. 343, l. 19, p. 344, l. 22.

215 *Ibid*., p. 345, ll. 30–31.

216 It is to the west of the former and the east of the latter. *Ibid*., p. 344, l. 29, p. 345, l. 30.

4

SUB-REGIONAL KINGDOMS AND LANDED MAGNATES

c. 550–800 AD

In the middle of the sixth century, Bengal witnessed the formation of sub-regional kingdoms in Vaṅga, Rāḍha and Puṇḍravardhana, while the making of hierarchical political structures in Samataṭa saw its intensification from the mid-seventh century onwards. In the first three sub-regions, the formation of sub-regional kingdoms went along with continuance of local participation in the process of land sale and donation, in which a change in power relations around rural society is detectable. This change was closely related to the agrarian development in each sub-region. In Samataṭa, the hierarchisation of rulers intensified with diverse power relations among them, in connection with the different levels of agrarian expansion and a new form of it, namely, the reclamation of wild forest tracts and settling of a large number of *brāhmaṇa*s en masse on the periphery. Following the chronological order, I first discuss the situation in Vaṅga, Rāḍha and Puṇḍravardhana.

*Adhikaraṇa*s under the sub-regional kingdoms

The formation of a sub-regional kingdom in Vaṅga in the mid-sixth century is attested by a series of copper plate inscriptions mentioning the kings with the title of *mahārājādhirāja*, denoting their sovereign status.[1] The reigns of at least four kings, Dvādaśāditya, Dharmāditya, Gopacandra and Samācāradeva, are confirmed by these documents.[2] Gopacandra and Samācāradeva are also known from gold coins bearing their names.[3] The extent of their control within Vaṅga and beyond is not necessarily clear. Gopacandra's power at least reached Vardhamānabhukti and Daṇḍabhukti of Rāḍha, as suggested by the Mallasarul and Jayarampur grants referring to his reign.[4] Puṇḍravardhana also witnessed the emergence of sub-regional kingdom, as shown by a new plate mentioning the reign of *mahārājādhirāja* Pradyumnabandhu.[5]

From the end of the sixth century to the first half of the seventh century, Śaśāṅka and Jayanāga ruled Rāḍha, as attested by a few copper plate inscriptions, their gold coins and the account of Chinese monk Xuanzang.[6] They held Gauḍa or northern Rāḍha as their main territory with the capital

Karṇasuvarṇa.[7] The extension of Śaśāṅka's rule towards the south-west is attested by the three copper plate inscriptions from Medinipur area mentioning his reign.[8] His influence reached southern Orissa at some point of time, as shown by the reference to his reign in the Ganjam plate of the Śailodbhava king Mādhavarāja.[9]

The administrative apparatus of these sub-regional kingdoms followed that of the Guptas. It was the same for their local administration both in terms of its organisation and interaction with local population through the *adhikaraṇa*. Puṇḍravardhanabhukti continued to be the highest administrative unit of the sub-region governed by an *uparika* appointed by the king.[10] Similarly, the administrative units of Navyāvakāśikā, Vardhamānabhukti and Daṇḍabhukti were established at the level immediately below the king and entrusted to governors with position of subordinate rulers.[11] The lower administrative units of *viṣaya* and *vīthī* were placed under them at supra-village level and managed by administrators like *viṣayapati*s. It was this level where the administration interacted with rural society through the organisation of *adhikaraṇa*.

Vārakamaṇḍalaviṣaya was an administrative unit belonging to an area called Navyāvakāśikā in Vaṅga.[12] According to the provenance of the inscriptions pertaining to this *viṣaya*, it covered the area around present Kotalipara *upazila* in Gopalganj district of Bangladesh.[13] It was governed by *rājānaka* Kṣasāma, *viṣayapati* Jajāva, *vyāpārakāraṇḍaya* Gopālasvāmin, *viniyuktaka* Vatsapālasvāmin and *viṣayapati* Pavitraka in chronological order.[14] Some of them are said to have been 'managing together' (*samvyavaharato*) with the *adhikaraṇa*.[15] This phrase denotes their collaboration with the organisation on administrative matters and the latter's location at the *viṣaya* headquarter, by analogy with the cases of *adhiṣṭhānādhikaraṇa*s in the previous period.[16] The *viṣayādhikaraṇa* was headed by the elder (*jyeṣṭha*) *kāyastha* or *adhikaraṇika*, a member of *adhikaraṇa*.[17] The terms 'elder' prefixed to their titles and 'headed by' (*pramukha*) qualifying the *adhikaraṇa* indicate the presence of other members of *adhikaraṇa* including *kāyastha*s or similar clerical functionaries headed by these elders. *Adhikaraṇikajana* in the Faridpur grant of the time of Gopacandra and *karaṇika*s in the Ghugrahati plate,[18] who were appointed to arbitrators (*kulavāra*s) executing the practical part of transactions, seem to have been such members. Thus, the *viṣayādhikaraṇa* in this locality was the organisation consisting of clerical group, collaborating with administrators and located outside rural society. Its membership seems to have been fixed to some extent, in view of *jyeṣṭhakāyastha* Nayasena who headed it in the two cases under the different kings (**Table 4.1**).

In Rāḍha, the three administrative units in different areas were involved with the *adhikaraṇa*s. The first was Vakkattakavīthī of Vardhamānabhukti, which was the venue of the case recorded in the Mallasarul grant. It can be located around the present Galsi *thana* of Bardhaman district according

Table 4.1 Receivers of petitions for land sales in Vārakamaṇḍalaviṣaya

Kotalipada CPI of the time of Dvādaśāditya, year 14 (Ryosuke Furui, 'The Kotalipada Copperplate Inscription of the Time of Dvādaśāditya, Year 14', *Pratna Samiksha: A Journal of Archaeology, New Series*, 2013, 4: 90–91, ll. 3–11, modified on re-reading.)
-*rājānaka* Kṣasāma.
-*Adhikaraṇa*.
-people beginning with (*ādayo prakṛtayaś*) (41): *viṣayamahattara* Dhṛticandra, *viṣayamahattara* Ghoṣacandra, *mahattara* Kolla, *mahattara* Ḍimva, *yājñiya* Amṛtakuṇḍa, *mahattara* Jinacandra, *mahattara* Guhayaśas, *mahattara* Thoḍḍa, *mahattara* Mitrasvāmin, *mahattara* Bhāśubha, *mahattara* Śīlacandra, *mahattara* Śubhasvāmin, *mahattara* Phālgurudra, *mahattara* Amṛta, *mahattara* Kula, *mahattara* Guhacandra, *mahattara* Goṇḍa, *mahattara* Śarvanandin, *mahattara* Keṇṭa, *mahattara* Bhāpaśu, *mahattara* Prabhasvāmin, *mahattara* Mahendra and Citracandra, *mahattara* Bhājayana, Vappabhaṭa, Sāryaka, Ḍimvāra, Śarvadāsa, *phalka* Umacandra, Śivadeva, Bṛhatkarṇa, Śubhadeva, Jayadatta, Śīlacandra, Śubhadeva, Dudhrāsara, *phalka* Śarvākāla, Gauḍacandra, Naradeva, Ṣuṅgākadevuka, Kulacandra.
Faridpur CPI of the time of Dharmāditya, year 3 (*SI* 1, p. 364, ll. 4–6.)
-*Adhikaraṇa*.
-people accompanied by (*purogā prakṛtayaś*) *viṣayamahattaras* (18): Iṭita, Kulacandra, Garuḍa, Vṛhaccaṭṭa, Aluka, Anācāra, Bhāśaitya, Śubhadeva, Ghoṣacandra, Animitra, Guṇacandra, Kālasakha, Kulasvāmin, Durlabha, Satyacandra, Arjuna, Bappa, Kuṇḍalipta.
Faridpur CPI of the time of Dharmāditya, ND (*SI* 1, p. 368, ll. 7–8.)
-*Adhikaraṇa* headed by *jyeṣṭhakāyastha* Nayasena.
-*mahattaras* of *viṣayas* (*viṣayānām*) accompanied by (*purassarāś*) *mahattara* Somaghoṣa.
Faridpur CPI of the time of Gopacandra, year 18 (*SI* 1, pp. 370–71, ll. 6–9, some parts are illegible.)
-*Adhikaraṇa* headed by *jyeṣṭhakāyastha* Nayasena.
-*mahattara* Viṣayakuṇḍa, Ghoṣacandra, Anācāra, Rājya –, *mahattarāḥ*, *pradhānavyāpāriṇaḥ*?
Ghugrahati CPI of the time of Samācāradeva, year 14 (Nalinikanta Bhattasali, 'The Ghugrahati Copper-Plate Inscription of Samachara-Deva', *Epigraphia Indica*, 1925–26 (1983), 18: 76, ll. 5–9.)
-*Adhikaraṇa* headed by *jyeṣṭhādhikaraṇika* Dāmuka.
-(6) *viṣayamahattara* Vatsakuṇḍa, *mahattara* Śucipālita, *mahattara* Vihitaghoṣa, Śūradatta, *mahattara* Priyadāsta, *mahattara* Janārdanakuṇḍa and so on, many other (*anye ca vahavaḥ*) *pradhānā vyavahārins*.

*Underlined names are mentioned in plural records

to the place names in the inscription.[19] The second was Ekatākakaviṣaya mentioned in the Panchrol plate, which is locatable around present Egra *thana* of East Medinipur district of West Bengal.[20] The third was Śvetavālikāvīthī belonging to Daṇḍabhukti, southernmost part of Rāḍha and locatable around present Baleswar district of Orissa, which appears in Jayarampur grant.

The administrators of Vakkattakavīthī and Ekatākakaviṣaya are not mentioned, while the officials including *kumārāmātya*s and *viṣayapati*s are among the addressees of the inscriptions.[21] In case of Śvetavālikāvīthī, *kumārāmātya rājanaka* Vijayavarman seems to have been the administrator, though he and other officials are also mentioned as addressees.[22] The relation between administrators and the *adhikaraṇa* in these localities is not mentioned clearly. So are the constituents of the *adhikaraṇa*, while it is the issuing authority of the copper plate inscriptions.[23] The reference to the organisation side by side with *mahattara*s and the other notables of rural society suggests that it did not include the latter as members (**Tables 4.2, 4.3, 4.4**). *Kāyastha*s (spelt *kāyata*) and *karaṇika*s, who are mentioned with

Table 4.2 **Receivers of petition for land sale in Mallasarul CPI of the time of Gopacandra, year 3** (*SI* 1, pp. 373–74, ll. 5–8.)

-People beginning with (*prabhutayo*) (13):

1. of Arddhakarakāgrahāra belonging to Vakkattakavīthī (1): *mahattara* Himadatta.
2. of Nirvṛtavāṭaka (1): *mahattara* Suvarṇayaśas.
3. of Kapisthavāṭakāgrahāra (1): *mahattara* Dhanasvāmin.
4. of Vaṭavallakāgrahāra (2): *mahattara* Ṣaṣṭhidatta, Śrīdatta.
5. of Koḍḍavīrāgrahāra (1): *bhaṭṭa* Vāmanasvāmin.
6. of Godhagrāmāgrahāra (2): Mahidatta, Rājyadatta.
7. of Śālmalivāṭaka (1): Jīvasvāmin.
8. of Vakkattaka (1) *khāḍgi* Hari.
9. of Madhuvāṭaka (1): *khāḍgi* Goika.
10. of Khaṇḍajoṭikā (1) *khāḍgi* Bhadranandin.
11. of Vindhyapura (1): *vāhanāyaka* Hari.

-*vīthyadhikaraṇa*.

Table 4.3 **Receivers of petition for land sale in Jayarampur CPI of the time of Gopacandra, year 1** (*IO*, p. 176, ll. 25–28, modified by my own reading of the original plate.)

-*viṣayādhikaraṇa*, *mahāmahattara*s, *gṛhasvāmin*s and so on (19):
(6): *mahāmahattara* Guhasvāmin, *mahattara* – svāmin, *mahattara* Bhavasvāmin, *mahattara* Dharmasvāmin, *mahattara* Devasvāmin, *mahattara* Indusvāmin.

1. Aśunapadraka (1): *pradhāna* Yogī –.
2. – padraka (1): Tanuka *prathāna* (*pradhāna*).
3. – padraka (1): Vauddhasvāmin.
4. Hulavaṇaja (1): *vettrakarmaṇimukhīya* (leader of cane workers?) *prathāna* Sāhu.
5. Śvetavāluka (2): – bhūṣaṇa, Dharmaprāṇa, *pradhāna* Gonāma.

kāyata (*kāyastha*) (2) Varāta, Vantīka.
karaṇika (3) *karaṇika* Dattanandin, *karaṇika* Anudatta, *karaṇika* Ādityadāsa.
pustapāla (2) Nāga –, Prabhaveṣṭa.

Table 4.4 **Receivers of petition for land sale in Panchrol CPI of the time of Śaśāṅka** (Ryosuke Furui, 'Panchrol (Egra) Copperplate Inscription of the Time of Śaśāṅka: A Re-edition', *Pratna Samiksha: A Journal of Archaeology, New Series*, 2011, 2: 121–22, ll. 8–16.)

-*Mahāmahattaras* and other dignitaries of twelve villages and *viṣaya* (32):

1. this habitation (*etad-ādhivāsya* = Ekatākaka) (2): *mahāmahattara* Skandasena, Nāgasena.
2. neighbouring (*praty*) *agrahāra* (1): Paṭa.
3. Ttrāṇekāgrahāra (2): Nāgadeva, Anantadeva.
4. Tarakkodakāgrahāra (2): *mahāmahattara* Dharmagupta, Yajña.
5. Vasuloḍḍovāgrahāra (2): *mahāmahattara* Somadeva, Guhadeva.
6. Akhavaṭayikāgrahāra (2): *mahāmahattara* Godhyakṣighoṣa, Mokṣadeva.
7. Viśatikhaḍḍāna (3): *mahāmahattara* Somarāta, Bhadrarāta, Chāttra.
8. Mṛgāṭī (1): *mahattara* Gomidatta.
9. Kharjūrapadraka (1): *bhaṭṭa* Dhanapāla.
10. Kāpalāśaka (1): *bhaṭṭa* Gopāladeva.
11. Sarṣapavāsinī (1): Mahādeva.
12. Vrāhmaṇapadraka (1): Raithisvāmin

Vaiṣayikānāma (of *viṣaya*, without name) (6): *mahāmahattara* Vatsaśarman, *mahāpradhāna* Udayacandra, *pradhāna* Jayadeva, *pradhāna* Dhruvada, *pradhāna* Yaśonāga, *pradhāna* Vanthavanāga.
karaṇika (3): Pravṛddhadatta, Samudradatta, Udyotasiṃha.
pustapāla (2): Jinasena, Ādāmaracita.
sthāyipāla (2): Śrīdharman, Svasti.

mahattaras but as a separate category in the Jayarampur and Panchrol plates,[24] may have been members of the *adhikaraṇa*, in view of the use of the word *karaṇa* as an abbreviation of *adhikaraṇa* in this sub-region.[25] They are mentioned together with *pustapālas* and *sthāyipālas* and seem to have belonged to clerical groups like them. Thus, the *adhikaraṇa* in Rāḍha may also have consisted of clerical groups.

Ghoṇādvīpakaviṣaya of Puṇḍravardhanabhukti seems to have been governed by *mahāpratīhāra* Avadhūta who is said to have obtained his *bhoga* in it.[26] While his relation with the *adhikaraṇa* of *viṣaya*, the issuing authority of the grant as indicated by the attached seal,[27] is not stated clearly, he was the applicant for land sale in the recorded case, whose petition was entertained by 'the ones belonging to *viṣaya*' (*vaiṣayikas*) beginning with *mahāmahattaras* and *mahattaras* residing in the *viṣaya*, accompanied by the *adhikaraṇa*.[28] The receivers of Avadhūta's petition are listed in the following part, and three *karaṇikas* and three *viṣayādhikaraṇikas* mentioned to its end seem to have been the members of the *adhikaraṇa* of the *viṣaya* (**Table 4.5**). Among them, *viṣayādhikaraṇikas* Śambudatta and Kṛṣṇadatta were probably identical with *kāraṇika* Śambudatta, the engraver of the grant, and *pustapāla* Kṛṣṇadatta who soldered the seal to the plate.[29] Thus the *adhikaraṇa* of Ghoṇādvīpakaviṣaya was also constituted by clerical

Table 4.5 **Receivers of petition for land sale in CPI of the time of Pradyumnabandhu, year 5** (Arlo Griffiths, 'New Documents for the Early History of Puṇḍravardhana: Copperplate Inscriptions from the Late Gupta and Early Post-Gupta Periods', *Pratna Samiksha: A Journal of Archaeology, New Series*, 2015, 6: 30, ll. 4–10.)

-the ones belonging to *viṣaya* beginning with *mahāmahattara*s and *mahattara*s residing in the *viṣaya*, with *adhikaraṇa* (36 = 4 *mahāmahattara*s, 5 *pāṭakamahattara*s, 16 *mahattara*s, 2 *brāhmaṇa*/*bhaṭṭa*s, 3 *karaṇika*s, 3 *viṣayādhikaraṇika*s and 3 others):

(7): *mahāmahattara* Ādityadeva, Jayadeva, Śivabhadra, *mahāmahattara* Śarvadeva, *pāṭakamahattara* Yaśodeva, Praśastarudra, Mitradeva.

1. residing in Bhiloṭa (3): *mahattara* Nātharudra, *pāṭakamahattara* Śāntirudra, Dharmarudra.
2. of Vārṣagrima (2): *mahattara* Pavitrasoma, Kṣemadeva.
3. residing in Ṣaṇḍadvīpa (2): *mahattara* Gorakakiraṇasvāmin, Rudrasvāmin.
4. residing in Pravaradvīpa (1): *brāhmaṇa* Guyaśas.
5. residing in Navadevakula (1): *mahattara* Śambhusvāmin.
6. resident of Pippalivanikā (1): *mahattara* Bhākideva.
7. of Pātravāṭa (1): *mahattara* Gopasoma.
8. of Śāṅkarapallikā (1): *bhaṭṭa* Dharmasvāmin.
9. residents of Śivanagara (3): Bhadrasvāmin, Śrīcandra, Kṣemaśarman.
10. of Dvīpaka (1): *mahattara* Amṛtaśāntanu.
11. residents of Varāhakoṭṭaka (2): *mahattara* Dharmakuṇḍa, Śivagupta.
12. residing in Khātaka (1): *mahattara* Jalla.
13. of Ārdralā (2): *mahattara* Jālacandra, Śyāmadeva.
14. of Audumvarikā (2): *mahattara* Abhinandana, Malayarudra.

karaṇika (3): Naradatta, Eḍitanu, Devasena.
viṣayādhikaraṇika (3): Śambhudatta, Kṛṣṇadatta, Paurudatta etc.

groups. In all the three sub-regions in this period, therefore, clerical groups constituted the *adhikaraṇa*s as members.

The *adhikaraṇa*s wielded the authority presiding over matters related to land sale and donation together with the rural magnates like *mahattara*s. Both are represented as an entity by the word 'we' and 'us' and addressed as such by plural 'you' by petitioners in those inscriptions.[30] They discussed or received the petition and verified the case together.[31] They also got united in this exercise.[32] As far as inferable from the cases pertaining to Vārakamaṇḍalaviṣaya, only where plural cases are known, the entity consisting of the *adhikaraṇa* and local notables was an irregular assembly to be convened for particular occasions, comparable to the *adhikaraṇa* of Śṛṅgaveravīthī in the previous period, for the number of named participants fluctuated and the only three among *mahattara*s participated in the plural cases (**Table 4.1**).[33]

The authority of the *adhikaraṇa* and associated local magnates seems to have been based on their position mediating the interests of both state and rural society, in a similar way to their counterpart in the previous period. This point is confirmed by the process of verification on which their decision in each case was based. In the cases in Vārakamaṇḍalaviṣaya, the conformity of a petition to 'the custom prevailing in the east' (*prākpravṛttā maryyādā*), 'the custom of eastern sea' (*prāksamudramaryyādā*), 'the custom of purchase in the east' (*prākkriyamāṇakamaryādā*) or 'the custom of behaviour in the east' (*prākpravṛttimaryādā*) was verified by *pustapālas*.[34] It seems to have been the local custom related to land sale transaction followed in this *viṣaya*. On the other hand, the king's acquisition of the one sixth of merit accruing from donations was also verified in case of both the grants of the time of Dvādaśāditya and Dharmāditya, year 3.[35] Similar concern for the royal share of merit and profit is present in the Ghugrahati, Mallasarul, Panchrol and Jayarampur plates, though they do not mention any local customs.[36] In the plate of the time of Pradyumnabandhu, both the local custom concerning sales of land plots and their donations to religious agents and the merit for the king were considered and verified by receivers of the petition.[37]

The interest of rural society was more clearly represented in the participation of local population in the transactions of land sale and donation. The character of participants and the forms of their participation, however, were different from those witnessed in North Bengal in the previous period. The difference was related to the changes in power relations within rural society, especially the ascendancy of *mahattara*s and other local magnates.

Ascendancy of *mahattara*s and other local magnates

The social groups which showed their strong presence in the procedures of land sale and donation in this period were *mahattara*s and other rural landed magnates, who constituted an assembly with the *adhikaraṇa* (**Tables 4.1–4.5**). In contrast, urban elites and *kuṭumbin*s, who had been involved in the transaction in various ways in the previous period, were conspicuous by their absence. The leaders of mercantile, artisanal and clerical groups had participated in the process of land sale and donation as members of *adhiṣṭhānadhikaraṇa* or as an applicant for land purchase.[38] However, leaders of the first two groups were not involved in the transactions in any right in this period, while clerical groups like *kāyastha*s still acted as members of the *adhikaraṇa*. The absence of these groups seems to indicate their exclusion from the rural affairs, while they may still have shown their presence in urban landscape.

In the rural context of contemporary inscriptions, the absence of *kuṭumbin*s all through the process is striking. In North Bengal in the previous period, *kuṭumbin*s residing in the concerned settlements had been informed of the land transactions as addressees and asked to execute the practical part of donations in some cases. The resourceful among them had participated in the process as petitioners for land sales and the dominant participated as decision makers.[39] In contrast, they are totally absent in the copper plate grants in this period. The Jayarampur, Mallasarul and Panchrol grants, only which have the sections mentioning addressees and issuing authority, are addressed to a number of officials in reference to their titles.[40] As for the petitioners, eight were dignitaries like military officer, administrators, subordinate rulers and close associate of the king,[41] and the other two were *brāhmaṇa*s.[42] The people participating in the decision making were limited to *mahattara*s and the other local magnates, as mentioned above. These facts point to the sidelining of *kuṭumbin*s from important affairs of rural society. *Kuṭumbin*s involved in the decision making in the previous period had surely been limited to their dominant section including *mahattaras*.[43] Their absence is, however, still notable and together with the stronger presence of *mahattaras*, it indicates the ascendancy of dominant groups in rural society which crystallised in sharper division between *mahattara*s and *kuṭumbin*s and the exclusion of the latter.

One element which contributed to the dominance of *mahattara*s was their establishment as landed magnates. Their character as substantial landholders is clear from the reference to the land plot belonging to *mahattara* Thoḍa in the Faridpur plate without date.[44] He had enough landholdings of which a part could be kept fallow for some time and then sold to a petitioner.[45] It confirms the clear differentiation between *mahattara*s and *kuṭumbin*s suggested above, and the rise of the former from the position held by their counterpart in the previous period, whose distinction from the latter had not been rigid.[46] On the other hand, the fact that Thoḍa had to keep some land fallow alludes to the limitation of labour power deployable for him and suggests that *mahattara*s had not gained full command over the labour of cultivators.

The ascendancy of landed magnates was accentuated by the growing inner difference. Its clearest indicator is the proliferation of subcategories of landed magnates and the hierarchical relation among them detectable in land sale grants. In the Kotalipada plate, the landed magnates wielding the titles of *viṣayamahattara*, *mahattara* and *phalka* are listed in descending order (**Table 4.1**). The last category, literally meaning 'one who has an expanded or extended body,'[47] seems to denote local magnate inferior to *mahattara*, according to the order of precedence. Similarly, the Jayarampur plate and the grant of the time of Pradyumnabandhu respectively list a *mahāmahattara*, *mahattara*s and *pradhāna*s and *mahāmahattaras*, *pāṭakamahattara*s and *mahattara*s as landed magnates, again in descending order (**Tables 4.3, 4.5**). More elaboration can be detected in the later Panchrol plate which mentions *mahāmahattara*s, a *mahattara*, a *mahāpradhāna* and *pradhāna*s (**Table 4.4**).

The inner difference of landed magnates was also resulted from the incorporation of diverse groups. In the Mallasarul plate, *khāḍgin*s and a *vāhanāyaka* are mentioned as constituents of an assembly, apart from *mahattaras* and a *brāhmaṇa* indicated by the honorific *bhaṭṭa* (**Table 4.2**). *Khāḍgin*, a derivative from the word *khaḍga*, 'sword,' may mean 'swordsman.' They could be a kind of military officers or guards wielding sword.[48] The fact that they are not mentioned among officials listed in the address of the grant but with *mahattaras* indicates their closeness to rural society and local notables. They may have been local influential people performing some kind of military function in the locality, probably with some landholdings. *Vāhanāyaka* may mean either 'superintendent of plough' or 'superintendent of transport.'[49] The appearance of this office in the forest area in process of reclamation through the creation of *agrahāra* settlements, which will be discussed below, makes the former a better interpretation.[50] Their appearance in the same manner as *mahattaras* and *khāḍgins* indicates their closeness to rural society.

The inner difference among landed magnates entailed particular power configuration among them, which in turn manifested itself in different forms of participation and representation in each locality. In Vārakamaṇḍalaviṣaya, local landed magnates working with the *adhikaraṇa* are represented only with their names and titles (**Table 4.1**). While the titles show their difference in status and locate them in a hierarchical order, their cohesion as a collective representing overall interest of the local community at the supra-village level of *viṣaya* is emphasised in this form.

The hierarchical order, on the other hand, led to more limited membership, though the emphasis on cohesion was sustained. In the Kotalipada plate, 'people' (*prakṛti*) beginning with 41 named *viṣayamahattaras*, *mahattaras* and *phalkas* received the petition with the *adhikaraṇa*.[51] In the Faridpur plate of the time of Dharmāditya, dated year 3, the number of named members accompanying *prakṛtis* decreased to 18, all categorised as *viṣayamahattara*.[52] Further reduction in number is clear in the following grants, in which only one to six are named among participants (**Table 4.1**).[53] *Phalkas* disappeared in the later grants and the term denoting unnamed members shifted from *prakṛtis* to *mahattaras* of *viṣayas*, principal *vyāpārins* or many other principal *vyavahārins*.[54] The appearance of the last two in almost the same context indicates their synonymous use in these cases.[55] As the description 'above written and other *vyavahārins*'[56] in the Ghugrahati plate suggests that six *mahattaras* mentioned in it are included in this category, it can be a general category of local landed groups involved in the management of some affairs around the *adhikaraṇa*, comparable with *samvyavahārins* of the previous period.[57] The term 'principal' (*pradhāna*) prefixed to it suggests that the only limited section of them participated in the transactions.

The tendency towards limited membership is further confirmed by the case of *mahattara* Thoḍa named in the Kotalipada plate as one of the members.[58] He is mentioned as the owner of a land plot in the Faridpur grant of the time of Dharmāditya without date, but not named as one of the recipients of petition. His land was expropriated by the *adhikaraṇa* and *mahattara*s for sale and donation and he had to comply with their decision through agreement or enforcement.[59] In view of these cases, especially the last one, the tendency towards limited membership points to the concentration of power and authority in the hand of a particular section of *mahattara*s excluding the others.

In Vakkattakavīthī, people including 13 named members and the *vīthyadhikaraṇa* received the petition and issued the grant (**Table 4.2**). Conspicuously, they are mentioned in reference to the 11 settlements. Their titles and names are prefixed by village names in the secondary derivative form indicating appurtenance or relation,[60] or village names suffixed with *agrahārīṇa*. As used side by side with village name in such a derivative form, the last term means 'of *agrahāra*' or 'belonging to *agrahāra*' and also denotes one's belonging to a settlement whose name ends with *agrahāra*.[61] Thus these adjectives indicate the settlements to which those members belong. The fact that only one or two persons are mentioned for a settlement points to their position representing each settlement. In cases of two members mentioned for a settlement, they share name endings and may be members of the same family, most probably father and son.[62]

Among the settlements represented by these people, Godhagrāma and Vaṭavallakāgrahāra were adjacent to Vettragarttā, the venue of land donation, and constituted the landmarks of its eastern, southern and northern borders.[63] The villages Khaṇḍajoṭikā, Vakkattaka, Śālmalivāṭaka, Koḍḍavīra, Kapisthavāṭaka, Nirvṛta and Vindhyapurī seem to have been located nearby these settlements.[64] Accordingly, the settlements represented were not limited to the vicinity of the concerned village but included villages clustering in a particular geographical stretch. On the other hand, Vettragarttā was not represented by these people.[65] Neither was Āmragarttikā, the neighbouring settlement to its west.[66] It indicates the hierarchy among settlements of which only important ones were represented and their representatives wielded authority over the others.[67]

While forming an assembly at supra-village level of *vīthī* in the same way as those in Vārakamaṇḍalaviṣaya, the landed magnates in Vakkattakavīthī asserted their distinction in reference to particular settlements more than their cohesion. It may have accrued from their stronger position with which they represent each village at the assembly, in contrast to their counterpart in Vārakamaṇḍalaviṣaya who had to emphasise their cohesion.

Subtle mingling of both propensities for cohesion and distinction is detectable in the other cases. In Śvetavālikāvīthī, a *mahāmahattara*, *mahattara*s, *pradhāna*s, *sītāla*s and an *adhikaraṇa* announced the present and future approached officials of the *vīthī* about the grant.[68] They seem to have been identical with *viṣayādhikaraṇa*, *mahāmahattara* and *gṛhasvāmin*s mentioned in the following part of the inscription as making preparation for land sales.[69] The latter consisted of 19 or more people who can be divided into the three categories: (1) six *mahattaras* beginning with *mahāmahattara* Guhasvāmin, (2) six people prefixed with five village names including *pradhānas* (*prathānas*) and a *brāhmaṇa* and (3) clerical groups including two *kāyasthas* (spelt *kāyata*), three *karaṇikas* and two *pustapālas* (**Table 4.3**).[70] 'The ones belonging to *viṣaya*,'[71] who received, discussed and decided on the petition in Ghoṇādvīpakaviṣaya, can also be divided into the three categories: (1) four *mahāmahattaras* and three *pāṭakamahattaras*, (2) two *pāṭakamahattaras*, 16 *mahattaras*, two *bhaṭṭa/brāhmaṇas* and three others mentioned in reference to the 14 settlements and (3) three *karaṇikas* and three *viṣayādhikaraṇikas* (**Table 4.4**). In case of the second group, one to three members are said to be residing (*nivāsin*) in, residents (*vāstavya*) of, or belonging to each settlement.

Of the three categories, the first and second consisted of landed magnates and the third was made up by clerical groups including members of the *adhikaraṇa*.[72] Those in the second category seem to represent each settlement on analogy of their counterpart in the Mallasarul plate, while the first indicates emphasis on cohesion representing the interest of whole locality at supra-village level like the ones in Vārakamaṇḍalaviṣaya. The superiority of those in the first category is inferable from the order of precedence and the title *mahāmahattara* held by their topmost members. Thus, the two tiers of landed magnates represented by different principles constituted assemblies together in these cases. Their relation could be laden with tension and the case in Ekatākakaviṣaya recorded in the Panchrol plate, which shows continuance of the same way of participation in the early seventh century, suggests one possible result.

In Ekatākakaviṣaya, the 32 named people, also dividable into the three categories, wielded full authority as issuers of the grant and receivers of the petition. The first category includes 19 people prefixed with names of villages to which they belong, with titles of *mahāmahattara*, *mahattara*, *bhaṭṭa* or none. The second category called *vaiṣayikānāma*, 'of *viṣaya*, without name,' consists of a *mahāmahattara*, a *mahāpradhāna* and four *pradhānas*. From the comparison of the styles, it is easily inferable that *anāma* here means that they have no village names prefixed to their own. Apart from those landed magnates, the clerical groups of *karaṇikas*, *pustapālas* and *sthāyipālas*, of whom the first could be the members of the *adhikaraṇa*, are listed as the third category (**Table 4.4**). While the composition of the three categories is the same as the two cases just mentioned above, the inverted order of the first and the second indicates the changed power relation among landed magnates. Those representing each settlement seem to have acquired stronger power overwhelming the others without such a position, despite that some of the latter wielded the titles of *mahāmahattara* and *mahāpradhāna*.

Those landed magnates interacted with state power through the *adhikaraṇa*. The *adhikaraṇa* in this period consisted of the clerical groups and did not include the landed magnates as its members.[73] It was located outside rural society like *viṣayādhikaraṇa* and *adhiṣṭhānādhikaraṇa* of the previous period, which had exercised its control through negotiations with the dominant section of rural society.[74] However, the relation of the *adhikaraṇa* and landed magnates in this period differed from that of the previous period. As discussed above, both constituted an entity presiding over the matters related to land transactions.[75] It suggests that the *adhikaraṇa* had to share the authority over local matters with the latter. While making clerical groups the agents in local administration as *adhikaraṇa* members, the state had to accommodate local landed magnates as co-authority. It was necessitated by ascendancy of the latter in rural society.

There could be some diversity in power equations between the landed magnates and the *adhikaraṇa*, though the presence of the former loomed large. The order of precedence in the inscriptions is an indicator. In the copper plate inscriptions pertaining to Vārakamaṇḍalaviṣaya, *viṣayādhikaraṇa* is mentioned the first among the authority over land transactions (**Table 4.1**). In contrast, the *vīthyadhikaraṇa* in the Mallasarul plate follows the landed magnates (**Table 4.2**). This difference shows the relative strength of landed magnates in relation to the *adhikaraṇa* and stronger authority held by the former in the second case. The same is observed in the contemporary Jayarampur plate in which the landed magnates are mentioned ahead of the *adhikaraṇa* as issuers of the grant.[76] The *mahattara*s and the others accompanied by the *adhikaraṇa* received the petition in the grant of the time of Pradyumnabandhu,[77] and the named local magnates and clerical groups acted as the authority of issuing grant and receiving petition in the Panchrol plate.[78] The last three cases, however, suggests more profound change occurring in rural society, namely, the formation of a dominant bloc by the nexus of landed magnates and literate groups.

The interaction between landed magnates and the *adhikaraṇa* occasioned collaborative relations between the former and the literate groups constituting the latter. Under the dominance of landed magnates in rural society, the collaboration of both groups resulted in their integration as a bloc through the incorporation of literate groups into the assembly of local magnates deciding on the cases of land sale. It is clear from the members of assemblies in the Jayarampur and Panchrol plates and the grant of the time of Pradyumnabandhu, among whom clerical groups like *karaṇika*s constituted the third category (**Tables 4.3–4.5**). It also included *pustapāla*s and *sthāyipāla*s, suggesting the incorporation of wider range of literates into the nexus of both groups (**Tables 4.3–4.4**).

Inclusion of *pustapāla*s in this nexus induced the appropriation of their function by the latter. *Pustapāla*s continued to fulfil the duty of verifying conformity of the petition to the local custom in the Kotalipada grant of the time of Dvādaśāditya and the three Faridpur plates.[79] The verification got simpler in the reign of Gopacandra and is described as 'rough verification of *pustapāla* Nayabhūti.'[80] In the Ghugrahati plate, even the reference to *pustapāla*s is missing and the verification of profit and merit of the king was made by the *vyavahārin*s, who were receivers of the petition in this context.[81] These cases show the continued involvement of *pustapāla*s in the early phase, and the gradual reduction of their importance and the appropriation of their function by the nexus of landed magnates and clerical groups in the later phase.

The process of appropriation was also detectable in Rāḍha. In the Jayarampur plate, *pustapāla* Bhogibhaṭa still made verification,[82] while the other *pustapāla*s prepared the donation with *mahattara*s.[83] In contrast, the verification was done by 'us,' the receivers of the petition, in the contemporary Mallasarul plate.[84] Similarly, it was mutually conducted by the people including the landed magnates and clerical groups in the Panchrol grant.[85] The verification in the grant of the time of Pradyumnabandhu was also done by the receivers of the petition, while *pustapāla* Kṛṣnadatta, who could also be a *viṣayādhikaraṇika*, soldered the seal to the plate.[86]

The nexus of landed magnates and clerical groups enhanced their power in rural society, as attested by its delegation in the form of the appointment of arbitrators called *kulavāra*s or *vārakṛta*s. In the Faridpur plate of the time of Gopacandra and the Ghugrahati plate, *kulavāra*s were especially appointed to execute practical parts of transactions like land measurement.[87] Some *adhikaraṇika*s were appointed by the *adhikaraṇa* as *kulavāra*s in the former, while *karaṇika* Nayanāga, Keśava and others were appointed by the receivers of the petition, namely, the *adhikaraṇa* and all the *vyavahārin*s, in the latter.[88] In the Mallasarul grant, *vārakṛta*s received money from the petitioner and divided the donated land plots.[89] They were called 'our' (*asman*) *vārakṛta*s, alluding to their appointment by landed magnates and the *adhikaraṇa*. *Viṣayavārika*s, who were made to receive money from the petitioner by the receivers of petition in the grant of the time of Pradyumnabandhu, could be compared with those arbitrators.[90]

The function performed by those arbitrators had been carried out by *kuṭumbin*s including their dominant section in North Bengal in the previous period. It had been an occasion in which some right over village land retained by *kuṭumbin*s could be negotiated with the external authority through the *adhikaraṇa*.[91] The performance of this duty by the entity of the *adhikaraṇa* and landed magnates in the Kotalipada grant of the time of Dvādaśāditya and the first Faridpur plate of the time of Dharmāditya shows that this right was appropriated by landed magnates who established their dominance. The delegation of *kulavāras/vārakṛta*s for this purpose indicates enhancement of their power with which they could unilaterally impose their decision upon rural society through the specialised functionaries. This aspect is especially clear in the Mallasarul plate, in which the order was executed in a village which was not represented in the assembly of landed magnates.[92] The nexus of landed magnates and literate groups brought out the combination of dominance of the former and specialised knowledge of the latter, both of which resulted in their enhanced power in rural society.

The landed magnates in this period included *brāhmaṇa*s, as indicated by titles of *bhaṭṭa* or *brāhmaṇa* prefixed to their names and suggested by name endings like Svāmin, Deva and Śarman (**Tables 4.1–4.5**). The growing importance of *agrahāra* settlements and their representatives on matters related to land transactions also attest to the growth of a part of *brāhmaṇa*s as landed magnates.[93] As such, they were also the constituents of the nexus between landed magnates and literate groups. However, they started to assert a distinct identity as *brāhmaṇa*s in this period. One symptom was minute descriptions of the *brāhmaṇa* donee with indicators of identity. The donees in the Faridpur and Mallasarul plates and the grant of the time of Pradyumnabandhu are mentioned with their *gotra*s and Vedic schools,[94] while the 14 or more *brāhmaṇa* donees of the Kotalipada plate are described as the noble *brāhmaṇa*s of various *gotra*s, schools, asceticism and recitation with mastery of Veda and Vedāṅga.[95] This is the same for the first Antla plate and the Maliadanga grant of Jayanāga, while the second Antla plate refers to the donee as *adhvaryu*, indicating his affiliation with Yajurveda.[96] In the Panchrol plate, *pravara* of the donee is also recorded.[97]

On the other hand, the cases of *brāhmaṇa*s who purchased land to donate to the other *brāhmaṇa*s suggest a new tendency. In the second Faridpur plate of the time of Dharmāditya, *brāhmaṇa* Vasudevasvāmin purchased and donated land to *brāhmaṇa* Somasvāmin belonging to Lauhitya *gotra* and Kāṇva Vājasaneya school.[98] In the Faridpur grant of the time of Gopacandra, Vatsapālasvāmin, who was *viniyuktaka* and belonged to Bhāradvāja *gotra*, purchased and donated land to *bhaṭṭa* Gomidattasvāmin belonging to the same *gotra* and school as Somasvāmin.[99] In these cases, *brāhmaṇa*s with the same indicators of identity, possibly even with kinship relation, were settled by the other *brāhmaṇa*s including an office bearer. As donors may have kept relation with donees, I may detect here the construction of social network among *brāhmaṇa*s in this particular area of Vārakamaṇḍalaviṣaya. Both tendencies, namely clearer identity and network building of *brāhmaṇa*s, would see their full-fledged development in the following period.

Change in power relation around rural society

In the areas of Bengal discussed above, the ascendancy of landed magnates and their nexus with clerical groups culminated in the establishment of their dominance in rural society. The new political context in this period, however, brought out a change in the power relation around it.

The political power present all through this period was the sub-regional kingship. While its administrative apparatus followed the Gupta provincial rule, its presence entrenched in the region was stronger than that of the Guptas who controlled North Bengal from afar through their administrative functionaries. This fact is attested by the list of officials informed of the land sale and donation in the Jayarampur, Mallasarul and Panchrol plates, which include six, 14 and seven official titles respectively.[100] Those mentioned in the lists are a high rank official called *kārtākṛtika*,[101] administrators like *uparika*, *kumārāmātya*, *viṣayapati* and *pattalaka*, tax collectors like *odraṅgika*, *oruṇasthānika* and *hiraṇyasāmudāyika*, lower rank subordinate rulers like *rājanaka* and *bhogapati*, officials of treasury (*bhāṇḍāgārādhikṛta*), police officer (*cauroddharaṇika*), superintendent of *agrahāra*s (*agrahārika*), and religious functionaries like *āvasathika* and *devadroṇīsambaddha*.

The agents representing the enhanced state presence in this period were officials and subordinate rulers under the king and literate groups deployed as members of the *adhikaraṇa*. Among them, the last was enticed by local landed magnates through the collaborative relation and constituted the nexus with them as discussed above. The first two, backed by the enhanced presence of the state, tried to extend their power over rural society. It resulted in a change of power relation around rural society, in which the main line of contention was drawn between officials and subordinate rulers on the one hand and the nexus of landed magnates and literate group on the other hand.

One symptom of the newly drawn line of contention was the redirection of notifications. The notifications of land sale and donation by the landed magnates and the *adhikaraṇa* were addressed to the officials and subordinate rulers, not to *kuṭumbin*s and other residents of a concerned settlement as was the case in the previous period. Under the sweeping authority of landed magnates and their clerical allies, *kuṭumbin*s were sidelined from the important affairs. The former did not need inform, involve and negotiate with the latter on the issues like land sale and donation any more. However, the increasing presence of officials and subordinate rulers brought local magnates to another front of negotiation. While establishing their dominance in rural society, the latter needed concurrence of the former, who were strengthening their presence.

The new line of contention was also reflected in the character of petitioners for land sale, who were mostly limited to officials and subordinate rulers.[102] Their monopolisation of land sale application underlined the confrontation between landed magnates and them, in contrast to the cases in the previous period when such applications had been made by wider range of social groups.[103] In the earlier period, the applications were made for legitimately acquiring personal stakes in rural society in the form of land rights. So were the applications by the administrators of lower units who petitioned the *adhikaraṇa* for land sale and donation.[104] What was detectable in the cases in this period, however, was different. It was rather an attempt of officials and subordinate rulers to legitimately extend their influence in rural society, which deserved to be called the thrust of their power into the latter.

This aspect was clearer in case of subordinate rulers. Their potential influence over rural society had been recognised by rural landed magnates from the beginning of this period. In the Kotalipada grant and the first Faridpur plate of the time of Dharmāditya, the *sāmanta*s and kings were requested to protect the donation, though none of them figured in the transaction in the latter inscription.[105] It makes a stark contrast with the similar injunction in the earlier grants, in which burden of the protection was laid on the shoulders of both administrators and local residents like *kuṭumbin*s.[106]

The actual case of a subordinate ruler extending his influence in rural society can be detected in the plate of the time of Pradyumnabandhu. *Mahāpratīhāra* Avadhūta was an administrator of Ghoṇādvīpakaviṣaya who acquired his *bhoga* in the *viṣaya*.[107] He was at the same time a petitioner for land sale who purchased Mastakaśvabhragrāma with citron grove and donated it to *brāhmaṇa* Jayadeva.[108] Interestingly, the local landed magnates who received his petition mentioned the amount of additional tax (*uparikara*) to be paid from the concerned village in future and the other income for the *viṣaya* to be equally burdened by them in their discussion, and claimed the lack of source and need of cash to pay for these charges. They were saved from difficulty by Avadhūta who paid 1,000 *cūrṇikā*s as price of the village.[109] On his side, Avadhūta could expand his power beyond his territory by this act of piety. The fact that he had to make application to the local magnates indicates that the village was not within his *bhoga* though under his jurisdiction as an administrator. By observing the formality of land sale grant and extracting the difficulty of local magnates, which could have been promulgated by using his position as an administrator charging taxes, he could extend his influence over the village and possibly incorporate it into his own territory.

The thrust of their power into rural society is evident in the Mallasarul plate. This inscription took the format common to the other land sale grants. The landed magnates with the *adhikaraṇa* acted as issuers of the document and receivers of the petition of *mahārāja* Vijayasena.[110] However, it refers to the messenger (*dūtaka*) at the end, with people who drafted the inscription and soldered a seal to the plate.[111] The seal attached to the grant is that of *mahārāja* Vijayasena, not of the *adhikaraṇa* as in the other cases.[112] The delegation of a messenger was rather common to royal grants like the Gunaighar plate and *sāndhivigrahika* who drafted the grant was a high rank official working under a king or a subordinate ruler.[113] From these points, it appears that Vijayasena practically executed preparation and issue of the grant with his subordinates, while keeping formality of petition and land purchase. Even the validity of the document depended on his authority embodied in his seal. I may detect here the encroachment upon the authority of the assembly of local landed magnates and the *adhikaraṇa* by a subordinate ruler. The power of landed magnates, who represented each settlement, was rather strong in this case and they were superior to the *adhikaraṇa*.[114] The thrust of Vijayasena's power was so strong that even they had to concede a part of their authority. At the same time, however, the power between both sides kept a delicate balance, as local landed magnates and the *adhikaraṇa* still wielded the authority to make decision and Vijayasena had to follow the prescribed protocol.

Tilting of the balance is discernible in the two Antla grants. In the earlier grant, dated year 8 of the regnal era of Śaśāṅka, the *adhikaraṇa* of Tāvīra with *brāhmaṇa*s and *pradhāna*s still issued the grant and *mahāpratihāra* Śubhakīrti, who governed Daṇḍabhukti, purchased the land from them.[115] In the other grant dated year 19, however, Prakīrṇadāsa, a minister (*amātya*) of *sāmantamahārāja* Somadatta who governed the same *bhukti* with Utkaladeśa, unilaterally conveyed Somadatta's message on his donation of the village, to the same *adhikaraṇa* united with people (*loka*).[116] Thus within 11 years, the balance had tilted to the side of the subordinate ruler, at least in Daṇḍabhukti. The fact that kings and subordinate rulers became sole authorities to issue copper plate inscriptions and that the grants recording land sale and participation of the members of rural society never appeared again indicates the similar situation in the other sub-regions.

The Maliadanga plate, a royal grant belonging to Rāḍha in the period just before or after the reign of Śaśāṅka, also shows some trace of this transition. It is a royal grant whose content is the order of *mahārājādhirāja* Jayanāga conveyed by *sāmanta* Nārāyaṇabhadra, who ruled Audumvarīkaviṣaya, to *vyavahārimahāpratihāra* Sūryasena, who managed the same *viṣaya*.[117] The political authority described in this plate is a well-defined hierarchy of a king and subordinate rulers. On the other hand, Sūryasena was ordered to give a copper plate grant with the seal of *viṣaya*, indicating that *viṣaya* was still considered a proper issuing authority.[118] The title of *vyavahārin* wielded by Sūryasena, a subordinate ruler with the title of *pratihāra*, is also suggestive. The former had been a general category of local people involved in the management of some local affairs around the *adhikaraṇa* in the earlier period.[119] It can be speculated that Sūryasena had belonged to the group of local notables and later got the position of a subordinate ruler through his association with the state authority and apparatus.

The last point leads us to another possibility, namely, an overlap between landed magnates and their clerical allies on the one hand and officials and subordinate rulers on the other hand. The authority of local landed magnates with their dominance in villages detectable in the cases in Rāḍha and Puṇḍravardhana made them close to petty subordinate rulers. It was possible that some of them, who established the power and distinction from their brethren, tried to get stronger power and authority through the association with state apparatus and succeeded to join the lower rank of administration or rather subordinate rulers, though there is no clear evidence on this account, except an uncertain case of Sūryasena mentioned above.

No matter what their origin was, emergent subordinate rulers established their presence in this period. A change in the power relation around rural society caused by their emergence and ascendancy of *mahattara*s was closely related to the forms of agrarian expansion and development witnessed in the respective sub-regions.

Forms of agrarian expansion and development

While the sedentary agriculture and complex society based on it had already emerged in the sub-regions of Bengal, further agrarian expansion and development were witnessed in this period, at least in some parts of these sub-regions mentioned in the contemporary copper plate inscriptions.

In Vaṅga, the situation in the area belonging to Vārakamaṇḍalaviṣaya is glimpsed from the five land sale grants. In case of the Faridpur plate of the time of Dharmāditya, dated year 3, and the other Faridpur grant of the time of Gopacandra, even the recorded events occurred in proximity as the border landmarks mentioned in both plates contain the common place names.[120] The border demarcation described in those inscriptions gives us clues to the environment and the form of agrarian expansion in this particular locality.

A geographical feature characteristic of the border landmarks mentioned in those plates was water bodies including navigable ones. The land plot donated in the Kotalipada grant was bordered by a boat landing on the opposite shore and the eastern embankment of dried lake on its southern and western sides.[121] Another plot mentioned in the Faridpur plate of the time of Dharmāditya, year 3, had three landing places (*trighaṭṭikā*), reservoir Śīlakuṇḍa connected to them and a boat harbour (*nāvātākṣeṇī*) to its south, west and north respectively.[122] In the other plate of the time of the same king, a lake (*taṭāka*) and boat path (*naudaṇḍaka*) flanked the donated plot on its western side.[123] The land donated in the Ghugrahati grant had a canal (*joṭikā*) as its southern border.[124] Also conspicuous were cultivated plots, especially donated ones. The second plot mentioned above had another donated plot (*tāmrapaṭṭa*) to its south, while the land tract (*pāṭaka*) of Himasena flanked its northern and eastern sides.[125] The third plot was neighboured by donated tracts (*tāmrapaṭṭa*s) of Soga and Gargasvāmin to its east and south respectively.[126]

These descriptions indicate the environment of low land adjacent to rivers, in which water transport was indispensable. The presence of cultivated tracts, together with cases of land donations, points to the agrarian expansion through the reclamation of such low land. One possible process of agrarian expansion is detectable in the cases of the Faridpur plates of the times of Dharmāditya, year 3 and Gopacandra, year 18. The land in village Dhruvilāṭī donated in the first grant was adjoined by Śīlakuṇḍa to its west, while the land donated in the second was flanked by Dhruvilāṭyāgrahāra and Śīlakuṇḍagrāma to the east and west respectively.[127] It is possible that Śīlakuṇḍa, a reservoir adjoining Dhruvilāṭī, had silted up in time being and then a new village named after it was established around there. The land plot donated in the second plate, located between the two villages, may have belonged to the land newly reclaimed after silting up.

Some extent of progress in agrarian expansion is attested by the fact that land plots donated in the two cases just cited above was cultivated ones (*kṣetra*).[128] Even in case of the Faridpur plate of the time of Dharmāditya without date, the donated land called *khila* was not an uncultivated waste but a fallow land, as it was donated from the land plot belonging to *mahattara* Thoḍa.[129] On the other hand, Vyāghracorakī, another *khila* land donated in the Ghugrahati plate, was deemed to be wild tract inhabited by beasts.[130] Together with Piśācaparkaṭī to the east, this land seems to have been a forest tract on a canal (*joṭikā*) at the fringe of village Gopendracorakagrāma, which was located to its north.[131] The presence of 3 *kulyavāpa*s of land previously donated by a land grant, which was excluded from the present donation,[132] in Vyāghracorakī suggests that the reclamation of wild forest tract was ongoing process in some area and it was facilitated by land grants.

The cases in Rāḍha pertained to several localities with different geographical conditions. One of them was the area belonging to Vakkattakavīthī of Vardhamānabhukti, which seems to have been a forest area according to the place names mentioned in the Mallasarul grant.[133] Another was the area belonging to Ekatākakaviṣaya. It had relatively low elevation and the border demarcation in the Panchrol grant points to a landscape characterised by several ponds.[134]

The information from both Mallasarul and Panchrol plates shows some phenomena common to those areas, in spite of their different ecological settings. First to mention is clustering of settlements. There were as many as 11 and 12 settlements respectively listed in these plates as locales of people involved in the land transactions (**Tables 4.2, 4.4**). The Mallasarul grant mentions two more villages.[135] Among the settlements which appear in this inscription, the five are still identifiable with present settlements located within Galsi block-2 of Barddhaman district.[136] It indicates clustering of these settlements within a limited area and the location of settlements in the Panchrol plate can be interpreted in the same line. What is remarkable is the high rate of *agrahāra*s among these settlements. Five each of the settlements mentioned in these inscriptions were *agrahāra*s (**Tables 4.2, 4.4**). It indicates the development of these areas through the establishment of *agrahāra*s and their resultant clustering.

Another common trait was an inclination towards clearer border demarcation by fixing pegs (*kīlaka*). In the Mallasarul plate, the donated tract was bordered by settlements on all sides and the pegs marked by lotus-shaped rosary were fixed to the four cardinal directions.[137] In the Panchrol grant, all borders were demarcated by pegs fixed beside the landmarks. The landmarks include *maṇḍala*s of Bhartrisvāmin and Vedamattasvāmin, which seem to have been the tracts donated to deities or *brāhmaṇa*s,[138] and water bodies like ditches (*garttā/garttikā*) and ponds (*puṣkariṇī*).[139] The locations of pegs are minutely indicated in relation to the landmarks, namely, to particular directions of a pond or a land tract,[140] at the corners (*koṇa*) beside a ditch or of a pond,[141] or on the wider sides (*mahāpadaka/mahāpakṣaka*) of ponds.[142] Together with clustering of settlements, such a tendency indicates well-settled condition of these areas.

Similar tendency in the coastal area of Daṇḍabhukti is suggested by the Jayarampur grant. The clustering of settlements in the area belonging to Śvetavālikāvīthī is attested by the reference to them as locales of people involved in the transaction, though they do not include *agrahāra*s (**Table 4.3**). Well-settled condition of this area is also shown by the border demarcations. Śvetavālikagrāma, the village donated by this grant, had a homestead land (*vāstu*), raised ground (*uddeśa*) and cultivated land plots (*kṣetra*) as landmarks to its west, north-west and north,[143] while a tree and bush, ponds belonging to village (*grāmapuṣkiraṇyaḥ)* and dried-up estuary (*utkirakhāṭikā*), and the ocean respectively constituted its north-eastern, eastern and southern borders.[144] Among the land plots, a homestead land and a cultivated plot are called Guṇadevamaṇḍalavāstu belonging to Daṅgagrāma and *maṇḍalakṣetra* of Bhagavat Goveśvara.[145] They seem to have been the donated tracts belonging to a *brāhmaṇa* and a deity respectively. This case points to the agrarian expansion towards coastal area.

What is discernible in these cases is the agrarian expansion to marshy low lands and forest tracts and some level of development reached in these enterprises. As was clearer in the cases in Rāḍha, donation to *brāhmaṇa*s, especially establishment of *agrahāra* settlements, seems to have been an element which prompted it. The agrarian expansion to such tracts, however, necessitated mobilisation of labour power with which large-scale works as draining of pond, excavation of tank and opening of forest tract could be made. The condition which enabled such mobilisation was the change in power relation around rural society, namely, ascendancy of *mahattara*s and other landed magnates including *brāhmaṇa*s. Their enhanced authority in rural society may have given them command over labour of *kuṭumbin*s and other residents. It makes a stark contrast with the condition in North Bengal in the previous period, in which the form of agrarian management based on family labour of *kuṭumbin*s limited the possibility of agrarian expansion to small-scale extension through the acquisition of *khila* land plots.[146] However, the command of landed magnates over labour of *kuṭumbin*s was not so strong in some area that they still had shortage of labour power like *mahattara* Thoḍa.[147]

The plate of the time of Pradyumanabndhu attests to the similar tendencies witnessed in an area of Puṇḍravardhanabhukti. The border demarcation of Mastakaśvabhragrāma, the settlement purchased and donated in the plate, shows that it was surrounded by water bodies like a stream (*srotikā*) with three landing places (*ghaṭṭikā*), a ditch (*khāta*), a canal (*joṭā*) and a lake (*villikā*) which were interconnected with each other, pointing to a village with plenty of water resource served with river traffics.[148] The term island (*dvīpa*) included in the names of the *viṣaya* and some settlements also points to a riverine tract.[149] Clustering of settlements in this area is, on the other hand, indicated by the 14 villages represented by the landed magnates in the grant (**Table 4.5**). Thus, the agrarian expansion to riverine low land with clustering of settlements similar to the other areas had proceeded in this area of Puṇḍravardhana. The ascendancy of landed magnates, the other common trend, and a new land relation brought by it may have contributed to this development.

This particular case also indicates the potential of *brāhmaṇas* in reclamation. As discussed above, the local magnates had difficulty paying the *viṣaya* some taxes charged on the village and sold the latter to *mahāpratīhāra* Avadhūta for cash.[150] The agrarian stagnancy resulting in deficiency of source is alluded to by a stereotyped statement that a land remaining empty does not make any profit for the king but would give visible and invisible results if donated once again, suggesting fallow condition of the village land.[151] The cause of stagnancy, which could be temporal or structural, is unclear from this single case. It should however be noted that both the application by Avadhūta, who seems to have intended to legitimately extend his influence,[152] and its acceptance by the landed magnates presupposed the potential of agrarian recovery through reclamation under the *brāhmaṇa* donee to whom the village was given. Their acts do not make sense without their common recognition of it.

On the other hand, the donation of a settlement, actually income from it, in this plate connotes a new land relation in which right to a share of product is separated from cultivation. The same can be said of the second Antla plate and the Maliadanga grant.[153] This tendency had already started in the previous period when local *kuṭumbin*s cultivated land for donees or were employed by petitioners managing donated tracts.[154] The ascendancy of landed magnates and the emergence of subordinate rulers in this period accelerated it by generating a stratified land relation in which a class of landlords partook in the share of production without engaging in cultivation. In this new land relation, the object of accumulation by the dominant sector shifted from land plots to the right to income from them or a settlement. Full-fledged development of this tendency would be, however, witnessed in the next period under the Pāla rule.

Now I would like to turn my attention to Samataṭa, which witnessed different patterns of agrarian development and local power relations.

Samataṭa: further development and formation of local power relations

From the early seventh century onwards, Samataṭa and neighbouring subregion of Śrīhaṭṭa saw the intensification of the agrarian development and the formation of local power relations, which were first attested by the two copper plate inscriptions of Vainyagupta in the early sixth century.[155] In the early seventh century, Bhāskaravarman, the king of Kāmarūpa, extended his control over some parts of this area, at least Śrīhaṭṭa as confirmed by his Nidhanpur grant.[156] In the middle of the same century, the Khaḍgas established their power in eastern Vaṅga and Samataṭa, where they issued land grants as sovereign rulers.[157] They were followed by the Devas, who ruled Samataṭa in the eighth and ninth centuries.[158] Meanwhile, the subordinate rulers like the Nāthas and the Rātas enjoyed semi-independent status under some overlords in the second half of the seventh century. They had subordinate rulers under themselves and issued their own grants.[159]

The political power constituted by these rulers was the sub-regional kingdom with hierarchy of subordinate rulers. It was comparable with that in contemporary Rāḍha, where the king and subordinate rulers were overpowering local landed magnates.[160] The issue of copper plate inscriptions was monopolised by the kings and stronger section of subordinate rulers. Local landed magnates and their clerical allies were not involved in the process of land grants in this area. Exceptionally, some local notables like *vyavahārin* and *kāyastha* were involved in border demarcation as 'giver of border' (*sīmāpradātṛ*) in the Nidhanpur plates.[161] However, they are mentioned with state functionaries like messenger, conveyer of order cum causer of its writing, tax-collector and engraver, including ones with titles of subordinate ruler.[162] It indicates incorporation of these local magnates into administrative machinery, rather than their autonomy in rural society as their counterparts in Vaṅga and Rāḍha in the earlier period.

On the other hand, the ponds of *vyavahārin* Khāsoka and of *mahattara* Ranaśubha respectively mentioned as border landmarks in the Nidhanpur and Tippera grants attest to the power of landed magnates in rural society enabling the labour mobilisation for the construction of such facilities.[163] It alludes to the agrarian development under their ascendancy as in the other sub-regions in the sixth and seventh centuries.[164] The copper plate grants issued by the political powers, however, show the three distinctive patters of agrarian development, in which the presence and agency of subordinate rulers were more important. They were reflected in the patterns of donations recorded in those documents.

The most conspicuous pattern witnessed in this area was the donation of unreclaimed tracts to a large number of *brāhmaṇas*. Such cases occurred in Śrīhaṭṭa and the periphery of Samataṭa. The number of *brāhmaṇa* donees settled by these donations is enormous. In case of the Nidhanpur plate, which pertains to Śrīhaṭṭa in the first half of the seventh century, the *agrahāra* land of Mayuraśālmala in Candrapuri viṣaya was given to at least 208 *brāhmaṇas* listed with their *gotra*, Vedic school and share of land or its product assigned to each of them.[165] The number must be more if we count the ones supposed to be listed in the missing fourth plate. The case of the Tippera plate belonging to Samataṭa in the second half of the same century shows similarity. It records a grant of the forest land plot (*āṭavībhūkhaṇḍa*) in Suvvuṅga-viṣaya to the *maṭha* of the deity Anantanārāyaṇa and *brāhmaṇas* studying the four Vedas.[166] The names of at least 192 *brāhmaṇa*s are listed with the size of land plots assigned to them.[167] The case of Kalapur plate belonging to Śrīhaṭṭa in the seventh century shares the basic structure with that of the last plate, though the detail is not clear due to corrosion of the plate. According to the information gathered from the legible lines, it records the donation of a land plot to the deity Anantanārāyaṇa and *brāhmaṇa*s studying the three Vedas for their daily rituals.[168]

The land tracts donated in these cases were unreclaimed lands adjacent to the existing settlements.[169] They had potential for further agrarian expansion. The tract donated by the Nidhanpur grant was surrounded by dried river Kauśikā, Ḍumbarīccheda (cleft)[170] and Gaṅginikā at all the directions except north, and the pit of potter (*kumbhakāragartta*) and the pond of *vyavahārin* Khāsoka were located to the north-west and north-east respectively.[171] It indicates the location of the land on the southern periphery of a settlement. Its potential for agrarian expansion is shown by the stipulation about the use of sedimentary land made by two rivers bordering the donated tract. According to it, the product of sedimentary land made by dried river Kauśikā belonged to *brāhmaṇa*s who were 'receivers' (*pratigrāhaka*), probably the representatives of *brāhmaṇa* donees including the holder of document (*paṭṭakapati*),[172] while the one made by Gaṅginikā should be equally distributed among *brāhmaṇa*s listed in the inscription.[173] Also in case of the Tippera plate, the donated land was located on the periphery of settlements as it was bordered by two villages to the south, donated land plots to the west and the pond of *mahattara* Ranaśubha to the north, while the eastern border was demarcated by a hill named Kaṇāmoṭikā.[174] Its potential for agricultural expansion as unreclaimed wild tract is clear from its description as 'forest land plot without differentiation between the artificial and natural' infested by various wild animals.[175] The land donated in the Kalapur inscription is also the wild tract described as 'land plot of water and forest' (*jalāṭavībhūkhaṇḍa*), though its location is not clear from the legible lines.[176]

As these unreclaimed tracts were to be reclaimed and settled by a large number of *brāhmaṇa*s, some arrangement was necessary to regulate relations of production. The minute assignment of a land plot or a share of product to each donee mentioned above was one of such arrangements. In case of the Tippera plate, the six people other than *brāhmaṇa* donees were also assigned land plots.[177] As they included a cook, a person who was supposed to speak something and a digger, they seem to have been a service group for the *maṭha* and *brāhmaṇa*s.[178] The stipulation on the use of sedimentary land made by rivers in the Nidhanpur plate could also have been such an arrangement for regulating land use and relations of production. These arrangements show the intention of the rulers to organise society of newly reclaimed tracts and to exhibit their authority through this act.

One interesting feature in these cases was the construction of shrine of deity in forest. In the Tippera plate, the donation was petitioned by *mahāsāmanta*

Pradoṣaśarman for the ritual service to the deity Anantanārāyaṇa installed by him in forest.[179] The Kalapur plate also records the donation of a land plot petitioned by *brāhmaṇa* Jayasvāmin for the ritual service to the deity Anantanārāyaṇa, who was installed and whose *maṭha* was constructed by him in the forest tract to be donated.[180] According to the description in the former plate, Anantanārāyaṇa seems to have been a form of Viṣṇu-Nārāyaṇa accompanied by deities and semi-divine beings adoring him.[181] Even though it was described as wild tract, the forest in this area may have been resided by forest dwellers subsisting on hunting and gathering. The installation of the deity with clear Brahmanical affiliation there alludes to the intention to encroach upon their territory by overwhelming these people through the religious system and authority unknown to them. The settling of large number of *brāhmaṇa*s can be understood in the same line. They were expected to be agents of the expansion of sedentary agrarian society to the territory of non-sedentary one.

Another notable factor was the initiative taken by subordinate rulers in the land donation through the petition to their superior ruler. The construction of a shrine by *mahāsāmanta* Pradoṣaśarman and his petition for donation in the Tippera plate have just been discussed. As the founder of shrine, he may have kept influence over the affairs in its donated tract. In case of the Nidhanpur plate, the donation was made as the reissue of copper plate grant and the resumption of *agrahāra* land given by Bhūtivarman, the great great grandfather of Bhāskaravarman, which was prompted by the information from *mahārāja* Jyeṣṭhabhadra. The latter informed that the *agrahāra* was yielding revenue as the original copper plate grant was lost.[182] In view of the other cases, this case can be interpreted differently. As an intermediary between *brāhmaṇa* donees and the king, the petitioner did favour to the former and it may have generated his influence over them. Even the lost copper plate given by Bhūtivarman can be fictitious, as no copper plate grant belonging to the period earlier than Bhāskaravarman's reign has yet been found and the same rhetoric of lost copper plate is used in his Dubi grant.[183] In their initiatives in land donation, I may detect the intention of subordinate rulers to extend their influence to the newly reclaimed land and even increase their own resource base through the channel of religious endowments and authority of their superior ruler.

A quite different pattern of land donation is discernible in the cases pertaining to western Samataṭa or eastern fringe of Vaṅga. It is the donation of cultivated land plots scattered around several settlements to the Buddhist *vihāra*s. What can be detected in these cases is the complicated land relation in the area with established sedentary society. Both Ashrafpur plates of Devakhaḍga, dated year 7 and 13 respectively,[184] belong to the second half of the seventh century and record the donation of land plots to the *vihāra*s of *ācārya* Saṃghamitra.[185] The nine plots in seven settlements and the nine plots in eight settlements were respectively donated by the two grants (**Table 4.6**).

Table 4.6 Land plots and tenure holders in the Ashrafpur CPIs of Devakhaḍga

Plot	*Settlement*	*Pa*	*Dv*	*Descriptions*
a. Year 7, G. M. Laskar, 'Ashrafpur Copper-Plate Grants of Devakhaḍga', *Memoirs of the Asiatic Society of Bengal*, 1904, 1(6): 90–91, ll. 7–14 (modified by own readings from the impression).				
9 plots in 7 settlements in Midikillikā Śālivadraka				
1	Talapāṭaka	1/2		with two homestead lands with areca nut trees, from *pāṭaka*s being enjoyed by Śakraka
2			20	enjoyed by *upāsaka*, being enjoyed by Svastiyoka
3	Markaṭāsīpāṭaka		27	being cultivated by Sulabdha and others
4			13	being cultivated by Rājadāsa and Durggaṭa
5	Vatsanāgapāṭaka-navaropya: Buddha-maṇḍapa-prāpi, given by Bṛhatparameśvara	1		given by śrī-Udīrṇakhaḍga, being enjoyed by Śatrughna
6	Peranātaṇanīla	1/2		
7	Darapāṭaka	1		
8	Dvārodaka	1/2		
9	Vārasuggakā	1/2		*cāṭa-prāpi*
	Sum	4	60	
	Sum mentioned in the grant	6	10	
b. Year 13, *SI* 2, p. 42, ll. 3–10 (modified by own readings from the impression attached as Plate II to *Proceedings of the Asiatic Society of Bengal* for March, 1885).				
9 plots in 8 settlements				
1	Jhāṭalyodyānikā-taralā-saṃ – –	2		being enjoyed by mahādevī-śrī-Prabhāvatī
2		?		being enjoyed by bhantarīko-Śubhaṃsukā
3	Śrīmitrāvalī in Kodāracoraka	1 1/2		being enjoyed by sāmanta-Vaṇṭiyoka
4	Relatalaka	1 1/2		being enjoyed by śrī-Netrabhaṭa
5	Peranāṭana-nādavarmi – tpalagarvbha		10	
6	Kṣivahradikā-śoggavarga	1/2		of a female dancer (nartakī)
7	__śrīmeta	1		being enjoyed by śrī-Śarvāntara, cultivated by mahattara-Śikhara and others. Two *vihāra-vāstu*s also.
8	Rollavāyikā-Ugravoraka	1		being enjoyed (?) by vandya-Jñānamani
9	Droṇimaṭhikā in Tīsanādajayadattakaṭaka	1		
	Sum	8 1/2	10	
	Sum mentioned in the grant	9	10	

The descriptions of these plots contain important information on the land relation in this area. Most of the land plots are mentioned with the tenure of particular holders apart from their size. The tenures include 'given' (*pratipādita*), 'being enjoyed' (*bhujyamānaka*), 'enjoyed' (*bhuktaka*) and 'being cultivated' (*kṛṣyamāṇaka*). These variations allude to the presence of hierarchical tenures over a particular land plot and some cases confirm this. 1 *pāṭaka* of land located in newly reclaimed land (*navaropya*, literally 'to be sown newly') of the settlement Vatsanāgapāṭaka was given by Udīrṇakhaḍga, probably a member of the royal family, and enjoyed by a person named Śatrughna, while the settlement itself had been given by Bṛhatparameśvara, probably denoting one of the former kings of the dynasty (**Table 4.6 a, Plot 5**).[186] Another *pāṭaka* of land mentioned in the grant dated year 13 was enjoyed by Śarvāntara and cultivated by *mahattara* Śikhara and others (**Table 4.6 b, Plot 7**).[187]

In these passages, at least four layers of tenure holders over a particular land plot are detectable: actual cultivators, enjoyers, a royal member who gave some part of land to an enjoyer and finally the king who gave whole the settlement. As enjoyers include Prabhāvatī, the chief queen of Devakhaḍga, *sāmanta* Vaṇṭiyoka and Netrabhaṭa, probably a member of the royal household (**Table 4.6 b, Plots 1, 3–4**),[188] the tenure of enjoyment seems to mean the right to extract some portion of product from a particular land plot as their share. The transferability of this tenure is connoted in the description of the 20 *droṇavāpa*s of land plot in Talapāṭaka, which had been enjoyed by an *upāsaka* and was currently enjoyed by Svastiyoka (**Table 4.6 a, Plot 2**).[189] As those land plots are said to have been given to the donee 'after taking away from an enjoyer in this way,'[190] the donations recorded in these documents were actually the transfers of the right of enjoyment to the religious institution and seem not to have affected the cultivators.

The so-called Devaparvata grant of Bhavadeva, dated year 2,[191] is related to Peranāṭanaviṣaya, the same locality mentioned in the Ashrafpur plates,[192] and belongs to the slightly later period, the eighth century. It records the donation of 7 1/2 *pāṭaka*s of land located in the four settlements to the Buddhist establishment in Veṇḍamatīvihārikā.[193] Though there is no reference to the stratified land rights in this inscription, the pattern of donation in which land plots scattered around several settlements are objects is similar to that of Ashrafpur plates.

The case of the Kailan plate of Śrīdhāraṇarāta, which belongs to the Samataṭa in the second half of the seventh century, can be placed between these two patterns. It has a format similar to the Tippera plate, though the donees were a Buddhist *saṃgha* and 13 *brāhmaṇa*s.[194] The donated land plots were located in well-settled marshy land according to the border landmarks, which contain water bodies like a lake (*villa*), rivers and embankments (*āli*) with facilities related to river traffics like boats harbour (*naupṛthvī*) and boat path (*naudaṇḍaka*),[195] and the land plots held by individual and institutional landholders.[196] One distinctive feature in this landscape was the land plots collectively held by groups like '150 sons of good families' and 'Malla blacksmiths beginning with Vendhana.'[197] The former seems to denote the land collectively held by people belonging to the higher class and reminds us of the settling of large number of *brāhmaṇa*s encountered in the first pattern, while the latter may be related to that of service groups. Existence of such group holdings indicates the reclamation of wild tracts and settling of people from which these settlements developed to the present state. This case thus shows a transitional phase between the first and second patterns.

The cases discussed above show the synchronic diversity of patterns of agrarian expansion and development within these sub-regions. It may come from the ecological diversity within the area. However, it can also be a result of the different levels of agrarian expansion experienced by each locality, in which a process of development is detectable. It is the development of newly reclaimed land tract to the area of established sedentary society, through which stratification of land relation would proceed. Riverine tracts of western Samataṭa or eastern Vaṅga had been reclaimed in the earlier period and developed to the well-settled area with complicated land rights, while marshy land connected with river traffics experienced the reclamation next to it and reached the transitional phase. The remote area of Śrīhaṭṭa and the fringe of Samataṭa just started to experience the intensive agrarian expansion.

One element conspicuous in these cases was the presence and agency of subordinate rulers as agents of reclamation or a part of stratified land relation. Their involvement in the agrarian expansion was both enabled and necessitated by the power relation in which they were entangled. It was the stratified power relations among layers of rulers, with inner tensions especially in the peripheral area.

Lokanātha and Śrīdhāraṇarāta were subordinate rulers of the common overlord, whose identity is unclear. The military service of the former is described in the seventh and eighth verses of the Tippera plate,[198] while the latter's position as a subordinate ruler is indicated by the title of *prāptapañcamahāśabda*.[199] However, they practically acted as independent rulers by issuing copper plate inscriptions without acknowledging the reign of the king. The use of the title Samataṭeśvara by both Śrīdhāraṇarāta and his father Jīvadhāraṇarāta also underlines their semi-independent status.[200] They were sometimes even rebellious. Lokanātha is described as 'in him the army of *parameśvara* went to annihilation many times.'[201] They also fought each other as described in the eighth and ninth verses of the Tippera plate.[202] Thus they were semi-independent rulers defying the authority of their overlord.

However, they still needed the royal authority in some matters. The ninth verse of the Tippera plate says that Jīvadhāraṇarāta stopped war and conceded his own *viṣaya* to Lokanātha, who obtained an auspicious document (*śrīpaṭṭa*). This document seems to have been the royal decree which guaranteed Lokanātha's possession of the *viṣaya* formerly held by Jīvadhāraṇarāta. It means that these subordinate rulers still needed authorisation of their rule by the king, even while they fought each other defying his authority. The format of their grant also shows their dependence. While it conveys their order, the document is issued by *kumārāmātya*s and their office (*adhikaraṇa*).[203] The seal authenticating the document is also that of *kumārāmātyādhikaraṇa* with so-called Gajalakṣmī emblem, on which these rulers stamped their own seal additionally.[204] The expression *śrīmatsamataṭeśvarapādānudhyāta* in the Kailan plate and its seal indicates the appointment of *kumārāmātya*s by Śrīdhāraṇarāta.[205] However, the use of common seal and their presence in the territories of different local rulers show the character of *kumārāmātya*s and their office as constituents of the central administrative apparatus under the king. The fact that the order was conveyed by the prince of local ruler acting as a messenger suggests that the function of this organisation mostly came under the control of these local rulers.[206] But they still had to keep the formality in the matter of land grant and this fact attests to the necessity of royal authority for them. While growing to semi-independence in this area, local rulers were yet to consolidate their power, which needed to be authorised and enhanced through their association with the king and his administrative apparatus.

The unconsolidated state of the control of local rulers gave their subordinates, against whom they may have needed authority and legitimacy provided by the king, an opportunity to extend their own interest. The petition for land donation by these subordinate rulers should be understood from this angle. As discussed above, these subordinate rulers may have extended their influence and even resource base in the donated tracts through the petition for donation. The second point is proved by the case of Kailan plate, in which *mahāsāndhivigrahādhikṛta* Jayanātha, the petitioner of the grant, clearly acquired some land plots as an alms giver (*bhikṣada*).[207] Such acts might have been against the interest of local rulers. But they had to accept the petition as far as it kept the required formality, for their power and authority also depended on their adherence to such a formality. Moreover, the donation of unreclaimed or reclaimed tracts by their order would have given them an opportunity to wield their authority in organising the relation of production, even though actual profit of the reclamation was extracted by the donee and the petitioner. What was observed in those cases of periphery was, therefore, a stratified power relation in which precarious balance was maintained between the king and his subordinate local rulers, and the latter and their subordinate rulers with tension among them. This stalemate prompted the subordinate rulers to extend their resource base and power to the unreclaimed tracts by the petition for land donation to religious agents. On the other hand, their position as local magnates enabled them to mobilise enough labour power to reclaim wild tracts or manage wider cultivated plots, in contrast to peasant householders (*kuṭumbin*) of the fifth century North Bengal who had purchased a small plot of *khila* land for extending their cultivation.[208]

The power relation in the well-settled area exhibits a sharp contrast in terms of the power balance, while it shows commonality as a stratified power relation. In the Ashrafpur plates, a subordinate ruler with the title of *sāmanta* appears as one of the enjoyers of product from a particular plot, side by side with members of the royal household and others (**Table 4.6 b, Plot 3**). The agency of subordinate rulers was invisible, and their incorporation into the stratified land relation topped by the king was rather conspicuous in these cases. The king wielded overarching authority in transferring the right of enjoyment from enjoyers to the donee. It indicates somehow established authority and control of the Khaḍga kings over subordinate rulers in this area. It was also confirmed by the fact that the Khaḍgas issued full-fledged royal grants with their own seals.[209] Such an established state of the Khaḍga rule seems to have emanated from the agrarian development in the core area of their territory, which provided them with stable resource base. On the other hand, the agency of subordinate rulers was latent under the established rule of the king and could surface in some occasions. In the Salban Vihara Plate of Balabhaṭa, the Khaḍga prince, the donation of 25 *pāṭaka*s of land scattered around several settlements seems to have been petitioned by a subordinate ruler with the titles of *mahāsāndhivigrahādhikṛta* and *prāptapañcamahāśabda*.[210] In the grant of Bhavadeva, the donation of land plots to the Buddhist establishment was petitioned by Vibhūtidāsa, a subordinate ruler, through the mediation of *mahāsāmantādhipati* Nandadhara as a messenger.[211] The established rule and authority of the Devas, who supplanted the Khaḍgas, is indicated not only by the issue of full-fledged royal grants but also by their use of the high-sounding titles of *parameśvara paramabhaṭṭāraka mahārājādhirāja*.[212] In this situation, the subordinate rulers tried to extend their interest and resource base by legitimately encroaching upon the king's authority and territory through the application for the donation in a stipulated manner, as agrarian expansion towards unreclaimed wild tract became difficult in such a well-settled area. The balance of power had tilted towards the king and the later history of this area witnessed further enhancement and establishment of royal authority under the Candras.

Harikela: state formation and agrarian expansion on the periphery

The sub-region of Harikela also witnessed the formation of sub-regional kingdom and the agrarian expansion in the eighth century, as attested by an inscription on a bronze vase now kept in the Bangladesh National Museum, dated year 77 presumably in the Burma era, corresponding to 715 AD.[213] It refers to the reign of king Devātideva and records the five occasions of land purchase and donation centred on a Buddhist *vihāra* called Haritakadharmasabhavihāra or Dharmasabhavihāra within the period of 14 years. Its contents and format similar to land sale grant suggest that the inscription is a copy of several earlier documents inscribed on the vase kept by the *vihāra*.[214]

The main inscription refers to the first case which took the form of full-fledged land sale grant and the others which were mostly land purchases by the residents of the *vihāra*. In the first case, the issuer was the *adhikaraṇa* (office) of all the Khaṣamaka accompanied by a *kumārāmātya*, four *mahābalādhikṛtas*, a *mahāmahattara bhaṭṭa*, a narrator of (*dharmapāṭha*), three *bhaṭṭas*, a *sāndhivigrahika*, three elders (*jyeṣṭha*), a *mudrapāla*, three *kāyasthas* and two *mahāvārikas*, and the addressees were all the *viṣayins* and all the king's servants (*rājakarmin*) who gathered at proper time in Khaṣamaka.[215] The members of the *adhikaraṇa* was ordered by *mahāpradhāna dauvārika* Saubhāgyakīrti to give a tenure of all the excessive enjoyment (*sarvātibhoga*) to 25 *pāṭakas* of land donated to a *vihāra* at Haritakadharmasabhavihāra, of which 22 *pāṭakas* were purchased from people of the two villages by *mahāpradhāna mantrimukhya* Nayaparākramagomin, and the remaining three were given by people of those villages.[216] The land was also given to *brāhmaṇas* belonging to the five *maṭhas*.[217] In the other cases, the land purchases were made by the residents of Dharmasabhavihāra including *bhikṣusaṃghācāryas* and *karaṇins* from residents of particular villages like goldsmiths and *mahāvārikas* in front of organisations called both *karaṇas* in Harikelā, with *sarvātibhoga* tenure.[218]

In many aspects, this inscription shows the progress in state formation and agrarian expansion. The reference to the reign of Devātideva, activities of officials like *kumārāmātya* and administrative units like *khaṇḍa* and *viṣaya* point to the establishment of a state with its administrative apparatus. The issue of a grant by the *adhikaraṇa* of all the Khaṣamaka in the first incident seems to indicate its function as an authority presiding over the land transactions including both sales and donations. Both *karaṇas* in Harikelā, in front of which land purchases were made in the other incidents, could also be such *adhikaraṇa* organisations. Such function of *adhikaraṇas* is comparable with that of *adhikaraṇas* in Puṇḍravardhana, Vaṅga and Rāḍha discussed above.[219]

The sustenance of state and its machinery depended on the surplus produced by advanced form of agriculture, and some extent of development on this account is attested by the references to land plots held by various landholders. The purchase of *khilakṣetra* mentioned in the fourth case,[220] on the other hand, indicates room for further agrarian expansion. It was also remarkable that landholders included artisans like goldsmiths and *brāhmaṇas* denoted by the titles of *bhaṭṭa* and *paṇḍita*.[221] The former indicates the development of artisanal and commercial activities, which is also attested by the use of currency called *taṇḍaka* in land transactions and the discovery of high-quality silver Harikela coins belonging to this period.[222] As for the latter, the presence of *brāhmaṇa* landholders and donations to *brāhmaṇa*s belonging to the five *maṭha*s in the first case show the settling of *brāhmaṇa*s in this area as both individuals and constituents of religious institutions.

It is remarkable that such phenomena occurred in the area called Khaṣamaka. Though the meaning of *maka* is unclear, the context suggests that Khaṣamaka denotes an area controlled by Devātideva and possibly related to *khasa*s. This name given to the area at least indicates the perception that it was an area inhabited by a group of tribal people who could be labelled as *khasa*s, which connotes a social group out of Brahmanical ambit but organised to the level of chiefdom.[223] Their incorporation into the sedentary agrarian society can be guessed from non-Sanskritic names like Oru and Ṭhihu found among landholders,[224] though it is not necessarily certain whether Devātideva and his lineage also belonged to the same group and were formerly their chiefs. On the other hand, Sanskritic village names like Candrabhaṭṭārikā attest to the establishment of new settlements instigated by the migration of *brāhmaṇas* and other members of sedentary agrarian society who were present among landholders.[225]

Like its counterpart in the other sub-regions, rural society of this sub-region also witnessed the ascendancy of landed magnates in alliance with literate groups, as attested by the collaboration of a *mahāmahattara bhaṭṭa* with *bhaṭṭa*s, *jyeṣṭha*s and *kāyastha*s in issuing land sale grant as the *adhikaraṇa* members. The remarkable was the fact that the members of the *adhikaraṇa* in the present case were not limited to these local notables. Among the other members, *kumārāmātya*, *mahābalādhikṛta* and *sāndhivigrahika* were royal officials, while *mahāvārika* could be an arbitrator chosen by local notables comparable to *kulavāra* or *vārakṛta*.[226] The narrator of *dharma* (*dharmapāṭha*) and the keeper of seal (*mudrapāla*) could be functionaries belonging to either state machinery or rural society depending on which *dharma* and seal are meant here. In any case, those members consisted of representatives of both administrative functionaries and local notables. The fact that the *adhikaraṇa* and its members functioned following the order of doorkeeper Saubhāgyakīrtti, a royal official, indicates their character as a part of administrative apparatus rather than an autonomous body, indicating assimilation of local magnates into the administrative machinery.

The incorporation of local magnates into the administrative apparatus could take a form of their conversion to office bearers. Both Saubhāgyakīrtti and leader of ministers Nayaparākramagomin are prefixed with the title *mahāpradhāna*. They may have originated from a class of local notables and acquired some position in the administration through their affinity with the king. Thus, the information in this inscription shows both the incorporation of local notables into a rank of administrative functionaries and transformation of their upper section into the constituents of the political powers.

The present inscription also gives us some information on Dharmasabhavihāra. The recorded incidents attest to its character as a large-scale landholder with its landed properties scattered around several villages in different administrative divisions (*khaṇḍa*) of Khaṣamaka. The phrase 'to be enjoyed as if it were a common patrimony' in the first incident suggests that those tracts were held by the institution as common property of members.[227]

The dependence of the institution on the patronage of temporal power was obvious in the first incident in which the largest part of land, 25 *pāṭaka*s, was donated by Nayaparākramagomin. However, the residents of the *vihāra* purchased land plots in all the other cases, either collectively or as a *saṃgha*. The members of the institution also contributed to its accumulation of landed properties independent of the patronages of the king and the others.

The composition of residents of the *vihāra* shows some aspects of its organisation.[228] The listed members are divided into two categories, namely, the *bhikṣu*s cum *ācārya*s of the *saṃgha* and the *pādamūlas* (servants) including two *karaṇin*s mentioned after them. While the former seems to have been eminent monks of the *saṃgha*, the latter could be functionaries or administrative staffs of the *vihāra*. The presence of the latter indicates the development of the institution which necessitated specialised staffs for its management. On the other hand, the collective action of both groups shows the function of managing body constituted by them in deciding on matters related to property of the *vihāra* and use of its wealth.

The description of border landmarks in the fourth incident shows the presence of another *vihāra* called Mahāyānavihāra, while the five Brahmanical *maṭha*s are mentioned in the first incident. [229] These references attest to the presence of several religious institutions apart from Dharmasabhavihāra, though how far they have developed as both organisations and large-scale landholders is unclear from the inscription.

Emergence of religious institutions as large-scale landholders

Before concluding this chapter, I would like to address one phenomenon which became evident in this period: the emergence of Buddhist *vihāra*s and other religious institutions as large-scale landholders. The donation to such institutions had already been witnessed in North Bengal in the fifth century, as shown by the Baigram, Jagadhishpur and Paharpur plates.[230] However, the land donated in these cases was rather small and seems to have been cultivated or managed by donors themselves. In contrast, the two inscriptions of Vainyagupta attest to the large-scale land donations to the Ājīvika and Mahāyāna Buddhist *saṃgha*s by the initiatives of kings or subordinate rulers in Samataṭa, which could have started as early as in the early fifth century.[231] They showed a tendency of religious institutions to accumulate landed properties, which would intensify in eastern Bengal after the middle of the seventh century.

This tendency was clearer for Buddhist establishments, as suggested by the cases of the Ashrafpur, Devaparvata and Kailan grants and the metal vase inscription discussed above.[232] In all but the case of the Kailan plate, in which a *saṃgha* acquired 4 1/2 *pāṭaka*s in one settlement,[233] the Buddhist establishments acquired land plots scattered around several settlements or right to enjoy product from those plots. In case of the Ashrafpur grants, the *vihāra* and the four *vihārikā*s of Saṃghamitra were given the right to enjoy product from 6 *pāṭaka*s 10 *droṇa*s in seven settlements and 9 *pāṭaka*s 10 *droṇa*s in eight settlements respectively (**Table 4.6**). In the Devaparvata plate, 7 1/2 *pāṭaka*s in four settlements were donated to the Buddhist establishment in Veṇḍamatīvihārikā.[234] In the cases recorded in the Bangladesh National Museum metal vase inscription, Dharmasabhavihāra acquired 30 *pāṭaka*s 23 *droṇavāpa*s of land in six settlements through donation by a royal official and purchases from individual residents.[235] Some managerial arrangement was necessary to bring these scattered plots under cultivation.

A clue to the form of land management by Buddhist establishment is provided by an account of Yijing, a Chinese monk who stayed in eastern India in the last quarter of the seventh century. In explaining the food and cloth necessary for monastic life, he mentions the management of agricultural land by Buddhist *saṃgha*. He first explains the relation between *saṃgha* and cultivators in theory:

> According to the teaching of the *Vinaya*, when cornfield is cultivated by the *Saṅgha* (the Brotherhood or community), a share in the product is to be given to the monastic servants or some other families by whom actual tilling has been done. Every product should be divided into six parts, and one-sixth should be levied by the *Saṅgha*; the *Saṅgha* has to provide the bulls as well as the ground for cultivation, while the *Saṅgha* is responsible for nothing else. Sometimes division of the product should be modified according to the seasons.[236]

He also refers to the case of some avaricious monks directly involved in observation of agricultural operation by giving out the work to servants.[237] Then he wrote of the actual case witnessed by him at a *vihāra* in Tāmralipti:

> When I for the first time visited Tāmralipti, I saw in a square outside the monastery some of its tenants who, having entered there, divided some vegetables into three portions, and, having presented one of the three to the priests, retired from thence, taking other portions with them. I could not understand what they did, and asked of the venerable Ta shang Tang (Mahāyāna Pradīpa) what was

> the motive. He replied: 'The priests in this monastery are mostly observers of precepts. As cultivation by the priests themselves is prohibited by the great Sage, they suffer their taxable lands to be cultivated by others freely, and partake of only a portion of products. Thus they live their just life, avoiding worldly affairs, and free from faults of destroying lives by ploughing and watering fields.'[238]

The first account indicates that a *saṃgha* should ideally make sharecropping with its own servants or other householders by leasing them land and cattle for ploughing and acquire the one sixth of product, without interfering with actual cultivation. Its practice in the western part of Bengal in this period is confirmed by the last account. On the other hand, the mention of avaricious monks alludes to the involvement of some section of monks in agrarian management. In either case, it was the employment of direct cultivators which provided labour power necessary to keep landholdings of Buddhist establishments under cultivation.

The consideration on the form of land management leads us to a condition which enabled the emergence of the Buddhist establishments as large-scale landholders. It was a new land relation emerging in this period. All the sub-regions witnessed the ascendancy of local landed magnates and the emergence of the class of subordinate rulers in this period. It resulted in a stratified land relation in which these groups held some form of superior right above direct cultivators. This intermediate right held by a wide range of non-cultivating landholders was the right to enjoy a part of agrarian product from a particular land plot, according to the cases of both Ashrafpur plates.[239] The last cases also show the alienability of the right as an object of donation. This new land relation enabled the Buddhist establishments to mobilise labour power of direct cultivators on the one hand and accumulate landholdings as superior right holders on the other hand.

The rise of the Buddhist establishments was also related to the royal patronage resulting in the emergence of a Buddhist centre in Lalmai hill range. The sealing discovered from Salban Vihara, a gigantic monastic complex on the range, indicates its establishment by king Bhavadeva.[240] The kingship with stable resource base as the Devas could afford such a huge project. The royal patronage in the form of land grants was also a major factor contributing to the accumulation of land plots by the Buddhist establishment.

The patronage to the Buddhist establishment seems to have been prompted by its function to legitimise royal power. In case of Samataṭa, a description in Yijing's account attests to it. In the biography of Sengzhe, who stayed at the *vihāra* of a king identifiable as Rājabhaṭa or Rājarājabhaṭa, Yijing describes the procession of the statue of Avalokiteśvara on a carriage, accompanied by monks and followed by the king, with pomp of banners, drum beats and music.[241] Such a procession can be interpreted as an occasion in which the authority of king is exhibited and legitimised through Buddhist ritual. Mutual interaction and dependence of kingship and *vihāra* is also discernible in the following description:

> In the royal city, there are around 4,000 monks and nuns. All of them receive offerings of the king. Every morning he orders (an official) to enter the *vihāra*, fold hands (to monks) in front of the cells and quickly make enquiry about disease. The great king asks the teacher of law and others whether they had peaceful night or not. They reply that they wish good health and long life of the great king and peace of the country. He makes (the official) reward (or reply to) them and then minutely discuss state affairs.[242]

Thus, while the kingship offers subsistence and welfare of monks, the latter give blessing to the king and his kingdom, and even provide counsel about state affairs for him in exchange.

The growth to large-scale landholders in this period was more prominent in case of the eminent Buddhist centres in neighbouring Magadha. Yijing mentions 201 villages and their households given eternally to Nālandāmahāvihāra by the generations of rulers.[243] He describes the details of the management of the institution including the personnel like the abbot chosen from the eldest of elders, the owner cum founder (*vihārasvāmin*), the custodian (*vihārapāla*) and the caretaker (*karmadāna*), the process of decision making through discussions of monks and the collective management of treasury with mutual check, suggesting its development as an organisation.[244]

Yijing also refers to the *vihāra*s of monks from different countries present around Mahābodhi, which kept interactions with their home countries, citing the examples of a *vihāra* of Kāpiśī resided by monks from the northern country and the other established by king Ādityasena beside the *vihāra* previously built by the Cālukya king, which was resided by many monks from the southern country.[245] It suggests the network of Buddhist *vihāra*s centred on the eminent sites, for which more concrete evidence is available in the later period. This network also constitutes one of the incentives for the patronage of political powers to these institutions, as will be discussed minutely in the next chapter.

The Buddhist establishments and their relation with political power would see further development under the Pālas and Candras, with the formation of their regional kingdoms and complicated power relation involving their subordinate rulers.

Notes

1 Ryosuke Furui, 'The Kotalipada Copperplate Inscription of the Time of Dvādaśāditya, Year 14', *Pratna Samiksha: A Journal of Archaeology, New Series*, 2013, 4: 89–98; Faridpur CPI of the Time of Dharmāditya, year 3, *SI* 1, pp. 363–67; of Dharmāditya, ND, *ibid.*, pp. 367–69; of Gopacandra, year 18, *ibid.*, pp. 370–72; Nalinikanta Bhattasali, 'The Ghugrahati Copper-plate Inscription of Samachara-Deva', *Epigraphia Indica*, 1925–26 (1983), 18: 74–86.

2 The genealogical relation of these kings is unclear. For their chronological order, see Furui, 'Kotalipada Copperplate', pp. 93–94. For a different opinion, see Sayantani Pal, 'Reconsidering the Chronology of the Rulers of Faridpur (6th Century)', *Journal of Bengal Art*, 2013, 18: 115–21.

3 B. N. Mukherjee, *Coins and Currency Systems of Post-Gupta Bengal: c. AD 550–700*, New Delhi: Munshiram Manoharlal, 1993, pp. 7–9, 39–40; Shariful Islam and Sayeeda Nasrin, 'A Fresh Assessment of Gopacandra in the Light of Numismatic Evidence', *Journal of the Asiatic Society of Bangladesh, Humanities*, 2014, 59(1): 32.

4 Mallasarul CPI of the time of Gopacandra, year 3, *SI* 1, pp. 372–77. N. G. Majumdar read its date as *saṃvvad* 3, while Sircar read as *saṃvva* 30 3. N. G. Majumdar, 'Mallasarul Copper-plate of Vijayasena', *Epigraphia Indica*, 1935–36 (1984), 23: 161, *SI*, 1, p. 377, l. 25. My own reading from the photograph of the plate supports Majumdar's opinion; Jayarampur CPI of the time of Gopacandra, year 1, S. N. Rajaguru, 'Jayarampur Copper-plate Inscription of the time of Gopachandra', *Orissa Historical Research Journal*, 1963, 11(4): 206–33, P. R. Srinivasan, 'Jayarampur Plate of Gopachandra', *Epigraphia Indica*, 1972 (1985), 39(5): 141–48, *IO*, pp. 174–79. I mostly rely on Tripathy's reading, with modification based on my own reading from the photographs of the original plate. As an opinion against identifying Gopacandra of the three plates, see Sayantani Pal, 'Jayarampur Plate of Gopacandra: Some Reconsideration', in Subrata Kumar Acharya (ed.), *Studies on Odishan Epigraphy*, Delhi: Pratibha Prakashan, 2015, pp. 65–71.

5 CPI of the time of Pradyumnabandhu, Arlo Griffiths, 'New Documents for the Early History of Puṇḍravardhana: Copperplate Inscriptions from the Late Gupta and Early Post-Gupta Periods', *Pratna Samiksha: A Journal of Archaeology, New Series*, 2015, 6: 27–33.

6 Mukherjee, *Coins and Currency Systems of Post-Gupta Bengal*, pp. 10–15, 40–42; Kyoto Teikoku Daigaku Bunka Daigaku (ed.), *Daitou Saiiki Ki*, Tokyo: Tosho Kankoukai, 1972 (reprint), fasc. 5, p. 4, Li Rongxi (tr.), *The Great Tang Dynasty Record of the Western Regions: Translated(sic.) by the Tripiṭaka-Master Xuanzang under Imperial Order Composed by Śramaṇa Bianji of the Great Zongchi Monastery (Taisho, Volume 51, Number 2087)*, Berkeley: Numata Center for Buddhist Translation and Research, 1996, p. 142; Lionel D. Barnett, 'Vappaghoshavata Grant of Jayanaga', *Epigraphia Indica*, 1925–26 (1983), 18: 60–64.

7 Karṇasuvarṇa is identified with the present site of Rajbadidanga in Murshidabad district. For the partial excavation of the site, see Sudhir Ranjan Das, *Rājbāḍīdāṅga: 1962 (Chiruṭī: Jadupur): An Interim Report on Excavations at Rājbāḍīdāṅga and Terracotta Seals and Sealings*, Calcutta: The Asiatic Society, 1968.

8 Ryosuke Furui, 'Panchrol (Egra) Copperplate Inscription of the Time of Śaśāṅka: A Re-edition', *Pratna Samiksha: A Journal of Archaeology, New Series*, 2011, 2: 119–30; Antla CPI of Śubhakīrtti, year 8, *SI* 2, pp. 24–26; of Somadatta, year 19, *ibid.*, pp. 26–27. For the actual provenances of these inscriptions rather

known as Egra and Midnapore plates, see Rajat Sanyal, 'Copperplate Inscriptions of West Bengal: Finding Find-spots and Locating Localities', *Pratna Samiksha: A Journal of Archaeology, New Series*, 2010, 1: 123–24.

9 E. Hultzsch, 'Plates of the Time of Sasankaraja; Gupta-Samvat 300', *Epigraphia Indica*, 1900–01 (1981), 6: 144, l. 3.

10 Griffiths 'New Documents', p. 29, ll. 1–2.

11 Navyāvakāśikā: Faridpur CPIs, *SI* 1, pp. 367–68, ll. 3–4 (Dharmāditya, ND), p. 370, ll. 3–4 (Gopacandra), Bhattasali, 'Ghugrahati Copper-plate', p. 76, ll. 3–4; Vardhamānabhukti: Mallasarul CPI, *SI* 1, p. 373, l. 3; Daṇḍabhukti: Jayarampur CPI, *IO*, p. 176, l. 23, Antla CPIs, *SI* 2, p. 25, ll. 5–6 (year 8), p. 26, ll. 4–5 (year 19). The control of *mahārāja* Vijayasena over the second is attested by his seal attached to the Mallasarul plate, though not clearly mentioned in the inscription itself. *SI* 1, p. 372.

12 Though the grant of Dvādaśāditya and the plate of Dharmāditya dated year 3 do not mention the name of the higher administrative unit, they refer to its governors. Furui, 'Kotalipada Copperplate', p. 90, ll. 2–3; *SI* 1, p. 364, ll. 2–3.

13 Ayoub Khan, 'Bengal Copperplates: Provenances and Preservation Data', *Pratnatattva*, 2007, 13: 7.

14 Furui, 'Kotalipada Copperplate', p. 90, l. 3; Faridpur CPIs, *SI* 1, p. 364, ll. 3–4 (Dharmāditya, year 3), p. 368, ll. 4–6 (Dharmāditya, ND), p. 370, ll. 4–6 (Gopacandra); Bhattasali, 'Ghugrahati Copper-plate', p. 76, ll. 4–5.

15 Faridpur CPI of the time of Dharmāditya, ND, *SI* 1, p. 368, ll. 5–6. The same phrase seems to be used in the plate of the time of Gopacandra. *Ibid.*, p. 370, ll. 5–6.

16 Supra Chapter 3.

17 *jyeṣrakāyasthanayasenapramukham adhikaraṇam*, Faridpur CPIs, *SI* 1, p. 368, l. 7 (Dharmāditya, ND), p. 370, l. 6 (Gopacandra); *jyeṣṭhādhikaraṇika* Dāmuka, Bhattasali, 'Ghugrahati Copper-plate', p. 76, ll. 5–6.

18 *SI* 1, p. 371, l. 18; Bhattasali, 'Ghugrahati Copper-plate', p. 77, l. 15.

19 Chitrarekha Gupta, 'Bengal Art and Bengal Inscriptions: An Approach Towards Co-relation – A Case Study with Punchra: A Village in the Vardhaman District, West Bengal', *Journal of Bengal Art*, 2002, 7: 87.

20 Furui, 'Panchrol (Egra) Copperplate', p. 127. For the reading 'Ekatākaka', see *ibid.*, p. 121, l. 5.

21 Mallasarul CPI, *SI* 1, p. 373, ll. 3–5; Furui, 'Panchrol (Egra) Copperplate', p. 121, ll. 6–7.

22 Jayarampur CPI, *IO*, p. 176, ll. 23–24. Cf. *ibid.*, p. 175, ll. 11–12.

23 Mallasarul CPI, *SI* 1, p. 374, l. 8; Furui, 'Panchrol (Egra) Copperplate', p. 121 (seal); Jayarampur CPI, *IO*, p. 175, l. 13.

24 *Ibid.*, p. 176, l. 28; Furui, 'Panchrol (Egra) Copperplate', p. 122, ll. 15–16.

25 In the Antla plates, both Tāvīrādhikaraṇa and Tāvīrakaraṇa are used synonymously. *SI* 2, p. 25, l. 7, p. 27, l. 9; R. C. Majumdar, 'Two Copper-plates of Śaśāṅka from Midnapore', *Journal of the Royal Asiatic Society of Bengal, Letters*, 1945, 11: 1 and Plate II (seal).

26 CPI of the time of Pradyumnabandhu, Griffiths, 'New Documents', pp. 29–30, l. 2.

27 *ghoṇādvīpakaviṣaye adhikaraṇasya*, *ibid.*, p. 29, primary seal.

28 *(e)tadviṣayanivāsimahāmahattaramahattarādayo v[ai]ṣayikās sādhikaraṇā*, *ibid.*, p. 30, ll. 2–3.

29 *l[i]khitaṃ kāraṇikaśam[budatte]na tāpitaṃ pustapālakṛṣṇadattena*, *ibid.*, l. 18.

30 *vayam*: Mallasarul CPI, *SI* 1, p. 374, l. 8, Griffiths, 'New Documents', p. 30, l. 12; *asmābhiḥ*: Furui, 'Kotalipada Copperplate', p. 91, ll. 13, 19–20, Faridpur CPI, time of Dharmāditya, year 3, *SI* 1, p. 364, l. 9, Mallasarul CPI, *ibid.*,

p. 374, l. 10, Jayarampur CPI, *IO*, p. 175, l. 20, Furui, 'Panchrol (Egra) Copperplate', p. 123, l. 22, Griffiths, 'New Documents', p. 30, l. 12; *asmākam:* Mallasarul CPI, *SI* 1, p. 375, l. 11; *bhavatām*: Furui, 'Kotalipada Copperplate', p. 91, l. 11, Faridpur CPIs, *SI* 1, p. 364, l. 7 (Dharmāditya, year 3), p. 368, l. 9 (Dharmāditya, ND), p. 371, l. 10 (Gopacandra); *bhavatā*: Bhattasali, 'Ghugrahati Copper-plate', p. 76, l. 9; *yuṣmad:* Jayarampur CPI, *IO*, p. 175, ll. 14–15.

31 *etad abhyarthanam adhikṛty*(*a*), Furui, 'Kotalipada Copperplate', p. 91, l. 13, Faridpur CPI, time of Dharmāditya, year 3, *SI* 1, p. 364, l. 9; *etad āvābhyarthānam adhikṛtty*(*a*), Faridpur CPI, time of Dharmāditya, ND, *ibid*., p. 368, ll. 12–13; *etad a(bhya)rthanam adhi*[*kkṛty*](*a*), Faridpur CPI, time of Gopacandra, *ibid*., p. 371, ll. 15–16; *enad abhyarthanam upalabhya*, Bhattasali, 'Ghugrahati Copper-plate', p. 76, l. 12; *vayam abhyarthitā*, Mallasarul CPI, *SI* 1, p. 374, l. 8; *prārthitā vayaṃ*, Jayarampur CPI, *IO*, p. 175, ll. 13–14; *yatosmābhir asyāb hyartha*(*na*)*yāvadhṛtam*, Mallasarul CPI, *SI* 1, p. 374, l. 10; (*a*)*smābhi*[*r yai*]*r uparilikhitaker anyonyāvadhāraṇayāvadhṛtam*, Furui, 'Panchrol (Egra) Copperplate', p. 123, ll. 22–23; *abhyarthitā*(*ḥ*), Griffiths, 'New Documents', p. 30, ll. 3, 4; *vijñāpayāma*, *ibid*., l. 4; *sanmantrayantī sm*(*a*), *ibid*., l. 10; *ity avadhṛtavanto vadhṛtya*, *ibid*., l. 13.

32 *akātyer bhutvā*, Faridpur CPI, time of Dharmāditya, year 3, *SI* 1, p. 364, l. 9. I followed Sircar's reconstruction of this passage as *aikātmye bhūtvā*. *Ibid*., note 9.

33 The three found in plural cases are Anācāra, Śubhadeva and Ghoṣacandra. For the *adhikaraṇa* of Śṛṅgaveravīthī, see supra Chapter 3.

34 Furui, 'Kotalipada Copperplate', p. 91, l. 14; Faridpur CPIs, *SI* 1, pp. 364–65, ll. 10–11 (Dharmāditya, year 3), p. 368, l. 13 (Dharmāditya, ND), p. 371, l. 16 (Gopacandra).

35 Furui, 'Kotalipada Copperplate', p. 91, ll. 15–16; *SI* 1, p. 365, l. 13.

36 Bhattasali, 'Ghugrahati Copper-plate', p. 77, ll. 13–14; *SI* 1, pp. 374–75, ll. 10–11; Furui, 'Panchrol (Egra) Copperplate', p. 123, ll. 23–25; *IO*, pp. 175–76, ll. 22–23.

37 Griffiths, 'New Documents', p. 30, ll. 10–12.

38 Table 3.1 (Koṭivarṣa); Paharpur CPI, *SI* 1, p. 359, l. 1 (Puṇḍravardhana). *Śreṣṭhin* Ribhupāla was the applicant in the case recorded in Damodarpur CPI of the time of Budhagupta, ND, *ibid*., p. 337, l. 5.

39 Supra Chapter 3.

40 *IO*, p. 175, ll. 11–12; *SI* 1, p. 373, ll. 3–5; Furui, 'Panchrol (Egra) Copperplate', p. 121, ll. 6–7.

41 military officer: *sādhanika* Vātabhoga in Faridpur CPI, time of Dharmāditya, year 3, *SI* 1, p. 364, l. 7; administrator: *viniyuktaka* Vatsapālasvāmin in Faridpur CPI, time of Gopacandra, *ibid*., p. 370, l. 5, p. 371, ll. 19–20; subordinate rulers: *rājānaka* Viviktasoma in Kotalipada CPI, Furui, 'Kotalipada Copperplate', p. 91, ll. 11, 12, *mahāsāmanta mahārāja* Acyuta in Jayarampur CPI, *IO*, p. 175, l. 14, *mahārāja* Vijayasena in Mallasarul CPI, *SI* 1, p. 374, l. 8, *mahāpratihāra* Śubhakīrti in Antla CPI of year 8, *SI* 2, p. 25, l. 8, *mahāpratīhāra* Avadhūta in CPI of the time of Pradyumnabandhu, Griffiths, 'New Documents', p. 30, l. 2; close associate: *antaraṅga* Doṣatuṅga in Furui, 'Panchrol (Egra) Copperplate', p. 122, l. 17.

42 Vasudevasvāmin in Faridpur CPI, ND, *SI* 1, p. 368, l. 6, p. 369, ll. 19–20; Supratīkasvāmin in Bhattasali, 'Ghugrahati Copper-plate', p. 76, l. 5.

43 Supra Chapter 3.

44 *SI* 1, p. 369, l. 17.

45 *Ibid*., p. 369, ll. 15–17.

46 Supra Chapter 3.

47 Monier Monier-Williams, *A Sanskrit-English Dictionary: Etymologically and Philologically Arranged with Special Reference to Cognate Indo-European Languages* (new ed.), Oxford: Oxford University Press, 2000 (reprint), p. 718, col. 1.
48 Sircar takes it the same as *khāḍgika*, which probably denotes a palace guard. *IEG*, p. 153.
49 *SI* 1, p. 374, note 2, *IEG*, p. 358.
50 Gupta, 'Bengal Art and Bengal Inscriptions', pp. 86–87.
51 Furui, 'Kotalipada Copperplate', pp. 90–91, ll. 3–11.
52 *SI* 1, p. 364, ll. 4–6.
53 In case of the grant of the time of Gopacandra, some more names must be written as the relevant part is illegible due to corrosion. *Ibid.*, pp. 370–71, ll. 6–9.
54 *viṣayāṇam mahattarā*, Faridpur CPI, time of Dharmāditya, ND, *ibid.*, p. 368, l. 8; *pradhānavyāpā[riṇaḥ]*, Faridpur CPI, time of Gopacandra, *ibid.*, p. 371, l. 9; *anye ca vahavaḥ pradhānā vyavahā(ri)ṇaś ca*, Bhattasali, 'Ghugrahati Copperplate', p. 76, ll. 8–9.
55 *Vyāpārin*, derived from vy-ā-√pṛ, 'to be occupied or engaged in', and *vyavahārin*, derived from vy-ava-√hṛ, 'to be active or busy, work', shared the connotation of engagement or dealing. Their interchangeable use in the same context is understandable.
56 *śaṃthoparilikhitānyair vyavahāribhiḥ*, *SI* 1, pp. 76–77, ll. 12–13. The engraver seems to have made mistake and overwritten *ya*. As a result, *yatho* got appearance like *śaṃtho*. *Ibid.*, p. 76, note 16.
57 Supra Chapter 3.
58 Furui, 'Kotalipada Copperplate', p. 90, l. 5.
59 *SI* 1, p. 369, l. 17.
60 In regular or Vṛddhi form with suffix – īya. For the form and meaning of secondary derivatives, see William Dwight Whitney, *Sanskrit Grammar: Including Both, the Classical Language and the Older Dialects of Veda and Brāhmaṇa*, Delhi: Motilal Banarsidass, 1994 (reprint), pp. 454–56, nos 1202–8. *Ibid.*, p. 464, no. 1215 for suffix – īya.
61 It is not a synonym of *agrahārin* suggested by Sircar, as the context shows. Cf. *SI* 1, p. 374, note 2. Suffix – īṇa can be a colloquial form of – īna, which also makes secondary derivatives. Whitney, *Sanskrit Grammar*, p. 469, no. 1223d.
62 *mahattara* Ṣaṣṭhidatta and Śrīdatta of Vaṭavallakāgrahāra, Mahidatta and Rājyadatta of Godhagrāmāgrahāra. Mallasarul CPI, *SI* 1, p. 374, ll. 6–7.
63 *Ibid.*, p. 375, ll. 14–15.
64 For the identification of some of these settlements with their modern counterparts and their location, see Gupta, 'Bengal Art and Bengal Inscriptions', p. 87 and Sanyal, 'Copperplate Inscriptions of West Bengal', p. 122. Some identifications need further philological explanation.
65 B. D. Chattopadhyaya, *Aspects of Rural Settlements and Rural Society in Early Medieval India*, Calcutta: K P Bagchi, 1990, p. 49.
66 *SI* 1, p. 375, l. 15.
67 Cf. Chattopadhyaya, *Aspects of Rural Settlements*, pp. 52–53.
68 Jayarampur CPI, *IO*, p. 175, ll. 10–13.
69 *Ibid.*, p. 176, l. 25.
70 Vauddhasvāmin of the second category can be a *brāhmaṇa*, according to his name ending.
71 Griffiths, 'New Documents', p. 30, ll. 2–3.
72 Supra.
73 Supra.
74 Supra Chapter 3.

75 Supra.
76 *IO*, p. 175, l. 13.
77 Griffiths, 'New Documents', p. 30, ll. 2–3.
78 Furui, 'Panchrol (Egra) Copperplate', pp. 121–22, ll. 8–17.
79 Furui, 'Kotalipada Copperplate', p. 91, l. 14; Faridpur CPIs, *SI* 1, pp. 364–65, ll. 10–11 (Dharmāditya, year 3), p. 368, l. 13 (Dharmāditya, ND), p. 371, l. 16 (Gopacandra).
80 I followed Sircar's reconstruction as *nayabhūtes tu sthūlāvadhāraṇayā*. *Ibid*., p. 371, ll. 17–18, note 4.
81 Bhattasali, 'Ghugrahati Copper-plate', pp. 76–77, ll. 12–15.
82 *yataḥ pustapālabhogibhaṭāvadhāraṇayā avadhṛtya*, *IO*, p. 176, l. 23. Modified by my own reading from the plate attached to Srinivasan, 'Jayarampur Plate'.
83 *IO*, p. 176, ll. 25–29.
84 *SI* 1, pp. 374–75, ll. 10–12.
85 *(a)smābhi[r yai]r uparilikhitaker anyonyāvadhāraṇayāvadhṛta[m]*', Furui, 'Panchrol (Egra) Copperplate', p. 123, ll. 22–23.
86 Griffiths, 'New Documents', p. 30, ll. 10–13, 18.
87 *SI* 1, p. 371, ll. 18–19; Bhattasali, 'Ghugrahati Copper-plate', p. 77, ll. 15–17.
88 *viṣayādhikaraṇenādhikaraṇakajñanakulavārān prakalpya*, *SI*, 1, p. 371, l. 18. I follow Sircar in reconstructing *adhikaraṇakajñana* as *adhikaraṇikajanān*. *Ibid*., note 5; Bhattasali, 'Ghugrahati Copper-plate', p. 77, l. 15.
89 *SI*, 1, p. 375, ll. 12–13.
90 Griffiths, 'New Documents', p. 30, l. 14, p. 36, note 33.
91 Supra Chapter 3.
92 Supra.
93 Chattopadhyaya, *Aspects of Rural Settlements*, pp. 51–53.
94 *SI* 1, p. 366, ll. 18–19, p. 368, ll. 10–11, p. 371, l. 13, p. 374, ll. 9–10. Griffiths, 'New Documents', p. 30, ll. 14–15. The name of donee's father is also given in the last case.
95 Furui, 'Kotalipada Copperplate', p. 91, ll. 21–24. Based on the modified reading, *nānāgotracaraṇatapasvādhyāya* in l. 21, suggested by Arlo Griffiths through personal communication.
96 *SI* 2, p. 25, ll. 10–11; Barnett, 'Vappaghoshavata Grant', p. 63, ll. 3–5; *SI* 2, p. 27, l. 12. For the actual provenance of the grant of Jayanāga, see Sanyal, 'Copperplate Inscriptions of West Bengal', p. 115.
97 Furui, 'Panchrol (Egra) Copperplate', p. 122, ll. 19–20.
98 *SI* 1, p. 368, ll. 6, 10–11.
99 *Ibid*., p. 370, l. 5, p. 371, ll. 13–14, 19.
100 *IO*, p. 175, ll. 11–12; *SI* 1, p. 373, ll. 3–5; Furui, 'Panchrol (Egra) Copperplate', p. 121, ll. 6–7.
101 Probably an official who reports the king about important matters. *IEG*, p. 149.
102 Supra.
103 Supra Chapter 3.
104 Supra.
105 Furui, 'Kotalipada Copperplate', p. 91, ll. 25–27; *SI* 1, p. 366, ll. 20–22. Chattopadhyaya, *Aspects of Rural Settlements*, p. 50.
106 Kalaikuri CPI, *SI* 1, p. 355, ll. 27–29; Damodarpur CPIs, *ibid*., p. 294, ll. 10–11 (year 128), p. 334, l. 11 (year 163), p. 338, l. 15 (time of Budhagupta, ND), p. 349, l. 19 (year 224); Baigram CPI, *ibid*., pp. 358–59, ll. 20–21; Jagadishpur CPI, *EDEP*, pp. 62–63, ll. 22–24; Nandapur CPI, *SI* 1, p. 383, l. 16.
107 Griffiths, 'New Documents', pp. 29–30, l. 2.

108 *Ibid.*, p. 30, ll. 3–4, 13–16.
109 *Ibid.*, ll. 12–14. For *cūrṇikā* as a currency unit equal to 100 cowrie-shells, see B. D. Chattopadhyaya, 'Currency in Early Bengal', *Journal of Indian History*, 1977, 55(3): 59.
110 *SI* 1, pp. 373–74, ll. 5–8.
111 *dūtakaḥ śubhadatto likhitaṃ sāndhivigrahikabhogacandreṇa tāpitaṃ pustapāla jayadāsena*, *ibid.*, p. 377, ll. 24–25.
112 (*mahā*)*rājavijaya*[*se*]*nasya*, *ibid.*, p. 372.
113 *Ibid.*, p. 343, ll. 15–16. For *sāndhivigrahika*s in royal grants, see supra Chapter 3.
114 Supra.
115 *SI* 2, p. 25, ll. 5–9.
116 *Ibid.*, p. 27, ll. 7–14.
117 Barnett, 'Vappaghoshavata Grant', p. 63, ll.1–4.
118 *Ibid.*, p. 63, ll. 6–7.
119 Supra.
120 *SI*,1, pp. 366–67, ll. 23–25, pp. 371–72, ll. 21–24.
121 Furui, 'Kotalipada Copperplate', p. 91, l. 33. The other landmarks were borders of villages Vaṇḍakhāṭakagrāma and Sragdhākaśoṭi to its east and north respectively. *Ibid.*, ll. 32, 33–34.
122 *SI* 1, pp. 366–67, ll. 24–25.
123 *Ibid.*, p. 369, ll. 22–23. I followed the reconstruction by Sircar. *Ibid*, note 8.
124 Bhattasali, 'Ghugrahati Copper-plate', p. 77, ll. 18–19.
125 *SI* 1, p. 366, ll. 23–24, p. 367, l. 25.
126 *Ibid.*, p. 369, ll. 21, 23.
127 *Ibid.*, p. 366, ll. 16, 23–24, p. 367, l. 25, p. 371, ll. 21–23, p. 372, l. 24.
128 *Ibid.*, p. 366, ll. 16–17, p. 371, l. 20.
129 *śrīmānmahattarathoḍa*[*samvaddha*]*kṣettrakhaṇḍalakāt*, *ibid.*, p. 369, l. 17.
130 *sāpaṭā śvāpadair juṣṭā*, Bhattasali, 'Ghugrahati Copper-plate', p. 77, l. 13.
131 *Ibid.*, ll. 18–20.
132 *prāktāmrapaṭṭīkṛtakṣettrakulyavāpatrayamm apāsya*, *ibid.*, ll. 15–16.
133 Gupta, 'Bengal Art and Bengal Inscriptions', p. 86.
134 Furui, 'Panchrol (Egra) Copperplate', pp. 123–24, ll. 30–35.
135 Vettragarttā and Āmragarttikā. *SI* 1, p. 374, l. 8, p. 375, l. 15.
136 *Ibid.*, p. 375, l. 13. Gupta, 'Bengal Art and Bengal Inscriptions', p. 87.
137 Godhagrāma (east and south), Vaṭavallakāgrahāra (north), Āmragarttikā (west), *SI* 1, p. 375, ll. 14–15. *kīlakāś cāttra kama*[*lā*]*kṣamālāṅkitā caturṣu dikṣu nyastā*, *ibid.*, pp. 375–76, ll. 15–16.
138 They are respectively located to the north and south. Furui, 'Panchrol (Egra) Copperplate', p. 124, ll. 32–33, 34.
139 Kaṇṭikārikagarttā or Kaṇṭikārigarttikā to the south. *Ibid.*, p. 123, l. 30, p. 124, ll. 35–36; Tālapuṣkariṇī to the south, *ibid.*, l. 31; Cālavahidakīyasṛṣṭodakapuṣkariṇī to the west, *ibid.*, l. 32; Cāṇḍālapuṣkariṇī to the east, ll. 33–34. Āmrapuṣkirāvabhaka, located to the west, also seems to be a pond. *Ibid.*, ll. 34–35.
140 [*cā*]*lavahidakīryasṛṣṭodakapuṣkiriṇyāṃ* (*pū*)*rvveṇa kīlaka*(*ḥ*), *ibid.*, l. 32; *vedamattasvāmimaṇḍale pūrveṇa kīlaka*(*ḥ*), *ibid.*, l. 34.
141 *kaṇṭikārikagarttāpaścimadakṣiṇe koṇe kīlaka*(*ḥ*), *ibid.*, pp. 123–24, ll. 30–31; *āmrapuṣkirāvabhakapaścimottarokkoṇe kīlake*, *ibid.*, p. 124, ll. 34–35.
142 *tālapuṣkiriṇyā*(*ḥ*) *paścimamahāpadakā dakṣiṇena kīlaka*(*ḥ*), *ibid.*, l. 31; *cāṇḍālapuṣkiriṇyā*(*ḥ*) *dakṣiṇamahāpakṣake kīlaka*(*ḥ*), *ibid.*, ll. 33–34.
143 Jayarampur CPI, *IO*, pp. 176–77, ll. 35–36.

144 *Ibid.*, p. 176, ll. 32–35, p. 177, l. 37. Tripathy erred in interpreting directions to which these landmarks were located. *Ibid.*, p. 179.
145 *daṅgagrāmīyaguṇadevamaṇḍalavāstu*, *ibid.*, p. 176, l. 35; *bhagavato goveśvarasya maṇḍalakṣ[etraṃ]*, *ibid.*, p. 177, l. 36. Modified by my own reading from the plate attached to Srinivasan, 'Jayarampur Plate'.
146 Supra Chapter 3.
147 Supra.
148 Griffiths, 'New Documents', p. 30, ll. 16–18.
149 Table 4.5 (3) Ṣaṇḍadvīpa, (4) Pravaradvīpa and (10) Dvīpaka.
150 Supra.
151 Griffiths, 'New Documents', p. 30, ll. 11–12. Also see *ibid.* p. 35, note 30 for the similar phrases in the contemporary and later land sale grants.
152 Supra.
153 *SI*, 2 p. 27, ll. 12–13; Barnett, 'Vappaghoshavata Grant', p. 63, l. 6.
154 Supra Chapter 3.
155 Supra Chapter 3.
156 P. N. Bhattacharya, 'Nidhanpur Copper Plates of Bhaskaravarman', *Epigraphia Indica*, 1913–14 (1982), 12: 65–79; idem, 'Two Lost Plates of the Nidhanpur Copper-plates of Bhaskaravarman', *Epigraphia Indica*, 1927–28 (1983), 19: 115–25; idem, 'A Third Lost Plate of the Nidhanpur Plates of Bhaskaravarman', *ibid.*: 245–50.
157 Ashrafpur CPI of Devakhaḍga, year 7, G. M. Laskar, 'Ashrafpur Copper-plate Grants of Devakhaḍga', *Memoirs of the Asiatic Society of Bengal*, 1904, 1(6): 88–91; year 13, *ibid.*: 89–90, *SI* 2, pp. 41–43.
158 Devaparvata CPI of Bhavadeva, D. C. Sircar, 'Copper-plate Inscription of King Bhavadeva of Devaparvata', *Journal of the Asiatic Society, Letters*, 1951, 17(2): 83–94. Rashid confirmed that this inscription had been recovered from the site of Ananda Vihara, Mainamati. M. Harunur Rashid, 'The Mainamati Inscriptions', in Enamul Haque (ed.), *Hakim Habibur Rahman Khan Commemoration Volume*, Dhaka: The International Centre for Study of Bengal Art, 2001, pp. 212–13.
159 Tippera CPI of Lokanātha, year [3]44, Radha Govinda Basak, 'Tipperah Copper-plate Grant of Lokanatha: The 44th Year', *Epigraphia Indica*, 1919–20 (1982), 15: 301–15, *SI* 2, pp. 28–35; Kailan CPI of Śrīdhāraṇarāta, year 8, D. C. Sircar, 'The Kailan Copper-plate Inscription of King Śrīdhāraṇa Rāta of Samataṭa', *The Indian Historical Quarterly*, 1947, 23(3): 221–41, *SI* 2, pp. 36–40; Kalapur CPI of Maruṇḍanātha, *CPS*, pp. 68–80.
160 Supra.
161 Bhattacharya, 'Nidhanpur Copper Plates', p. 75, ll. 48–49 (pl. 6).
162 *ājñāśatāprāpayitā prāptapañcamahāśavdaśrīgopāla*, *ibid.*, p. 75, ll. 47–48 (pl. 6); *śāsaītā lekhayitā ca vasuvarṇṇabhāṇḍāgārādhikṛtamahāsāmantadivākaraprabha*, *ibid.*, l. 50 (pl. 6); *utkheṭayitā dattakārapurṇṇo* | *sekyakārakāliyā*, *ibid.*, l. 51 (pl. 6). For the peculiar last term mainly found in the inscriptions from Assam, see *IEG*, p. 354.
163 Bhattacharya, 'Nidhanpur Copper Plates', p. 75, ll. 46–47 (pl. 7); *SI* 2, p. 32, l. 31.
164 Supra.
165 For details, see Ryosuke Furui, '*Brāhmaṇa*s in Early Medieval Bengal: Data of Inscriptional References', in Nobuhiro Ota (ed.), *Zen-kindai Minami-Ajia Shakai Ni Okeru Matomari To Tsunagari* (*Clustering and Connections in Pre-Modern South Asian Society*), Tokyo: Research Institute for Languages and Cultures of Asia and Africa, Tokyo University of Foreign Studies, 2017, pp. 207–12, Appendix Table 2.

166 *SI* 2, pp. 28–35.
167 For details, see Furui, '*Brāhmaṇa*s in Early Medieval Bengal: Data', pp. 213–15, Appendix Table 3.
168 *CPS*, pp. 68–80.
169 Suchandra Ghosh, 'Economy of Samataṭa in the Early Medieval Period: A Brief Overview', in Gerd J. R. Mevissen and Arundhati Banerji (eds), *Prajñādhara: Essays on Asian Art, History, Epigraphy and Culture in Honour of Gouriswar Bhattacharya*, New Delhi: Kaveri Books, 2009, p. 354.
170 P. N. Bhattacharya interpreted Ḍumbarīccheda as 'a (piece of) hewn fig tree.' Bhattacharya, 'Two Lost Plates', p. 121. However, as it demarcates the south-eastern, southern and south-western borders and has confluence (*samvedyā*) with Kauśikā and Gaṅginikā, it should be interpreted as a cleft (*cheda*) or riverbed named Ḍumbarī, connected with these rivers.
171 *Ibid.*, p. 120, ll. 54–55 (pl. 6), Bhattacharya, 'Nidhanpur Copper Plates', p. 75, ll. 45–47 (pl. 7).
172 Idem, 'Two Lost Plates', p. 118, ll. 10–11, 12. Furui, '*Brāhmaṇa*s in Early Medieval Bengal: Data', p. 207, Appendix Table 2, nos 1 and 8.
173 Bhattacharya, 'Two Lost Plates', p. 120, ll. 52–54 (pl. 6).
174 *SI* 2, p. 32, ll. 30–31.
175 *kṛtākṛtāviruddhāṭavībhūkhaṇḍa*, *ibid.*, p. 31, ll. 22, 25, p. 32, l. 31.
176 *CPS*, p. 70, l. 21.
177 *SI* 2, p. 34, ll. 55–56, Furui, '*Brāhmaṇa*s in Early Medieval Bengal: Data', pp. 214–15, Appendix Table 3, nos 193–98.
178 *pācakavasu dro* 20, *SI* 2, p. 34, l .55. *–vācakatvena sudhāna*(?) *dro* 20, *utkhātakāmananaradattasya dro* 10 9, *ibid.*, l. 56.
179 *Ibid.*, p. 31, ll. 22–24.
180 *CPS*, p. 70, 1. 17–19, p. 71, 2. 7–8.
181 *SI* 2, p. 31, ll. 23–24.
182 Bhattacharya, 'Two Lost Plates', p. 118, 1. 6–7 (pl. 3).
183 *SI* 2, p. 14, ll. 110–12.
184 Laskar, 'Ashrafpur Copper-plate', pp. 88–91; *Ibid.*, pp. 89–90, *SI* 2, pp. 41–43. The reading of date of the former is based on Ganguly's reading. D. C. Ganguly, 'Date of Ashrafpur Plate', *Epigraphia Indica*, 1941–42 (1985), 26: 125–26.
185 *śālīvardajaācāryasaṃghamittrasya vihāre*, Ashrafpur CPI, year 7, my own reading from the impression attached as Plate VII. Cf. Laskar, 'Ashrafpur Copper-plate', p. 91, l. 16; *ācāryavandyasaṃghamittrapādai(ḥ) kāri(ta)–vihāravihārikācatuṣṭayam*, Ashrafpur CPI, year 13, *SI* 2, p. 42, ll. 13–14.
186 *vuddhamaṇḍapaprāpivṛhatparameśvareṇa pratipāditakavatsanāgapāṭaka-navaropye śrīudīrṇakhaḍgena pratipādita śattrughnena bhujyamānaka pāṭaka*, Ashrafpur CPI, year 7, my own reading from the impression attached as Plate VII. Cf. Laskar, 'Ashrafpur Copper-plate', p. 90, ll. 11–12.
187 – *śrīmete śrīśarvāntareṇa bhujyamānaka*(*ḥ*) *mahattaraśikharādibhiḥ kṛṣyamā*(*ṇakap*)*āṭaka*(*ḥ*), Ashrafpur CPI, year 13, *SI* 2, p. 42, ll. 8–9.
188 [*mahā*]*devīśrīprabhāvatyā bhujyamāṇakapāṭakadvayaṃ*, *ibid.*, p. 42, l. 4. Prabhāvatī is clearly mentioned as the chief queen of Devakhaḍga in the Deulbadi image inscription. Nalinikanta Bhattasali, 'Some Image Inscriptions from East Bengal', *Epigraphia Indica*, 1923–24 (1983), 17: 359, l. 2. *sāmantavaṇṭiyokena bhujyamānakadvyardha*(*pāṭakaḥ*), *SI* 2, p. 42, l. 5. *śrīnetrabhaṭena bhujyamānakadvyardhapāṭaka*, *SI* 2, p. 42, l. 6. The name ending Bhaṭa is shared by prince Rājarājabhaṭa, son of Devakhaḍga.
189 *upāsakena bhuktakādhunā svastiyokena bhujyamānakaviṃśatir droṇavāpā*, Laskar, 'Ashrafpur Copper-plate', p. 90, ll. 8–9.

190 *yathābhuñjanād apanīya*, Laskar, 'Ashrafpur Copper-plate', p. 91, l. 16. The same sentence is written in the other plate with the last part illegible. *SI* 2, p. 42, l. 12.
191 Sircar, 'Copper-plate Inscription of King Bhavadeva', pp. 83–94.
192 Laskar, 'Ashrafpur Copper-plate', p. 91, l. 13; *SI* 2, p. 42, l. 6.
193 Sircar, 'Copper-plate Inscription of King Bhavadeva', p. 94, ll. 56–59.
194 *SI* 2, p. 38, ll. 22–24, p. 40, ll. 45–48.
195 Sircar interpreted the last as the same as a Bengali term *nāodāṃrā* used in central Bengal in the sense of a path for boats made on the moss-covered waters of *bil* (lake) etc. Sircar, 'The Kailan Copper-plate', pp. 236–37.
196 *svatāmraṃ*, *SI* 2, p. 39, l. 33; *mahākāyasthabhāskaracandratāmram*, *ibid.*, l. 38; *devīma[ṭhatāmram]*, *ibid.*, l. 35; *mitravalavihāratāmram*, *ibid.*, ll. 35–36; *daṇḍajayasenakṣetraṃ*, *ibid.*, l. 33; *śrītāpasadhanadevakṣetrañ ca*, *ibid.*, l. 39.
197 *(a)rddhattrikaśatakulaputtrakānāṃ kṣetraṃ*, *ibid.*, ll. 33–34; *vendhanādī(nāṃ) mallakarmmakārānāṃ kṣetraṃ*, *ibid.*, ll. 37–38.
198 *Ibid.*, p. 30, ll. 12–14.
199 Kailan CPI, *ibid.*, p. 37, l. 14. For the use of *pañcamahāśabda* as a privilege conferred on a subordinate ruler, see *IEG*, pp. 230–31.
200 Kailan CPI, *SI* 2, p. 37, ll. 9–10, 14.
201 *yasmiñ chrīparameśvarasya vahuśo yātaṃ kṣayam sainikam*, Tippera CPI, *ibid.*, p. 30, l. 13.
202 *Ibid.*, pp. 30–31, ll. 13–15.
203 *kumārāmātyā adhikaraṇañ ca*, Tippera CPI, *ibid.*, p. 29, l. 1; *chrīmatsamataṭeśvarapādānudhyātāḥ kumārāmātyā adhikaraṇañ ca*, Kailan CPI, *ibid.*, p. 37, ll. 3–4.
204 *Ibid*, pp. 29, 36. This is common to the plate of Maruṇḍanātha. *CPS*, p. 69.
205 For *pādānudhyāta*, see Cédric Ferrier and Judit Törzsök, 'Meditating on the King's Feet? Some Remarks on the Expression *pādānudhyāta*', *Indo-Iranian Journal*, 2008, 51(2): 100–2.
206 *tatsutarājapu[tra]lakṣmīnātha[dūta]kenā[jñā?]*, Tippera CPI, *SI* 2, p. 31, ll. 15–16; *ājñāśataprāpiṇo yuvarājaprāptapañcamahāśavdaśrībaladhāraṇarātabhaṭṭārakasya mukhena*, Kailan CPI, *ibid.*, p. 38, ll. 17–18.
207 Of 25 *pāṭaka*s, he obtained 7 1/2, while the Buddhist establishment and *brāhmaṇa* group got 4 1/2 and 13 respectively. *Ibid.*, p. 40, ll. 45–49.
208 Supra Chapter 3.
209 *śrīmaddevakhaḍga(ḥ)*, Laskar, 'Ashrafpur Copper-Plate', p. 85.
210 Salban Vihara CPI of Balabhaṭa, l. 28. Read from the photographs. His name is not clear from the photographs, though Gupta read it as Yajñavarman. Kamalakanta Gupta, 'Two Mainamati Copper-plate Inscriptions of the Khadga and Early-Deva Times (7th and 8th centuries A. D.)', *Bangladesh Archaeology*, 1979, 1(1): 144.
211 Sircar, 'Copper-plate Inscription of King Bhavadeva', p. 94, ll. 53–56. Vibhūtidāsa's position as a subordinate ruler is indicated by eulogies of his family. *Ibid.*, pp. 93–94, ll. 45–54.
212 *Ibid.*, p. 93, ll. 42–43.
213 Gouriswar Bhattacharya, 'A Preliminary Report on the Inscribed Metal Vase from the National Museum of Bangladesh', in Debala Mitra (ed.), *Explorations in Art and Archaeology of South Asia: Essays Dedicated to N. G. Majumdar*, Calcutta: Directorate of Archaeology and Museums, 1996, pp. 237–47.
214 Ryosuke Furui, 'Bangladesh National Museum Metal Vase Inscription of the Time of Devātideva and its Implications for the Early History of Harikela', *Puravritta*, 2019, 2: 43–51.
215 *Ibid.*, pp. 44–45. For details of the issuers, see *ibid.*, p. 49, Appendix 1. Cf. Bhattacharya, 'A Preliminary Report', p. 243, ll. 2–4.

216 *Ibid.*, ll. 5–8.
217 *Ibid.*, pp. 243–44, ll. 9–10.
218 *Ibid.*, pp. 244–45, ll. 11–19.
219 Supra Chapters 3 and 4.
220 Bhattacharya, 'A Preliminary Report', p. 244, ll. 13–14.
221 For the names and titles of residents, see Furui 'Bangladesh National Museum Metal Vase', pp. 49–50, Appendix 2.
222 Michael Mitchiner, *The Land of Water: Coinage and History of Bangladesh and Later Arakan circa 300 BC to the Present Day*. London: Hawkins Publications, 2000, pp. 64–70.
223 Furui, 'Bangladesh National Museum Metal Vase', p. 47.
224 Bhattacharya, 'A Preliminary Report', p. 243, l. 6.
225 *Ibid.*, l. 14.
226 Furui, 'Bangladesh National Museum Metal Vase', p. 47.
227 *yathaikam api paitrikān paribhogyam*, Bhattacharya, 'A Preliminary Report', p. 243, l. 9.
228 *Ibid.*, ll. 11–13.
229 *Ibid.*, ll. 16, 10.
230 Supra Chapter 3.
231 Supra Chapter 3.
232 Supra.
233 *SI* 2, p. 40, l. 45.
234 Sircar, 'Copper-plate Inscription of King Bhavadeva', p. 94, ll. 56–59.
235 Bhattacharya, 'A Preliminary Report', p. 243, ll. 5–6, 7–8, p. 244, ll. 12, 14, 15–17, pp. 244–45, ll. 18–19.
236 I-tsing, J. Takakusu (tr.), *A Record of the Buddhist Religion as Practised in India and the Malay Archipelago (AD 671–695)*, New Delhi: Munshiram Manoharlal, 1998 (reprint), p. 61. Italicisation is mine.
237 *Ibid.*
238 *Ibid.*, p. 62. For the original text of the cited portions, see Yìjìng, Wáng Bāng-Wéi (ed., annot.), *Nánhǎijìguīnèifǎchuán Jiàozhù*, Běijīng: Zhōnghúashūjú, 1995, text, pp. 82–83. Dachengdeng (Ta shang Tan, Mahāyānapradīpa) was a monk from Aizhou in present Vietnam who came to Tāmralipti earlier than Yijing, had studied there for 12 years and then went to 'Middle India', connoting present Bihar region for Chinese monks, with him. For his biography, see Kiroku Adachi (ed., tr., annot.), *Daitou Saiiki Guhou Kousou Den*, Tokyo: Iwanami Shoten, 1942, pp. 77–79, I-Ching, Latika Lahiri (tr.), *Chinese Monks in India: Biography of Eminent Monks Who Went to the Western World in Search of the Law during the Great T'ang Dynasty*, Delhi: Motilal Banarsidass, 1986, pp. 40–43. Lahiri's translation is inaccurate in some parts.
239 Supra.
240 Abu Imam, *Excavations at Mainamati: An Exploratory Study*, Dhaka: The International Centre for Study of Bengal Art, 2000, p. 25.
241 Adachi, *Daitou*, p. 161, I-Ching, Lahiri, *Chinese Monks*, p. 85. The carriage, which Lahiri translated as 'royal carriage', is rather the one prepared for the statue according to the context.
242 Adachi, *Daitou*, p. 161. My own translation. Lahiri's translation shows several misunderstandings of terms and contexts in this paragraph. I-Ching, Lahiri, *Chinese Monks*, pp. 85–86.
243 Adachi, *Daitou*, p. 93, I-Ching, Lahiri, *Chinese Monks*, p. 61.
244 Adachi, *Daitou*, p. 91, I-Ching, Lahiri, *Chinese Monks*, pp. 54–55.
245 Adachi, *Daitou*, p. 89, I-Ching, Lahiri, *Chinese Monks*, pp. 48–49.

5

GROWING CONTRADICTIONS

c. 800–1100 AD

In the period from the second half of the eighth century to the end of the 11th century, Bengal witnessed the establishment of strong dynasties which ruled wider territories covering several sub-regions and beyond. They were the Pālas and the Candras.

The Pālas, who originated from Varendra, extended their dominion to Rāḍha and then to eastern Bihar. In their early political career, especially during the reign of Dharmapāla around the end of the eighth century, their power occasionally stretched westwards as far as Kānyakubja and they were involved in the struggles for the hegemony over it against the Gurjara-Pratihāras and the Rāṣṭrakūṭas. Their conflict on the western front continued against the Gāhaḍavālas and the Kalacuris in the following period, while they kept their control over Varendra, northern Rāḍha and eastern Bihar until the end of the 11th century.[1]

The origin of the Candras is not clear. What we can be sure is that they were the rulers of Candradvīpa or Vaṅgāla, approximately corresponding to the present Bakarganj area, under the suzerainty of the kings of Harikela, who might have been the Devas. In the reign of Śrīcandra, which fell to the first half of the tenth century, they established their position as sovereign rulers of almost all the eastern Bengal with Vaṅga, Samataṭa and Śrīhaṭṭa under their control.[2]

In the same period, the peripheral areas of southern Rāḍha and Harikela witnessed occasional rise of independent political powers in a smaller scale. The Kāmbojas ruled Daṇḍabhukti, an area bordering present Orissa, and some kings with the name ending Deva showed their presence in Harikela, both as sovereign rulers.

Under the rules of these dynasties, the state and its administrative apparatus strengthened their control over rural society, while the formation of a power structure centred on subordinate rulers intensified in this period and a new line of contention was drawn between the king and them. Two religious authorities, religious institutions and *brāhmaṇas*, also enhanced their presence in rural society by the patronage of political powers and their own network building. Rural society, meanwhile, saw the intensification of inner stratification. The new power structure within and outside it had close relation with diverse forms of agrarian development. In this situation, the two forms of social reorganisation were attempted.

In this chapter, I will discuss the power relation and deepening contradictions around rural society, which finally saw their culmination in the *Kaivarta* rebellion resulting in the temporary ouster of the Pālas from Varendra.

Enhanced state control and social stratification

Power relations around rural society had seen a drastic change by the eighth century. First of all, it manifested itself in the character of copper plate inscriptions. From the eighth century onwards, the issue of these documents became a royal monopoly. In a standardised format, they convey unilateral orders of the king to his subordinates and local residents, informing them of the donation of land plots or villages to religious agents either instigated by the king or petitioned by his subordinates. Unlike the land sale grants in Varendra, Vaṅga and Rāḍha in the period between the fifth and seventh centuries, the influential section of rural society took no part in the decision making on donations.[3] The subordinate rulers, some of whom practically wielded authority to issue land and village grants in Rāḍha and Samataṭa in the seventh century,[4] also lost such a power, while they were involved in the process of donations as petitioners. The royal monopoly of land and village grants points to the enhanced state control over rural society, with which the state could realise its claim over territorial land as unilateral imposition of its decision superseding the authority of local notables and the autonomy of subordinate rulers.

The enhancement of state control is discernible in the privileges conferred on the grantees. In the Pāla grants in Bengal, the following terms and conditions are listed in common. The extent of the donated tract is 'as far as own borders, grass land and pasture.'[5] The donation is accompanied by flat land (*satala*), raised ground (*soddeśa*),[6] trees (*sapādapa*)[7] or more specifically mango and mahua trees (*sāmramadhūka*), watering place (*sajalasthala*),[8] ditches and saline land (*sagarttoṣara*), additional tax (*soparikara*),[9] right to levy fines of ten offences (*sadaśāpacāra*) and right to catch thieves (*sacauroddharaṇa*). The donated land or settlements are also exempted from all the labour charges (*parihṛtasarvapīḍa*) and kept free from entrance of *cāṭa*s and *bhaṭa*s (*acāṭabhaṭapraveśa*). Nothing should be taken (*akiñcitpragrāhya*) from donees and all the dues like *bhāga*, *bhoga*, *kara* and *hiraṇya* accompany the tenure.[10] These dues may respectively be the share of agricultural products, periodical offerings, taxes in grain and cash.[11] Apart from them, the privileges especially include small market, landing place and ferry, toll at the gates, and market and landing place in cases of the Khalimpur, Jagajjibanpur, Jajilpara and Rangpur plates.[12]

Almost the same privileges are listed in the Candra grants, with alternative or additional clauses like 'with mango and jackfruit trees' (*sāmrapanasa*), 'with areca nut and coconut trees' (*saguvākanālikera*) and 'with salt' (*salavaṇa*), which seem to accrue from the ecological character of Vaṅga and Samataṭa.[13] The privileges conferred on donees by the Kāmboja grants are as exhaustive as those in the Pāla grants, and even include night-soil deposit (*avaskarasthāna*) and salt mine (*lavaṇākara*) in both the Irda and Kalanda plates of Nayapāla, and market, boat landing (*haṭṭaghaṭṭa*) and ferry (*tara*) in the former.[14]

As evident from the descriptions above, the privileges conferred on donees were extensive. They exhaustively covered the sources of income and resources in a rural space. They especially contained the rights over commons like grass land, pasture and watering place which would otherwise have been controlled by the community of local residents. The authority of local policing was also conceded to donees as rights to charge fines and catch thieves, while the donated land and settlements were made immune to the interference by mercenaries called *cāṭa*s and *bhaṭa*s. Donated tracts were exempted from the charges in the form of labour and product, probably imposed by the king and his administrative apparatus, and donees were entitled to several types of income supposed to go to the king. Thus, donees were given the right to income and resources from the donated tracts with relegation of some administrative powers.

Donees also acquired the authority to mobilise labour power of cultivators. In these documents, there is an injunction by which local cultivators are requested to obey the order of the donee and properly offer him specific dues. It is stipulated in the Pāla grants that the offering of all the dues like tax (*kara*) and food (*piṇḍaka*)[15] or share of agricultural products (*bhāga*), periodical offerings (*bhoga*), taxes in grain and cash (*karahiraṇya*)[16] should be made by the residing cultivators after becoming the ones who are enjoined to listen to the order of the donee. In the same manner, residing cultivators are told in the Candra grants to obey the order of the donee and offer dues as declared.[17] Similarly, *vyavahārin*s with *karaṇa*s and cultivators with local residents are told in the Kāmboja grants to offer the tribute to the donee after becoming submissive to him and to live comfortably in the locality.[18]

The privileges and power bestowed on donees point to their strong presence in rural society and the enhanced state control which guarantees their position. In view of the formalised character of the copper plate grants, the enhanced control represented in these privileges and powers could be notional and just a claim by the state. The degree of actual control may have varied in each locality. However, such a claim was never made in the previous period, when the arrangement for cultivation of donated tracts was not made in the grants and seems to have been left to the negotiation between donees and local residents. Its appearance suggests the stronger power of state in relation to rural society, especially in view of its claim on commons and labour power of cultivators.

The change of power relation between state and rural society is also detectable in the address of copper plate inscriptions. The enhanced presence of the former is evident in large number of offices and titles listed for royal subordinates 'associated with' (*samupagata*) land plots or villages to be donated (**Table 5.1–5.3**). It increased enormously compared with that in the previous period.[19] The minute analysis of these addresses, on the other hand, gives us an insight into different power equations, both within and outside rural society, experienced in each sub-region.

In the address of the Pāla grants in Varendra, declining power of rural society and growing stratification within it are traceable. The earliest grants, the Indian Museum plate and the Khalimpur grant of Dharmapāla assignable to the beginning of the ninth century, are addressed to the four categories of people. The first is 'dependants of the royal favour' (*rājapādaprasādopajīvin*) or 'dependants of the king' (*rājapādopajīvin*) which respectively include 20 and 24 titles consisting of royal officials and subordinate rulers like *rāja*, *rājanaka* and *rājaputra*. The second is the others belonging to (*jātīya*) *cāṭa*s and *bhaṭa*s.[20] The third is *viṣayavyavahārin*s being in the position at the proper time (*yathākālādhyāsino*), with *karaṇa*. They are mentioned as beginning with *jyeṣṭhakāyastha*, *mahāmahattara*, *mahattara* and *dāśagrāmika* in the second plate.[21] The fourth is 'residing cultivators', mentioned with homage to *brāhmaṇa*s beforehand (**Table 5.1 a,5.1 b**). The next grant from the same sub-region, the Jagajjibanpur plate of Mahendrapāla belonging to the mid-ninth century, is also issued to the four categories of addressees almost the same as those of the Indian Museum Plate of Dharmapāla (**Table 5.1 c**).[22]

From the reign of Gopāla II in the second half of the ninth century, the address of the Pāla grants got standardised. His Mohipur plate is issued to the two categories of people related to the village to be donated. The first is the 'royal officials' (*rājapuruṣa*) or 'dependants of the king' including 43 offices and titles which consist of royal officials, subordinate rulers like *rāja*, *rājanaka*, *rājaputra* and *mahāsāmanta*, and *cāṭa bhaṭa* servants including Gauḍas, Mālavas, Khaśas, Hūṇas, Kulikas, Karṇātas and Lāṭas. The second category is residents, of whom *brāhmaṇa*s are foremost, headed by *mahattama*s and *kuṭumbin*s, reaching to *meda*s, *andhraka*s and *caṇḍāla*s (**Table 5.1 d**). With addition of *uttama* between *mahattama* and *kuṭumbin* and slight difference in listed offices, this standardised address is used in almost all the Pāla grants in Varendra following the Jajilpara plate of Gopāla III, which belongs to the second half of the tenth century.[23]

The more or less standardised form of the address consisting of two categories had already been adopted in Magadha even during the reign of Dharmapāla. His Nalanda plate is addressed to 37 'dependants of (my) own lotus-like feet' (*svapādapadmopajīvin*) including subordinate rulers, royal officials and *bhaṭa cāṭa* servants of Gauḍa, Mālava, Khaśa, Kulika and Hūṇa origin, and residents, of whom *brāhmaṇa*s are foremost, headed by *mahattama*s and *kuṭumbin*s, reaching to *meda*s, *andhra*s and *caṇḍāla*s.[24] The Monghyr and Nalanda grants of Devapāla, his son, also have a similar standardised description of the address, with increase of the number of

Table 5.1 Addresses in the Pāla grants

a. **Indian Museum CPI of Dharmapāla, year 26** (Ryosuke Furui, 'Indian Museum Copper Plate Inscription of Dharmapala, Year 26: Tentative Reading and Study', *South Asian Studies*, 2011, 27(2): 153, ll. 40–45.)

-All the dependants on royal favour (*sarvarājapādaprasādopajīvins*) (20): *rājanaka*, *rājaputra*, *kumārāmātya*, *bhuktipati*, *viṣayapati*, *bhogin*, *senāpati*, *uparika*, *tadāyuktaka*, *viniyuktaka*, *dāṇḍika*, *dāṇḍapāśika*, *cauroddharaṇika*, *dauḥsādhasādhanika*, *khola*, *dūta*, *gamāgamika*, *abhitvaramāṇa*, *hastyaśvoṣtranaubalavyāpṛtaka*, *gomahiṣyajāvikavaḍavādhyakṣa* etc.
-Others belonging to *cāṭa*s and *bhaṭa*s (*anyāṃś ca cāṭabhaṭajātīyān*).
-*Viṣayavyavahārins* in position in the proper time, with *karaṇa* (*yathākālādhyāsiviṣayavyavahāriṇaḥ sakaraṇān*).
-With homage to *brāhmaṇa*s beforehand (*brāhmaṇamānanāpūrvakam*), residing cultivators (*prativāsinaḥ kṣetrakarāṃś ca*).

b. **Khalimpur CPI of Dharmapāla, year 32** (*SI*, 2, p. 68, ll. 44–48.)

-All the dependants of the king (*rājapādopajīvins*) (24): *rāja*, *rājanaka*, *rājaputra*, *rājāmātya*, *senāpati*, *viṣayapati*, *bhogapati*, *ṣaṣṭhādhikṛta*, *daṇḍaśakti*, *dāṇḍapāśika*, *cauroddharaṇika*, *daussādhasādhanika*, *dūta*, *khola*, *gamāgamika*, *abhitvaramāṇa*, *hastyaśvagomahiṣyajāvikādhyakṣa*, *naukādhyakṣa*, *balādhyakṣa*, *tarika*, *śaulkika*, *gaulmika*, *tadāyuktaka*, *viniyuktaka* etc.
-Others unnamed (*anyāṃś cākīrttitān*) belonging to *cāṭa*s and *bhaṭa*s.
-*Viṣayavyavahārins* being in the position in proper time, beginning with *jyeṣṭhakāyastha*, *mahāmahattara*, *mahattara*, *dāśagrāmika*, with *karaṇa*.
-Residing cultivators, with homage to *brāhmaṇa*s beforehand.

c. **Jagajjibanpur CPI of Mahendrapāla, year 7** (Suresh Chandra Bhattacharya, 'The Jagjibanpur Plate of Mahendrapaala Comprehensively Re-edited,' *Journal of Ancient Indian History*, 2005–06 (2007), 23: 69, ll. 35–39.)

-All the dependants of the king (*rājapādopajīvins*) (19): *rājanaka*, *rājaputra*, *kumārāmātya*, *bhuktipati*, *viṣayapati*, *senāpati*, *uparika*, *tadāyuktaka*, *viniyuktaka*, *dāṇḍika*, *daṇḍapāśika*, *cauroddharaṇika*, *dau(ḥ)sādhyasādhanika*, *khola*, *dūta*, *gamāgamika*, *abhitvaramāṇa*, *hastyaśvoṣṭranaubalavyāpṛtaka*, *gomahiṣyajāvikavaḍavādhyakṣa* etc.
-Others belonging to *cāṭa*s and *bhaṭa*s.
-*Viṣayavyavahārins* being in the position in proper time, with *karaṇa*s.
-With homage to *brāhmaṇa*s beforehand, residing cultivators.

d. **Mohipur CPI of Gopāla II, year 3** (Ryosuke Furui, 'A New Copper Plate Inscription of Gopala II', *South Asian Studies*, 2008, 24: 73, ll. 41–46.)

-All the royal officials (*rājapuruṣa*s)/dependants of the king (*rājapādopajīvins*) (43): *rāja*, *rājanaka*, *rājaputra*, *rājāmātya*, *mahāsāmanta*, *mahāsenāpati*, *mahāsāndhivigrahika*, *mahākṣapaṭalika*, *mahāpratīhāra*, *mahādaṇḍanāyaka*, *mahārājasthānīya*, *uparika*, *mahākārttākṛtika*, *mahādaussādhyasādhanika*, *dāṇḍika*, *dāṇḍapāśika*, *śaulkika*, *gaulmika*, *kṣetrapa*, *prāntapāla*, *koṭṭapāla*, *khaṇḍarakṣa*, *tadāyuktaka*, *viniyuktaka*, *hastyaśvoṣṭranaubalavyāpṛtaka*, *kiśoravaḍavāgomahiṣyajāvikādhyakṣa*, *dūta*, *preṣaṇika*, *gamāgamika*, *abhitvaramāṇa*, *viṣayapati*, *tarapati*, *tarika*, Gauḍa, Mālava, Khaśa, Hūṇa, Kulika, Karṇāṭa, Lāṭa, *cāṭa*, *bhaṭa*, *sevaka* etc. and unnamed others.
-Residents, of whom *brāhmaṇa*s are foremost, headed by *mahattama*s and *kuṭumbin*s, reaching to *meda*s, *andhraka*s and *caṇḍāla*s (*prativāsinaś ca brāhmaṇottarām mahattamakuṭumbipurogamedāndhrakacaṇḍālaparyantān*).

e. Belwa CPI of Vigrahapāla III, year 11 (D. C. Sircar, 'Two Pala Plates from Belwa', *Epigraphia Indica*, 1951–52 (1987), 29: 11–12. ll. 29–37.)

-All the royal officials/dependants of the king (45): *rāja*, *rājanyaka*, *rājaputra*, *rājāmātya*, *mahāsāndhivigrahika*, *mahākṣapaṭalika*, *mahāsāmanta*, *mahāsenāpati*, *mahāpratīhāra*, *dauḥsādhasādhani(ka)*, *mahādaṇḍanāyaka*, *mahākumārāmātya*, *rājasthāna*, *uparika*, *dāśāparādhika*, *cauroddharaṇika*, *dāṇḍika*, *dāṇḍapāśika*, *saulkika*, *gaulmika*, *kṣetrapa*, *prāntapāla*, *koṭapāla*, *aṅgarakṣa*, *tadāyuktaka*, *viniyuktaka*, *hastyaśvoṣṭranaubalavyāpṛtaka*, *kiśora-vaḍavāgomahiṣyajāvikādhyakṣa*, *dūta*, *preṣaṇika*, *gamāgamika*, *abhitvaramāṇa*, *viṣayapati*, *grāmapati*, *tarika*, Gauḍa, Mālava, Khasa, Hūṇa, Kulika, Karṇāṭa, Lāṭa, *cāṭa*, *bhaṭa*, *sevaka* etc. and unnamed others.

-Residents, of whom *brāhmaṇas* are foremost, headed by *mahattamas*, *uttamas* and *kuṭumbins*, reaching to *medas*, *andhrakas* and *caṇḍālas*.

officials in both plates[25] and substitution of *mahattara* for *mahattama* in the first.[26] Nevertheless, the peculiar form of address was used in contemporary Varendra and it must have reflected a particular social situation in the sub-region in the ninth century. The adoption of the standard address in the Mohipur plate in turn suggests a change in this situation.

Among the four categories of addressees mentioned in the three earliest grants, the second and the third show difference from the standard address. The second category consists of people belonging to *cāṭas* and *bhaṭas*. Though its meaning is not clear, *cāṭa* is often described as rogues committing misdeeds in rural areas.[27] *Bhaṭa* means a soldier or a warrior and is also described as harassing rural population.[28] Both are often mentioned together in the contemporary copper plate grants and exemption from their entrance is listed as a privilege conferred on donees, as mentioned above. In the other Pāla grants, they are prefixed with ethnic labels like Gauḍa, Mālava, Karṇāta and so on.[29] These references suggest that they were irregular troops or mercenaries including people from Bengal and the other regions, who were employed for war or police duty in rural area and tended to disturb residents.[30] Their categorisation separate from the other royal subordinates indicates their loose connection with the king and ambiguous position standing between state administration and rural society.

The third category is *vyavahārins* of *viṣaya*. As discussed in the previous chapter, *vyavahārin* was a general category of local people who were involved in the management of some local affairs related to the *adhikaraṇa* and belonged to the dominant section of a locality.[31] The description in the Khalimpur plate shows that they were local notables including a chief scribe and landed magnates like *mahattaras*. The expression 'with *karaṇa*,' conditioning them, has an important meaning if we recall that *karaṇa* was sometimes used as an abbreviation for *adhikaraṇa* in the previous period.[32] Though it is synonymous with *kāyastha*, the mention of *jyeṣṭhakāyastha* as a constituent of *vyavahārins* excludes this connotation in the present case. Thus, these *vyavahārin*s were local notables with their *adhikaraṇa* organisation functioning at the level of *viṣaya*. As the plate of the time of Pradyumnabandhu shows, Varendra also saw the ascendancy of rural notables with inner differentiation and their involvement in local affairs through the organisation of *adhikaraṇa* in the previous period, in the same manner as their counterparts in Vaṅga and Rāḍha.[33] The appearance of *viṣayavyavahārin*s in those Pāla plates points to the continuing presence and activity of those notables in Varendra at least in the early phase of the Pāla rule. Their differentiation from the other residing cultivators indicates their superiority to the ordinary cultivators.

In general terms, the rearrangement of categories mentioned above can be interpreted as absorption of the middle categories into the first and the last. In case of *cāṭa*s and *bhaṭa*s, their inclusion in the category of royal officials or dependants means a tighter control over them by the king and his administrative apparatus, or at least the latter's intention to impose it. The change of suffix from the 'belonging to' (*jātīya*) to 'servant' (*sevaka*) subtly expresses this tendency. At the same time, the appearance of various ethnic groups among them may mean employment of the mercenaries from the other regions, which started earlier in the western territory of the Pālas. As social groups without roots in the locality, they may have been more dependent on their employer, the king, until they established their position as subordinate rulers after some generations, as did the Senas from Karṇāta in Rāḍha.

In case of *viṣayavyavahārin*s, the category itself disappeared and some of their constituents were incorporated into the category of local residents. In the copper plate inscriptions from the reign of Gopāla II onwards, local residents are almost uniformly described as 'residents, of whom *brāhmaṇa*s are foremost, headed by *mahattama*s, *uttama*s and *kuṭumbin*s, reaching to *meda*s, *andhra*s and *caṇḍāla*s' (**Table 5.1 d–5.1 e**). Among these social groups, *mahattama*s and *uttama*s seem to have been the upper strata of landholders who constituted *viṣayavyavahārin*s of the earlier inscriptions, while *kuṭumbin*s were peasant householders. *Meda*s, *andhra*s and *caṇḍāla*s are the terms used to denote social groups placed at the bottom of the society for some time. In the *Manusmṛti*, *meda*s and *andhra*s are described as mixed *jāti*s who should stay outside a village and engage in hunting wild animals in forest.[34] *Caṇḍāla*s are described in the same text as a mixed *jāti* kept out of a village and engaging in carrying corpse and execution.[35] Thus it is a stereotyped expression which comprehends all the members of rural society by indicating the groups placed at both ends of social hierarchy.

The change in categories of addressees related to rural society points to the weakening authority of local notables in relation to the state power. In the early phase of the Pāla rule in Varendra, they were distinguished from the other local residents and kept *adhikaraṇa* organisations, even though they were not involved in the process of land grants as active participants any more. They lost such a distinguished position and were categorised together with the others as the uppermost section of rural residents in the later grants from the reign of Gopāla II onwards. While they upheld their dominance over other members of rural society, the local notables lost their distinction.

The change of address also alludes to the intensified stratification among rural residents. Though the expression employed in the standard address can be rhetorical, its adoption by the Pāla regime instead of 'residing cultivators' points to the recognition of social stratification in rural society. Needless to say, the mention of *meda*s, *andhra*s and *caṇḍāla*s does not necessarily mean the existence of the same social groups as the composer of the *Manusmṛti* in the much earlier period perceived in Madhyadeśa. Rather, some non-sedentary social groups newly incorporated into the fold of sedentary society may have been labelled by these terms used for denoting similar groups in the past. The references to *ḍombī*s in the *Caryāgīti*, to be discussed below, confirm it.

The address of the Candra grants related to Vaṅga, Samataṭa and Śrīhaṭṭa does not show much change throughout the period between the tenth and mid-11th centuries. In almost all the Candra plates, four categories of people are listed as addressees (**Table 5.2**). The first category is royal officials (*rājapuruṣa*) or dependants (*rājapādopajīvin*) including queen (*rājñī*), subordinate rulers like *rāṇaka* and *rājaputra*, officials and others. The titles listed here are more irregular than those in the Pāla grants, as their number fluctuates between 16 and 23 without any recognisable tendency (**Table 5.2 a –5.2 b**).[36] The second is persons who are 'declared of the position as officials, unnamed here,'[37] which may mean the other royal officials not listed in the inscription. The third is people belonging to *cāṭa*s and *bhaṭa*s.[38] The fourth is *janapada*s and cultivators, of whom *brāhmaṇa*s are foremost.[39] Except the Madanpur grant, which has only two categories of subordinates of the king and the ones of whom *brāhmaṇa*s are foremost (*brāhmaṇottarān*) (**Table 5.2 b**), all the other Candra plates accessible to us employ these four categories, with slight difference in titles of the listed officials.[40]

Among these categories, the first two can be interpreted as royal officials and subordinate rulers who constituted the state administrative apparatus. The expression used for the third category of *cāṭa*s and *bhaṭa*s is much the same as the early Pāla grants of Dharmapāla and Mahendrapāla. The separate category for them may connote their ambiguous position as discussed above.

The fourth category is related to residents of rural society. The presence of *brāhmaṇa*s as a leading section of rural society is evident in the expression *brāhmaṇottara*. *Janapada*s, mentioned beside cultivators (*kṣetrakara*), seem to denote non-agrarian members of rural society. They possibly include mercantile, clerical and artisanal groups who are mentioned in some inscriptions. The Baghaura and Narayanpur image inscriptions refer to merchants

Table 5.2 Addresses in the Candra grants

a. Paschimbhag CPI of Śrīcandra, year 5 (*EDEP*, pp. 66–67, ll. 28–33.)

-All the dependants of the king (*rājapādopajīvins*) (23): *rājñī, rāṇaka, rājaputra, mahāsāndhivigrahika, mahāsainyapati, mahāmudrādhikṛta, mahākṣapaṭalika, pādamūlaka, mahāpratīhāra, mahātantrādhikṛta, mahāsarvādhikṛta, mahābalādhikaraṇika, mahāvyūhapati, maṇḍalapati, koṭṭapāla, daussādhanika, cauroddharaṇika, naubalahastyaśvagomahiṣājāvikādivyāpṛtaka, gaulmika, śaulkika, dāṇḍapāsika, dāṇḍanāyaka, viṣayapati* etc. and others (*anyāṃś ca*).
-(Those) declared of the position as officials, unnamed here (*adhyakṣapracāroktān ihākīrtitān*).
-*cāṭabhaṭajātīyān.*
-People and cultivators, of whom *brāhmaṇa*s are foremost (*janapadān kṣetrakarāṃś ca brāhmaṇottarān*).

b. Madanpur CPI of Śrīcandra, year 46 (R. G. Basak, 'Madanpur Plate of Srichandra, year 44,' *Epigraphia Indica*, 1949–50 (1985), 28: 57, ll. 21–25.)

-(16) *rājñī, rāṇaka, rājaputra,* (*rājapu*)*rohita, mahāsāndhivigrahika, mahāsenāpati, mahāsāmanta,* (*mahādharmmā?*)*dhyakṣa, mahāsarvādhikṛta, mahātantrādhyakṣa, mahāpīlupati, goccha*[*ka*]*pati, ardhanauvāṭaka, nauvāṭaka, dussādhyasādhanika, gomahiṣyājād*(*yadhya?*)*kṣa* and others undeclared (*anyāṃś cānuktān*).
-*brāhmaṇottarān.*

c. Mainamati CPI of Laḍahacandra, year 6 (no. 1) (*EDEP*, p. 74, ll. 45–50.)

-All the royal officials (*rājapuruṣa*s)/all the dependants of the king (*sakalarājapādopajīvins*) (18): *rājñī, rāṇaka, rājaputra, rājāmātya, mahāvyūhapati, maṇḍalapati, mahāsāndhivigrahika, mahāsenāpati, mahākṣapaṭalika, mahāsarvādhikṛta, mahāpratihāra, koṭṭapāla, daussādhasādhanika, cauroddharaṇika, naubalahastyaśvagomahiṣājāvikādivyā-pṛtaka, gaulmika, śaulkika, viṣayapati* etc. and others.
-(Those) declared of the position as officials, unnamed here.
-*cāṭabhaṭajātīyān.*
-People and cultivators, of whom *brāhmaṇa*s are foremost.

living in a village named Vilakīndaka or Vilikhandaka in Samataṭa towards the end of the tenth century,[41] while the Paschimbhag plate of Śrīcandra lists scribes, artisans and musicians and so on as service groups to whom some land plots were assigned as a part of the large-scale donation to *maṭha*s and *brāhmaṇa*s in Śrīhaṭṭa in the early tenth century.[42] The last case, on the other hand, proves the landholdings by those groups, which are also attested by the descriptions of border landmarks in the Mainamati grants of Laḍahacandra, pertaining to Samataṭa in the 11th century, including lands and village of cook (*sūpakāra*), carpenter (*vardhaki*) and brazier (*kaṃsāra*).[43] Their involvement in cultivation is unclear and they may have their land plots tilled either by family members or by the other cultivators. The second possibility entails a layered land relation among rural residents, which had been observed in Samataṭa in the previous period.[44] However, the two categories of *janapada*s and *kṣetrakara*s, which do not convey much sense of hierarchy, show that the social stratification if any did not yet reach the level to be taken seriously by the state, compared with that in the Pāla territory reflected in the address of the grants.

The address of the two grants of the Kāmboja king Nayapāla, pertaining to Daṇḍabhukti of Rāḍha in the second half of the tenth century, is divided into two parts (**Table 5.3**). In the first part, the king 'orders, with worship of *brāhmaṇa*s and so on beforehand,' *vyavahārin*s accompanied by *karaṇa*s and cultivators accompanied by residents in a village and inform them of the donation.[45] They are told to be submissive to the donee and offer him tributes.[46] In the second part, the king 'looks, talks to and orders' or 'with favours, declares, talks to and orders' his subordinates,[47] who are sub-divided into seven groups, and 'future kings connected with own *tīrtha*,' which may denote future kings of his own lineage.[48] The king asked them to protect the donation eternally.[49] The reference to *vyavahārin*s with *karaṇa*s is similar to that of the early Pāla grants. *Karaṇa* stands for *adhikaraṇa* in these cases too, as it is used to denote office of officials (*adhyakṣa*) in the second address.[50] The position of *vyavahārin*s as local notables is well expressed by their differentiation from the royal subordinates and by their superiority to other cultivators and residents expressed by their precedence in the order. The reference to them with their *karaṇa*s shows the continuance of their activity and ascendancy, which was witnessed in the sixth and seventh centuries in this area.[51] The fact that the king exclusively informs *vyavahārin*s and cultivators about the donation and asks royal subordinates only its protection indicates importance given to the former by the king and their relatively strong position.

Table 5.3 Addresses in the Kāmboja grants

Irda CPI of Nayapāla, year 13 (N. G. Majumdar, 'Irda Copper-Plate of the Kamboja King Nayapaladeva', *Epigraphia Indica*, 1933–34 (1984), 22: 155, ll. 20–22; 156, ll. 32–36.)

(A) -*Vyavahārin*s with *karaṇa*s (*karaṇair vyavahāriṇaḥ samaṃ*)

-cultivators with residents, with homage to *brāhmaṇa*s and so on beforehand (*kṛṣakāṃñ caiva nivāsibhis tathā dvijapūjādipūrvvam*).

(B) -Queen, crown prince and councillor (*mahiṣīyuvarājamantriṇaḥ*).

-likewise *purohita* accompanied by *ṛtvij*s (*saha ṛtvigbhir a*[*tho*] *purohitaṃ*).
- –*niyogin*s and the ones knowing *dharma* accompanied by magistrates (*dharmmajñāṃś ca sa*[*maṃ*] *pradeṣ*[*tṛ*]*bhiḥ*).
-all the group of officials accompanied by *karaṇa*s (*adhyakṣavargam akhilaṃ karaṇais sametāṃ*).
-general accompanied by leaders of corporation of soldiers (*senāpatiñ ca saha sainikasaṅghamukhyaiḥ*).
-messengers with secret officials accompanied by keepers of *mantra* (*dūtān sagūḍhapuruṣān saha man*[*tra*]*pālair*).
-other subordinates of the king (*anyān api kṣitipater anujīvinaś ca*).
-future kings connected with own *tīrtha* (*āgāmino pi nṛpatīn nijatīrthayuktān*).

The inscription of *rājādhirāja* Attākaradeva on a metal vase, datable to the early tenth century, is so far the only one inscription which sheds light on rural society of contemporary Harikela.[52] It records the two occasions of land grant to a Buddhist establishment and is addressed to present and future kings, *rājaputras*, *rāṇakas* and *ṭhakkuras*, and all the royal officials like *akṣapaṭalika* in Harikelāmaṇḍala, with homage to *brāhmaṇas* beforehand.[53] The absence of local residents, with possible exception of *brāhmaṇas*, is conspicuous in this address. However, individual residents are mentioned as holders of donated land plots. The land plots of *kārada* Indranātha and *bhārada* Amhela are mentioned among the land plots donated in the first occasion.[54] The land donated in the second occasion, recorded on the rim of the vase, includes a small garden of areca nut trees and so on belonging to Nāgadatta.[55] *Kārada* and *bhārada*, respectively meaning giving tax and giving labour, may indicate two categories of landholders who offer tribute to the political powers either by their production or labour service. On the other hand, Nāgadatta shows the case of an individual resident possessing resources like garden of valuable trees. Their presence attests to the difference among landholders in rural society. It should be noted, however, that the overarching authority of the king was exercised in donating their landed properties.

The information in the copper plate grants and the other inscription shows the enhancement of state control over rural society as a general tendency, with various power equations between both sides. It also indicates social stratification within the latter in different degrees in each subregion. These phenomena can be corroborated by the contemporary literary sources, namely verses in Sanskrit and Old Bengali compiled as anthologies, though their character does not allow us to pinpoint their location both in time and space, except that they belong to Bengal in this period. They especially show the stratification in rural society of Bengal by references to subordinate cultivators.

Some verses in the *Subhāṣitaratnakoṣa* and the *Saduktikarṇāmṛta* depict a social group called *pāmaras*. Their differentiation from other cultivators is discernible in a verse in which *pāmaras* call out to the other group of cultivators (*karṣakajana*) when they find out and chase a pair of rabbits during the harvest.[56] Another verse describes a *pāmara* as being summoned by a *hālika* and reluctantly coming to a field.[57] It shows the subordinate position of the former to the latter. *Hālikas* are described as peasant householders whose houses 'become worthy' (*arghanti*) after the first harvest of winter rice,[58] even if the term rather denotes subordinate agriculturalist in the sources of the other regions.[59] In case of *pāmaras*, the context of their appearance is rather their collective labour at agricultural field and threshing floor,[60] though they are also mentioned with their house, as small as being thrust through by a bull,[61] in which a *pāmara* woman rotates a hand-mill.[62] Thus *pāmaras* can be labelled as agricultural labourers collectively working for peasant householders.[63] Their presence and subservient position show the stratification among cultivators in rural society.

The other tendency, the enhanced presence of state power, is also detectable in a verse in the *Subhāṣitaratnakoṣa*. It describes a merciless *bhogapati* as a causeless disaster afflicting families in a village, because of whom only some families retain their land as 'land of own lineage' (*nijavaṃśabhū*) and villages become desolate.[64] *Bhogapati*, listed as one of royal subordinates,[65] constitutes a part of state machinery either as an official in charge of an administrative unit or tax called *bhoga*, or as a holder of some land tenure (*bhoga*). The possibility of his interference with donated land tracts is presumed in the Paschimbhag grant, which asks *bhogapati*s, instead of future kings, to protect the donation.[66] What is important is the description that some families retain their land because they are 'measured/investigated' (*mita*) as holding land of own lineage.[67] We may detect here the enhancement of state control over rural society through ascertaining land rights of peasant families, which could also incite interference and harassment by agents of state power.

The *Caryāgīti*, esoteric verses composed by Buddhist *siddhācārya*s and collected at one time, offers some glimpses of one aspect of the social stratification, namely, the incorporation of non-sedentary groups into rural society. In verses included in the collection, *ḍomba* women (*ḍombī*) are often referred to as a metaphor of Śūnyatā or Nairātmā, the goddess embodying voidness. They are described as low class women living on the fringe of rural society, with some interaction with other members in rural society like sexual relations with male members,[68] providing commodities like loom and bamboo basket, and working as a ferry woman.[69] On the other hand, both *mātaṅgī* and *caṇḍālī* are interchangeably used as synonym of *ḍombī* in some verses.[70] Those descriptions indicate that fringe groups which can be labelled as *ḍomba*s were somehow incorporated into rural society, while the names denoting them were imposed by the latter which recognised them as such. The last point may explain the appearance of *caṇḍāla*s in the Pāla copper plate inscriptions as discussed above.

The new power relation around rural society which emerged in this period can be summarised as the enhancement of state control over rural society with a range of power equations and the stratification of the latter in different degrees according to the locality. In this relation, the line of contention shifted from the confrontation of state and rural society to the negotiation among constituents of state power, especially between the king and subordinate rulers called *sāmanta*s, to be discussed in the next section.

Shifting line of contention: rise of *sāmanta*s

Among agents of the state control, subordinate rulers called *sāmanta*s gained prominence in the early phase of this period. Though the enhanced state control did not allow them to hold semi-independent status as their counterpart in the seventh century Samataṭa,[71] they still kept territorial control over a particular area. While they served the king as a part of his administrative apparatus especially in military and administrative capacity, they had their own agenda and stakes in rural society. It resulted in the tension and negotiation between the king and them, which are discernible in their activities recorded in their own inscriptions and the royal grants issued on their petition. The cases mostly pertained to Varendra in the early phase of the Pāla rule.

The genealogies of subordinate rulers included in these inscriptions show that they were a composite group with various origins, which included merchants, local chiefs and notables, and *brāhmaṇa* and non-*brāhmaṇa* literates. The great grandfather of *mahāsāmanta* Bhadraṇāga was a trader.[72] Pāhila, a subordinate of Devapāla, belonged to a family of local chieftains which shifted their allegiance from Yaśovarman to the Pālas.[73] Vajradeva, a general of Mahendrapāla, seems to have originated from a local notable family, while Kokkāka, a general of Gopāla II, belonged to a family of *sāmanta*s which had served Samataṭa kings and then shifted to Varendra to serve the Pāla kings.[74] The Badal pillar inscription of Guravamiśra records the deeds of a *brāhmaṇa* family, of which five generations were associated with the six Pāla kings by serving them mostly as political advisors and occasionally as priests or generals.[75] The Bhaturiya stone inscription of Yaśodāsa, on the other hand, attests to the rise of a family of non-*brāhmaṇa* literates located in rural society to that of councillor and minister through the marriage alliance, the association with king Rājyapāla, and the religious and public activities in locality.[76] Adding to them, the *Rāmacarita* of Sandhyākaranandin mentions the Rāṣṭrakūṭas of Aṅga,[77] which seems to have been a collateral branch of the famous royal lineage having settled in eastern Bihar, and forest chiefs called *āṭavika*s, which are glossed as *aṭavīyasāmanta*s in a near contemporary commentary, as subordinate rulers of Rāmapāla.[78] *Kaivarta* chiefs, who led the rebel *sāmanta*s against the Pāla kings, may have had a similar social background of tribal chieftains heading peasantised fisherfolks or boatmen settled in a particular area of Varendra as the latter.[79] Whatever were their origins, they acquired the position of subordinate rulers through their association with the Pāla kings in the forms of military or other services and the appointment to administrative positions.[80]

The tension and negotiation between those *sāmanta*s and the king can be detected in one of their activities, namely, the construction of religious institutions followed by the petition for donation of land plots or villages. In the Khalimpur grant, *mahāsāmantādhipati* Nārāyaṇavarman petitioned Dharmapāla to give four villages to the deity Nannanārāyaṇabhaṭṭāraka, who was installed by Nārāyaṇavarman at the temple constructed by him in Śubhasthalī, and to the attendants of the deity (*pādamūla*) like Lāṭa *brāhmaṇa* priests protecting him, for the worship and attendance.[81] The four donated villages belonged to the two *viṣaya*s in Vyāghrataṭīmaṇḍala of Puṇḍravardhanabhukti.[82] This *maṇḍala* could be the territory of Nārāyaṇavarman, as Balavarman, who mediated the petition by king Bālaputradeva of Suvarṇadvīpa as a messenger and was called Vyāghrataṭīmaṇḍalādhipati in the Nalanda grant of Devapāla, seems to have been his son.[83] This is thus the case of a subordinate ruler having donated villages within his own territory to the religious institution established by him, probably in the same territory.

In similar terms, the Jagajjibanpur and Mohipur plates record donations to Buddhist *vihāra*s constructed by generals. In the former, Vajradeva petitioned Mahendrapāla to give Nandadīrghikodraṅga to the Buddhist *vihāra* constructed by him in the same locality.[84] In the latter, Kokkāka petitioned Gopāla II to give village Kaṅkāvāsaka to the *vihāra* constructed by him in the same village.[85] The construction of *vihāra*s in each locality points to its control by these subordinate rulers and their resources accruing from it, which enabled such an enterprise. The establishment of religious institutions with personal connection and the donation of villages to them may have contributed to the extension of local influence of the subordinate rulers, for these institutions were enhancing their presence in rural society.

Implication of their action is, however, not limited to this. There is an additional clause to the purposes of donation listed in these documents, which include worship of the Buddha and other divinities, copying of scriptures, provision to the *bhikṣusaṃgha* and repairs of buildings.[86] It says that others wished by the petitioner would also partake in the donation, in the ratio decided by him, for complete usufruct (*anavadyabhoga*, literally 'unobjectionable enjoyment').[87] This clause alludes to the involvement of petitioners in the management of donated property and their following influence over it. In view of this, the action of these subordinate rulers can be interpreted as an attempt to secure for the properties under their influence the status of *śāsana* land, immune to revenue charges and other interferences by the king. The case of the Khalimpur plate can also be understood in the same manner. While accepting claim of the king on land in his territory and exclusive right of its disposal, *sāmanta*s could legitimately encroach upon his power and enhance their own through the construction of religious institutions and the petition for grants. Here we can detect the negotiation between *sāmanta*s and the king.

The relation and power equation between the king and his subordinate rulers were complicated and diverse. The case of the Indian Museum grant of Dharmapāla rather shows the subtlety of their relation. In this record, *mahāsāmanta* Bhadraṇāga petitioned for donation of several land plots to a *vihāra* constructed by him in Antarāvanikā and a perfume chamber (*gandhakuṭī*) and a *vihārikā* established respectively by him and his wife Saṇhāyikā at Somapuramahāvihāra.[88] As far as the first *vihāra* is concerned, this case is similar to the cases of Jagajjibanpur and Mohipur plates mentioned above. Bhadraṇāga established a *vihāra* in village Antarāvanikā which included in its premise two land plots respectively belonging to his *vihāra* and *vihārikā*.[89] It is the case of a *sāmanta* enhancing his local control through the establishment of a religious institution within his own territory and legitimately encroaching upon the royal power through the petition for grant.

The construction of facilities in Somapuramahāvihāra, however, indicates something else. As will be discussed in the next section, the involvement of Dharmapāla in the establishment of this *mahāvihāra* is well-known. The contribution of some facilities to it may indicate the intention of Bhadraṇāga to cultivate a close connection with Dharmapāla, his overlord, through this act. It is endorsed by the inclusion of the king among those whose merit is purported to increase by donation, a feature not encountered in the other inscriptions.[90] The land plots donated to these facilities were most probably located within the territory of Bhadraṇāga, though the portion mentioning them is illegible due to corrosion.[91] The presence of these plots belonging to the eminent religious institution may enhance his authority in the locality by showing his connection with it and its founder Dharmapāla.

Thus, we can detect in this particular case two different manoeuvres executed by a subordinate ruler to enhance his power in the locality. He tried to enhance his authority and resource base by encroaching upon the royal authority, while strengthening his tie with the king at the same time. This contradictory behaviour indicates a complicated power relation in which Bhadraṇāga is located. He owed his position and authority to the king, while he needed to extend control and resource base in his own territory. Though dependence on the royal power was the same for his counterparts appearing in the contemporary and slightly later Pāla grants mentioned above, they seem to have had better position in which they could concentrate on one kind of manoeuvre, namely, the establishment of religious institutions within their own territories.

The cases in the later inscriptions allude to the reclaiming of power attempted by the kings in their negotiation with subordinate rulers. In the Bhagalpur plate, king Nārāyaṇapāla donated a village to the temple of Śiva established by him and to the assembly of scholars of the Pāśupata sect.[92] What should be noted is the additional clause to purposes of donation, which prescribes complete usufruct for others wished by the king in the ratio fixed by him.[93] It is almost the same as the clauses found in the Jagajjibanpur and Mohipur plates and indicates the involvement of the king in management of the institution. By adopting the practice initiated by subordinate rulers, the king tried to counter their attempt to encroach upon his power. It later developed into the royal patronage of Brahmanical religious institutions with which the kings had personal connections. It became conspicuous during the reigns of Mahīpāla I and Nayapāla in the 11th century, according to the Bangarh and Siyan stone inscriptions of the time of the latter.[94]

The effort of the king to block the encroachment by *sāmanta*s is clearer in the Bhaturiya stone inscription belonging to the mid-tenth century. According to the inscription, Yaśodāsa constructed a Śaiva temple complex and installed a *liṅga* at the main high building (*prāsāda*) surrounded by eight shrines.[95] Then king Rājyapāla gave village Madhusrava to the deity after withholding the tax (*nikara*) of 100 *purāṇa*s.[96] This is a case of *karaśāsana*, by which a land plot or a village is given on condition that certain amount of tax would continue to be paid to the king.[97] Accordingly, the grant did not give full immunity. Though it is not clearly mentioned, Yaśodāsa may have petitioned the king for the bestowal of a *śāsana* land with the issue of a copper plate grant. The fact that this inscription was engraved on the stone slab and not issued as a copper plate grant points to the failure of Yaśodāsa. The king succeeded to limit Yaśodāsa's control over the donated tract and keep some interest in it.

The attempt to reclaim royal power is further reflected in the changed patterns of land and village grants. The grants of *śāsana* land to religious institutions established by *sāmanta*s disappeared after the reign of Gopāla II in the late ninth century. Instead, the royal grants to individual *brāhmaṇa*s became a norm from his reign onwards. The donees of royal grants in this period were highly qualified *brāhmaṇa*s with clearer identity, who were in the process of building their own networks with establishment of Brahmanical centres in Varendra and Rāḍha.[98] Land grants to them prompted their network building through their settling in rural society and enabled the king to spread his claim of control through this network.[99] Some of the *brāhmaṇa*s were specialists of propitiatory rites (*śānti*) serving the king, as indicated by their title of *śāntivārika*.[100] They could be better representatives of the royal authority than *sāmanta*s, including those of *brāhmaṇa* origin, who had their own territorial power and agenda.

The change in patterns of donations coincided with the introduction of new practices. They were the land measurement and the reference to 'standard' (*pramāṇa*) of particular settlements. The earliest case of land measurement is found in one of the two grants of Gopāla II dated year 4. In this inscription, the donated portion (*aṅśa*) and whole the village of Bhūtabhada measure 1 *kulya* 1 *droṇa* 1 *āḍhavāpa* 2 *pāda*s 3 *kākinī*s and 9 1/2 *kulya*s 1 *pāda* respectively.[101] Kuñjabhaddhikādāma, one of the settlements donated in the Rangpur grant of Mahīpāla I dated year 5, measure 41 *kulyavāpa*s 1 *āḍhavāpa*.[102] The Belwa grant of Vigrahapāla III belonging to the second half of the 11th century records the donation of a half of village Lovanikāma excluding some land tract.[103] Both donated and excluded portions are mentioned with the standard of 3 *kulya*s 7 1/2 *droṇa*s 11 *udamāna*s and 1 *kulya* 2 *droṇa*s 3 1/4 *āḍhavāpa*s 3 1/2 *udamāna*s respectively.[104] In the Amgachi plate of the same king, the donated village, Viṣamapurāṃśa with Daṇḍatraheśvara belonging to Brāhmaṇīgrāmamaṇḍala, is mentioned with standard of 6 *kulya*s 2 *droṇa*s 2 *udamāna*s 3 *kākinī*s.[105] While the size of donated land plots was generally mentioned in the previous period, the measurement of the whole village, even when only a part of it is donated, was unprecedented.

The reference to standard of settlements first appeared in the two grants of Gopāla II dated year 4. Suvarṇakārikādaṇḍa, a settlement or an administrative unit from which some land plots were donated in two separate occasions, is mentioned as the standard (*pramāṇa*) of 4,000 without any specification of unit.[106] The donated portions are mentioned as the standard of 457 with 9 *paṇa*s accompanied by 10 *gaṇḍaka*s in the first plate and 450 in the second plate.[107] As both *paṇa* and *gaṇḍaka* were units of currency,[108] it is easily inferable that the unspecified standard was also in a currency unit. The similar description is used in the Belwa grant of Mahīpāla I dated year 2 for the three donated villages. [109] Osinnakaivarttavṛtti, Nandisvāminī and Gaṇeśvarasametagrāmapuṣkiriṇī are described as 210 *pramāṇa*s, 493 *pramāṇa*s 6 *paṇa*s 5 *kāṇḍaka*s[110] and 151 *pramāṇa*s respectively.[111] In the Biyala plate of the same king, the donated village Palāśavṛnda is mentioned with the standard of 1,000 *purāṇa*s.[112] As will be discussed below, *purāṇa* is a unit of silver currency.[113] In view of the last case, the unspecified currency unit used in the first three inscriptions must also be *purāṇa*. The reference to 5,910 *parimāṇa* (measure) in relation to Rājikāgrāmodraṅga, a settlement donated in the Rangpur grant of Mahīpāla I, can be the indication of standard in the same unit.[114]

The standard in numerals in these cases seems to be the estimated production of a village calculated in currency units, in consideration of the similar description in the Bangaon grant of Vigrarahapāla III, where the donated portion, land of half the village of Vasukāvarta, is said to be a part of 500 by production.[115] This conjecture is supported by the descriptions in the two Rajibpur plates of Gopāla IV and Madanapāla, in which donated tracts are estimated to be 300 in production.[116]

The estimation of production in currency units could be a measure taken by the Pāla kings to enhance their control over rural settlements by computing production by a uniform standard. Its application in tax administration is proved by the case recorded in the Bhaturiya stone inscription which refers 100 *purāṇa*s as tax withheld by king Rājyapāla.[117]

Both practices, the measurement of land of the whole village and the assessment of estimated production in currency units, show the attempt at enhanced control over rural society and settlements of which the administrative machinery would gather information and keep records. It makes a stark contrast with the early Pāla grants, especially the ones petitioned by subordinate rulers, in which these practices are absent. The implementation of such measures was not necessarily thorough in this period, as settlements donated in the Jajilpara grant of Gopāla III and the Bangarh plate of Mahīpāla I have no indications of land measurement or estimated production.[118] Its full-fledged development will be witnessed in the later period under the Sena rule.

The royal effort to reclaim power and enhance local control may have given the king a stronger position in relation to subordinate rulers and rural society. It however did not lessen but rather heightened the tensions among these parties. The manifold tensions and conflicts culminated in the *Kaivarta* rebellion, to be discussed below.

In Vaṅga and Samataṭa under the Candras, from the first half of the tenth century to the middle of the 11th century, subordinate rulers kept their appearance low-key and were almost invisible with possible exception of Karmāntapāla Kusumadeva and his son Bhāvudeva who installed an image of the deity Narteśvara during the reign of Laḍahacandra.[119] There is no case of subordinate rulers petitioning the king for land or village grants and the reference to them is limited to the address of the inscriptions (**Table 5.2**). The phenomena discernible in the Candra plates were rather similar to those in the later Pāla grants which were connected with the efforts of the king to enhance his control, namely, royal grants to individual *brāhmaṇa*s and detailed land measurement.

All the grants of Śrīcandra except the Paschimbhag plate, which constitutes a special case to be discussed separately, are land grants to individual *brāhmaṇa*s.[120] In the Dhulla and Rampal grants, donees wielded the title of *śāntivārika* and received land plots as rewards for performing *adbhutaśānti* ritual in the four times of *homa* held by the king and for attending *koṭihoma* respectively.[121] *Adbhutaśānti* is a propitiatory rite against evil omens,[122] while *koṭihoma* is a kind of *navagrahahoma*, propitiatory rites to pacify bad effects of planets.[123] *Śāntivārika* is a *brāhmaṇa* priest specialised in such propitiatory rites. The donee of an undated plate was also granted a land plot for attending *koṭihoma*.[124] Thus these were the grants to *brāhmaṇas* for their ritual services to the king. In the Madanpur plate, on the other hand, the king is especially mentioned as 'born in the same country' as *brāhmaṇa* Śukradeva, the donee.[125] In these cases, donees had a personal association with the king through the ritual service to him or the shared origin with him. The imposition of such *brāhmaṇa*s as donees may have contributed to the extension of the influence of the king in rural society.

While the measurement of land plots to be donated had already been a regular feature in the time of Śrīcandra,[126] the progress in this custom occurred in the reign of Laḍahacandra as discernible in his two Mainamati plates. The first grant records the donation of a land plot and two villages with reference to their respective sizes.[127] Minute descriptions of border landmarks are given for the last two villages.[128] Suravorakagrāma, which was donated by the second grant, is also mentioned with its size and border demarcations.[129] The measurement of not only a land plot but also a whole village paralleled the phenomenon observed in the Pāla grants from the reign of Gopāla II onwards, which suggests the attempt at enhanced control over rural society, together with estimation of production.[130]

In Daṇḍabhukti of Rāḍha in the tenth century delineable from the two Kāmboja plates, subordinate rulers were conspicuous by their absence. Even the list of royal subordinates in the address of the grants does not contain any titles denoting them, though councillor (*mantrin*) and general (*senāpati*) may be of their kind.[131] It makes a stark contrast with the situation of the seventh century when subordinate rulers were visible in the copper plate grants.[132] However, as many as seven *sāmanta*s of Rāḍha, including Jayasiṃha of Daṇḍabhukti, were included in the army of Rāmapāla according to the commentary of the *Rāmacarita*.[133] Though invisible in the Kāmboja grants, they seem to have kept their presence in the sub-region to re-emerge in the later period.

The pattern of grants by Nayapāla conforms to that of the contemporary Pāla and Candra grants, namely, settling highly qualified *brāhmaṇa*s by donating villages to them.[134] The Kāmbojas also seem to have tried to extend their influence by implanting these agents of state authority in rural society.

The presence of subordinate rulers in the early tenth-century Harikela is clear in the address of the metal vase inscription of Attākaradeva, which includes *rājaputra*s, *rāṇaka*s and *ṭhakkura*s.[135] Furthermore, land plots were donated for worship of the Buddha installed in a cell (*maṭhikā*) constructed by *prāptapañcamahāśabda mahāpratīhāra* Sahadeva, provision for the *bhikṣusaṃgha* of Velavihāra and repairs of the abode (*āyatana*).[136] As the cell most probably belonged to the *vihāra*, this was the case in which a subordinate ruler constructed a facility of *vihāra* and the king donated land to it. Though not stated clearly, the *vihāra* may have been constructed by the king and the application of Sahadeva prompted his donation. It indicates an attempt by a subordinate ruler to cultivate a close connection with his overlord, comparable with the case recorded in the Indian Museum plate of Dharmapāla in one aspect.[137]

The discussion made above shows rise of *sāmanta*s and the line of contention drawn between them and the kingship with various power equations in sub-regions of Bengal. The cases recorded in the Pāla grants especially shows negotiation and changing power relation between both sides, in which prevailed the efforts of the king to curb the attempts of subordinate rulers at legitimate encroachment upon his authority and to enhance his control over rural society. The focus of their negotiation, and also of the relation among political powers in the other sub-regions, was the religious agents including both institutions and *brāhmaṇa*s, which saw a new phase of their presence in this period through their nexus with political powers.

Two religious agents: institutions and *brāhmaṇa*s

Buddhist *vihāra*s, which had emerged as large-scale landholders earlier,[138] grew to prominence in this period, as attested by the gigantic monuments left as archaeological sites to date. In Bihar, Mahābodhi temple in present Bodhgaya and Nālandāmahāvihāra continued to be the important Buddhist centres,[139] while Vikramaśīlamahāvihāra, identifiable with the excavated site of Antichak, emerged as their match.[140] Somapuramahāvihāra and Paṭṭikerāmahāvihāra, respectively identified with the present site of Paharpur and the Buddhist complex around Lalmai hill range, were the prominent Buddhist centres of Bengal in this period,[141] to which newly excavated site of Jagaddala identifiable with the *mahāvihāra* of the same name can be added.[142] Apart from them, moderate scale *vihāra*s of the period are known from excavations at sites like Sitakot, Vasu Bihar and Jagajjibanpur.[143]

The most important element which contributed to the growth of those *vihāra*s was patronage of temporal powers, especially the regional kingships of the Pālas and Candras with Buddhist leanings. Devapāla and Dharmapāla are respectively credited with the foundations of *mahāvihāra*s of Somapura and Vikramaśīla by the later Tibetan chroniclers beginning with Tāranātha.[144] The involvement of Dharmapāla in the foundation of the former is attested by the clay sealings discovered from the site of Paharpur.[145] His patronage to the same *mahāvihāra* in the form of land grant is known from his Indian Museum grant, and the donations of villages to Nālandāmahāvihāra by him and his son Devapāla are recorded in their copper plates discovered from the site, though the first and last cases were made on applications by a *sāmanta* and the king of Suvarṇadvīpa respectively.[146] Rāmapāla is credited with the foundation of Jagaddalamahāvihāra in the *Rāmacarita*.[147]

There is so far no clear evidence of the patronage of the Candras to Buddhist *vihāra*s. However, the presence of landed property of the Buddhist establishment and its protection by excluding it from donation to Brahmanical *maṭha*s and *brāhmaṇa*s in the Paschimbhag grant of Śrīcandra indirectly attest to his patronage to Buddhist institutions in Śrīhaṭṭa.[148] The same can be said of Laḍahacandra, whose second plate mentions *śāsanabhūmi* of Lokanāthabhaṭṭāraka as one of border landmarks of the donated village in Samataṭa.[149] His establishment of a Brahmanical shrine in Paṭṭikera, the premise of Lalmai hill,[150] presupposed the long term association of the Candras with the Buddhist establishment of Mainamati. King Attākaradeva of the neighbouring sub-region of Harikela also donated land plots to Velavihāra through the elder (*sthavira*) Dharmadatta.[151]

The religious institutions which flourished by royal patronage in this period were not limited to Buddhist *vihāra*s. The Mirzapur plate of Śūrapāla records the donation of four villages in Nagarabhukti to the temple of Māhaṭeśvara constructed by his mother Māhaṭā in Vārāṇasī and to the congregation (*pariṣad*) of Śaiva *ācārya*s there.[152] The Bhagalpur plate of Nārāyaṇapāla records the donation of a village in the same *bhukti* to the temple of Śiva constructed by the king and to the *pariṣad* of Pāśupata *ācārya*s.[153] Mahīpāla I and his son Nayapāla are known for their patronage to the order of Śaiva ascetics of whom the two served the latter king as his *rājaguru*s.[154] The Siyan inscription mentioning the reign of Nayapāla gives a glimpse of the Brahmanical institutions in diverse locations of

Bengal like Devīkoṭa (Koṭīvarṣa) and Gaṅgāsāgara, which generations of the Pāla kings established and patronised.[155] Among the Candra kings, Śrīcandra donated a huge land tract to the nine *maṭha*s of Brahmanical deities and 6,000 *brāhmaṇa*s, while Laḍahacandra established the shrine of Laḍahamādhava, Viṣṇu named after himself, and donated a land plot and villages to it.[156] Govindacandra also donated a plot to Naṭṭeśvara, Śiva in dancing form.[157]

Subordinate rulers also patronised religious institutions. The inscription of Pāhila records his construction of a Vaiṣṇava *maṭha*.[158] As mentioned above, the grants of Dharmapāla, Mahendrapāla and Gopāla II, which were issued on application of Nārāyaṇavarman, Bhadraṇāga, Vajradeva and Kokkāka, and the Bhaturiya inscription of Yaśodāsa attest to the construction of Buddhist *vihāra*s and Brahmanical temples by those subordinate rulers.[159] In Harikela, *prāptapañcamahāśabda mahāpratīhāra* Sahadeva constructed a cell of a *vihāra*.[160]

The patronage to these religious institutions could be prompted by their potential to legitimise and enhance temporal powers by rituals and the other means, which were emphasised in Tantric religions of both Buddhist and Śaiva strands.[161] It is also inferable that these institutions with massive edifices functioned as symbols of the power and authority of rulers, especially when the deities installed in these institutions were named after the rulers, like Nannanārāyaṇa and Laḍahamādhava,[162] or the founders were clearly mentioned in the names of *vihāra*s impressed on the sealings.[163] As embodiments of temporal powers, their presence in rural society was also strengthened in proportion to the enhanced state control in this period.[164]

The stronger presence of religious institutions was accompanied by their growth as large-scale landholders resulting from the patronage of temporal powers. Their landed properties scattered over wide space may have functioned as outposts of the authority of temporal powers who established and continued to be involved with them. It in turn encouraged rulers to patronise these institutions further, as the networks connecting the institution and its landholdings could work as channels to disseminate their claim of control.[165] In view of such characters of their presence, it is understandable that the religious institutions became a focus of negotiations between the king and subordinate rulers under him.

Mutual interactions of the religious institutions, on the other hand, constituted the networks covering wider area. The Buddhist *vihāra*s in eastern India were connected with each other through the movement of monks. An inscription on the Buddha image from Bodhgaya describes the donor Vīryendra as an eminent Mahāyānist from Samataṭa and a *sthavira* (elder) belonging to Somapuramahāvihāra.[166] The Nalanda stone inscription of monk Vipulaśrīmitra similarly records his meritorious deeds including establishment of a Tārā shrine at Somapura and donation of a *vihārikā* at Nālandā, indicating his shift from the former to the latter.[167] Their networks covered a vast area beyond eastern India and even the subcontinent. The Ghosravan stone inscription of the time of Devapāla records the eulogy of Vīradeva, who was a son of a *brāhmaṇa* in Nagarahāra in Kabul valley, became a Buddhist *bhikṣu* at the *mahāvihāra* of Kaniṣka and shifted to Mahābodhi and then to Nālandā.[168] It is especially mentioned that he came to the *vihāra* of Yaśovarmapura at Mahābodhi to see *bhikṣus* from his homeland, suggesting the regular interaction between the north-western part of the subcontinent and the *vihāras* of eastern India.[169] Inscriptions on the metal images and other objects discovered from Kurkihar in Gaya district, Bihar, mention at least 13 people, mostly monks, from Kāñcī as donors.[170] One of them was a *sthavira* of Kāñcī originating from Keraladeśa.[171] The presence of *sthavira* Pūrṇadāsa from Sindhu at Pāḍikramavihāra in present Bihar is also attested by the inscriptions on the two Buddha statues kept at Indian Museum.[172] The inscription on an image of the Buddha from Bodhgaya mentions Buddhasena, a Mahāyāna monk from Siṃhaladvīpa, as the donor.[173] The network connecting religious institutions was not limited to Buddhist *vihāras*. The eulogy of Śaiva ascetic Mūrtiśiva in the stone slab inscription from Bangarh records the deeds of six ascetics of Mattamayūra sect originating from Golagīmaṭha, whose activity extended from Golagī to Vārāṇasī, Koṭīvarṣa and Dhārā.[174] Indraśiva, the third in their scholarly lineage, was given a temple and a *maṭha* by Mahīpāla I at present Bangarh.[175] Golagīmaṭha further expanded to Rāḍha and then to Āndhra under the Kākatīyas in the later period.[176]

The networks of these institutions could work as channels through which fame and prestige of the rulers were disseminated. This potential is fully attested by the Nalanda grant of Devapāla, which records the donation of five villages to a *vihāra* at Nālandā established by Bālaputradeva, the Śailendra king of Suvarṇadvīpa, on petition of the latter.[177] It is remarkable that the document took the same form as the grants petitioned by subordinate rulers.[178] The network of Buddhist *vihāras* occasioned the interaction of the Pāla king and the Śailendra king and enabled the former to nominally claim his suzerainty, despite that he had no control over the remote territory of the latter.

The changing pattern of the later Pāla grants and the overall tendency of the Candra and Kāmboja grants highlight the growing importance of the other religious agent, namely, *brāhmaṇas*.[179] As the address of royal grants show (**Tables 5.1–5.3**), they continued to be a dominant section of rural residents in this period. The position of *brāhmaṇa* donees, however, changed drastically with extensive privileges conferred on them through the village and land grants.[180] They held a strong position approximating that of landlords in rural society, with command over the resources and labour power of cultivators.[181]

Such a privileged sector of *brāhmaṇas* intensified the construction of their identity and networks. Their keener sense of identity is exhibited by the increased indicators of their academic qualification and kinship relations. The Vedic school of a donee is mentioned in all the Pāla, Candra and Kāmboja grants, while the later Pāla grants have additional references to the name of teacher and the branches of knowledge mastered by the donee including *mīmāṃsā*, *vyākaraṇa*, *tarka* and *vidyā*. As for his kinship relation, *gotra*, three or five *pravara*s and genealogy of three or four generations are regular features.[182] Their academic qualification distinguishes them from the other *brāhmaṇa*s residing in rural society, while the indicators of kinship relations points to the acute consciousness on this matter accruing from the development of kinship relation among them and necessity of its regulation.[183]

The construction of networks by qualified *brāhmaṇa*s seem to have been facilitated by their geographical spread through migrations, as indicated by the references to the original and residential villages of *brāhmaṇa* donees in the Pāla grants from the reign of Gopāla II onwards and the Kāmboja grants.[184] The one grant of Śrīcandra mentions the original village of the donee.[185] With addition of the donated villages, these cases attest to the involvement of a donee with at least three *village*s through migrations. Their migrations were not only incited by royal grants, but also made voluntarily as shown by the Silimpur stone inscription, in which serial migrations of *brāhmaṇa*s are expressed as genealogies of villages and themselves.[186] Such migrations coincided with the emergence of Bahmanical centres like Tarkāri, Kroḍāñca and Hastipadagrāma in Śrāvasti, the area locatable to present Hilli-Balurghat area of South Dinajpur district, in Varendra, and Siddhalagrāma in Rāḍha. Those centres seem to have owed their establishment to the migration of *brāhmaṇa*s from Madhyadeśa, as most of them were named after its eminent Brahmanical centres and the last village was known as an abode of *brāhmaṇa*s of Sāvarṇa *gotra* originating from the region. As abodes of qualified *brāhmaṇa*s eligible for royal grants, these Brahmanical centres functioned as nodes of the networks built by migrations of those *brāhmaṇa*s.[187]

As already stated above, those highly qualified *brāhmaṇa*s with their networks established in sub-regions of Bengal could be better representatives of the royal authority, especially when they had close connection with the king as ritual specialists serving him. Their importance for kingship grew as the latter negotiated with subordinate rulers over local control with religious institutions in focus.[188] It led to the intensive royal patronage, which contributed to the establishment of Brahmanical authority in rural society with the formation of their networks.

The changed and changing power relations among rural residents, political powers and religious agents discussed above brought out a configuration in which a new form of agrarian development proceeded side by side with another phenomenon in rural society, namely, the commercialisation of its economy.

Agrarian development and commercialisation of rural economy

A new form of agrarian development was the most visible in Varendra, where relatively large number of the copper plate grants and the other inscriptions shed light on it. The changed power relation around rural society, especially its intensified stratification, produced the condition in which the limit of agrarian development imposed by the inherent contradictions of agrarian relations based on family labour of peasant householders, characterising the earlier period and receding afterwards,[189] could be overcome. The emergence of lower social strata providing agrarian labourers solved the problem of labour shortage, while the social stratification and the enhancement of state control weakened communal restriction on which infringement by the state power was expressed as bestowal of right to commons on donees.[190]

The resultant agrarian expansion is detectable in the rural landscape described in the royal grants. In the Indian Museum, Khalimpur and Jagajjibanpur plates, donated settlements are described with border landmarks. The most characteristic of them are water bodies and related facilities including river (*gaṅginikā/nadī*), stream/canal (*śrotā/śrotikā/joṭā/joṭikā*), lake/pond/reservoir (*puṣkariṇī/ādhāra*), embankment (*āli/bandha/bandhāka*) and ditch (*khātaka/avakhātaka*).[191] The landscape delineable from them is a riverine tract marked by ponds and criss-crossed by watercourses. The village Kaṅkāvāsaka donated in the Mohipur plate, which was accompanied by 'land of both banks' (*pārāvārabhūmi*), may also have been in such a landscape.[192] What is notable is the presence of artificial water bodies or facilities prefixed with personal names like 'pond of Rahayyāditya' and 'embankment of Viṭaka.'[193] They indicate enterprise of local magnates in agrarian expansion through construction of such facilities. It is clearer in the case of 'embankment made by *rājaputra* Devaṭa.'[194] Those descriptions show the agrarian expansion in low land facilitated by enterprise of local landed magnates including the lowest rank of subordinate rulers like *rājaputra*s. The new situations in the contemporary rural society allowed such an enterprise.

The agrarian expansion seems to have resulted in the extension of settled area leading to the rearrangement of administrative units in Varendra. Under the Pāla rule, a unit called *maṇḍala* was established at the tier between *viṣaya/vīthī* and settlement. Some *maṇḍala*s contain the term *grāma* as an element of their names.[195] They could have been named after the settlements on which *maṇḍala*s centred. Such arrangement indicates the establishment of a *maṇḍdala* necessitated by the expansion of settled area around a central village. The same can be said of Caṇḍagrāmaviṣaya mentioned in the two grants of Gopāla II dated year 4.[196] Caṇḍagrāma was a village mentioned in the Damodarpur plate of year 163 GE.[197] In the last plate, the *aṣṭakulādhikaraṇa* located in village Palāśavṛndaka and some of its residents presided over the case of sale and donation of a land plot in

Caṇḍagrāma, which apparently did not have such an organisation.[198] The emergence of a *viṣaya* named after it indicates growth of the previously insignificant settlement to the centre of a locality.[199] On the other hand, Palāśavṛnda, identical with Palāśavṛndaka, appears in the Biyala grant as a village belonging to Amalakīmaṇḍala of Koṭīvarṣaviṣaya.[200] This can be a case in which settlement expansion changed the geographical context of a village, resulting in its loss of centrality and reconfiguration of an administrative setting around it.

Names of the other *maṇḍala*s also have an implication for agrarian expansion. Most of them are unheard of in the earlier records and named after particular fauna and flora like Vyāghrataṭī (tiger shore) and Amalakī (Āmalakī) (Emblic Myrobalan).[201] Their establishment can be connected with the expansion of settled area through the reclamation of uninhabited tracts with which wild animals and trees are related.[202]

Some aspects of the process of agrarian expansion on the frontier are discernible in a series of copper plate grants pertaining to Phāṇitavīthī, corresponding to the area around present Belwa in Palsa union, Ghoraghat *upazila* of Dinajpur district in Bangladesh. They are the three grants of Mahīpāla I and Vigrahapāla III belonging to the period between the end of the tenth century and the second half of the 11th century. In the Rangpur plate, the earliest of them, one of the donated villages seems to have included a tract related to a hill and tamarind tree, where *kirāta*s took some actions.[203] Together with the resting place of elephants in the same village, the reference to *kirāta*s, a generic term denoting any forest tribes, points to the proximity of donated tract to the forest area and the agrarian expansion through its reclamation.[204] Remarkably, the same village was located in a place called Uddhannakaivartavṛttivahikala.[205] Similarly, one of the settlements donated in the Belwa plate of Mahīpāla I was called Osinnakaivartavṛtti.[206] *Kaivarta*s, who were deemed to be fishers or boatmen in the *Manusmṛti* and the *Subhāṣitaratnakoṣa*,[207] first appeared in a grant of Gopāla II as one of the lowest categories of rural residents, side by side with *meda*s, *andhra*s and *caṇḍāla*s.[208] The reference to their *vṛtti*, a land given for livelihood or some service,[209] connotes their settling in agrarian frontier and the growth of some section to a class of landholders. This phenomenon suggests the agrarian expansion through peasantisation of non-agrarian groups in the lower social strata like *kaivarta*s. The agrarian expansion resulted in the extension of settled area, as the growth of Phāṇitavīthī to Phāṇitavīthīviṣaya by the reign of Vigrahapāla III illustrates.[210]

Agrarian expansion in Varendra was accompanied by another phenomenon, namely, commercialisation of rural economy implied by the spread of rural markets (*haṭṭa*) and monetary transactions. *Haṭṭa* had already appeared in the Damodarpur plate of year 128 GE as an accompaniment of the donated plot.[211] It is mentioned more frequently from the ninth century onwards in relation to village grants. A small market (*haṭṭikā*) accompanies the four donated villages in the Khalimpur plate of Dharmapāla.[212] *Haṭṭa* also constitutes a place name as is the case of Bṛhaddhaṭṭa in the Bhaturiya stone inscription.[213] A clause 'with market' (*sahaṭṭa*) is listed as one of the privileges conferred on donees in the Rangpur and Ramganj grants.[214] Those references attest to the spread of *haṭṭa*s in rural area.

The clause *sahaṭṭa* in the last cases is an indicator of commercialisation of rural space. It seems to denote the entitlement to tax on markets and is feasible as a privilege only with thriving commercial activities around them. The agreement by members of the association of merchants (*vaṇiggrāma*) belonging to the three markets recorded in the Rajbhita stone inscription of the time of Mahīpāla I attests to such activities by merchants located in rural area.[215] The names of Deśihaṭṭa and Gauḍahaṭṭa among those markets show involvement of diverse merchant groups including both locals and outsiders in markets of a particular area.[216] While the case of Ajāhaṭṭa (goat market) in the British Museum stone inscription of the time of Mahendrapāla shows the presence of a *haṭṭa* as a rural market where foodstuffs and other commodities of daily use are exchanged,[217] the references to 'income at the gate' (*dvārikādāna*) in relation to the donated villages in the Jajilpara plate and income from boat landing (*ghaṭṭa*) as one of the donee's privileges in the Jagajjibanpur, Rangpur and Ramganj grants point to the connection of rural markets with wider trade networks.[218]

The spread of monetary transactions in rural society is the most visible in the assessment of production of particular villages and land plots in currency units like *purāṇa*, *paṇa* and *gaṇḍa*, which was discussed above as a measure taken by the Pālas to enhance their control over rural society.[219] The application of such a measure was viable only when rural residents were somehow accustomed to the use of currency units and transactions involving them. In view of this, the practice points to penetration of monetary economy into rural society. What was the medium of exchange sustaining such an economy is the next question.

Purāṇa and *paṇa* are respectively units of silver and copper coins. *Gaṇḍa* or its synonym *gaṇḍaka* denotes a unit consisting of four cowrie-shells. In relation to cowrie-shells, each of them has 1,280, 80 and four times of value, according to the later Bengali arithmetical tables cited by Sircar.[220] The same rate for *purāṇa* and *paṇa* against a cowrie-shell is found in Utpala's commentary on the *Bṛhatsaṃhitā* (79. 12–13) which gives equation of 1 *purāṇa* = 4 *caturtha*s = 16 *paṇa*s = 64 *kākiṇī*s = 1,280 *śvetikā*s.[221] What to note is the absence of corresponding coined currencies circulating in Bengal under the Pālas and the Senas. The account of Arab merchant Sulaymān and the others compiled in 851 AD reports the use of cowrie-shells as a medium of exchange in the Pāla territory, and this is endorsed by a hoard of cowrie-shells found at the site of Paharpur.[222] *Kapardakapurāṇa* in the Sena plates, on the other hand, denotes a notional or theoretical unit of account representing the value of *purāṇa* counted in cowrie-shells.[223] The currency units mentioned in the Pāla inscriptions can be understood in the same way. In the absence of metallic coins, transactions requiring physical money could be mediated by cowrie-shells.[224] The soldiers were remunerated by cowries (*kapardaka*) and bread (*roṭi*) in the army of Madanapāla, according to the *Rāmacarita*.[225] The use of cowries in a market is attested by the British Museum inscription of the time of Mahendrapāla, which mentions one cowrie-shell (*varāṭikā*) each charged at fish shops of Ajāhaṭṭa.[226] They could mediate large-scale transactions in bulk, if we believe the account of Minhāj al-Sirāj Jūzjānī mentioning donation of *lakh*s of cowries by Lakṣmaṇasena.[227] Actual case of bulk payment in cowries is recorded in the Gaya stone inscription of the time of Govindapāla, year 1232 VS (1174–75 AD), in which 50 *kārṣāpaṇa*s of religious endowment was made and paid in cowrie-shells.[228] It amounts to 80,000 pieces, if we take the rate of 20 *paṇa*s for a *kārṣāpaṇa* mentioned by Utpala's commentary on the *Bṛhatsaṃhitā* (79. 12–13).[229]

Earlier, the lack of coins and exclusive use of cowrie-shells were thought to be the evidence of stagnancy of trade and commerce.[230] However, cowrie-shells, which were abundantly caught in Maldives according to the contemporary Arab merchants,[231] themselves attest to the Bengal's connection with thriving maritime trade. The later account of Ibn Baṭṭūṭa says that cowrie-shells were imported from the islands to Bengal in exchange for rice.[232] The continued importation of cowrie-shells suggests increasing demand for them due to vigorous commercial activities and other monetary transactions, which may have been stimulated by the spread of those activities to rural society. It was comparable with the prevalent use of debased silver coins in the early medieval North India to cater for the thriving trade in paucity of silver supply.[233]

The circulation and use of currencies in both gold and silver were known in Varendra in the fifth and sixth centuries, as attested by the land sale grants.[234] Payment in *cūrṇikā*, which possibly means a sum of the value of 100 *kaparda*s or cowries, is also mentioned in the grant of the time of Pradyumnabandhu, datable to the late sixth or the early seventh century.[235] However, the use of these currencies was limited to high value transactions involving land and the price was fixed by local customs, rather than by its exchange value.[236] Compared with that, the monetary transaction in this period shows an advanced state in which rural residents were more accustomed to the use of money so that production of a particular village or land plot could be calculated in currency unit, though actual payment of revenue may not have been commuted to cash payment.

The level to which the commercialisation of rural economy reached is attested by the Rajbhita stone inscription. It records an agreement by the association of all the merchants belonging to the three markets, in relation to some members who grew areca nut and coconut trees at land plots in the four villages belonging to the donated tract of a deity called

Sonnakādevīmādhava. It is agreed that they would annually pay in cash (*hiraṇya*) three *paṇa*s per coconut tree and one *paṇa* per areca nut tree respectively for worship of the deity.[237] This transaction implies that some merchants of the association leased plots in the revenue-free tracts of the deity and cultivated fruit-bearing trees on them. The activity of those merchants amounted to commercial cropping and presupposed the spread of monetary economy to rural society, in which agrarian products could be sold for some form of cash.

The interconnection of the two phenomena observed in Varendra, namely the agrarian expansion with new form of land relation and the commercialisation of rural economy, can be hypothesised in the following manner. The early urban centres like Puṇḍravardhana and Koṭivarṣa continued to be occupied in the early medieval period, as the excavated data of Mahasthangarh and Bangarh show.[238] Though absent in epigraphic sources, they may have continued to supply necessities of rural area in proximity. However, the agrarian expansion and the enlargement of settled area resulting from it rendered those cities insufficient to fulfil the needs of rural settlements beyond their ambit. The newly created demand of rural residents may have been catered for by the spread of *haṭṭa*s and vigorous mercantile activities around them.

The hypothesis made above, however, does not answer one fundamental question: what was the market demand of rural society, which had to be supported by commercial activities around rural markets and circulation of cowrie-shells as a medium of exchange? One answer to this question can be found in the changed structure of rural society. As discussed above, rural society of Varendra saw social stratification and its intensification from the late ninth century onwards, resulting in the rise of landed magnates including the upper section of rural residents, subordinate rulers and religious agents. Their landholdings, actually rights to production from land, and dominance within rural society enabled them to accumulate wealth beyond their own consumption. The accumulated wealth created the demand of landed magnates for commodities from outside with which its surplus would be exchanged. On the other hand, their wealth contained diverse resources including fruits and other agrarian products, if we take the extensive list of privileges conferred on donees of religious endowments as an indicator of resources available for the privileged sectors in rural society. Some of those resources constituted commodities to be exchanged. Thus, we see possible demand of landed magnates for market both as consumers and suppliers of commodities.

The demand of landed magnates necessitated circulation of imported cowrie-shells as a medium facilitating vigorous exchanges. The importation and circulation of vast numbers of cowrie-shells would in turn have stimulated exchanges. Further, demand for commodities was not limited to the upper class, as fish shops at Ajāhaṭṭa in the British Museum stone inscription and sales of coconuts and areca nuts probably at the three markets in the Rajbhita inscription suggest.[239] The spread of monetary economy and transactions to rural society in this period can be understood in this overall context.

Vaṅga, Samataṭa and Śrīhaṭṭa under the Candras, where the stratification of rural society was not so acute, show different pictures. All the donations recorded in the copper plate inscriptions of Śrīcandra pertaining to Vaṅga and Samataṭa were grants of land plots to individual *brāhmaṇa*s. As shown by the privileges transferred to a donee covering vast range of local resources and the instructions to local residents to obey his order and pay tributes to him,[240] what was actually donated in these cases was not a land plot itself but a right to income from the plot and a certain level of administrative power over it. In Vaṅga, the relatively small plots of 8 *droṇa*s 8 *gaṇḍa*s in Bhāṇḍāriyaka belonging to Vaṅgasāgara and 1 *pāṭaka* in Nehakāṣṭhigrāma of Nāvyamaṇḍala were donated by the Madanpur and Rampal grants respectively.[241] Even when a large size of land, 19 *hala*s 6 *droṇa*s in total, was donated in the Dhulla grant, it had to be secured from five settlements in two *viṣaya*s as five land plots of sizes ranging from 2 *hala*s 6 *droṇa*s to 7 *hala*s.[242] The limited availability of land plots reflected in their relatively small size and scattered condition indicates the limit of agrarian development reached in this sub-region, which had earlier seen reclamation of riverine low land.[243] The limit was yet to be overcome in the contemporary social condition.

In Samataṭa, the land plots of 1 *pāṭaka* in Vyāghravoraka of Śrīnagaraviṣaya and 10 *pāṭaka*s in Turadiśā of Gaṇagiriviṣaya were respectively donated in the two grants of Śrīcandra.[244] The large size of the plot in the second case indicates more availability and less congested condition of land in this sub-region, where reclamation of forest tract had been an ongoing process in the seventh century.[245] There still seems to have been room for agrarian development, and the village name Vyāghravoraka in the first case alludes to reclamation of a wild tract having resulted in the settlement formation. This room was extracted in the following period, as the two grants of Laḍahacandra in the early 11th century show. In his first grant, a land plot and two villages, namely a land of 5 3/4 *droṇa*s named Campāvaṇī in Phullahāḍā, Bappasiṅhavorakagrāma consisting of 8 *pāṭaka*s 4 3/4 *droṇa*s 5 *yaṣṭi*s 3 *kāka*s 2 *bindu*s in Ḍollavayikā and Mahādevagrāma of 3 *pāṭaka*s 9 *droṇa*s 1 *kāka*s in Guptīnāṭana, were donated to the deity Laḍahamādhava, while Suravorakagrāma of 8 *pāṭaka*s 1 1/2 *droṇa*s 29 *yaṣṭi*s in Peranāṭanaviṣaya was donated to the same deity in the second grant.[246] The donation of whole villages to a religious institution was a new phenomenon. The location of those villages in Guptīnāṭana and Peranāṭana, which had been mentioned in the grants of the seventh and eighth centuries,[247] suggests the intensified agrarian development in the area which had already seen high level of development with complicated land relation.[248] However, the size of the villages, which was remarkably small even compared with the land plots donated earlier in this sub-region, and their border demarcations, which were clearly defined by embankments (*āli*) and pegs (*kīlaka*) in reference to neighbouring villages, donated tracts and several kinds of land plots,[249] point to the congestion of settlements in these particular areas and the limit of agrarian expansion reached in this period, which did not allow further reclamation of wild tracts. The potential of agrarian expansion was exhausted then under the particular social condition of less stratified rural society, which seems not to have changed yet when Govindacandra donated 2 *pāṭaka*s of land plot in Sāharatalāka of the same Peranāṭanaviṣaya to another deity Naṭṭeśvara.[250]

In Śrīhaṭṭa, the large-scale donation accompanied by settling of vast number of *brāhmaṇa*s, which had been observed in the seventh century,[251] continued in this period. The Paschimbhag plate of Śrīcandra records the creation of a Brahmanical settlement (*brahmapura*) named Śrīcandrapura by merging three *viṣaya*s of Garalā, Pogāra and Candrapura, of which the last seems to have been identical with Candrapuriviṣaya, the venue of the earlier large-scale grant recorded in the Nidhanpur plates,[252] and the donation of this vast tract to the nine *maṭha*s and 6,000 *brāhmaṇa*s.[253]

The donees can be divided into three categories. The first was the *maṭha* of Brahmā to which 120 *pāṭaka*s of land were donated. Among them, 73 *pāṭaka*s were assigned to 81 people related to the *maṭha* including a grammarian of Candra school, ten students for their food and chalk, five guest *brāhmaṇa*s for everyday meal and service groups like garland makers, potters, musicians, servants and so on, while 47 *pāṭaka*s were earmarked for repairs. The second was the two sets of four *maṭha*s of Vaiśvānara (Agni), Yogeśvara, Jaimani (Jaimini) and Mahākāla, each of which belonged to Vaṅgāla or the other country (*deśāntarīya*). 280 *pāṭaka*s were donated to them with minute assignments to each of 170 people related to those *maṭha*s and for their repairs in a similar manner. The third is 6,000 *brāhmaṇa*s settled by *Vaiṣṇava* Vināyaka who was born in Kālīgrāma.[254] The remaining lands were donated in equal division to those *brāhmaṇa*s, of whom 37 were named. Finally, land belonging to a Buddhist establishment (*ratnatrayabhūmi*) and 52 *pāṭaka*s belonging to the quay (*naubandha*) of Indreśvara were excluded from the donated land (**Table 5.4**).

As shown by the presence of the excluded lands and the inclusion of *janapada*s and cultivators in addressees of the grant,[255] the area had settlements within its ambit and was not an uncultivated tract as opined by B. D. Chattopadhyaya,[256] though it also had enough room for agrarian expansion to accommodate enormous number of *brāhmaṇa*s. What transpires from this case is a reorganisation of rural society through the land grant to the *maṭha*s and settling of *brāhmaṇa*s. This is discernible in the detailed description of land assignments to the service groups for the *maṭha*s. A distinction was

Table 5.4 Donees and land plots in Paschimbhag CPI of Śrīcandra (*EDEP*, pp. 67–68, ll. 36–51, p. 68, l. 54.)

Donee/Use	*Heads*	*Pāṭaka (each)*	*Pāṭaka (sum)*
1. Brahmā and its *maṭha*			
Candravyākaraṇopadhyāya (grammarian of Candra school)	1	10	10
10 pupils (*chātra*), for meal (*pāli*) and chalk (*ghuṭṭaka*)	10		10
Daily meal (*bhakta*) for 5 guest (*apūrva*) *brāhmaṇa*s	5		5
Brāhmaṇa who has place made (*adhiṣṭhāyakārayitur*)	1	1	1
Gaṇaka (astrologer)	1	1	1
Kāyastha	1	2 1/2	2 1/2
*Mālākāra*s (garland makers)	4	1/2	2
*Tailika*s (oil pressers)	2	1/2	1
*Kumbhakāra*s (potters)	2	1/2	1
*Kāhalika*s (*kahala* drum player)	5	1/2	2 1/2
*Śaṅkhavādaka*s (conch blowers)	2	1/2	1
*Ḍhakkāvādaka*s (*ḍhakkā* drum players)	2	1/2	1
*Drāgaḍika*s (*drāga* drum players)	8	1/2	4
*Karmakara*s, *carmmakāra*s (labourers, leather workers)	22	1/2	11
Naṭa (dancer)	1	2	2
*Sūtradhāra*s (carpenters)	2	2	4
*Sthapati*s (architects)	2	2	4
*Karmakāra*s (black smiths)	2	2	4
*Ceṭṭikā*s (female servants)	8	3/4	6
For repairs (*navakarmanimitta*)			47
Subtotal	81		120
2. Vaiśvānara, Yogeśvara, Jaimani and Mahākāla of 4 *maṭha*s belonging to the other countries (*deśāntarīya*), 4 Vaṅgālamaṭhas			
Scholars of Ṛg, Yajus, Sāma, Atharva attached to both *maṭha* groups	8	10	80
5 pupils of each *maṭha*	40	5 (each *maṭha*)	40
*Mālākāra*s (garland makers)	8	1/2	4
*Nāpita*s (barbers)	8	1/2	4
*Tailika*s (oil pressers)	8	1/2	4
*Rajaka*s (washermen)	8	1/2	4
*Kammakara*s, *carmakāra*s (labourers, leather workers, 8 each)	64	1/2	32
*Ceṭṭikā*s (female servants, 2 each)	16	3/4	12
Repairs of each *maṭha*		10	80
*Mahattarabrāhmaṇa*s at each 4 *maṭha*s	2	2	4
*Vārika*s (manager)	2	1 1/2	3
*Kāyastha*s	2	2 1/2	5
*Gaṇaka*s (astrologers)	2	1	2
*Vyaidya*s (*vaidya*s, physicians)	2	3	6
Subtotal	170		280

3. 6,000 *brāhmaṇas* of various *gotras*, *pravaras*, *caraṇas* and *śākhās*: remaining land in equal division
37 Named People
(1) Vāvasadatta, (2) Harṣa, (3) Śekhara, (4) Viśvarūpa, (5) Bhānudatta, (6) Īśāna, (7) Dhanyanāga, (8) Nandayaśas, (9) Caṅga, (10) Govardhana, (11) Siṅghadatta, (12) Kamalanandin, (13) Savitāra, (14) Māṇikya, (15) Kāmuka, (16) Bhīmapāla, (17) Antaga, (18) Vatsadhara, (19) Nandaghoṣa, (20) Śrīdhara, (21) Rāma, (22) Śivavandhu, (23) Maṅgala, (24) Vedo, (25) Ghavala, (26) Bihnudatta, (27) Śāntidāman, (28) Gargaśarman, (29) Mahīndrasoma, (30) Ravikara, (31) Bhānu, (32) Nārāyaṇa, (33) Gargagupta, (34) Śasidatta, (35) Hari, (36) Jayadatta (37) Garga
4. Excluded land

Name	*Pāṭaka*
Ratnatrayabhūmi	
Indreśvaranauvandhaprativaddha	52

* 1 *pāṭaka* = 10 *droṇas* (*EDEP*, p. 67, ll. 36–37, p. 68, l. 54)

made between two categories of artisanal and service groups.[257] Garland makers, oil pressers, potters, drummers, conch-shell blowers, labourers and leather workers, barbers and washermen received only 1/2 *pāṭaka* per person, while a dancer, carpenters, architects and blacksmiths received 2 *pāṭakas* per person and even female servants received the 3/4. *Kāyasthas* and *vaidyas* received 2 1/2 and 3 respectively (**Table 5.4**). The differentiated ordering of the various communities in this case could have been derived from the pattern of differentiation already in existence in rural society.[258] However, the same size of plots equally assigned to various kinds of service groups and the larger size of plots given to female servants indicate that the size of assigned land plots rather depended on the importance of their service for the *maṭhas*. Those service groups must have come from settlements within the donated tract and been embedded in the social order of these villages, which was stratified to some extent. The attachment of these groups to the *maṭhas* and the assignment of land plots to them according to their relation with the latter can be interpreted as the re-definition of social relations centred on the *maṭhas*. It inevitably interfered with the existing social order of the locality. Apart from that, settling of a large number of *brāhmaṇas* must have affected the existing rural society which had to bear the burden of offering dues and surrendering resources to which the donees were entitled.[259] Thus the case of the Paschimbhag grant can be interpreted as a reorganisation of rural society initiated by the king. It could be enacted due to the peripheral character of the sub-region carried over from the previous period.

The information on agrarian condition in Harikela obtainable from the only one source, namely the metal vase inscription of Attākaradeva, is rather meagre, due to the severe damage on the relevant part of the vase. Still, the presence of land plots measured by a unit called *pāda*, held by some individuals and including a garden of areca nut trees can be confirmed.[260] It attests to the agrarian development in some part of the sub-region continuing from the previous period glimpsed from the other metal vase inscription of the early eighth century.[261] Its extent and intensity, however, cannot be guessed from the inscription alone.

The three sub-regions of eastern Bengal commonly experienced the circulation of high-quality silver coins with some local variations between the seventh and the tenth centuries. These Harikela coins originated from present Chittagong area and then spread to Samataṭa.[262] Following the motif and weight standard of the coins of the Candras of Arakan,[263] they may have mainly catered for the high-value interregional trade. The presence of the coins with fractional weights from one sixteenth to a half of the standard weight, on the other hand, could indicate wider use to which they were put.[264] Though the one sixteenth of standard silver coin is still large a denomination compared with cowrie-shells,[265] the use of *paṇa* with equal value for transactions in rural society is attested by the Rajbhita inscription pertaining to Varendra.[266] Considering this fact with Dhṛtipurahaṭṭikā included in Mahādevagrāma of the first grant of Laḍahacandra, the merchants residing in a settlement of Samataṭa mentioned in the two image inscriptions and a garden of areca nut trees donated in the Metal vase inscription of Attākaradeva,[267] it can be conjectured that rural society of eastern Bengal also experienced some level of commercialisation and monetisation of economy, if not as intensive as in contemporary Varendra discussed above. The assignment of land plots to professional groups for their service in the Paschimbhag grant, on the other hand, indicates less monetised condition of the peripheral sub-region of Śrīhaṭṭa (**Table 5.4**).

The agrarian development in Daṇḍabhukti of Rāḍha seems to have reached some level, as far as we can delineate from the Kāmboja grants. The two villages donated in them are said to have been demarcated by confirmed borders on all sides, while Bṛhacchattivannāgrāma of the Irda plate was neighboured by the three villages.[268] The donations accompanied reservoir (*jalādhāra*) and night-soil deposit (*avaskarasthāna*), suggesting efforts at intensive cultivation.[269] On the other hand, the inclusion of income from market (*haṭṭa*), boat landing (*ghaṭṭa*) and ferry (*tara*) as privileges conferred on the donee in the Irda plate somehow points to the spread of commercial activities in the rural space,[270] though we have no evidence for the level of their monetisation.

In the context of changed power relations, new form of agrarian development and commercialisation of economy, rural society of Bengal witnessed trials of social reorganisation of which two directions explored by different social groups are detectable in the contemporary sources.

Trials of social reorganisation

As is clear from the discussions made above, rural society of the period was confronting two problems, namely, the social stratification within itself and the enhanced control over it by political powers and religious agents patronised by them. Monetisation of rural economy, which gave the kings another means to enhance their local control through estimation of production, aggravated the problems.[271] Members of rural society tried to counter those challenges through the two forms of social reorganisation. The first of them was an attempt to keep cohesion of rural society, especially among peasant householders. It is detectable in the *Kṛṣiparāśara*, a Sanskrit treatise on agriculture composed in the mid-11th century, most probably in Bengal.[272]

Rural society depicted in the text is an agrarian society that almost exclusively consists of cultivators without clear inner differences. Almost all the instructions, except the ones for cowherds (*gopāla*) during the cattle festival (*goparva/gopūjā*), are given to cultivators (*kṛṣaka/karṣaka/kṛṣāna*).[273] They are supposed to have first-hand engagement in agricultural operations, probably with family labour in a moderate scale.[274] Cooperative works are prescribed for assembling a plough and making a ritual post (*medhi*), [275] and alluded to for sowing.[276] Cultivators are recognised as a collective entity, namely, people bound by common interests.[277] There is no reference to agricultural labourers or their employment by the other cultivators in this text, while the *Kāśyapīyakṛṣisūkti*, a near-contemporary agricultural treatise in Sanskrit probably belonging to the South Indian tradition,[278] refers to dependants (*anujīvika*), attendants (*anucara*) and servants (*bhṛtya)* as agricultural labourers differentiated from cultivators (*kṛṣīvala*) in the context of harvest and threshing.[279] The image of rural society in the *Kṛṣiparāśara* gives a strong impression of homogeneity.

Arbitrariness of this image of homogeneous agrarian society is clear when we compare it with rural society described in the other contemporary sources like the Pāla grants, which are addressed to rural residents including both dominant landholders and people of the lowest rank, and the anthologies of Sanskrit poems which mention *pāmaras*.[280] Furthermore, the two occasions described in the *Kṛṣiparāśara*, cattle festival (*goparva*) and *Puṣyayātrā* betray inconsistency in the image of a homogeneous agrarian society.

Cattle festival is prescribed for the health of cattle on the first day of the month Kārttika.[281] In this festival, cowherds play a leading role in the procession of a leader bull through the village, with their bodies and cattle well decorated and accompanied by music. Then a cultivator puts oil mixed with turmeric on the body of cattle and gathers with other cultivators.[282] The former part of the prescription is an injunction for cowherds, unlike the other parts of the text where cultivators are agents even in the matters concerning cattle. The injunction for a cultivator just after it, especially a reference to the gathering of cultivators, suggests that this is an occasion in which cowherds and cultivators interact with each other and reconfirm their relation annually. The leading role of cowherds can be interpreted as a temporary inversion of hierarchy or power relations. On the other hand, these verses remind us of the total absence of injunctions on pasturage in which cowherds could have appeared. This absence is understandable in view of the character of the text as a manual for cultivators. The relation with cowherds was, however, so important that the composer of the text still could not avoid prescribing an occasion for its reconfirmation. In any case, these verses show the presence of a group which cannot be accommodated in the image of a homogeneous agrarian society.

Puṣyayātrā is another festival prescribed for the month of Pauṣa before harvesting and threshing. It should be 'mutually' performed by people near an agricultural field.[283] The first procedure prescribed in the text is a feast in which all the people feed each other special cuisine prepared from various kinds of materials including fish and meat.[284] As shown by the reference to 'all the people' (*janāḥ sarve*) and the use of verb 'feed' (*bhojayuḥ*), it is a communal feast attended by all the local population. The use of 'all the people' instead of cultivators, in contrast to the other parts of the text, indicates incorporation of various social groups apart from cultivators in this category. It is plausible that this festival was a special occasion in which restrictions on social interaction were temporarily eschewed, or at least the composer constructed it as such.

The next procedure is besmearing of each other with sandal paste, *catuḥsama* (unguent of sandal, agallochum, saffron and musk) and oil boiled with good perfume, and making each other bite agreeable betel leaf scented with camphor and filled with incense. The great festival of dance and music follows them.[285] It is significant that these acts are prescribed to be done to 'each other' or 'mutually' (*anyonyaṃ*). The context suggests that all the people, including a variety of social groups, intermingle and perform such merrymaking all together. In view of the fact that it is held before harvest, which needs the collaboration of rural population, *Puṣyayātrā* could be an occasion in which the cohesion of rural society is reconfirmed through gathering and temporary discarding of differences among all the social groups.

The intention of reconfirming cohesion or oneness is connoted by the incantation, whose recital is prescribed afterwards:

> In the field with yet harvested paddy, she who is revered by us all, the giver of welfare (Śubhapradā), must protect us as a result of *Puṣyayātrā*. All of them, who are opposing us by action, mind and word, must be stilled as a result of *Puṣyayātrā*. Increase of paddy, increase of fame, welfare of wife and son, increase of the honour

> of king, growth of cattle, increase of *mantra* and *śāsana* (land?), increase of wealth, day and night, always they should be to us as long as the year has not completed.[286]

The use of 'us' in this incantation shows consciousness as a group to be shared by all the participants. In *Puṣyayātrā* also, the allusion to the local population possibly covering a wider social range contradicts the image of a homogeneous agrarian society. Again, the importance of such an occasion did not allow the composer of the text to ignore it. Due importance given to *Puṣyayātrā* by him is attested by the statement that Parāśara made this festival for the welfare of whole the world or people (*sarvaloka*) in ancient time.[287] His emphasis on maintenance of cohesion, on the other hand, leads us to an answer to the question why the image of homogeneous agrarian society was constructed.

The concluding remarks on *Puṣyayātrā* include the following verse: 'The people proud of wealth do not perform *Puṣyayātrā*. For them, there is no cessation of obstacles. Then how there can be any pleasure (for them) in the year?'[288] It suggests that the composer recognised social differentiation in the contemporary rural society and interpreted it as a result of accumulation of wealth by some members. It also shows his disagreement with such a tendency. The image of homogeneous agrarian society could be interpreted as a social norm constructed by him due to his strong inclination towards social cohesion and due to his intention to gloss over diversity and divisiveness of the society. Both composer and intended audience of the text may have belonged to dominant groups in rural society, as inferable from their character as rural literates constituting the notable group.[289] In this period, they were confronted with the social stratification within and the growing control of the external powers including both temporal and religious authorities. With their authority on decline, local notables needed to re-establish the solidarity of rural society, especially wide range of peasant groups who constituted its main part, to counter the outside authorities. For this purpose, it was necessary for them to check the intensification of social stratification and to emphasise their cohesion as a single category of cultivators. The collaboration of the peasant group as a whole was also necessary to sustain their authority over the other rural population. The representation of rural society as a homogeneous agrarian society may have been worked out to fulfil these requirements. The instruction on the cattle festival shows another way to keep their authority through the regulation of the relation with the other social groups. The injunctions on *Puṣyayātrā*, on the other hand, show the strong intension to uphold cohesion of rural society as a whole, including the wider range of social groups, with cognition of the presence of the latter.

An attempt at social reorganisation towards cohesion of rural society discernible in the *Kṛṣiparāśara*, however, seems not to have borne fruit, as the social stratification continued to be expressed in the address of copper plates in this period. Another attempt in this direction would be made under Brahmanical hegemony in the following period, to be discussed in the next chapter.

The other form of social reorganisation witnessed in this period was the construction of identities and networks of social groups based on common occupations and their consolidation towards *jātis*. This tendency was the most evident among literate groups, especially *brāhmaṇa*s, whose activities were well recorded in inscriptions. As discussed above and elsewhere, highly qualified *brāhmaṇa*s with clearer sense of their identity, both in terms of academic qualification and kinship relations, were constructing their networks by the geographical spread through migration and by the establishment of Brahmanical centres which would function as nodes.[290]

The similar tendency is found among the other literate groups like *kāyastha*s in the inscriptions left by them, if not as clear as that of *brāhmaṇa*s. Their consolidation as groups is inferable from marriage alliances among them. The Kosham Shahar image inscription of the time of Vigrahapāla II records the installation of an image of Gaurī, in the form of mother and child, by Catuḥsamā, the wife of *mudrādhikārin* Līlānandin. It describes Vāyilanandin, the father of Līlānandin, as *sāndhivigrahika* of king Rājyapāla, while Catuḥsamā as the daughter of *kāyastha* Subhaṅgaladatta and Sumānuṣī.[291] The family of Līlānandin was that of royal officials in charge of documentary administration, as *mudrādhikārin* could be an official in charge of the royal seal. They may have belonged to a non-*brāhmaṇa* literate group. Thus, the marriage of Līlānandin and Catuḥsamā was a marriage alliance between the two families belonging to a literate group. It is not clear how common such marriage alliances were among those literate groups. What is clear is the establishment of the identity of the groups as *karaṇa* by the end of the 11th century as discernible in the *Rāmacarita*. In his own eulogy, Sandhyākaranandin describes his father Prajāpati as the foremost among *karaṇa*s, who got the position of *sāndhivigrahika*.[292] *Karaṇa* had become a term denoting an occupational group that is differentiated from official designations like *sāndhivigrahika*.[293] It also ceased to be an abbreviation for *adhikaraṇa*.[294]

The geographical spread of non-*brāhmaṇa* literate groups through migration is connoted in the Bhaturiya inscription, in which Aṭṭamūla, the original place of the Dāsas, a lineage of subordinate rulers originating from non-*brāhmaṇa* literate group, is said to have derived from Bṛhaddhaṭṭa, another settlement.[295] This description is similar to the depiction of the expansion of Brahmanical settlements as genealogies of villages in the Silimpur inscription and the Bangaon plate.[296] Bṛhaddhaṭṭa could also be the birthplace of Sandhyākaranandin, according to the emendation of Bṛhadvaṭu in a verse of the *Rāmacarita* by Gudrun Melzer in consideration of metre and similarity of *akṣaras*.[297] It seems to have been a centre of *kāyastha*s and functioned as a node of their network facilitated by migrations, like the contemporary Brahmanical centres.

The cases of some families engaging in engraving of copper plate grants show the geographical spread and the other aspects of such literate groups. Dakkadāsa, son of Jayadāsa and the engraver of the Mohipur plate of Gopāla II, is said to be 'born to a good person of Samataṭa origin' (*satsāmataṭajanman*).[298] In view of the chronological proximity, he seems to be identical with his namesake who engraved the inscription of Pāhila and the Mirzapur plate of Śūrapāla.[299] He gained the position of *sāmanta* according to the description in the latter inscription.[300] Maṅghadāsa and his son Vimaladāsa, respectively the engravers of the Bhagalpur plate of Nārāyaṇapāla and the Jajilpara plate of Gopāla III,[301] may have belonged to the same family, as almost the same expression of *satsamataṭajanma* and the same name ending of Dāsa are used for them. These cases show the long term activity of a migrant family of scribes as engravers of the Pāla royal grants, which covers a wide geographical stretch from Mudgagiri, the issuing place of the Mirzapur grant, to south-eastern corner of Varendra, where the inscription of Pāhila was discovered.[302] It is remarkable that they retained their origin from Samataṭa as an indicator of their identity, even after shifting to Varendra. It indicates their presence as a scribal group differentiated from the others by their origin from the other sub-region. A similar case is observable in the Paschimbhag grant of Śrīcandra, of which the messenger was *mahāmudrādhikṛta* Śubhāṅga from Sāra (core) Varendrī.[303] The Bangarh inscription of the time of Nayapāla and the Silimpur inscription, both of which belong to the 11th century Varendra, were respectively engraved by Lakṣmīdhara and Someśvara from Magadha.[304] These cases show the mobility of the literate group in this period.

The other group of engravers show another aspect of their geographical spread, namely, the establishment of their centre. The artisans (*śilpin*) from Poṣalīgrāma are known to be the engravers of the six grants of Mahīpāla I and Vigrahapāla III. They are Puṣyāditya, the son of Candrāditya, Bharadeva, the son of Śūdradeva, Mahīdhara, the son of Vikramāditya and Dāmāditya, the son of Candrāditya in the Belwa, Rangpur, Bangarh and Biyala plates of Mahīpāla I,[305] and Śaśideva, the son of Mahīdharadeva and Śaśideva, the son of Mānhrīdeva in the Amgachi and Bangaon grants of Vigrahapāla III.[306] Among them, Puṣyāditya and Dāmāditya seem to be the brothers with the same father, Candrāditya. As suggested by Sircar, Mānhrīdeva could be a misspelling of Mahīdeva and the same as Mahīdharadeva,[307] so that we have a lineage of three generations, namely, Vikramāditya, Mahīdhara/Mahīdharadeva and Śaśideva. With Śūdradeva and Bhavadeva of the Rangpur grant, there were the three families from the same village, whose members worked as engravers under the two Pāla kings. The shared name endings of Āditya and Deva may indicate their kinship relation. What is important, however, is the existence of a village which provided families of artisans especially skilled in engraving royal grants. Poṣalīgrāma could be identical with Poṣalī *gāñī* of the Rāḍhīya *brāhmaṇas*, which has been identified with modern Poshela about 5 miles to the southeast of Mangalkot in Barddhaman district.[308] It is not clear whether the village had already established its position as a Brahmanical centre in this period. But the cases cited above show that it was a centre of artisans with special skill and literacy, whose activity covered Varendra and even Mithilā, with this centre as a hub. Tinniḍāgrāma, from which the father of *śilpin* Pṛthvīdeva who engraved the Belwa plate of Vigrahapāla III originated, may have been another centre of the same kind.[309]

With the commercialisation of rural economy,[310] merchants extended their residence and activities to rural space. While some merchant families converted themselves to lineages of subordinate rulers like that of *sārthavāha* Balanāga recorded in the Indian Museum grant of Dharmapāla,[311] the others continued their mercantile activities as hereditary occupations in rural society. This is glimpsed from some inscriptions on images and a stone pillar from eastern Bihar and Bengal, datable to the period between the ninth and 12th centuries.[312] Their hereditary character is clear from the expression 'merchant family' (*vaṇikakula*) in the Nalanda pillar inscription of the time of Rājyapāla and the title *vaṇika* prefixed to the names of both father and son in the Narayanpur image inscription of the time of Mahīpāla I.[313] Their location in rural space is discernible in the names of their residence like Etrahāgrāma in the Chandimau image inscription of the time of Rāmapāla and Vilakīndaka/Vilikandhaka of Samataṭa in the Baghaura and Narayanpur image inscriptions of the time of Mahīpāla I,[314] though Kṛmilā, the residence of the donor mentioned in the Rajauna image inscription, was rather an urban settlement called *adhiṣṭhāna*.[315] The first case also attests to the shift of merchant family from city to rural settlement, as the donor *vaṇika sādhu* Saharaṇa is said to have originated from Rājagṛha and resided in Etrahāgrāma.[316]

The presence of the merchant group in rural society, inferable from the pattern of donations limited to installation of images or erection of a pillar, was rather weak, compared with their predecessors in the fifth and sixth century North Bengal who had been urban elites involved in land transactions both as donors and decision makers.[317] A new form of their social organisation is, however, detectable in the Rajbhita stone inscription of the time of Mahīpāla I, which records an agreement by the *vaṇiggrāma* consisting of all the merchants belonging to the three markets (*haṭṭa*). The reference to the *haṭṭa*s to which merchants belonged suggests that the affiliation with particular *haṭṭa*s was an important element of their identity. The names of those *haṭṭa*s, Deśi, Jaya and Gauḍa, indicate the difference in their character and constituents.[318] The merchants organized themselves as a collective in spite of their affiliations with different markets and probable differences in specialisation.

The position of the *vaṇiggrāma* representing the collective interest of merchants is implied in the inscribed agreement made in its name, which prescribes payment of stipulated amount of cash to Sonnakādevīmādhava by its members leasing land plots of the deity.[319] Its intervention in the relationship between the members and the deity, an institutional landholder, suggests that the association negotiated with the latter on behalf of the former. This form of collective representation may have strengthened the bargaining power of merchants in relation to the temple authority. On the other hand, it entailed the imposition of inner regulation. The members had to accept the terms set by the association while leasing, as individuals, land plots from the deity. For collective interest to be represented and pursued, cohesion of the association had to be maintained through the regulation of its members.[320] Thus the case recorded in the Rajbhita inscription shows the organisation of merchants into an association which kept its cohesion by inner regulation and dealt with the external authority as a collective.

Artisanal groups are also mentioned as donors in the image and votive inscriptions from eastern Bihar in this period. The occupations of donors or their fathers recorded in them include oil presser (*tailika*), potter (*kumbhakāra*), leather worker (*carmakāra*), gold smith (*suvarṇakāra*) and vintner (*śauṇḍika*).[321] These references attest to the presence of artisan groups in rural society with distinctive identities based on their occupations. The presence of such groups in Śrīhaṭṭa is clear in the Paschimbhag plate of Śrīcandra, in which various artisans are included in the service groups for the *maṭha*s (**Table 5.4**).

The cases discussed above show an inclination of various groups in rural society towards construction of clearer identity based on occupation. *Brāhmaṇa*s and the other literate groups were constructing their networks through geographical expansion and marriage alliances, with the establishment of centres which would function as nodes. On the other hand, merchants organised themselves into an association with inner regulation. In different ways, those occupational groups were consolidating themselves as groups, which would develop into *jāti*s in the later period.

The two forms of social reorganisation were attempted by rural society confronting its own contradiction of inner stratification and the encroachment by external authorities which were also experiencing the growing contradictions among themselves. These contradictions culminated in the *Kaivarta* rebellion.

Culmination of contradictions: *Kaivarta* rebellion[322]

The *Kaivarta* rebellion, which occurred in the last quarter of the 11th century and gave a main theme to Sandhyākaranandin's *Rāmacarita*, was a critical event in the early history of Bengal. It temporarily ousted the Pālas from their ancestral territory of Varendra and decisively weakened their control over subordinate rulers.

According to the descriptions in the *Rāmacarita* and its near contemporary commentary, the rebellion proceeded in the five phases. The first was the battle between Mahīpāla II, the reigning king and the elder brother of Rāmapāla, and the rebel army led by Divya the *kaivarta* chief, which resulted in the death of the king and ouster of the Pālas from Varendra. The second was the mustering of the aid of *sāmanta*s by Rāmapāla for the reconquest of Varendra. The third was the advance raid by Śivarāja, a subordinate and relative of the king, which resulted in the devastation and occupation of a part of Varendra and prepared for the following attack by the main army led by the king. The fourth was the invasion of Varendra by Rāmapāla and his confrontation with Bhīma, the nephew of Divya, who was captured at first but escaped later. The fifth and last phase was the defeat of Bhīma's army resulting in his execution.

The first phase of the rebellion can surely be taken as a revolt of *sāmanta*s against the king, as discernible in the description of the death of Mahīpāla II in the commentary. He is said to have died in the battle in which his disarrayed army was surrounded by a circle (*cakra*) of uncountable *sāmanta*s. There is no reference to how the revolt started but the cause of his failure in war is said to be reckless deployment of army disregarding the advice of his councillors.[323] In view of the circumstance of his death in which his army was totally outnumbered by the enemy troops, it was at least sure that the majority of *sāmanta*s in Varendra took stand against the king. Divya or Divvoka, the *kaivarta* chief, seems to have been one of these *sāmanta*s, as he is described as a subordinate (*bhṛtya*) of the king.[324] A reference to him as the enemy *kaivarta* king ruling the earth, namely Varendra, after killing Mahīpāla II indicates his leading position among the rebel *sāmanta*s.[325] Varendra was occupied by him and then ruled by his nephew Bhīma.[326]

Śūrapāla II and Rāmapāla, the younger brothers who had been imprisoned by Mahīpāla II in suspicion, escaped Varendra after his death. Rāmapāla ascended the throne after the short reign of Śūrapāla II and prepared for the reconquest of Varendra. The rebellion proceeded to the second phase with his preparation. He travelled around the territories of *sāmanta*s for asking their military aid in recovering the lost territory.[327] As described in the next canto, they were mostly *sāmanta*s of eastern Bihar and western Bengal.[328] It should be noted that they are described as *vyāla* and *āṭavika*. In the commentary, *vyāla*, meaning 'wicked,' is glossed as *āgrahārika*, 'the one who appropriates *agrahāra*' and *vaiṣayika* which may also denote an appropriator of *viṣaya* in analogy. *Āṭavika* on the other hand is equated with *aṭavīyasāmanta* and connotes a forest chief.[329] These words suggest that those *sāmanta*s consisted of some who had exploited weakened governmental control in appropriating land of donated tracts or lower administrative units, and the others who were forest chiefs under weaker control from the beginning. Rāmapāla had to appease them with gift of land and enormous movable wealth for gaining their support.[330] Thus the control of the Pālas over their *sāmanta*s was weak even in their remaining territory.

Still reliable among those *sāmanta*s was the Rāṣṭrakūṭas of Aṅga, the maternal relative of the king. Mahaṇa or Mathana, the maternal uncle of Rāmapāla, joined him with his two sons, *mahāmāṇḍalika* Kāhnaradeva and Suvarṇadeva, and his nephew *mahāpratīhāra* Śivarājadeva.[331] The advance raid by Śivarāja made up the third phase of the rebellion. Having crossed the Ganga on elephant-back with army, he devastated and then occupied a part of Varendra, and broke the defence arrangement of Bhīma.[332] What should be noted in this section is the description of Varendra under Bhīma as miserable because of the confusion of *viṣaya* and *grāma*.[333] The commentary explains it as follows: 'for the protection of the land of *deva*s and *brāhmaṇa*s, questions as "what is this *viṣaya*, what is this *grāma*, whose is this *bhukti*" followed afterwards.'[334] What is described in the concerned verse was thus the confusion of ownership, which had to be ascertained after the occupation. The reference to the protection of land of *deva*s and *brāhmaṇa*s alludes to the occurrence of encroachment upon the land donated to them. The usurpation of donated tracts reminds us of the commentary to *vyāla sāmanta*s as appropriators of *agrahāra*s and *viṣaya*s.[335] In analogy, it can be assumed that the perpetrators of encroachment were rebel *sāmanta*s who overturned the Pāla rule.

The advance raid by Śivarāja paved the way to the fourth phase, namely, the invasion of Varendra by Rāmapāla leading his army with four divisions (horse, elephant, foot and boat) joined by *sāmanta*s and his sons.[336] A verse emphasising his reliance on himself and his Rāṣṭrakūṭa kinsmen alludes to his tenuous position against his own *sāmanta*s, who were just won over by gift of land and treasure.[337] He then crossed the Ganga by a fleet of boats and encountered with Bhīma's army.[338] The clash of both armies is described as a fierce battle fought by infantry, cavalry and elephant troops with many kinds of weapons.[339] It is depicted as a confrontation between the equals, both equipped and trained properly. Bhīma, the enemy king, is also eulogised for his valour and virtues.[340] Though defeated, he was treated with honour in his captivity by Vittapāla, the son of Rāmapāla.[341] In view of these descriptions, the rebellion until this phase can be interpreted as a revolt of *sāmanta*s with proper military capability, which had to be confronted with adequate military strength. It should be noted that such strength was available for the king only by deploying the other *sāmanta*s, though they were not as dependable as his own kinsmen.

The fifth and the last phase, however, showed a quite different character. Hari, Bhīma's friend, regrouped his army and the second round of the confrontation between Bhīma, who seems to have escaped from the captivity, and Rāmapāla ensued.[342] This time, however, Bhīma's army was enlarged by the deployment of ill-equipped 'naked army' (*kīśabala*), which was ill-trained and disarrayed in confusion.[343] Unlike the previous one, the battle is described as one-sided in which only the death of Bhīma's soldiers is depicted and Vittapāla is said to have exhausted golden pitchers for war-gifts (*vigrahadāna*) to reward *sāmanta*s.[344] At the end, Bhīma was brutally executed, after being forced to witness the beheading of his kin.[345]

The poor condition of Bhīma's army in this phase alludes to the mobilisation of the lower social strata and the depiction of army riding on buffaloes, casting bundle of large arrows,[346] enhances this allusion, even though with some exaggeration. It is remarkable that the army is said to have been 'agreeable to the people agitated by tax' (*karakṣobhirucita*).[347] This expression connotes the support for the rebellion by some groups afflicted by taxation. The party which imposed the tax seems to have been the Pāla regime, not the rebels as Bhīma is rather praised for bringing out prosperity to the whole world and enlivening it by his generosity.[348] These elements indicate the wider range of participation in the rebellion, especially in its last phase.

The phases of the rebellion analysed above show its overall character as a revolt of *sāmanta*s of Varendra, in which main line of contention was drawn between them and the Pāla kings. As far as its suppression was possible only by deploying another group of *sāmanta*s, it was also a conflict among *sāmanta*s who took sides of either the king or the rebel chief. Another line of contention revealed in the rebellion was the one between *sāmanta*s and religious institutions over donated land tracts. As the control over donated tracts by religious institutions depended on the royal authority, of which the weakening resulted in the encroachment upon the tracts by *sāmanta*s, the two lines of contention were actually interconnected. The core of this interconnection was the grant to religious institutions, which was royal monopoly under the Pālas. As discussed above, the changing forms of royal grants had implications for the power relation between the Pāla kings and their *sāmanta*s.[349]

On the other hand, the support for rebels and the participation of wider range of social groups witnessed in the last phase of the rebellion point to its character as popular uprising. The reason of support given as the agitation by tax, presumably imposed by the Pāla regime, suggests the popular resentment which was latent whole through the rebellion but revealed only in its last phase. The resentment necessitated Rāmapāla to appease people of Varendra by mild taxation (*mṛdukara*) and bring back prosperity by restarting regular cultivation.[350] The depth of popular dissent is revealed by the confusion of villages still observed in the reign of Madanapāla.[351] Thus the rebellion had an element of popular protest, which was triggered by the revolt of *sāmanta*s. The heavy taxation, which caused the popular resentment, was connected with the intensification of local control attempted by the Pālas.[352] It was also connected with their policy of settling highly qualified *brāhmaṇa*s, whose presence in rural society became dominant and even oppressive with enormous privileges given to them.[353]

The analyses just made above show that the multiple social changes and contradictions accruing from them constituted the context, which conditioned the occurrence and sustenance of the rebellion. The tension between the Pāla kings and their subordinate rulers over local control, which manifested itself as the attempts of the latter to encroach upon the royal authority and as the countermeasures taken by the former, did not subside in spite of some level of success attained by the former. Connected with this was growing presence of qualified *brāhmaṇa*s with close connection with the kingship. Their dominant presence guaranteed by the royal patronage and its geographical expansion enhanced the state control and dented the local rule of *sāmanta*s. The encroachment upon donated tract following the overturning or weakening of the Pāla rule can be understood as the reaction of *sāmanta*s against the religious agents counterpoised to them. The growing presence of *brāhmaṇa*s with a dominant position in rural areas could also mean heavier burden on its residents, adding to increased fiscal charges enabled by the tighter grip through better estimation of production. It may explain the popular dissent which constituted an important element of the rebellion.

The other element of the social context was the growth of *kaivarta*s. As discussed above, some section of *kaivarta*s, who had been fisherfolks or boatmen deemed to belong to the lowest ranks of rural society, were settled on the periphery of Varendra and grew to a class of landholders, in the context of a new phase of agrarian expansion.[354] The emergence of *kaivarta* chiefs like Divya and Bhīma should be understood as an extension of this process. The continued presence of *kaivarta*s as landholders and their consolidation as a social group, even after the rebellion, are confirmed by the Rajibpur grant of Madanapāla, year 22, which mentions enclosed land (*vṛti*) of *kaivarta*s included in a royal estate (*rājabhoga*). They were presumably assigned such land in lieu of the service to the king, like *carmakāra*s mentioned together.[355]

For the Pālas, the rebellion was an 'unfortunate disturbance of *dharma*' to be repelled by Rāmapāla.[356] The *dharma* disturbed by the incident was the order which was considered proper and upheld by the kingship. With the weakened royal power, its recovery was an arduous task and necessitated measures of reconciliation and reorganisation, apart from appeasement of people. While executing Bhīma and his kin, Rāmapāla put chief Hari, a friend of Bhīma who regrouped his army, on the 'position invested with great power.'[357] He also made reorganisation of *viṣaya*s, which was said to have been necessitated by the rule of Divya.[358] The efforts brought out temporary recovery of the Pāla authority, which enabled Rāmapāla to deal with neighbouring political powers by conciliation and military means. However, their heavy dependence on *sāmanta*s, revealed through the rebellion, was evident even in the military actions taken in the aftermath.[359] It finally led to the rise of the Senas as sovereign power and the final expulsion of the Pālas from Bengal by their hands.

Some tendencies and attempts witnessed in this period would see their development in the following period, as will be discussed in the next chapter.

Notes

1 For the latest political history of the Pālas incorporating new evidences, see Rajat Sanyal, 'The Pala-Sena and Others', in Dilip K. Chakrabarti and Makkhan Lal (eds), *History of Ancient India, vol. 5: Political History and Administration (c AD. 750–1300)*, New Delhi: Vivekananda International Foundation and Aryan Books International, 2014, pp. 171–93.

2 For the political history of the Candras, see Abdul Momin Chowdhury, *Dynastic History of Bengal (c. 750–1200 A. D.)*, Dacca: The Asiatic Society of Pakistan, 1967, pp. 154–89.

3 For their participation, see supra Chapters 3 and 4.

4 Supra Chapter 4.

5 *svasīmātṛṇayūtigocaraparyantāḥ*, Belwa CPI of Mahīpāla I, D. C. Sircar, 'Two Pala Plates from Belwa', *Epigraphia Indica*, 1951–52 (1987), 29: 8, l. 41. Sometimes *yūti* is spelt *pūti*.

6 *Tala* and *uddeśa* are interpreted as 'surface of ground' and 'space above the ground' by Sircar. *IEG*, pp. 404–5. However, the mention of *talapāṭaka* in the Khalimpur CPI of Dharmapāla suggests that *tala* is rather a land usable for agricultural purpose. *SI* 2, p. 68, l. 51. In this light, 'flat land' is better interpretation for *tala*. Accordingly, *uddeśa* may denote 'raised ground' meant for house stead and garden. These interpretations better suit the geographical context of Bengal.

7 Mohipur CPI of Gopāla II, Ryosuke Furui, 'A New Copper Plate Inscription of Gopala II', *South Asian Studies*, 2008, 24: 73, l. 52.

8 *Jalasthala* is interpreted as 'land and water' by Sircar. *IEG*, p. 399. If we consider that the land is already connoted in *tala* and *uddeśa*, 'watering place' can be more reasonable interpretation.

9 From the reign of Mahīpāla I, this privilege ceased to appear in the Pāla grants.

10 As an example of these privileges, see Pramatha Nath Misra and R. C. Majumdar, 'The Jājilpārā Grant of Gopāla II, Year 6', *Journal of the Asiatic Society, Letters*, 1951, 17(2): 143, ll. 31–33.

11 *IEG*, p. 401.

12 *atratyahaṭṭikātalapāṭakasametān*, Khalimpur CPI, *SI* 2, p. 68, ll. 51–52; *saghaṭṭataropetaḥ*, Suresh Chandra Bhattacharya, 'The Jagjibanpur Plate of Mahendrapāla Comprehensively Re-edited', *Journal of Ancient Indian History*, 2005–06 (2007), 23: 69, l. 46; *atratya ābhāvya | dvārikādānasametayoḥ*, Misra and Majumdar, 'Jājilpārā Grant', p. 142, l. 23; *sahaṭṭaghaṭṭaḥ*, Ryosuke Furui, 'Rangpur Copper Plate Inscription of Mahīpāla I, year 5', *Journal of Ancient Indian History*, 2010–11 (2011), 27: 241, l. 39.

13 Ex. D. C. Sircar, 'Dhulla Plate of Srichandra', *Epigraphia Indica*, 1959–60 (1987), 33: 140, ll. 30–33.

14 N. G. Majumdar, 'Irda Copper-plate of the Kamboja King Nayapaladeva', *Epigraphia Indica*, 1933–34 (1984), 22: 155, ll. 22–25; K. V. Ramesh and S. Subramonia Iyer, 'Kalanda Copper Plate Charter of Nayapāladeva', *Epigraphia Indica*, 1975–76 (1989), 41: 203, ll. 23–26.

15 *prativāsibhiḥ kṣetrakaraiś cājñāśravaṇavidheyair bhūtvā samucitakarapiṇḍakādi-sarvvapratyāyopanayaḥ kārya*, Khalimpur CPI, *SI* 2, p. 68, l. 55. In the Mohipur CPI, tribute is just mentioned as *sarvvapratyāyopanayaḥ*, Furui, 'A New Copper Plate Inscription of Gopala II', p. 73, ll. 56–57.
16 Ex. *prativāsibhiś ca kṣetrakarair ājñāśravaṇavidheyībhūya yathākālaṃ samucita bhāgabhogakarahiraṇyādisarvvapratyāyopanayaḥ kārya*, Misra and Majumdar, 'Jājilpārā Grant', p. 144, ll. 39–40.
17 *nivāsibhiḥ kṣetrakaraiś ca ājñāśravaṇavidheyībhūya ya*[*tho*]*ci*[*tapratyā*]*y-opanayaḥ kāryya*, Sircar, 'Dhulla Plate', p. 140, l. 40.
18 *tad*[*y-*]*pratyāyaṃ samagram tasmai vidheyatāṃ gatvā kālocitaṃ* [*dadānāḥ*] *sukhena nivasatheha*, Majumdar, 'Irda Copper-plate', p. 156, ll. 31–32. Almost the same phrase is found in the Kalanda CPI. Ramesh et al., 'Kalanda Copper Plate', p. 204, ll. 31–32.
19 For example, the Devaparvata grant of Bhavadeva is addressed to only present and future *viṣayapati*s, *karaṇika*s and *daśagrāmika*s. D. C. Sircar, 'Copper-plate Inscription of King Bhavadeva of Devaparvata', *Journal of the Asiatic Society, Letters*, 1951, 17(2): 93, ll. 43–44.
20 In Khalimpur CPI, 'unnamed' (*akīrttita*) is added to others. *SI* 2, p. 68, ll. 46–47.
21 *Ibid.*, l. 47.
22 Difference lies in the fact that the first category does not include *bhogin* in the Jagajjibanpur plate. Bhattacharya, 'Jagjibanpur Plate', p. 69, ll. 35–39.
23 Misra and Majumdar, 'Jājilpārā Grant', pp. 142–43, ll. 23–30. Ex. Belwa CPI of Vigrahapāla III, Table 5.1 e.
24 P. N. Bhattacharyya, ''Nalanda Plate of Dharmapaladeva', *Epigraphia Indica*, 1935–36 (1984), 23: 291, ll. 7–17.
25 The Monghyr CPI lists 45 titles including Karṇāta and Lāṭa. Lionel D. Barnett, 'The Mungir Plate of Devapaladeva: Samvat 33', *Epigraphia Indica*, 1925–26 (1983), 18: 306, ll. 31–36. The Nalanda CPI lists 42 titles which do not include Lāṭa. *SI* 2, p. 75, ll. 28–32.
26 Barnett, 'Mungir Plate of Devapaladeva', p. 306, l. 36.
27 Abhay Kant Choudhary, *Early Medieval Village in North-Eastern India (A. D. 600–1200) [Mainly a Socio-economic Study]*, Calcutta: Punthi Pustak, 1971, pp. 116–17.
28 *Ibid.*, p. 117.
29 Ex. Barnett, 'Mungir Plate of Devapaladeva', p. 306, ll. 35–36.
30 Sircar compares them to modern rural polices like *paik*. *IEG*, pp. 51, 67–68.
31 Supra Chapter 4.
32 Ex. Antla plates of the seventh century, *SI* 2, pp. 24–27.
33 Supra Chapter 4.
34 Patrick Olivelle (ed., tr.), *Manu's Code of Law: A Critical Edition and Translation of the Mānava-Dharmaśāstra*, New Delhi: Oxford University Press, 2006, 10. 36, 48.
35 Olivelle, *Manu's Code of Law*, 10. 51, 55, 56.
36 23 in the Paschimbhag CPI and 16 in the Madanpur CPI, both belong to the reign of Śrīcandra. *EDEP*, p. 67, ll. 28–33; R. G. Basak, 'Madanpur Plate of Srichandra, year 44', *Epigraphia Indica*, 1949–50 (1985), 28: 57, ll. 21–25.
37 *adhyakṣapracāroktān ihākīrttitān*, Paschimbhag CPI, *EDEP*, p. 67, l. 33.
38 *cāṭabhaṭajātīyān*, *ibid.*
39 *janapadān kṣetrakarāṃś ca brāhmaṇottarān*, *ibid.* In the Rampal CPI, *janapadas* are not mentioned. *IB*, p. 5, l. 22.

40 The Idilpur CPI of Śrīcandra, of which only abstract was published, and the Dhaka CPI of Kalyāṇacandra, which has not yet been edited, are out of purview on this matter. Nalini Kanta Bhattasali, 'The Kedarpur Plate of Sri-Chandra-Deva', *Epigraphia Indica*, 1923–24 (1983), 17: 189–90. The Kedarpur CPI of Śrīcandra contains only eulogies of the Candra kings and does not have any address. It seems to be a blank copper plate prepared for future use. *Ibid.*, pp. 188–92.

41 Nalinikanta Bhattasali, 'Some Image Inscriptions from East Bengal', *Epigraphia Indica*, 1923–24 (1983), 17: 355, ll. 2–3; D. C. Sircar, 'Nārāyaṇpur Vināyaka Image Inscription of King Mahīpāla.-Regnal Year 4', *Indian Culture*, 1942, 9(1), Miscellanea: 125, ll. 2–4.

42 *EDEP*, pp. 67–68, ll. 38–47.

43 *sūpakāravoraka*, *EDEP*, p. 73, l. 38; *valeśvaravardhakivorakabhūmi*, *ibid.*, l. 39; *kaṃsārākaddapolakagrāma*, *ibid*, p. 75, l. 10. For the interpretation of *voraka* as land on which *boro*, a sort of rice for swampy ground, is sown, see *ibid.*, p. 57.

44 Supra Chapter 4.

45 Majumdar, 'Irda Copper-plate', p. 155, ll. 20–22; Ramesh et al., 'Kalanda Copper Plate', p. 203, ll. 21–23.

46 Majumdar, 'Irda Copper-plate', p. 156, ll. 31–32. Cf. Ramesh et al., 'Kalanda Copper Plate', p. 204, ll. 31–32.

47 *vīkṣati voḍaty anuśāsati*, Majumdar, 'Irda Copper-plate', p. 156, l. 36. [*snehena*] *vicakṣati vadaty anu*(*śāsati*) *cāpi*, Ramesh et al., 'Kalanda Copper Plate', p. 204, l. 35.

48 Majumdar, 'Irda Copper-plate', p. 156, ll. 32–36; Ramesh et al., 'Kalanda Copper Plate', p. 204, ll. 32–35.

49 Majumdar, 'Irda Copper-plate', p. 156, ll. 36–37; Ramesh et al., 'Kalanda Copper Plate', p. 204, l. 36.

50 *adhyakṣavarggam akhilaṃ karaṇais sametāṃ*, Majumdar, 'Irda Copper-plate', p. 156, l. 34; Ramesh et al., 'Kalanda Copper Plate', p. 204, l. 33.

51 Supra Chapter 4.

52 Gouriswar Bhattacharya, 'An Inscribed Metal Vase Most Probably from Chittagong, Bangladesh', in Adalbert J. Gail and Gerd J. R. Mevissen (eds), *South Asian Archaeology 1991: Proceedings of the Eleventh International Conference of the Association of South Asian Archaeologists in Western Europe held in Berlin 1–5 July 1991*, Stuttgart: Franz Steiner Verlag, 1993, pp. 323–38. Another inscription, the Chittagong plate of Kāntideva datable to the first half of the ninth century contains only eulogy, name of the king and address of 'future kings in Harikelamaṇḍala.' R. C. Majumdar, 'Chittagong Copper-plate of Kantideva', *Epigraphia Indica*, 1941–42 (1985), 26: 313–18.

53 *iheva harikelāmaṇḍale yathākālabhāvino bhūpatīn rājaputrarāṇakaṭhakkurān ākṣapaṭalikādisarvvarājakarmmiṇo brāhmaṇamānanāpūrvvakaṃ*, Bhattacharya, 'An Inscribed Metal Vase', p. 333, ll. 3–4.

54 *kārada-indranāthasaṃpapañcadaśapadāni* | *bhārada-ambelasadadavalaṣapañca daśapadāni*, *ibid.*, p. 335, l. 14.

55 *nāgadattasambaddhaguvāvṛkṣādivāṭikā*, *ibid.*, p. 336, rim, l. 2.

56 D. D. Kosambi and V. V. Gokhale (eds), *The Subhāṣitaratnakoṣa*, Cambridge, MA: Harvard University Press, 1957, v. 300; Sures Chandra Banerji (ed.), *Sadukti-Karṇāmṛta of Śrīdharadāsa*, Calcutta: Firma KLM, 1965, 2. 173. 5.

57 *Sadukti*, 2. 73. 4.

58 *Subhāṣita*, v. 314; *Sadukti*, 2. 173. 2

59 B. N. S. Yadava, 'Terminological Analysis and Social Change: Locating the Peasants in Early Medieval North India', in Vijay Kumar Thakur and Ashok

Aounshuman (eds), *Peasants in Indian History vol. 1: Theoretical Issues and Structural Enquiries (Essays in Memory of Professor Radhakrishna Chaudhary)*, Patna: Janaki Prakashan, 1996, pp. 201–2.

60 *Subhāṣita*, v. 300; *Sadukti*, 2. 173. 5 (agricultural field). *Subhāṣita*, v. 318 (threshing floor).

61 *Subhāṣita*, v. 1176 (*pāmarāgāra*).

62 *Ibid.*, v. 1173. The term used in this verse is *geha*.

63 Choudhary, *Early Medieval Village*, pp. 98–99.

64 *Subhāṣita*, v. 1175.

65 Ex. Khalimpur CPI of Dharmapāla, *SI* 2, p. 68, l. 44. Table 5.1 b.

66 *EDEP*, p. 68, ll. 57–58.

67 *Subhāṣita*, v. 1175. Literally, families (*kula*) are 'investigated (*mita*) as "lands of own lineage" (*nijavaṃśabhū*)'. I add 'holding' to make a sense from it.

68 Per Kvaerne, *An Anthology of Buddhist Tantric Songs: A Study of the Caryāgīti* (3rd ed.), Bangkok: Orchid Press, 2010, Caryā 10, p. 113 (having relation with a *brāhmaṇa*); Caryā 18, p. 151 (relation with a high rank *brāhmaṇa* connoted); Caryā 19, p. 155 (marriage of Kāhṇupāda with a *ḍombī*).

69 *Ibid.*, Caryā 10, p. 113 (selling loom and bamboo basket); Caryā 14, p. 131 (working as a ferry woman).

70 *Ibid.*, Caryā 14, p. 131 (*mātaṅgī* and *ḍombī*); Caryā 18, p. 151, Caryā 47, p. 255 (*caṇḍālī* and *ḍombī*).

71 Supra Chapter 4.

72 Ryosuke Furui, 'Indian Museum Copper Plate Inscription of Dharmapala, Year 26: Tentative Reading and Study', *South Asian Studies*, 2011, 27(2): 153, ll. 46–48, v. 14.

73 Gouriswar Bhattacharya, 'Bangladesh National Museum Praśasti of Pāhila', in Samaresh Bandyopadhyay (ed.), *Prācyaśikṣāsuhāsinī: Seventy-Fifth Anniversary Celebration Volume of the Department of Ancient Indian History and Culture*, Calcutta: University of Calcutta, 1999, p. 389, ll. 5–11, vv. 4–9.

74 Bhattacharya, 'Jagjibanpur Plate', p. 70, ll. 54–56, vv. 22–23; Furui, 'A New Copper Plate Inscription of Gopala II', p. 74, ll. 62–63, 67–68, vv. 28, 34–35.

75 *SI* 2, pp. 87–91. Suresh Chandra Bhattacharya convincingly pointed out indirect references to Mahendrapāla and Gopāla II contained in this eulogy. Suresh Chandra Bhattacharya, 'Pāla Kings in the Badal Praśasti – A Stock-Taking', *Journal of Ancient Indian History*, 2007–08 (2008), 24: 73–82.

76 D. C. Sircar, 'Bhaturiya Inscription of Rajyapala', *Epigraphia Indica*, 1959–60 (1987), 33: 153–54, ll. 2–14, vv. 2–10.

77 Haraprasad Sastri (ed.), Radhagovinda Basak (rev., tr., notes), *Rāmacaritam of Sandhyākaranandin*, Calcutta: The Asiatic Society, 1969, 2. 8, commentary, 4. 18–21.

78 *Ibid.*, 1. 43, commentary, 2. 5, commentary.

79 Ryosuke Furui, 'Characteristics of Kaivarta Rebellion Delineated from the *Rāmacarita*', *Proceedings of Indian History Congress*, 2015, 75: 96.

80 For details of all those cases, see Ryosuke Furui, 'Subordinate Rulers under the Pālas: Their Diverse Origins and Shifting Power Relation with the King', *The Indian Economic and Social History Review*, 2017, 54(3): 341–45.

81 *SI* 2, p. 68, ll. 49–52.

82 Mahantāprakāśaviṣaya: Krauñcaśvabhra, Māḍhāśāmmalī and Pālitaka; Sthālīkaṭaviṣaya: Gopippalīgrāma included in Āmraṣaṇḍikāmaṇḍala. *Ibid.*, p. 67, ll. 31, 37–38, 40, 41–42.

83 *Ibid.*, p. 77, ll. 50–51.

84 Bhattacharya, 'Jagjibanpur Plate', p. 69, ll. 39–44. The site of the *vihāra* was excavated at Jagajjibanpur, the findspot of the plate. Amal Roy, Shiharan Nandy (photo.), *Jagjivanpur 1996–2005 Excavation Report*, Kolkata: Directorate of Archaeology and Museums, Govt. of West Bengal, 2012. It was known as 'Nandadīrghīvihāra caused to make by Vajradeva', according to the legend of sealings excavated from the site. Amal Roy, 'Nandadirghi-vihara: A Newly Discovered Buddhist Monastery at Jagajjibanpur, West Bengal', in Gautam Sengupra and Sheena Panja (eds), *Archaeology of Eastern India: New Perspectives*, Kolkata: Centre for Archaeological Studies and Training, Eastern India, 2002, p. 566.

85 Furui, 'A New Copper Plate Inscription of Gopala II', p. 73, ll. 47–51.

86 Bhattacharya, 'Jagjibanpur Plate', p. 69, ll. 41–43; Furui, 'A New Copper Plate Inscription of Gopala II', p. 73, ll. 48–50.

87 *anyeṣām api mamābhimatānām matparikalpitavibhāgenānavadyabhogārtham*, Bhattacharya, 'Jagjibanpur Plate', p. 69, ll. 43–44. Almost the same in Mohipur plate, except the addition of *ādy* after *bhoga*. Furui, 'A New Copper Plate Inscription of Gopala II', p. 73, l. 50.

88 Furui, 'Indian Museum Copper Plate', p. 154, ll. 57–66.

89 *Ibid.*, p. 153, ll. 29–32.

90 *Ibid.*, p. 154, l. 61.

91 *Ibid.*, p. 153, ll. 32–40.

92 *SI* 2, p. 84, ll. 38–44.

93 *anyeṣām api svābhimatānāṃ* I *svaparikalpitavibhāgena* I *anavadyabhogārthañ ca*, *ibid.*, ll. 40–41.

94 D. C. Sircar, 'Bāṇgaḍh Stone Inscription of the Time of Nayapāla', *Journal of Ancient Indian History*, 1973–74 (1975), 7: 135–58, idem, 'Mūrtiśiva's Bangarh Prasasti of the Time of Nayapāla', *Journal of Ancient Indian History*, 1980–82 (1983), 13(1–2): 34–56; idem, 'Siyan Stone Slab Inscription of Nayapala', *Epigraphia Indica*, 1971 (1982), 39(2): 39–56.

95 Sircar, 'Bhaturiya Inscription', p. 154, ll. 14–16, v. 11.

96 *Ibid.*, ll. 16–17, v. 12. For this currency unit, see infra.

97 D. C. Sircar, *Studies in the Political and Administrative Systems in Ancient and Medieval India*, Delhi: Motilal Banarsidass, 1974, pp. 74–75.

98 Ryosuke Furui, '*Brāhmaṇa*s in Early Medieval Bengal: Construction of Their Identity, Networks and Authority', *Indian Historical Review*, 2013, 40(2): 229–36.

99 For the grants to *brāhmaṇa*s as acts of extending and strengthening royal authority, see Hermann Kulke, 'Some Observations on the Political Functions of Copper-plate Grants in Early Medieval India', in Bernhard Kölver (ed.), *Recht, Staat und Verwaltung im klassischen Indien (The State, the Law, and Administration in Classical India)*, München: R. Oldenbourg Verlag, 1997, pp. 241–43.

100 Ryosuke Furui, 'Re-reading Two Copper Plate Inscriptions of Gopāla II, Year 4', in Gerd J. R. Mevissen and Arundhati Banerji (eds), *Prajñādhara: Essays on Asian Art, History, Epigraphy and Culture in Honour of Gouriswar Bhattacharya*, New Delhi: Kaveri Books, 2009, p. 325, ll. 42–43, p. 328, l. 41.

101 Furui, 'Re-Reading Two Copper Plate Inscriptions', p. 325, ll. 27–28. For these units of land measurements and their interrelation discernible in the Sena plates of the later period, see Chitrarekha Gupta, 'Land-measurement and Land-revenue System in Bengal under Senas', in Debala Mitra (ed.), *Explorations in Art and Archaeology of South Asia: Essays Dedicated to N. G. Majumdar*, Calcutta: Directorate of Archaeology and Museums, 1996, pp. 578–83.

102 Furui, 'Rangpur Copper Plate', p. 240, ll. 29–30.
103 Sircar, 'Two Pala Plates', p. 11, ll. 27–29. Ardhalovanikāma is treated as a village. *Ibid.*, p. 12, l. 38
104 *Ibid.*, p. 11, ll. 27–29.
105 R. D. Banerji, 'The Amgachhi Grant of Vigraha-Pala III: The 12th Year', *Epigraphia Indica*, 1919–20 (1982), 15: 297, ll. 24–26. The donated part is also treated as a village. *Ibid.*, l. 32.
106 Furui, 'Re-Reading Two Copper Plate Inscriptions', p. 325, l. 26; p. 327, ll. 25–26.
107 *Ibid.* p. 325, ll. 26–27, p. 327, l. 26.
108 *IEG*, pp. 110–11(*gaṇḍā, gaṇḍaka*), 228–29 (*paṇa*).
109 The date of the plate is read by D. C. Sircar as [5]. Sircar, 'Two Pala Plates', p. 8, l. 49. It is 2 according to my own reading from a digital photograph provided by Bangiya Sahitya Parishad.
110 *pañcakāṇḍakādhikaṣaṭṭapaṇopetatrinavatyuttaracatuḥśatapramāṇanandisvāminī*, my own reading from the photograph. Cf. Sircar, 'Two Pala Plates', p. 7, ll. 29–30. *Kāṇḍaka* seems to be an equivalent of *gaṇḍaka*.
111 *Ibid.*, ll. 28–31. Though the last one sounds like a pond belonging to a village, all the three are collectively mentioned as 'three villages written above' (*yathoparilikhitāḥ trigrāmāḥ*). *Ibid.*, p. 8, l. 41.
112 *palāśavṛnde sahasrapurāṇapramāṇe*, Ryosuke Furui, 'Biyala Copperplate Inscription of Mahīpāla I', *Pratna Samiksha: A Journal of Archaeology, New Series*, 2010, 1: 104, l. 28.
113 Infra.
114 *ḍaṣottaranavaśatādhike pañcasahasraparimāṇe*, Furui, 'Rangpur Copper Plate', p. 240, ll. 28–29. The first two *akṣara*s should be emended to *daśo*.
115 *vasukāvarttāt* | *yathotpatyā pañcaśatikā[ṃ]śe*, D. C. Sircar, 'Bangaon Plate of Vigrahapala III; Regnal Year 17', *Epigraphia Indica*, 1951–52 (1987), 29: 55, l. 25.
116 Ryosuke Furui, 'Rajibpur Copperplate Inscriptions of Gopāla IV and Madanapāla', *Pratna Samiksha: A Journal of Archaeology, New Series*, 2015, 6: 43, ll. 37–38; 45, l. 51; 53, l. 48.
117 Sircar, 'Bhaturiya Inscription', p. 154, l. 16.
118 Misra and Majumdar, 'Jājilpārā Grant', p. 142, ll. 22–23; R. D. Banerji, 'The Bangarh Grant of Mahi-Pala I: The 9th Year', *Epigraphia Indica*, 1917–18 (1982), 14: 327, ll. 31–32.
119 Bharella image inscription, Bhattasali, 'Some Image Inscriptions', p. 351.
120 The Kedarpur CPI, which has only the eulogy of kings, is out of purview. Bhattasali, 'Kedarpur Plate'.
121 Sircar, 'Dhulla Plate', p. 139, ll. 35–36; *IB*, p. 5, ll. 28–29.
122 P. V. Kane, *History of Dharmaśāstra (Ancient and Medieval Religious and Civil Law)*, vol. 5 pt. 2 (2nd ed.), Poona: Bhandarkar Oriental Research Institute, 1977, pp. 761–63.
123 P. V. Kane, *History of Dharmaśāstra (Ancient and Medieval Religious and Civil Law)*, vol. 5 pt. 1 (2nd ed.), Poona: Bhandarkar Oriental Research Institute, 1974, p. 290.
124 Benjamin J. Fleming, 'New Copperplate Grant of Śrīcandra (no. 8) from Bangladesh', *Bulletin of the School of Oriental and African Studies*, 2010, 73(2): 234, l. 30.
125 *ekadeśabhavas tasmai smitapūrvvābhibhāṣiṇe śrīmate śukradevāya śrīcand ranṛpa(tir dda)dau*, R. G. Basak, 'Madanpur Plate of Srichandra, Year 44', *Epigraphia Indica*, 1949–1950 (1985), 28: 58, ll. 35–36.

126 Sircar, 'Dhulla Plate', p. 139, ll. 20–23, 40, l. 30; Fleming, 'New Copperplate Grant of Śrīcandra', p. 233, ll. 18, 24; E. M. Mills, 'A Copper Plate from the Reign of Śrīcandra (Bangladesh National Museum Accession Number 77.1478)', *South Asian Studies*, 1993, 9: 79, ll. 20–21; Basak, 'Madanpur Plate', p. 57, ll. 20–21, 26; *IB*, p. 5, ll. 17, 23.
127 *EDEP*, pp. 73–74, ll. 37–45, p. 74, ll. 50–51.
128 *Ibid.*, pp. 73–74, ll. 37–44.
129 *Ibid.*, pp. 75–76, ll. 8–11, p. 76, l. 17.
130 Supra.
131 Majumdar, 'Irda Copper-plate', p. 156, ll. 32–35; Ramesh et al., 'Kalanda Copper Plate', p. 204, ll. 32–35.
132 Supra Chapter 4.
133 *Rāmacarita*, 2. 5–6, commentary. For their identifications, see Chowdhury, *Dynastic History of Bengal*, pp. 117–20.
134 Majumdar, 'Irda Copper-plate', pp. 155–56, ll. 25–30; Ramesh et al., 'Kalanda Copper Plate', p. 203, ll. 26–29.
135 Bhattacharya, 'An Inscribed Metal Vase', p. 333, ll. 3–4.
136 *Ibid.*, pp. 334–35, ll. 6–9.
137 Furui, 'Indian Museum Copper Plate', p. 151.
138 Supra Chapter 4.
139 For these sites, see D. R. Patil, *The Antiquarian Remains in Bihar*, Patna: K. P. Jayaswal Research Institute, 1963, pp. 59–70, 300–35.
140 For the site and its excavation report, see B. S. Verma, *Antichak Excavations-2 (1971–1981)*, New Delhi: Archaeological Survey of India, 2011.
141 K. N. Dikshit, *Excavations at Paharpur, Bengal*, New Delhi: Archaeological Survey of India, 1999 (reprint). For the overview of the result of later excavations, see Md. Shafiqul Alam, 'Post-Liberation Excavations at Paharpur World Heritage Site', in idem (ed.), *Proceedings of the International Seminar on Elaboration of an Archaeological Research Strategy for Paharpur World Heritage Site and its Environment (Bangladesh): 20–25 March, 2004*, Dhaka: Department of Archaeology, Ministry of Cultural Affairs, Govt. of Bangladesh and UNESCO Dhaka, 2004, pp. 52–57. For the sites on Lalmai range, see Abu Imam, *Excavations at Mainamati: An Exploratory Study*, Dhaka: The International Centre for Study of Bengal Art, 2000.
142 Md. Abul Hashem Miah, 'Archaeological Excavations at Jagaddala Vihara: A Preliminary Report', *Journal of Bengal Art*, 2003, 8: 147–66.
143 M. Harunur Rashid, 'Excavation', *Bangldesh Archaeology*, 1979, 1(1): 21–67; Roy, *Jagjivanpur 1996–2005*.
144 Debiprasad Chattopadhyaya (ed.), Lama Chimpa and Alaka Chattopadhyaya (trs), *Tāranātha's History of Buddhism in India*, Delhi: Motilal Banarsidass, 1990, pp. 266–67, 274–75. The genealogy of the Pālas recorded by Tāranātha has some confusion. Devapāla is described as the son of Gopāla and the grandfather of Dharmapāla, and wrongly credited with the construction of a *vihāra* at Somapurī.
145 *śrīsomapure śrīdharmapāladevamahāvihārīyāryabhikṣusaṅghasya*, Dikshit, *Excavations at Paharpur*, p. 90, P. 304.
146 Furui, 'Indian Museum Copper Plate'; Nalanda CPI of Dharmapala, Bhattacharya, 'Nalanda Plate'; Nalanda CPI of Devapāla, *SI* 2, pp. 71–79.
147 *Rāmacarita*, 3. 7.
148 *EDEP*, p. 58, l. 54.
149 *Ibid.*, p. 75, reverse ll. 8–9.
150 *Ibid.*, p. 74, l. 53, p. 76, l. 20.

151 Bhattacharya, 'An Inscribed Metal Vase', p. 335, l. 16.
152 D. C. Sircar, 'Lucknow Museum Copper-plate Inscription of Surapala I, Regnal Year 3', *Epigraphia Indica*, 1973 (1986), 40(1): 15, ll. 58–60.
153 *SI* 2, p. 84, ll. 39–40.
154 Sircar, 'Bāṇgaḍh Stone Inscription'; idem, 'Mūrtiśiva's Bangarh Prasasti'.
155 Sircar, 'Siyan Stone Slab Inscription', p. 53, l. 18, p. 54, l. 25, p. 55, ll. 28–29.
156 *EDEP*, pp. 67–68, ll. 36–51, p. 68, l. 54; pp. 73–74, ll. 37–45, p. 74, l. 53; p. 75, ll. 8–11, p. 76, l. 20.
157 *Ibid.*, p. 80, ll. 35–36, 42–43, 46.
158 Bhattacharya, 'Bangladesh National Museum Praśasti', pp. 389–90, ll. 12–14, v. 11.
159 Supra.
160 Bhattacharya, 'An Inscribed Metal Vase', p. 333, ll. 6–7.
161 Ronald M. Davidson, *Indian Esoteric Buddhism: A Social History of the Tantric Movement*, Delhi: Motilal Banarsidass, 2004; Alexis Sanderson, 'The Śaiva Age – The Rise and Dominance of Śaivism during the Early Medieval Period – ', in Shingo Einoo (ed.), *Genesis and Development of Tantrism*, Tokyo: Institute of Oriental Culture, University of Tokyo, 2009, pp. 254–60.
162 Khalimpur CPI of Dharmapāla, *SI* 2, p. 68, l. 50; Mainamati CPIs of Laḍahacandra, *EDEP*, p. 74, l. 53, p. 76, l. 20.
163 Dikshit, *Excavations at Paharpur*, p. 90, P. 304; Roy, 'Nandadirghi-vihara', p. 566.
164 Supra.
165 The networks centred on royal temples are more clearly observable in Tamil South under the Coḷas. James Heitzman, *Gifts of Power: Lordship in an Early Indian State*, Delhi: Oxford University Press, 1997, pp. 121–42.
166 *SI* 2, p. 59, pt. 2, ll. 1–3.
167 *Ibid.*, pp. 61–62, ll. 6–12, vv. 5–10.
168 *GL*, pp. 47–49, ll. 3–12, vv. 3–10.
169 *Ibid.*, p. 48, ll. 9–10, v. 8.
170 Parmeshwari Lal Gupta (ed.), *Patna Museum Catalogue of Antiquities (Stone Sculptures, Metal Images, Terracottas and Minor Antiquities)*, Patna: Patna Museum, 1965, pp. 128–29, no. 14, p. 129, no. 15, p. 129, no. 17, p. 130, nos 19, 21, pp. 134–35, no. 49, pp. 139–40, no. 79, p. 146, nos 114–15, p. 155, no. 164, p. 156, nos 165–66, p. 159, nos 205–8.
171 *Ibid.*, p. 156, no. 165.
172 *iha vihāranaivāsikasindhurddeśavinirgatapāḍikramaṇavihāravṛddhapariṣadhya dhadeśiṇa sthavirapūrṇṇadāsena*, my own reading of the inscription on the image of the Buddha, Acc. No. 3764, ll. 3–4. Cf. Nilmani Chakravartti, 'Pāla Inscriptions in the Indian Museum', *Journal and Proceedings of the Asiatic Society of Bengal, New Series*, 1908, 4(3): 108.
173 Debala Mitra, 'Image of Buddha of the 11th Regnal Year of King Mahīpāla', *Indian Museum Bulletin*, 1991, 26: 8.
174 Sircar, 'Mūrtiśiva's Bangarh Prasasti'.
175 *Ibid.*, p. 44, ll. 8–9, v. 9.
176 Amitabha Bhattacharyya, 'The Maṭhas of Eastern India in the Early Medieval Period', in idem, *Selected Essays*, Kolkata: Centre for Archaeological Studies and Training, Eastern India, 2004, p. 16.
177 *SI* 2, pp. 71–79.
178 Supra.
179 Supra.
180 Supra.

181 Furui, '*Brāhmaṇa*s in Early Medieval Bengal: Construction', pp. 230–31.
182 For details, see Ryosuke Furui, '*Brāhmaṇa*s in Early Medieval Bengal: Data of Inscriptional References', in Nobuhiro Ota (ed.), *Zen-kindai Minami-Ajia Shakai Ni Okeru Matomari To Tsunagari* (*Clustering and Connections in Pre-Modern South Asian Society*), Tokyo: Research Institute for Languages and Cultures of Asia and Africa, Tokyo University of Foreign Studies, 2017, pp. 196–202, Appendix Table 1, nos 22–36 (Pālas), 38–42 (Candras), 43–44 (Kāmbojas).
183 Furui, '*Brāhmaṇa*s in Early Medieval Bengal: Construction', pp. 231–32.
184 Idem, '*Brāhmaṇa*s in Early Medieval Bengal: Data', pp. 196–200, 202, Appendix Table 1, nos 23–26, 28–36 (Pālas), 43–44 (Kāmbojas).
185 Fleming, 'New Copperplate Grant of Śrīcandra', p. 234, l. 29.
186 Radha Govinda Basak, 'Silimpur Stone-slab Inscription of the Time of Jayapaladeva', *Epigraphia Indica*, 1915–16 (1982), 13: 283–95. Furui, '*Brāhmaṇa*s in Early Medieval Bengal: Construction', pp. 233–34.
187 *Ibid*., pp. 234–35.
188 Supra.
189 Supra Chapters 3 and 4.
190 Supra.
191 Furui, 'Indian Museum Copper Plate', p. 153, ll. 30–32; Khalimpur CPI, *SI* 2, pp. 67–68, ll. 31–43; Bhattacharya, 'Jagjibanpur Plate', pp. 68–69, ll. 31–35.
192 Furui, 'A New Copper Plate Inscription of Gopala II', p. 73, ll. 40–41.
193 *rahayyādityapuṣkariny*, Furui, 'Indian Museum Plate', p. 153, l. 31; *viṭakāli*, Khalimpur CPI, *SI* 2, p. 67, l. 33.
194 *rājaputtradevaṭakṛtāli*, *ibid*., l. 32.
195 Udragrāmamaṇḍala, *ibid*., p. 68, ll. 42–43; Trapatagrāmamaṇḍala, Śivagrāmamaṇḍala, Furui, 'Rangpur Copper Plate', p. 240, ll. 26, 29; Brāhmaṇīgrāmamaṇḍala, Banerji, 'Amgachhi Grant', p. 297, ll. 24–25.
196 Furui, 'Re-reading Two Copper Plate Inscriptions', p. 324, l. 25, p. 327, l. 25.
197 *SI* 1, p. 333, l. 3.
198 Supra Chapter 3.
199 For the archaeological research which can support this possibility, see Swadhin Sen, 'The Transformative Context of a Temple in Early Medieval Varendri: Report of the Excavation at Tileshwarir Aara in Dinajpur District, Bangladesh', *South Asian Studies*, 2015, 31(1): 71–110.
200 Furui, 'Biyala Copperplate', p. 104, ll. 27–28.
201 Khalimpur CPI, *SI* 2, p. 67, l. 31; Furui, 'Biyala Copperplate', p. 104, l. 27.
202 This phenomenon and its possible connection with agrarian expansion are pointed out by Rajat Sanyal through personal communication.
203 Furui, 'Rangpur Copper Plate', p. 240, ll. 27–29.
204 *Ibid*., p. 237.
205 *Ibid*., p. 240, l. 27.
206 Sircar, 'Two Pala Plates from Belwa', p. 7, ll. 28–29.
207 Olivelle, *Manu's Code of Law*, 10. 34; *Subhāṣita*, v. 1351.
208 Furui, 'Re-reading Two Copper Plate Inscriptions', p. 325, l. 36.
209 *IEG*, p. 381.
210 Belwa CPI of Vigrahapāla III, Sircar, 'Two Pala Plates from Belwa', p. 11, l. 27.
211 *SI* 1, p. 194, l. 11.
212 *SI* 2, p. 68, ll. 51–52.
213 Sircar, 'Bhaturiya Inscription', p. 153, l. 2.
214 Furui, 'Rangpur Copper Plate', p. 241, l. 39; Ramganj CPI, *IB*, p. 154, ll. 24–25.

215 Ryosuke Furui, 'Merchant Groups in Early Medieval Bengal: With Special Reference to the Rajbhita Stone Inscription of the Time of Mahīpāla I, Year 33', *Bulletin of the School of Oriental and African Studies*, 2013, 76(3): 391–412.
216 *Ibid.*, p. 393, l. 1. The other market is named Jayahaṭṭa.
217 Gouriswar Bhattacharya, 'The British Museum Stone Inscription of Mahendrapāla', *South Asian Studies*, 2007, 23: 69–74.
218 Misra and Majumdar, 'Jājilpārā Grant', p. 142, l. 23; Bhattacharya, 'Jagjibanpur Plate', p. 69, l. 46; Furui, 'Rangpur Copper Plate', p. 241, l. 39; Ramganj CPI, *IB*, p. 154, ll. 24–25.
219 Supra.
220 D. C. Sircar, *Early Indian Numismatic and Epigraphical Studies*, Calcutta: Indian Museum, 1977, pp. 51–52.
221 Acyutananda Jha (comm.), Ramachandra Pandey (intro.), *Varāhamihirakṛtā Bṛhatsaṃhitā: 'bhaṭṭotpalavivṛti' samanvita 'vimalā' hindīvyākhyāyutā*, uttarārddhā, Varanasi: Chaukhamba Vidyabhavan, 2005, p. 353. B. N. Mukherjee, 'Commerce and Money in the Western and Central Sectors of Eastern India (c. A. D. 750–1200)', *Indian Museum Bulletin*, 1982, 17: 68.
222 *Akhbār Al-Ṣīn Wa'l-Hind* by Sulaymān al-Tājir et al in S. Maqbul Ahmad (tr.), *Arabic Classical Accounts of India and China*, Shimla: Indian Institute of Advanced Study, 1989, p. 44. Dikshit, *Excavations at Paharpur*, p. 33.
223 Mukherjee, 'Commerce and Money', pp. 68–69.
224 John S. Deyell, 'Cowries and Coins: The Dual Monetary System of the Bengal Sultanate', *The Indian Economic and Social History Review*, 2010, 47(1): 73.
225 *Rāmacarita*, 4. 36.
226 Bhattacharya, 'British Museum Stone Inscription', p. 72, ll. 5–6.
227 H. G. Raverty (tr.), *Tabakat-i-Nasiri: A General History of the Muhammadan Dynasties of Asia Including Hindustan from A. H. 194 (810 A. D.) to A. H. 658 (1260 A. D.) and the Irruption of the Infidel Mughals in Islam*, 2 vols, Calcutta: The Asiatic Society, 1995 (reprint), vol. 1, pp. 555–56; Deyell, 'Cowries and Coins', pp. 65–66.
228 D. C. Sircar, 'Three Pala Inscriptions', *Epigraphia Indica*, 1964 (1963), 35(5): 233–38.
229 Jha and Pandey, *Bṛhatsaṃhitā*, p. 353. Equating *purāṇa* with *kārṣāpaṇa*, Mukherjee counts 64,000 cowries for the present case. Mukherjee, 'Commerce and Money', p. 68.
230 R. S. Sharma, *Indian Feudalism: c. A.D. 300–1200* (2nd ed.), Delhi: Macmillan India, 1980, pp. 105–6.
231 Maqbul Ahmad, *Arabic Classical Accounts*, p. 34.
232 Mahdi Husain (tr., comm.), *The Reḥla of Ibn Baṭṭūṭa: India, Maldive Islands and Ceylon*, Baroda: Oriental Institute, 1953, p. 201.
233 John S. Deyell, *Living without Silver: The Monetary History of Early Medieval North India*, Delhi: Oxford University Press, 1990.
234 Supra Chapter 3.
235 Arlo Griffiths, 'New Documents for the Early History of Puṇḍravardhana: Copperplate Inscriptions from the Late Gupta and Early Post-Gupta Periods', *Pratna Samiksha: A Journal of Archaeology, New Series*, 2015, 6: 30, ll. 13–14.
236 Supra Chapter 3.
237 Furui, 'Merchant Groups in Early Medieval Bengal', pp. 393–94, ll. 1–5.
238 Vincent Bernard, Marie-Françoise Boussac, Jean-Yves Breuil and Jean-François Salles, 'Excavations at the Eastern Rampart Site (1993–1998) Preliminary Report of the French Team', in Md. Shafiqul Alam and Jean-François Salles (eds), *France=Bangladesh Joint Venture Excavations at Mahasthangarh:*

First Interim Report 1993–1999, Dhaka: Department of Archaeology, 2001, pp. 154–56; Kunja Govinda Goswami, *Excavations at Bangarh (1938–41)*, Calcutta: University of Calcutta, 1948, pp. 6–9.

239 Bhattacharya, 'British Museum Stone Inscription', p. 72, l. 6; Furui, 'Merchant Groups in Early Medieval Bengal', p. 404.

240 Supra.

241 Basak, 'Madanpur Plate', p. 57, ll. 20–21; Rampal CPI, *IB*, p. 5, l. 17.

242 Sircar, 'Dhulla Plate', p. 139, ll. 20–23.

243 Supra Chapter 4.

244 Fleming, 'New Copperplate Grant of Śrīcandra', pp. 232–33, ll. 17–18; Mills, 'A Copper Plate from the Reign of Śrīcandra', p. 79, ll. 20–21.

245 Supra Chapter 4.

246 *EDEP*, pp. 73–74, ll. 36–45, p. 74, ll. 50–51, 53; *Ibid.*, pp. 75–76, ll. 8–11, p. 76, ll. 17, 20. For the units of land measurement and their mutual relations, see *ibid.*, p. 56 and Gupta, 'Land Measurement', pp. 580–83.

247 Guptīnāṭana: Kailan CPI of Śrīdhāraṇarāta, *SI* 2, p. 37, l. 4; Peranāṭana: Ashrafpur CPI of Devakhaḍga, year 7, my own reading from the impression attached as Plate VII to *Memoirs of the Asiatic Society of Bengal*, 1905, 1. Cf. G. M. Laskar, 'Ashrafpur Copper-plate Grants of Devakhaḍga', *Memoirs of the Asiatic Society of Bengal*, 1904, 1(6): 90–91, ll. 12–13; Ashrafpur CPI of year 13, my own reading from the impression attached as Plate II to *Proceedings of the Asiatic Society of Bengal* for March, 1885. Cf. *SI* 2, p. 42, l. 6; D. C. Sircar, 'Copper-plate Inscription of King Bhavadeva of Devaparvata', *Journal of the Asiatic Society, Letters*, 1951, 17(2): 93, ll.43–44, 94, l. 56.

248 Supra Chapter 4.

249 *EDEP*, pp. 73–74, ll. 38–44, pp. 75–76, ll. 8–11.

250 Mainamati CPI of Govindacandra, *ibid.*, p. 80, ll. 35–36, 46.

251 Supra Chapter 4.

252 P. N. Bhattacharya, 'Two Lost Plates of the Nidhanpur Copper-plates of Bhaskaravarman', *Epigraphia Indica*, 1927–28 (1983), 19: 118, pl. 3, 1. 5.

253 *EDEP*, pp. 67–68, ll. 35–51.

254 *Ibid.*, p. 69, l. 64.

255 *Ibid*, p. 67, l. 33. Table 5.2 a.

256 B. D. Chattopadhyaya, *Aspects of Rural Settlements and Rural Society in Early Medieval India*, Calcutta: K P Bagchi, 1990, p. 55.

257 *Ibid.*, pp. 55–56.

258 *Ibid.*, p. 57.

259 *EDEP*, p. 68, ll. 52–54, 56–57

260 Bhattacharya, 'An Inscribed Metal Vase', p. 335, ll. 9–15, p. 336, rim inscription.

261 Supra Chapter 4.

262 Nicholas G. Rhodes, 'Trade in South-East Bengal in the First Millennium CE: The Numismatic Evidence', in Rila Mukherjee (ed.), *Pelagic Passageways: The Northern Bay of Bengal Before Colonialism*, Delhi: Primus Books, 2011, pp. 268–69.

263 For the Arakan coins, see Robert S. Wicks, *Money, Markets, and Trade in Early Southeast Asia: The Development of Indigenous Monetary Systems to AD 1400*, Ithaca: Southeast Asia Program, Cornell University, 1992, p. 86.

264 Vasant Chowdhury, 'Harikela Coins: Some New Interpretations', *Indian Museum Bulletin*, 1996, 31: 36.

265 Sircar, *Early Indian Numismatic and Epigraphical Studies*, pp. 51–52.

266 Furui, 'Merchant Groups in Early Medieval Bengal', p. 395.

267 *EDEP*, p. 74, l. 45; Baghaura image inscription, Bhattasali, 'Some Image Inscriptions', p. 355, ll. 2–3, Sircar, 'Nārāyaṇpur Vināyaka Image Inscription', p. 125, ll. 2–4; Bhattacharya, 'An Inscribed Metal Vase', p. 336, rim inscription.
268 Majumdar, 'Irda Copper-plate', p. 155, ll. 21, 22–23; Ramesh et al., 'Kalanda Copper Plate', p. 203, ll. 23–24.
269 Majumdar, 'Irda Copper-plate', p. 155, ll. 23–24; Ramesh et al., 'Kalanda Copper Plate', p. 203, l. 24.
270 Majumdar, 'Irda Copper-plate', p. 155, l. 25.
271 Supra.
272 For a minute discussion on the date of the text, see Lallanji Gopal, 'The Date of the Krsi-Parasara', *Journal of Indian History*, 1973, 50: 151–68.
273 Ryosuke Furui, 'The Rural World of an Agricultural Text: A Study on the *Kṛṣiparāśara*', *Studies in History, New Series*, 2005, 21(2): 160–61.
274 *Ibid.*, pp. 160–62.
275 Girija Prasanna Majumdar and Sures Chandra Banerji (ed., tr.), *Kṛṣi-Parāśara*, Kolkata: The Asiatic Society, 2001 (reprint), vv. 119, 215.
276 *Kṛṣiparāśara*, v. 181. Furui, 'The Rural World', p. 164.
277 *Ibid.*
278 Gyula Wojtilla, (ed., introductory study), *Kāśyapīyakṛṣisūkti: A Sanskrit Work on Agriculture*, Wiesbaden: Harrassowitz Verlag, 2010, pp. 11–19.
279 *Ibid.*, vv. 478, 480, 484.
280 Supra.
281 *Kṛṣiparāśara*, vv. 99–104.
282 *Ibid.*, vv. 100–2. For a translation see Furui, 'The Rural World', p. 167.
283 *Kṛṣiparāśara*, v. 221.
284 *Ibid.*, vv. 222–24. For a translation see Furui, 'The Rural World', pp. 167–68.
285 *Kṛṣiparāśara*, vv. 225–28. For a translation, see Furui, 'The Rural World', p. 168.
286 *Kṛṣiparāśara*, vv. 229–32.
287 *Ibid.*, v. 234.
288 *Ibid.*, v. 236.
289 Furui, 'The Rural World', pp. 153–63.
290 Furui, '*Brāhmaṇa*s in Early Medieval Bengal: Construction', pp. 231–36.
291 Gouriswar Bhattacharya, 'The Munificence of Lady Catuḥsamā', in idem (ed.), *Akṣayanīvī: Essays Presented to Dr. Debala Mitra in Admiration of her Scholarly Contributions*, Delhi: Sri Satguru Publications, 1991, p. 317.
292 *Rāmacarita*, Kavipraśasti, v. 3.
293 Chitrarekha Gupta, *The Kāyasthas: A Study in the Formation and Early History of a Caste*, Calcutta: K P Bagchi, 1996, p. 39.
294 For its use as an abbreviation for *adhikaraṇa*, see Supra Chapter 4.
295 Sircar, 'Bhaturiya Inscription', p. 153, ll. 2–3; Furui, 'Subordinate Rulers', p. 344.
296 Furui, '*Brāhmaṇa*s in Early Medieval Bengal: Construction', pp. 233, 235.
297 *Rāmacarita*, Kavipraśasti, v. 1. Gudrun Melzer, 'A Dancing Cāmuṇḍā Named Siddheśvarī from the Time of Mahīpāla I', in Mokammal H. Bhuiyan (ed.), *Studies in South Asian Heritage: Essays in Memory of M Harunur Rashid*, Dhaka: Bangla Academy, 2015, p. 103.
298 Furui, 'A New Copper Plate Inscription of Gopala II', p. 74, l. 76.
299 Bhattacharya, 'Bangladesh National Museum Praśasti', p. 390, l. 16; Sircar, 'Lucknow Museum Copper-plate', p. 16, l. 72.
300 *utkirṇṇam idaṃ śāśanaṃ sāmantadakkadāsavairocanadāsābhyāṃ, ibid.*
301 Bhagalpur CPI of Nārāyaṇapāla, *SI* 2, p. 85, ll. 53–54; Misra and Majumdar, 'Jājilpārā Grant', p. 144, l. 46.

302 Sircar, 'Lucknow Museum Copper-plate', p. 14, l. 48. The stone inscription of Pāhila was discovered in Nimgachi *thana*, Sirajganj district, Bangladesh, according to the information provided by Bangladesh National Museum.
303 *EDEP*, p. 68, ll. 54–55, 63.
304 Sircar, 'Mūrtiśiva's Bangarh Prasasti', p. 49, ll. 34–35; Basak, 'Silimpur Stone-slab Inscription', p. 292, ll. 24–25.
305 Sircar, 'Two Pala Plates from Belwa', p. 9, ll. 57–58; Furui, 'Rangpur Copper Plate', p. 241, l. 56; Banerji, 'The Bangarh Grant', p. 328, l. 62; Furui, 'Biyala Copperplate', p. 105, ll. 55–56.
306 Banerji, 'The Amgachhi Grant', p. 298, l. 49; Sircar, 'Bangaon Plate', p. 57, ll. 48–49.
307 *Ibid*., pp. 51, 57 note 4.
308 Sircar, 'Two Pala Plates from Belwa', p. 6. *Gāñī*s or *gain*s are surnames of *kulīna brāhmaṇa*s of the later period, based on names of villages which they were supposed to have received as gifts. N. K. Dutt, *Origin and Growth of Caste in India* (Volumes 1 and 2 Combined), Calcutta: Firm KLM, 1986, pp. 210–11.
309 Sircar, 'Two Pala Plates from Belwa', p. 13, l. 54.
310 Supra.
311 Furui, 'Indian Museum Copper Plate', p. 153, ll. 46–55.
312 For details, see Furui, 'Merchant Groups in Early Medieval Bengal', pp. 401–2.
313 Nalanda pillar inscription of the time of Rājyapāla, D. C. Sircar, 'Two Pillar Inscriptions', *Journal of the Royal Asiatic Society of Bengal, Letters*, 1949, 15(1): 3; idem, 'Nārāyaṇpur Vināyaka image inscription', p. 125, ll. 3–4.
314 Chandimau image inscription, R. D. Banerji, 'The Pālas of Bengal', *Memoirs of the Asiatic Society of Bengal*, 1915, 5(3): 93, l. 1; Bhagaura image inscription, Bhattasali, 'Some image inscriptions', p. 355, ll. 2–3; Sircar, 'Nārāyaṇpur Vināyaka Image Inscription', p. 125, ll. 2–3.
315 Rajauna image inscription of the time of Śūrapāla, Priyatosh Banerjee, 'Some Inscriptions from Bihar', *Journal of Ancient Indian History*, 1973–74 (1975), 7(1–2): 107, pt. 2.
316 Chandimau image inscription, Banerji, 'The Pālas of Bengal', p. 93, ll. 1–2.
317 Supra Chapter 3.
318 Furui, 'Merchant Groups in Early Medieval Bengal', p. 396.
319 *Ibid*., p. 395.
320 *Ibid*., p. 397.
321 *tailika*: National Museum image inscription of the time of Devapāla, year 25, Gouriswar Bhattacharya, 'A Dated Avalokiteśvara Image of the Devapāla Period', in Natasha Eilenberg, M. C. Subhadradis Diskul and Robert L. Brown (eds), *Living A Life In Accord With Dharma: Papers In Honor Of Professor Jean Boisselier On His Eightieth Birthday*, Bangkok: Silpakorn University, 1997, p. 88; *kumbhakāra* (*kumhāra*, *kumhārī*): Nalanda votive inscription of the time of Devapāla, Hirananda Sastri, *Nalanda and Its Epigraphic Material*, New Delhi: Archaeological Survey of India, 1999 (reprint), p. 88; *carmakāra*: Gaya Museum image inscription of the time of Śūrapāla, year 12, Susan L. Huntington, *The "Pāla-Sena" Schools of Sculpture*, Leiden: E. J. Brill, 1984, p. 211, No. 16a; *suvarṇakāra*: Kurkihar image inscription of the time of Mahīpāla I, year 31, Gupta, *Patna Museum Catalogue*, p. 149, no. 133, Indian Museum image inscription of the time of Vigrahapāla III, year 13, Banerji, 'The Pālas of Bengal', p. 112; *śauṇḍika*: Naulagarh image inscription of the time of Vigrahapāla III, year 24, D. C. Sircar, 'Some Inscriptions from Bihar', *Journal of the Bihar Research Society*, 1951, 37(3–4): 4.

322 This section was earlier published as Ryosuke Furui, 'Characteristics of Kaivarta Rebellion Delineated from the *Rāmacarita*', *Proceedings of Indian History Congress*, 75, 2015, pp. 93–98.
323 *Rāmacarita*, 1. 31, commentary.
324 *Ibid.*, 1. 38, commentary.
325 *Ibid.*, 1. 29, commentary.
326 *Ibid.*, 1. 38–39.
327 *Ibid.*, 1. 43–45.
328 *Ibid.*, 2. 5–6, commentary. For their identification, see Chowdhury, *Dynastic History of Bengal*, pp. 117–20.
329 *Rāmacarita*, 1. 43, commentary.
330 *Ibid.*, 1. 45.
331 *Ibid.*, 2. 8, commentary.
332 *Ibid.*, 1. 46–50.
333 *Ibid.*, 1. 48.
334 *Ibid.*, commentary.
335 *Ibid.*, 1. 43, commentary.
336 *Ibid.*, 2. 5–7 and commentary.
337 *Ibid.*, 2. 8 and commentary.
338 *Ibid.*, 2. 10–11.
339 *Ibid.*, 2. 13–19.
340 *Ibid.*, 2. 23–27.
341 *Ibid.*, 2. 36–37.
342 *Ibid.*, 2. 37–38.
343 *Ibid.*, 2. 39–41.
344 *Ibid.*, 2. 42–43.
345 *Ibid.*, 2. 45–49.
346 *kāsaravāhanakavalakṣiptamahāśarakalāpam*, *ibid*, 2. 42.
347 *Ibid.*, 2. 40.
348 *Ibid.*, 2. 24–25.
349 Supra.
350 *Rāmacarita*, 3. 27.
351 *Ibid.*, 4. 23.
352 Supra.
353 Furui, '*Brāhmaṇa*s in Early Medieval Bengal: Construction', pp. 230–31.
354 Supra.
355 Furui, 'Rajibpur Copperplate', p. 58.
356 *anīkaṃ dharmaviplavaṃ*, *Rāmacarita*, 1. 24.
357 *mahādraviṇaveṣṭitapratiṣṭhā*, *ibid.*, 3. 32.
358 *Ibid.*, 4. 1–2.
359 *Ibid.*, 3. 46–47.

6

TOWARDS BRAHMANICAL SYSTEMATISATION

c. 1100–1250 AD

From the last quarter of the 11th century, Bengal witnessed the rise of the dynasties originating from the other regions with the strong inclination to Brahmanical traditions, while the Pāla control was steadily declining after the reign of Rāmapāla. Among those dynasties, the Varmans, who may have originated from Kaliṅga, established their stronghold in Vaṅga after the Candras for a short period from c. 1080 to 1150 AD.[1] The Senas, who originated from Karṇāta, first established their position as a *sāmanta* of the Pālas in Rāḍha. They expanded their territory to Vaṅga and a part of Varendra in the reign of Vijayasena assignable to the period between 1096 and 1159 AD. They integrated almost all the sub-regions of Bengal by ousting the Pālas from Varendra sometime after 1165 AD,[2] though just for a short period before losing their western and northern territories to the Turkish army led by Muhammad Bakhtiyār Khaljī at the beginning of the 13th century. The Senas continued their rule in Vaṅga until the middle of the same century,[3] while several royal lineages showed their presence in Samataṭa and Śrīhaṭṭa in the 13th century. Dāmodaradeva ruled Samataṭa in the second quarter of the same century and Daśarathadeva, his son, extended their power to Vaṅga after the decline of the Senas.[4] Keśavadeva and Īśānadeva of the other lineage were the contemporary rulers of Śrīhaṭṭa.[5]

In this period, *brāhmaṇa*s enhanced their presence as a dominant group in rural society, as a result of their network building and the royal patronage, especially of the Senas. Under their stronger influence, the tendencies witnessed in the previous period, namely, the enhanced power of the political and religious authorities over rural society, the agrarian development with stratified land relation and commercialisation of rural economy, and the two forms of social reorganisation took another turn. In this chapter, I will discuss these historical changes and their culmination, that is, an attempt at social reorientation and systematisation based on the Brahmanical view represented by the texts like *Dharmanibandha*s and local *Purāṇa*s. The first to discuss is the further efforts of political powers to enhance their local control.

Efforts towards enhanced control

The reorganisation of the Pāla administration in Varendra after the *Kaivarta* rebellion is discernible in some verses of the *Rāmacarita* and its contemporary commentary. The confusion of land ownership due to the encroachment upon the landholdings of religious institutions and *brāhmaṇa*s by the rebel *sāmanta*s required its ascertainment after the recovery of the territory.[6] Rāmapāla also had to reorganise *viṣaya*s and appease his subjects by moderate taxation.[7]

The continued effort of the Pāla kings in keeping local control through the assessment of production is attested by the Rajibpur plate of Gopāla IV and Madanapāla dated year 2, and the Manahali and Rajibpur grants of Madanapāla dated years 8 and 22 respectively, all of which record the donations of villages in an administrative unit called Halāvartamaṇḍala in Koṭīvarṣaviṣaya of Puṇḍravardhanabhukti to individual *brāhmaṇas*.[8] In these plates, the donated tracts are respectively estimated 300, 320 and 300, presumably in the currency unit of *purāṇa*.[9] The 'standard of ploughed land and house' (*kṛtahalakulapramāṇa*), by which the production of the village donated in the first Rajibpur grant was estimated, suggests the assessment of production based on the size of cultivated tracts and the number of households.

The administrative reorganisation by the Pāla kings in the last phase of their rule is also discernible in those inscriptions. What to note is the reference to granary (*koṣṭhāgāra*) in the last two grants. In the second Rajibpur plate, the donated tracts are said to belong to the southern neighbourhood (*dakṣiṇāvadhi*) attached to the granary of Devīkoṭa.[10] 'Attached' (*pratibaddha*) in this description seems to indicate a fiscal arrangement by which revenue from the area called southern neighbourhood was assigned to the granary of Devīkoṭa, the city identical with Koṭīvarṣa.[11] A similar expression is also found in the Manahali grant, in which the donated land or village is said to belong to a granary.[12] Such descriptions absent in the first Rajibpur plate or any of the earlier Pāla grants point to a new fiscal arrangement adopted by Madanapāla to tighten the control over his territory, which was shrinking in front of the parallel kingship of Gopāla IV, who then ruled some parts of Varendra and eastern Bihar, and the growing power of the Senas.[13] Such efforts to consolidate the remaining territory are also noticeable in the exclusion of the royal estates (*rājasambhoga*), including enclosed land (*vṛti*) of the Buddhist establishment (*ratnatraya*), *kaivarta*s and *carmakāra*s, from the donated tracts in the same inscriptions.[14]

In spite of their efforts, the distress of the Pāla kings remained in the reign of Madanapāla, who continued the policy of reconciliation and sought the alliance with an unnamed king due to confusion in the villages.[15] Furthermore, the Pāla rule in Bengal was declining in front of rising *sāmanta*s, whose power was enhanced by the heavy dependence of the Pālas on them in the repression of the *Kaivarta* rebellion.[16] The dependence continued in the aftermath of the rebellion. Rāmapāla was helped by a subordinate ruler called *aśvapati* in a battle and served by another in conquering Kāmarūpa and the other areas.[17] The unchanged importance of the Rāṣṭrakūṭas of Aṅga for the Pāla kings is pronounced in the extensive depiction of *maṇḍalādhipati* Candradeva, the son of Suvarṇadeva, and his association with Madanapāla in the *Rāmacarita*.[18] The heavy dependence of Madanapāla on *sāndhivigrahika* Bhīmadeva, the messenger of the two Rajibpur grants and the Manahali plate,[19] is evident in the Rajghat stone inscription of the latter. It says that Maṅgadeva was *mahāsāndhivigrahika* of the Gauḍa king and that his son Caṃgadeva gained the position of *rāṇaka*.[20] Bhīmadeva, son of the latter, also became *mahāsāndhivigrahaka* of the Gauḍa king and is said to have supported the kingdom of Gauḍa-Varendra which moved like a sinking ship in the ocean of enemy troops.[21]

In proportion to the weakening of the Pāla control, *sāmanta*s became more autonomous and even independent. The Chaprakot stone inscription records autonomous deeds of a *sāmanta* family under the later Pāla kings from Vigarahapāla III to Gopāla IV, including the establishment of a *mahāvihāra* at Kuṭumvavilla.[22] In the reign of Kumārapāla, Kāmarūpa was ruled by a subordinate ruler called Tiṃgyadeva.[23] As he showed a rebellious tendency, Vaidyadeva, another subordinate ruler born to a lineage of hereditary ministers, who served the king as a minister and won a naval battle in southern Vaṅga,[24] was sent against Tiṃgyadeva and appointed to the ruler of Kāmarūpa after defeating him.[25] Then Vaidyadeva himself became an independent king as attested by the issue of his own grant and the titles of *mahārājādhirāja*, *parameśvara* and *paramabhaṭṭāraka* wielded by him.[26] More decisive was the case of the Senas. Vijayasena is identified with Vijayarāja of Nidrāvalī, one of the *sāmanta*s who helped Rāmapāla in his reconquest of Varendra.[27] His acquisition of land by helping Rāmapāla in recovery of Varendra is alluded to in the Deopara stone inscription.[28] As evident from the presence of this inscription, which records the construction of a temple complex by him, in present Rajshahi district,[29] Vijayasena expanded his territory to the southern part of Varendra at the cost of the Pālas. He claimed the sovereign status for himself with titles of *parameśvara*, *paramabhaṭṭāraka* and *mahārājādhirāja*, as shown in his Barrackpur grant.[30] The Senas finally finished the Pāla rule in Varendra sometime after 1165 AD as mentioned above. The efforts of the Pāla kings to enhance their local control and consolidate their territory did not bear fruit in the changed balance of power between them and their *sāmanta*s.

A glimpse of the Varman rule in Vaṅga is obtainable from the three grants and one stone inscription so far discovered in eastern Bengal.[31] The extensive privileges conferred on the donees by the grants, comparable with those in the Pāla and Candra ones, suggest the enhanced state control in rural society.[32] The enhancement of control is also discernible in the address of these grants consisting of the four categories in the same way as that of the Candra plates. The number of royal subordinates listed in the address increased from 19 in the Samantasar grant of Harivarman, datable to the end of the 11th century or the first half of the 12th century, to 27 in that of Bhojavarman belonging to the mid-12th century, suggesting more strengthened presence of state administrative apparatus (**Table 6.1**). With *mahāsarvādhikṛta* and *śaulkika* subtracted and *mahāmudrādhikṛta*, *daṇḍapāśika* and *daṇḍanāyaka* added, the former list is similar to that of the Mainamati plate of Laḍahacandra, which includes 18 titles and offices (**Tables 5.2 c, 6.1 a**). The latter list shows a close affinity with that of the Barrackpur plate of Vijayasena, which contains 25 officials excluding *pīṭhikāvitta* and *mahābhogika* (**Tables 6.1 b, 6.2 a**). The similarity in the first case indicates the inheritance of administrative apparatus of the preceding dynasty by the Varmans, while that in the second shows their efforts towards consolidation of local control, which would be realised under the Senas.

On the other hand, a stone inscription of the time of Bhojavarman from Sujanagar, Munshiganj district of Bangladesh shows presence and activity of a subordinate ruler under the Varman rule. It records a donation made by *mahāsāmanta* Avūdeva, the son of *pāñcakulika* Hāsī.[33] The donation seems to have been necessitated by the withdrawal of capital in cash deposited to conch-shell workers, of which interest was supposed to be assigned to a religious agent. The withdrawal was made with the assent of all the

Table 6.1 Addresses in the Varman grants

a. Samantasar CPI of Harivarman (N. K. Bhattasali, 'Two Grants of Varmans of Vanga', *Epigraphia Indica*, 30, 1953–54 (1987), 30: 257–58, 2. 3–8.)

-All the royal officials/dependants of the king (19): *rājñī*, *rāṇaka*, *rājaputra*, *rājāmātya*, *mahāvyūhapati*, *maṇḍalapati*, *mahāsāndhivigrahika*, *mahāsenāpati*, *mahākṣapaṭalika*, *mahāmudrādhikṛtya*, *mahāpratīhāra*, *koṭṭapāla*, *dauḥsādhasādhanika*, *cauroddharaṇika*, *naubalahastyaśvagomahiṣājāvikādivyāpṛtaka*, *gaulmika*, *daṇḍapāśika*, *daṇḍanāyaka*, *viṣayapati* etc. and others.
-(Those) declared of the position as officials, unnamed here (*adhyakṣapracāroktān ihākīrttitān*).
-anyāṃś ca ācaṭṭabhaṭṭajātīyān.
-janapadān kṣetrakarāṃś ca brāhmaṇottarān.

b. Belava CPI of Bhojavarman, year 5 (*IB*, pp. 20–21, ll. 29–36.)

-All the dependants of the king (27): *rāja*, *rājanyaka*, *rājñī*, *rāṇaka*, *rājaputra*, *rājāmātya*, *purohita*, *pīṭhikāvitta*, *mahādharmādhyakṣa*, *mahāsāndhivigrahika*, *mahāsenāpati*, *mahāmudrādhikṛta*, *antaraṅga*, *bṛhaduparika*, *mahākṣapaṭalika*, *mahāpratīhāra*, *mahābhogika*, *mahāvyūhapati*, *mahāpīlupati*, *mahāgaṇastha*, *daussādhika*, *cauroddharaṇika*, *naubalahastyaśvagomahiṣājāvikādivyāpṛtaka*, *gaulmika*, *daṇḍapāśika*, *daṇḍanāyaka*, *viṣayapati* etc. and others.
-(Those) declared of the position as officials, unnamed here.
-caṭṭabhaṭṭajātīyān.
-janapadān kṣetrakarāṃś ca brāhmaṇān brāhmaṇottarān.

Table 6.2 Addresses in the Sena grants

a. Barrackpur CPI of Vijayasena, year 62 (*IB*, p. 63, ll. 25–30.)

-All the dependants of the king (25) *rāja, rājanyaka, rajñī, rāṇaka, rājaputra, rājāmātya, purohita, mahādharmādhyakṣa, mahāsāndhivigrahika, mahāsenāpati, mahāmudrādhikṛta, antaraṅga, bṛhaduparika, mahākṣapaṭalika, mahāpratīhāra, mahāvyūhapati, mahāpīlupati, mahāgaṇastha, dauḥsādhika, cauroddharaṇika, naubalahastyaśvagomahiṣājāvikādivyāpṛtaka, gaulmika, daṇḍapāśika, daṇḍanāyaka, viṣayapati* etc. and others.
-*(a)dhyakṣapracāroktān ihākīrttitāna.*
-*caṭṭabhaṭṭajātīyāna.*
-*janapadān kṣetrakarāṃś ca brāhmaṇāna brā[(hma)ṇottarān.*

b. Saktipur CPI of Lakṣmaṇasena, year 6 (Dhirendra Chandra Ganguly, 'Saktipur Copper-Plate of Lakshmanasena', *Epigraphia Indica*, 1931–32 (1984), 21: 217–18, ll. 19–24.)

-All the dependants of the king (25) *rāja, rājanyaka, rajñī, rāṇaka, rājaputra, rājāmātya, mahāpurohita, mahādharmādhyakṣa, mahāsāndhivigrahika, mahāsenāpati, mahāmudrādhikṛta, antaraṅga, bṛhaduparika, mahākṣapaṭalika, mahāpratīhāra, mahābhogika, mahāpīlupati, mahāgaṇastha, dauḥsādhika, cauroddharaṇika, naubalahastyaśvagomahiṣājāvikādivyāpṛtaka, gaulmika, daṇḍapāśika, daṇḍanāyaka, viṣa(ya)patyādīn anyāṃś ca.*
-*(a)dhyakṣapracāroktān ihākīrttitān.*
-*caṭṭabhaṭṭajātīyān.*
-*kṣetrakarāṃś ca brāhmaṇān brāhmaṇottarān.*

c. Madanapada CPI of Viśvarūpasena, year 14 (D. C. Sircar, 'Madanapada Plate of Visvarupasena', *Epigraphia Indica*, 1959–60 (1987), 33: 324, ll. 38–41.)

-All the dependants of the king (17) *rāja, rājanyaka, rājñī, rāṇaka, rājaputra, rājāmātya, mahāpurohita, mahādharmādhyakṣa, mahāsāndhivigrahika, mahāsenāpati, dauḥsādhika, cauroddharaṇika, naubalahastyaśvagomahiṣājāvikādivyāpṛta, gaulmika, daṇḍapāśika, daṇḍanāyaka, viṣayapatyādīn anyāṃś ca.*
-*(a)dhyakṣapravarān.*
-*caṭṭabhaṭṭajātīyān.*
-*brāhmaṇān brāhmaṇottarāṃś ca.*

kinsmen belonging to the other countries,[34] suggesting their contribution to the original capital. Hāsī, the father of Avūdeva, was *pāñcakulika*, a leader or a member of *pañcakula* which denotes an urban administrative organisation in charge of documentary works and custom house (*maṇḍapikā*), mainly consisting of urban influential people in the early medieval western India.[35] As implied by the monetary contribution by kinsmen dispersed in abroad, possibly constituting a network, and the position of his father as an urban elite, Avūdeva could have belonged to a merchant family and been given a position of *mahāsāmanta* by the Varman king. He at least held right to levy tax on a market (*haṭṭa*) as his own *bhoga* (enjoyment) of *mahāsāmanta*,[36] which was donated instead of withdrawn capital. On the other hand, the administration by *adhikṛta* Jīvasena mentioned in reference to the time of donation,[37] side by side with the date and reign of the king, alludes to the incorporation of a territory of *sāmanta*s in an administrative unit governed by an official appointed by the king and also to some form of control imposed on the *sāmanta*s under his jurisdiction. It corresponds with the tendency towards stronger local control detected in the Varman grants discussed above.

The copper plate inscriptions of the Senas show their firm intention and effort to enhance their control over rural society. The fiscal arrangement similar to that found in the last phase of the Pāla rule is discernible in the Saktipur grant of Lakṣmaṇasena, in which Rāghavahaṭṭapāṭaka, one of the donated hamlets, is said to have been detached from Madhugirimaṇḍala and attached to Kumbhīnagara.[38] More important, however, were their attempt and failure to implement a uniform standard of land measurement in the different sub-regions of Bengal under their control.

In the Barrackpur grant of Vijayasena, the donated tract measures 4 *pāṭaka*s by a *nala* of Samaṭata (Samataṭīyanala).[39] The plate was discovered from a village nearby Barrackpur cantonment in 24 Parganas, and Khāḍīviṣaya, to which the concerned village belonged, can be located in the Diamond Harbour sub-division of this modern administrative unit.[40] This locality could not have belonged to Samataṭa. Though Chitrarekha Gupta suggests that this standard could have been used in the deltaic parts of Bengal during the time of the Candras,[41] no Candra grants mention such a standard, and their territorial expansion towards the present 24 Parganas area also lacks any substantial evidence. In the present condition of evidence, the introduction of the standard of Samataṭa had better be attributed to Vijayasena, as his Barrackpur grant is so far the first record mentioning it. The application of the standard of land measurement prevalent in one sub-region to the other attests to the intention of Vijayasena to implement a uniform standard all over his territory.

The attempt of Vijayasena and its inheritance by the following kings are discernible in a standard named Vṛṣabhaśaṅkaranala used in the grants of Vallālasena and Lakṣmaṇasena. Vṛṣabhaśaṅkara or Arivṛṣabhaśaṅkara was an epithet of Vijayasena, as evident from a verse in the Barrakpur grant which mentions the king by this name in describing his nomination of a messenger.[42] The introduction of this standard can be attributed to Vijayasena, after whom it was named, though it is unclear whether the standard was identical with Samataṭīyanala and came to be known by this name in his reign or later.[43] Vṛṣabhaśaṅkaranala appears in the Naihati grant of Vallālasena and the Anulia and Saktipur plates of Lakṣmaṇasena.[44] The first and last inscriptions pertain to Uttara Rāḍha, which first belonged to Vardhamānabhukti and then to Kaṅkagrāmabhukti,[45] and the second to Vyāghrataṭī of Pauṇḍravardhanabhukti.[46] The former corresponds to the area west to the Bhagirathi and north to the Ajay.[47] If Vyāghrataṭī mentioned in the Anulia grant was identical with Vyāghrataṭīmaṇḍala, the territory of subordinate rulers of the Pālas mentioned in the Khalimpur plate of Dharmapāla and the Nalanda grant of Devapāla,[48] it can be located somewhere in North Bengal, though the plate was discovered in Nadia district of West Bengal.[49] As Rāḍha is mentioned as the territory of the early Sena rulers in the Naihati grant,[50] it is probable that the Senas tried to apply a uniform standard first in their old territory and then to impose it on a part of North Bengal to which they started to extend their power during the reign of Vijayasena.

The incompleteness or failure in applying a uniform standard is, however, suggested by the simultaneous use of diverse standards of land measurement in the other grants of Lakṣmaṇasena. In the Govindapur plate dated year 2, which pertained to Veṭaḍḍacaturaka of Paścimakhāṭikā in Vardhamānabhukti, identifiable with present Biral-Dhamnagar in Gobindapur *thana* of Howrah district,[51] land was assessed by a *nala* measured by 56 cubits (*hastas*), which was a practice of the locality.[52] Similarly, land was measured by a '*nala* which was custom of this country' in the Tarpandighi grant of year 2, which was related to Varendrī of Pauṇḍravardhanabhukti.[53] The phrases used in these plates show the prevalence of local customs on the standards of land measurement. In the Dighirpar-Bakultala plate dated year 2, the land is calculated by a unit of *unmāna* measured by 32 cubits, which is in turn measured by a cubit added with 12 finger-breadths marked by the pillar of the deity Ugramādhava.[54] The standard of land measurement was fixed against a pillar belonging to a local deity, endorsing the local character of such a standard. The relevant part in the Rajavadi plate dated year 27, which pertains to the area corresponding to present Sripur *upazila* of Gazipur district in Bangladesh,[55] mentions a *nala* measured by 22 cubits as a standard of land measurement.[56]

These cases surely show that the different types of *nalas* were used for measuring land in different parts of the Sena dominion.[57] However, the contrast between Vṛṣabhaśaṅkaranala, which had connection with the Sena kingship, and the other *nalas* related to local customs alludes not only to the coexistence of various local standards of land measurement but also to the intention and failure of the Senas to impose a uniform standard and supplant the local ones. The difficulty of imposition is indicated by the use of different standards even in the same area where Vijayasena introduced Samataṭīyanala and in its vicinity, as indicated by the cases of the Barrackpur and Dighirpar-Bakultala plates, both pertaining to Khāḍīviṣaya/-maṇḍala, and of the Govindapur plate related to the neighbouring area. The abandonment of the effort of standardisation is detectable in the absence of any references to the standards of land measurement in the Madhainagar plate of Lakṣmaṇasena and the Madhyapada grant of Viśvarūpasena.[58] In the Idilpur and Madanapada plates of the latter, even size of land plots is not mentioned.[59]

Compared with the failed imposition of a uniform standard of land measurement, the assessment of annual production of settlements or land plots in a uniform currency unit was thoroughly applied by the Sena kings. It provided them with leverage for enhancing their control over rural society.

A unit of currency named *kapardakapurāṇa* was used for estimating production of particular villages or land plots in the Sena grants. In the Barrackpur grant of Vijayasena, 4 *pāṭaka*s of land plot in Bhāṭṭavaḍāgrāma is said to be production of 200 *kapardakapurāṇas*.[60] Similar descriptions in the Naihati plate of Vallālasena and the Tarpandighi, Anulia, Rajavadi and Madhainagar grants of Lakṣmaṇasena with words *pratyabdaṃ*, *vatsareṇa* and *samvatsareṇa* show that what is calculated in this currency unit is annual production.[61] The unit mentioned as *purāṇa* in the Govindapur and Dighirpar-Bakultala plates of the last king and the unspecified unit in his Saktipur grant most probably indicate the same, in view of the similarity in phrases.[62] In the Govindapur grant, the rate of 15 *purāṇa*s per *droṇa* is also provided as the basis of calculation.[63] Similarly, the rates of *hiraṇya* per *udāna* of homestead and cultivated land are given by abbreviations for the two plots in the Madhyapada plate.[64]

Kapardakapurāṇa seems to denote a theoretical unit of account representing the value of a *purāṇa*, a unit of silver currency, counted in cowrie-shells.[65] *Purāṇa* and *cūrṇī* synonymously used in the grants of Viśvarūpasena, especially in his Madanapada grant, also seem to denote the same unit, while *hiraṇya* and its abbreviated form *hi* used side by side with them represents cash counted in it.[66] As discussed above, the use of such a notional unit of currency was known in the earlier period in Varendra under the Pāla rule, against the background of maritime trade which brought cowrie-shells to Bengal and of commercialisation of rural economy.[67] Its use in the other subregions of Bengal indicates the progress in spread of monetary transactions and commercialisation of rural economy, to be discussed below.

The use of currency unit enabled the Sena kings to assess the quantum of production from rural settlements by a common unit regardless of the local difference in standards of land measurement, and to keep information and control over revenue from them. The Saktipur grant recording the donation of six hamlets (*pāṭaka*s) to *brāhmaṇa* Kuvera shows the efficacy of this system. The six hamlets measured 89 *droṇa*s in total by Vṛṣabhaśaṅkaranala and the annual income from them was estimated to be 500, probably in *kapardakapurāṇa*.[68] It is said that those were given in exchange for the donated tract named Kṣatrapāṭaka with production of 500 received by *gayālabrāhmaṇa* Haridāsa from Vallālasena.[69] This description suggests the following sequence of events: first, the land with production of 500, previously given to Haridāsa by Vallālasena, was mistakenly donated to Kuvera. Informed of this fact, probably by Haridāsa, Lakṣmaṇasena gave another land with the same value in production to Kuvera in the form of the six hamlets in the two neighbouring clusters.[70] Such an arrangement was possible only through the estimation of the value in a common unit. The *kapardakapurāṇa* functioned as such a unit and the assessment of annual production in it enabled the Senas to overcome the difference in standards of land measurement.[71]

While the Sena grants show the tendency towards the enhanced local control by the kingship and its administrative apparatus, the presence and activity of *sāmanta*s are less visible in these documents. The titles denoting them like *rāja*, *rājanyaka*, *rāṇaka* and *rājaputra* are included in the address of the grants (**Table 6.2**). However, their appearance is limited to that of holders of landed property, or more precisely, of tenure in the stratified land relation to be discussed below. In the Madhyapada plate of Viśvarūpasena, *sāndhivigrahika* Nāñīsiṃha donated the superior right over a particular land plot to a *brāhmaṇa* donee who had purchased inferior right on the same plot from a group of people.[72] The members of royal household like princes Sūryasena and Puruṣottamasena also appeared side by side with him as the donors of the superior right in the same grant.[73] Those tenures seem to have been assigned to them by the king in view of the case recorded in the Madanapada grant, in which king Viśvarūpasena donated a land plot 'belonging to (king's) own dependant,'[74] indicating the reassignment of tenure from one holder to another by the king.

Some aspects of those assignees and their tenures are revealed by the cases related to Vilāsadevī, the chief queen of Vijayasena and the mother of Vallālasena. She performed the rituals of *kanakatulāpuruṣamahādāna* and *hemāśvamahādāna*, according to the Barrackpur and Naihati grants which record donations of a land plot and a village to *brāhmaṇa*s as rewards for their services.[75] In the second plate, it is clearly stated that the village was first given (*utsṛṣṭa*) by her and then donated (*pradatta*) by the king after making a copper plate grant.[76] The last verse of the royal eulogy also endorses this fact.[77] Thus Vilāsadevī seems to have provided for not only the cost of ritual but also the reward for an officiating *brāhmaṇa* from her own assigned landed property, and the king upgraded the donated tract to a revenue-free *śāsana* village. The donation in the Barrackpur plate which king Vijayasena 'caused her to give' can also be understood in the same manner.[78] It should be noted, on the other hand, that the land plot donated in the last grant, presumably assigned to Vilāsadevī, was located in village Bhāṭṭavaḍāgrāma, an estate (*sambhoga*) of Ghāsa who seems to have been a subordinate of the king.[79] Similarly, the plots donated by Sūryasena and Nāñīsiṃha in the Madhyapada plate belonged to Deūlahastī, a single village where the land established by the king on both eastern and western sides of a river was also present.[80] Those cases suggest that the superior land rights assigned to members of the royal household and subordinates were created over land plots scattered around plural settlements where the plots assigned to different tenure holders existed side by side. The subordinate rulers like Nāñīsiṃha, who depended on such scattered land assignments, could not compare with their counterparts in the previous period, who held consolidated territories and negotiated with the kingship.[81] This fact is also endorsed by the absence of the eulogy of *sāmanta*s in any royal grants or inscriptions, unlike those in the earlier period which include their genealogies.[82]

However, there could still have been subordinate rulers with own territories in some parts of the Sena domain. This possibility is indicated by an exceptional case of a *sāmanta* who showed an open defiance by issuing his own copper plate grant. The Rakshaskhali grant was issued by Ḍommaṇapāla, who was the son of a *mahāmāṇḍalika* and wielded the titles including '*sāmanta* hostile to *mahārājādhirāja*' (*mahārājādhirājavipakṣasāmanta*).[83] As this inscription is dated year 1118 SE (1196 AD), the concerned *mahārājādhirāja* must have been Lakṣmaṇasena. The case recorded in this grant pertained to the area named Pūrvakhāṭikā, which is said to have been acquired by the Pāla lineage originating from Ayodhyā.[84] It is locatable to the east side of the Bhagirathi, adjacent to Paścimakhāṭikā mentioned in the Govindapur plate of Lakṣmaṇasena as his territory.[85] Unlike the last inscription, the Rakshaskhali grant has no reference to land assessment, suggesting that the system of assessment was not introduced in the hereditary territory of this *sāmanta* lineage. It should also be noted that the donee of the grant was *mahārāṇaka* Vāsudevaśarman, a *brāhmaṇa* with the position of a subordinate ruler who was given a village excluding land of the Buddhist establishment (*triratna*) as a gift for friend (*mitradāna*).[86] The latter seems to have succeeded in extending his territory using his position as a *brāhmaṇa*. This case, in which a *sāmanta* showed a defiance and his subordinate ruler exercised the own agency, both with exceptional visibility, paradoxically proves how well the Senas could keep their subordinates under control in the areas where they imposed the system of land assessment as discussed above.

The political powers of Samataṭa and Śrīhaṭṭa present in the 13th century are known from their copper plate grants. *Mahāśvanibandhika* Dadhieva issued his own grant dated year 1141 SE (1220 AD) to donate a land plot to Durgottārāvihārī established in Paṭṭikeranagarī.[87] He seems to have ruled the area around present Lalmai hill as a subordinate ruler of Raṇavaṅkamalla Harikāladeva, who is described as his master and whose regnal era is used in the plate.[88] The issue of his own grant indicates the status of Dadhieva as a semi-independent ruler.

More concrete evidence is available for the rule of Dāmodaradeva in Samataṭa by his grants recording land donations to *brāhmaṇas*. The well defined administrative hierarchy with four layers of units consisting of *bhukṭi*, *maṇḍala*, *viṣaya* and *khaṇḍala* is discernible in his Mehar and Sobharampur plates, dated years 1156 and 1158 SE (1234 and 1236 AD) respectively.[89] However, the address only available for the Mehar grant lists no royal subordinates or officials but prominent *janapada*s and *mahattara*s residing in Mehāragrāma.[90] It indicates the relatively weak power of the kingship which had to depend on the prominent section of rural population for its control over rural society. The same plate, on the other hand, shows the efforts of Dāmodaradeva towards enhanced control. It mentions type and number of mound (*ṭīkara*), size in *droṇa* and production in a currency unit of *purāṇa/hiraṇya* for each of 20 donated land plots, attesting to the practice of land assessment like the preceding Sena rule (**Table 6.3**).

Table 6.3 Donees and land plots in Mehar CPI of Dāmodaradeva (*SI* 2, pp. 142–43, ll. 17–32)

No.	*Donee*	*Type of mound*	*Number of ṭī*	*Type of land*	*Homestead*	*Cultivated land*	*hiraṇya*
1	Sāvarṇya-sagotra *paṃ* śrī-Kāpaḍīka	*gṛha-vāṭik-ādi-ṭī* with income of 25 *purāṇas*	3	*vyā-bhū*	1/2		25
2	*vrā* śrī-Śāṅkoka	*ca-ṭī*, income of 5 *pu*	1	*vyā-bhū*		1/8	5
3	*vrā* śrī-Sudoka	*ca-ṭī*	1	*vyā-bhū*		3/16	8
4	*vrā* Kālemīka	*ṭī*	1	*vyā-bhū*	1/8		4
5	*vrā* Tārāpati	*ca-ṭī*	1	*vyā-bhū*		9/64	4 1/2
6	Bharadvāja-sagotra *paṃ* śrī-Pāṇḍoka	*gṛ-ṭī*	1	*vyā-bhū*	13/64		10 1/8
7	*vrā* śrī-Deḍaka	*gṛha-ṭī*	1	*vyā-bhū*	9/64		4
8	*vrā* śrī-Sudoka	*gṛha-ṭī*	1	*vyā-bhū*	1/4		8 7/16
9	Kāṇṭāmaṇīya *vrā* śrī-Keśava	*gṛ-ṭī*	1	*vyā-bhū*	1/8		4 7/8
		mu-ṭī	1	*vyā-bhū*	5/64		9/16
10	*vrā* śrī-Vrahmoka	*gṛ-ṭī*	1	*vyā-bhū*	3/16		2
		mu-ṭī	1	*vyā-bhū*	1/8		1 1/4
				nā-bhū		1/2	2
11	*vrā* śrī-Siroka	*gṛha-ṭī*	1	*vyā-bhū*	9/64		5 3/4
12	Pūrvagrāmīya *vrā* śrī-Dharaṇika	Guṇombh-ārddha-*ca-ṭī*	1	*vyā-bhū*		3/32	2 1/2
13	Sidhalagrāmīya *paṃ* śrī-Pāuka	*ca-ṭī*	1	*vyā-bhū*		1/4	4
14	Ātreya-gotra *vrā* śrī-Śāṅkoka			*nā-bhū*		1/4	1 1/4
15	Diṇḍisāyīya *vrā* śrī-Prajāpati			*gṛha- vāṭyāṃ bhū*	1/16		3 1/4
16	*gṛhi-paṃ* śrī-Nāthoka			*nā-bhū*		5/16	1 1/4
	grā-hi of *vrā* śrī-Jaloka (excluded)						-1 1/8
17	*vrā* śrī-Viśvarūpa	*gṛ-ṭī*	1	*vyā-bhū*	9/64		3 3/8
18	*vrā* śrī-Mādhoka	*ci-khi-mu-ṭī*	1	*vyā-bhū*	1/4		
19	Keśarakoṇīya *vrā* śrī-Śṛpati	*śāsana-ca-ṭī* made by *mahāsāndhivigrahika* śrī-Munidāsa	1	*vyā-bhū*		3/16	
20	*vrā* śrī-Śṛvatsa	*śāsana-gṛ-ca-ṭī* made by *mahākṣapaṭalika* śrī-Dalaeva	1	*vyā-bhū*	5/16		
	Sum		21		2 41/64	2 3/64	100
	Sum in CPI		16		2 11/16	2	100

*Unit of area is *droṇa*. *Hiraṇya* indicates annual production

Abbreviations: *vrā* = *brāhmaṇa*; *ṭī* = *ṭikara* (mound); *gṛ-ṭī*, *gṛha-ṭī* = homestead mound; *ca-ṭī* = cultivated mound; *mu-ṭī* = uncultivated mound; *ci-khi*: *cira-khila*: barren for

The same practice seems to have been followed in Vaṅga under the rule of Daśarathadeva, the son of Dāmodaradeva, according to his Adavadi grant which is said to mention income from the land plots distributed to 15 *brāhmaṇa*s, about 500 *purāṇa*s in sum.[91] The execution of the practice was, however, not thorough or systematic. The Sobharampur and Nasirabad grants of Dāmodaradeva do not record production in currency unit, though the minute descriptions of border landmarks and the size of plots provided in them point to some forms of local assessment.[92] The Mainamati grant of Vīradharadeva, the other king who ruled an area of Samataṭa in the 13th century, also attests to the incompleteness of the implementation, as it does not refer to production or border landmarks of the donated tracts.[93]

The rule of the other Deva lineage in Śrīhaṭṭa is glimpsed from the Bhatera plates of Keśavadeva and his son Īśānadeva.[94] The grant of Keśavadeva records his donation of 375 of cultivated land plots (*bhūhala*) and 296 of gardens (*vāṭī*) in various villages, and also diverse attendants and *jāti*s of people in great number, to the deity Vaṭeśvara located in Bhaṭṭapāṭaka.[95] Notably, the grant lists the 64 properties including cultivated land plots (*bhūhala/hala*), gardens, 'land' (*bhūke*) of the other kind and various categories of houses (*gṛha*) as detailed contents of the donated objects, with their locations, in reference to border landmarks in some cases, and names of owners for houses (**Table 6.4**). Numerals given for each item, without any specification of unit, seem to denote size of land for *bhūhala/hala*, *vāṭī* and *bhūke*, and number of houses for *gṛha*. The minute information contained in this plate points to the assessment of the concerned area with attempt at better control.

Apart from the effort of local control through land assessment, the agency of subordinate rulers in administrative functions and donative acts is commonly observed in both sub-regions in this period. In all the three grants of Dāmodaradeva, subordinates are mentioned in the verses following the royal eulogy. Among them, Gautamadatta, the official in charge of the seal (*mudrādhikārin*) and minister (*saciva*) of the Sobharampur plate, was a petitioner of grant and so could be Gaṅgādharadeva, the chief of elephant troop of the Mehar plate.[96] Guṇadhara, the sole chief of all the ministers (*sarvāmātyaikamukhya*), acted as a conveyer of royal order in the Nasirabad plate.[97] The *śāsana* plots 'caused to make by' (*kārita*) *mahāsāndhivigrahika* Munidāsa and *mahākṣapaṭalika* Dalaeva are included in the donated tracts in the Mehar grant (**Table 6.3, nos 19, 20**). The Bhatera plate of Īśānadeva was issued to assure the royal grant which had been made on the petition of *ākṣapaṭalika* Vanamālikara of the lineage of *vaidya*, described as an elder sonless *rājaputra*, and to order the wife of this late *rājaputra* and a child installed as their son to protect the donated land plots.[98] The conveyer of the order was Vīradatta, the chief (*adhinātha*) of Pūtalā.[99] In the other Bhatera plate of Keśavadeva, Syahuṇa, one of the treasurers (*koṣṭhin*) who seemed to have confirmed the grant, is mentioned as *mahāsācūḍo*, which could be an abbreviation of *mahāsāmantacūḍāmaṇi*.[100] What is remarkable in these

Table 6.4 Land plots and houses in the Bhatera CPI of Keśavadeva (*CPS*, pp. 159–61, ll. 29–51, modified by readings from the photographs.)

No.	*Location*	*Bhūhala*	*Hala*	*Vāṭī*	*Bhūke*
1	Bhāṭapaḍā-devavandha	35 1/2		110	
2	Vaḍagāma	12			
3	Mahurāpura			1	
4	Iṭākhālāka	7		6	
5	N. of Degigāva	1			
6	Varapañcāla	5		4	
7	Āmatarīkha		2		
8	Sihaḍara			1	
9	Bhāmanāṭeṅgārika				6
10	Guḍāvayīka			2	
11	Kāṭāraha	2			
12	Ākhālikula		7		
13	Parākoṇāka			1	
14	Pithāyinagara	17		4	
15	Venūragāma			2	
16	Yoḍātithāka, prūtakara-saṃ		2	11	
17	Kaivāma		8	1	
18	Vāndesīgāma		5		
19	W. of Navahāṭī		2		
20	Śūghara		5	1	
21	Bhothilahāṭāka	5		8	
22	S. of Ka-udiyā, E. of Gosvayā, N. of Govaṭa, W. of Varuṇī	18			
23	S. of Savaśānadī	5		3	
24	N. of the same river (*tathānadyuttara*)	35		12	
25	N. of the same river, E. of Nāṭīvasta			1	
26	N. of the same river, W. of landing place (*ghaṭābhū*), S. of *garvarabhū*	7			
27	N. of Kāliyāṇīnadī, E. of Phomphāṇiyā	8 1/2		7	
28	S. of the same river, E. of Kharasontī, W. of Bhāskaraṭeṅgarī	45		81	
29	Jagāpāntara, two villages (*grāmadvaya*) of Nāṭayāna	5		20	
30	Salācāpaḍāka, E. of Mulīkāndhī, W. of Sāgara	10			
31	S. and N. of Kāliyāṇīnadī	8 1/2			
32	S. of Dhāmāyinadī	5		10	
33	N. of Bhogāḍabhurāḍaḍa	4		4	
34	W. of Nathośāsana, N. of *haṭṭavara*	7		10	
35	S. of Sātakopā, E. of Vaḍasoḍa		10		
36	Ceṅgaccuḍīka	2		1	

No.	Location	Bhūhala	Hala	Vāṭī	Bhūke
37	Āḍāgakāndhīka			8	4
38	Māṅgalapāvīka			8	
39	Meghāparāka			1	6
40	E. of Paṃsidho, N. of Āndhārī	80		1	
41	Onaḍakuṭīgāma			8	
42	The same *gāma*, N. of Thāmanadī			6	4
43	E. of Gosvayākhāta, N. of cattle track (*gopatha*), S. of Jūḍīgāṅga, W. of Elaṅgajoṭṭī, Karagāsana		5		
44	Dohāliyā ākhālichaḍāka	10			
45	E. of Vāsudevaśāsana	5			
46	S. of Vovācchaḍā, N. of Jogāvaniyā			1	
	Sum	339 1/2	46	334	20
	Sum mentioned in the grant	375		296	

No.	Location	Owner	Gṛha	Type
47	Bhāṭapaḍāka	Kedāk-ādi	10	*vāva*
48	The same place (*tathāka*)	Amṛtāk-ādi	1	*gopa*
49	Just the same place (*tathāke hi*)	Vaṭṭayāk-ādi	5	*te*
50	The same place (*tathāka*)	Kāsyagovindā	1	
51	Vaḍagāma	Gopasadā	1	*
52	The same place	Ārupānāk-ādi	7	*vāva*
53	Jogā uttārāni	Dhisākaśvaphya	8	*te*
54	Bhāṭapaḍā Iṭākhālāni	Kṛṣṇagaṭāk-ādi	7	
55	Bhāṭapaḍā Vavapañcāla Iṭākhālāni	Divākavāk-ādi	6	*mālā*
56	Bhāṭapaḍā	Simerāk-ādi	5	*go*
57	Bhāṭapaḍāni	*nāpita* Govindā	1	
58		*rajaka* Sirupā	1	
59	Vovācchaḍāni	Vaṃvāṭayipāk-ādi	5	
60	The same place (*tathāni*)	Dotthaveṭṭapāk-ādi	5	
61	Navahāṭīni	Dosyamāṭipāk-ādi	2	
62	Bhāṭapaḍāni	Vāndhapāk-ādi	2	*haddiya*
63	Pindāyinagara, Dyokha	Navikāk-ādi	2	
64	Siṃha-uragrāma	*dantavāra* Vajari	1	*gā* (*go*)
	Sum		70	

*Not mentioned as *gṛha*

cases is the active participation of subordinate rulers in the process of royal land grants, like their counterparts in the early phase of the Pāla rule.[101] The relatively weak state control over rural society, in spite of the effort to enhance it by assessment, seems to have created a room for subordinate rulers to exercise their agency latent under the stronger state control of the Candras in the previous period.[102]

Except eastern peripheries, the *sāmanta*s of this period kept their presence rather in a low key. In contrast, the other social group got prominent with the enhanced state control of rural society. It was *brāhmaṇa*s who were consolidating their position both at royal court and in rural society.

Establishment of Brahmanical authority

*Brāhmaṇa*s were establishing their authority at royal court and trying to consolidate their dominance in rural society, though the latter was a protracted and complicated process which would not see its completion within the period covered by the present study. At the court, the establishment of their authority took the form of the closer association of kingship with *brāhmaṇa*s and the adoption of particular Brahmanical norms by the former.

The highly qualified *brāhmaṇa*s continued to be the main recipients of land and village donations. In this period, however, rewarding their ritual service became a main reason for donations. The rituals performed by the kings with their service were *mahādāna*s and *śānti*s. Both the Rajibpur plates of Gopāla IV and Madanapāla record village grants as rewards (*dakṣiṇā*) for performing the ritual of *hemāśvamahādāna*, donation of a golden horse.[103] The Varman grants do not have any direct references to such rituals, but the donees of the Samantasar and Belava grants wield the titles of *śāntivārika* and *śāntyāgārādhikṛta* respectively.[104] The former appeared as a specialist of *śānti* in the previous period and latter also seems to be a priest in charge of it.[105] Their appearance as donees alludes to the performance of *mahāśānti*s by the Varman kings and the grant of land as a reward for the ritual service.

The Sena grants record donations occasioned by various Brahmanical rituals performed by the kings and members of the royal household. The Barrackpur grant of Vijayasena refers to the *kanakatulāpuruṣamahādāna*, distribution among *brāhmaṇa*s of gold which is weighed against a person, performed by chief queen Vilāsadevī, and to the land grant as a reward for *homa* performed in it.[106] The same queen is credited with the performance of *hemāśvamahādāna* in the Naihati grant of her son Vallālasena.[107] The Govindapur plate of Lakṣmaṇasena records a village grant at the time of coronation ceremony (*rājyābhiṣeka*),[108] while his Tarpandighi plate mentions a land grant as a reward on the occasion of *hemāśvarathamahādāna*, donation of a golden chariot with seven or four horses.[109] The Madhainagar plate of the same king seems to mention 'original coronation' (*mūlābhiṣeka*) and *aindrīmahāśānti* as the occasion of a village grant.[110] According to a passage in the *Adbhutasāgara* citing the *Matsyapurāṇa* (228. 20), the latter is a propitiatory rite prescribed in coronation ceremonies when invasion from an enemy circle is apprehended, when one's own territory is divided, and for killing one's enemy.[111] The case in the last plate could be the reworking of the original coronation ceremony with the performance of this propitiatory rite against the invasion and conquest of Nadia by the army of Muhammad Bakhtiyār Khaljī.[112] Adding to them, the plot donated to *śāntyāgārika* Kṛṣṇadharadevaśarman in the Dighirpar-Bakultala grant of Lakṣmaṇasena was bordered by two donated tracts (*śāsana*) and a sugarcane field (*gaḍolībhūmi*) held by the other *śāntyāgārika*s, showing the importance of specialists of *śānti* rituals acknowledged by the kings through land grants.[113]

The ritual service of *brāhmaṇa*s in *śānti*s arranged by the kings was known in the previous period.[114] However, the frequent mentions of their participations in *śānti*s and the other rituals in the royal grants show enhanced presence of *brāhmaṇa*s as ritual specialists at the court and their strengthened connection with the kingship.

*Brāhmaṇa*s also enhanced their presence at the court as an authority of *dharma*. The Varmans and the Senas are known for patronising eminent authors of the *Dharmanibandha*s. *Bhaṭṭa* Bhavadeva is known as the author of works like the *Prāyaścittaprakaraṇa* and the *Sambandhaviveka*.[115] His association with king Harivarman as a minister (*saciva*) is attested by the Bhubaneswar stone inscription.[116] Aniruddha is another *nibandhakāra* credited with the authorship of the *Hāralatā* and the *Pitṛdayitā*.[117] He held the position of *dharmādhyakṣa*[118] and was a preceptor (*guru*) of Vallālasena, as stated in the introduction of the *Dānasāgara*.[119] Halāyudha, an eminent scholar, was also associated with the Senas.[120] According to the description in his *Brāhmaṇasarvasva*, Lakṣmaṇasena conferred on him a position of *dharmādhikāra*,[121] otherwise called *mahādharmādhyakṣa*, *mahādharmādhikṛta*, *dharmādhyakṣa* or *dharmādhikṛta* in the same work.[122] His father Dhanañjaya also held the position of *dharmādhyakṣa*.[123]

The office of *mahādharmādhyakṣa* had special bearing for the Varmans and the Senas. From the reign of Bhojavarman to the end of the Sena regime, this office was regularly mentioned as one of the addressees in the grants (**Tables 6.1b, 6.2**). It makes a stark contrast with the Pālas who never include this office in the address of their plates despite that Mahādevarāta, the great grandfather of Maheśvararātaśarman, the donee of the Rajibpur grant of year 22, is mentioned with the title of *mahādharmādhikaraṇika*.[124] It indicates the growing importance of this office under the Varman and Sena regimes, which corresponds to their close association with the eminent *nibandhakāra*s.

What transpires from the enhanced presence of *brāhmaṇa*s as ritual specialists and an authority of *dharma* and their closer association with kings is the acceptance of particular Brahmanical norms by the kingship. These are the norms based on the *Dharmaśāstra*s and the *Purāṇa*s, as is clear from the patronage of *nibandhakāra*s by the Varmans and the Senas. In case of the Senas, the kings themselves took the initiative in compiling *Dharmanibandha*s. Vallālasena compiled the *Dānasāgara* and the *Adbhutasāgara*, and Lakṣmaṇasena took over the compilation of the latter and completed it.[125]

The acceptance of Puranic norms is evident in the performance of *mahādānas*, which were first codified in the *Matsyapurāṇa* in the period between 550 and 650 AD.[126] These rituals seem to have been enacted in a particular social context of the state formation and acculturation in West Deccan and performed by various kings located in the peripheral regions for their function of validating royal power.[127] The adoption of *mahādānas* by kings of Bengal in this period indicates their acceptance of the religious principles which permeate in these rituals and are propagated by the texts. The acceptance of the *Purāṇas* as their guideline by the Senas is also attested by the Madanapada plate of Viśvarūpasena, which mentions the acquisition of merit of land donation propagated by the *Śivapurāṇa* as a reason for the grant.[128] The extensive use of the *Purāṇas* by Vallālasena for his *Dānasāgara* and *Adbhutasāgara* also confirms this point.[129] The prevalence of these norms points to the establishment of the authority of *brāhmaṇas* at the royal court with their stronger presence and association.

The establishment of Brahmanical authority was not a matter limited to the royal court but an ongoing process in rural society, connected with the progress in their network building. The networking through the multiple migrations continued through the early 12th century as attested by the inscriptions of Gopāla IV, Madanapāla, Bhojavarman and Vijayasena. The two Rajibpur grants of Gopāla IV and Madanapāla show the migration of a *brāhmaṇa* family from Sammārjanī to Devīkoṭa, then to Vudhavadākhāma.[130] The Belava grant of Bhojavarman records the case in which a *brāhmaṇa* belonging to a family originating from Madhyadeśa and having settled in Siddhalagrāma, a Brahmanical centre in Uttara Rāḍha, migrated to Vaṅga due to the patronage of the Varman king.[131] The donee of the Barrackpur grant of Vijayasena is said to have originated from Madhyadeśa and belonged to Kāntijoṅgī, and received a land plot in Bhāṭṭavaḍāgrāma belonging to Khāḍīviṣaya, locatable in the present Diamond Harbour division in West Bengal.[132]

On the other hand, a case recorded in the contemporary Manahali grant of Madanapāla shows a new tendency emerging in this period. Vaṭeśvarasvāmiśarman, the donee of the grant, is said to both belong to and reside in Campāhiṭṭī, without any reference to the original place of his family.[133] It seems to be identical with Cāmpahaṭṭī, to which *nibandhakāra* Aniruddha belonged,[134] and to have been a Brahmanical centre in Varendra. The present case shows that some *brāhmaṇa* family chose to settle and take root in a particular locality, rather than to migrate further. It indicates the level of progress in the construction of Brahmanical networks, at which the migration and creation of centres slowed down and the consolidation of their presence in each locality became important. The diminishing importance of migration is also discernible in the Sena grants. In all their grants after the reign of Vijayasena, references to the origin and residence of the donee are conspicuous by their absence.[135] On the other hand, the reference in the

Mehar grant of Dāmodaradeva to Pūrvagrāma, Sidhala(Siddhala)grāma, Diṇḍisāya and Keśarakoṇa, Brahmanical centres in Rāḍha to be included in later *gāñīs*, as settlements to which some of donee *brāhmaṇa*s belonged, suggests the continuance of migrations of *brāhmaṇa*s in the peripheral sub-region of Samataṭa as late as in the 13th century.[136]

One result of the networking of *brāhmaṇa*s is discernible in the contemporary text. In his discussion on Vedic studies among the contemporary *brāhmaṇa*s in the *Brāhmaṇasarvasva*, Halāyudha mentions Rāḍhīya and Vārendra as categories of *brāhmaṇa*s, together with Utkalas and Pāścattyas.[137] While the last two categories indicate the presence of *brāhmaṇa* groups with distinctive identities as migrants respectively from Utkala, the north-eastern sub-region of present Orissa,[138] and 'West,' connoting Madhyadeśa, the first two categories show the making of identities based on their sub-regional affiliations among *brāhmaṇa*s in Bengal. It is remarkable that Rāḍha and Varendra appear in this context, while Vaṅga and Samataṭa do not. It can be assumed that this difference comes from the existence of Brahmanical centres. The progress in the migration and networking of *brāhmaṇa*s with these centres as their nodes, which was witnessed in the previous period,[139] culminated in their cognition as groups with sub-regional identities.

The construction of Brahmanical networks also resulted in settling and incorporation of qualified *brāhmaṇa*s in rural society. The shifting meaning of the term *brāhmaṇottara* in this period alludes to it. In the address of the Pāla and Candra grants, the word means 'of whom *brāhmaṇa*s are foremost' and conditions local residents to denote the inclusion of *brāhmaṇa*s among the latter (**Tables 5.1 d – e, 5.2**). The shift of meaning is observable in the Varman plates. In the Samantasar grant of Harivarman, the earliest of them, the relevant portion is the same as that of the Candra plates.[140] In the Vajrayogini Plate of Sāmalavarman and the Belava Plate of Bhojavarman, however, the term *brāhmaṇa* is inserted between cultivators (*kṣetrakara*) and *brāhmaṇottara*, so that *brāhmaṇottara* is converted from a term conditioning local residents to a category different from *brāhmaṇa* (**Table 6.1**).[141] In the last cases, *brāhmaṇottara* means 'higher *brāhmaṇas*' differentiated from the other ordinary *brāhmaṇa*s. Their appearance among addressees of the grants indicates the incorporation of qualified *brāhmaṇa*s into rural society. This expression with two categories of *brāhmaṇa*s is regularly employed in the Sena grants (**Table 6.2**).

The clue to the position of those *brāhmaṇa*s in rural society is offered by the descriptions in the grants. The resources and privileges conferred on donees were as extensive as they had been in the previous period, even with additions.[142] It was the same for the early Sena grants.[143] The number of privileges, however, decreased from the reign of Lakṣmaṇasena onwards. A clause about king's dues accompanying the tenure was also absent.[144] The decrease of resources and privileges could be interpreted as an evidence of the declining authority of *brāhmaṇa* donees and the state which guarantee them. However, its implication may have been different in the context of settling of qualified *brāhmaṇa*s and their incorporation into rural society. Enhancement of their dominance in rural society is suggested by the address in the later Sena plates, which mention only *brāhmaṇa*s and *brāhmaṇottara*s among rural residents.[145] *Brāhmaṇa*s seems to have established their dominance in rural society so well that the king need not announce the donation to the other members. With such dominance, the lack of minute description of royal dues assigned to the donee rather implies unspecified and arbitrary character of extraction. Arbitrariness of the tenure is indicated by a clause in the Idilpur and Madhyapada grants of Viśvarūpasena, which says that donation was made for the donee 'to enjoy' donated property 'with enjoyment at own will' as a hereditary right.[146]

One aspect of Brahmanical dominance in rural society is shown by the Madhyapada plate of Viśvarūpasena.[147] This grant records the donation of the 11 land plots scattered over the six villages in the three administrative units, which measure 336 1/2 *udāna*s in total with production of 500 *hiraṇya*s, to *brāhmaṇa* Halāyudhaśarman (**Table 6.5**). Its contents reveal the actual aim of the grant to upgrade those land plots, which had been acquired by Halāyudhaśarman on the six occasions recorded minutely, to *śāsana* land exempted from revenue and the other charges.

The detailed information about land plots provided in this inscription offers a rare glimpse of multi-layered land tenures, which constitutes a topic of the next section. For current discussion, the activities of Halāyudhaśarman gleaned from the record are important. Modes of land acquisition adopted by him and mentioned in the grant include not only donations by the king and the other political powers but also purchases by the donee himself. Among the 11 land plots acquired by him, the four are mentioned as *paṭṭolī* purchased from groups of people (**Table 6.5, nos 6–9**). *Paṭṭolī* originally means 'deed of purchase' and denotes land purchased by such a purchase deed.[148] These *paṭṭolī* lands are located in the two villages belonging to the different administrative units, and the three of them include homestead lands with areca nut trees.[149] A land plot in Ajikulāpāṭaka is especially mentioned with annual income from the sales of 3,000 areca nuts from the areca nut plantation (*kalana*) belonging to it (**Table 6.5, no. 6**). Apart from them, a *śāsana* land held by *rājapaṇḍita* Mahesara in village Ghāgharakāṭṭī belonging to Urācaturaka of Phandradvīpa was purchased by Halāyudhaśarman (**Table 6.5, no. 10**).

What transpires from these cases is the presence of this highly qualified *brāhmaṇa* as a large-scale landholder involved in the acquisition and management of his landholdings. As a *brāhmaṇa* with credentials of Vedic study, the title of *paṇḍita* and laudable family background indicated by his *gotra*, *pravara* and genealogy,[150] he was eligible for donations and was actually donated some land plots (**Table 6.5, nos 1–4, 11**). He however seems not to have been satisfied so much with them that he vigorously accumulated

Table 6.5 Details of land plots donated in Madhyapada CPI of Viśvarūpasena (*IB*, pp. 146–47, ll. 42–59.)

No.	*Place*	*History*	*Land Type*	*udāna*	*hi/u*	*hiraṇya*
Rāmasiddhipāṭaka in Nāvya						
1	SE of Varāhakuṇḍa		Homestead	34 3/4		
2	E of Devahāra, 4 mounds		Mixed Arable	4 1/4 26 3/4	1 3/8	
3	N of Devahāra		Arable	2	1 1/8	
	Subtotal			67 3/4		80 5/16
4	7 units (*khaṃ*) in 2 lots: 4 new *varaja*s (betel vine plantations) of the group of Nāko, Lokta, Gāñīka etc. and 3 *varaja*s of the group of Śremano, Udayi, Apara, Loktaka					19 11/16
	Total (1–4): donated on the occasion of the summer solstice in the year 13					100
5	In Vinayatilakagrāma in Nāvya-E: *samudra*, S: Pranullī-bhū, W: *jaṅghāla*, N: *śāsana*		land with homestead	25		60
6	Ajikulāpāṭaka in Navasaṃgrahacaturaka, Madhukṣīrakāvṛtti	*Paṭṭolī* purchased by Halāyudha from Śauvasā, Kirito, Maito, Ucchoka etc.	land with homestead	165		100
	Price/year of 3,000 areca nuts belonging to *kalana* (areca nut plantation) in the residential plot					40
	Subtotal (6)					140
Deūlahastī in Lāuhaṇḍācaturaka, Vikramapurabhāga						
7	Land established by the king on both E. and W. sides of the river	*Paṭṭolī* purchased by Halāyudha from the group of Āranto, Kāmya, Piṇṭhanāga etc.	land with homestead	25		50
	Total (5–7): donated when the queen mother saw the lunar eclipse, with price of areca nuts					250

(*Continued*)

Table 6.5 (Continued)

No.	*Place*	*History*	*Land Type*	*udāna*	*hilu*	*hiraṇya*
8	In the same village: *paṭṭolī* purchased by Halāyudha from the group of Vrahmo, Amṛtoka: donated by prince Sūryasena on his birthday		Arable	7		
			Homestead with areca nut trees	3		
	Subtotal (8)		land with homestead	10		25
9	In the same village: *paṭṭolī* purchased by Halāyudha from the group of Kano, Amṛtoka: donated by *sāndhivigrahika* Nāñīsiṃha		Arable	3		
			Homestead with areca nut trees	4		
	Subtotal (9)		land with homestead	7		25
Phandradvīpa						
10	Ghāgharakāṭṭīpāṭaka, E of Jayajāhaḍā, in Urācaturaka	*Śāsana* purchased by Halāyudha from *rājapaṃ* Mahesara	land with homestead	12 3/4		50
11	Pātilādivīka	Belonging to the income enjoyed by prince Puruṣottamasena: donated by him on 12th, former half of Kārttika, year 14	land with homestead	24		50
	Total (1–11)			336 1/2		500

landholdings through purchases and had them upgraded to *śāsana* land. It is also notable that he especially purchased homestead lands with areca nut trees, of which the profitability would have been further enhanced by his possession of the seven betel vine plantations (*varaja*) in one of the donated land plots (**Table 6.5, no. 4**). These facts indicate his interest in the management of landholdings through the accumulation of profitable land plots. Thus the case of Halāyudhaśarman shows the presence and activities of a *brāhmaṇa* in rural society as a landlord, in the same way as subordinate rulers under the Senas, who became the assignees of superior land tenure scattered over several land plots.[151] This could be an exceptional case, as the other Sena grants are silent about such activities of donees, while some of them received land plots with similar or higher value.[152] However, the fact that the *paṭṭolī*s purchased by Halāyudhaśarman were recognised and upgraded to *śāsana* land by the king without any reservation suggests that the active involvement of *brāhmaṇa*s in land acquisition and management was rather a normal phenomenon which would not have made any problems for the political powers.

Thus, the dominance of *brāhmaṇa*s in rural society was underscored by their position as large-scale landholders. It was in turn enabled by the social stratification resulting in a layered land relation incorporating residents of rural society.

Social stratification and organisation of occupational groups

Stratification of rural society is evident in the Pāla grants of this period. In the three plates of Gopāla IV and Madanapāla, local residents from *mahattama*s or *mahattara*s, *uttama*s, *kuṭumbin*s to *caṇḍāla*s, of whom *brāhmaṇa*s are foremost, are informed of the land grants.[153] As discussed in the previous chapter, this can be a stereotyped expression which comprehends all the members of a rural society by indicating the groups placed at both top and bottom ends of social hierarchy and shows an intensified state of social stratification, resulting partly from the incorporation of non-sedentary social groups.[154] What is notable here is a simplification of the bottom rank, which in the previous period generally consisted of *meda*s, *andhra*s and *caṇḍāla*s (**Table 5.1 c – d**), with *kaivarta*s in one case,[155] to *caṇḍāla*s only. While the omission of *kaivarta*s could be explained by the upward social mobility of a part of them to a landholding group with their own chief,[156] there is no evidence of such social mobility for *meda*s and *andhra*s. The simplification rather suggests the changed perception of the Pāla administration, for which the distinction among the lowest social groups became less important. In contrast, groups to the upper end are much the same as before (**Tables 5.1, c – d**). It shows the importance of those dominant groups in rural society for the Pāla administration. In the aftermath of the *Kaivarta* rebellion, the dependence of the Pāla kings on them as well as subordinate rulers for controlling rural society grew, in spite of their efforts for the administrative reorganisation and the consolidation of their remaining territory.[157]

The rural residents are simply mentioned as people (*janapada*) and cultivators (*kṣetrakara*) in the address of the Varman and Sena grants, without any reference to the stratification among them (**Tables 6.1, 6.2, a - b**). However, the stratified land relation incorporating rural residents is detectable in some grants. The Madanapada plate refers to a land plot of *padāti* Śāpāmārka belonging to Kandarpaśaṅkarāśrama, excluded from the donated tract.[158] He seems to have been assigned a plot from the landholdings of the *āśrama* for his service as a foot soldier or a peon. There could be one more layer in this relation, if he had his plot tilled by the other cultivators.

Fuller view of the stratified land relation is provided by the Madhyapada plate of Viśvarūpasena related to the sub-region of Vaṅga.[159] As mentioned above, it records upgrading of the 11 land plots acquired by Halāyudhaśarman on the six occasions to *śāsana* land (**Table 6.5**). Descriptions of the land plots and occasions of their acquisition show diverse patterns of landholdings.

The four plots donated by the king without any reference to intermediaries could be the land under his direct control (**Table 6.5, nos 1–3, 5**). The indication of annual income from them is preceded by either *grāmapatyā* or *nānāpatyā*,[160] which seems to denote an agent of revenue collection, either the head of village or that of its diverse subdivisions.[161] The other three plots donated by the king and mentioned with plural people, who held betel vine plantations (*varaja*) or from whom the donee purchased the plots as *paṭṭolī* (**Table 6.5, nos 4, 6–7**), seem to be the royal land held and managed by those people. Among the plots, the one has an indication of income preceded by the words *nānāpatyā* and *ucchannatvāt* (**Table 6.5, no. 6**).[162] The reference to the agents of revenue collection, which was given for the land under direct royal control in the other cases, could be necessitated by the condition of 'lost,' connoting a crop failure in view of low income of tract for its size, 100 *hiraṇya*s for 165 *udāna*s.

The three plots donated by princes Sūryasena, Puruṣottamasena and *sāndhivigrahika* Nāñīsiṃha could be the lands assigned to them as their estates. The plots under Sūryasena and Nāñīsiṃha were held by the groups of people from whom the donee purchased them as *paṭṭolī*, while the other under Puruṣottamasena seems to have been managed by himself (**Table 6.5, nos 8–9, 11**). The last to mention is the plot of *rājapaṇḍita* Mahesara purchased by the donee, which was a *śāsana* tract (**Table 6.5, no. 10**).

The patterns of landholdings described above make us detect the three layers of tenures on a particular land plot. The highest was the power to confer the status of *śāsana* to a land plot, which was exclusively wielded by the king. The second was the superior right over a land plot expressed as power to dispose it for donations, exercised by the king, princes and a subordinate ruler. The third was the right of landholding and management, kept by the above three or people under them. We can add the fourth level, the right of cultivation, assuming the presence of actual cultivators under landholders.

Of those tenures, the third level, the right of landholding, was substantial, as this was what Halāyudhaśarman sought after. It seems to have entitled the holder to some share of production from the land, as can be assumed from the description of a plot as 'belonging to the income enjoyed by prince illustrious Puruṣottamasena',[163] and to the power to have it cultivated, as the holders of this tenure including the king and prince Puruṣottamasena needed the service of cultivators for land management. The king and the prince are deemed to have held this tenure on the land under their direct control, and the same can be said of *rājapaṇḍita* Mahesara, a *śāsana* holder.[164] In the five plots under the king and the other political powers, this tenure was held by the untitled people who seem to have been local residents. Among these plots, the four were jointly held by groups of people whose names are prefixed with a term *vāra*, which indicates their collectivity as will be discussed below (**Table 6.5, nos 4, 7–9**). The remaining one plot of land with homestead, 165 *udāna*s in size held by Śauvāsa, Kirito, Maito, Ucchoka and others, seems not to have been a single plot but a collection of plots held by each of them, as it is much larger than any other plots, and those people are not prefixed with *vāra* (**Table 6.5, no. 6**).[165] The tenure was transferable and Halāyudhaśarman acquired it through donations by the king and the prince or purchases from a *śāsana* holder and groups of local people.

The character of the second level as a superior land right is clear from the cases in which the king, Sūryasena and Nāññīsiṃha donated the land plots which were purchased by Halāyudhaśarman from groups of landholders.[166] The fact that the land donated by princes and a subordinate needed to be upgraded to a *śāsana* land by the king show that this right was inferior to the power held by the king and did not entail immunity and privileges of *śāsana* lands. Accordingly, it seems to have been the right to some portion of production, possibly accompanying some administrative power, assigned to members of royal household and king's subordinates. It accompanied the obligation of revenue payment and the other duties, which could be exempted by the issue of a *śāsana*.

The first level, the king's power to make *śāsana* land, indicates his overarching authority which notionally covered all his territory. He could even confiscate and donate land plots under his subordinate, as shown by the case of the land of king's own dependant mentioned in the Madanapada grant.[167] Such a power of the king may have been based on the enhanced state control over rural society discussed above.[168] The case of the plot of *rājapaṇḍita* Mahesara shows that *śāsana* land could be sold to the other *brāhmaṇa* but had to be reconfirmed of its status as such by another royal grant.

Members of rural society were embedded in such a stratified land relation prominently as landholders in estates of the king and the other political powers or as agents of revenue collection in the land under direct royal control. The reference to a village head (*grāmapati*) and a head of the diverse (*nānāpati*), most provably subdivisions of a village, in the latter capacity attests to the presence of local notables put to such positions representing local residents.

The presence of landholders was, on the other hand, characterised by their collective landholding. In village Rāmasiddhipāṭaka, the four new betel vine plantations (*varaja*) in a lot were held by Nāko, Lokta, Gāñīka and others, and three betel vine plantations in another lot by Śremano, Udayi, Apara and Loktaka (**Table 6.5, no. 4**). Each group is prefixed with a term *vāra*,[169] which, according to Sircar, means 'collection' and indicates that each group of betel vine plantations were jointly held by a group of people.[170] Similarly, each of three land plots with homestead land in the village Deūlahastī, two of which include areca nut trees, was held by a group of people prefixed with *vāra*. Among them, a plot with homestead land measuring 25 *udāna*s was held by Āranto, Kāmya, Piṇṭhanāga and others (**Table 6.5, no. 7**).[171] The other plot consisting of 7 *udāna*s of arable land and 3 *udāna*s of homestead land with areca nut trees was held by Vrahmo and Amṛtoka (**Table 6.5, no. 8**).[172] The last plot constituted by 3 *udāna*s of arable land and 4 *udāna*s of homestead land with areca nut trees was held by Kano and Amṛtoka (**Table 6.5, no. 9**).[173] What transpires from these cases is the collectivity and connection of a few landholders based on their joint landholding. As joint holders of a land plot, they seem to have shared both production from it and burden imposed on it by the superior tenure holders.

It was remarkable that some people belonged to plural landholding groups simultaneously. In case of the betel vine plantations of Rāmasiddhipāṭaka, Lokta and Loktaka, who respectively belonged to the groups holding new and old *varaja*s, could be one and the same person.[174] As for the plots in Deūlahastī, Amṛtoka was a member of two landholding groups. Thus, a landholder was able to hold stakes in plural land plots located in the same village as a member of different landholding groups. Though the relation among different landholding groups were not clear in the context of the present grant, some kind of connection may have been facilitated by the presence of a common member, alluding to the horizontal social relation of landholders at a village level.

Though the information on those landholders is limited to their names and insufficient to guess their social position, their position superior to cultivators, who are invisible in the grant in spite of their indispensability in managing agrarian tracts, can be recognised. It points to the stratification among agrarian groups of rural society, which is glossed over by the label of cultivator (*kṣetrakara*) or its absence in the Sena plates including the present one (**Table 6.2**).

In the Mehar grant of Dāmodaradeva pertaining to Samataṭa, the stratification of rural society is clearly expressed by the prominent *janapada*s and *mahattara*s mentioned as addressees.[175] The grant also attests to the stratified land relation by references to *śāsana* land plots made by subordinates and donated by the king (**Table 6.3, nos 19, 20**). Thus, the stratification of rural society in the layered land relation was also witnessed in this sub-region in the 13th century.

While the agrarian groups embedded in the layered land relation experienced social stratification of themselves, the artisans, merchants and the other professional groups were in the process of social organisation based on their occupations. Their activities are not described minutely in the contemporary inscriptions, compared with those of their counterparts in the previous period.[176] Though *śilpin* Tathāgatasara is credited with engraving the grants of Gopāla IV and Madanapāla,[177] no information regarding his identity other than his title and name is given, unlike the engravers of the earlier Pāla plates.[178] On the other hand, the involvement of professional groups in some form of landholdings is discernible in the Rajibpur plate of year 22, which mentions enclosed land (*vṛti*) of the *kaivarta*s and *carmakāra*s included in the royal estate.[179] They seem to have been assigned a part of royal estate for some services to the king, showing their consolidation as collectives.

The Varman and Sena grants do not mention names of the engravers. The Deopara stone inscription of Vijayasena, however, describes Śūlapāṇi, the engraver, as 'a crest jewel of the *śilpigoṣṭhī* of Varendra,' with his genealogy of four generations and title of *rāṇaka*.[180] The presence of artisan families who were specialised in engraving royal inscriptions, acquiring the status of *sāmanta* or having a particular village as their centre, was known in the earlier Pāla grants.[181] What is remarkable here is the reference to a corporate body of such artisans based on sub-regional identity. The making of such an organisation can be compared with *vaṇiggrāma* consisting of merchants centred on rural markets in the 11th century.[182] Its formation in the framework of sub-region shows, however, a close affinity with the making of sub-regional identities among *brāhmaṇa*s resulting from the establishment of Brahmanical centres and networks.[183] The *śilpigoṣṭhī* of Varendra could have also emanated from the horizontal networking of a group of artisans through their mobility and establishment of their centres.

As for the other professional groups, fragmentary but interesting information is available from some inscriptions. The Sujanagar stone inscription of the time of Bhojavarman mentions conch-shell worker(s) (*śaṃkhakara*) given cash in cowrie-shells, without any clue to their social organisation.[184] In the same inscription, the kinsmen of *mahāsāmanta* Avūdeva, who all together contributed to the cash deposit presumably for a religious purpose and later assented to its withdrawal, are said to have belonged to the other countries.[185] As Avūdeva seems to have belonged to a merchant family,[186] his kinsmen could have been engaged in commercial activities and constituted a trans-regional trade network based on their kinship tie. Their collectivity in both building up monetary capital for religious endowment and agreeing with its liquidation suggests the presence of their kinship organisation. How far it can be connected with the later development of mercantile *jāti*s is unclear, for they could rather be foreign merchants staying in Vaṅga as suggested by their support for a *vihāra* protected by Allahabhaṭṭārakasvāmin, which may denote a *madrasa*.[187]

The Bhatera grant of Keśavadeva, datable to the 13th century, also gives information on some occupational groups. In detailing 'various attendants' and '*jāti*s of people in great number' who were donated to the deity with cultivated land plots and gardens, it lists 'houses' (*gṛha*), 70 in total, belonging to particular individuals (**Table 6.4, nos 47–64**). The donation of houses of individuals seems to denote the assignment of the service of their households to a religious institution. While most of the 'owners' of houses are mentioned with their names only, the three are prefixed with occupational signifiers of *nāpita* (barber), *rajaka* (washerman) and *dantavāra*, possibly a mistake for *dantakāra* (ivory worker) (**Table 6.4, nos 57–58, 64**).[188] Apart from them, *gopa*, *mālā* and *haddiya* among the terms prefixed to *gṛha* to indicate its type may connote the occupational groups to which the owners belong (**Table 6.4, nos 48, 55, 62**).

The reference to those groups reminds us of the tenth-century Paschimbhag plate pertaining to the same sub-region of Śrīhaṭṭa, in which the members of occupational groups serving Brahmanical *maṭha*s are assigned some land plots (**Table 5.4**). While the case of the last plate suggests service tenure through which labour of occupational groups was redirected to the service remunerated by the assignment of landholdings, the case of the Bhatera plate of Keśavadeva points to the transfer of labour of these groups already bonded in a service relation with one authority, the king in this case, to the other. It indicates the subservient position of those including occupational groups and the others who could be actual cultivators. Thus, the present case confirms the social stratification in Śrīhaṭṭa in the 13th century, though it does not show how the professional groups organised themselves. The presence of hereditary occupational groups to be perceived by *brāhmaṇa*s as *jāti*s is detectable in the narrative of *Varṇasaṃkara* unfolded in the *Bṛhaddharmapurāṇa*, to be discussed in the last section of this chapter.

The social stratification and the organisation of occupational groups in rural society in this period discussed above were closely connected with a new phase of the economic phenomena witnessed in the previous period, namely, agrarian development and commercialisation of rural economy.

New phase of agrarian development and commercialisation

The social stratification and layered land relation, which had enabled mobilisation of labour power of subordinate cultivators and constituted the conditions for agrarian development in the previous period, especially in Varendra,[189] continued in this period and spread to the eastern sub-regions as discussed above. However, the agrarian development observed in the sub-regions of Bengal took diverse forms and did not necessarily follow the same course as that in the earlier period, due to some new elements emerging in this period.

The sub-region of Varendra was in the process of recovery from the devastation caused by the *Kaivarta* rebellion and its suppression. Rāmapāla encouraged the restart of cultivation with moderate tax and excavated a large pond (*puṣkariṇī*).[190] Though the confusion of villages were still observed in the reign of Madanapāla,[191] the three grants of Gopāla IV and Madanapāla, which pertain to the same locality of Halāvartamaṇḍala and record the donations of villages with production of 300 or 320 *purāṇa*s to individual *brāhmaṇa*s, attest to the some level of recovery in this particular area around the mid-12th century.[192] However, the deemed village donated in the Rajibpur grant of year 22 was actually a sum of tracts consisting of 35 *āḍhāvāpa*s of land in the land plots (*khaṇḍakṣetra*) of Vāṭhuṇḍavallī, Kusumuṇḍā, Piśācakuleya and Vivudhapallī, and the other land belonging to Vaṅgaḍī.[193] As the individual villages with similar production could be donated in the two earlier plates,[194] it suggests limited availability of cultivated land tracts for donations, which could be primarily due to the shrinkage of the Pāla territory, but have some implications for a limit of agrarian expansion near to be reached.

The progress of this trend, namely the agrarian development reaching a limit of expansion, is discernible in the three Sena grants pertaining to Varendra. First of all, plots or a settlement donated in the Tarpandighi, Anulia and Madhainagar plates of Lakṣmaṇasena are relatively small in size, 120 *āḍhāvāpa*s 5 *unmāna*s, 1 *pāṭaka* 9 *droṇa*s 1 *āḍhāvāpa* 37 *unmāna*s 1 *kākinī* and 100 *khāḍī*s 91 *khāḍikā*s respectively.[195] Though the difference in measuring standard and units makes it difficult to compare them with the other plots or settlements,[196] the productions of 150, 100 and 163 *kapardakapurāṇa*s each confirm their relatively small sizes.[197]

The descriptions of border landmarks in those grants confirm the aforementioned trend of agrarian development. The land plot donated in the Tarpandighi plate was bordered by the eastern embankment of 1 *āḍhāvāpa* of the tax-free donated land of the deities of the Buddha *vihārī* to the east and by a pond (*puṣkariṇī*), a reservoir (*kuṇḍī*) and a canal (*khāḍī*) to the remaining three directions.[198] Water bodies both natural and artificial surrounding the concerned tract and the donated land of the other religious agent lying within it are notable, and the existence of the last is also confirmed by a clause excluding land without income such as that of deities and cattle tracks.[199] The border landmarks of the land plot donated in the Anulia grant were an *aśvattha* tree, Jalapillā which could be a watercourse or a river, a *śāsana* of *śānti* Gopī and a garden (*vāṭī*) of Mālāmañca to the four cardinal directions.[200] The presence of a donated tract and a garden in this landscape should be noted. Dāpaṇiyāpāṭaka, the donated settlement in the Madhainagar grant, is demarcated by the lands of settlements Caḍaspasāpāṭaka, Gayanagara, Guṇḍīsthirāpāṭaka and Guṇḍīdāpaṇiyā to the four cardinal directions.[201] Remarkably, the well-defined borders are provided in reference not only to the neighbouring settlements but also to the lands within them. The name of the last settlement, which consists of the elements of the names of the donated settlement and its western neighbour, suggests its establishment by migrants from both settlements. Adding to them, the presence of previously donated tracts within Dāpaṇiyāpāṭaka is suggested by a clause excluding land of deities and *brāhmaṇa*s similar to that of the Tarpandighi plate mentioned above.[202]

What transpires from these border descriptions is the process of agrarian development through the establishment of artificial water bodies and the expansion by migration to neighbourhood, which resulted in the formation of a settlement cluster. However, the relatively small size of each plot or settlement, the strict and minute demarcation of its border and the presence of several donated lands within a limited space, even within the donated tract itself, indicate the congestion of agrarian tracts brought out by the limit of agrarian expansion coming closer.

The agrarian landscape of northern (Uttara) Rāḍha under the Senas is glimpsed from the two plates. The border of Vāllahiṭṭhāgrāma donated in the Naihati grant of Vallālasena is clearly demarcated by the river Siṅgaṭiānadī skirting the three *śāsana*s to its south and east and by border embankments (*sīmāli*) and cattle tracks (*gopatha*) on a canal called Āūhāgaṭṭiā, on the two settlements and on the three *śāsana*s to its north and west.[203] The two tracts consisting of six hamlets donated in the Saktipur plate of Lakṣmaṇasena are also mentioned with minute border descriptions. The first tract, Rāghavahaṭṭapāṭaka accompanied by Vārahakoṇāpāṭaka, Vāllihitāpāṭaka and a land plot of Nimāpāṭaka, was bordered by the watercourse Aparājolī and a land adjacent to the reservoir Mālikuṇḍa to the east, land plot of Bhāgaḍī belonging to Brahmasthalī to the south, the cattle track of Acchamā to the west and the river Moranadī to the north. The second tract, Vijahārapurapāṭaka with Dāmaravaḍāpāṭaka, was surrounded by three *jolī*s to the east, south and west respectively and by the cattle track of Parajāṇa to the north.[204] What is discernible from them is the agrarian development in riverine tracts with both natural and artificial water bodies, resulting in the concentration of *śāsana* tracts and the other settlements demarcated by the well-defined borders.

The size of Vāllahiṭṭhāgrāma, 7 *pāṭaka*s 9 *droṇa*s 1 *āḍhaka* 40 *unmāna*s 3 *kāka*s,[205] indicates the availability of such a large tract as a single settlement in the early phase of development. The size of the two tracts in the Saktipur grant, 89 *droṇa*s in total,[206] is still not small but the fact that they had to be secured as six hamlets shows the congestion of agrarian tracts, which is also implied in a clause excluding the land of deities and *brāhmaṇa*s, suggesting their presence within the donated tracts.[207] These hamlets were donated in exchange for the other tract with the same production previously given to another donee by Vallālasena.[208] It means that land of the same production available as a single tract in the earlier period had to be procured as a collection of small hamlets, showing the progress of agrarian development with which the expansion was reaching a limit resulting in the congestion of agrarian tracts.

When Varendra and Uttara Rāḍha saw the agrarian development and the stagnation of expansion resulting from it, a new phase of agrarian expansion was proceeding in the areas which had not experienced the agrarian development. One area was lower Bengal, more precisely the Bhagirathi estuary, as attested by the copper plate inscriptions discovered from the present areas of Howrah and 24 Parganas, even including Sundarbans, which pertain to the administrative units of Khāḍīmaṇḍala/-viṣaya and Paścimakhāṭikā.[209] The settlement formation in riverine tracts is discernible in the descriptions of border landmarks in those grants. A plot of 4 *pāṭaka*s in Bhāṭṭavaḍāgrāma donated in the Barrackpur plate of Vijayasena was surrounded by a half of water of Tikṣahaṇḍa, which could be a stream, to its south, west and north.[210] Village Viḍḍāraśāsana, 60 *droṇa*s 17 *unmāna* in size, in the Govindapur grant of Lakṣmaṇasena was bordered by the river Jāhnavī to the east, the small pavilion or shrine (*maṇḍapī*) of Leṅghadeva to the south, a cultivated land of Ḍālimva to the west and village Dharmanagara to the north.[211] A small plot of 3 *droṇa*s 1 *khāḍikā* 23 *unmāna*s 2 1/2 *kākiṇī*s donated in the Dighirpar-Bakultala grant of the same king was demarcated by the donated tract of *śāntyāgārika* Prabhāsa to the east, a half of canal (*khāta*) of Citāḍi to the south, the eastern side of the donated tract of *śāntyāgārika* Rāmadeva to the west and the sugar cane field (*gaḍolībhūmi*) of *śāntyāgārika* Viṣṇupāṇi and that of Keśava to the north.[212]

It is notable that Bhāṭṭavaḍāgrāma was estate (*sambhoga*) of Ghāsa, a subordinate of the king, and included the land assigned to the queen within it.[213] The reclamation and development of the settlement seems to have been undertaken by him to whom the king assigned it. We may find here the agency of assignees of unreclaimed tract, a royal subordinate in this case, in reclaiming such a tract and the attempt of the king to pursue agrarian expansion through it. A *brahmadeya* village grant to *mahārāṇaka* Vāsudevaśarman in the Rakshaskhali plate pertaining to this area can be understood in the same manner.[214] The agents of reclamation were not limited to subordinate rulers, and the concentration of *śāsana*s of *śāntyāgārika*s in the area mentioned in the Dighirpar-Bakultala grant could indicate the royal attempt at agrarian expansion through the agency of a particular kind of *brāhmaṇa*s connected with the kingship by ritual service.[215] The agents of reclamation could also include religious institutions like a Buddhist establishment, of which the land was excluded from the village donated in the Rakshaskhali grant.[216]

The other area of agrarian expansion was the area close to Madhupur tract, where the two land tracts in villages Vāsumaṇḍana and Mādisāhaṃsa within Vasuśrīcaturaka belonging to Vāṇḍanāvṛtti of Pauṇḍravardhanabhukti were donated by the Rajavadi grant of Lakṣmaṇasena.[217] The descriptions of these tracts show their complicated structures in composition or surroundings. Rāpaśvakoṭamajagaharttarāka, the first tract bordered by Poñceṣādāṇḍi to the east, Jaladāṇḍi to the south and Majanadī to the west and north, was accompanied by the land plots (*khaṇḍakṣetra*) of Kavilkī, Cuñcalī, Gāṇḍolī and Dehiyā.[218] A small area (*kiyadekadeśa*) of Mādisāhaṃsagrāma, the second tract, was demarcated by two strips (*sūtra*) of land connected to Guḍahāsa, Siṃhajāvilkī, the western part of Kematagrāvāṭi and a watercourse down to four strips of land connected to Jaladāṇḍi to the east, Jaladāṇḍi to the south and west and Vānahāranada to the north.[219] The landscape of cultivated land tracts divided into small plots and strips surrounded by water bodies like rivers (*nadī/nada*) and watercourses (*dāṇḍi* and *jāṇa*) can be read in this description.[220] The land consisting of the two tracts seemingly in close proximity was 6 *pāṭaka*s 1 *droṇa* 28 *kākinī*s in size and 400 *purāṇa*s in production, relatively large and high in value.[221] The presence of such tracts attests to the ongoing agrarian expansion in this area.

The situation in Vaṅga, which had seen the limit of agrarian development in the previous period,[222] did not change much in the 12th century, as far as it is discernible from the Samantasar and Belava grants of the Varman kings recording donations of rather small land plots without any border demarcations.[223] However, the later Sena grants show a new round of agrarian development in Vaṅga in the 13th century. A land plot with production of 200 *hiraṇya*s in the Idilpur grant of Viśvarūpasena was surrounded by Satrakādvīgrāma to the east, a land of villages Sāṅkarapasā and Govindakeli to the south, Vāśeśvaragrāma in Pañcakoṇa to the west and a land cultivated by Vāgulīvittagada to the north.[224] Piñjokāṣṭhīgrāma, a village of 500 *hiraṇya*s donated in the Madanapada plate of the same king, was bordered by a land of embankment (*jaṅghāla*) of Aṭhayāgagrāma to the east, a land of Vārayipaḍāgrāma to the south, a land of Uñcokāṭṭīgrāma to the west and an embankment of Vīrakāṭṭī to the north.[225] In the last inscription, a land plot of 132 *purāṇa*s belonging to *padāti* Śāpāmārka of Kandarpaśaṅkarāśrama was excluded from the donated village, and the land plot of 127 *hiraṇya*s belonging to the king's own protégée (*svakīyapālyasvaṃ*) in Nāraṇḍapagrāma within the land assigned to the same *āśrama* was given instead.[226] The landscape of well-developed agrarian settlements is obtainable from both cases, while the minute border demarcation and the land of the other agent present within the donated village observed in the second plate show symptoms of congestion.

The mature phase of agrarian development in Vaṅga is clearer in the Madhyapada plate. The landscape of some plots like the three in

Rāmasiddhipāṭaka scattered among reservoir, river, an estate of deity (*devabhoga*) and a land of the other area, and the one in Deūlahastī established by the king on both sides of a river suggests the agrarian development on riverine tracts, even on the seaside as shown by a plot in Vinayatilakagrāma demarcated by the ocean to the east (**Table 6.5, nos 1–3, 5, 7**).[227] The fact that Halāyudhaśarman could accumulate his landholdings by purchases and donations of many cultivated and homestead land plots also confirms the agrarian development initiated by the different kinds of landholders including the king, princes, his subordinates, religious agents and local notables set in the stratified land relations.[228] However, that he had to acquire them as 11 plots dispersed over the six settlements in the four administrative units suggests the congestion of settled land tracts and the emerging limit of agrarian expansion resulting from the development (**Table 6.5**).

Samataṭa also saw the limit of agrarian expansion in the 13th century. The Maninamati grant of Dadhieva records the donation of 20 *droṇa*s of land plots to a Buddhist *vihāra* in Paṭṭikeranagarī.[229] The size of land much smaller than those donated in the earlier grants of the same area under the Candras is conspicuous.[230] The same limit was observed in the other areas of Samataṭa, as shown by the almost contemporary grants of Dāmodaradeva. The Mehar plate issued 14 years later in relation to Vāyisagrāmakhaṇḍala of Paralāyiviṣaya shows an extreme case in which homestead and cultivated land, 4 11/16 *droṇa*s in total, were donated and distributed to 20 *brāhmaṇa*s (**Table 6.3**). The size of each plot is minuscule from 1/16 to 1/2 *droṇa*s so that those plots must have been additional to landed property of each donee, which supposedly scattered over a wide area. The land plots donated in the Sobharampur and Nasirabad plates of the same king were also small, 15 and 5 *droṇa*s respectively. Even such small land plots had to be procured by merging three settlements of Sundaraya, Diśāga and Vāṇḍura belonging to Chātiharakhaṇḍala of Miḍillīviṣaya in the former,[231] or by accumulating three plots in two villages of Kāmanāpiṇḍiyāka and Ketaṅgapālā in Ḍāmvāraḍāma in the latter.[232] The borders were also clearly defined for each plot.[233] Thus the wider areas of Samataṭa experienced the limit of agrarian expansion and the congestion of land. Due to the lack of evidence, it is difficult to say whether this agrarian condition was the continuance of the limit experienced in the 12th century,[234] or the result of intensive agrarian development in the intervening period.

One case exceptional to this trend was the land grant recorded in the Mainamati plate of Vīradharadeva. It was the donation of 17 *pāṭaka*s of land in the three villages belonging to the two *viṣaya*s of Vātagaṅgā and Gaṅgāmaṇḍala,[235] which may not have been far away from the Mainamati area, as the donee Laḍahamādhava was the same deity established by Laḍahacandra on Lalmai hill.[236] The large size of land plot makes a stark contrast with the earlier Candra grants and the near contemporary grant of Dadhieva, which also pertain to the area close to Mainamati.[237] The first *viṣaya* seems to have been created in the area along the river Vātagaṅgā, which had already experienced the early agrarian development in the fifth century, with establishment of extensive cultivated tracts held by individual and collective landholders.[238] It is difficult to guess what occurred in the 700 years or so between the year 184 GE, the date of the grant of Vainyagupta which approved the earlier grant in this area, and the time of the present plate, due to the lack of any other sources. The well-developed state of the area in the 13th century is attested by the market, boat landing, ferry, gate, *malaṅga*, areca nut trees and so on accompanying the land plots.[239] However, the availability of large size of plots for donation indicates the less complicated land relation and room for agrarian expansion, which in turn points to the recent development. In view of its location on the large and mighty river labelled *gaṅgā*, the area could have experienced many rounds of reclamations for the recovery from floods. The same can be said of Gaṅgāmaṇḍalaviṣaya according to its name. Thus, the exceptional case found in the grant of Vīradharadeva can be explained from the character of the area and its probable history of repeated reclamations.

Śrīhaṭṭa, which had room for agrarian expansion accompanying a large-scale grant in the first half of the tenth century,[240] saw a new phase of agrarian development in the 13th century, as shown by the Bhatera plate of Keśavadeva. It lists the 46 plots, including cultivated land (*bhūhala*), garden (*vāṭī*) or both within them, as objects of donation (**Table 6.4**). They were scattered over many settlements and some were located in reference to the neighbouring settlements or landmarks like markets, rivers, landing places, lake, cattle track and donated tracts.[241] Those settlements were well populated, and the labour service of 70 households of people in the nine settlements was assigned to the donee (**Table 6.4, nos 47–64**). Those facts show the emergence of an area with developed agrarian settlements in the sub-region which had been characterised for long time by large-scale donations accompanying social rearrangement based on the room for agrarian expansion.[242]

Thus, the sub-regions of Bengal experienced in different timelines a new phase of agrarian development and a limit of agrarian expansion resulting from it. The former was connected with the stratification of land rights which enabled the agrarian development through the mobilisation of subordinate labour power by the assignees of upper land rights. The agrarian expansion, however, reached a limit for some reasons, which can be the limitation of labour power, technology or both. It resulted in the congestion of agrarian tracts and necessitated the dispersal of assigned land.

This agrarian condition brought out a tendency, common to almost all the sub-regions, towards intensive use of landed property with emphasis on homestead land and gardens for growing products with commercial value, especially areca nuts and betel leaves. The Belava grant of Bhojavarman has a special reference to the donated land plot as 'accompanied by areca nut trees and so on,' apart from the common clause of 'with areca nut and coconut trees.'[243] The Idilpur and Madhyapada grants of Viśvarūpasena pertaining to the same sub-region of Vaṅga say that the tracts were donated 'after making shrines, ponds and so on, after planting areca nut and coconut trees and so on.'[244] As the land plots donated in both grants lay in well-developed agrarian tracts, these acts could be interpreted as additional investment aimed at their intensive use.

The land plots donated in the last grant include seven betel vine plantations (*varaja*) and three homestead land with areca nut trees (*guvākavāstubhū*) (**Table 6.5, nos 6, 8–9**). In view of this, homestead land accompanying the donated tracts of the Naihati and Saktipur plates pertaining to northern Rāḍha and Dighirpar-Bakultala grant related to the Bhagirathi estuary could also denote such land meant for plantations.[245]

Importance of homestead land and gardens is also discernible in the grants pertaining to Samataṭa and Śrīhaṭṭa in the 13th century. The land plots donated in the Mehar plate of Dāmodaradeva include the one with mound of homestead and garden (*vāṭikā*) and the land in homestead and garden (*gṛhavāṭyāṃ bhū*), which have high annual production of 50 and 52 *hiraṇya*s per *droṇa* respectively (**Table 6.3, nos 1, 15**). The land tract donated in the Sobharampur plate was combined with homestead land and bordered by house and garden of betel grower (*vārajika*) Guṇo to the south.[246] Similarly, the plots in the Nasirabad grant also included homestead and cultivated land, and a plot of 3 *droṇa*s among them was bordered by a garden of an *āśrama*.[247] One of the tracts donated in the Mainamati plate of Vīradharadeva, 12 *droṇa*s in villages Meśvāñcā and Athavasā, was accompanied by areca nut trees.[248] The Bhatera grant of Keśavadeva pertaining to Śrīhaṭṭa mentions many *vāṭī*s as a category separate from *bhūhala*s. Their size is substantial, in total 296 as mentioned in the grant and 334 according to my own calculation, and comparable with *bhūhala*s, which are 375 or 339 1/2 in total (**Table 6.4**). 2 *bhūhala*s of land confirmed of the donation to Viṣṇu temple in the other Bhatera grant of Īśānadeva included *vāstu* within it, in spite of its small size.[249]

Commercial cropping of areca nuts and coconuts had already been practiced by merchants in Varendra in the 11th century.[250] The spread of this practice to the other sub-regions, discernible from the emphasis on homestead land and gardens especially with areca nut trees and betel vines in the inscriptions mentioned above, was interconnected with the other phenomenon, namely, the commercialisation of rural economy which had also started earlier in Varendra and observed in the wider area of Bengal in this period. This is the most evident in the spread of monetary transaction attested by the assessment of annual production in a currency unit of *kapardakapurāṇa*, *purāṇa* or *hiraṇya* in the copper plate inscriptions of Gopāla IV and Madanapāla, all the Sena grants and the Mehar and Adavadi plates of Dāmodaradeva and Daśarathadeva, which cover the sub-regions of Varendra, Rāḍha, Vaṅga and Samataṭa.[251]

The depth of monetisation of rural economy is exhibited by the activities of Halāyudhaśarman recorded in the Madhyapada plate. He could purchase landholdings from groups of landholders by purchase deeds (*paṭṭolī*), and *śāsana* land from the other *brāhmaṇa* (**Table 6.5, nos 6–9, 10**). Such transactions are viable only when both sides are accustomed to some form of monetary system. Even though it did not take the form of payment in cash, accumulated wealth of the purchaser was calculated in a currency unit, and his payment could be accepted by sellers as such. The reference to the price of 3,000 areca nuts annually produced from areca nut plantation (*kalana*) belonging to one of the land plots also indicates routine monetary transaction, which includes sales of nuts (**Table 6.5, no. 6**).[252]

The commercialisation of rural economy is also attested by the presence of markets (*haṭṭa*) and commercial activities around them. Rāghavahaṭṭapāṭaka, one of the settlements which constituted the donated tract in the Saktipur plate, could have originated from such a market.[253] The two land plots donated in the Mainamati grant of Vīradharadeva were accompanied by markets and so on, and the first tract was also by boat landing (*ghaṭṭa*) and ferry (*tara*), indicating commercial activities facilitated by river traffics.[254]

More information on commercialisation of rural economy is available from the Sujanagar stone inscription, which records two transactions by *mahāsāmanta* Avūdeva. The first was the withdrawal of cash capital deposited to conch-shell workers, from which interest must have been generated and spent on religious matters. Avūdeva did it for the protection of sureties, with the assent of all the kinsmen belonging to the other countries.[255] It first of all presupposes the sales of manufactured products by conch-shell workers and the market for these staffs. As discussed above, the assent of kinsmen in abroad for this transaction points to their contribution to the cash capital and also to the possibility of commercial network constituted by them.[256] The second was the donation of right to levy tax on a market, which was his 'own enjoyment of *mahāsāmanta*', for repairs of a *vihāra* protected by Allahabhaṭṭārakasvāmin.[257] What was meant by this action seems to have been the transfer of the tax from a market, which was assigned by the king to Avūdeva for his service, to the religious institution, necessitated by the liquidation of the fund deposited to conch-shell workers. This deal presupposed vigorous trade activities around the market generating income. Thus, the two transactions recorded in the Sujanagar inscription attest to the commercialisation of rural economy in Vaṅga in the mid-12th century.

The social stratification and organisation of occupational groups in rural society, interconnected with the economic conditions discussed above, provoked the intervention of *brāhmaṇa*s in the two forms of social reorganisation attempted in the previous period, namely, the maintenance of cohesion of rural society and the consolidation of social groups based on common occupations.[258] Their initiatives and efforts in reorganisation of society are discernible in the *Purāṇa*s composed in Bengal in this period.

Puranic festivals: efforts towards social cohesion by Brahmanical initiative

The effort of *brāhmaṇa*s towards social cohesion is detectable in the prescriptions of festivals at special occasions in annual calendar. The most important and minutely described among them is the autumn goddess festival held in the month of Āśvina, which is called by names like *Durgotsava*, *Mahāṣṭamī* or *Navarātra* in the *Purāṇa*s. This is a festival centred on worship of the goddess known by Durgā and the other names by animal sacrifices and the other offerings on the eighth and ninth days of bright fortnight of the month Āśvina. Its procedure is described in several *Purāṇa*s and there are some variations among them, even between different sections of the same *Purāṇa*.[259] What is conspicuous in the accounts of this festival in the *Purāṇa*s compiled in Bengal in this period like the *Devībhāgavatapurāṇa*, the *Mahābhāgavatapurāṇa* and the *Bṛhaddharmapurāṇa*, and in the *Kālikāpurāṇa*, which seems to have been compiled in Assam or the part of Bengal near to it in the tenth or the first half of the 11th century,[260] is the character of the festival as a social gathering with temporary suppression of differences and subversion of the normal order.

According to the *Bṛhaddharmapurāṇa*, the festival starts with the invocation of the goddess on the ninth day of the dark fortnight in the month Āśvina.[261] It continues for 15 days until the ninth of the bright fortnight of the same month, and she is worshipped in the form of Vilva tree for the first 13 days.[262] On the seventh day of the bright fortnight, the goddess is brought to a house, and her worship with various kinds of animal sacrifice (*bali*) and overnight vigil (*jāgaraṇa*) is made in the following two days.[263] It especially prescribes fasting on the eighth and animal sacrifice on the ninth.[264] The *Mahābhāgavatapurāṇa* also mentions similar procedures starting with the invocation of the goddess in Vilva tree[265] and continues for 15 days, until the tenth of the bright fortnight.[266] According to the text, she should be worshipped in the earthen image from the seventh of the bright fortnight until the ninth.[267]

The *Bṛhaddharmapurāṇa* makes special instructions for the worship during the two days between the eighth and the ninth. The worship should be made by all the people, and *brāhmaṇa*s, *kṣatriya*s, *vaiśya*s and *śūdra*s with devotion would be always connected with profit and wisdom in the gathering, after discarding worldly duties, injuring, strife and selfishness. No teaching, studying, battle, purchase and sale, reception of a guest (*argha*) nor agriculture (*karṣa*) should be done at this time. A song with names of female and male genitals, with words of eroticism, should be sung and one should feed *brāhmaṇa*s and satisfy women.[268] Similarly, the *Devībhāgavatapurāṇa* prescribes great merrymaking (*mahotsava*) consisting of songs, music and dance during *Navarātra*[269] and the *Mahābhāgavatapurāṇa* mentions the release of the goddess image in a stream with a huge merrymaking (*sumahotsava*) on the tenth day.[270]

The merrymaking mentioned in the *Bṛhaddharmapurāṇa* and the *Mahābhāgavatapurāṇa* may correspond to *śāvarotsava* described in the *Kālikāpurāṇa*. The latter contains as many as eight accounts of the festival with variations according to the contexts and the forms of the goddess.[271] Among them, the two mention *śāvarotsava* and prescribe it at the time of dismissal of the goddess on the tenth day.[272] Jīmūtavāhana explains it in his *Kālaviveka* as follows:

> Being as if (one is) *śavara varṇa*, after becoming one whose body is covered by leaves and so on and smeared with mud and so on, who is devoted to jump, dance, song, instrumental music and so on connected with various ways. This is the meaning of the word *śāvarotsava*.[273]

Its contents are minutely explained in the *Kālikāpurāṇa*:

> With married women and young girls, with prostitutes, with actors, with sound of conch-shell and instruments, with drums, with kettle drums. With many kinds of banners and clothes, with scattered perched grains and flowers, with dust and mud slinging, with play (*krīḍā*), festivity (*kautuka*) and auspicious acts (*maṅgala*), with names of male and female genitals, with songs of male and female genitals, with pronouncement of male and female genitals and so on, people should play thoroughly. One who is not insulted by others and one who does not insult others, to him angry Bhagavatī gives a very terrible curse.[274]

This is thus a merrymaking made by people disguising themselves as *śavara*s, with much emphasis on obscenity and sexual acts. It is remarkable that this element of merrymaking is shared by the near contemporary *Purāṇa*s of Bengal and the *Kālikāpurāṇa*, although the latter contains the other accounts which show its emphasis on kingship indicated by the centrality of the king in rituals and the incorporation of the procession of army with 'lustration' (*nīrājana*) to the procedure.[275]

One characteristic of the social gathering during the goddess festival depicted in those *Purāṇa*s is a confirmation of solidarity through the temporary suppression of differences. The *Mahābhāgavatapurāṇa* claims that there is no consideration of sovereignty/power (*ādhipatya*) and *varṇa*s of devotees for the goddess.[276] The stipulations in the *Bṛhaddharmapurāṇa* about the worship on the eighth and ninth days mentioned above clearly show this character. Especially important is the prohibition of daily duties during the festival. These duties, teaching and study, battle, purchase and sale, reception of a guest and agriculture, seem to represent duties of four *varṇa*s. On the other hand, they can also be interpreted as the actions which differentiate people. They divide people into teachers and students, winners and losers, buyers and sellers, and guests and hosts. Agriculture also contains the element of domination and subordination between landholders and cultivators in the context of stratified land relations in this period.[277] Thus injunctions against those activities during the festival connote a temporary suppression of difference and power relation among members of rural society. It is comparable with *Puṣyayātrā* prescribed in the *Kṛṣiparāśara*, which was discussed in the previous chapter.[278] The prescription of merrymaking (*utsava*) with dance and music is also common to both, though merrymaking in the *Purāṇa*s contains more subversive elements of obscenity and sexual acts.

However, there are some critical differences between them. First, the temporary suppression of difference and participation by all the members prescribed in the *Purāṇa*s presuppose a difference of social ranks in the framework of four *varṇa*s. It is different from a social view asserted in the *Kṛṣiparāśara*, which tries to gloss over difference among cultivators and never mentions any *varṇa* or *jāti*.[279] This difference could be connected with the formation and consolidation of diverse social groups based on commonality of occupations.[280] The society, of which cohesion should be maintained, did not consist of idealised peasant householders but of diverse occupational groups consolidating themselves as *jāti*s. The application of the four *varṇa* scheme shows the intention of *brāhmaṇa*s to impose their social norms, even if notionally.

The second to note is the involvement of *brāhmaṇa*s in the festival. In the *Bṛhaddharmapurāṇa* and the *Mahābhāgavatapurāṇa*, their involvement is expressed as a stipulation of their feeding during the festival.[281] In case of the *Devībhāgavatapurāṇa*, *brāhmaṇa*s are first invited at the night on the new moon day after preparation of the place of worship (*maṇḍapa*).[282] Then they make recitation of scriptures and utter the word of welcome to the goddess according to *mantras* of the *Veda*, after being honoured by gift of clothes and ornaments and so on.[283] Though it is not clearly mentioned whether all the ritual procedures are officiated by *brāhmaṇa* priests in those accounts, their involvement makes a clear contrast to *Puṣyayātrā*, in which the recitation of *mantra* after merrymaking should be done by all the participants, without any intervention of priests.[284]

Similar tendency is noticeable in the other festivals described in the *Bṛhaddharmapurāṇa*. *Dīpānvitā* is a festival for worshipping goddess Kālī at the next new moon night after the full moon day of the month Āśvina.[285] In this festival, the goddess should be worshipped in the manner of *Mahāṣṭamī* festival or in Tantric way with animal sacrifice, offering of rice and so on.[286] It is also said that high-minded people who have subdued senses, desire for food and sleepiness should worship the goddess with offering of various kinds of clothes, ornaments, rice and *pāyasa*, and with songs, instrumental music and dance, accompanied with a row of candles.[287] Those people are also described as being delighted in Mālasī songs and mentioning female and male genitals.[288] The element of subversive merrymaking with obscenity is remarkable in these descriptions. On the other hand, the involvement of *brāhmaṇa*s as priests is obvious in the description that *brāhmaṇa*s should worship the goddess and the god, Kālī and Śiva, by abundant offerings of animals, flowers and honouring water,[289] and in the reference to the reward (*dakṣiṇā*) for four *prahara*s (a division of time corresponding to around three hours) of worship.[290] They should also be fed on the next day.[291]

Rāsotsava is a festival held on the full moon day of month Kārttika, in which Kṛṣṇa and *gopī*s (cowheardess) are worshipped in images. While this festival otherwise called *Gopikotsava* contains merrymaking with dance, song and instrumental music,[292] *brāhmaṇa*s should be invited and honoured by seats and washing of their feet for welcome, and by offering of various food, clothes, decorations, ornaments and so on before the worship.[293] They should be worshipped, rewarded and satisfied before the dismissal of the images, after which they should also be fed with sweets.[294]

All those festivals contain both characters of the social gathering with subversive merrymaking and the ritual involving *brāhmaṇa*s. What transpires here is the attempt of *brāhmaṇa*s to incorporate and regulate the festivals with popular elements, which may have functioned as occasions for reconfirming solidarity and cohesion of rural society, in a way which enables them to keep their authority and control. They tried to attain this aim by inserting themselves in the festivals at least as receivers of honour, even when they could not establish their position as officiating priests. They also tried to keep subversive elements under their control by limiting them to a specific period and even then by imposing some regulations. In the other chapter of the *Bṛhaddharmapurāṇa*, it is said that one should not utter the sound denoting female and male genitals to people belonging to other families (*paragocara*, literally 'other pasture') and should utter it during the days of *mahāpūjā* in the month Āśvina.[295] Even then, he should not utter it in front of his mothers and daughters, or female disciples who have not yet been initiated to *Śakti* worship.[296] We may detect here an ambiguous position of *brāhmaṇa*s concerning such subversive elements and a delicate balance struck by them.

The description of the other festival, *Śivamahotsava* held in month Caitra, alludes to the difficulty accompanying the attempt of *brāhmaṇa*s. This is a festival in which devotees worship Śiva with great merrymaking of dance and songs, by disguising themselves as he.[297] Its ecstatic and violent character is indicated by the mention of self-torment among devotees beginning with *kṣatriya*s.[298] In view of the absence of groups claiming *kṣatriya* status in the contemporary Bengal, the last category may indicate *ugra*s or the other groups engaging in military occupations,[299] including tribals who would participate in the festival. In this festival, *brāhmaṇa*s are conspicuous by their absence. They seem to have had much difficulty to penetrate into the festival, so that they tried to segregate it by limiting its venue to the outside of a village.[300]

Thus, we can see the efforts towards social cohesion by the initiative of *brāhmaṇas* in those festivals. Their attempts may be backed up by their enhanced position in rural society. However, their difficulty to accommodate popular elements is detectable in the accounts of festivals in the *Purāṇas* themselves. It is a process to be followed by further attempts in the later period.

Brahmanical systematisation of social order[301]

The attempt at social reorganisation based on professions, which started in the previous period and continued in this period, seems to have resulted in the making of various *jātis*. The presence of such groups is attested by the narrative of *Varṇasaṃkara* in the *Bṛhaddharmapurāṇa*. What this narrative conveys is, however, not an objective account of those groups. A careful reading of the narrative reveals an attempt of *brāhmaṇas* at comprehension of stratified and variegated social reality and its systematisation.

The concept of *Varṇasaṃkara*, that is, the mixture or intermarriage of different *varṇas* resulting in their progeny with inferior status and particular professions, was introduced by the *Dharmasūtras* and had been employed to comprehend and explain the presence of social groups other than the four *varṇas* in the texts of the following period.[302] What is characteristic of the narrative in the *Bṛhaddharmapurāṇa* is the combination of the theory of *Varṇasaṃkara* with the story of king Veṇa, which is narrated in the *Mahābhārata* and the early *Purāṇas* to explain the origin of Niṣādas.[303] In the present text, *Varṇasaṃkara* is depicted as a result of evil deed of the king.

The narrative is unfolded in the 13th and 14th chapters of Uttarakhaṇḍa of the *Bṛhaddharmapurāṇa*, as the narration by Vyāsa to Jāvāli. The narration of Vyāsa starts with the genealogy of Veṇa, followed by his evil deeds as a prince, which resulted in the abdication of his father Aṅga and Veṇa's accession to the throne.[304] As Veṇa disturbed *dharma*, the sages came to admonish him and explained the result of abandonment of *dharma*.[305] They mentioned the confusion of ownership of property, women and house as its result.[306] They also explained that a country with unrighteous king is the same as a country without king and there would be the intercourse with the other's wife and the mixture of *varṇas*.[307] They finally warned Veṇa that the mixture (*saṃkara*) is the way to the hell.[308] Provoked by this statement by the sages, he forced members of the different *varṇas* intermarry and made them produce mixed progeny. He further made the mixed progeny produce their offspring.[309] As a result of the mixture of *varṇas*, the three ranks of *saṃkaras* were produced (**Table 6.6**).

Among the *saṃkaras*, the 20 resulted from the mixtures of four *varṇas*, except one between a *śūdra* father and a *brāhmaṇa* mother, were ranked

Table 6.6 Varṇasaṃkaras in the Bṛhaddharmapurāṇa (Haraprasad Shastri (ed.), *Bṛhaddharmapurāṇam* (2nd ed.), Varanasi: Krishnadas Academy, 1974.)

No.	*Father*	*Mother*	*Offspring*	*Ref.*	*Occupation*	*Ref.*
			Uttama (20)			
1	*Vaiśya*	*Śūdra*	*Karaṇa*	3. 13. 34	Duty of king.	3. 14. 34
2	*Brāhmaṇa*	*Vaiśya*	*Ambaṣṭha* (*Vaidya*)	3. 13. 35	Medicine.	3. 14. 48
3			*Gandhiko Vaṇik* (*Vaṇik*)	3. 13. 35	Sales of condiments,	3. 14. 63
4	*Brāhmaṇa*	(*Vaiśya*)	*Kaṃsakāra*	3. 13. 35	Works on copper and brass etc.	3. 14. 65
5			*Śaṅkhakāra* (*Śāṅkhika*)	3. 13. 35	Conch-shell ornament.	3. 14. 65
6	*Kṣatriya*	*Vaiśya*	*Ugra*	3. 13. 36	*Kṣatravṛtti*.	3. 14. 55
7			*Rājaputra*	3. 13. 36		
8	(*Brāhmaṇa*)	*Kṣatriya*	*Kumbhakāra*	3. 13. 36	Clay works.	3. 14. 65
9			*Tantravāya*	3. 13. 36	Garment production.	3. 14. 63
10	*Śūdra*	*Kṣatriya*	*Karmakāra*	3. 13. 37	Iron smithy.	3. 14. 64
11			*Dāsa*	3. 13. 37	Agricultural works (*kṛṣikarmāṇi*)	3. 14. 66
12	*Vaiśya*	*Kṣatriya*	*Māgadha*	3. 13. 37	Admirer of *brāhmaṇa* and *kṣatriya*, carrier of their documents, superintendent of *kṣatraveda*.	3. 14. 58–59
13			*Gopa*	3. 13. 37	Writing.	3. 14. 63
14	*Kṣatriya*	*Śūdra*	*Nāpita*	3. 13. 38	Shaving	3. 14. 63
15			*Modaka*	3. 13. 38	Molasses making	3. 14. 66
16	*Brāhmaṇa*	*Śūdra*	*Vārajīvin* (betel vine grower)	3. 13. 38		
17	*Kṣatriya*	*Brāhmaṇa*	*Sūta*	3. 13. 39	Help for *dāsa*.	3. 14. 66
18			*Mālākāra*	3. 13. 39	Flower plucking for *devapūjā* of all.	3. 14. 66–67
19	*Vaiśya*	*Brāhmaṇa*	*Tāmbūli*	3. 13. 39	Sales of betel leaves.	3. 14. 60*
20			*Taulika* (*Tailika*)	3. 13. 39	Sales of areca nuts.	3. 14. 64
			Madhyama (12)			
21	*Karaṇa*	*Vaiśya*	*Takṣan* (carpenter)	3. 13. 41		
22			*Rajaka* (washerman)	3. 13. 41		
23	*Ambaṣṭha*	*Vaiśya*	*Svarṇakāra*	3. 13. 41	Examination of gold and silver ornaments etc.	3. 14. 67
24			*Svarṇavaṇik* (*Kānako Vaṇik*)	3. 13. 41	Inspection of genuineness of gold, silver ornaments etc.	3. 14. 68

25	*Gopa*	*Vaiśya*	*Ābhīra* (cowherd)	3. 13. 42		
26			*Tailakāraka* (oil presser)	3. 13. 42		
27	*Gopa*	*Śūdra*	*Dhīvara* (fisher/boatman)	3. 13. 42		
28			*Śauṇḍika* (vintner)	3. 13. 42		
29	*Mālākāra*	*Śūdra*	*Naṭa* (actor)	3. 13. 43		
30			*Śāvāka* (*Śrāvaka*)	3. 13. 43		
31	*Māgadha*	*Śūdra*	*Śekhara*	3. 13. 43		
32			*Jālika* (fisher)	3. 13. 43		
			Adhama/Antyaja (8)			
33	*Svarṇakāra*	*Vaidya*	*Malegrahin* (sweeper)	3. 13. 44		
34	*Svarṇavaṇik*	*Vaidya*	*Kuḍava*	3. 13. 45		
35	*Śūdra*	*Brāhmaṇa*	*Cāṇḍāla*	3. 13. 45		
36	*Ābhīra*	*Gopa*	*Varuḍa*	3. 13. 46		
37	*Takṣan*	*Vaiśya*	*Carmakāra* (leatherworker)	3. 13. 46		
38	*Rajaka*	*Vaiśya*	*Ghaṇṭajīvin* (*Ghaṭṭajīvin*, ferryman)	3. 13. 47		
39	*Tailakāra*	*Vaiśya*	*Dolāvāhin* (palanquin bearer)	3. 13. 47		
40	Dhīvara	*Śūdra*	*Malla* (wrestler)	3. 13. 48		
41			*Devala/Śākadvīpī dvija*	3. 13. 52		
42	*Devala*	*Vaiśya*	*Gaṇaka* (*Grahavipra*)	3. 13. 52	*Jyotiḥśāstra.*	3. 14. 71
43			*Vādaka* (speaker)	3. 13. 52		
			Outsiders (9)			
44	Veṇa		Mleccha	3. 13. 53		
45	Mleccha		Pulinda	3. 13. 53		
46	Mleccha		Pukkaśa	3. 13. 53		
47	Mleccha		Khaśa	3. 13. 53		
48	Mleccha		Yavana	3. 13. 53		
49	Mleccha		Suhma	3. 13. 54		
50	Mleccha		Kamboja	3. 13. 54		
51	Mleccha		Śavara	3. 13. 54		
52	Mleccha		Khara	3. 13. 54		

*This verse is included in Panchanana Tarkaratna (ed.), *Bṛhaddharmmapurāṇa*, Calcutta: Navbharat Publishers, 1396 BS (1989) (reprint).

as *Uttama* (the best) (**Table 6.6, nos 1–20**).[310] The 12 offspring from the unions of *karaṇa*, *ambaṣṭha*, *gopa* fathers and *vaiśya* mothers, and of *gopa*, *mālākāra*, *māgadha* fathers and *śūdra* mothers was called *Madhyama* (middle) (**Table 6.6, nos 21–32**).[311] The third rank called *Adhama* (the lowest) or *Antyaja*s were resulted from the mixtures of *Madhyama*s, *Madhyama* fathers and *vaidya*, *gopa*, *vaiśya* or *śūdra* mothers, with an exception of *cāṇḍāla* who was from a *śūdra* father and a *brāhmaṇa* mother (**Table 6.6, nos 33–40**).[312] They were declared to be outside the *varṇāśramadharma*.[313] All those *saṃkara*s were mentioned as 'the 36 natural occupations with additions.'[314] The description of *saṃkara*s is followed by the reference to *devala*, who was brought from Śākadvīpa by Suparṇa (Garuḍa) and called *śākadvīpī vipra* (*brāhmaṇa*), and to *gaṇaka* and *vādaka* born to him and a *vaiśya* woman (**Table 6.6, nos 41–43**).[315] Then it is said that Mleccha was born from Veṇa's body and the sons like Pulinda, Pukkaśa, Khaśa, Yavana, Suhma, Kamboja, Śavara and Khara were born from him (**Table 6.6, nos 44–52**).[316] After seeing the destruction of *dharma* by Veṇa, the group of sages came to him and killed him by their word. Then they created king Pṛthu, who was Viṣṇu himself, and his consort from Veṇa's body, and the order was restored under him.[317]

The 14th chapter starts with the summoning of *brāhmaṇa*s by Pṛthu, who could not get the comfort of his mind while governing his kingdom righteously, because the earth did not yield food for people.[318] *Brāhmaṇa*s answered his enquiry and said that the earth did not yield food because she bore the burden of pain made by *saṃkara*s roaming around on her.[319] They offered the solutions to the king, who asked them how to deal with those *saṃkara*s.[320] They first told him to stop further mixture of *jāti*s and *saṃkara*s.[321] Then they advised him to summon *saṃkara*s and hold 'the gathering of *dharma*' (*dharmasaṃgraha*) to decide on their occupations.[322] Following their advice, Pṛthu summoned and interrogated the group of *saṃkara*s. After their initial defiance towards the king and the following subjugation through punishment, *saṃkara*s obeyed him.[323] The king requested the *brāhmaṇa*s to decide *varṇa*s and occupations of *saṃkara*s. The *brāhmaṇa*s interrogated *saṃkara*s after declaring that those '36 *jāti*s' were *śūdra*s.[324]

Among the *saṃkara*s, *karaṇa* talked to *brāhmaṇa*s at first and showed humility and submission by admitting their stupidity, low-origin and lack of wisdom.[325] Delighted by his word, *brāhmaṇa*s said to the king that *karaṇa* should do the duty of king (*rājakārya*) as he was furnished with discipline and good behaviour, spoke excellently, and knew policy (*nīti*).[326] They declared him to be a *satśūdra* because of his devotion to *brāhmaṇa*s and deities. They also claimed that devotion to *brāhmaṇa*s, homage to deities, lack of envy (*amātsarya*) and good discipline (*suśīlatva*) were criteria of a *satśūdra*.[327] Then *brāhmaṇa*s directed *karaṇa*, who bowed to them, to be suitable for king's duty and skilful in writing (*lipikarma*), to show devotion to *brāhmaṇa*s, to discard envy and so on. They guaranteed him that his descendant would be equal to himself.[328] The decision on *ambaṣṭha* followed the case of *karaṇa*. *Brāhmaṇa*s first performed the initiatory rite (*saṃskāra*) for *ambaṣṭha* and made him as if he were reborn, because he committed the sin of making offspring with *vaiśya* woman who belonged to the same *varṇa* as his mother.[329] Then they created *Āyurveda* with the help of Aśvins and gave it and the name *vaidya* to *ambaṣṭha*.[330] They assigned medicine (*cikitsā*, *vaidika*) as his occupation, with warning against neglecting *Āyurveda* and reciting (learning) other scriptures like *Purāṇa*s.[331] Then *brāhmaṇa*s assigned powerful and ferocious *ugra* the occupation of *kṣatriya* (*kṣatravṛtti*) due to his suitability for combat, and tried to put *māgadha* to the same duty.[332] *Māgadha* rejected it and asked royal activities (*rājakarman*) other than occupation of war (*yuddhavṛtti*). *Brāhmaṇa*s assigned him duties as an admirer of *brāhmaṇa* and *kṣatriya*, a conveyer (*voḍhā*) of their documents and a superintendent of knowledge of *kṣatriya* (*kṣatraveda*).[333] Then *brāhmaṇa*s decided the occupations of the remaining *Uttamasaṃkara*s, and *svarṇakāra* and *svarṇavaṇik*.[334] After deciding occupations of *saṃkara*s, *brāhmaṇa*s bestowed *Jyotiḥśāstra*s to *gaṇaka* and made him *grahavipra* (astrologer).[335] Then *saṃkara*s asked *brāhmaṇa*s who would preside over their *Vaidika*, *Smārta* and *Āgamika* rituals. *Brāhmaṇa*s replied that *śrotriya*s themselves would be the priests for the 20 *Uttamajāti*s and fallen *brāhmaṇa*s would be the priests for the 16 other *jāti*s.[336] Thus everything was settled and Pṛthu could make the earth yield crops again.[337]

The general framework of the narrative, which combines *Varṇasaṃkara* and the myth of Veṇa and Pṛthu, might show the emphasis of *brāhmaṇa*s on the centrality of the king and the importance of proper marriage for the maintenance of the order.[338] However, a minute scrutiny of the text enables us to read the intention and effort of the *brāhmaṇa*s to comprehend various social groups in contemporary Bengal and redefine their positions in a hierarchical order, with their own dominance kept over the others.

All the *saṃkara*s are deemed to be *śūdra*s and this supposition results in the *varṇa* composition devoid of the two intermediate *varṇa*s.[339] Their absence might reflect the situation in contemporary Bengal, which witnessed neither the rise of political powers legitimised by their claim of authentic *kṣatriya* status nor the dominance of merchant groups, unlike in western India.[340] The dichotomy of *brāhmaṇa*s and *śūdra*s can otherwise be interpreted as claim of superiority over any other social groups by *brāhmaṇa*s, which was made possible by their dominance in rural society. The theory of *Varṇasaṃkara* thus enabled the *brāhmaṇa*s to legitimise and explain the absence of the two intermediate *varṇa*s and their dominance without any contenders.

The employment of this scheme also offered them a way to explain and impose a social hierarchy on the other members of rural society in conformity with Brahmanical social view. Three ranks of *Uttama*, *Madhyama* and

Adhama/Antyaja may be based on the actual social hierarchy perceived by *brāhmaṇa*s, though the status of *svarṇakāra* and *svarṇavaṇik* show some ambiguity. By the scheme of *Varṇasaṃkara*, this hierarchy could be converted into the ritual ranks which can be explained by the Brahmanical social view of four *varṇa*s and the extent of their mixture. The ranks of *Uttama* and *Madhyama* are explained as results of intermarriages among four *varṇa*s and *pratiloma* liaisons between *Uttamasaṃkara* men and *vaiśya*, *śūdra* women respectively, while the origin of *Adhama* rank is attributed to *pratiloma* marriages between *Madhyamasaṃkara* men and *Uttamasaṃakara*, *vaiśya*, *śūdra* women, except *cāṇḍālas* born to *śūdra* father and *brāhmaṇa* mother (**Table 6.6**). This system of three ranks is complemented by another system of ritual status in relation to the service of *brāhmaṇa*s. It differentiates *Uttamasaṃkara*s as *satśūdra*s deserving ritual services of highly qualified *śrotriya brāhmaṇa*s, from the others to be served by fallen *brāhmaṇa*s with the same status as themselves. This system of ritual status makes the relation with *brāhmaṇa*s a decisive factor for the position of the other groups in the social hierarchy.

The other social groups listed as Veṇa's descendants seem to be outsiders to the Brahmanical fold, including foreigners and non-sedentary groups. The story of king Veṇa, which narrated the creation of Niṣādas from his left thigh in the earlier texts,[341] enabled *brāhmaṇa*s to comprehend them as outsiders of the *Varṇasaṃkara* scheme. The ambiguous position of *gaṇaka*s, who are included in neither *saṃkara*s nor outsiders, seems to be related to their position as a literate group, as will be discussed below.

The claim of authority by *brāhmaṇa*s can be read in the episode of the gathering of *dharma* (*dharmasaṃgraha*), which decides occupations of *saṃkara*s. What is notable is that the *brāhmaṇa*s take the initiative in the decision, while the gathering is convened by king Pṛthu following their advice.[342] They claim themselves to be the custodians of *dharma*, the proper social order, while admitting the royal authority.

The sequence of defiance and subjugation of *saṃkara*s, which occurs at the beginning of the gathering, provides an interesting view about their claim of authority and control. It begins with the remark of the king about *saṃkara*s. He described them as deformed (*vikṛtākāra*), ill-clothed (*kucela*), dirty-faced (*malinānana*), withered (*śīrṇa*) and very weak (*sudurbala*), and lamented what kind of knowledge he would hear from them.[343] *Saṃkara*s countered his remarks by claiming themselves as clean-formed (*śubhākāra*), well-clothed (*sucela*), clean-faced (*vimalānana*), clean-bodied (*śubhāṅga*) and strong (*subala*), and claimed him to be blind.[344] They declared that they were the same as Veṇa, protected and produced by him, and that even the deities like Brahmā and Viṣṇu were not superior to them.[345] Hearing these words, the *brāhmaṇa*s laughed at them and the infuriated king bound them. Tormented and bound, *saṃkara*s asked the king to protect them.[346] They agreed to obey the king's order and asked him to convert them from deformed to clean-formed, decide their *varṇa*s, occupations and names, and destroy their offence due to foolish knowledge of Veṇa.[347]

This episode can be interpreted as a textual representation of the subjugation of the other social groups by *brāhmaṇa*s. It explains and legitimises the subordinated and 'disciplined' condition of *saṃkara*s, in which they accept the authority of *brāhmaṇa*s and their discourse.[348] One important aspect of the process of subjugation is the exercise of coercive power (*daṇḍa*). The defiance of *saṃkara*s makes an occasion for the use of *daṇḍa* by the king to subdue them. It is preceded by the advice of *brāhmaṇa*s not to kill but to punish errant people.[349] This event indicates the acceptance of the royal authority by *brāhmaṇa*s. However, his power is limited to the maintenance and imposition of the social order stipulated by *brāhmaṇa*s who take the initiative all through this narrative. We may detect here an intention of *brāhmaṇa*s to define kingship as a necessary but secondary power under Brahmanical authority.

Another aspect is the imposition of perception as a form of subjugation. The remarks on *saṃakara*s made by Pṛthu can be interpreted as representation of an image of the subordinate group perceived by the dominant. Importantly, the defiance of *saṃkara*s takes a form of word-for-word denial and counterclaim against this perception. The subjugation is also expressed by the acceptance of 'deformed' (*vikṛtākāra*), one of those remarks, as their own image.[350] Thus the perception is conceived as a point of contention between the dominant and the subordinate, and the imposition of perception of the former upon the latter constitutes an indispensable element of subjugation. This point is endorsed by the expression that *saṃkara*s become beautiful (*cārurūpa*) and intelligent (*subuddhi*) after *brāhmaṇa*s put them to their proper occupations,[351] which is a result of their acceptance of the authority of *brāhmaṇa*s and the social order enacted by them. The importance of this aspect should be emphasised from the fact that the aim of whole the episode narrated here can be interpreted as the imposition of a social image perceived by *brāhmaṇa*s on the other groups.

The interrogations of *saṃkara*s by *brāhmaṇa*s, through which their occupations are fixed, show the social groups over whom *brāhmaṇa*s tried to establish their authority, and a delicate balance with which they achieved their aim. The social groups of which occupations are decided in the 14th chapter of the text are limited to the 21, including all the *Uttamasaṃkara*s except *rājaputra* and *vārajīvin*, *svarṇakāra* and *svarṇavaṇik* among *Madhyamasaṃkara*s, and *gaṇaka* (**Table 6.6, nos 1–6, 8–15, 17–20, 23–24, 42**). The emphasis on *Uttamasaṃkaras* is clear. This category includes groups with literacy (*karaṇa*, *ambaṣṭha*, *māgadha*, *gopa*) and administrative function (*karaṇa*, *ugra*, *māgadha*), and merchants specialised in particular commodities (*gandhika*, *tāmbūli*, *taulika*), apart from agriculturists, artisans and the other service groups (**Table 6.6, nos 1–20**).[352] They can be considered the people who wield some authority in rural society because of their superiority in terms of knowledge, power and wealth. *Brāhmaṇa*s might have needed their compliance to keep their own authority in rural society. Their intention to establish the authority over these groups is discernible in the references to qualities of *satśūdra*s synonymous with *Uttamasaṃkara*s. In these references, devotion (*bhakti*) to *brāhmaṇa*s and lack of envy (*amātsarya*) are especially listed as criteria of a *satśūdra*.[353]

The cases of *svarṇakāra*, *svarṇavaṇik* and *gaṇaka*, on the other hand, show some ambiguity. Among *Madhyamasaṃkara*s, *svarṇakāra* and *svarṇavaṇik* are especially mentioned in the context of decision of occupations, while the others are not. It may be due to their wealth accruing from their involvement with craft and trade in gold and other precious metals that *brāhmaṇa*s cannot ignore them as the others included in this category. However, the occupations assigned to them are examination (*nirūpaṇa*) and inspection of genuineness (*tattvaparīkṣā*) of gold and silver ornaments and so on,[354] and not craft and trade of those staffs as inferable from their names. We may detect here the intension of *brāhmaṇa*s to restrict these wealthy groups in terms of both their ritual status and occupations. In case of *gaṇaka*, their special treatment may be due to their character as a literate group.

The effort of *brāhmaṇa*s to maintain their authority and a delicate balance which they struck in this exercise are the most evident in their treatment of literate groups. In the episode of *dharmasaṃgraha*, *karaṇa*, *ambaṣṭha* and *māgadha* are mentioned with special plots of which each consists of eight to 14 verses.[355] The case of *gaṇaka* is described by a full verse.[356] They make a stark contrast with the other cases, in which occupations of two to four *jāti*s are explained in each verse.[357]

Karaṇa is listed at the foremost of *saṃkara*s and depicted as their representative, who spoke out first.[358] He is also described as a paradigmatic *satśūdra*, for the explanation of *satśūdra* in general follows the description of his good characters and *satśūdra* status.[359] He is also assigned to the king's duty, which seems to mean administrative functions, due to his knowledge of policy. These statements indicate the admission of his prominent position in rural society by *brāhmaṇa*s. On the other hand, the depiction of his humility and submission to *brāhmaṇa*s and appraisal of his devotion to them as virtue common to *satśūdra*s allude to their intention to assign him a subordinate position. In case of *ambaṣṭha*, his dependence on *brāhmaṇa*s is represented by their *saṃskāra* which cleansed him of sin and their creation and bestowal of *Āyurveda*, while his high position is admitted and expressed as his origin from a *brāhmaṇa* father.[360] The special character of his knowledge is also acknowledged by a reference to the help of Aśvins for its creation, which contradicts the credit claimed by *brāhmaṇa*s.[361] *Māgadha*'s dependence on *brāhmaṇa*s is expressed in their duties as an admirer of *brāhmaṇa*s and *kṣatriya*s, and as conveyer of their documents, while another duty as a custodian of *kṣatraveda* implies their admission of his special knowledge.[362] *Gaṇaka* occupies a special position. Though his foreign origin is alluded to by mentioning *śākadvīpī brāhmaṇa* as his father,[363] he is not bundled together with the other foreign groups who are claimed to be Veṇa's descendants. He is not categorised as *saṃkara* either. However, his importance is duly acknowledged with his occupation as an astrologer decided by *brāhmaṇa*s like that of *Uttama*s. On the other hand, the bestowal of his knowledge, *Jyotiḥśāstra*s, is credited to *brāhmaṇa*s.[364]

These groups are literates with alternative knowledge, or at least recognised as such by *brāhmaṇa*s. The caution of *brāhmaṇa*s in these groups is discernible in a warning to *ambaṣṭha* against learning other scriptures like *Purāṇa*s.[365] The mention of *Purāṇa*s in this context points to the anxiety of *brāhmaṇa*s about a potential encroachment by these groups upon their intellectual domain. Confronting this challenge, *brāhmaṇa*s concede the possession of a particular branch of specialised knowledge by each of those literate groups. *Brāhmaṇa*s also admit their prominent position among *saṃkara*s. Both *ambaṣṭha* and *māgadha* are addressed as 'the best of *saṃkara*s' (*saṃkarottama*),[366] while *karaṇa* is described as a representative of all the *saṃkara*s as discussed above. Admission of *gaṇaka*'s prominence is reflected in his ambiguous position between *saṃkara*s and outsiders. On the other hand, *brāhmaṇa*s claim the authority over these literates through the emphasis of their dependence on *brāhmaṇa*s. The rhetoric especially employed for this purpose is the bestowal of knowledge by *brāhmaṇa*s, as is the case of *ambaṣṭha* and *gaṇaka*. What is discernible here is the intention and effort of *brāhmaṇa*s to accommodate literate groups and secure their cooperation through concession, while maintaining the authority over those groups.

The narrative discussed above can be seen as an attempt to design a framework of social systematisation by *brāhmaṇa*s through which they give a meaning and explanation to the social reality perceived by them and try to impose a social order compatible with their own worldview. The tension between them and the other social groups accompanying this attempt is recognisable in the fact that the text needs to include the episode of the defiance and subjugation of the *saṃkara*s for legitimising the authority of *brāhmaṇa*s to decide matters related to these social groups. This episode and the interactions between *brāhmaṇa*s and *saṃkara*s also suggest the negotiation between both sides. In this negotiation, the emphasis is laid on securing compliance of the upper section of rural society, especially the literate groups with alternative knowledge. It conforms to the Brahmanical way to accommodate local cultures in what Kunal Chakrabarti calls Puranic process in the context of the early medieval Bengal.[367]

The result of the negotiation, or the extent of the success of *brāhmaṇa*s in their attempt, is not clear from the contemporary sources, as texts like the *Dharmanibandha*s rather maintain the four *varṇa* scheme. For example, Jīmūtavāhana discusses shares of inheritance for the sons born to mothers of different *varṇa*s by this scheme in his *Dāyabhāga*.[368] Only once he mentions 'between (different) *varṇas*' (*varṇāntarāla*) and 'mixed origin' (*saṃkīrṇajāta*) in a vague manner.[369]

The continuance of such an attempt in the later period is attested by another narrative related to *Varṇasaṃkara* in the *Brahmavaivartapurāṇa*.[370] Many social groups which appeared in the *Bṛhaddharmapurāṇa* are mentioned in this text, with additions of the other groups, and the three-layered ranks are loosely followed without systematisation.[371] However, a totally different approach is taken in the narrative concerning *Varṇasaṃkara* in the text. The origin of *saṃkara*s is connected not only with marriage among different *varṇa*s and *jāti*s, but also with divine genealogy. The nine *jāti*s of artisans (*śilpakārin*) are claimed to be born to Viśvakarman and *apsaras* Ghṛtācī, who were born as a *brāhmaṇa* man and a *śūdra* woman because of the curse cast on each other.[372] The different approaches of the two texts show that the systematisation of social order attempted by *brāhmaṇa*s was a process which required their multiple trials and long term effort. The attempt detectable in the *Bṛhaddharmapurāṇa* could be the first step taken by them.

The two forms of social reorientation and systematisation by the initiative of *brāhmaṇa*s discussed above are complementary to each other. The Brahmanical festivals for social cohesion were necessary to integrate diverse social groups consolidating themselves as organisations, which were defined as *jāti*s and arranged in a hierarchical order. The socio-economic changes of the period, the social stratification and the organisation of occupational groups interconnected with the stratified land relation and commercialisation of rural economy provoked the Brahmanical intervention in these forms, which were in turn enabled by the establishment of Brahmanical authority.

Notes

1 For their history, see Abdul Momin Chowdhury, *Dynastic History of Bengal (c. 750–1200 A. D.)*, Dacca: The Asiatic Society of Pakistan, 1967, pp. 189–201.

2 As the Rajibpur CPI of Madanapāla is dated year 22 of his reign which began 1143 AD, he surely kept a part of Varendra until 1165 AD. Ryosuke Furui, 'Rajibpur Copperplate Inscriptions of Gopāla IV and Madanapāla', *Pratna Samiksha: A Journal of Archaeology, New Series*, 2015, 6: 56.

3 For the history of the Senas, see Chowdhury, *Dynastic History of Bengal*, pp. 204–64.

4 *Ibid*., pp. 263–64.

5 Their reigns and genealogy are known from the two Bhatera grants. *CPS*, pp. 153–203.

6 Haraprasad Sastri (ed.), Radhagovinda Basak (rev., tr., notes), *Rāmacaritam of Sandhyākaranandin*, Calcutta: The Asiatic Society, 1969, 1. 48, commentary.

7 *Rāmacarita*, 4. 1, 3. 27.

8 Furui, 'Rajibpur Copperplate', p. 43, ll. 37–38; N. N. Vasu, 'Copper-plate Inscription of Madanapāla', *Journal of the Asiatic Society of Bengal*, 1900, 69(1): 71, ll. 32–33; Furui, 'Rajibpur Copperplate', p. 51, ll. 32–35.

9 *Ibid.*, p. 43, ll. 37–38, p. 45, l. 51; Vasu, 'Copper-plate Inscription of Madanapāla', p. 71, ll. 32–33; Furui, 'Rajibpur Copperplate', p. 53, l. 48.
10 *Ibid.*, p. 51, l. 33.
11 *Ibid.*, p. 58.
12 Vasu, 'Copper-plate Inscription of Madanapāla', p. 71, l. 32. Vasu read the relevant part as *kāṣṭhagirisaṃ*, which can be easily corrected to *koṣṭhāgārasaṃ* by presuming that he missed a stroke to the left of *ka* and mistook a stroke indicating vowel *ā* to the right of *ṣṭha* and *ga* for a vowel sign *i* to the left of *ga* and *ra*.
13 Furui, 'Rajibpur Copperplate', pp. 56–58.
14 Vasu, 'Coppr-plate Inscription of Madanapāla', p. 72, l. 41; Furui, 'Rajibpur Copperplate', p. 53, ll. 43–44.
15 *Rāmacarita*, 4. 22–23.
16 Supra Chapter 5.
17 *Rāmacarita*, 3. 46–47.
18 *Ibid.*, 4. 18–21.
19 Furui, 'Rajibpur Copperplate', p. 45, ll. 62–63, p. 53, ll. 59–60; Vasu, 'Copper-plate Inscription of Madanapāla', p. 73, ll. 56–57.
20 D. C. Sircar, 'Rajghat Inscription of Bhimadeva', *Epigraphia Indica*, 1957–58 (1987), 32: 281, ll. 1–3, vv. 1–2.
21 *Ibid.*, p. 281, ll. 6–8, v. 5.
22 Ryosuke Furui, 'Chaprakot Stone Inscription of the Time of Gopāla IV, Year 9', in Alamgir Muhammad Serajuddin, Nazrul Islam, Sultana Shafee, Syed Manzoorul Islam and Syed Mohammad Shaheed (eds), *Centenary Commemorative Volume (1913–2013)*, Dhaka: Bangladesh National Museum, 2013, pp. 110–17.
23 Kamauli CPI of Vaidyadeva, Arthur Venis, 'Copper-plate Grant of Vaidyadeva, King of Kāmarūpa', *Epigraphia Indica*, 1894 (1984), 2: 351, ll. 19–20, v. 13.
24 *Ibid.*, pp. 350–51, ll. 3–19, vv. 3–12.
25 *Ibid.*, pp. 351–52, ll. 19–22, vv. 13–14.
26 *Ibid.*, p. 353, ll. 47–48.
27 *Rāmacarita*, 2. 6, commentary. For his identification, see Chowdhury, *Dynastic History of Bengal*, pp. 119–20.
28 *dattvā divyabhuvaḥ pratikṣitibhṛtām urvvīm urīkurvvatā vīrāsṛglipilāñchito 'sir amunā prāg eva pattrīkṛtaḥ*, *IB*, p. 48, l. 18, v. 19ab. As is correctly pointed out by Chowdhury, *divyabhū* connotes 'land of Divya', that is, Varendra occupied by Divya the *kaivarta* chief in double entendre. Chowdhury, *Dynastic History of Bengal*, pp. 221–22.
29 *IB*, p. 42.
30 *Ibid.*, p. 62, ll. 23–24.
31 Samantasar CPI of Harivarman and Vajrayogini CPI of Sāmalavarman, N. K. Bhattasali, 'Two Grants of Varmans of Vanga', *Epigraphia Indica*, 1953–54 (1987), 30: 255–63; Belava CPI of Bhojavarman, *IB*, pp. 14–24; Sujanagar stone inscription of the time of Bhojavarman, year 7, Shariful Islam, 'Unpublished Stone Inscription of the Seventh Regnal Year of Bhojavarman', *Journal of the Asiatic Society of Bangladesh, Humanities*, 2010, 55(1): 113–19.
32 Samantasar CPI, Bhattasali, 'Two Grants of Varmans', p. 258, 2. 9–11, 15, Vajrayogini CPI, *ibid.*, p. 263, 2. 4–6, 10–11; Belava CPI, *IB*, p. 21, ll. 37–41, 47–48. For discussions on the previous period, see Supra Chapter 5.
33 *pāñcakulikahāsī[su]tamahāsāmantaśrīavūdevena*, Sujanagar stone inscription, ll. 3–4, my own reading from the photograph. Cf. Islam, 'Unpublished Stone Inscription', p. 117, ll. 3–4. Islam could not actually read the inscription so that he made several untenable conjectures and unnecessary discussions.
34 *pāradeśikasamastajñātīnām anumatyā*, Sujanagar stone inscription, ll. 2–3.

35 For the interpretation of *pañcakula* based on inscriptional sources, see Masahiko Mita, 'Panchakula To Mahājana: Chūseishoki Rājasthān-Gujarāt No Toshigyōsei To Shūkaisoshiki' (*Pañcakula* and *Mahājana*: Urban Administration and Assembly Organisation in Early Medieval Rajasthan and Gujarat) (in Japanese), in Nobuhiro Ota (ed.), *Zen-kindai Minami-Ajia Shakai Ni Okeru Matomari To Tsunagari* (*Clustering and Connections in Pre-Modern South Asian Society*), Tokyo: Research Institute for Languages and Cultures of Asia and Africa, Tokyo University of Foreign Studies, 2017, pp. 62–72. Cf. *IEG*, p. 230.

36 *svakīyamahāsāmantabhogahaṭṭagrahakḷptaṃ ca dattam iti*, Sujanagar stone inscription, ll. 6–7.

37 *adhikṛtaśrījīvasenavyāpāre*, *ibid.*, l. 2.

38 *śrīmadhugirimaṇḍalāvacchinnakumbhīnagarapratīvaddhaḥ*, Dhirendra Chandra Ganguly, 'Saktipur Copper-plate of Lakshmanasena', *Epigraphia Indica*, 1931–32 (1984), 21: 218, ll. 26–27.

39 *IB*, p. 63, l. 33.

40 Amitabha Bhattacharyya, *Historical Geography of Ancient and Early Medieval Bengal*, Calcutta: Sanskrit Pustak Bhandar, 1977, p. 76.

41 Chitrarekha Gupta, 'Land-measurement and Land-revenue System in Bengal under Senas', in Debala Mitra (ed.), *Explorations in Art and Archaeology of South Asia: Essays Dedicated to N. G. Majumdar*, Calcutta: Directorate of Archaeology and Museums 1996, p. 576.

42 *nṛpagaṇanāgrimarekhaḥ śrīmān arivṛṣabhaśaṅkaraḥ kṛtavā*[*n*] (|) *udayakaraśāsanadāne śālāḍḍanāgam iha dūtaṃ* (||), *IB*, p. 64, ll. 48–49.

43 Abhay Kant Choudhary, *Early Medieval Village in North-Eastern India (A. D. 600–1200) [Mainly a Socio-economic Study]*, Calcutta: Punthi Pustak, 1971, p. 127.

44 Naihati CPI, *IB*, p. 74, ll. 44–45; Anulia CPI, *ibid.*, p. 87, ll. 36–37; Ganguly, 'Saktipur Copper-plate', p. 218, ll. 35–36.

45 Naihati CPI, *IB*, p. 74, ll. 37–38; Ganguly, 'Saktipur Copper-plate', p. 218, ll. 26–27.

46 Anulia CPI, *IB*, p. 87, ll. 34–35.

47 Supra Chapter 2.

48 Khalimpur CPI, *SI* 2, p. 67, l. 31; Nalanda CPI, *ibid.*, p. 77, l. 51.

49 *IB*, p. 81.

50 *Ibid.*, pp. 71–72, ll. 5–7, v. 3.

51 Rajat Sanyal, 'Copperplate Inscriptions of West Bengal: Finding Find-spots and Locating Localities', *Pratna Samiksha: A Journal of Archaeology, New Series*, 2010, 1: 125–26.

52 *taddeśīyasaṃvyavahāraṣaṭpañcāśatahastaparimitanalena*, *IB*, p. 96, ll. 36–37.

53 *tatratyadeśavyavahāranalena*', *ibid.*, p. 102, l. 36.

54 *śrīmadugaramādhavapādīyastambhāṅkitadvādaśāṅgulādhikahastena* (?) *dvātriṃśaddhastaparimitonmānenodhastayā* (?), *ibid.*, p. 171. For the findspot of the plate, see Sanyal, 'Copperplate Inscriptions of West Bengal', pp. 127–28.

55 N. K. Bhattasali, 'The Rājāvāḍī (Bhāwāl) Plate of Lakṣmaṇa Sena Deva', *Journal of the Royal Asiatic Society of Bengal, Letters*, 1942, 8(1): 7–17; Ayoub Khan, 'Bengal Copperplates: Provenances and Preservation Data', *Pratnatattva*, 2007, 13: 18, no. 9.

56 *dvāviṃśatihastaparimitanalena*, Bhattasali, 'The Rājāvāḍī (Bhāwāl) Plate', p. 36, 2. 10–11.

57 Gupta, 'Land-measurement and Land-revenue System', p. 578.

58 Madhainagar CPI, *SI* 2, pp. 124–30; Madhyapada CPI, *IB*, pp. 140–48. For the findspot of the latter, which is generally called the Vangiya Sahitya Parishad plate, see Khan, 'Bengal Copperplates', p. 18.

59 Idilpur CPI, *IB*, pp. 118–31; D. C. Sircar, 'Madanapada Plate of Visvarupasena', *Epigraphia Indica*, 1959–60 (1987), 33: 315–26.

60 *kaparddakapurāṇaśatadvayotpattiḥ*, Barrackpur CPI, *IB*, p. 63, ll. 33–34.

61 *pratyavdaṃ kaparddakapurāṇapañcaśatotpattikaḥ*, Naihati CPI, *ibid.*, p. 74, l. 46; *saṃvvatsareṇa kaparddakapurāṇasārddhaśataikotpattiko*, Tarpandighi CPI, *ibid.*, p. 102, ll. 37–38; *saṃvatsareṇa kaparddakapurāṇaśataikotpattikaṃ*, Anulia CPI, *ibid.*, p. 87, l. 38; *samvatsareṇa kaparddakapurāṇaśatacatuṣṭayotpattika*, Bhattasali, 'The Rājāvāḍī (Bhāwāl) Plate', p. 36, 2. 12; *saṃvatsareṇa kaparddakāṣṭaṣaṣṭipurāṇādhikaśatamūlyotpattiko*, Madhainagar CPI, *SI* 2, p. 128, ll. 43–44.

62 *vatsareṇa navaśatotpattikaḥ*, Govindapur CPI, *IB*, p. 96, ll. 38–39; *samvatsareṇa pañcāśatpurāṇotpattikaḥ*, Dighirpar-Bakultala CPI, *ibid.*, p. 171; *samvatsareṇa sārddhaśatadvayotpattikaḥ*, *samvatsareṇa sārddhaśatadvayotpattiko*, *samvatsareṇa pañcaśatotpattikaṃ*, Ganguly, 'Saktipur Copper-plate', p. 218, ll. 30, 33–34, 36.

63 *pratidroṇe pañcadaśapurāṇa utpattiniyame*, Govindapur CPI, *IB*, p. 96, l. 38.

64 *vāstu u p*[*r*]*ati hi* 1 3/8, *nāla u p*[*r*]ati hi 1 1/8, D. C. Sircar, 'Vaṅgīya Sāhitya Pariṣad Plate of Viśvarūpasena', *Journal of the Asiatic Society, Letters*, 1954, 20(2): 202, l. 44. Cf. *IB*, p. 146, l. 44.

65 B. N. Mukherjee, 'Commerce and Money in the Western and Central Sectors of Eastern India (c. A. D. 750–1200)', *Indian Museum Bulletin*, 1982, 17: 68–69.

66 *kandarppaśaṅkarāśramīyapadātiśāpāmarkasāṃ*(*d*)*v*(*ā*)*triṃśatpurāṇottaracūrṇṇīśataika* 132 *vahiḥ sāṃ bhū hi* 500, Sircar, 'Madanapada Plate', pp. 324–25, ll. 43–44.

67 Supra Chapter 5.

68 Ganguly, 'Saktipur Copper-plate', p. 218, ll. 34–38, p. 219, ll. 46–48.

69 *Ibid.*, p. 219, ll. 44–49.

70 Those hamlets are located in the two clusters with two separate border descriptions, both of which belong to the same *caturaka*. *Ibid.*, p. 218, ll. 26–34.

71 In a different context of the early modern Deccan, Frank Perlin convincingly discusses how monetisation facilitated organisation of a uniform administrative system despite local variations of measurement and so on. Frank Perlin, *The Invisible City: Monetary, Administrative and Popular Infrastructures in Asia and Europe, 1500–1900*, Hampshire: Variorum, 1993, pp. 46–48.

72 *IB*, p. 147, ll. 54–55.

73 *Ibid*, ll. 53–54, 57–58.

74 *nāraṇḍapagrāme svakīyapālyasvaṃ*, Sircar, 'Madanapada Plate', p. 325, ll. 44–45.

75 Barrackpur CPI, *IB*, p. 63, ll. 33–34, 37–43; Naihati CPI, *ibid.*, p. 74, ll. 44–46, 51–54.

76 Naihati CPI, *ibid.*, p. 74, ll. 52, 54.

77 *Ibid.*, p. 73, ll. 27–28, v. 14.

78 Barrackpur CPI, *ibid.*, p. 62, ll. 20–22, v. 10.

79 *ghāsasambhogabhāṭṭavaḍāgrāme*, *ibid.*, p. 63, l. 32.

80 *deūlahastyāṃ nadīpūrvvapaścime rājahitā*, *ibid.*, p. 146, l. 51; Plots donated by Sūryasena and Nāñīsiṃha, *ibid.*, p. 147, ll. 53–56.

81 Supra Chapter 5.

82 Ryosuke Furui, 'Subordinate Rulers under the Pālas: Their Diverse Origins and Shifting Power Relation with the King', *The Indian Economic and Social History Review*, 2017, 54(3): 341–44.

83 Ramesh K. Ghoshal, 'Rakshaskhali Island Plate of Madommanapala; Saka 1118', *Epigraphia Indica*, 1947–48 (reprint 1985), 27: 122, ll. 1–3.

84 *ayodhyāvinihsṛtapālānvayopārjjitapūrvvakhāṭikāntaḥpāti*, *ibid*, l. 3.

85 *IB*, p. 96, l. 34. Bhattacharyya, *Historical Geography*, p. 80.

86 Ghoshal, 'Rakshaskhali Island Plate', pp. 328–29, ll. 9–11.
87 Dinesh Chandra Bhattacharyya, 'The Maināmati Copper-plate of Raṇavaṅkamalla Harikāladeva (1141 Śaka).', *The Indian Historical Quarterly*, 1933, 9(1): 287, ll. 12–20.
88 *Ibid.*, p. 287, ll. 9–12, v. 5, ll. 22–24.
89 Mehar CPI, *SI* 2, p. 142, l. 15; Ahmad Hasan Dani, 'Sobharampur Plate of Damodaradeva, Saka 1158', *Epigraphia Indica*, 1953–1954 (1987), 30: 188, ll. 27–28.
90 *mehāragrāmanivāsiyathāpradhānajanapadān mahattarāṃś ca*, *SI* 2, p. 142, ll. 15–16.
91 *IB*, p. 181. He is mentioned as the son of Dāmodaradeva in the Pakamura grant. D. C. Sircar, *Śilālekha-Tāmraśāsanādir Prasaṅga*, Calcutta: Sahityaloka, 1982, p. 167. Both plates of Daśarathadeva are yet to be edited properly and only summaries are published so far.
92 Dani, 'Sobharampur Plate', p. 188, ll. 19, 27–34; Nasirabad CPI, *IB*, p. 161, ll. 24–34.
93 S. C. Bhattacharyya, 'Mainamati Copper Plate of Vīradharadeva', *Journal of Ancient Indian History*, 1983–84 (1984), 14(1–2): 26, ll. 11–16.
94 *CPS*, pp. 157–61, 184–86. The interpretation of these plates is based on the modified readings from the photographs of the original plates taken by myself.
95 *Ibid.*, p. 159, ll. 25–29.
96 Dani, 'Sobharampur Plate', p. 187, ll. 15–18, v. 7; Mehar CPI, *SI* 2, p. 142, ll. 11–13, v. 7. For the possibility that Gaṅgādharadeva was the petitioner, see D. C. Sircar, 'Epigraphic Notes', *Epigraphia Indica*, 1953–54 (1987), 30: 52–53.
97 *IB*, pp. 160–61, ll. 18–24, vv. 6–7.
98 *CPS*, p. 186, ll. 24–28, vv. 16–18.
99 *Ibid.*, ll. 28–29, v. 19.
100 *Ibid.*, p. 161, ll. 52–53.
101 Supra Chapter 5.
102 Supra Chapter 5.
103 Furui, 'Rajibpur Copperplate', p. 45, ll. 50–51, p. 53, ll. 47–48. For the ritual, see P. V. Kane, *History of Dharmaśāstra (Ancient and Medieval Religious and Civil Law)*, vol. 2, pt. 2 (2nd ed.), Poona: Bhandarkar Oriental Research Institute, 1974, p. 875.
104 Samantasar CPI, Bhattasali, 'Two Grants of Varmans', p. 258, 2. 13; Belava CPI, *IB*, p. 21, l. 45.
105 Supra Chapter 5. *IEG*, p. 299.
106 *IB*, p. 63, ll. 39–41. For the ritual, see Kane, *History of Dharmaśāstra*, vol. 2, pt. 2, p. 869.
107 *IB*, p. 74, ll. 51–52.
108 *Ibid.*, p. 96, l. 46.
109 *Ibid.*, p. 102, l. 46. For this ritual, see Kane, *History of Dharmaśāstra*, vol. 2, pt. 2, p. 875.
110 *SI* 2, p. 128, ll. 49–50.
111 *bhaviṣyaty abhiṣeke ca paracakrabhayeṣu ca* || *svarāṣṭrabhede 'rivadhe aindrī śāntis tatheṣyate*, Muruli Dhara Jha (ed.), *Adbhutasāgara*, Benares Cantt.: The Prabhakari and Co., 1905, p. 734.
112 Bhattasali, 'The Rājāvāḍī (Bhāwāl) Plate', pp. 19–20.
113 *pūrvve śāntyāgārikaprabhāsaśāsanaṃ sīmā, paścime śāntyāgārikarāmadeva-śāsanapūrvvapārśvaḥ sīmā, uttare śāntyāgārikaviṣṇupāṇigaḍolīkeśavagaḍolī-bhūmi sīmā*, *IB*, p. 171.
114 Supra Chapter 5.

115 P. V. Kane, *History of Dharmaśāstra (Ancient and Medieval Religious and Civil Law)*, vol. 1, pt. 2 (2nd ed.), Poona: Bhandarkar Oriental Research Institute, 1975, pp. 639–52.
116 *SI* 2, p. 108, ll. 10–11, v. 16. According to D. C. Sircar, this inscription may have originated from some temple in Bengal and mistakenly returned to Ananta-Vāsudeva temple at Bhubaneswar, where it lies now. *Ibid.*, p. 110, note 1.
117 Kane, *History of Dharmaśāstra*, vol. 1, pt. 2, pp. 727–30.
118 Kamalakanta Smrtitirtha (ed.), *Hāralatā of Aniruddha Bhaṭṭa*, Calcutta: The Asiatic Society of Bengal, 1909, p. 214, colophon.
119 Bhabatosh Bhattacharya (ed.), *Dānasāgara of Ballāla Sena*, fasc. 1, Calcutta: The Asiatic Society of Bengal, 1953, p. 2, Upakramaṇikā, vv. 6–7.
120 Kane, *History of Dharmaśāstra*, vol. 1, pt. 2, pp. 622–39.
121 Durgamohan Bhattacharya (ed.), *Brāhmaṇa-Sarvasva: A Pre-Sāyaṇa Vedic Commentary by Halāyudha*, Calcutta: Sanskrit Sahitya Parishad, 1960, p. 2, opening verse 12.
122 *mahādharmādhyakṣa*: *ibid.*, pp. 17, 26; *mahādharmādhikṛta*: *ibid.*, pp. 85, 123, 140, 170, 187, 204; *dharmādhyakṣa*: *ibid.*, p. 198; *dharmādhikṛta*: *ibid.*, pp. 145, 331.
123 *Ibid.*, p. 1, opening verse 5.
124 Furui, 'Rajibpur Copperplate', p. 53, l. 46.
125 Kane, *History of Dharmaśāstra*, vol. 1, pt. 2, pp. 730–35.
126 R. C. Hazra, *Studies in the Purāṇic Records on Hindu Rites and Customs* (2nd ed.), Delhi: Motilal Banarsidass, 1975, pp. 44–45.
127 Vijay Nath, '*Mahādāna*: The Dynamics of Gift-economy and the Feudal Milieu', in D. N. Jha (ed.), *The Feudal Order: State, Society and Ideology in Early Medieval India*, New Delhi: Manohar, 2000, pp. 411–40.
128 *śivapurāṇoktabhūmidānaphalaprāptikāmanayā*, Sircar, 'Madanapada Plate', p. 325, ll. 46–47.
129 R. C. Hazra, 'Purāṇa Literature as Known to Ballālasena', *Purāṇa*, 1985, 27(1): 41–59.
130 Furui, 'Rajibpur Copperplate', p. 43, l. 37, p. 44, l. 44, p. 45, ll. 48–49, p. 51, ll. 33–35, p. 53, ll. 41, 46, p. 59.
131 *IB*, p. 20, ll. 27–29, p. 21, ll. 37, 43–45.
132 *Ibid.*, p. 63, ll. 31–34, 37.
133 *campāhiṭṭīyāya campāhiṭṭīvāstavyāya*, Vasu, 'Copper-plate Inscription of Madanapāla', p. 72, ll. 43–44.
134 *cāmpahaṭṭīyamahopadhyāyadharmmādhyakṣaśrīmadaniruddha*, *Hālaratā*, p. 214, colophon.
135 Ryosuke Furui, '*Brāhmaṇa*s in Early Medieval Bengal: Data of Inscriptional References', in Nobuhiro Ota (ed.), *Zen-kindai Minami-Ajia Shakai Ni Okeru Matomari To Tsunagari* (*Clustering and Connections in Pre-Modern South Asian Society*), Tokyo: Research Institute for Languages and Cultures of Asia and Africa, Tokyo University of Foreign Studies, 2017, pp. 203–6, Appendix Table 1, nos 49–59.
136 The other settlement is Kāṇṭāmaṇi. *SI* 2, p. 142, l. 22, p. 143, ll. 25–27, 30. Table 6.4, nos 9, 12–13, 15 and 19. For inclusion of these villages in *gāñī*s of Rāḍhī *brāhmaṇa*s, see Ronald B. Inden, *Marriage and Rank in Bengali Culture: A History of Caste and Clan in Middle Period Bengal*, New Delhi: Vikas Publishing House, 1976, p. 39, Table 2.
137 *Brāhmaṇasarvasva*, p. 8.
138 D. C. Sircar, *Studies in the Geography of Ancient and Medieval India* (2nd ed.), Delhi: Motilal Banarsidass, 1971, pp. 173–74.

139 Ryosuke Furui, '*Brāhmaṇa*s in Early Medieval Bengal: Construction of Their Identity, Networks and Authority', *Indian Historical Review*, 2013, 40(2): 233–35.
140 *janapadān kṣetrakarāṃś ca vrāhmaṇottarān*, Bhattasali, 'Two Grants of Varmans', p. 258, 2. 7–8.
141 *(kṣetra)karāṃś ca vrāhmaṇāna vrāhmaṇottarāna*, Vajrayogini CPI, *ibid*., p. 263, 2. 1–2; *janapadān kṣetrakarāṃś ca vrāhmaṇān vrāhmaṇottarān*, Belava CPI, *IB*, p. 21, l. 36.
142 A clause 'with forest and shrub' (*sajhāṭaviṭapa*) is added in the Pāla plates. Furui, 'Rajibpur Copperplate', p. 44, l. 45, p. 53, l. 42; Vasu, 'Copper-plate Inscription of Madanapāla', p. 72, l. 40. Privileges listed in the Varman plates are almost the same as those in the Candra grants. Bhattasali, 'Two Grants of Varmans', p. 258, 2. 9–11, 2. 15; *IB*, p. 21, ll. 37–41, 47–48. The latter does not include *sacauroddharaṇa*.
143 Barrackpur CPI of Vijayasena, *ibid*., p. 63, ll. 33–37. Almost the same privileges are listed in the Naihati CPI of Vallālasena with replacement of *satala* and *soddeśa* by *savāstunālakhilādi* and of *savanā* by *sajhāṭaviṭapa*. *Ibid*., p. 74, ll. 44–45, 47–49.
144 Ex. Tarpandighi CPI of Lakṣmaṇasena, *ibid*., p. 102, ll. 38–41.
145 Idilpur CPI, *ibid*., p. 124, l. 46; Sircar, 'Madanapada Plate', p. 324, l. 41. Table 6.2 c; Madhyapada CPI, *IB*, p. 146, l. 41.
146 *putrapautrādisantatikrameṇa svacchandopabhogenopabhoktum*, *IB*, p. 125, ll. 52–53, p. 147, l. 61.
147 *Ibid*., pp. 140–48. D. C. Sircar provides the modified reading and interpretation, which are mostly accepted. Sircar, 'Vaṅgīya Sāhitya Pariṣad Plate', pp. 201–8.
148 *Ibid*., p. 205.
149 One is located in Ajikulāpāṭaka belonging to Navasaṃgrahacaturaka of Madhukṣīrakāvṛtti and the other three are in Deūlahastī belonging to Lāuhaṇḍācaturaka of Vikramapurabhāga. Table 6.5, nos 6, 7–9.
150 *IB*, p. 147, ll. 61–64.
151 Supra.
152 In Madanapada CPI of the same king, the donee received land plots of which production was valued 627 *purāṇa*s per annum. Sircar, 'Madanapada Plate', p. 325, l. 45.
153 *prativāsino vrāhmaṇottarān mahattarottamakuṭumbipurogamacaṇḍālaparyantān*, Furui, 'Rajibpur Copperplate', p. 44, l. 43. Almost the same in *ibid*., p. 53, l. 40 and Vasu, 'Copper-plate Inscription of Madanapāla', p. 72, l. 38, with *mahattama* in place of *mahattara*.
154 Supra Chapter 5.
155 Ryosuke Furui, 'Re-reading Two Copper Plate Inscriptions of Gopāla II, year 4', in Gerd J. R. Mevissen and Arundhati Banerji (eds), *Prajñādhara: Essays on Asian Art, History, Epigraphy and Culture in Honour of Gouriswar Bhattacharya*, New Delhi: Kaveri Books, 2009, p. 325, l. 36.
156 Supra Chapter 5.
157 Supra.
158 Sircar, 'Madanapada Plate', pp. 324–25, ll. 43–44.
159 Sircar, 'Vaṅgīya Sāhitya Pariṣad Plate', p. 201. *pauṇḍravarddhanabhuktyantaḥpātivaṅge*, *IB*., p. 146, l. 42.
160 *grāmapatyā sāṃ hi* 80 5/16, Sircar, 'Vaṅgīya Sāhitya Pariṣad Plate', p. 202; *nānāpatyā sāṃ hi* 60, *ibid*., p. 204. Cf. *IB*, p. 146, ll. 45, 48.
161 According to Sircar, these are the abbreviations for *grāmajanapatitvāt* and *nānāgrāmajanapatitvāt*, and respectively indicate that the tenants of land plots

are inhabitants of the village in which land plots are located or of villages of the neighbourhood. Sircar, 'Vaṅgīya Sāhitya Pariṣad Plate', pp. 203–4. Though interesting, this hypothesis is overstretched without any concrete evidence and cannot explain the absence of these terms for any other plots except one.

162 *udāna* 165 *nānāpatyā ucchannatvāt sāṃ hi* 100, *IB*, p. 146, l. 50.

163 *kumāraśrīpuruṣottamasenabhujyamānāyasaṃ*, *IB*, p. 147, ll. 57–58, modified on Sircar, 'Vaṅgīya Sāhitya Pariṣad Plate', p. 207.

164 Table 6.5, nos 1–3, 5 (king), 10 (Mahesara), 11 (Puruṣottamasena).

165 Sircar, 'Vaṅgīya Sāhitya Pariṣad Plate', p. 205.

166 Table 6.5, nos 4, 6–7 (king), 8 (Sūryasena), 9 (Nāñīsiṃha).

167 Sircar, 'Madanapada Plate', p. 325, ll. 44–45.

168 Supra.

169 *vāranākoloktagāñīkādīnāṃ*, *IB*, p. 146, l. 45; *vāraśremanoudayiaparalokta-kānāṃ*, *ibid.*, ll. 45–46. Modified on Sircar, 'Vaṅgīya Sāhitya Parishad Plate', p. 202.

170 *Ibid.*, p. 204.

171 *vāraārantokāmyapiṇṭhanāgādīnāṃ*, *IB*, pp. 146–47, ll. 51–52. Modified on Sircar, 'Vaṅgīya Sāhitya Parishad Plate', p. 205.

172 *vāravrahmoamṛtokayoḥ*, *IB*, p. 147, l. 53. Modified on Sircar, 'Vaṅgīya Sāhitya Parishad Plate', p. 206.

173 *vārakanoamṛtokayoḥ*, *IB*, p. 147, l. 55. Modified on Sircar, 'Vaṅgīya Sāhitya Parishad Plate', p. 206.

174 *Ibid.*, p. 204.

175 *SI* 2, p. 142, ll. 15–16.

176 Supra Chapter 5.

177 Furui, 'Rajibpur Copperplate', p. 45, l. 63, p. 53, l. 60; Vasu, 'Copper-plate Inscription of Madanapāla', p. 73, ll. 56–57.

178 Supra Chapter 5.

179 Furui, 'Rajibpur Copperplate', p. 53, ll. 43–44.

180 *dharmmopraṇaptā manadāsanaptā vṛhaspateḥ sūnur imāṃ praśastiṃ* | *cakhāna vārendrakaśilpigoṣṭhīcūḍāmaṇī rāṇakaśūlapāṇiḥ* ||, *IB*, p. 49, l. 32, v. 36.

181 Supra Chapter 5.

182 Supra Chapter 5.

183 Supra.

184 Sujanagar stone inscription, ll. 4–5.

185 *Ibid.*, ll. 2–3. Supra.

186 Supra.

187 Sujanagar stone inscription, ll. 5–6.

188 *nāpita* Govinda, *rajaka* Sirupā and *dantavāra* Vajari, *CPS*, p. 161, ll. 49 and 51.

189 Supra Chapter 5.

190 *Rāmacarita*, 3. 27, 42.

191 *Ibid.*, 4. 23.

192 Furui, 'Rajibpur Copperplate', p. 43, ll. 37–38, p. 45, l. 51; Vasu, 'Copper-plate Inscription of Madanapāla', p. 71, ll. 32–33; Furui, 'Rajibpur Copperplate', p. 53, l. 48.

193 *Ibid.*, p. 51, ll. 33–35.

194 Rajibpur CPI, year 2, *ibid.*, p. 43, ll. 37–38; Manahali CPI, Vasu, 'Copper-plate Inscription of Madanapāla', p. 71, ll. 32–33.

195 Tarpandighi CPI, *IB*, p. 102, ll. 36–37; Anulia CPI, *ibid.*, p. 87, ll. 36–38; Madhainagar CPI, *SI* 2, p. 128, ll. 42–43.

196 For the difference of standard, see supra.

197 Tarpandighi CPI, *IB*, p. 102, ll. 37–38; Anulia CPI, *ibid.*, p. 87, l. 38; Madhainagar CPI, *SI* 2, p. 128, l. 43.
198 *IB*, p. 102, ll. 33–38.
199 *devagopathādyasārabhūvahiḥ*, *ibid.*, l. 36.
200 *Ibid.*, p. 87, ll. 35–36.
201 *SI* 2, p. 128, ll. 40–42.
202 *devavrāhmaṇapālyabhavadbhiḥ*, *ibid.*, l. 42. Sircar emends *bhavadbhiḥ* as *svabahiḥ*. It can be better emended to *bhūvahiḥ*.
203 *IB*, p. 74, ll. 38–44.
204 Ganguly, 'Saktipur Copper-plate', p. 218, ll. 27–38.
205 Naihati CPI, *IB*, p. 74, ll. 44–46.
206 Ganguly, 'Saktipur Copper-plate', p. 218, ll. 35–38.
207 *devavrāhmaṇādibhūvahi*(*ḥ*), *ibid.*, l. 35.
208 *Ibid.*, p. 219, ll. 44–46. Supra.
209 Khāḍīviṣaya: Barrackpur CPI, *IB*, p. 63, ll. 31–32; Paścimakhāṭikā: Govindapur CPI, *ibid.*, p. 96, l. 34; Khāḍīmaṇḍala: Dighirpar-Bakultala CPI, *ibid.*, p. 171.
210 *Ibid.*, p. 63, l. 33.
211 *Ibid.*, p. 96, ll. 34–36.
212 *Ibid.*, p. 172.
213 Barrackpur CPI, *ibid.*, p. 63, l. 32. Supra.
214 Ghoshal, 'Rakshaskhali Island Plate', pp. 328–29, ll. 7–11. Supra.
215 For the growing importance of *śānti*s for kingship, see supra.
216 *ratnatrayavahiḥ*, Ghoshal, 'Rakshaskhali Island Plate', p. 328, l. 7.
217 Bhattasali, 'The Rājāvāḍī (Bhāwāl) Plate', pp. 35–36, 2. 4–13.
218 *Ibid.*, pp. 35–36, 2. 5–7.
219 *Ibid.*, p. 36, 2. 7–10.
220 The meanings of *dāṇḍi* and *jāṇa* are unclear but their connotation as water courses is guessed from the linearity of Jaladāṇḍi and *jalanirgammajāṇa* in their description.
221 Bhattasali, 'The Rājāvāḍī (Bhāwāl) Plate', p. 36, 2. 10–13.
222 Supra Chapter 5.
223 Samantasar CPI, Bhattasali, 'Two Grants of Varmans', p. 257, 2. 2–3; Belava CPI, *IB*, p. 20, ll. 28–29.
224 *Ibid.*, pp. 124–25, ll. 46–49, p. 125, l. 57. Modified on reading from the facsimile attached to *Journal of the Asiatic Society of Bengal*, 1838, 7(2).
225 Sircar, 'Madanapada Plate', p. 324, ll. 42–43.
226 *Ibid.*, pp. 324–25, ll. 43–45.
227 *IB*, p. 146, ll. 42–44, 47–48, 51, Sircar, 'Vaṅgīya Sāhitya Pariṣad Plate', pp. 202–4.
228 Supra.
229 Bhattacharyya, 'The Maināmati Copper-plate of Raṇavaṅkamalla Harikāladeva', p. 287, ll. 14–16.
230 Supra Chapter 5.
231 Dani, 'Sobharampur Plate', p. 188, ll. 19, 27–28, 33–34.
232 3 *droṇa*s in Kāmanāpiṇḍiyāka, two plots in Ketaṅgapālā, of which each measures 1 *droṇa*. Nasirabad CPI, *IB*, p. 161, ll. 24–26, 31–33.
233 Dani, 'Sobharampur Plate', p. 188, ll. 27–31; Nasirabad CPI, *IB*, p. 161, ll. 26–33.
234 Supra Chapter 5.
235 12 *pāṭaka*s in Meśvāñcā and Athavasā of Vātagaṅgāviṣaya and 5 *pāṭaka*s in Nāroraka of Gaṅgāmaṇḍalaviṣaya. Bhattacharyya, 'Mainamati Copper Plate of Vīradharadeva', p. 26, ll. 11–16.

236 *Ibid.*, p. 25, ll. 1–2; Mainamati CPIs of Laḍahacandra, *EDEP*, p. 74, l. 53, p. 76, l. 20.
237 Supra Chapters 5 and 6.
238 Supra Chapter 3.
239 *haṭṭaghaṭṭataravalajamalaṅgaguvākādisameta*, reading from the photographs taken by myself. Cf. Bhattacharyya, 'Mainamati Copper Plate of Vīradharadeva', p. 26, ll. 12–13. The meaning of *malaṅga* is unclear.
240 Supra Chapter 5.
241 Table 6.4, nos 19 and 34 (*hāṭī*, *haṭṭavara*), 22 (Varuṇī), 23–26 (Savaśānadī), 27–28, 31 (Kaliyāṇīnadī), 32 (Dhāmāyinadī), 42 (Thāmanadī), 43 (Jūḍīgāṅga), 26 (*ghaṭābhū*), 30 (*sāgara*), 43 (*gopatha*), 34 (Nathośāsana), 45 (Vāsudevaśāsana).
242 Supra Chapters 4 and 5.
243 *guvākādisameta*, *IB*, p. 20, l. 28. Cf. *saguvākanālikerā*, *ibid.*, p. 21, ll. 38–39.
244 *devakulapuṣkariṇyādikaṃ kārayitvā guvākanārikelādikaṃ laggāvayitvā*, Idilpur CPI, *ibid.*, p. 125, ll. 51–52, Madhyapada CPI, *ibid.*, p. 147, ll. 60–61.
245 *savāstunālakhilādibhiḥ*, Naihati CPI, *IB*, p. 74, l. 45; *vāstubhūsahitaṃ*, Ganguly, 'Saktipur Copper-plate', p. 218, l. 35; *savāstucihnaḥ*, Dighirpar-Bakultala CPI, *IB*, p. 171.
246 *vāstubhūyutān*, Dani, 'Sobharampur Plate', p. 188, l. 19; *dakṣiṇe vārajikaguṇogṛhavāṭī*, *ibid.*, l. 29.
247 *savāstubhūdroṇa* 3, *IB*, p. 161, l. 29; *savānābhūdro* 1, *ibid.*, ll. 32, 33; *savānābhūdroṇa* 5, *ibid.*, ll. 33–34. *lavanotsavāśramasamvādhā vāṭī sīmā*, *ibid.*, ll. 27–28.
248 Bhattacharyya, 'Mainamati Copper Plate of Vīradharadeva', p. 26, ll. 12–13.
249 *CPS*, p. 186, l. 26.
250 Supra Chapter 5.
251 Supra.
252 *tathaitadvāstubhūmau kalanasaṃsā(ṃ)guvākaśata* 30 *etan mūlyaṃ hi* 40, *IB*, p. 146, ll. 50–51. I followed Sircar for the reading of this part and interpretation of *kalana*. Sircar, 'Vaṅgīya Sāhitya Pariṣad Plate', pp. 204–5.
253 Ganguly, 'Saktipur Copper-plate', p. 218, ll. 31, 36.
254 Bhattacharyya, 'Mainamati Copper Plate of Vīradharadeva', p. 26, ll. 12–16.
255 Sujanagar stone inscription, ll. 2–5.
256 Supra.
257 *allahabhaṭṭārakasvāmijaṅśitavihārapratikaraṇārthaṃ svakīyamahāsāmantabhogahaṭṭagrahakḷptaṃ ca dattam*, Sujanagar inscription, ll. 5–7.
258 Supra Chapter 5.
259 For the minute descriptions of procedures of this festival in the *Purāṇa*s, see Shingo Einoo, 'The Autumn Goddess Festival: Described in the Purāṇas', in Masakazu Tanaka and Musashi Tachikawa (eds), *Living with Śakti: Gender, Sexuality and Religion in South Asia*, Osaka: National Museum of Ethnology, 1999, pp. 33–70. Apart from the *Purāṇa*s consulted by Einoo, the chapter 45 of the *Mahābhāgavatapurāṇa* has a description of the festival. Panchanana Tarkaratna (ed.), *Śrīmahābhāgavatam*, Calcutta: Navbharat Publishers, 1995 (reprint), 45, especially 45. 34–43.
260 R. C. Hazra, *Studies in the Upapurāṇas*, vol. 2, Calcutta: Sanskrit College, 1963, pp. 232, 245.
261 Haraprasad Shastri (ed.), *Bṛhaddharmapurāṇam* (2nd ed.), Varanasi: Krishnadas Academy, 1974, 1. 22. 17. Unless mentioned otherwise, the text used in this chapter is this edition.
262 *Ibid.*, 1. 22. 26.
263 *Ibid.*, 1. 22. 27.

264 *Ibid.*, 1. 22. 27ab.
265 *Mahābhāgavata*, 45. 1.
266 *Ibid.*, 45. 42–43.
267 *Ibid.*, 45. 34.
268 *Bṛhaddharma*, 1. 22. 30–33.
269 *Śrīdevībhāgavatapurāṇam*, Delhi: Nag Publishers, 1986 (reprint), 3. 26. 36.
270 *Mahābhāgavata*, 45. 42
271 Biswanarayan Shastri (ed.), *The Kālikāapurāṇa (Text, Introduction & Translation in English)*, 3 pts, Delhi: Nag Publishers, 1991–92, 60. 6–11, 12–16 (goddess with 10 arms), 17–21 (with 18 arms), 22–25 (Vaiṣṇavī), 25cd – 32 (battle between Rāma and Rāvaṇa), 33–54 (*nīrājana* of Indra), 55–80 (slaying of Mahiṣa), 61. 14cd – 30 (mentioning offering of human flesh).
272 *Ibid.*, 60. 32cd, 61. 17–18.
273 Pramathanatha Tarkabhusana, *The Kāla-Viveka (A Part of Dharmaratna) by Jīmūutavāhana*, Calcutta: The Asiatic Society of Bengal, 1905, p. 514.
274 *Kālikā*, 61. 19cd – 23ab.
275 *durgātantreṇa mantreṇa kuryād durgāmahotsavam* | *mahānavamyāṃ śaradi balidānaṃ nṛpādayaḥ* ||, *ibid*, 60. 1; *balanīrājanaṃ rājā kuryād balavivṛddhaye* ||, *ibid.*, 60. 43cd. Also *ibid.*, 60. 21, 33, 36. For details of *nīrājana* described in the *Viṣṇudharmottarapurāṇa* and the *Agnipurāṇa*, see Einoo, 'The Autumn Goddess Festival', p. 52 Table 11 and p. 53 Table 12.
276 *nādhipatyavicaro'sti na vā varṇavicāraṇā* | *tasyāṃ yasya matiḥ puṇyā tasyaiva sulabhā tu sā* ||, *Mahābhāgavata*, 43. 86.
277 Supra.
278 Supra Chapter 5.
279 Ryosuke Furui, 'The Rural World of an Agricultural Text: A Study on the *Kṛṣiparāśara*', *Studies in History, New Series*, 2005, 21(2): 158.
280 Supra.
281 *Bṛhaddharma*, 1. 22. 33cd; *Mahābhāgavata*, 46. 17, 19.
282 *Devībhāgavata*, 3. 26. 12.
283 *Ibid.*, 3. 26. 14–17.
284 Girija Prasanna Majumdar and Sures Chandra Banerji (ed., tr.), *Kṛṣi-Parāśara*, Kolkata: The Asiatic Society, 2001 (reprint), v. 228.
285 *Bṛhaddharma*, 1. 23. 4cd.
286 *Ibid.*, 1. 23. 19.
287 *Ibid.*, 1. 23. 10–12ab.
288 *mālasīgānaniratā bhagaliṅgābhiśabdinaḥ* |, *ibid.*, 1. 23. 11ab. According to Sukumar Sen, Mālasī are songs on Durgā and Śiva, which were generally sung in the melody of the same name. Sukumar Sen, *An Etymological Dictionary of Bengali: c. 1000–1800 A. D.*, Calcutta: Eastern Publishers, 1971, p. 760.
289 *atastām atra vai bhaktyā devadevīṃ dvijātayaḥ* | *pūjayeyur mudā śyāmāṃ paśupuṣpārghyasampadā* ||, *Bṛhaddharma*, 1. 23. 9.
290 *catuṣpraharapūjāyā dadyād vipuladakṣiṇām* |, *ibid.*, 1. 23. 20cd.
291 *paratrāhani vai viprān bhojayed bhaktitatparaḥ* ||, *ibid.*, 1. 23. 20ef.
292 *nṛtyagītādivādyaiś ca kārayed gopikotsavam* ||, *ibid.*, 1. 22. 32cd.
293 *svāgatāsanapādyādyair naivedyair vividhair api* || *vastrālaṅkārabhūṣādyair āhūya brāhmaṇān api* |, *ibid.*, 1. 23. 31cd – 32ab.
294 *saṃpūjya dakṣiṇān dattvā brāhmaṇān paritoṣya ca* | *visarjayet tāḥ pratimāḥ paratrāhani tūtsavaiḥ* || *bhojayet brāhmaṇān miṣṭaṃ kṛtvaivaṃ vidhim uttamam* |, *ibid.*, 1. 23. 33–34ab.
295 *bhagaliṅgādiśabdañ ca noccaret paragocaram* || *uccared āśvine māsi mahāpūjādineṣu hi* |, *ibid.*, 3. 6. 81cd – 82ab.

296 *mātṝṇāñ ca sutānāñ ca samīpe na tadāpi ca* || *aśaktidīkṣitāyāś ca śiṣyāyāḥ sannidhau na ca* |, *ibid.*, 3. 6. 82cd – 83ab.
297 *caitre śivotsavaṃ kuryyān nṛtyagītamahotsavaiḥ* |, *ibid.*, 3. 9. 41ab; *śivasvarūpatāṃ yāti śivaprītikaraḥ paraḥ* |, *ibid.*, 3. 9. 42ab; *nānāvidhair mahāvādyair nṛtyaiś ca vividhair api* || *nānāveśadharair nṛtyaiḥ prīyate śaṅkaraḥ prabhuḥ* |, *ibid.*, 3. 9. 44cd – 45ab.
298 *kṣatriyādiṣu yo martyo dehaṃ saṃpīḍya bhaktitaḥ* ||, *ibid.*, 3. 9. 42cd.
299 For the assignment of *kṣatravṛtti* to *ugras*, see *ibid.*, 3. 14. 55.
300 *grāmād vahir imaṃ śambhor utsavaṃ kārayen mudā* |, *ibid.*, 3. 9. 47ab.
301 This section was earlier published as Ryosuke Furui, 'Finding Tensions in the Social Order: a Reading of the Varṇasaṃkara Section of the Bṛhaddharmapurāṇa', in Suchandra Ghosh, Sudipa Ray Bandyopadhyay, Sushmita Basu Majumdar and Sayantani Pal (eds), *Revisiting Early India: Essays in Honour of D. C. Sircar*, Kolkata: R. N. Bhattacharya, 2013, pp. 203–18.
302 For the theory and descriptions of *Varṇasaṃkara* in the *Dharmasūtras* and the early *Smṛtis*, see Gen'ichi Yamazaki, *The Structure of Ancient Indian Society: Theory and Reality of the Varṇa System*, Tokyo: The Toyo Bunko, 2005, pp. 8–10, 214–18.
303 Aloka Parasher, *Mlecchas in Early India: A Study in Attitudes Towards Outsiders Upto AD 600*, New Delhi: Munshiram Manoharlal, 1991, p. 200.
304 *Bṛhaddharma*, 3. 13. 4–18.
305 *Ibid.*, 3. 13. 19–27.
306 *tyaktadharmme jane bhūte dhanaṃ yasya na tasya tat* | *yasya strī tasya na strī ca gṛhaṃ yasya na tadgṛham* ||, *ibid.*, 3. 13. 24.
307 *Ibid.*, 3. 13. 25–26.
308 *saṃkaro narakāyaiva kulaghnānāṃ kulasya ca* | *evaṃ dharmmasya vaiṣamyaṃ duṣṭarājye bhavaty uta* ||, *ibid.*, 3. 13. 27.
309 *Ibid.*, 3. 13. 30–34ab.
310 *Ibid.*, 3. 13. 34cd – 40.
311 *Ibid.*, 3. 13. 41–43.
312 *Ibid.*, 3. 13. 44–48.
313 *ity ādayo'ntyajāḥ proktā varṇāśramavahiṣkṛtāḥ* ||, *ibid.*, 3. 13. 48cd.
314 *ṣaṭtriṃśajjātakarmmāṇi sādhikāḥ kathitās tava* |, *ibid.*, 3. 13. 49ab.
315 *Ibid.*, 3. 13. 52.
316 *Ibid.*, 3. 13. 53–54.
317 *Ibid.*, 3. 13. 55–60.
318 *Ibid.*, 3. 14. 2–3.
319 *Ibid.*, 3. 14. 4–6.
320 *Ibid.*, 3. 14. 7–10.
321 *Ibid.*, 3. 14. 11–12.
322 *ye tu jātā hi saṃkīrṇās teṣāṃ vṛttīś ca kalpaya* | *tān āhūya kuruta ca nirṇayaṃ dharmmasaṃgraham* ||, *ibid.*, 3. 14. 13.
323 *Ibid.*, 3. 14. 18–25.
324 *Ibid.*, 3. 14. 26–29.
325 *Ibid.*, 3. 14. 30–31.
326 *Ibid.*, 3. 14. 32–34ab.
327 *Ibid.*, 3. 14. 34–36.
328 *Ibid.*, 3. 14. 37–39.
329 *Ibid.*, 3. 14. 41–43. For the origin of *ambaṣṭha* from *brāhmaṇa* father and *vaiśya* mother, and his progeny from *vaiśya* woman, see Table 6.6, nos 2, 23, 24.
330 *Bṛhaddharma*, 3. 14. 44–45.
331 *Ibid.*, 3. 14. 47–50ab.

332 *Ibid.*, 3. 14. 55.
333 *Ibid.*, 3. 14. 56–59.
334 *Ibid.*, 3. 14. 62cd – 68. For details, see Table 6.6, nos 3–5, 8–11, 13–15, 17–20.
335 *Bṛhaddharma*, 3. 14. 71.
336 *Ibid.*, 3. 14. 73–75.
337 *Ibid.*, 3. 14. 78–79.
338 Inden, *Marriage and Rank in Bengali Culture*, p. 52.
339 *Bṛhaddharma*, 3. 14. 28.
340 For the case of *rājpūt* clans in Rajasthan, see B. D. Chattopadhyaya, *The Making of Early Medieval India*, Delhi: Oxford University Press, 1994, pp. 57–88. For merchants in the same region, see *ibid.*, pp. 89–119.
341 Parasher, *Mlecchas in Early India*, pp. 200–1.
342 *Bṛhaddharma*, 3. 14. 13.
343 *pṛthur uvāca* I *katham vai vikṛtākārāḥ kucelā malinānanāḥ* I *śīrṇā sudurvvalā yūyaṃ kathaṃ vedaṃ śṛṇomi vaḥ* II, *ibid.*, 3. 14. 18.
344 *saṅkarā ūcuḥ* I *vayaṃ sarvve śubhākārāḥ sucelā vimalānanāḥ* I *śubhāṅgāḥ subalāḥ sarvve dṛṣṭihīnaḥ kathaṃ bhavān* II, *ibid.*, 3. 14. 19.
345 *vayaṃ veṇasamāḥ sarvve veṇena pratipālitāḥ* I *veṇena janitaś cāpi sa cāsīd rājasattamaḥ* II *brahmaviṣṇvādiyo devā nāsmatto hy adhikāḥ kvacit* II, *ibid.*, 3. 14. 20–21.
346 *śrutvaivaṃ vacanaṃ jahasur brāhmaṇādayaḥ* I *rājā tu krodham āviṣṭas tān babandha kṛtāgasaḥ* II *tadā te pīḍitā baddhā mlānavaktrāḥ kucelakāḥ* I *rakṣa rakṣa mahāvāho iti bhāṣākulānanāḥ* II, *ibid.*, 3. 14. 22–23.
347 *saṃkarā ūcuḥ* I *rājaṃs tavājñāvaśagāḥ vayaṃ sarvve yathāyatham* I *sarvvān no vikṛtākārān śubhākārān kuruṣva ca* II *dharmmātman kalpayāsmākaṃ varṇaṃ vṛttiñ ca nāma ca* I *mūrkhāṇāṃ veṇabuddhīnām aparādhaṃ kṣamasva naḥ* II, *ibid.*, 3. 14. 24–25.
348 *Brāhmaṇa*s talked to *saṃkara*s, who were disciplined after this event. *teṣāṃ vṛttyādikalpārthaṃ tān ūcur vinayānvitān* II, *ibid.*, 3. 14. 27cd.
349 *Ibid.*, 3. 14. 14–16.
350 *Ibid.*, 3. 14. 24.
351 *tenaivaite babhūvur hi cārurāpā subuddhayaḥ* I *brāhmaṇānāṃ śubhājñābhir yathā vṛttim upasthitāḥ* II, *ibid*, 3. 14. 69.
352 The half stanza mentioning the occupation of *tāmbūli* is not included in the text edited by Shastri, but in the other edition by Tarkaratna. Panchanana Tarkaratna (ed.), *Bṛhaddharmmapurāṇa*, Calcutta: Navbharat Publishers, 1396 BS (1989) (reprint), 3. 14. 60ab.
353 *brāhmaṇe bhaktimāś caiva deveṣv api bhavatv api* II *eṣa eva hi satśūdro bhavaty eva na saṃśayaḥ* II, *Bṛhaddharma*, 3. 14. 34cd – 35; *brāhmaṇe bhaktimat tvantu devatārādhane matiḥ* I *amātsaryyaṃ saśīlatvam etat satśūdralakṣaṇam* II, *ibid.*, 3. 14. 36.
354 *svarṇakāre svarṇarūpyabhūṣaṇādinirūpaṇam* II *teṣāṃ tattvaparīkṣāyai kalpitaḥ kānako vaṇik* I, *ibid.*, 3. 14. 67cd – 68ab.
355 *Karaṇa*: *ibid.*, 3. 14. 30–40; *ambaṣṭha*: *ibid.*, 3. 14. 41–54; *māgadha*: *ibid.*, 3. 14. 55–62.
356 *Ibid.*, 3. 14. 71.
357 Ex. *tantravāye vastrasṛṣṭiṃ vaṇijāṃ gandhavikrayam* I *nāpite kṣaurakarmmādād gope likhanam eva ca* II, *ibid.*, 3. 14. 63.
358 *Ibid.*, 3. 13. 34, 3. 14. 30–31.
359 *Ibid.*, 3. 14. 33–35.
360 *asmābhir asya saṃskāraḥ karttavyo viprajanmanaḥ* I *yenāsau saṃskṛto bhūtvā punarjāta ivāstu ca* II, *ibid.*, 3. 14. 43.

361 *ity uktvā te dvijagaṇāḥ smṛtvā nāsatyadasrakau* ǀ *tayor anugrahād vipra dayāvanto dvijātayaḥ* ǁ *āyurvedaṃ dadus tasmai vaidyanāma ca puṣkalam* ǀ, *ibid.*, 3. 14. 44–45ab.
362 *Ibid.*, 3. 14. 58–59.
363 *Ibid.*, 3. 13. 52.
364 *gaṇakāya dadus teṣu jyotiḥśāstrāṇi sarvvaśaḥ* ǀ *grahavipram akurvvaṃs te sarvve brāhmaṇapuṅgavāḥ* ǁ, *ibid.*, 3. 14. 71.
365 *āyurvedas tu yo dattas tubhyam ambaṣṭha bhūsuraiḥ* ǀ *tena pramatto naivānyat purāṇādi vadiṣyasi* ǁ *āyurvedāt paraṃ nānyad yuṣmākaṃ vācyam arhati* ǀ, *ibid.*, 3. 14. 49–50ab.
366 *ambhaṣṭha*: *ibid.*, 3. 14. 47; *māgadha*: *ibid.*, 3. 14. 59.
367 Kunal Chakrabarti, *Religious Process: The Purāṇas and the Making of a Regional Tradition*, New Delhi: Oxford University Press, 2001, pp. 316–18.
368 Ludo Rocher (ed., tr., intro., annot.), *Jīmūtavāhana's Dāyabhāga: The Hindu Law of Inheritance in Bengal*, New York: Oxford University Press, 2002, pp. 329–35.
369 *Ibid.*, p. 314, 6. 1. 36.
370 J. L. Shastri (ed.), Satkari Mukhopadhyaya (index, intro.), *Brahmavaivartapurāṇa of Kṛṣṇa Dvaipāyana Vyāsa*, pt. 1, Delhi: Motilal Banarsidass, 1983, 1. 10. Hazra dates most parts of the text to the period between the 10th and 16th centuries and concludes that Smṛti-chapters except 4. 8 and 26, including the present one, are very late additions. Hazra, *Studies in the Purāṇic Records*, pp. 166–67.
371 For those groups, see Niharranjan Ray, John W. Hood (tr.), *History of Bengali People (Ancient Period)*, Calcutta: Orient Longman, 1994, pp. 196–97.
372 *Brahmavaivarta*, 1. 10. 19–95.

7

CONCLUSION

The historical process unfolded in rural society of early medieval Bengal can be summarised in the following manner.

In the fifth and sixth centuries, rural society of Puṇḍravardhana, the northern sub-region of Bengal under the provincial administration of the Guptas, was characterised by the activities of peasant householders called *kuṭumbin*s centred on the organisation of *adhikaraṇa*, a local body established at diverse administrative divisions and constituted by the dominant section of *kuṭumbin*s or the urban elites. As members of the *adhikaraṇa*s in rural area, dominant *kuṭumbin*s including their upper section called *mahattara*s wielded authority to decide on the important local matters, especially the sales of waste/fallow land. Their authority was based on the position as both representatives of the interest of rural society and agents of local administration, which compelled the Gupta kingship to seek their collaboration in governing the area away from its core territory. The *adhikaraṇa*s also functioned as a venue for the dominant section of *kuṭumbin*s to reconfirm their solidarity against and authority over the ordinary *kuṭumbin*s and the other social groups, and as an arena for the latter to negotiate with the former. On the other hand, the *adhikaraṇa*s located outside rural society gave urban elites and officials the authority to decide on the affairs in rural society and the opportunity to extend their own interest there. In this exercise, they confronted and negotiated with rural society including dominant *kuṭumbin*s.

The dominant form of agrarian production based on family labour of *kuṭumbin*s, among whom the inner differentiation was in progress but yet to produce a sharp division, necessitated the agrarian expansion through the acquisition and management of a moderate size of waste/fallow land. This form of agrarian development had inherent contradictions. The available labour power confined to family labour put a limit on further expansion. The remnant of communal land control over waste/fallow land restricting its reclamation by dominant *kuṭumbin*s could not be overcome, as long as their authority and eminence depended on their capacity to represent the interest of rural society. They also had to keep their solidarity as a community to confront with the external authority. The resolutions of these contradictions would be brought out by the social changes resulting in a new agrarian relation with subjection of cultivators, of which some symptoms started to emerge in the later phase of this period.

Samataṭa, the eastern sub-region, saw different forms of political power and agrarian development, namely the subordinate rulers under the Gupta suzerainty growing to semi-independence and the settlement formation and agrarian expansion through the reclamation of riverine tracts. Land plots were held individually or collectively by landholders with difference in wealth and occupations but without hierarchical relations developing among them. Rural society consisting of less stratified landholders was, instead, imposed of the control of religious institutions and state apparatus with inner contention among its constituents, the king and subordinate rulers.

From the mid-sixth century to the early seventh century, rural society in Vaṅga, Rāḍha and Puṇḍravardhana, respectively the southern, western and northern sub-regions, saw the continued activities of local people around the *adhikaraṇa*, under the rule of rising sub-regional kingships. What characterised their activities was the ascendancy of *mahattara*s as landed magnates, shown by the appearance of their sub-categories and the presence of some with positions representing particular settlements. Excluding *kuṭumbin*s, they wielded authority to decide on the cases of land sale and donation with the *adhikaraṇa* constituted by clerical groups like *kāyastha*s. The collaboration brought out a nexus between landed magnates and literate groups, which culminated in their dominance in rural society. They confronted with the agents of state control including officials and subordinate rulers who, backed by the enhanced presence of state, tried to extend their power over rural society. The delicate power balance maintained between both sides through the period tilted towards political powers, especially subordinate rulers who could also have incorporated the upper section of local landed magnates in their lowest rung.

With changed power relation around rural society, those sub-regions witnessed the agrarian expansion to marshy low lands and forest tracts, which reached some level of development as exhibited by the clustering of settlements and the minute border demarcations. The mobilisation of labour power necessary for the reclamation of such tracts was made possible by the ascendancy of *mahattara*s and other landed magnates including *brāhmaṇa*s, who got command over labour of *kuṭumbin*s and other residents.

In the seventh and eighth centuries, Samataṭa and the neighbouring subregion of Śrīhaṭṭa saw the intensification of the agrarian development and the formation of local power relations. The former manifested itself as the synchronic existence of the three phases of agrarian expansion, from the reclamation of wild forest tracts by settling a large number of *brāhmaṇa*s to the establishment of stratified land relation in relatively developed area, through the transitional phase. The latter was represented by the presence of subordinate rulers with diverse power equation in relation to the king, from the autonomous local rulers having to deal with their own aspiring subordinates who tried to extend power and resource base by reclaiming forest tracts, to those incorporated in the stratified land relation as superior tenure holders under the established royal control. Harikela, the other eastern sub-region, also witnessed the formation of sub-regional kingdom and the agrarian expansion in the eighth century.

The emergence of Buddhist *vihāra*s and the other religious institutions as large-scale landholders was the other phenomenon witnessed in this period. Their presence as such was enabled by the stratified land relation in which they acquired superior land right above cultivators. The royal patronage contributed to the rise of these institutions, which legitimised the temporal power through the rituals and the inter-regional network.

In the period between the ninth and 11th centuries, rural society of Bengal came under the rule of the regional kingships, namely, the Pālas in the northern and western sub-regions and the Candras in the eastern half. The state control was enhanced under them as attested by the royal monopoly of land and village grants. The extensive privileges conferred on donees consisted of the rights to income and resources including commons, the relegation of administrative power including local policing and the authority to mobilise labour power of cultivators, all of which point to the strong presence of donees guaranteed by the enhanced state power. In rural society losing its autonomy against the state control, the social stratification intensified, especially in Varendra, North Bengal, partially due to the incorporation of non-sedentary groups like *ḍomba*s in sedentary agrarian society as agrarian labourers categorised as *pāmara*s.

In the changed balance of power, the main line of contention shifted from the confrontation of the state and rural society to the negotiation between the king and rising subordinate rulers generally called *sāmanta*s, with various power equations. In Varendra, *sāmanta*s under the early Pāla kings tried to enhance their power and resource base by legitimately encroaching upon the king's authority through the application for royal land and village grants to the religious institutions established by them. The later Pāla kings countered such attempts and reclaimed their power especially by settling highly qualified *brāhmaṇa*s, who could be better representatives of the royal authority with which they had close connection especially as ritual specialists, in rural society through village grants and by tightening local control through land measurement and estimation of production in currency units. *Sāmanta*s were less visible in the other sub-regions under the Candras and the Kāmbojas, where the patronage to *brāhmaṇa*s by the royal initiative like the cases in the later Pāla rule was a norm.

The two kinds of religious agents, institutions and *brāhmaṇa*s, were the focus of negotiations between the king and *sāmanta*s. Buddhist *vihāra*s and the other religious institutions reached prominence by the patronage of temporal powers prompted by the potential of the former to legitimise and enhance the latter. The mutual interactions of those institutions formed networks which could function as channels disseminating the fame and prestige of rulers. *Brāhmaṇa* donees of royal grants were those with clear identities in terms of both academic qualification and kinship relations, which differentiated them from the other *brāhmaṇa*s residing in rural area. They were building their networks through the multiple migrations, either made voluntarily or facilitated by royal village grants, and through the establishment of Brahmanical centres named after those in Madhyadeśa, the Gangetic heartland, in Varendra and Rāḍha.

The intensified stratification of rural society and the stronger presence of political and religious authorities were conductive of a new form of agrarian expansion by producing the condition with which the limit imposed in the earlier period could be overcome in Varendra. The sub-region saw the agrarian expansion in riverine tracts by the enterprise of local magnates, with the resultant administrative reorganisation. The remarkable was the agrarian expansion in a particular area through the peasantisation of non-agrarian groups, especially *kaivarta*s of whom some section grew to landholding group with their own chief. The agrarian expansion was accompanied by the commercialisation of rural economy implied by the spread of markets and monetary transactions mediated by notional currency unites and imported cowrie-shells, which catered for the demand of rural landed magnates. In Vaṅga and Samataṭa, the reclamation of riverine tracts which had started earlier reached a limit yet to be overcome in the less stratified condition of rural society, while the agrarian expansion through the large-scale land grants and social reorganisation continued in Śrīhaṭṭa. The eastern sub-regions including Harikela also experienced commercialisation of rural economy, especially circulation of silver currency, if not as intensive as that in Varendra.

In a new context of power relations and economic conditions, the two forms of social reorganisation were attempted. The first was the effort to keep the cohesion of peasant householders against the inner social stratification and the enhanced control of external authorities by representing themselves as a homogeneous group and prescribing festive occasions for temporary suppression of their difference, without much success. The second was the construction of identities and networks based on common occupations towards groups to be consolidated later as *jāti*s. Following *brāhmaṇa*s, non-*brāhmaṇa* literates built up their networks and sub-regional centres, while merchants shifted centres of their activities to rural space and organised themselves into associations based on rural markets.

The growing contradictions, including both the tension between the king and subordinate rulers and the intensified stratification of rural society, culminated in the *Kaivarta* rebellion, which temporarily ousted the Pālas from

Varendra in the last quarter of the 11th century. The rebellion, which started as a revolt of *sāmanta*s led by the *kaivarta* chief against the reigning king, was followed by their encroachment upon the landed property of religious agents. It saw the participation of the wider range of social groups in its last phase. The rebellion decisively weakened the Pāla power, which could recover its home territory only through the aid of *sāmanta*s, and made it more dependent on them.

In the period from the last quarter of the 11th century to the middle of 13th century, rural society of Bengal experienced a new phase of socio-economic change under the authority of *brāhmaṇa*s and the political powers with strong inclination towards Brahmanical traditions. While the Pāla power, heavily dependent on subordinate rulers, declined despite its effort to reorganise and tighten local control in the shrinking territory of Varendra, the Varmans somehow consolidated their rule in Vaṅga, especially by keeping control over subordinate rulers. The Senas, who integrated almost all the sub-regions of Bengal, tried to enhance their control over rural society by the introduction of a uniform standard of land measurement and the assessment of production in the uniform currency unit of *kapardakapurāṇa*, of which the latter was implemented thoroughly and contributed to the enhancement of their local control. Under the Sena rule, subordinate rulers were mostly incorporated in the stratified land relation topped by the king as superior tenure holders, side by side with members of the royal household.

The highly qualified *brāhmaṇa*s established their authority at the royal courts as specialists of Puranic rituals of *śānti*s and *mahādāna*s, for which they received land and village grants, and as an authority of *dharma* composing the *Dharmanibandha*s. It shows the royal acceptance of the particular Brahmanical norms explicated in the *Purāṇa*s and the *Dharmaśāstra*s. The *brāhmaṇa*s also tried to consolidate their dominance in rural society. The construction of their networks through multiple migrations and establishment of Brahmanical centres reached the level at which both processes slowed down and the consolidation of their presence in each locality became more important. It resulted in the formation of their sub-regional identities, Rāḍhīya and Vārendra, and the settling down and incorporation of highly qualified *brāhmaṇa*s in rural society. Their dominance accrued not only from the privileges and powers conferred and guaranteed by the enhanced state power but also from their position as landlords embedded in the stratified land relation of the period.

While the stratification of rural society was still visible in Varendra under the Pāla rule, it was rather glossed over by simpler categories of residents like *janapada* and *kṣetrakara* under the Varmans and the Senas. However, some occasional references attest to the stratified land relation, in which cultivators were overburdened with as many as three levels of tenure holders, including the king, the superior tenure holders like royal family members and subordinate rulers, and the individual and collective landholders. While the agrarian groups embedded in such a stratified land relation were divided into landholders and cultivators, the professional groups like merchants and artisans were in the process of social organisation based on their occupations.

The stratification of rural society and the formation of occupational groups were closely connected with the two economic developments. The sub-regions of Bengal, including Varendra in the process of recovery from the devastation, witnessed a new round of agrarian development in different timelines. The most remarkable was the agrarian expansion to the Bhagirathi estuary and the area near to Madhupur tract. The social stratification resulting in layered land relation, which enabled the assignees of upper tenures to mobilise labour power of subject cultivators, was conductive for the agrarian enterprise. However, the agrarian expansion in those sub-regions reached a limit which could not be overcome in the contemporary conditions, possibly both social and technological. It resulted in the congestion of land and dispersal of landed properties. In this situation, all the sub-regions commonly saw the tendency towards intensive use of landed property with emphasis on the cultivation of commercially valuable products, especially areca nuts and betel leaves. The prevalence of such commercial cropping was connected with the commercialisation of rural economy, which spread to the wider area beyond Varendra in this period.

Confronting the social stratification and the formation of occupational groups in a new economic context, *brāhmaṇa*s, backed by their enhanced authority, tried to intervene in the two forms of reorganisation of rural society which had been attempted in the previous period, through the composition of the local *Purāṇa*s. For the cohesion of rural society, they prescribed the festivals in annual calendar, of which the most important was the autumn festival for the goddess. Those festivals were crafted as the social gatherings of all the members for confirming their solidarity through the temporary suppression of inner differences and the subversive merrymaking. Notable was the intention of *brāhmaṇa*s to insert themselves in those festivals with popular elements as officiating priests or recipients of material benefits and honour. As for the construction of occupational groups, *brāhmaṇa*s tried to explain the emergence of diverse groups by their own social view consisting of four *varṇa* scheme and reorganise those groups in a hierarchical *jāti* order by the narrative of *Varṇasaṃkara* combined with Veṇa-Pṛthu myth. In this exercise, they had to negotiate with the literate groups like *karaṇa*s, *ambaṣṭha*s and *gaṇaka*s, to whom they conceded special positions, and the mercantile groups, whom they tried to contain in an ambiguous position. The two forms of social reorientation and systematisation by the initiative of *brāhmaṇa*s were complementary to each other, in that the festivals for social cohesion were necessary to integrate diverse social groups consolidating themselves towards *jāti*s arranged in a hierarchical order.

The historical process delineated above consisted of several strands with which multiple agencies were involved; in terms of power relation, it was the process in which the authority over rural society wielded by the dominant section of *kuṭumbin*s shifted to the nexus of *mahattara*s and literates, which was confronted by the growing presence of the external political powers. With the emergence and establishment of regional kingships, the focus of power struggle shifted to the contradictions between the king and subordinate rulers, which were centred on religious agents patronised by both sides. The contradictions culminated in the *Kaivarta* rebellion, the heavy dependence of the Pāla kings on subordinate rulers and the incorporation of the latter in stratified land relation under the firmer royal control of the Senas. In this changing power relation, rural society experienced the growing stratification of agrarian members towards stratified land relation, especially the emergence of subject cultivators, and the organisation of hereditary occupational groups of clerical, mercantile and artisanal characters and the systematisation of their mutual relations towards a *jāti* order. The growth of *brāhmaṇa*s as a group through the formation of clearer identity and networks, the establishment of their authority and their intervention in social reorganisation constituted another pillar of the historical process. Those political and social processes constituted as well as were constituted by the economic processes of agrarian development, with forms changing from management by family labour to mobilisation of subject cultivators, and commercialisation of rural economy through the spread of markets and monetary transactions mediated by currency units and cowrie-shells. The interconnection of all those strands brought out the social formations which evolved in Bengal through the long period of 800 years dealt with in the present study. Their history defies the application of any simplistic model or the attribution to any single cause, as is clear from the discussions made above.

The social formation resulting from the historical process of the period formed the basis for another process to unfold in the following period, in the changed political context of the Turkish conquest and the establishment of the Sultanate and Mughal rules. The stratified land relation continued and evolved with the introduction of new administrative systems, in which old literate elites of *brāhmaṇa*s, *kāyastha*s and *vaidya*s constituted a part of local landed magnates side by side with newly induced military, mercantile and religious elites.[1] Though the rise of *kāyastha*s and *vaidya*s as such could be attributed to their service to the new political power, which was later followed by *brāhmaṇa*s,[2] the presence of those groups as landed magnates had root in the social change of the early medieval period. The systematisation of hereditary occupational groups as a *jāti* order continued with plural attempts in different logics, and the version constructed in the *Bṛhaddharmapurāṇa* finally prevailed to become the standard one accepted widely, with the protracted process of its imposition on and acceptance by the wider range of social groups.

*Brāhmaṇa*s, who tried to maintain their authority by inventing a new system of inner regulation like *samāja* and *kulīna* status,[3] continued their efforts of social reorganisation with adjustment to a new context. Raghunandana, the eminent *nibandhakāra* of the 16th century, reformulated *Durgāpūjā* as domestic festival for reproduction and prosperity to cater for the demand of the local landed gentry, new patrons.[4] The ensued effort and struggle of *brāhmaṇas* to insert themselves in popular festivals can be glimpsed from *Gājan* festival, the modern equivalent of *Śivamahotsava*, in which the actions of self-tormenting *sannyāsins* are predominant but *brāhmaṇas* still have roles to play as priests.[5]

Agrarian expansion further proceeded in both western and eastern fringes of Bengal through the incorporation of marginal groups into sedentary agrarian society, with the mediation of the cults of minor deities and the Sufistic Islam respectively.[6]

Thus, the historical process in the medieval or the early modern period, critical for the formation of Bengal society, was welded to the earlier process discussed in the present work. Like its predecessor, it must have consisted of plural strands of changes involving multiple agencies interacted with each other, so did its successor under the huge impact of modernisation.

Notes

1 Ratnalekha Ray, *Change in Bengal Agrarian Society: c1760–1850*, New Delhi: Manohar, 1979, pp. 13–72.
2 Reena Bhaduri, *Social Formation in Medieval Bengal*, Kolkata: Bibhasa, 2001, pp. 70–78.
3 Ronald B. Inden, *Marriage and Rank in Bengali Culture: A History of Caste and Clan in Middle Period Bengal*, New Delhi: Vikas Publishing House, 1976.
4 Bihani Sarkar, 'The Rite of Durgā in Medieval Bengal: An Introductory Study of Raghunandana's *Durgāpūjātattva* with Text and Translation of the Principal Rites', *Journal of the Royal Asiatic Society*, 2012, 22(2): 325–90.
5 Ralph W. Nicholas, *Rites of Spring: Gājan in Village Bengal (With an Essay by David Curley)*, New Delhi: Chronicle Books, 2008.
6 Jawhal Sircar, *The Construction of the Hindu Identity in Medieval Western Bengal?: The Role of Popular Cults*, Kolkata: Institute of Development Studies, 2005; Richard M. Eaton, *The Rise of Islam and the Bengal Frontier, 1204–1760*, Berkeley: University of California Press, 1993, pp. 194–227.

APPENDIX: LIST OF INSCRIPTIONS

a. Copper plate inscriptions

1 Dhanaidaha CPI, year 113 GE: Basak, 'Dhanaidaha Copper-Plate Inscription of the Time of Kumaragupta I: The Year 113' (1923–24); *SI* 1, pp. 287–89; *CBI*, pp. 41–44; *CII* 3 (rev.), pp. 273–76.

2 Kalaikuri-Sultanpur CPI, year 120 GE: Sircar, 'Kalaikuri Copper-plate Inscription of the Gupta Year 120 (=A.D. 439)' (1943); Sanyal, 'Sultanpur Copper-Plate Inscription' (1955–56); *SI* 1, pp. 352–55.

3 Damodarpur CPI of the Time of Kumāragupta I, year 124 GE: Basak, 'The Five Damodarpur Copper-Plate Inscriptions of the Gupta Period' (1919–20), pp. 129–32; *SI* 1, pp. 290–92; *CBI*, pp. 45–47; *CII* 3 (rev.), pp. 282–87.

4 Damodarpur CPI of the Time of Kumāragupta I, year 128 GE: Basak, 'Five Damodarpur Copper-Plate', pp. 132–34; *SI* 1, pp. 292–94; *CBI*, pp. 47–49; *CII* 3 (rev.), pp. 288–91.

5 Baigram CPI, year 128 GE: Basak, 'Baigram Copper-Plate Inscription of the [Gupta]-Year 128' (1931–32); *SI* 1, pp. 355–59; *CBI*, pp. 49–53.

6 Jagadishpur CPI, year 128 GE: Sircar, 'Jagadishpur Plate of the Gupta Year 128' (1970); *EDEP*, pp. 61–63.

7 Mahatiraktamala CPI, year 159 GE: Griffiths, 'New Documents for the Early History of Puṇḍravardhana: Copperplate Inscriptions from the Late Gupta and Early Post-Gupta Periods' (2015), pp. 16–27.

8 Paharpur CPI, year 159 GE: Dikshit, 'Paharpur Copper-Plate Grant of the [Gupta] Year 159' (1929–30); *SI* 1, pp. 359–63; *CBI*, pp. 53–58.

9 Damodarpur CPI of the Time of Budhagupta, year 163 GE: Basak, 'Five Damodarpur Copper-Plate', pp. 134–37; *SI* 1, pp. 332–34; *CBI*, pp. 58–61; *CII* 3 (rev.), pp. 335–39.

10 Nandapur CPI, year 169 GE: Majumdar, 'Nandapur Copper-Plate of the Gupta Year 169' (1935–36); *SI*, 1, pp. 382–84.

11 Damodarpur CPI of the Time of Budhagupta, ND: Basak, 'Five Damodarpur Copper-Plate', pp. 137–41; *SI* 1, pp. 336–39; *CBI*, pp. 61–64; *CII* 3 (rev.), pp. 342–45.

12 CPI of Vainyagupta, year 184 GE: Furui, 'Ājīvikas, Maṇibhadra and Early History of Eastern Bengal: A New Copperplate Inscription of Vainyagupta and its Implications' (2016).

13 Gunaighar CPI of Vainyagupta, Year 188 GE: Bhattacharyya, 'A Newly Discovered Copperplate from Tippera [The Gunaighar Grant of Vainyagupta: The Year 188 Current (Gupta Era)]' (1930); *SI* 1, pp. 340–45; *CBI*, pp. 65–70.

14 Damodarpur CPI, Year 224 GE: Basak, 'Five Damodarpur Copper-Plate', pp. 141–45; *SI* 1, pp. 346–50; *CBI*, pp. 70–74; *CII* 3 (rev.), pp. 360–63.

15 CPI of the Time of Pradyumnabandhu, year 5, Griffiths, 'New Documents', pp. 27–33.

16 Kotalipada CPI of the Time of Dvādaśāditya, year 14: Islam, 'Koṭālipāḍā Copper Plate of Dvādaśāditya' (2011); Furui, 'The Kotalipada Copperplate Inscription of the Time of Dvādaśāditya, Year 14' (2013).

17 Faridpur CPI of the Time of Dharmāditya, year 3: Pargiter, 'Three Copper-Plate Grants from East Bengal' (1910), pp. 193–98; *SI* 1, pp. 363–67; *CBI*, pp. 74–79.

18 Faridpur CPI of the Time of Dharmāditya, ND: Pargiter, 'Three Copper-Plate', pp. 199–202; *SI* 1, pp. 367–69; *CBI*, pp. 79–83.

19 Jayarampur CPI of Gopacandra, year 1: Rajaguru, 'Jayarampur Copper-Plate Inscription of the Time of Gopachandra' (1963); Srinivasan, 'Jayarampur Plate of Gopachandra' (1972); *IO*, pp. 174–79.

20 Mallasarul CPI of Vijayasena, of the Time of Gopacandra, year 3: Majumdar, 'Mallasarul Copper-Plate of Vijayasena' (1935–36); Chhabra, 'Note on Mallasarul Charter of Vijayasena' (1953–54); *SI* 1, pp. 372–77; *CBI*, pp. 87–95.

21 Faridpur CPI of the Time of Gopacandra, year 18: Pargiter, 'Three Copper-Plate', pp. 203–5; *SI* 1, pp. 370–72; *CBI*, pp. 83–87.

22 Ghugrahati CPI of the Time of Samācāradeva, year 14, Banerji, 'The Koṭwalipārā Spurious Grant of Samācāra Deva' (1910); Pargiter, 'Ghāgrāhāṭi (Koṭwālipāṛā) Grant and Three other Copper-Plate Grants' (1911), pp. 475–502; Bhattasali, 'The Ghugrahati Copper-Plate Inscription of Samachara-Deva' (1925–26).

23 Maliadanga CPI of Jayanāga: Barnett, 'Vappaghoshavata Grant of Jayanaga' (1925–26); Banerji, 'A Note on the Vappaghoshavata Grant of Jayanaga' (1927–28).

24 Panchrol CPI of the Time of Śaśāṅka: Sircar, 'Egra Plate of the Time of Sasank' (1974); *STP*, pp. 59–64; Furui, 'Panchrol (Egra) Copperplate Inscription of the Time of Śaśāṅka: A Re-edition' (2011).

25 Antla CPI of Śubhakīrti, year 8: Majumdar, 'Two Copper-Plates of Śaśāṅka from Midnapore' (1945), p. 9; *SI*, 2, pp. 24–26.

26 Antla CPI of Somadatta, year 19, Majumdar, 'Two Copper Plates of Śaśāṅka', pp. 1–8; *SI* 2, pp. 26–27.

27 Ganjam CPI of Mādhavarāaja, year 300 GE: Hultzsch, 'Plates of the Time of Sasankaraja; Gupta-Samvat 300' (1900–01).
28 Nidhanpur CPI of Bhāskaravarman: Bhattacharya, 'Nidhanpur Copper Plates of Bhaskaravarman' (1913–14); idem, 'Two Lost Plates of the Nidhanpur Copper-Plates of Bhaskaravarman' (1927–28); idem, 'A Third Lost Plate of the Nidhanpur Plates of Bhaskaravarman' (1927–28); *CPS*, pp. 7–67; *IAA*, pp. 38–81.
29 Dubi CPI of Bhāskaravarman: Sircar, 'Dubi Plates of Bhaskaravarman' (1953–54); *IAA*, pp. 10–32; *SI* 2, pp. 1–15.
30 Tippera CPI of Lokanātha, year [3]44(?): Basak, 'Tipperah Copper-Plate Grant of Lokanatha: the 44th Year' (1919–20); *SI* 2, pp. 28–35.
31 Kalapur CPI of Maruṇḍanātha: *CPS*, pp. 68–80; *EDEP*, pp. 14–18.
32 Kailan CPI of Śrīdhāraṇarāta, year 8: Sircar, 'The Kailan Copper-plate Inscription of King Śrīdhāraṇa Rāta of Samataṭa' (1947); *SI* 2, pp. 36–40.
33 Uriswar CPI of Śrīdhāraṇarāta: Islam, 'Uḍīśvara Copper Plate of Śrīdhāraṇarāta' (2012).
34 Ashrafpur CPI of Devakhaḍga, year 7: Laskar, 'Ashrafpur Copper-Plate Grants of Devakhaḍga' (1904), pp. 88–91.
35 Ashrafpur CPI of Devakhaḍga, year 13: Laskar, 'Ashrafpur Copper-Plate', pp. 89–90; *SI* 2, pp. 41–43.
36 Salban Vihara CPI of Devakhaḍga: Rashid, 'The Mainamati Inscriptions' (2001), p. 201.
37 Salban Vihara CPI of Khaḍgas: Rashid, 'Mainamati Inscriptions', p. 201.
38 Salban Vihara CPI of Balabhaṭa: Gupta, 'Two Mainamati Copper-Plate Inscriptions of the Khadga and Early-Deva Times (7th and 8th centuries A. D.)' (1979), pp. 141–44.
39 Salban Vihara CPI of Ānandadeva, year 39 and Bhavadeva, year 2: Gupta, 'Two Mainamati Copper-Plate Inscriptions', pp. 145–48.
40 Devaparvata (Salban Vihara) CPI of Bhavadeva, year 2: Sircar, 'Copper-Plate Inscription of King Bhavadeva of Devaparvata' (1951).
41 Indian Museum CPI of Dharmapāla, year 26: Bhattacharya, 'The Murshidabad (Indian Museum) Copper-Plate Grant of Dharmapāla and the Somapura Mahāvihāra' (2006–07); Furui, 'Indian Museum Copper Plate Inscription of Dharmapala, Year 26: Tentative Reading and Study' (2011); Bhattacharya, 'Murshidabad (Indian Museum) Copper Plate of Dharmapāla: The Complete Version' (2013).
42 Khalimpur CPI of Dharmapāla, year 32: Kielhorn, 'Khalimpur Plate of Dharmapaladeva' (1896–97); *GL*, pp. 9–28; *SI* 2, pp. 63–70; *CBI*, pp. 95–110.
43 Nalanda CPI of Dharmapāla: Bhattacharyya, 'Nalanda Plate of Dharmapaladeva' (1935–36).
44 Monghyr CPI of Devapāla, year 33: *GL*, pp. 33–44; Barnett, 'The Mungir Plate of Devapaladeva: Samvat 33' (1925–26); *CBI*, pp. 114–31.

45 Nalanda CPI of Devapāla, year 39: Shastri, 'The Nalanda Copper-Plate of Devapaladeva' (1923–24); Majumdar, *Nālandā Copper-Plate of Devapāladeva* (1926); *SI* 2, pp. 71–79.
46 Chittagong CPI of Kāntideva, Majumdar, 'Chittagong Copper-Plate of Kantideva' (1941–42).
47 Jagajjibanpur CPI of Mahendrapāla, year 7: Ramesh and Subramonia Iyer, 'Māldā District Museum Copper-Plate Charter of Mahendrapāladeva, year 7' (1977–78); Mukherji, 'The Jagajjivanpur Copper-plate Inscription of King Mahendrapāla (of the Pāla Dynasty), regnal year 7 (857 A. D.)' (1997–99); Bhattacharya, 'A Note on the Jagjibanpur Inscription of Mahendrapāla' (1997–99); Bhattacharya, 'The Jagjibanpur Plate of Mahendrapāla Comprehensively Re-edited' (2005–06).
48 Mirzapur CPI of Śūrapāla, year 3: Sircar, 'Lucknow Museum Copper-Plate Inscription of Surapala I, Regnal Year 3' (1973).
49 Mohipur CPI of Gopāla II, year 3: Furui, 'A New Copper Plate Inscription of Gopala II' (2008).
50 Suvarnakarikadanda CPI of Gopāla II, year 4 (no. 1): Mukherji, 'Two New Copper-plate Inscriptions (Nos. 1 and 2) of King Gopāla II, Pāla Dynasty of Bengal and Bihar, regnal year 4 (Circa 878 A. D.)' (1997–99); Furui, 'Re-reading Two Copper Plate Inscriptions of Gopāla II, year 4' (2009).
51 Suvarnakarikadanda CPI of Gopāla II, year 4 (no. 2), Mukherji, 'Two New Copper-plate Inscriptions (Nos. 1 and 2) of King Gopāla II'; Furui, 'Re-reading Two Copper Plate Inscriptions'.
52 Bhagalpur CPI of Nārāyaṇapāla, year 17: *GL*, pp. 55–69; *CBI*, pp. 163–84; *SI* 2, pp. 80–86.
53 Bharat Kala Bhavan CPI of Rājyapāla, year 2: Mishra, 'Bharat Kala Bhavan Copper-Plate Grant of Rājyapāla (Regnal Year 2)' (1981); Subramonia Iyer, 'Bharat Kala Bhavan Copper Plate Charter of Rajyapaladeva, Year 2' (2011–12); Furui, 'Bharat Kala Bhavan Copper Plate Inscription of Rājyapāla, year 2: Re-edition and Reinterpretation' (2016).
54 Paschimbhag CPI of Śrīcandra, year 5: *CPS*, pp. 81–152; Sircar, 'Paschimbhag Plate of Srichandra, Year 5' (1968); *EDEP*, pp. 63–69; *SI* 2, pp. 92–100.
55 Dhulla CPI of Śrīcandra, year 8: Sircar, 'Dhulla Plate of Srichandra' (1959–60).
56 Rampal CPI of Śrīcandra: Basak, 'Rampal Copper-Plate Grant of Srichandradeva' (1913–14); *IB*, pp. 1–9; *CBI*, pp. 221–29.
57 Bangladesh National Museum CPI of Śrīcandra, year 46: Mills, 'A Copper Plate from the Reign of Śrīcandra (Bangladesh National Museum Accession Number 77.1478)' (1993).
58 Madanpur CPI of Śrīcandra, year 46: Basak, 'Madanpur Plate of Srichandra, year 44' (1949–50); Sircar, 'Epigraphic Notes' (1949–50), pp. 337–39.

59 Kedarpur CPI of Śrīcandra: Bhattasali, 'The Kedarpur Plate of Sri-Chandra-Deva' (1923–24); *IB*, pp. 10–13; *CBI*, pp. 229–34.
60 Idilpur CPI of Śrīcandra, Bhattasali, 'Kedarpur Plate', pp. 189–90 (abstract).
61 Bogra(?) CPI of Śrīcandra: Fleming, 'New Copperplate Grant of Śrīcandra (no, 8) from Bangladesh' (2010).
62 Jajilpara CPI of Gopāla III, year 6: Misra and Majumdar, 'The Jājilpārā Grant of Gopāla II, Year 6' (1951).
63 Irda CPI of Nayapāla, year 13: Majumdar, 'Irda Copper-Plate of the Kamboja King Nayapaladeva' (1933–34).
64 Kalanda CPI of Nayapāla, year 14: Ramesh and Subramonia Iyer, 'Kalanda Copper Plate Charter of Nayapāladeva' (1975–76).
65 Belwa CPI of Mahīpāla I, year 2: Gupta, 'The Two Pāla Copper-Plate Inscriptions of Belwā' (1951), pp. 117–31; Sircar, 'Two Pala Plates from Belwa' (1951–52), pp. 1–9.
66 Rangpur CPI of Mahīpāla I, year 5: Furui, 'Rangpur Copper Plate Inscription of Mahīpāla I, Year 5 (2010–11).
67 Bangarh CPI of Mahīpāla I, year 9: Kielhorn, 'The Dinājpur Copper-Plate Inscription of Mahīpāla' (1892); *GL*, pp. 91–100; Banerji, 'The Bangarh Grant of Mahi-Pala I: The 9th Year' (1917–18); *CBI*, pp. 197–208.
68 Biyala CPI of Mahīpāla I, year 35: Bhattacharya, 'Prathama Mahīpāladeber Biyālā Tāmraphalaka' (1987); Furui, 'Biyala Copper-plate Inscription of Mahīpāla I' (2010).
69 Panchbibi CPI of Mahīpāla I: Bhattacharya, 'Newly Discovered Copper Plate Grants of the Pāla Dynasty' (1994), p. 206.
70 CP of Nayapāla: Bhattacharya, 'An Incomplete Copper-Plate Grant Belonging to the Pāla Ruler Nayapāla' (1996).
71 Mainamati CPI of Laḍahacandra, year 6 (no. 1): Dani, 'Mainamati Plates of the Candras' (1966), pp. 37–46; Sircar, 'Mainamati Plates of the Chandra Kings', (1970), pp. 201–7; *EDEP*, pp. 69–75.
72 Mainamati CPI of Laḍahacandra, year 6 (no. 2), Dani, 'Mainamati Plates', pp. 47–49; Sircar, 'Mainamati Plates', pp. 207–9; *EDEP*, pp. 75–76.
73 Mainamati CPI of Govindacandra, Dani, 'Mainamati Plates', pp. 50–55; Sircar, 'Mainamati Plates', pp. 209–14; *EDEP*, pp. 77–81.
74 Belwa CPI of Vigrahapāla III, year 11: Gupta, 'Two Pāla Copper-Plate', pp. 131–35; Sircar, 'Two Pala Plates from Belwa', pp. 9–13.
75 Amgachi CPI of Vigrahapāla III, year 12: *GL*, pp. 121–26; Banerji, 'The Amgachhi Grant of Vigraha-Pala III: the 12th Year' (1919–20); *CBI*, pp. 192–97.
76 Bangaon CPI of Vigrahapāla III, year 17: Sircar, 'Bangaon Plate of Vigrahapala III; Regnal Year 17' (1951–52).
77 Ramganj CPI of Īśvaraghoṣa, year 35: *IB*, pp. 149–57; *CBI*, pp. 361–70.

78 Samantasar CPI of Harivarman: Bhattasali, 'Two Grants of Varmans of Vanga' (1953–54), pp. 255–59.
79 Vajrayogini CPI of Sāmalavarman: Bhattasali, 'Two Grants of Varmans', pp. 259–63.
80 Belava CPI of Bhojavarman, year 5: Basak, 'Belava Copper-Plate of Bhojavarmadeva. The Fifth Year' (1913–14); *IB*, pp. 14–24; *CBI*, pp. 234–44.
81 Kamauli CPI of Vaidyadeva, year 4: Venis, 'Copper-Plate Grant of Vaidyadeva, King of Kāmarūpa' (1894); *GL*, pp. 127–46; *CBI*, pp. 370–86; *IAA*, pp. 273–90.
82 Rajibpur CPI of Gopāla IV, year 2 and Madanapāla, year 2: Furui, 'Rajibpur Copperplate Inscriptions of Gopāla IV and Madanapāla' (2015), pp. 40–48.
83 Manahali CPI of Madanapāla, year 8: Vasu, 'Copper-plate Inscription of Madanapāla' (1900); *GL*, pp. 147–58; *CBI*, pp. 209–19.
84 Barrackpur CPI of Vijayasena, year 62: Banerji, 'Barrackpur Grant of Vijayasena: The 32nd Year' (1919–20); *IB*, pp. 57–67.
85 Rajibpur CPI of Madanapāla, year 22: Furui, 'Rajibpur Copperplate', pp. 49–56.
86 Naihati CPI of Vallālasena, year 11: Banerji, 'The Naihati Grant of Vallala-Sena; The 11th Year' (1917–18); *IB*, pp. 68–80; *CBI*, pp. 258–71.
87 Govindapur CPI of Lakṣmaṇasena, year 2: *IB*, pp. 92–98; *CBI*, pp. 271–77.
88 Tarpandighi CPI of Lakṣmaṇasena, year 2: *IB*, pp. 99–105; *CBI*, pp. 295–302.
89 Dighirpar-Bakultala CPI of Lakṣmaṇasena, year 2: *IB*, pp. 169–72; *CBI*, pp. 290–94.
90 Anulia CPI of Lakṣmaṇasena, year 3: *IB*, pp. 81–91; *CBI*, pp. 302–12.
91 Saktipur CPI of Lakṣmaṇasena, year 6: Ganguly, 'Saktipur Copper-Plate of Lakshmanasena' (1931–32).
92 Rakshaskhali CPI of Ḍommaṇapāla, year 1118 SE: Sen and Ghosh, 'A Dated Copper-Plate Grant from Sundarban' (1934); Ghoshal, 'Rakshaskhali Island Plate of Madommanapala; Saka 1118' (1947–48); Sircar, 'Epigraphic Notes' (1953–54), pp. 42–46; idem, 'Epigraphic Notes' (1963), pp. 98–99.
93 Rajavadi CPI of Lakṣmaṇasena, year 27: Bhattasali, 'The Lost Bhowal Copper-Plate of Lakṣmaṇa Sena Deva of Bengal' (1927); Randle, 'India Office Plate of Lakshmanasena' (1941–42); Bhattasali, 'The Rājāvāḍī (Bhāwāl) Plate of Lakṣsmaṇa Sena Deva' (1942); idem, 'The Rājāvāḍī (Bhāwāl) Plate of Lakṣmaṇa Sena Deva (Additions and Corrections)' (1942).
94 Madhainagar CPI of Lakṣmaṇasena: *IB*, pp. 106–15; *CBI*, pp. 277–89; *SI* 2, pp. 124–30.
95 Idilpur CPI of Viśvarūpasena, year 3?: Banerji, 'Edilpur Grant of Kesavasena' (1914); *IB*, pp. 118–31; *CBI*, pp. 333–49.

96 Madanapada CPI of Viśvarūpasena, year 14: *IB*, pp. 132–39; Sircar, 'Madanpāṛā Plate of Viśvarūpasena' (1954); idem, 'Madanapada Plate of Visvarupasena' (1959–60); *CBI*, pp. 312–21; *SI* 2, pp. 131–39.

97 Madhyapada CPI of Viśvarūpasena, years 13 and 14: *IB*, pp. 140–48; Sircar, 'Vaṅgīya Sāhitya Pariṣad Plate of Viśvarūpasena' (1954), pp. 201–8; *CBI*, pp. 321–32.

98 Mainamati CPI of Harikāladeva, year 1141 SE, 17 RE: Bhattacharyya, 'The Maināmati Copper-plate of Raṇavaṅkamalla Harikāladeva (1141 Śaka).' (1933); idem, 'The Mainamati Copper-plate of Ranavankamalla Harikaladeva: 1141 Saka' (1934).

99 Mainamati CPI of Dāmodaradeva, year 1155 SE: Unpublished (Photographed).

100 Mehar CPI of Dāmodaradeva, year 1156 SE, 4 RE: Barua and Chakravarti, 'Mehar Plate of Damodaradeva' (1947–48); Sircar, 'Epigraphic Notes' (1953–54), pp. 51–58; *SI* 2, pp. 140–45.

101 Sobharampur CPI of Dāmodaradeva, year 1158 SE, 6 RE: Dani, 'Sobharampur Plate of Damodaradeva, Saka 1158' (1953–54).

102 Mainamati CPI of Dāmodaradeva, year 1159 SE: Unpublished (Photographed).

103 Nasirabad CPI of Dāmodaradeva, year 1165 SE: *IB*, pp. 158–63.

104 Adavadi CPI of Daśarathadeva, year 3: *IB*, pp. 181–82 (abstract).

105 Pakamura CPI of Daśarathadeva: *STP*, pp. 165–68 (abstract).

106 Mainamati CPI of Vīradharadeva, year 15: *EDEP*, pp. 57–59, 81; Bhattacharyya, 'Mainamati Copper Plate of Vīradharadeva' (1983–84); Bhattacharjee, 'Mainamati Copper Plate of Sri Viradharadeva' (1994).

107 Bhatera CPI of Govindakeśavadeva: *Proceedings of the Asiatic Society of Bengal*, August 1880: 141–53; Gupta, 'The Bhatera Copper-Plate Inscription of Govinda-Kesavadeva (C. 1049 A.D.)' (1927–28); Chaudhuri, 'Some Observations on Two Copper-plate Grants from Bhāṭerā, Sylhet District, Assam' (1941), *CPS*, pp. 153–80.

108 Bhatera CPI of Īśānadeva: Chaudhuri, 'Some Observations on Two Copper-plate Grants'; *CPS*, pp. 181–203.

b. Other inscriptions

1 Mahasthan Brahmi Inscription: Bhandarkar, 'Mauryan Brahmi Inscription of Mahasthan' (1931–32); *SI* 1, pp. 79–80; *CBI*, pp. 39–40.

2 Susuniya Rock Inscription of Candravarman: *SI* 1, pp. 351–52; *CBI*, pp. 40–41.

3 Allahabad Stone Pillar Inscription of Samudragupta: *SI* 1, pp. 262–68; *CII* 3 (rev.), pp. 203–20.

4 Mehrauli Iron Pillar Inscription of Candra: *SI* 1, pp. 283–85; *CII* 3 (rev.), pp. 257–59.

5 Deulbadi Image Inscription of Mahādevī Prabhāvatī, Queen of Devakhaḍga: Bhattasali, 'Some Image Inscriptions from East Bengal' (1923–24), pp. 357–59.

6 Bangladesh National Museum Metal Vase Inscription of the Time of Devātideva, year 77: Bhattacharya, 'A Preliminary Report on the Inscribed Metal Vase from the National Museum of Bangladesh' (1996).

7 Dudhpani Rock Inscription of Udayamāna: Kielhorn, 'Dudhpani Rock Inscription of Udayamana' (1894).

8 Nalanda Inscription of the Time of Dharmapāla, year 4: Subramonia Iyer, 'Nālandā Inscription of Dharmapāladeva, Year 4' (1977–78).

9 Bodhgaya Inscription of the Time of Dharmapāla, year 26: *GL*, pp. 29–32; *CBI*, pp. 110–14.

10 Valgudar Image Inscription of the Time of Dharmapāla: Sircar, 'Three Inscriptions from Valgudar' (1949–50): pp. 137–40, 144–45.

11 Nalanda Image Inscription of the Time of Devapāla, year 3: Sastri, *Nalanda and Its Epigraphic Material* (1999), p. 87.

12 Linden Museum Bronze Śivaliṅga Inscription of the Time of Devapāla, year 4: Bhattacharya, 'Two Inscribed Bronze Ekamukha-liṅgas of the Devapāla Period' (2007).

13 Kurkihar Image Inscription of the Time of Devapāla, year 9: Banerji-Sastri, 'Ninety-Three Inscriptions on the Kurkihar Bronzes' (1940), p. 251; Gupta, *Patna Museum Catalogue of Antiquities (Stone Sculptures, Metal Images, Terracottas and Minor Antiquities)* (1965), pp. 152–53, no. 149.

14 Hilsa Inscription of Devapāla, year 25: Majumdar Sastri, 'The Hilsa Statue Inscription of the Thirty-fifth Year of Devapala' (1924); Gupta, *Patna Museum Catalogue*, pp. 63–64, no. 58; Huntington, *The "Pāla-Sena" Schools of Sculpture* (1984), pp. 209–10, no. 12.

15 National Museum Image Inscription of the Time of Devapāla, year 25: Bhattacharya, 'A Dated Avalokiteśvara Image of the Devapāla Period' (1997).

16 Berlin Museum of Indian Art Image Inscription of the Time of Devapāla, year 31: Bhattacharya, 'A Second Dated Tārā Image of the Reign of Devapāla' (1982).

17 Nalanda Votive Inscription of the Time of Devapāla: Sastri, *Nalanda and Its Epigraphic Material*, p. 88; Huntington, *The "Pāla-Sena" Schools*, p. 207, no. 8.

18 Nalanda Image Inscription of the Time of Devapāla: Sastri, *Nalanda and Its Epigraphic Material*, pp. 88–89; Ghosh, 'A Bronze Image Inscription from Nalanda' (1939–40); Huntington, *The "Pāla-Sena" Schools*, pp. 207–8, no. 9.

19 Ghosravan Rock Inscription of the Time of Devapāla: *GL*, pp. 45–54; *CBI*, pp. 131–41.

20 Asutosh Museum Pedestal Inscription of the Time of Devapāla: *Annual Report of Indian Epigraphy*, 1949–50, p. 20, B. 2.

21 Bangladesh National Museum Inscription of Pāhila: Biswas, 'Pālarāja Debapāler Samasāmayika Śrīpāhiler Ekṭi Aprakāśita Prastaralipi' (1994); Bhattacharya, 'Bangladesh National Museum *praśasti* of Pāhila (9th century A. D.)' (1997); idem, 'Bangladesh National Museum Praśasti of Pāhila' (1999).

22 British Museum Stone Inscription of the Time of Mahendrapāla, year 2: Bhattacharya, 'The British Museum Stone Inscription of Mahendrapāla' (2007).

23 Berlin Museum of Indian Art Image Inscription of the Time of Mahendrapāla, year 2: Bhattacharya, 'Two Inscribed Buddhist Images from the Museum of Indian Art, Berlin' (1986), pp. 32–38; Sanyal, 'Dedicatory Inscriptions of the Time of Mahendrapāla: A Fresh Appraisal' (2009), pp. 304–5.

24 Indian Museum Image Inscription of the Time of Mahendrapāla, year 4, *Annual Report of Archaeological Survey of India*, 1923–24, pp. 101–2; Sanyal, 'Dedicatory Inscriptions', p. 305.

25 Bihar-Sharif Image Inscription of the Time of Mahendrapāla, year 4: Sastri, *Nalanda and Its Epigraphic Material*, pp. 105–6; Sanyal, 'Dedicatory Inscriptions', p. 305.

26 Paharpur Stone Inscription of the Time of Mahendrapāla, year 5: Dikshit, *Excavations at Paharpur Bengal* (1999), p. 75; Sanyal, 'Dedicatory Inscriptions', p. 306.

27 Itakhauri Image Inscription of the Time of Mahendrapāla, year 8: Huntington, *The "Pāla-Sena" Schools*, p. 241, no. 63, fig. 40; Sanyal, 'Dedicatory Inscriptions', pp. 306–7.

28 Ramgaya Inscription of the Time of Mahendrapāla, year 8: Banerji, 'The Pālas of Bengal' (1915), pp. 63–64; Sanyal, 'Dedicatory Inscriptions', p. 307.

29 Gunariya Image Inscription of the Time of Mahendrapāla, year 9: Banerji, 'The Pālas of Bengal', p. 64; idem, 'The Pratīhāra Occupation of Magadha' (1918), p. 110; Sanyal, 'Dedicatory Inscriptions', pp. 307–8.

30 British Museum Pedestal Inscription of the Time of Mahendrapāla, year 9: Bhattacharya, 'A Puzzling Report on a British Museum Buddhist Pedestal Inscription' (1990); Sanyal, 'Dedicatory Inscriptions', p. 308.

31 Mahisantosh Image Inscription of the Time of Mahendrapāla, year 15: Sircar, 'Mahisantosh Image Inscription of Mahendrapala, Year 15' (1968); Sanyal, 'Dedicatory Inscriptions', pp. 308–9.

32 Nalanda Votive Inscription of the Time of Mahendrapāla: Sastri, *Nalanda and Its Epigraphic Material*, p. 106; Sanyal, 'Dedicatory Inscriptions', p. 310.

33 Indian Museum Image Inscription of the Time of Śūrapāla, year 3: Chakravartti, 'Pāla Inscriptions in the Indian Museum' (1908), pp. 107–8.

34 Rajauna Image Inscription of the Time of Śūrapāla, year 5: Banerjee, 'Some Inscriptions from Bihar' (1973–74), pp. 102–8; Huntington, *The "Pāla-Sena" Schools*, pp. 210–11, no. 15, fig. 36.
35 Gaya Museum Image Inscription of the Time of Śūrapāla, year 12: Huntington, *The "Pāla-Sena" Schools*, p. 211, no. 16a.
36 Nalanda Inscription of Śūrapāla: Sircar, 'Notes and Queries' (1953), pp. 301–2.
37 Mandhuk Image Inscription of the Time of Gopāla II, year 1: Sircar, 'Pāla Rule in the Tippera District' (1952); Bhattacharya, 'Nalanda Vāgīśvarī and Mandhuk Gaṇeśa: Are They of the Same Period?' (1999).
38 Sarnath Inscription of Jayapāla: *Annual Report of Archaeological Survey of India*, 1907–08, p. 75, no. 6.
39 Gaya Inscription of the Time of Nārāyaṇapāla, year 7: Sircar, 'Three Pala Inscriptions' (1964), pp. 225–28.
40 Indian Mueum Inscription of the Time of Nārāyaṇapāla, year 9: Banerji, 'The Pālas of Bengal', pp. 61–62.
41 Bihar Sharif Image Inscription of the Time of Nārāyaṇapāla, year 54: Banerji, 'The Pratīhāra Occupation', pp. 109–10.
42 Badal Stone Pillar Inscription of Guravamiśra in the Time of Nārāyaṇapāla: Kielhorn, 'Badal Pillar Inscription of the Time of Narayanapala' (1894); *GL*, pp. 70–85; *CBI*, pp. 150–63; *SI* 2, pp. 87–91.
43 Nalanda Stone Pillar Inscription of the Time of Rājyapāla, year 24: Banerji, 'The Pratīhāra Occupation', p. 111; Sircar, 'Two Pillar Inscriptions' (1949), pp. 7–8.
44 Kurkihar Image Inscription of the Time of Rājyapāla, year 28: Banerji-Sastri, 'Ninety-Three Inscriptions', pp. 246–47; Gupta, *Patna Museum Catalogue*, p. 155, no. 164.
45 Kurkihar Image Inscription of the Time of Rājyapāla, year 31: Banerji-Sastri, 'Ninety-Three Inscriptions', p. 250; Gupta, *Patna Museum Catalogue*, p. 153, no. 153.
46 Kurkihar Image Inscription of the Time of Rājyapāla, year 32 (no.1): Banerji-Sastri, 'Ninety-Three Inscriptions', pp. 247–48; Gupta, *Patna Museum Catalogue*, pp. 149–50, no. 134.
47 Kurkihar Image Inscription of the Time of Rājyapāla, year 32 (no.2): Banerji-Sastri, 'Ninety-Three Inscriptions', p. 248; Gupta, *Patna Museum Catalogue*, p. 150, no. 135.
48 Victoria and Albert Museum Image Inscription of the Time of Rājyapāla, year 37: Huntington, *The "Pāla-Sena" Schools*, p. 216, no. 24.
49 Bhaturiya Stone Inscription of Yośodāsa in the Time of Rājyapāla: Lahiri, 'Bhāturiyā Inscription of Rājyapāla' (1955); Sircar, 'Bhaturiya Inscription of Rajyapala' (1959–60).
50 Chittagong(?) Metal Vase Inscription of Attākaradeva: Bhattacharya, 'An Inscribed Metal Vase Most Probably from Chittagong, Bangladesh' (1993).

51 Nalanda Image Inscription of the Time of Gopāla III, year 1: Chakravartti, 'Pāla Inscriptions in the Indian Museum', pp. 105–6; *GL*, pp. 86–87; *CBI*, pp. 187–88, 191–92; Bhattacharya, 'Nalanda Vāgīśvarī and Mandhuk Gaṇeśa'.

52 Bodhgaya Stone Inscription of the Time of Gopāla III: *GL*, pp. 88–90; *CBI*, pp. 184–87, 189–91.

53 Kolagallu Inscription of Khottiga, year 889 SE: Rao, 'Kolagallu Inscription of Khottiga; Saka 889' (1931–32).

54 Kosham Shahar Image Inscription of the Time of Vigrahapāla II: Bhattacharya, 'The Munificence of Lady Catuḥsamā' (1991), pp. 315–22.

55 Dinajpur Pillar Inscription mentioning Kambojas: Chanda, 'Dinājpur Pillar Inscription' (1911).

56 Baghaura Image Inscription of the Time of Mahīpāla I, year 3: Bhattasali, 'Some Image Inscriptions', pp. 353–55.

57 Narayanpur Image Inscription of the Time of Mahīpāla I, year 4: Sircar, 'Nārāyaṇpur Vināyaka Image Inscription of King Mahīpāla.-Regnal Year 4 (1942); *STP*, pp. 81–84.

58 Bodhgaya Inscription of the Time of Mahīpāla I, year 11: Banerji, 'The Pālas of Bengal', p. 75; Mitra, 'Image of Buddha of the 11th Regnal Year of King Mahīpāla' (1991).

59 Nalanda Inscription of the Time of Mahīpāla I, year 11, Chakravartti, 'Pāla Inscriptions in the Indian Museum', pp. 106–7; *GL*, pp. 101–3; *CBI*, pp. 208–9.

60 Nimdighi Image Inscription of the Time of Mahīpāla I, year 23: Bhattacharya, 'A Dated Viṣṇu Image of the Mahīpāla (I) Period' (1998).

61 Thalta Majhgram Image Inscription of the Time of Mahīpāla I, year 29: Melzer, 'A Dancing Cāmuṇḍā Named Siddheśvarī from the Time of Mahīpāla I' (2015).

62 Kurkihar Image Inscription of the Time of Mahīpāla I, year 31: Banerji-Sastri, 'Ninety-Three Inscriptions', p. 245; Gupta, *Patna Museum Catalogue*, p. 149, no. 133.

63 Rajbhita Stone Inscription of the Time of Mahīpāla I, year 33: Hok and Kuddus, 'Prathama Mahīpāler Rājabhiṭā Śilālipi: Pāṭhoddhāra o Biśleṣaṇa' (1412 BS); Furui, 'Merchant Groups in Early Medieval Bengal: With Special Reference to the Rajbhita Stone Inscription of the Time of Mahīpāla I, Year 33' (2013).

64 Imadpur Image Inscription of the Time of Mahīpāla I, year 48 (no. 1): Majumdar and Banerjea, 'Two Inscribed Images of Imadpur' (1950); Sircar, 'Date of the Imādpur Image Inscriptions of Mahipāla I' (1954).

65 Imadpur Image Inscription of the Time of Mahīpāla I, year 48 (no. 2): Majumdar and Banerjea, 'Two Inscribed Images'; Sircar, 'Date of the Imādpur Image Inscriptions'.

66 Sarnath Inscription of Mahīpāla I, year 1083 VS: Hultzsch, 'The Sarnath Inscription of Mahipala' (1885); *GL*, pp. 104–9; *CBI*, pp. 219–21.

67 Shantipur Image Inscription of the Time of Mahīpāla I: Mitra, 'A Fragmentary Bejewelled Image of Buddha of the Time of Mahipala from Shantipur' (1995–96).
68 Tetrawan Image Inscription of the Time of Mahīpāla I: Gupta, *Patna Museum Catalogue*, pp. 75–76, no. 113.
69 Chopra Image Inscription of the Time of Mahīpāla I: Pal, 'The Chopra Image Inscription of Mahīpāla' (2010).
70 Bodhgaya Image Inscription of Vīryendra: *SI* 2, p. 59.
71 Bharella Image Inscription of the Time of Laḍahacandra, year 18, Bhattasali, 'Some Image Inscriptions', pp. 349–52.
72 Kulkudi Image Inscription of the Time of Govindacandra, year 12: Bhattasali, 'Two Inscriptions of Govindacandra, King of Vanga' (1947–48), pp. 24–26.
73 Betka Image Inscription of the Time of Govindacandra, year 23: Sircar, 'Pāīkpāṛā Vāsudeva Image Inscription of King Govindacandra of Bengal – Regnal Year 23' (1941); Bhattasali, 'Two Inscriptions of Govindacandra', pp. 26–27; *STP*, pp. 149–53; *SI* 2, p. 101.
74 Tirumalai Rock Inscription of Rājendra Coḷa: Hultzsch, 'Tirumalai Rock Inscription of Rajendra-Chola I' (1907–08).
75 Rajauna Image Inscription of the Time of Nayapāla, year 13: Banerjee, 'Some Inscriptions from Bihar', pp. 108–9.
76 Kawaya Image Inscription: Banerjee, 'Some Inscriptions from Bihar', pp. 109–10.
77 Gaya Stone Inscription of Viśvāditya, year 15 of Nayapāla: *GL*, pp. 110–20; Sircar, 'Inscriptions of Two Brahman Rulers of Gaya' (1965), pp. 84–86; *CBI*, pp. 141–50.
78 Gaya Stone Inscription of Viśvarūpa, year 15 of Nayapāla: Sircar, 'Inscriptions of Two Brahman Rulers', pp. 86–88.
79 Gaya Fragmentary Stone Inscription: Sircar, 'Inscriptions of Two Brahman Rulers', pp. 88–89.
80 Bangarh Stone Inscription of the Time of Nayapāla: Sircar, 'Bāṇgaḍh Stone Inscription of the Time of Nayapāla' (1973–74); idem, 'Mūrtiśiva's Bangarh Prasasti of the Time of Nayapāla' (1980–82).
81 Siyan Stone Inscription of the Time of Nayapāla: Sircar, 'Siyan Stone Slab Inscription of Nayapala' (1971); *STP*, pp. 102–22.
82 Kurkihar Image Inscription of the Time of Vigrahapāla III, year 3: Banerji-Sastri, 'Ninety-Three Inscriptions', p. 240; Gupta, *Patna Museum Catalogue*, pp. 131–32, no. 30.
83 Mandoil Image Inscription of the Time of Vigrahapāla III, year 4: Rahman, *Sculpture in the Varendra Research Museum: A Descriptive Catalogue* (1998), pp. 97–98, no. 251.
84 Gaya Fragmentary Inscription of Viśvarūpa or Viśvāditya, year 5 of Vigrahapāla III, Sircar, 'Inscriptions of Two Brahman Rulers', pp. 89–92.

85 Bihar Terracotta Plaque Inscription of the Time of Vigrahapāla III, year 8: Banerji-Sastri, 'Terra Cotta Plaque of Vigrahapāla-Deva' (1940).

86 Indian Museum Image Inscription of the Time of Vigrahapāla III, year 13: Banerji, 'The Pālas of Bengal', p. 112; Huntington, *The "Pāla-Sena" Schools*, p. 212, no. 17.

87 Kurkihar Image Inscription of the Time of Vigrahapāla III, year 19 (no. 1): Banerji-Sastri, 'Ninety-Three Inscriptions', p. 239; Gupta, *Patna Museum Catalogue*, p. 133, no. 34.

88 Kurkihar Image Inscription of the Time of Vigrahapāla III, year 19 (no. 2): Banerji-Sastri, 'Ninety-Three Inscriptions', p. 240; Gupta, *Patna Museum Catalogue*, p. 133, no. 33.

89 Naulagarh Image Inscription of the Time of Vigrahapāla III, year 24: Sircar, 'Some Inscriptions from Bihar' (1951), pp. 1–4.

90 Silimpur Stone Inscription of the Time of Jayapāla of Kāmarūpa: Basak, 'Silimpur Stone-slab Inscription of the Time of Jayapala-deva' (1915–16).

91 Gaya Stone Inscription of Yakṣapāla: Sircar, 'Inscriptions of Two Brahman Rulers', pp. 92–94; *SI* 2, pp. 102–4.

92 Tetrawan Image Inscription of the Time of Rāmapāla, year 2: Alexander Cunningham, *Archaeological Survey of India Reports*, 1871–72, 3: 124; Chakravartti, 'Pāla Inscriptions in the Indian Museum', pp. 108–9.

93 Rajauna Image Inscription of the Time of Rāmapāla, year 9: Sanyal, 'Another Inscribed Image of the Reign of Rāmapāla from South Bihar' (2012).

94 Uren Image Inscription of the Time of Rāmapāla, year 14: Banerjee, 'Some Inscriptions from Bihar', pp. 110–11.

95 Arma Pedestal Inscription of the Time of Rāmapāla, year 26: *Annual Report of Indian Epigraphy*, 1960–61, p. 64. B. 117.

96 Samsarpokhari Pedestal Inscription of the Time of Rāmapāla, year 37, *Annual Report of Indian Epigraphy*, 1949–50, p. 21, B. 26.

97 Chandimau Image Inscription of the Time of Rāmapāla, year 42: Banerji, 'The Pālas of Bengal', pp. 93–94.

98 Uren Image Inscription of the Time of Rāmapāla, Banerjee, 'Some Inscriptions from Bihar', p. 111.

99 Asutosh Museum Image Inscription of the Time of Rāmapāla, *Annual Report of Indian Epigraphy*, 1949–50, p. 20, B. 1.

100 Bhubaneswar Stone Inscription of Bhavadeva: *IB*, pp. 25–41; *CBI*, pp. 349–61; *SI* 2, pp. 105–11.

101 Sujanagar Stone Inscription of the Time of Bhojavarman, year 7: Biswas, 'Jātīya Jādughare Rakṣita Bhojabarmār 1ma Rājyavarṣer Ekṭi Śilālekha' (2007); Islam, 'Unpublished Stone Inscription of the Seventh Regnal Year of Bhojavarman' (2010).

102 Chaprakot Stone Inscription of the Time of Gopāla IV, year 9: Mukherji, 'Bangladesh National Museum Stone Slab Inscription of King Gopāla

IV (?). Regnal Year 9 (1137 A. D. ?)' (2001); Furui, 'Chaprakot Stone Inscription of the Time of Gopāla IV, Year 9' (2013).

103 Rajibpur Image Inscription of the Time of Gopāla IV, year 14: Bhattasali, 'Two Inscriptions of Gopāla III of Bengal' (1941), pp. 217–22; Sircar, 'Indological Notes No. 30. Rājībpur Sadāśiva Image Inscription of Gopāla III, Year 14' (1980–82); *STP*, pp. 128–31.

104 Nimdighi Stone Inscription mentioning Gopāla IV: Bhattasali, 'Two Inscriptions of Gopāla III', pp. 208–16; Sircar, 'Three Pala Inscriptions', pp. 228–33.

105 Nalanda Stone Inscription of Vipulaśrīmitra: Majumdar, 'Nalanda Inscription of Vipulasrimitra' (1931–32); *SI* 2, pp. 60–62.

106 Nongadh Pedestal Inscription of the Time of Madanapāla, year (1)201 VE: Sircar, 'Three Inscriptions from Bihar' (1965), pp. 41–42.

107 Bihar Hill Image Inscription of the Time of Madanapāla, year 3, Cunningham, *Archaeological Survey of India Reports*, 1871–72, 3: 124; Banerjee, 'Two Medieval Inscriptions' (1953), pp. 105–6; Huntington, *The "Pāla-Sena" Schools*, pp. 235–36, no. 53.

108 Arma Stone Inscription of the Time of Madanapāla, year 14: Sircar, 'Three Inscriptions from Bihar', pp. 42–44.

109 Jaynagar Pedestal Inscription of the Time of Madanapāla, year 14, Cunningham, *Archaeological Survey of India Reports*, 1871–72, 3: 125; Majumdar, 'Some Dates in the Pāla and Sena Records' (1941), p. 216.

110 Valgudar Image Inscription of the Time of Madanapāla, year 18 RE, 1083 SE: Sircar, 'Three Inscriptions from Valgudar', pp. 137–41, 145.

111 Rajghat Stone Inscription of Bhīmadeva: Sircar, 'Rajghat Inscription of Bhimadeva' (1957–58); idem, 'Note on Rajghat Inscription of Bhimadeva' (1968); *SI* 2, pp. 112–14.

112 Kandi Image Inscription of *rāṇaka* Samudrāditya: Sircar, 'Some Inscriptions from Bihar', pp. 7–10.

113 Gaya Stone Inscription mentioning Govindapāla, past year 14 RE and year 1232 VE: Sircar, 'Three Pala Inscriptions', pp. 233–38.

114 Lai Pedestal Inscription of Vikramadevī, year 32: Sircar, 'Inscriptions from Bihar' (1953–54), pp. 82–84.

115 Jaynagar Image Inscription of the Time of Palapāla, year 35: Banerji, 'Pala Chronology' (1928), p. 496; D. C. Sircar, 'Jayanagar Image Inscription of Year 35' (1955); Huntington, *The "Pāla-Sena" Schools*, pp. 239–40, no. 59.

116 Antichak Stone Pillar Inscription of Māsanikeśa: Sircar, 'Three East Indian Inscriptions of the Early Medieval Period' (1972–73), pp. 53–59; idem, *Some Epigraphical Records of the Medieval Period from Eastern India* (1979), pp. 23–29.

117 Madavpur Fragmentary Inscription, year 368: Mukherjee and Ray, 'Madavpur Fragmentary Inscription of the Year 368' (1991).

118 Deopara Stone Inscription of Vijayasena: *IB*, pp. 42–56; *CBI*, pp. 244–58; *SI* 2, pp. 115–22.
119 Paikore Image Inscription mentioning Vijayasena: *IB*, p. 168.
120 Sanokhar Inscription of the Time of Vallālasena, year 9: Sircar, 'Inscriptions from Bihar', pp. 78–82; *SI* 2, p. 123.
121 Rampal Image Inscription of the Time of Lakṣmaṇasena, year 3: Bhattasali, 'Some Image Inscriptions', pp. 359–62; *IB*, pp. 116–17.
122 Bagbari Stone Inscription of Lakṣmaṇasena: Hok and Kuddus, 'Lakṣmaṇasener Bāgabāḍi Praśasti: Barendra Gabeṣaṇā Jādughare Eka Mūlyabāna Saṃyojana' (1412 BS).
123 Keoar Image Inscription: Bhattasali, 'Some Image Inscriptions', pp. 355–56.
124 Bodhgaya Stone Inscription of the Time of Aśokacalla, year 51 Lakṣmaṇasena Era: Vidyavinoda, 'Two Inscriptions from Bodh-Gaya' (1913–14); *SI* 2, pp. 146–48.
125 Bodhgaya Stone Inscription of the Time of Aśokacalla, year 74 Lakṣmaṇasena Era: Vidyavinoda, 'Two Inscriptions'; *SI* 2, pp. 149–50.
126 Patna Museum Stone Inscription of Jayasena, year 83: Majumdar, 'Patna Museum Inscription of Jayasena' (1919).
127 Bodhgaya Stone Slab Inscription of Buddhasena, year 83 Lakṣmaṇasena Era: Sircar, 'Three East Indian Inscriptions', pp. 47–53; idem, *Some Epigraphical Records*, pp. 29–34.
128 Bihar Inscribed Terracotta Plaque, year 67: Sircar, 'Inscriptions from Bihar', pp. 85–87.

SELECT BIBLIOGRAPHY

1. Primary sources

a. Epigraphical sources

Bhandarkar, D. R. (rev.), B. Ch. Chhabra and G. S. Gai (eds), *Corpus Inscriptionum Indicarum, vol. 3 (rev.): Inscriptions of the Early Guptas*, New Delhi: Archaeological Survey of India, 1981.

Gupta, Kamalakanta (ed.), *Copper-plates of Sylhet, vol. 1 (7th–11th Century A. D.)*, Sylhet: Lipika Enterprises, 1967.

Maitreya, Akshay Kumar (ed.), *Gauḍalekhamālā*, Rajshahi: The Varendra Research Society, 1912 (reprint, Kolkata: Sanskrit Pustak Bhandar, 2004).

Majumdar, Nani Gopal, *Nālandā Copper-plate of Devapāladeva*, Rajshahi: The Varendra Research Society, 1926.

——— (ed.), *Inscriptions of Bengal Volume III: Containing Inscriptions of the Chandras, the Varmans and the Senas, and of Īśvaraghosha and Dāmodara*, Rajshahi: The Varendra Research Society, 1929.

Mukherjee, Ramaranjan and Sachindra Kumar Maity (eds), *Corpus of Bengal Inscriptions: Bearing on History and Civilization of Bengal*, Calcutta: Firma KLM, 1967.

Sastri, Hirananda, *Nalanda and Its Epigraphic Material*, New Delhi: Archaeological Survey of India, 1999 (reprint).

Sharma, Mukunda Madhava, *Inscriptions of Ancient Assam*, Gauhati: Department of Publication, Gauhati University, 1978.

Sircar, D. C. (ed.), *Select Inscriptions Bearing on Indian History and Civilization Vol. 1: From the Sixth Century B. C. to the Sixth Century A. D.* (2nd ed.), Calcutta: University of Calcutta, 1965.

———, *Epigraphic Discoveries in East Pakistan*, Calcutta: Sanskrit College, 1973.

———, *Some Epigraphical Records of the Medieval Period from Eastern India*, New Delhi: Abhinav Publications, 1979.

———, *Śilālekha-Tāmraśāsanādir Prasaṅga*, Calcutta: Sahityaloka, 1982.

——— (ed.), *Select Inscriptions Bearing on Indian History and Civilization Vol. 2: From the Sixth to the Eighteenth Century A. D.*, Delhi: Motilal Banarsidass, 1983.

Tripathy, Snigdha, *Inscriptions of Orissa vol. 1: Circa Fifth-Eighth Centuries A. D.*, Delhi: Motilal Banarsidass, 1997.

b. Purāṇas

Brahmavaivartapurāṇa: Shastri, J. L. (ed.), Satkari Mukhopadhyaya (index, intro.), *Brahmavaivartapurāṇa of Kṛṣṇa Dvaipāyana Vyāsa*, 2 pts, Delhi: Motilal Banarsidass, 1983, 1985; Tarkaratna, Panchanana (ed.), *Brahmavaivarttapurāṇam*, Calcutta: Vangavasi Press, 1827 SE (1905).

Bṛhaddharmapurāṇa: Shastri, Haraprasad (ed.), *Bṛhaddharmapurāṇam* (2nd ed.), Varanasi: Krishnadas Academy, 1974; Tarkaratna, Panchanana (ed.), *Bṛhaddharmapurāṇa*, Calcutta: Navbharat Publishers, 1396 BS (1989) (reprint).

Devībhāgavatapurāṇa: *Śrīmaddevībhāgavatapurāṇam*, Delhi: Nag Publishers, 1986 (reprint).

Kālikāpurāṇa: Shastri, Biswanarayan (ed.), *The Kālikāpurāṇa (Text, Introduction & Translation in English)*, 3 pts, Delhi: Nag Publishers, 1991–92.

Mahābhāgavatapurāṇa: Kumar, Puspendra (ed.), *The Mahābhāgavata Purāṇa (An Ancient Treatise on Śakti Cult)* Delhi: Eastern Book Linkers, 1983; Tarkaratna, Panchanana (ed.), *Śrīmahābhāgavatam*, Calcutta: Navbharat Publishers, 1995 (reprint).

c. Dharma *texts*

Adbhutasāgara of Vallālasena: Jha, Muruli Dhara (ed.), *Adbhutasāgara*, Benares Cantt.: The Prabhakari and Co., 1905; Jha, Sivakant (ed., annot.), *Adbhutasāgaraḥ, śrīmadvallālasenadevapraṇītaḥ*, Varanasi: Chaukhamba Surbharati Prakashan, 2006.

Baudhāyanadharmasūtra: Olivelle, Patrick (ed., note, tr.), *Dharmasūtras: The Law Codes of Āpastamba, Gautama, Baudhāyana, and Vasiṣṭha*, Delhi: Motilal Banarsidass, 2000, pp. 191–345, 569–630.

Brāhmaṇasarvasva of Halāyudha: Bhattacharya, Durgamohan (ed.), *Brāhmaṇa-Sarvasva: A Pre-Sāyaṇa Vedic Commentary by Halāyudha*, Calcutta: Sanskrit Sahitya Parishad, 1960.

Dānasāgara of Vallālasena: Bhattacharya, Bhabatosh (ed.), *Dānasāgara of Ballāla Sena*, fascs 1–4, Calcutta: The Asiatic Society of Bengal, 1953, 1955, 1956.

Dāyabhāga of Jīmūtavāhana: Rocher, Ludo (ed., tr., intro., annot.), *Jīmūtavāhana's Dāyabhāga: The Hindu Law of Inheritance in Bengal*, New York: Oxford University Press, 2002.

Hāralatā of Aniruddha: Smrtitirtha, Kamalakanta (ed.), *Hāralatā of Aniruddha Bhatta*, Calcutta: The Asiatic Society of Bengal, 1909.

Kālaviveka of Jīmūtavāhana: Tarkabhushana, Pramathanatha (ed.), *The Kāla-Viveka (A Part of Dharmaratna) by Jīmūtavāhana*, Calcutta: The Asiatic Society of Bengal, 1905.

Manusmṛti: Olivelle, Patrick (ed., tr.), *Manu's Code of Law: A Critical Edition and Translation of the Mānava-Dharmaśāstra*, New Delhi: Oxford University Press, 2006.

Nāradasmṛti: Lariviere, Richard W. (ed., tr., annot.), *The Nāradasmṛti*, 2 pts, Philadelphia: Department of South Asia Regional Studies, Pennsylvania University, 1989.

Prāyaścittaprakaraṇa of Bhavadeva: Vedantatirtha, Girish Chandra (ed.), Nani Gopal Majumdar (intro.), *The Prayaschitta Prakaranam (A Text on Expiatory Rites) by Bhatta Bhavadeva*, Rajshahi: The Varendra Research Society, 1927.

Sambandhaviveka of Bhavadeva: Banerji, Suresh Chandra, 'The Sambandha-Viveka of Bhavadeva Bhatta (Introduction)' *New Indian Antiquary*, 1943–44, 6: 97–102, idem, 'The Sambandha-Viveka of Bhavadeva Bhatta: Critically edited for the first time with Introduction, English Translation, Index etc.', *ibid.*, pp. 252–60.

Vyavahāramātṛkā of Jīmūtavāhana: Mookerjee, Asutosh, 'The Vyavahāra Mātrikā of Jimutavāhana', *Memoirs of the Asiatic Society of Bengal*, 1912, 3(5): 277–353; Chatterjee Sastri, Heramba (ed.), *Vyavahāramātṛkā of Jīmūtavāhana*, Part 1, Calcutta: The Sanskrit Sahitya Parishat, 1996.

d. Other texts in Sanskrit and Old Bengali

Āryāsaptaśatī of Govardhanācārya: Prasad, Durga, Kasinath Pandurang Parab and Vasudev Laxman Sastri Pansikar (eds), *The Āryāsaptaśatī of Govardhanāchārya with The Commentary Vyaṅgyārtha-dīpanā of Ananta=Paṇḍit*, Delhi: Nag Publishers, 1988 (reprint).

Bṛhatsaṃhitā of Varāhamihira, with commentary of Utpala: Jha, Acyutananda (comm.), Ramachandra Pandey (intro.), *Varāhamihirakṛtā Bṛhatsaṃhitā: 'bhaṭṭotpalavivṛti' samanvita 'vimalā' hindīvyākhyāyutā*, Varanasi: Chaukhamba Vidyabhavan, 2005.

Caryāgīti: Kvaerne, Per, *An Anthology of Buddhist Tantric Songs: A Study of the Caryāgīti* (3rd ed.), Bangkok: Orchid Press, 2010; Mojumdar, Atindra (ed.) *Caryāpada* (3rd ed.), Calcutta: Naya Prokash, 1993; idem (ed., tr.), *The Caryāpadas* (2nd ed.), Calcutta: Naya Prokash, 1973; Sen, Nilratan (ed.), *Caryāgītikoṣa: Facsimile Edition*, Simla: Indian Institute of Advanced Study, 1977; Sen, Sukumar (ed.), *Caryāgīti-Padāvali*, Vardhaman: Anand Publishers, 1995 (reprint); Shastri, Haraprasad (ed.), Bratindra Nath Mukherji (intro.), *Hajār Bacharer Purāṇa Vāṅgālā Bhāṣāy Bauddhagān O Doha (Caryācaryāviniścaya, Sarojavajrer Dohākoṣa, Kāṅhapāder Dohākoṣa O Ḍākārṇava)*, Calcutta: Mahabodhi Book Agency, 2000.

Kāśyapīyakṛṣisūkti: Wojtilla, Gyula (ed., introductory study), *Kāśyapīyakṛṣisūkti: A Sanskrit Work on Agriculture*, Wiesbaden: Harrassowitz Verlag, 2010.

Kṛṣiparāśara: Majumdar, Girija Prasanna and Sures Chandra Banerji (ed., tr.), *Kṛṣi-Parāśara*, Calcutta: The Asiatic Society, 2001 (reprint).

Pavanadūta of Dhoyī: Chakravarti, Chintaharan (ed.), *Pavanadūtam of Dhoyī*, Calcutta: The Sanskrit Sahitya Parishat, 1926.

Raghuvaṃśa of Kālidāsa: Devadhar, C. R. (ed.), *Raghuvaṃśa of Kālidāsa*, Delhi: Motilal Banarsidass, 1985.

Rāmacarita of Sandhyākaranandin: Brocquet, Sylvain, *La geste de Rāma: poème à double sens de Sandhyākaranandin (Introduction, texte, traduction, analyse)*, Pondichéry: Institut français de Pondichéry, École française d'Extrême-Orient, 2010; Majumdar, R. C., Radhagovinda Basak and Nanigopal Banerji (eds), *The Rāmacaritaṃ of Sandhyākaranandin*, Rajshahi: The Varendra Research Museum, 1939; Sastri, Haraprasad (ed.), Radhagovinda Basak (rev., tr., notes), *Rāmacaritam of Sandhyākaranandin*, Calcutta: The Asiatic Society, 1969.

Saduktikarṇāmṛta of Śrīdharadāsa: Banerji, Sures Chandra (ed.), *Sadukti-Karṇāmṛta of Śrīdharadāsa*, Calcutta: Firma KLM, 1965.

Subhāṣitaratnakoṣa of Vidyākara: Kosambi, D. D. and V. V. Gokhale (eds), *The Subhāṣitaratnakoṣa*, Cambridge, MA: Harvard University Press, 1957.

e. Foreign accounts

Faxian: Nagasawa, Kazutoshi (ed., tr., annot.), *Hokkenden Yakuchu Kaisetsu: Hokusou-bon, Nansou-bon, Kourai Daizoukyou-bon, Ishiyamadera-bon Yonshu Eiin To Sono Hikaku Kenkyu*, Tokyo: Yuzankaku, 1996; Legge, James (tr., annot.), *A Record of Buddhistic Kingdom: Being an Account by the Chinese Monk Fa-Hien of Travels in India and Ceylon (AD 399–414) in Search of the Buddhist Books of Discipline*, New Delhi: Munshiram Manoharlal, 1998 (reprint); Li, Rongxi (tr.), 'The Journey of the Eminent Monk Faxian: Translated from the Chinese of Faxian (Taishō Volume 51, Number 2085)', in *Lives of Great Monks and Nuns*, Berkeley: Numata Center for Buddhist Translation and Research, 2002.

Ibn Baṭṭūṭa: Husain, Mahdi (tr., comm.), *The Reḥla of Ibn Baṭṭūṭa: India, Maldive Islands and Ceylon*, Baroda: Oriental Institute, 1953.

Ibn Khurdādhbih, Sulaymān et al.: Maqbul Ahmad, S. (tr.), *Arabic Classical Accounts of India and China*, Shimla: Indian Institute of Advanced Study, 1989.

Minhāj al-Sirāj Jūzjānī: Raverty, H. G. (tr.), *Tabakat-i-Nasiri: A General History of the Muhammadan Dynasties of Asia Including Hindustan from A. H. 194 (810 A. D.) to A. H. 658 (1260 A. D.) and the Irruption of the Infidel Mughals in Islam*, 2 vols, Calcutta: The Asiatic Society, 1995 (reprint).

Periplus Maris Erythraei: Casson, Lionel (ed., tr., intro., comm.), *The Periplus Maris Erythraei*, Princeton, NJ: Princeton University Press, 1989.

Tāranātha: Chattopadhyaya, Debiprasad (ed.), Lama Chimpa and Alaka Chattopadhyaya (trs), *Tāranātha's History of Buddhism in India*, Delhi: Motilal Banarsidass, 1990.

Xuanzang: Kyoto Teikoku Daigaku Bunka Daigaku (ed.), *Daitou Saiiki Ki*, Tokyo: Tosho Kankoukai, 1972 (reprint); Beal, Samuel (tr.), *Si-Yu-Ki: Buddhist Records of the Western World: Translated from the Chinese of Hiuen Tsiang (A. D. 629)*, Delhi: Motilal Banarsidass, 1981 (reprint); Li Rongxi (tr.), *The Great Tang Dynasty Record of the Western Regions: Translated(sic.) by the Tripiṭaka-Master Xuanzang under Imperial Order Composed by Śramaṇa Bianji of the Great Zongchi Monastery (Taisho, Volume 51, Number 2087)*, Berkeley: Numata Center for Buddhist Translation and Research, 1996; Utsunomiya, Kiyoyoshi (ed.), *Daitou Daijionji Sanzouhoushi Den Oyobi Koui Sakuin*, Kyoto: Houyu Shoten, 1979; Beal, Samuel (tr.), *The Life of Hiuen-Tsiang by the Shaman Hwui Li* (2nd ed.), New Delhi: Munshiram Manoharlal, 1973 (reprint); Li Rongxi (tr.), *A Biography of the Tripiṭaka Master of the Great Ci'en Monastery of the Great Tang Dynasty: Translated from the Chinese of Śramaṇa Huili and Shi Yancong (Taishō, Volume 50, Number 2053)*, Berkeley: Numata Center for Buddhist Translation and Research, 1995.

Yijing: Adachi, Kiroku (ed., tr., annot.), *Daitou Saiiki Guhou Kousou Den*, Tokyo: Iwanami Shoten, 1942; I-Ching, Latika Lahiri (tr.), *Chinese Monks in India: Biography of Eminent Monks Who Went to the Western World in Search of the Law During the Great T'ang Dynasty*, Delhi: Motilal Banarsidass, 1986; Yìjìng, Wáng Bāng-Wéi (ed., annot.), *Nánhǎijìguīnèifǎchuán Jiàozhù*, Běijīng: Zhōnghúashūjú,

1995; I-Tsing, J. Takakusu (tr.), *A Record of the Buddhist Religion as Practised in India and the Malay Archipelago (AD 671–695)*, New Delhi: Munshiram Manoharlal, 1998 (reprint).

f. Archaeological data

Alam, Md. Shafiqul, 'Post-Liberation Excavations at Paharpur World Heritage Site', in idem (ed.), *Proceedings of the International Seminar on Elaboration of An Archaeological Research Strategy for Paharpur World Heritage Site and Its Environment (Bangladesh) 20–25 March, 2004*, Dhaka: Department of Archaeology, Ministry of Cultural Affairs, Govt. of Bangladesh and UNESCO Dhaka, 2004, pp. 52–57.

Baidya, T. J. and Shantanu Maity, 'Excavation at Bangarh 2008–2009', *Pratna Samiksha: A Journal of Archaeology, New Series*, 2010, 1: 35–37.

Bernard, Vincent, Marie-Françoise Boussac, Jean-Yves Breuil and Jean-François Salles, 'Excavations at the Eastern Rampart Site (1993–1998) Preliminary Report of the French Team', in Md. Shafiqul Alam and Jean-François Salles (eds), *France=Bangladesh Joint Venture Excavations at Mahasthangarh: First Interim Report 1993–1999*, Dhaka: Department of Archaeology, 2001, pp. 74–160.

Bloch, T., 'Excavations at Basarh', *Annual Report of Archaeological Survey of India*, 1903–04 (1906): 81–122.

Chakrabarti, Dilip K., Gautam Sengupta, R. K. Chattopadhyay and Nayanjot Lahiri, 'Balck-and-Red Ware Settlements in West Bengal', *South Asian Studies*, 1993, 9: 123–35.

Das, Sudhir Ranjan, *Rājbāḍīdāṅga: 1962 (Chiruṭī: Jadupur): An Interim Report on Excavations at Rājbāḍīdāṅga and Terracotta Seals and Sealings*, Calcutta: The Asiatic Society, 1968.

Dikshit, K. N., *Excavations at Paharpur, Bengal*, New Delhi: Archaeological Survey of India, 1999 (reprint).

Goswami, Kunja Govinda, *Excavations at Bangarh (1938–41)*, Calcutta: University of Calcutta, 1948.

Imam, Abu, *Excavations at Mainamati: An Exploratory Study*, Dhaka: The International Centre for Study of Bengal Art, 2000.

Miah, Md. Abul Hashem, 'Archaeological Excavations at Jagaddala Vihara: A Preliminary Report', *Journal of Bengal Art*, 8, 2003, pp. 147–66.

Nag, Arun K., 'Spatial Analysis of Pre- and Proto-Historic Sites in Ajay-Damodar Valley', in B. M. Pande and B. D. Chattopadhyaya (eds), *Archaeology and History: Essays in Memory of Shri A. Ghosh*, Delhi: Agam Prakashan, 1987, pp. 265–80.

Patil, D. R., *The Antiquarian Remains in Bihar*, Patna: K. P. Jayaswal Research Institute, 1963.

Rashid, M. Harunur, 'Excavations', *Bangladesh Archaeology*, 1979, 1(1): 20–91.

Roy, Amal, 'Nandadirghi-vihara: A Newly Discovered Buddhist Monastery at Jagajjibanpur, West Bengal', in Gautam Sengupta and Sheena Panja (eds), *Archaeology of Eastern India: New Perspectives*, Kolkata: Centre for Archaeological Studies and Training, Eastern India, 2002, pp. 557–611.

Roy, Amal, Shiharan Nandy (photo.), *Jagjivanpur 1996–2005 Excavation Report*, Kolkata: Directorate of Archaeology and Museums, Govt. of West Bengal, 2012.

Sen, Swadhin, 'The Transformative Context of a Temple in Early Medieval Varendri: Report of the Excavation at Tileshwarir Aara in Dinajpur District, Bangladesh', *South Asian Studies*, 2015, 31(1): 71–110.

Spooner, D. B., 'Excavations at Basarh, 1911–1912', *Annual Report of Archaeological Survey of India*, 1913–14: 98–185.

Verma, B. S., *Antichak Excavations-2 (1971–1981)*, New Delhi: Archaeological Survey of India, 2011.

2. Secondary sources

Agrawal, Ashvini, *Rise and Fall of Imperial Guptas*, Delhi: Motilal Banarsidass, 1989.

Banerjee, Priyatosh, 'Two Medieval Inscriptions', *Journal of the Asiatic Society, Letters*, 1953, 19(1): 105–7.

———, 'Some Inscriptions from Bihar', *Journal of Ancient Indian History*, 1973–74 (1975), 7(1–2): 102–11.

Banerji, Rakhal Das, 'The Koṭwalipārā Spurious Grant of Samācāra Deva', *Journal and Proceedings of the Asiatic Society of Bengal, New Series*, 1910, 6(9): 429–36.

———, 'The Pālas of Bengal', *Memoirs of the Asiatic Society of Bengal*, 1915, 5(3): 43–113.

———, 'Edilpur Grant of Kesavasena', *Journal and Proceedings of the Asiatic Society of Bengal, New Series*, 1914 (1918), 10: 97–104.

———, 'The Pratīhāra Occupation of Magadha', *Indian Antiquary*, 1918, 47: 109–11.

———, 'The Bangarh Grant of Mahi-Pala I: The 9th Year', *Epigraphia Indica*, 1917–18 (reprint 1982), 14: 324–30.

———, 'The Naihati Grant of Vallala-Sena; The 11th Year', *Epigraphia Indica*, 1917–18 (reprint 1982), 14: 156–63.

———, 'The Amgachhi Grant of Vigraha-Pala III: the 12th Year', *Epigraphia Indica*, 1919–20 (reprint 1982), 15: 293–301.

———, 'Barrackpur Grant of Vijayasena: The 32nd Year', *Epigraphia Indica*, 1919–20 (reprint 1982), 15: 278–86.

———, 'A Note on the Vappaghoshavata Grant of Jayanaga', *Epigraphia Indica*, 1927–28 (reprint 1983), 18: 286–87.

———, 'Pala Chronology', *Journal of the Bihar and Orissa Research Society*, 1928, 14(4): 489–538.

Banerji-Sastri, A., 'Ninety-Three Inscriptions on the Kurkihar Bronzes', *Journal of the Bihar and Orissa Research Society*, 1940, 26(3): 236–51.

———, 'Terra Cotta Plaque of Vigrahapāla-Deva', *Journal of the Bihar and Orissa Research Society*, 1940, 26(1): 35–39.

Barnett, Lionel D., 'The Mungir Plate of Devapaladeva: Samvat 33', *Epigraphia Indica*, 1925–26 (reprint 1983), 18: 304–7

———, 'Vappaghoshavata Grant of Jayanaga', *Epigraphia Indica*, 1925–26 (reprint 1983), 18: 60–64.

Barua, B. M. and Pulin Behari Chakravarti, 'Mehar Plate of Damodaradeva', *Epigraphia Indica*, 1947–48 (reprint 1985), 27: 182–91.

Basak, Radha Govinda, 'Belava Copper-plate of Bhojavarmadeva. The Fifth Year', *Epigraphia Indica*, 1913–14 (reprint 1982), 12: 37–43.

———, 'Rampal Copper-plate Grant of Srichandradeva', *Epigraphia Indica*, 1913–14 (reprint 1982), 12: 136–42.
———, 'Silimpur Stone-slab Inscription of the Time of Jayapala-deva', *Epigraphia Indica*, 1915–16 (reprint 1982), 13: 283–95.
———, 'The Five Damodarpur Copper-plate Inscriptions of the Gupta Period', *Epigraphia Indica*, 1919–20 (reprint 1982), 15: 113–45.
———, 'Tipperah Copper-plate Grant of Lokanatha: the 44th Year', *Epigraphia Indica*, 1919–20 (reprint 1982), 15: 301–15.
———, 'Dhanaidaha Copper-plate Inscription of the Time of Kumaragupta I: The Year 113', *Epigraphia Indica*, 1923–24 (reprint 1983), 17: 345–48.
———, 'Baigram Copper-plate Inscription of the [Gupta]-Year 128', *Epigraphia Indica*, 1931–32 (reprint 1984), 21: 78–83.
———, 'Madanpur Plate of Srichandra, year 44', *Epigraphia Indica*, 1949–1950 (reprint 1985), 28: 51–58.
Bhaduri, Reena, *Social Formation in Medieval Bengal*, Kolkata: Bibhasa, 2001.
Bhandarkar, D. R. 'Mauryan Brahmi Inscription of Mahasthan', *Epigraphia Indica*, 1931–32 (reprint 1984), 21: 83–91.
Bhattacharjee (Bhattacharya), Swapan Bikash, 'Prathama Mahīpāladeber Biyālā Tāmraphalaka', *Bangladesh Asiatic Society Patrika*, 1987, 5: 1–9.
———, 'Mainamati Copper Plate of Sri Viradharadeva', *Journal of the Asiatic Society of Bangladesh, Humanities*, 1994, 39(2): 71–75.
Bhattacharya, Gouriswar, 'A Second Dated Tārā Image of the Reign of Devapāla', *Indian Museum Bulletin*, 1982, 17: 21–23.
———, 'Two Inscribed Buddhist Images from the Museum of Indian Art, Berlin', in idem (ed.), *Deyadharma: Studies in Memory of Dr. D. C. Sircar*, Delhi: Sri Satguru Publications, 1986, pp. 29–45.
———, 'A Puzzling Report on a British Museum Buddhist Pedestal Inscription', *South Asian Studies*, 1990, 6: 39–42.
———, 'The Munificence of Lady Catuḥsamā', in idem (ed.), *Akṣayanīvī: Essays Presented to Dr. Debala Mitra in Admiration of her Scholarly Contributions*, Delhi: Sri Satguru Publications, 1991, pp. 313–22.
———, 'An Inscribed Metal Vase Most Probably from Chittagong, Bangladesh', in Adalbert J. Gail and Gerd J. R. Mevissen (eds), *South Asian Archaeology 1991: Proceedings of the Eleventh International Conference of the Association of South Asian Archaeologists in Western Europe held in Berlin 1–5 July 1991*, Stuttgart: Franz Steiner Verlag, 1993, pp. 323–38.
———, 'Newly Discovered Copper Plate Grants of the Pāla Dynasty', in Nalini Balbir and Joachim K. Bautze (eds), *Festschrift Klaus Bruhn: zur Vollendung des 65. Lebensjahres dargebracht von Schulern, Freunden und Kollegen*, Reinbek: Dr. Inge Wezler, 1994, pp. 195–224.
———, 'An Incomplete Copper-plate Grant Belonging to the Pāla Ruler Nayapāla', *Berliner Indologische Studien*, 1996, 9–10: 315–25.
———, 'A Preliminary Report on the Inscribed Metal Vase from the National Museum of Bangladesh', in Debala Mitra (ed.), *Explorations in Art and Archaeology of South Asia: Essays Dedicated to N. G. Majumdar*, Calcutta: Directorate of Archaeology and Museums, 1996, pp. 237–47.
———, 'Bangladesh National Museum *praśasti* of Pāhila (9th Century A. D.)', *Journal of Bengal Art*, 1997, 2: 111–20.

———, 'A Dated Avalokiteśvara Image of the Devapāla Period', in Natasha Eilenberg, M. C. Subhadradis Diskul and Robert L. Brown (eds), *Living a Life in Accord With Dharma: Papers in Honor of Professor Jean Boisselier on His Eightieth Birthday*, Bangkok: Silpakorn University, 1997, pp. 83–90.

———, 'A Dated Viṣṇu Image of the Mahīpāla (I) Period', *Journal of Bengal Art*, 1998, 3: 151–55.

———, 'Bangladesh National Museum Praśasti of Pāhila', in Samaresh Bandyopadhyay (ed.), *Prācyaśikṣāsuhāsinī: Seventy-Fifth Anniversary Celebration Volume of the Department of Ancient Indian History and Culture*, Calcutta: University of Calcutta, 1999, pp. 384–90.

———, 'A Note on the Jagjibanpur Inscription of Mahendrapāla', *Pratna Samiksha*, 1997–99 (1999), 6–8: 88–90.

———, 'Nalanda Vāgīśvarī and Mandhuk Gaṇeśa: Are They of the Same Period?', *Journal of Bengal Art*, 1999, 4: 373–80.

———, 'The British Museum Stone Inscription of Mahendrapāla', *South Asian Studies*, 2007, 23: 69–74.

———, 'Two Inscribed Bronze Ekamukha-liṅgas of the Devapāla Period', *Tribus (Jahrbuch, Linden-Museum Stuttgart)*, 2007, 56: 55–59.

Bhattachary(y)a, Padma Nath, 'Nidhanpur Copper Plates of Bhaskaravarman', *Epigraphia Indica*, 1913–14 (reprint 1982), 12: 65–79.

———, 'Two Lost Plates of the Nidhanpur Copper-plates of Bhaskaravarman', *Epigraphia Indica*, 1927–28 (reprint 1983), 19: 115–25.

———, 'A Third Lost Plate of the Nidhanpur Plates of Bhaskaravarman', *Epigraphia Indica*, 1927–28 (reprint 1983), 19: 245–50.

———, 'Nalanda Plate of Dharmapaladeva', *Epigraphia Indica*, 1935–36 (reprint 1984), 23: 290–92.

Bhattachary(y)a, Suresh Chandra, 'Mainamati Copper Plate of Vīradharadeva', *Journal of Ancient Indian History*, 1983–84 (1984), 14(1–2): 17–28.

———, 'The Jagjibanpur Plate of Mahendrapāla Comprehensively Re-edited', *Journal of Ancient Indian History*, 2005–06 (2007), 23: 61–125.

———, 'The Murshidabad (Indian Museum) Copper-plate Grant of Dharmapāla and the Somapura Mahāvihāra', *Journal of Bengal Art*, 2006–07 (2008), 11–12: 237–50.

———, 'Pāla Kings in the Badal Praśasti – A Stock-Taking', *Journal of Ancient Indian History*, 2007–08 (2008), 24: 73–82.

———, 'Murshidabad (Indian Museum) Copper Plate of Dharmapāla: The Complete Version', in Suchandra Ghosh, Sudipa Ray Bandyopadhyay, Sushmita Basu Majumdar and Sayantani Pal (eds), *Revisiting Early India: Essays in Honour of D. C. Sircar*, Kolkata: R. N. Bhattacharya, 2013, pp. 117–34.

Bhattacharyya, Amitabha, *Historical Geography of Ancient and Early Medieval Bengal*, Calcutta: Sanskrit Pustak Bhandar, 1977.

———, 'The Maṭhas of Eastern India in the Early Medieval Period', in idem, *Selected Essays*, Kolkata: Centre for Archaeological Studies and Training, Eastern India, 2004, pp. 13–22.

Bhattacharyya, Dinesh Chandra, 'A Newly Discovered Copperplate from Tippera [The Gunaighar Grant of Vainyagupta: The Year 188 Current (Gupta Era)]', *The Indian Historical Quarterly*, 1930, 6(1): 45–60.

——, 'The Mainămati Copper-plate of Raṇavaṅkamalla Harikāladeva (1141 Śaka)', *The Indian Historical Quarterly*, 1933, 9(1): 282–89.
——, 'The Mainamati Copper-plate of Ranavankamalla Harikaladeva: 1141 Saka', *Varendra Research Society's Monographs*, 1934, 5: 10–16.
Bhattasali, Nalini Kanta, 'The Kedarpur Plate of Sri-Chandra-Deva', *Epigraphia Indica*, 1923–24 (reprint 1983), 17: 188–92.
——, 'Some Image Inscriptions from East Bengal', *Epigraphia Indica*, 1923–24 (reprint 1983), 17: 349–62.
——, 'The Ghugrahati Copper-plate Inscription of Samachara-Deva', *Epigraphia Indica*, 1925–26 (reprint 1983), 18: 74–86.
——, 'The Lost Bhowal Copper-plate of Lakṣmaṇa Sena Deva of Bengal', *The Indian Historical Quarterly*, 1927, 3(1): 89–96.
——, 'Two Inscriptions of Gopāla III of Bengal', *The Indian Historical Quarterly*, 1941, 17(2): 207–22.
——, 'The Rājāvāḍī (Bhāwāl) Plate of Lakṣmaṇa Sena Deva', *Journal of the Royal Asiatic Society of Bengal, Letters*, 1942, 8(1): 1–39.
——, 'The Rājāvāḍī (Bhāwāl) Plate of Lakṣmaṇa Sena Deva (Additions and Corrections)', *Journal of the Royal Asiatic Society of Bengal, Letters*, 1942, 8(2): 381–83.
——, 'Two Inscriptions of Govindacandra, King of Vanga', *Epigraphia Indica*, 1947–48 (reprint 1985), 27: 24–27.
——, 'Two Grants of Varmans of Vanga', *Epigraphia Indica*, 1953–54 (reprint 1987), 30: 255–63.
Biswas, Swapan Kumar, 'Pālarāja Debapāler Samasāmayika Śrīpāhiler Ekṭi Aprakāśita Prastaralipi', *Bangladesh Asiatic Society Patrika*, 1994, 12(2): 13–21.
——, 'Jātīya Jādughare Rakṣita Bhojabarmār 1ma Rājyavarṣer Ekṭi Śilālekha', *Jādughar Mamācār (Baṅladeś Jātīya Jādughar)*, January-March 2007: 13.
Bourdieu, Pierre, Richard Nice (tr.), *Outline of a Theory of Practice*, Cambridge: Cambridge University Press, 1977.
——, *The Logic of Practice*, Stanford, CA: Stanford University Press, 1990.
Chakrabarti, Kunal, *Religious Process: the Purāṇas and the Making of a Regional Tradition*, New Delhi: Oxford University Press, 2001.
Chakravarti, Ranabir, 'Kutumbikas of Early India', in Vijay Kumar Thakur and Ashok Aounshuman (eds), *Peasants in Indian History vol. 1: Theoretical Issues and Structural Enquiries (Essays in Memory of Professor Radhakrishna Chaudhary)*, Patna: Janaki Prakashan, 1996, pp. 179–98.
——, *Trade and Traders in Early Indian Society*, New Delhi: Manohar, 2002.
Chakravartti, Nilmani, 'Pāla Inscriptions in the Indian Museum', *Journal and Proceedings of the Asiatic Society of Bengal, New Series*, 1908, 4(3): 101–9.
Champakalakshmi, R., 'Peasant State and Society in Medieval South India', *The Indian Economic and Social History Review*, 1981, 18(3–4): 411–26.
Chanda, Rama Prasad, 'Dinājpur Pillar Inscription', *Journal and Proceedings of the Asiatic Society of Bengal, New Series*, 1911, 7(9): 615–19.
Chatterjee, Kumkum, 'Communities, Kings and Chronicles: The *Kulagranthas* of Bengal', *Studies in History, New Series*, 2005, 21(2): 173–213.
Chatterji, Suniti Kumar, *The Origin and Development of the Bengali Language*, New Delhi: Rupa & Co., 1993 (reprint).

Chattopadhyaya, B. D., 'Trade and Urban Centres in Early Medieval North India', *Indian Historical Review*, 1974, 1: 203–19.
———, 'Currency in Early Bengal', *Journal of India History*, 1977, 55(3): 41–60.
———, *Aspects of Rural Settlements and Rural Society in Early Medieval India*, Calcutta: K P Bagchi, 1990.
———, *The Making of Early Medieval India*, Delhi: Oxford University Press, 1994.
———, 'Introduction: The Making of Early Medieval India', in idem, *The Making of Early Medieval India*, Delhi: Oxford University Press, 1994, pp. 1–37.
———, 'Political Process and the Structure of Polity in Early Medieval India', in idem, *The Making of Early Medieval India*, Delhi: Oxford University Press, 1994, pp. 183–222 (originally Presidential Address, Ancient India Section, Indian History Congress 44th session, 1983).
———, 'State and Economy in North India: Fourth Century to Twelfth Century', in Romila Thapar (ed.), *Recent Perspectives of Early Indian History*, Bombay: Popular Prakashan, 1995, pp. 309–37.
Chaudhuri, Umesh Chandra, 'Some Observations on Two Copper-plate Grants from Bhāṭerā, Sylhet District, Assam', *Journal of the Royal Asiatic Society of Bengal, Letters*, 1940 (1941), 6(2): 73–77.
Chhabra, Bahadur Chand, 'Diplomatic of Sanskrit Copper-plate Grants', *The Indian Archives*, 1951, 5(1): 1–20.
———, 'Note on Mallasarul Charter of Vijayasena', *Epigraphia Indica*, 1953–54 (reprint 1987), 30: 161–63.
Choudhary, Abhay Kant, *Early Medieval Village in North-Eastern India (A. D. 600–1200) [Mainly a Socio-economic Study]*, Calcutta: Punthi Pustak, 1971.
Chowdhury, Abdul Momin, *Dynastic History of Bengal* (*c. 750–1200 A. D.*), Dacca: The Asiatic Society of Pakistan, 1967.
Chowdhury, Vasant, 'Harikela Coins: Some New Interpretations', *Indian Museum Bulletin*, 1996, 31: 35–41.
Cohn, Bernard S., 'African Models and Indian Histories', in Richard G. Fox (ed.), *Realm and Region in Traditional India*, New Delhi: Vikas Publishing House, 1977, pp. 90–113.
Curley, David L., *Poetry and History: Bengali Mangal-kābya and Social Change in Precolonial Bengal*, New Delhi: Chronicle Books, 2008.
Dani, Ahmad Hasan, 'Sobharampur Plate of Damodaradeva, Saka 1158', *Epigraphia Indica*, 1953–1954 (reprint 1987), 30: 184–88.
———, 'Mainamati Plates of the Candras', *Pakistan Archaeology*, 1966, 3: 22–55.
Dasgupta, Shashibhushan, *Obscure Religious Cults* (3rd ed.), Calcutta: Firma KLM, 1969.
Davidson, Ronald M., *Indian Esoteric Buddhism: A Social History of the Tantric Movement*, Delhi: Motilal Banarsidass, 2004.
Deshpande, Madhav M., *Sociolinguistic Attitudes in India: An Historical Reconstruction*, Ann Arbor: Karoma Publishers, 1979.
Deyell, John S., *Living without Silver: The Monetary History of Early Medieval North India*, Delhi: Oxford University Press, 1990.
———, 'Cowries and Coins: The Dual Monetary System of the Bengal Sultanate', *The Indian Economic and Social History Review*, 2010, 47(1): 63–106.
Dikshit, K. N., 'Paharpur Copper-plate Grant of the [Gupta] Year 159', *Epigraphia Indica*, 1929–30 (reprint 1983), 20: 59–64.

Dutt, Nripendra Kumar, *Origin and Growth of Caste in India (Volumes 1 and 2 Combined)*, Calcutta: Firm KLM, 1986.
Eaton, Richard M., *The Rise of Islam and the Bengal Frontier, 1204–1760*, Berkeley: University of California Press, 1993.
Einoo, Shingo, 'The Autumn Goddess Festival: Described in the Purāṇas', in Masakazu Tanaka and Musashi Tachikawa (eds), *Living with Śakti: Gender, Sexuality and Religion in South Asia*, Osaka: National Museum of Ethnology, 1999, pp. 33–70.
Eschmann, Anncharlott, Hermann Kulke and Gaya Charan Tripathi (eds), *The Cult of Jagannath and the Regional Tradition of Orissa*, New Delhi: Manohar, 1978.
Ferrier, Cédric and Judit Törzsök, 'Meditating on the King's Feet? Some Remarks on the Expression *pādānudhyāta*', *Indo-Iranian Journal*, 2008, 51(2): 93–113.
Fleming, Benjamin J., 'New Copperplate Grant of Śrīcandra (no. 8) from Bangladesh', *Bulletin of the School of Oriental and African Studies*, 2010, 73(2): 223–44.
Furui, Ryosuke, 'The Rural World of an Agricultural Text: A Study on the *Kṛṣiparāśara*', *Studies in History, New Series*, 2005, 21(2): 149–71.
———, 'A New Copper Plate Inscription of Gopala II', *South Asian Studies*, 2008, 24: 67–75.
———, 'Re-reading Two Copper Plate Inscriptions of Gopāla II, Year 4', in Gerd J. R. Mevissen and Arundhati Banerji (eds), *Prajñādhara: Essays on Asian Art, History, Epigraphy and Culture in Honour of Gouriswar Bhattacharya*, New Delhi: Kaveri Books, 2009, pp. 319–30.
———, 'Biyala Copperplate Inscription of Mahīpāla I', *Pratna Samiksha: A Journal of Archaeology, New Series*, 2010, 1: 99–106.
———, 'Indian Museum Copper Plate Inscription of Dharmapala, Year 26: Tentative Reading and Study', *South Asian Studies*, 2011, 27(2): 145–56.
———, 'Panchrol (Egra) Copperplate Inscription of the Time of Śaśāṅka: A Re-edition', *Pratna Samiksha: A Journal of Archaeology, New Series*, 2011, 2: 119–30.
———, 'Rangpur Copper Plate Inscription of Mahīpāla I, Year 5', *Journal of Ancient Indian History*, 2010–11 (2011), 27: 232–45.
———, 'Agrarian Expansion and Local Power Relation in the Seventh and Eighth Century Eastern Bengal: A Study on Copper Plate Inscriptions', in Ratnabali Chatterjee (ed.), *Urbanity and Economy: The Pre Modern Dynamics in Eastern India*, Kolkata: Setu Prakashani, 2013, pp. 96–110.
———, '*Brāhmaṇa*s in Early Medieval Bengal: Construction of their Identity, Networks and Authority', *Indian Historical Review*, 2013, 40(2): 223–48.
———, 'Chaprakot Stone Inscription of the Time of Gopāla IV, Year 9', in Alamgir Muhammad Serajuddin, Nazrul Islam, Sultana Shafee, Syed Manzoorul Islam and Syed Mohammad Shaheed (eds), *Centenary Commemorative Volume (1913–2013)*, Dhaka: Bangladesh National Museum, 2013, pp. 110–17.
———, 'Finding Tensions in the Social Order: A Reading of the Varṇasaṃkara Section of the Bṛhaddharmapurāṇa', in Suchandra Ghosh, Sudipa Ray Bandyopadhyay, Sushmita Basu Majumdar and Sayantani Pal (eds), *Revisiting Early India: Essays in Honour of D. C. Sircar*, Kolkata: R. N. Bhattacharya, 2013, pp. 203–18.
———, 'The Kotalipada Copperplate Inscription of the Time of Dvādaśāditya, Year 14', *Pratna Samiksha: A Journal of Archaeology, New Series*, 2013, 4: 89–98.
———, 'Merchant Groups in Early Medieval Bengal: With Special Reference to the Rajbhita Stone Inscription of the Time of Mahīpāla I, Year 33', *Bulletin of the School of Oriental and African Studies*, 2013, 76(3): 391–412.

———, 'Rajibpur Copperplate Inscriptions of Gopāla IV and Madanapāla', *Pratna Samiksha: A Journal of Archaeology, New Series*, 2015, 6: 39–61.

———, 'Characteristics of Kaivarta Rebellion Delineated from the Rāmacarita', *Proceedings of Indian History Congress*, 2015, 75: 93–98.

———, 'Ājīvikas, Maṇibhadra and Early History of Eastern Bengal: A New Copperplate Inscription of Vainyagupta and Its Implications', *Journal of the Royal Asiatic Society*, 2016, 26(4): 657–81.

———, 'Bharat Kala Bhavan Copper Plate Inscription of Rājyapāla, Year 2: Re-edition and Reinterpretation', *Puravritta*, 2016, 1: 41–56.

———, '*Brāhmaṇa*s in Early Medieval Bengal: Data of Inscriptional References', in Nobuhiro Ota (ed.), *Zen-kindai Minami-Ajia Shakai Ni Okeru Matomari To Tsunagari (Clustering and Connections in Pre-Modern South Asian Society)*, Tokyo: Research Institute for Languages and Cultures of Asia and Africa, Tokyo University of Foreign Studies, 2017, pp. 181–215.

———, 'Subordinate Rulers under the Pālas: Their Diverse Origins and Shifting Power Relation with the King', *The Indian Economic and Social History Review*, 2017, 54(3): 339–59.

———, 'Variegated Adaptations: State Formation in Bengal from the Fifth to the Seventh Century' (rev.), in Karashima Noboru and Hirosue Masashi (eds), *State Formation and Social Integration in Pre-modern South and Southeast Asia: A Comparative Study of Asian Society*, Tokyo: The Toyo Bunko, 2017, pp. 73–87.

———, 'Bangladesh National Museum Metal Vase Inscription of the Time of Devātideva and Its Implications for the Early History of Harikela', *Puravritta*, 2019, 2: 43–51.

Gadgil, Madhav and Ramacandra Guha, *This Fissured Land: An Ecological History of India*, Delhi: Oxford University Press, 1992.

Ganguly, Dhirendra Chandra, 'Saktipur Copper-plate of Lakshmanasena', *Epigraphia Indica*, 1931–32 (reprint 1984), 21: 211–19.

———, 'Date of Ashrafpur Plate', *Epigraphia Indica*, 1941–42 (reprint 1985), 26: 125–26.

Ghosh, A., 'A Bronze Image Inscription from Nalanda', *Epigraphia Indica*, 1939–40 (reprint 1985), 25: 334–35.

Ghosh, Suchandra, 'Economy of Samataṭa in the Early Medieval Period: A Brief Overview', in Gerd J. R. Mevissen and Arundhati Banerji (eds), *Prajñādhara: Essays on Asian Art, History, Epigraphy and Culture in Honour of Gouriswar Bhattacharya*, New Delhi: Kaveri Books, 2009, pp. 352–58.

Ghoshal, Ramesh K., 'Rakshaskhali Island Plate of Madommanapala; Saka 1118', *Epigraphia Indica*, 1947–48 (reprint 1985), 27: 119–24.

Gopal, Lallanji, *The Economic Life of Northern India: c. A.D. 700–1200*, Delhi: Motilal Banarsidass, 1965.

———, 'The Date of the Krsi-Parasara', *Journal of Indian History*, 1973, 50: 151–68.

Griffiths, Arlo, 'New Documents for the Early History of Puṇḍravardhana: Copperplate Inscriptions from the Late Gupta and Early Post-Gupta Periods', *Pratna Samiksha: A Journal of Archaeology, New Series*, 2015, 6: 15–38.

Gupta, Chitrarekha, 'Early Brahmanic Settlement in Bengal – Pre Pala Period', in B. N. Mukherjee, D. R. Das, S. S. Biswas and S. P. Singh (eds), *Sri Dinesacandrika: Studies in Indology (Shri D. C. Sircar Festschrift)*, Delhi: Sundeep Prakashan, 1983, pp. 215–24.

——, '"Khila-kṣetra" in Early Bengal Inscriptions', in Debala Mitra and Gouriswar Bhattacharya (eds), *Studies in Art and Archaeology of Bihar and Bengal: Nalinīkānta Śatavārṣikī, Dr. N. K. Bhattasali Centenary Volume (1888–1988)*, Delhi: Sri Satguru Publications, 1989, pp. 271–83.
——, 'Evolution of Agrarian Society in Kamarupa in Early Medieval Period', *Indian Historical Review*, 1992–93 (1996), 19(1–2): 1–20.
——, *The Kāyasthas: A Study in the Formation and Early History of a Caste*, Calcutta: K P Bagchi, 1996.
——, 'Land-measurement and Land-revenue System in Bengal under Senas', in Debala Mitra (ed.), *Explorations in Art and Archaeology of South Asia: Essays Dedicated to N. G. Majumdar*, Calcutta: Directorate of Archaeology and Museums, 1996, pp. 573–93.
——, 'Bengal Art and Bengal Inscriptions: An Approach Towards Co-relation – A Case Study with Punchra: A Village in the Vardhaman District, West Bengal', *Journal of Bengal Art*, 2002, 7: 83–100.
Gupta Kamalakanta, 'Two Mainamati Copper-plate Inscriptions of the Khadga and Early-Deva Times (7th and 8th Centuries A. D.)', *Bangladesh Archaeology*, 1979, 1(1): 141–48.
Gupta, K. M., 'The Bhatera Copper-plate Inscription of Govinda-Kesavadeva (C. 1049 A.D.)', *Epigraphia Indica*, 1927–28 (reprint 1983), 19: 277–86.
Gupta, Monoranjon, 'The Two Pāla Copper-plate Inscriptions of Belwā', *Journal of the Asiatic Society, Letters*, 1951, 17(2): 117–35.
Gupta, Parmeshwari Lal (ed.), *Patna Museum Catalogue of Antiquities (Stone Sculptures, Metal Images, Terracottas and Minor Antiquities)*, Patna: Patna Museum, 1965.
——, *The Imperial Guptas*, 2 vols, Varanasi: Vishwavidyalaya Prakashan, 1973, 1979.
Gupta, Swarupa, *Notions of Nationhood in Bengal: Perspectives on Samaj, c. 1867–1905*, Leiden: Brill, 2009.
Gurukkal, Rajan, 'From Clan and Lineage to Hereditary Occupations and Caste in Early South India', *Indian Historical Review*, 1993–94 (1996), 20: 22–33.
——, *Social Formations of Early South India*, New Delhi: Oxford University Press, 2010.
Hazra, R. C., *Studies in Upapurāṇas*, 2 vols, Calcutta: Sanskrit College, 1958, 1963.
——, *Studies in the Purāṇic Records on Hindu Rites and Customs* (2nd ed.), Delhi: Motilal Banarsidass, 1975.
——, 'Purāṇa Literature as Known to Ballālasena', *Purāṇa*, 1985, 27(1): 41–59.
Heitzman, James, *Gifts of Power: Lordship in an Early Indian State*, Delhi: Oxford University Press, 1997.
Hindess, Barry and Paul Q. Hirst, *Pre-Capitalist Modes of Production*, London, Henley and Boston: Routledge and Kegan Paul, 1975.
Hok, M. Monirul and M. Abdul Kuddus, 'Lakṣmaṇasener Bāgabāḍi Praśasti: Barendra Gabeṣaṇā Jādughare Eka Mūlyabāna Saṃyojana', *IBS Journal*, 1412 BS (2005), 11: 7–20.
——, 'Prathama Mahīpāler Rājabhiṭā Śilālipi: Pāṭhoddhāra o Biśleṣaṇa', *IBS Journal*, 1412 BS (2005), 13: 7–18.
Hultzsch, E., 'The Sarnath Inscription of Mahipala', *Indian Antiquary*, 1885, 14: 139–40.

———, 'Plates of the Time of Sasankaraja; Gupta-Samvat 300', *Epigraphia Indica*, 1900–01 (reprint 1981), 6: 143–46.
———, 'Tirumalai Rock Inscription of Rajendra-Chola I', *Epigraphia Indica*, 9, 1907–08 (reprint 1981), 9: 229–33.
Hunter, W. W., *A Statistical Account of Bengal, vol. 7: Districts of Maldah, Rangpur, and Dinajpur*, Delhi: Concept Publishing Company, 1984 (reprint).
———, *A Statistical Account of Bengal, vol. 8: Districts of Rajshahi and Bogra*, Delhi: Concept Publishing Company, 1984 (reprint).
Huntington, Susan L., *The "Pāla-Sena" Schools of Sculpture*, Leiden: E. J. Brill, 1984.
Husain, A. B. M., 'History, Society and Culture', in A. B. M. Husain, M. Harunur Rashid, Abdul Momin Chowdhury and Abu H. Imamuddin (eds), *Gawr-Lakhnawati*, Dhaka: Asiatic Society of Bangladesh, 1997, pp. 9–28.
Inden, Ronald B., *Marriage and Rank in Bengali Culture: A History of Caste and Clan in Middle Period Bengal*, New Delhi: Vikas Publishing House, 1976.
Ingalls, Daniel H. H., 'A Sanskrit Poetry of Village and Field: Yogeśvara and His Fellow Poets', *Journal of the American Oriental Society*, 1954, 74: 119–31.
Islam, Shariful, 'Unpublished Stone Inscription of the Seventh Regnal Year of Bhojavarman', *Journal of the Asiatic Society of Bangladesh, Humanities*, 2010, 55(1): 113–19.
———, 'Koṭālipāḍā Copper Plate of Dvādaśāditya', *Journal of the Asiatic Society*, 2011, 53(4): 71–82.
———, 'Uḍīśvara Copper Plate of Śrīdhāraṇarāta', *Journal of the Asiatic Society of Bangladesh, Humanities*, 2012, 57(1): 61–72.
Islam, Shariful and Sayeeda Nasrin, 'A Fresh Assessment of Gopacandra in the Light of Numismatic Evidence', *Journal of the Asiatic Society of Bangladesh, Humanities*, 2014, 59(1): 31–37.
Jahan, Shahnaj Husne, 'Samandar: An Important Centre for Maritime Activities in Bengal', *Journal of Bengal Art*, 2000, 5: 223–43.
Jha, D. N., 'Relevance of Peasant State and Society to Pallava-Cola Times', *Indian Historical Review*, 1981–82 (1982), 8(1–2): 74–94.
——— (ed.), *Feudal Social Formation in Early India*, Delhi: Chanakya Publications, 1987.
——— (ed.), *The Feudal Order: State, Society and Ideology in Early Medieval India*, New Delhi: Manohar, 2000.
———, 'Editor's Introduction', in D. N. Jha (ed.), *The Feudal Order: State, Society and Ideology in Early Medieval India*, New Delhi: Manohar, 2000, pp. 1–58.
Jha, Vishwa Mohan, 'Settlement, Society and Polity in Early Medieval Rural India', *Indian Historical Review*, 1996, 20: 34–65.
Kane, P. V., *History of Dharmaśāstra (Ancient and Medieval Religious and Civil Law)*, vol. 2 2 pts (2nd ed.), Poona: Bhandarkar Oriental Research Institute, 1974.
———, *History of Dharmaśāstra (Ancient and Medieval Religious and Civil Law)*, vol. 5 pt. 1 (2nd ed.), Poona: Bhandarkar Oriental Research Institute, 1974.
———, *History of Dharmaśāstra (Ancient and Medieval Religious and Civil Law)*, vol. 1 pt. 2 (2nd ed.), Poona: Bhandarkar Oriental Research Institute, 1975.
———, *History of Dharmaśāstra (Ancient and Medieval Religious and Civil Law)*, vol. 5 pt. 2 (2nd ed.), Poona: Bhandarkar Oriental Research Institute, 1977.
Karashima, Noboru, *South Indian History and Society: Studies from Inscriptions, A.D. 850–1800*, Delhi: Oxford University Press, 1984.

Khan, Ayoub, 'Bengal Copperplates: Provenances and Preservation Data', *Pratnatattva*, 2007, 13: 5–36.

Kielhorn, F. 'The Dinājpur Copper-plate Inscription of Mahīpāla', *Journal of the Asiatic Society of Bengal*, 1892, 61(1): 77–87.

———, 'The Mungir Copper-plate Grant of Devapaladeva', *Indian Antiquary*, 1892, 21: 253–58.

———, 'Badal Pillar Inscription of the Time of Narayanapala', *Epigraphia Indica*, 1894 (reprint 1984), 2: 160–67.

———, 'Dudhpani Rock Inscription of Udayamana', *Epigraphia Indica*, 2, 1894 (reprint 1984), 2: 343–47.

———, 'Khalimpur Plate of Dharmapaladeva', *Epigraphia Indica*, 1896–97 (reprint 1979), 4: 243–54.

Knutson, Jesse Ross, *Into the Twilight of Sanskrit Court Poetry: The Sena Salon of Bengal and Beyond*, Berkeley, Los Angeles and London: University of California Press, 2014.

Kosambi, D. D., *An Introduction to the Study of Indian History* (Revised 2nd ed.), Bombay: Popular Prakashan, 1975.

———, 'Scientific Numismatics', in idem, *Indian Numismatics*, New Delhi: Orient Longman, 1981, pp. 145–56.

———, 'Living Prehistory in India', in D. D. Kosambi, B. D. Chattopadhyaya (comp., ed., intro.), *The Oxford India Kosambi: Combined Methods in Indology and Other Writings* (2nd ed.), New Delhi: Oxford University Press, 2009, pp. 30–48.

Kulke, Hermann, 'Royal Temple Policy and the Structure of Medieval Hindu Kingdom', in Anncharlott Eschmann, Hermann Kulke and Gaya Charan Tripathi (eds), *The Cult of Jagannath and the Regional Tradition of Orissa*, New Delhi: Manohar, 1978, pp. 125–37.

———, 'Introduction: The Study of the State in Pre-modern India', in Hermann Kulke (ed.), *The State in India 1000–1700*, Delhi: Oxford University Press, 1995, pp. 1–47.

———, 'The Early and the Imperial Kingdom: A Processural Model of Integrative State Formation in Early Medieval India', in Hermann Kulke (ed.), *The State in India 1000–1700*, Delhi: Oxford University Press, 1995, pp. 233–62.

———, 'Some Observations on the Political Functions of Copper-plate Grants in Early Medieval India', in Bernhard Kölver (ed.), *Recht, Staat und Verwaltung im klassischen Indien (The State, the Law, and Administration in Classical India)*, München: R. Oldenbourg Verlag, 1997, pp. 237–43.

Lahiri, Nayanjot, 'Landholding and Peasantry in the Brahmaputra Valley C. 5th–13th Centuries AD', *Journal of the Economic and Social History of Orient*, 1990, 33(2): 157–67

———, *Pre-Ahom Assam: Studies in the Inscriptions of Assam between the Fifth and the Thirteenth Centuries AD*, New Delhi: Munshiram Manoharlal, 1991.

Lahiri, Siva Prasanna, 'Bhāturiyā Inscription of Rājyapāla', *The Indian Historical Quarterly*, 1955, 31(3): 215–31.

Laskar, G. M., 'Ashrafpur Copper-plate Grants of Devakhaḍga', *Memoirs of the Asiatic Society of Bengal*, 1904, 1(6): 85–91.

Maity, Sachindra Kumar, *Economic Life in Northern India in the Gupta Period (Cir. A. D. 300–550)* (2nd ed.), Delhi: Motilal Banarsidass, 1970.

Majumdar, Nani Gopal, 'Patna Museum Inscription of Jayasena', *Indian Antiquary*, 1919, 48: 43–48.

———, 'Nalanda Inscription of Vipulasrimitra', *Epigraphia Indica*, 1931–32 (reprint 1984), 21: 97–101

———, 'Irda Copper-plate of the Kamboja King Nayapaladeva', *Epigraphia Indica*, 22, 1933–34 (reprint 1984), 22: 150–59.

———, 'Mallasarul Copper-plate of Vijayasena', *Epigraphia Indica*, 1935–36 (reprint 1984), 23: 155–61.

———, 'Nandapur Copper-plate of the Gupta Year 169', *Epigraphia Indica*, 1935–36 (reprint 1984), 23: 52–56.

Majumdar, Ramesh Chandra, 'Some Dates in the Pāla and Sena Records', *Journal of the Royal Asiatic Society of Bengal, Letters*, 1941, 7: 215–18.

———, 'Chittagong Copper-plate of Kantideva', *Epigraphia Indica*, 1941–42 (reprint 1985), 26: 313–18.

——— (ed.), *History of Bengal vol. 1: Hindu Period*, Dacca: The University of Dacca, 1943.

———, 'Two Copper-plates of Śaśāṅka from Midnapore', *Journal of the Royal Asiatic Society of Bengal, Letters*, 1945, 11(1): 1–9.

———, *History of Ancient Bengal*, Calcutta: Bharadwaj & Co., 1971.

Majumdar, R. C. and J. N. Banerjea, 'Two Inscribed Images of Imadpur', *Journal of the Royal Asiatic Society of Bengal, Letters*, 1950, 16(2): 247–51.

Majumdar Sastri, Surendranath, 'The Hilsa Statue Inscription of the Thirty-fifth Year of Devapala', *Journal of the Bihar and Orissa Research Society*, 1924, 10(1–2): 31–36.

Mazumdar, Bhakat Prasad, *Socio-Economic History of Northern India: 1030–1194 A.D.*, Calcutta: Firma KLM, 1960.

Melzer, Gudrun, 'A Dancing Cāmuṇḍā Named Siddheśvarī from the Time of Mahīpāla I', in Mokammal H. Bhuiyan (ed.), *Studies in South Asian Heritage: Essays in Memory of M Harunur Rashid*, Dhaka: Bangla Academy, 2015, pp. 95–123.

Mills, E. M., 'A Copper Plate from the Reign of Śrīcandra (Bangladesh National Museum Accession Number 77.1478)', *South Asian Studies*, 1993, 9: 77–86.

Mishra, R. S., 'Bharat Kala Bhavan Copper-plate Grant of Rājyapāla (Regnal Year 2)', in Anand Krishna (ed.), *Chhavi-2: Rai Krishnadasa Felicitation Volume*, Banaras: Bharat Kala Bhavan, 1981, pp. 221–30.

Misra, Pramatha Nath and R. C. Majumdar, 'The Jājilpārā Grant of Gopāla II, Year 6', *Journal of the Asiatic Society, Letters*, 1951, 17(2): 137–44.

Mita, Masahiko, 'Panchakula To Mahājana: Chūseishoki Rājasthān-Gujarāt No Toshigyōsei To Shūkaisoshiki' (*Pañcakula* and *Mahājana*: Urban Administration and Assembly Organisation in Early Medieval Rajasthan and Gujarat) (in Japanese), in Nobuhiro Ota (ed.), *Zen-kindai Minami-Ajia Shakai Ni Okeru Matomari To Tsunagari* (*Clustering and Connections in Pre-Modern South Asian Society*), Tokyo: Research Institute for Languages and Cultures of Asia and Africa, Tokyo University of Foreign Studies, 2017, pp. 55–95.

Mitchiner, Michael, *The Land of Water: Coinage and History of Bangladesh and Later Arakan circa 300 BC to the present day*, London: Hawkins Publications, 2000.

Mitra, Debala, 'Image of Buddha of the 11th Regnal Year of King Mahīpāla', *Indian Museum Bulletin*, 1991, 26: 7–12.

———, 'A Fragmentary Bejewelled Image of Buddha of the Time of Mahipala from Shantipur', *Pratna Samiksha*, 1995–96 (1996), 4–5: 165–72.

Monier-Williams, Monier, *A Sanskrit-English Dictionary: Etymologically and Philologically Arranged with Special Reference to Cognate Indo-European Languages* (new ed.), Oxford: Oxford University Press, 2000 (reprint).

Morrison, Barrie M., 'Region and Subregion in Pre-Muslim Bengal', in David Kopf (ed.), *Bengal Regional Identity*, East Lansing: Asian Studies Center, Michigan State University, 1969, pp. 3–20.

———, *Political Centers and Cultural Regions in Early Bengal*, Tucson: University of Arizona Press, 1970.

Mukherjee, B. N., 'Commerce and Money in the Western and Central Sectors of Eastern India (c. A. D. 750–1200)', *Indian Museum Bulletin*, 1982, 17: 65–83.

———, *Coins and Currency Systems of Post-Gupta Bengal: c.AD 550–700*, New Delhi: Munshiram Manoharlal, 1993.

———, 'A Survey of the Samataṭa and Harikela Coinages', *Journal of Bengal Art*, 2003, 8: 199–212.

Mukherjee, B. N. and P. Ray, 'Madavpur Fragmentary Inscription of the Year 368', *Indian Museum Bulletin*, 1991, 26: 42–45.

Mukherji, S. C., 'The Jagajjivanpur Copper-plate Inscription of King Mahendrapāla (of the Pāla Dynasty), regnal year 7 (857 A. D.)', *Pratna Samiksha*, 1997–99 (1999), 6–8: 58–70.

———, 'Two New Copper-plate Inscriptions (Nos. 1 and 2) of King Gopāla II, Pāla Dynasty of Bengal and Bihar, regnal year 4 (Circa 878 A. D.)', *Pratna Samiksha*, 1997–99 (1999), 6–8: 71–80.

———, 'Bangladesh National Museum Stone Slab Inscription of King Gopāla IV (?). Regnal Year 9 (1137 A. D.?)', *Journal of Bengal Art*, 2001, 6: 61–63.

Mukhia, Harbans, 'Peasant Production and Medieval Indian Society', *The Journal of Peasant Studies*, 1985, 12(2–3): 228–51.

———, 'Was There Feudalism in Indian History?', in Hermann Kulke (ed.), *The State in India 1000–1700*, Delhi: Oxford University Press, 1995, pp. 86–133 (originally Presidential Address, Medieval Section, Indian History Congress 40th Session, 1979).

———, (ed.), *The Feudalism Debate*, New Delhi: Manohar, 1999.

Nandi, Ramendra Nath. *State Formation, Agrarian Growth and Social Change in Feudal South India: c. A. D. 600–1200*, New Delhi: Manohar, 2000.

Nath, Vijay, '*Mahādāna*: The Dynamics of Gift-economy and the Feudal Milieu', in D. N. Jha (ed.), *The Feudal Order: State, Society and Ideology in Early Medieval India*, New Delhi: Manohar, 2000, pp. 411–40.

Nicholas, Ralph W., *Rites of Spring: Gājan in Village Bengal (With an Essay by David Curley)*, New Delhi: Chronicle Books, 2008.

Niyogi, Puspa, *Brahmanic Settlements in Different Subdivisions of Ancient Bengal*, Calcutta: Indian Studies: Past and Present, 1967.

Pal, Sayantani, 'The Chopra Image Inscription of Mahīpāla', *Pratna Samiksha: A Journal of Archaeology, New Series*, 2010, 1: 95–98.

———, 'Reconsidering the Chronology of the Rulers of Faridpur (6th Century)', *Journal of Bengal Art*, 2013, 18: 115–21.

———, 'Jayarampur Plate of Gopacandra: Some Reconsideration', in Subrata Kumar Acharya (ed.), *Studies on Odishan Epigraphy*, Delhi: Pratibha Prakashan, 2015, pp. 65–71.

Parasher, Aloka, *Mlecchas in Early India: A Study in Attitudes Towards Outsiders Upto AD 600*, New Delhi: Munshiram Manoharlal, 1991.

Pargiter, F. E., 'Three Copper-plate Grants from East Bengal', *Indian Antiquary*, 1910, 39: 193–216.

———, 'Ghāgrāhāṭi (Koṭwālipāṛā) Grant and Three Other Copper-plate Grants', *Journal and Proceedings of the Asiatic Society of Bengal, New Series*, 1911, 7(8): 475–502.

Perlin, Frank, *The Invisible City: Monetary, Administrative and Popular Infrastructures in Asia and Europe, 1500–1900*, Hampshire: Variorum, 1993.

Pollock, Sheldon, 'The Sanskrit Cosmopolis, 300–1300: Transculturation, Vernacularization, and the Question of Ideology', in Jan E. M. Houben (ed.), *Ideology and Status of Sanskrit: Contributions to the History of the Sanskrit Language*, Leiden: E. J. Brill, 1996, pp. 197–247.

———, *The Language of the Gods in the World of Men: Sanskrit, Culture, and Power in Premodern India*, Delhi: Permanent Black, 2007.

Rahman, Mukhlesur, *Sculpture in the Varendra Research Museum: A Descriptive Catalogue*, Rajshahi: Varendra Research Museum, University of Rajshahi, 1998.

Rajaguru, Shri Satyanarayan, 'Jayarampur Copper-plate Inscription of the Time of Gopachandra', *Orissa Historical Research Journal*, 1963, 11(4): 206–33.

Ramesh, K. V. and S. Subramonia Iyer, 'Kalanda Copper Plate Charter of Nayapāladeva', *Epigraphia Indica*, 1975–76 (reprint 1989), 41: 199–205.

———, 'Māldā District Museum Copper-plate Charter of Mahendrapāladeva, year 7', *Epigraphia Indica*, 1977–78 (reprint 1992), 42: 6–29.

Randle, H. N., 'India Office Plate of Lakshmanasena', *Epigraphia Indica*, 1941–42 (reprint 1985), 26: 1–13.

Rao, N. Laksminarayan, 'Kolagallu Inscription of Khottiga; Saka 889', *Epigraphia Indica*, 1931–32 (reprint 1984), 21: 260–67.

Rashid, Haroun Er, *Geography of Bangladesh* (2nd ed.), Dhaka: University Press Ltd., 1991.

Rashid, M. Harunur, 'The Mainamati Inscriptions', in Enamul Haque (ed.), *Hakim Habibur Rahman Khan Commemoration Volume*, Dhaka: The International Centre for Study of Bengal Art, 2001, pp. 193–224.

Ray, Niharranjan, John W. Hood (tr.), *History of Bengali People (Ancient Period)*, Calcutta: Orient Longman, 1994.

Ray, Rajat and Ratna Ray, 'Zamindars and Jotedars: A Study of Rural Politics in Bengal', *Modern Asian Studies*, 1975, 9(1): 81–102.

Ray, Ratnalekha, *Change in Bengal Agrarian Society: c1760–1850*, New Delhi: Manohar, 1979.

Raychaudhuri, Tapan, *Bengal under Akbar and Jahangir: An Introductory Study in Social History*, New Delhi: Munshiram Manoharlal, 1969.

Rhodes, Nicholas G., 'Trade in South-East Bengal in the First Millennium CE: The Numismatic Evidence', in Rila Mukherjee (ed.), *Pelagic Passageways: The Northern Bay of Bengal Before Colonialism*, Delhi: Primus Books, 2011, pp. 263–75.

Rocher, Ludo, *The Purāṇas*, Wiesbaden: Otto Harrassowitz, 1986.

Sahu, Bhairabi Prasad, 'Aspects of Rural Economy in Early Medieval Orissa', *Social Scientist*, 1993, 21(1–2): 48–68.

———, 'Agrarian Changes and the Peasantry in Early Medieval Orissa (c. A. D. 400–1100)', in Vijay Kumar Thakur and Ashok Aounshuman (eds), *Peasants in Indian History vol. 1: Theoretical Issues and Structural Enquiries* (Essays in Memory of Professor Radhakrishna Chaudhary), Patna: Janaki Prakashan, 1996, pp. 283–311.

———, *The Changing Gaze: Regions and the Constructions of Early India*, New Delhi: Oxford University Press, 2013.

Sanderson, Alexis, 'The Śaiva Age – The Rise and Dominance of Śaivism During the Early Medieval Period – ', in Shingo Einoo (ed.), *Genesis and Development of Tantrism*, Tokyo: Institute of Oriental Culture, University of Tokyo, 2009, pp. 41–349.

Sanyal, Hitesranjan, 'Mallabhum', in Surajit Sinha (ed.), *Tribal Polities and State Systems in Pre-Colonial Eastern and North-Eastern India*, Calcutta: K P Bagchi, 1987, pp. 73–142.

Sanyal, Niradbandhu, 'Sultanpur Copper-plate Inscription', *Epigraphia Indica*, 1955–56 (reprint 1987): 31: 57–66.

Sanyal, Rajat., 'Dedicatory Inscriptions of the Time of Mahendrapāla: A Fresh Appraisal', in Gerd J. R. Mevissen and Arundhati Banerji (eds), *Prajñādhara: Essays on Asian Art, History, Epigraphy and Culture in Honour of Gouriswar Bhattacharya*, New Delhi: Kaveri Books, 2009, pp. 302–18.

———, 'Copperplate Inscriptions of West Bengal: Finding Find-spots and Locating Localities', *Pratna Samiksha: A Journal of Archaeology, New Series*, 2010, 1: 107–34.

———, 'Another Inscribed Image of the Reign of Rāmapāla from South Bihar', *Pratna Samiksha: A Journal of Archaeology, New Series*, 2011, 2: 139–44.

———, 'The Pala-Sena and Others', in Dilip K. Chakrabarti and Makkhan Lal (eds), *History of Ancient India, Vol. 5: Political History and Administration (c AD. 750–1300)*, New Delhi: Vivekananda International Foundation and Aryan Books International, 2014, pp. 165–213.

Sarkar, Bihani, 'The Rite of Durgā in Medieval Bengal: An Introductory Study of Raghunandana's *Durgāpūjātattva* with Text and Translation of the Principal Rites', *Journal of the Royal Asiatic Society*, 2012, 22(2): 325–90.

Sarkar, Himanshu Bhusan, 'Bengal and her Overland Routes in India and Beyond', *Journal of the Asiatic Society*, 1974, 16: 92–119.

Sen, Benoy Chandra and Devaprasad Ghosh, 'A Dated Copper-plate Grant from Sundarban', *The Indian Historical Quarterly*, 1934, 10(2): 321–31.

Sen, Sukumar, *An Etymological Dictionary of Bengali: c. 1000–1800 A. D.*, Calcutta: Eastern Publishers, 1971.

Sengupta, Gautam, 'Archaeology of Coastal Bengal', in Himanshu Prabha Ray and Jean-François Salles (eds), *Tradition and Archaeology: Early Maritime Contact in the Indian Ocean*, New Delhi: Manohar, 1996, pp. 115–28.

Sharma, R. S., *Indian Feudalism: c.300–1200*, Calcutta: Calcutta University Press, 1965.

———, *Social Changes in Early Medieval India (Circa A. D. 500–1200)*, New Delhi: People's Publishing House, 1969.

———, *Indian Feudalism: c. A.D. 300–1200* (2nd ed.), Delhi: Macmillan India, 1980.

———, 'The Kali Age: A period of social crisis', in S. N. Mukherjee (ed.), *India: History and Thought* (Essays in Honour of A. L. Basham), Calcutta: Subarnarekha, 1982, pp. 186–203.

———, *Urban Decay in India (c.300 – c.1000)*, New Delhi: Munshiram Manoharlal, 1987.

———, 'How Feudal was Indian Feudalism? (revised and updated, 1992)', in Hermann Kulke (ed.), *The State in India 1000–1700*, Delhi: Oxford University Press, 1995, pp. 48–85.

———, *Early Medieval Indian Society: A Study in Feudalisation*, New Delhi: Orient Longman, 2001.

Shastri, Hirananda, 'The Nalanda Copper-plate of Devapaladeva', *Epigraphia Indica*, 1923–24 (reprint 1983), 17: 310–27.

Shomer, Karine, Joan L. Erdman, Deryck O. Lodrick and Lloyd I. Rudolph (eds), *The Idea of Rajasthan: Explorations in Regional Identity*, 2 vols, New Delhi: Manohar, 2001.

Singh, Upinder, *Kings, Brāhmaṇas and Temples in Orissa: An Epigraphic Study AD 300–1147*, New Delhi: Munshiram Manoharlal, 1994.

Sinha Kapur, Nandini, *State Formation in Rajasthan: Mewar during the Seventh-Fifteenth Centuries*, New Delhi: Manohar, 2002.

Sircar, D. C., 'Pāīkpāṛā Vāsudeva Image Inscription of King Govindacandra of Bengal – Regnal Year 23', *Indian Culture*, 1941, 7(4): 405–16.

———, 'Nārāyaṇpur Vināyaka Image Inscription of King Mahīpāla.-Regnal Year 4', *Indian Culture*, 1942, 9(1), Miscellanea: 121–25.

———, 'Kalaikuri Copper-plate Inscription of the Gupta Year 120 (=A.D. 439)', *The Indian Historical Quarterly*, 1943, 19(1): 12–26.

———, 'The Kailan Copper-plate Inscription of King Śrīdhāraṇa Rāta of Samataṭa', *The Indian Historical Quarterly*, 1947, 23(3): 221–41.

———, 'Two Pillar Inscriptions', *Journal of the Royal Asiatic Society of Bengal, Letters*, 1949, 15(1): 5–8.

———, 'Epigraphic Notes', *Epigraphia Indica*, 1949–50 (reprint 1985), 28: 335–41.

———, 'Three Inscriptions from Valgudar', *Epigraphia Indica*, 1949–50 (reprint 1985), 28: 137–45.

———, 'Copper-plate Inscription of King Bhavadeva of Devaparvata', *Journal of the Asiatic Society, Letters*, 1951, 17(2): 83–94.

———, 'Some Inscriptions from Bihar', *Journal of the Bihar Research Society*, 1951, 37(3–4): 1–13.

———, 'Bangaon Plate of Vigrahapala III; Regnal Year 17', *Epigraphia Indica*, 1951–52 (reprint 1987), 29: 48–57.

———, 'Two Pala Plates from Belwa', *Epigraphia Indica*, 1951–52 (reprint 1987), 29: 1–13.

———, 'Pāla Rule in the Tippera District', *The Indian Historical Quarterly*, 1952, 28(1): 51–57.

———, 'Notes and Queries', *The Indian Historical Quarterly*, 1953, 29(3): 294–303.

———, 'Dubi Plates of Bhaskaravarman', *Epigraphia Indica*, 1953–54 (reprint 1987), 30: 287–304.

———, 'Epigraphic Notes', *Epigraphia Indica*, 1953–54 (reprint 1987), 30: 42–58.
———, 'Inscriptions from Bihar', *Epigraphia Indica*, 1953–54 (reprint 1987), 30: 78–87.
———, 'Date of the Imādpur Image Inscriptions of Mahipāla I', *The Indian Historical Quarterly*, 1954, 30(4): 382–87.
———, 'Vaṅgīya Sāhitya Pariṣad Plate of Viśvarūpasena', *Journal of the Asiatic Society, Letters*, 1954, 20(2): 201–8.
———, 'Madanpāṛā Plate of Viśvarūpasena', *Journal of the Asiatic Society, Letters*, 1954, 20(2): 209–17.
———, 'Jayanagar Image Inscription of Year 35', *Journal of the Bihar Research Society*, 1955, 41(2): 143–53.
———, 'Rajghat Inscription of Bhimadeva', *Epigraphia Indica*, 1957–58 (reprint 1987), 32: 277–82.
———, 'Bhaturiya Inscription of Rajyapala', *Epigraphia Indica*, 1959–60 (reprint 1987), 33: 150–54.
———, 'Dhulla Plate of Srichandra', *Epigraphia Indica*, 1959–60 (reprint 1987), 33: 134–40.
———, 'Madanapada Plate of Visvarupasena', *Epigraphia Indica*, 1959–60 (reprint 1987), 33: 315–26.
———, 'Epigraphic Notes', *Epigraphia Indica*, 1963, 35(2): 95–102.
———, 'Three Pala Inscriptions', *Epigraphia Indica*, 1964 (1963), 35(5): 225–38.
———, 'Inscriptions of Two Brahman Rulers of Gaya', *Epigraphia Indica*, 1965 (1964), 36(2): 81–94.
———, *Indian Epigraphy*, Delhi: Motilal Banarsidass, 1965.
———, 'Three Inscriptions from Bihar', *Epigraphia Indica*, 1965 (1964), 36(1): 39–44.
———, *Indian Epigraphical Glossary*, Delhi: Motilal Banarsidass, 1966.
———, 'Mahisantosh Image Inscription of Mahendrapala, Year 15', *Epigraphia Indica*, 1968 (1969), 37(5): 204–8.
———, 'Note on Rajghat Inscription of Bhimadeva', *Epigraphia Indica*, 1968 (1970). 37(6): 245–46.
———, 'Paschimbhag Plate of Srichandra, Year 5', *Epigraphia Indica*, 1968 (1970), 37(7): 289–304.
———, *Landlordism and Tenancy in Ancient and Medieval India as Revealed by Epigraphical Records*, Lucknow: University of Lucknow, 1969.
———, 'Mainamati Plates of the Chandra Kings', *Epigraphia Indica*, 1970 (1976), 38(5): 197–214.
———, 'Jagadishpur Plate of the Gupta Year 128', *Epigraphia Indica*, 1970 (1979), 38(6): 247–52.
———, 'Siyan Stone Slab Inscription of Nayapala', *Epigraphia Indica*, 1971 (1982), 39(2): 39–56.
———, *Studies in the Geography of Ancient and Medieval India* (2nd ed.), Delhi: Motilal Banarsidass, 1971.
———, 'Three East Indian Inscriptions of the Early Medieval Period', *Journal of Ancient Indian History*, 1972–73 (1973), 6: 39–59.
———, 'Lucknow Museum Copper-plate Inscription of Surapala I, Regnal Year 3', *Epigraphia Indica*, 1973 (1986), 40(1): 4–16.

———, 'Bāṇgaḍh Stone Inscription of the Time of Nayapāla', *Journal of Ancient Indian History*, 1973–74 (1975), 7: 135–58.

———, 'Egra Plate of the Time of Sasank', *Epigraphia Indica*, 1974 (1986), 40(4): 133–38.

———, *Studies in the Political and Administrative Systems in Ancient and Medieval India*, Delhi: Motilal Banarsidass, 1974.

———, *Early Indian Numismatic and Epigraphical Studies*, Calcutta: Indian Museum, 1977.

———, 'Indological Notes No. 30. Rājībpur Sadāśiva Image Inscription of Gopāla III, Year 14', *Journal of Ancient Indian History*, 1980–82 (1983), 13(1–2): 123–27.

———, 'Mūrtiśiva's Bangarh Prasasti of the Time of Nayapāla', *Journal of Ancient Indian History*, 1980–82 (1983), 13(1–2): 34–56.

———, 'Political History', in H. K. Barpujari (ed.), *The Comprehensive History of Assam vol. 1: Ancient Period*, Guwahati: Publication Board Assam, 1990, pp. 94–171.

Sircar, Jawhar, *The Construction of the Hindu Identity in Medieval Western Bengal?: The Role of Popular Cults*, Kolkata: Institute of Development Studies, 2005.

Sivathamby, K., 'Early South Indian Society and Economy: The Tinai Concept', *Social Scientist*, 1974, 3(5): 20–37.

Spate, O. H. K. and A. T. A. Learmonth, *India and Pakistan: A General and Regional Geography* (3rd ed.), New Delhi: Munshiram Manoharlal, 1984 (reprint).

Srinivasan, P. R., 'Jayarampur Plate of Gopachandra', *Epigraphia Indica*, 1972 (1985), 39(5): 141–48.

Stein, Burton, 'The Segmentary State in South Indian History', in Richard G. Fox, *Realm and Region in Traditional India*, New Delhi: Vikas Publishing House, 1977, pp. 3–51.

———, *Peasant State and Society in Medieval South India*, Delhi: Oxford University Press, 1980.

———, 'The Segmentary State: Interim Reflections', in Hermann Kulke (ed.), *The State in India 1000–1700*, Delhi: Oxford University Press, 1995, pp. 134–61.

Subramonia Iyer, S., 'Nālandā Inscription of Dharmapāladeva, Year 4', *Epigraphia Indica*, 1977–78 (reprint 1992), 42: 104–5.

———, 'Bharat Kala Bhavan Copper Plate Charter of Rajyapaladeva, Year 2', *Epigraphia Indica*, 2011–12 (2011), 43(1): 25–39.

Talbot, Cynthia, *Precolonial India in Practice: Society, Region and Identity in Medieval Andhra*, New Delhi: Oxford University Press, 2001.

Tarafdar, M. R., 'Trade and Society in Early Medieval Bengal', *Indian Historical Review*, 1978, 4(2): 274–86.

Tirumalai, R., *Land Grants and Agrarian Reactions in Coḷa and Pāṇḍya Times*, Madras: University of Madras, 1987.

Vasu, N. N., 'Copper-plate Inscription of Madanapāla', *Journal of the Asiatic Society of Bengal*, 1900, 69(1): 66–73.

Veluthat, Kesavan, *The Political Structure of Early Medieval South India*, New Delhi: Orient Longman, 1993.

———, 'The Structure of Land-rights and Social Stratification in Early Medieval South India', in Vijay Kumar Thakur and Asok Aounshuman (eds), *Peasants in Indian History vol. 1: Theoretical Issues and Structural Enquiries (Essays in Memory of Professor Radhakrishna Chaudhary)*, Patna: Janaki Prakashan, 1996, pp. 312–30.

——, *The Early Medieval in South India*, New Delhi: Oxford University Press, 2009.

Venis, Arthur, 'Copper-plate Grant of Vaidyadeva, King of Kāmarūpa', *Epigraphia Indica*, 1894 (reprint 1984), 2: 347–58.

Vidyavinoda, Vinoda Vihari, 'Two Inscriptions from Bodh-Gaya', *Epigraphia Indica*, 1913–14 (reprint 1982), 12: 27–30.

Whitney, William Dwight, *Sanskrit Grammar: Including Both, the Classical Language and the Older Dialects of Veda and Brāhmaṇa*, Delhi: Motilal Banarsidass, 1994 (reprint).

Wicks, Robert S., *Money, Markets, and Trade in Early Southeast Asia: The Development of Indigenous Monetary Systems to AD 1400*, Ithaca: Southeast Asia Program, Cornell University, 1992.

Yadava, B. N. S., *Society and Culture in Northern India in the Twelfth Century*, Allahabad: Central Book Depot, 1973.

——, 'The Accounts of the Kali Age and the Social Transition from Antiquity to the Middle Ages', *Indian Historical Review*, 1979, 5(1–2): 31–63.

——, 'Terminological Analysis and Social Change: Locating the Peasants in Early Medieval North India', in Vijay Kumar Thakur and Ashok Aounshuman (eds), *Peasants in Indian History vol. 1: Theoretical Issues and Structural Enquiries (Essays in Memory of Professor Radhakrishna Chaudhary)*, Patna: Janaki Prakashan, 1996, pp. 199–219.

——, 'The Problem of the Emergence of Feudal Relations in Early India', in D. N. Jha (ed.), *The Feudal Order: State, Society and Ideology in Early Medieval India*, New Delhi: Manohar, 2000, pp. 249–301 (originally Presidential Address, Ancient India Section, Indian History Congress 41st session, 1980).

Yamazaki, Gen'ichi, *The Structure of Ancient Indian Society: Theory and Reality of the Varṇa System*, Tokyo: The Toyo Bunko, 2005.

Yamazaki, Toshio, '5, 6 Seiki Bengal No Tochibaibaimonjo Ni Tsuiteno Jakkan No Kousatsu' (Some considerations on the land sale documents of the fifth and sixth century Bengal) (in Japanese), *Toyo Bunka Kenkyujo Kiyo*, 1959, 18: 89–133.

——, 'Some Aspects of Land-Sale Inscriptions in Fifth and Sixth Century Bengal', *Acta Asiatica*, 1982, 43: 17–36.

INDEX

Note: page numbers in **bold** indicate a table on the corresponding page.

For Product Safety Concerns and Information please contact our EU representative GPSR@taylorandfrancis.com
Taylor & Francis Verlag GmbH, Kaufingerstraße 24, 80331 München, Germany

www.ingramcontent.com/pod-product-compliance
Ingram Content Group UK Ltd.
Pitfield, Milton Keynes, MK11 3LW, UK
UKHW020018200926
475702UK00014B/1950

* 9 7 8 0 3 6 7 7 8 5 9 2 5 *